HC 135 .C44

Changing structure of
Mexico

Date Due

DEC 1 3 2006			
SEP 1 8 2012			

CHANGING STRUCTURE OF MEXICO

COLUMBIA UNIVERSITY SEMINAR SERIES

Robert Belknap, Director

CHANGING STRUCTURE OF MEXICO

POLITICAL, SOCIAL, AND ECONOMIC PROSPECTS

SECOND EDITION

LAURA RANDALL

EDITOR

M.E.Sharpe
Armonk, New York
London, England

Copyright © 2006 by M.E. Sharpe, Inc.

Editor's Note

The chapters in this volume were written between January 2004 and October 2005. The editor wrote the introductory paragraphs in italics at the front of each chapter and translated chapters 3, 10, 12, 15, 22, 26, and 29.

Library of Congress Cataloging-in-Publication Data

Changing structure of Mexico : political, social, and economic prospects / [edited by] Laura Randall.—2nd ed.
   p. cm. — (Columbia University seminar series)
Includes bibliographical references and index.
ISBN 0-7656-1404-9 (hardcover : alk. paper)
   1. Mexico—Economic conditions—1994– 2. Mexico—Social conditions—1970– 3. Mexico—Economic policy. 4. Mexico—Social policy. 5. Mexico—Politics and government—1988– I. Randall, Laura. II. Series.

HC135.C44 2006
972.08′4—dc22   2004029098

Printed in the United States of America

The paper used in this publication meets the minimum requirements of American National Standard for Information Sciences Permanence of Paper for Printed Library Materials, ANSI Z 39.48-1984.

∞

BM (c)   10   9   8   7   6   5   4   3   2   1

Contents

I. Introduction and Overview

II. Current Policy Issues

III. Changes in Sectors

IV. Resources and the Environment

Boxes, Figures, Maps, and Tables

Maps

Tables

Acronyms

CAFTA	Central America Free Trade Agreement
CIDE	Centro de Investigacíon y Docencia Económicas
CONACYT	National Council of Science and Technology
FDI	foreign direct investment
EOC	economic overhead capital
EZLN	Zapatista National Liberation Army (Ejército Zapatista de Liberación Nacional)
FOBAPROA	Fondo Bancario de Protección al Ahorro (Bank Savings Protection Fund)
FTA	Free Trade Area
FTAA	Free Trade Areas of the Americas
GATT	General Agreement on Tariffs and Trade
GDP	gross domestic product
GKF	gross capital formation
IMP	Instituto Mexicano del Petróleo
INEGI	Instituto Nacional de Estadística, Geografía e Informática
IPAB	(successor to FOBAPROA) Institute for the Protection of Bank Savings (Instituto de Protección al Ahorro Bancario)
JIT	just-in-time
LOPPE	Ley Federal de Organizaciones, Procesos y Participación Electorales
NAFTA	North American Free Trade Agreement
NEG	New Economic Geography
OAS	Organization of American States
OC	public investment
OECD	Organization for Economic Cooperation and Development
Pacto	Economic Stability Pact
PAN	Partido Acción Nacional (Nacional Action Party)
PCD	Partido de Convergencia Democrática
PEMEX	Petróles Mexicanos (Mexican national oil company)
PI	private investment
PMS	Partido Mexicano Socialista
PNR	National Revolutionary Party
PNUD-OT	Programa da Nações Unidas para o Desenvolvimento (National Program for Urban Development and Territorial Planning)

PPP	Plan Puebla-Panamá
PPS	Partido Popular Socialista (Popular Socialist Party)
PRD	Partido de la Revolución Democrática (Democratic Revolution Party)
PRI	Partido Revolucionario Institucional (Institutional Revolutionary Party)
PRN	Mexican Revolutionary Party
PRONALEES	National Program for the Strengthening of Reading and Writing in Primary Education
PRONASOL	Programa Nacional de Solidaridad (National Solidarity Program)
PSE	Pacto de Solidaridad Económica (Economic Solidarity Pact)
PSUM	Partido Socialista Unificado de Mexico (Communist Party)
PT	Partido del Trabajo (Labor Party)
PVEM	Partido Verde Ecologista de México (Mexican Green Ecology Party)
SEDESOL	Secretaría de Desarrolio Social (Ministry of Welfare)
SOC	social overhead capital
SHCP	Secretaríat de Hacienda y Crédito Público (Ministry of Finance and Public Credit)
SOC	social infrastructure
UNAM	National Autonomous University of Mexico
UNPAN	United Nations Online Network in Public Administration and Finance
VAT	value added tax

Contributors

Dr. Adrián Guillermo Aguilar, Director, Instituto de Geografía, Universidad Nacional Autónoma de México (UNAM); adrian@servidor.unam.mx

Gabriela Angeles-Serrano, Associate Researcher, Center for Research on North America Universidad Nacional Autónoma de México (UNAM); ganserr@servidor.unam.mx

Fernando Barceinas Paredes, Professor, Economics Department, doctoral coordinator in economics, Universidad Autónoma Metropolitana (deceased)

Rodrigo Barros, doctoral student in economics, Stanford University; rbarros@stanford.edu

Miguel Basáñez, pollster; WAPOR president (1998–2000); president of Global Quality Research Corporation; professor, Instituto Tecnológico Autónomo de México (ITAM); mb@mx.inter-net

Mariano Bauer E., Researcher, Instituto de Fisica, Universidad Autonoma de Mexico. bauer@fisica.unam.mx

Roberto Blancarte, Professor/Researcher and Academic Coordinator of the Centro de Estudios Sociológicos, Colegio de Mexico; blancart@colmex.mx

David Barton Bray, Associate Professor, Department of Environmental Studies at Florida International University; brayd@fiu.edu

Consuelo Castro, Coordinadora de Profesionalización y Asesoría Jurídica, (Legal Advisory Coordinator) Centro Mexicano para la Filantropía; ccastro@cemefi.org

Jennifer Catino, M.P.H., Regional Program Coordinator, Population Council, Regional Office for Latin America and the Caribbean, Mexico City, Mexico; jcatino@popcouncil.org.mx

Hugo A. Concha Cantú, Professor/Researcher, Instituto de Investigaciones Jurídicas, UNAM; editor of *Reforma Judicial: Revista Mexicana de Justicia*; hacc@servidor.unam.mx

Oscar F. Contreras, Professor/Researcher and director of the Ph.D. Program in Social Sciences of El Colegio de Sonora; ocontre@conson.edu.mx

Melissa Cornejo, M.S., Department of Environmental Studies, Florida International University; mcornejo26@hotmail.com

Eugenia Correa, Postgraduate of Department of Economics; Professor, UNAM; correa@servidor.unam.mx

Dr. Silke Cram, Senior Researcher A, Physical and Chemical Environmental Analysis Laboratory, Instituto de Geografía, UNAM; silke@servidor.unam.mx

Graciana del Castillo, Managing Director, Macroeconomics Advisory Group (MAG); Adjunct Professor of Economics, School of International and Public Affairs, Columbia University; gracianadelcastillo@macroadvisory.com

Dr. Javier Delgado, Senior Researcher A, Social Geography Department, Instituto de Geografía, UNAM; jdelgado@igiris.igeograf.unam.mx

Carlos Elizondo Mayer-Serra, Professor/Researcher, CIDE; carlos.elizondo@amadeus.cide.edu

Sara Gordon Rapoport, Investigadora Titular "C" T.C., Definitiva, Instituto de Investigaciones Sociales; gordon@servidor.unam.mx

Boris Graizbord, Coordinator, Programa de Estudios Avanzados en Desarrollo Sustentable y Medio Ambiente, LEAD–México, El Colegio de México; graizbord@lead.colmex.mx

Marcos Hernández, M.A. in government and public affairs, UNAM; Ph.D. candidate in public policy; marcos_hrl@hotmail.com

Dr. Aron Jazcilevich D., Researcher, Centro de Ciencias de la Atmosfera, UNAM; jazcilev@servidor.unam.mx

Joseph L. Klesner, Professor, Chair, Department of Political Science, Kenyon College; klesner@kenyon.edu

Ana Langer, M.D., President, EngenderHealth, alanger@engenderhealth.org

Soledad Loaeza, Professor/Researcher, Centro de Estudios Internacionales, El Colegio de México; maloa@colmex.mx

Jordy Micheli Thirión, Professor/Researcher, Department of Economics, Universidad Autónoma Metropolitana (UAM), Azcapotzalco; jomicheli@correo.azc.uam.mx

Skya Rose Murphy, M.S. candidate, Department of Environmental Studies at Florida International University; skya.murphy@fiu.edu

Rubén Oliver Espinoza, Researcher, Center of Economic, Administrative, and Social Research Instituto Politécnico Nacional (IPN); roliver@ipn.mx

Pia M. Orrenius, Senior Economist, Research Department, Federal Reserve Bank of Dallas; Pia.Orrenius@dal.frb.org

Juan Quintanilla Martínez, Research Staff, Departamento de Cómputo para la Investigación, Dirección General de Servicios de Cómputo Académico, UNAM; juaquin@servidor.unam.mx

Fernando Reimers, Associate Professor of education, Graduate School of Education, Harvard University; reimerfe@gse.harvard.edu

Naxhelli Ruiz, Ms.C. in regional studies, Ph.D. candidate in development studies, University of East Anglia (UEA); n.ruiz@uea.ak.uk

Dr. Christina Siebe, Senior Researcher B, Soil Science Department, Instituto de Geología, UNAM; siebe@servidor.unam.mx

Fernanda Somuano, Professor and Academic Coordinator, Centro de Estudios Internacionales, El Colegio de México; fsomuano@colmex.mx

Pamela K. Starr, Analyst, Latin America, Eurasiagroup.net; Starr@eurasiagroup.net

Rafael Tamayo-Flores, Professor, Economics Department, Tecnológico de Monterrey, Mexico City Campus, and Researcher, Public Policy and Administration Department, CIDE; rafael.tamayo@amadeus.cide.edu

María Luisa Tarrés, Professor/Researcher, Center of Sociological Studies, El Colegio de México; mtarres@colmex.mx

José F. Ursúa, doctoral student in economics, Harvard University; jfursua@fas.harvard.edu

Sidney Weintraub, Simon Chair in Political Economy, Center for Strategic and International Studies (CSIS); SWeintraub@csis.org

Alejandro M. Werner, Director of Economic Policy, Ministry of Finance, Mexico; alejandro_werner@hacienda.gob.mx

Scott Whiteford, Director, Center for Latin American and Caribbean Studies, Michigan State University; whitefo1@msu.edu

Margaret Wilder, Assistant Professor, Latin American Studies and Geography, University of Arizona; mwilder@email.arizona.edu

Antonio Yúnez-Naude, Professor, Centro de Estudios Económicos, and Coordinator of Program for the Studies of Economic Change and the Sustainability of Mexican Agriculture; ayunez@colmex.mx

Francisco Zapata Professor, Centro de Estudios Sociológicos, El Colegio de México; Zapata@colmex.mx

I
Introduction and Overview

Map 1.1   **States and Regions of Mexico**

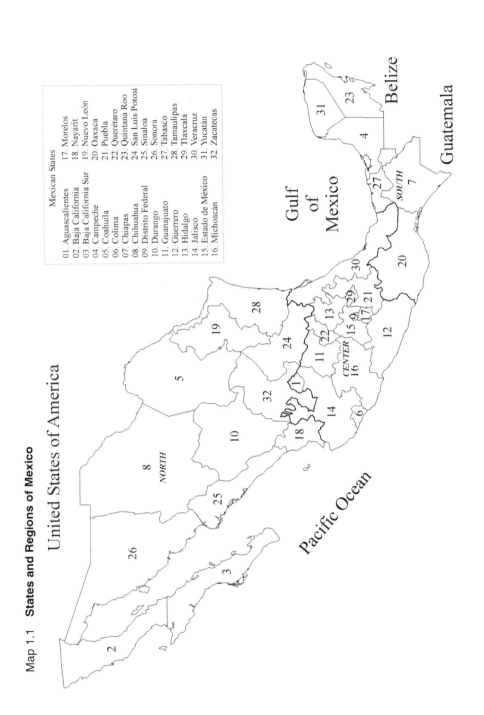

Mexican States

01. Aguascalientes
02. Baja California
03. Baja California Sur
04. Campeche
05. Coahuila
06. Colima
07. Chiapas
08. Chihuahua
09. Distrito Federal
10. Durango
11. Guanajuato
12. Guerrero
13. Hidalgo
14. Jalisco
15. Estado de México
16. Michoacán

17. Morelos
18. Nayarit
19. Nuevo León
20. Oaxaca
21. Puebla
22. Querétaro
23. Quintana Roo
24. San Luis Potosí
25. Sinaloa
26. Sonora
27. Tabasco
28. Tamaulipas
29. Tlaxcala
30. Veracruz
31. Yucatán
32. Zacatecas

United States of America

Gulf of Mexico

Pacific Ocean

Belize

Guatemala

NORTH

CENTER

SOUTH

LAURA RANDALL

Reinventing Mexico

Modernization in an International Context

"Reinventing Mexico" is the theme of this book. The text differs from news reports that often are written as if there is a single "Mexican" view, or a single explanation of an event. In contrast, there are many explanations of the political, social,
and economic conditions of Mexico and their future prospects. During the last
decades, diminished governmental control of newspapers and the increased availability of television and Internet sources of information have ended the "suspension of disbelief" in official explanations of Mexican history. Competing
government, political party, and academic explanations of Mexican events abound.
They differ so greatly from earlier ways of describing the changes taking place in
Mexico that through these diverse views, Mexico is reinventing itself.

Mexico is reinvented by individuals in the society whose values have shifted
from the traditional values still held by older, poorer, and less educated Mexicans.
The traditional values are being challenged by Mexicans who are younger, more
educated, have higher incomes, and have more modern values.[1] The change in
values reflects both a pragmatic adaptation to the nation's needs and an increased
opening to international influences that are broader than the interchange of values
between Mexico and its neighbors that result from migration and tourism. Mexico's
opening to foreign influence is not solely the result of its relationship with the
United States. For almost half a century, the Mexican government has sent its civil
servants and elites to a wide range of nations for advanced study.

This is particularly beneficial because Western Europe (excluding Ireland) and
Japan have more secular-rational values than those of the United States. A result of
European influence has been, for example, that Mexico based its 1977 political
reform law, designed to promote a multiparty system, on the Spanish Law of Political Associations of 1976. Mexico joined the Organization for Economic Cooperation and Development (OECD) on May 18, 1994—an important step in Mexico's
policy of transforming its institutions to improve its integration into the world
polity and economy. Major changes in attitude began in 1997 just before the Mexican government approved the Agreement of Economic Association, Political and

Cooperation with the European Union and initiated the negotiations to sign up a general free trade agreement with this entity. This required the inclusion of the "democratic clause," which made explicit reference to democratic governance and human rights as essential parts of the agreement. This clause was adopted as a result of pressure by domestic and international nongovernmental organizations that forced a change in the Mexican government's initial position of rejecting it.

Mexico's membership in the OECD gave the nation access to advice on a wide range of issues. For example, it adopted the recommendations of the OECD for national science and technology policy. The inclusion of environmental issues in international treaties added to the domestic reasons to protect the environment: exhaustion of resources and degradation of the environment cost 11 percent of gross domestic product in 2002. Government spending on protecting the environment rose to 0.6 percent of gross domestic product in 1999–2002, and a political party that is ostensibly devoted to the environment holds a little more than 3 percent of the seats in the Chamber of Deputies. This has not resulted in improved definition of environmental tasks, delineation of responsibilities, or administration of rules intended to improve the environment, despite the OECD analysis of how to do so.

Domestic Economic Policy in an International Context

Macroeconomic Policies: Taxes

Mexican economic policy during the last decade has primarily been directed to using macroeconomic policies to provide a stable context for a more competitive economy that is increasingly integrated into world markets. This policy is consistent with some of the values reported by the 2000 World Values Survey for Mexico: Mexicans wish to have a stable economy, have an increasingly strong work ethic, value stability more than growth, and feel that people should take more responsibility for themselves.

The transition from a closed to an open and more competitive economy undertaken to achieve these goals is difficult: per capita income in pesos of constant purchasing power grew at an annual rate of 1.59 percent under President Salinas (1988–1994), 3.23 percent under President Zedillo (1994–2000), and at an estimated 0.95 percent during the first four years of President Fox's administration (2000–) (see Table 1.1), although a real per capita growth rate of 2.7 percent was predicted for 2004. Mexican economic performance was only partly consistent with public opinion, which criticized the damage caused to the most vulnerable Mexicans during the transition. This is consistent with the increasing calls for economic and political reforms to strengthen Mexican institutions. Tax reform may be the most pressing reform that is needed. Among the thirty states that were members of the OECD in 2000, Mexico had the lowest tax revenue of all: the total income of the federal government was 15.4 percent of gross domestic product (GDP). This includes tax and nontax revenue, the latter mainly royalties paid by the state-run oil company, PEMEX

Table 1.1

Real Per Capita Growth Rates, 1988–2004, 1993 Prices

	Gross domestic product[a]				Disposable national income[a]			
	Total		Per capita		Total		Per capita	
Year	Millions of 1993 pesos[b]	Real annual growth (%)	Millions of 1993 pesos[b]	Real annual growth (%)	Millions of 1993 pesos[b]	Real annual growth (%)	Millions of 1993 pesos[b]	Real annual growth (%)
1988	1,042,066	n.d.	12.714	n.d.	896,243	n.d.	10.935	n.d.
1989	1,085,815	4.2	12.977	2.1	950,218	6.0	11.356	3.9
1990	1,140,848	5.1	13.363	3.0	1,015,926	6.9	11.899	4.8
1991	1,189,017	4.2	13.655	2.2	1,062,128	4.5	12.198	2.5
1992	1,232,162	3.6	13.882	1.7	1,102,028	3.8	12.416	1.8
1993	1,256,196	2.0	13.893	0.1	1,118,109	1.5	12.366	-0.4
1994	1,311,661	4.4	14.251	2.6	1,164,118	4.1	12.648	2.3
1995	1,230,771	-6.2	13.149	-7.7	1,049,886	-9.8	11.216	-11.3
1996	1,294,197	5.2	13.608	3.5	1,118,674	6.6	11.763	4.9
1997	1,381,839	6.8	14.314	5.2	1,216,151	8.7	12.598	7.1
1998	1,451,351	5.0	14.822	3.5	1,276,811	5.0	13.039	3.5
1999	1,503,930	3.6	15.151	2.2	1,333,419	4.4	13.433	3.0
2000	1,602,640	6.6	15.936	5.2	1,430,198	7.3	14.221	5.9
2001	1,602,711	0.0	15.740	-1.2	1,435,627	0.4	14.099	-0.9
2002 p	1,613,206	0.7	15.656	-0.5	1,449,770	1.0	14.070	-0.2
2003 p	1,633,076	1.3	15.670	0.2	n.d.	n.d.	n.d.	n.d.
2004 p	1,688,020	3.8	16.023	2.7	n.d.	n.d.	n.d.	n.d.

Source: 4o Informe de Gobierno, p. 177.

[a]Based on figures at market prices. Until 2002, data are taken from Cuentas de Bienes y Servicios, volumes 1 and 2, various issues. From 2003, the figures are based on the calculation of Quarterly Domestic Product; for 2004, figures for Gross Domestic Product at current prices for the first quarter and at current and 1993 prices are reported for the first semester. The per capita calculations are based on estimations and projections of the mid–year population from CONAPO brought up to date with definitive data from the XII Census of Population and Housing of 2000.

[b]Calculated with the implicit price index for gross domestic product, 1993 = 100.

p = Preliminary figures.

n.d. = Not available.

(Petróleos Mexicanos). The resulting limited resources of the federal government are shared with municipal and state governments, and also are used to pay interest and amortization on Mexico's large public debt. The government has cut its expenditures. The political parties have not yet agreed on tax reform at the municipal, state, or federal level that would increase the share of gross domestic product that is collected in taxes and facilitate the greatly needed increase in social expenditure and spending on public goods. A recent initiative toward resolution of these problems involved the consultations leading to the signing of the National Fiscal Accord[2] by representatives of different levels of the executive and legislative branches of government. The Accord strengthens aspects of tax administration and suggests reforms that await legislation.

Macroeconomic Policy: Changing Forms of Debt

Tax revenues from domestic sources are not sufficient to achieve Mexico's goals. Additional funds for the public sector are therefore obtained by borrowing at home and abroad. However, in order to provide access to international money markets and international finance, reduce the share of traditionally measured foreign debt of the public sector, and improve the terms upon which it is obtained, the Mexican government has run a surplus in its public sector. Some of the improvement in the level of traditionally measured foreign debt reflects a shift in how imports are financed: the energy sector now can obtain imports under long-term arrangements for investment and repayment called PIDIREGAS (Proyectos de Impacto Diferido en el Registro de Gasto), which are reflected in only the first two years when repayment is due, after which it is assumed that the invested funds will be sufficient to meet repayment obligations. The result is that traditional debt measures are notably smaller than a broad measure of the public debt.

A large share of these PIDIREGAS agreements is the result of the state oil company's need for finance. In 2002, PEMEX provided 38 percent of government fiscal revenues. It is anticipated that Mexico's modernization of energy sector and the consequent reduction of imports of oil and gas products would require the investment of an estimated US$168 billion from 2002 to 2011; that may require changes in government ownership and control of the energy sector to permit this investment. Although the war in Iraq led to an increase in oil prices, the increased government revenue from oil sales is unlikely to be sufficient to meet the increasing development needs of the oil sector, especially in view of newly announced potential—but not yet proven—oil reserves that will require both foreign technology and investment for their development.

Macroeconomic Policy: Money and Banking

Tax policy has not been sufficient to promote growth, and inadequate money and banking policy can prevent it. In order to improve money and banking policy and conditions, in 1993 the Mexican government granted autonomy to the Central Bank, which was no longer required to finance the government deficit. The government deregulated the stock market and permitted the expansion of foreign ownership of banks. This was not enough to provide a safe banking environment. The mid-1990s economic crisis led many banks into technical bankruptcy. The bailout of these banks by increased lending by the Central Bank and the assumption of the bad loans of commercial banks by the institutions designed to maintain bank solvency and protect depositors cost well over $100 billion, to be paid over several years. Congress has not yet passed legislation to improve bank lending practices or to increase the cost to debtors of default.

The private banking sector is profitable, but the rest of the economy has not grown adequately. Monetary policy has succeeded in stabilizing prices, but high interest rates have contributed to a contraction of domestic investment.

International Treaties, Trade, and the Development of Agriculture and Industry

Mexico's economy is increasingly integrated with those of many nations, and the successive trade treaties with nations that compete with each other for trade tend to increasingly lower barriers to trade. In the mid-1980s Mexico's low-key foreign policy was formulated with the goal of encouraging U.S. willingness to help minimize the costs of Mexico's 1982 economic crisis. Mexico's increasing opening to trade and investment was accompanied by a strengthening of its alliances with other Latin American nations. To this end, the Contadora Group was formed to demand a negotiated solution to Central America's civil wars. Other steps taken were the signing of several free trade treaties in the 1990s, as well as the sponsoring of regional representation in international forums. An attempt to broaden the North American Free Trade Agreement (NAFTA) and reach a bilateral migration agreement with the United States has been restricted by U.S. electoral politics and preoccupation with worldwide terrorism. Thus, the Fox administration overestimated the extent to which democratization in Mexico would create shared interests with the United States because of the shift in U.S. priorities.

Mexican trade is tightly bound to the United States, and the impact of the NAFTA accord between Mexico, the United States, and Canada has increased Mexican trade by $322 billion over the past ten years. In 2002, intra-NAFTA trade accounted for 45 percent of the total trade of the three countries. In 2003, provisional figures indicate that trade with the United States and Canada accounted for 77.3 percent of Mexico's total trade; 61.9 percent of imports and 89 percent of exports were with the United States. However, in 2003 and the first half of 2004, Mexico lost its position to China as the second-biggest exporter—after Canada—to the United States after China joined the World Trade Organization on November 11, 2001. NAFTA by itself does not determine which country has the largest exports to the United States.

Thus, the fact that Mexico has grown at only around 1 percent per capita in real terms since NAFTA began is not the result of the almost tripling of Mexican exports during this period. Instead, it reflects the political stalemate that has impeded structural reforms, especially those of educational and fiscal policy. Moreover, NAFTA-related growth is part of a longer-term trend; however, NAFTA did have differing impacts on regions and sectors within Mexico. During the last decade, growth in Mexico, except for the South, has increasingly depended on growth in the Pacific region of the United States. The South of Mexico, although poorer than the rest of the nation, is less benefited or harmed by changes in the U.S. economy. The expansion of the domestic and foreign market for Mexican goods and the increased openness of the Mexican economy, largely because of NAFTA, together may have increased foreign direct investment in Mexico by about 70 percent. The future impact of NAFTA, however, may be weakened as Mexico signs increasing numbers of trade agreements. By mid-September 2004, Mexico was one of Latin America's most open economies with eleven free trade agreements, including thirty-two countries around the world, and an agreement with Japan enacted in March 2005. This has broadened into support for extending free trade agreements with individual nations to a proposed Free Trade of the Americas among the thirty-four North, Central and South American nations: in October 2004, polls indicated that 62 percent of Mexicans and 59 percent of respondents in the United States supported this proposal.[3]

Similarly, the impact of NAFTA may be overestimated for agriculture: a large share of economic growth in agriculture is a result of long-term trend rather than of the NAFTA agreement. Moreover, the government's best known domestic agricultural policy has had little impact on landownership so far: the government has long viewed small properties, whether privately owned or held as *ejidos* (lands owned by the nation; the right to work them was granted to villages), as inefficient. The Constitution was amended in 1992 to facilitate sale of ejido land to private owners, but only 5 percent of ejidos were sold by 2001 because a large share of ejido land has low productive value except for nonagricultural uses. Change in land ownership did not provide a major explanation for structural change in agriculture from 1994 to 2002. In addition, a disproportionate amount of environmental damage results from agricultural production. Preventing environmental degradation by the use of sustainable development production methods, however, is only adopted and maintained when these methods are profitable; successful examples are provided by small farmers and coffee producers, who have found new markets for environmentally based products, and by some community-based forestry enterprises. This is not yet a major feature of agricultural policy or practice in Mexico.

The impact of free trade in general on Mexican agriculture differs somewhat from the impact of NAFTA alone. Both better prices for some exports under NAFTA and lower prices due to competition from Chilean producers because of the free trade agreement with Chile have led to shifts in cultivation to crops that require more water, which leads to environmental problems. An additional complication is that crops like water-intensive asparagus are produced by private farmers, while the less water-intensive grapes are produced by farmers on ejidos. Some trade is for niche markets, formed by those who favor environmentally friendly, organic, fair trade and sustainable agricultural production. Organic coffee now accounts for 10 percent of Mexican coffee production because there is an export market for it. However, it has been more difficult to introduce sustainable agricultural techniques for traditional crops, even when this is profitable. It is possible that among small farmers, it may be that only those who have found new markets for environmentally based production will survive in the medium term.

The impact of free trade on industry began in 1965, before the signing of NAFTA, with the establishment of free trade zones in the North of Mexico for duty-free imports on components that were worked on in Mexico and then exported under special programs, such as that for maquiladoras in Northern Mexico. A similar program was established for most other regions of Mexico on May 3, 1990. All of Mexico became a free trade area with the signing of NAFTA.

From 1985 to 2000, the maquiladoras became the main source of creation of industrial jobs, and the second most important source of foreign exchange. For U.S. enterprises that established maquila operations in Mexico, this scheme was very advantageous because it allowed them to dramatically reduce their labor costs.

During the 1970s and first years of the 1980s, maquiladoras were simple assembly plants in which unskilled manual labor, a low level of technology, and low salaries predominated. In 2002, maquiladoras used increasingly advanced technology and incorporated larger shares of skilled technicians, engineers, and managers in their labor force.

Beginning in 2000, a worldwide increase in free trade eroded Mexico's ability to compete in the United States because other nations covered by free trade agreements had labor costs much lower than those of Mexico, which had not developed an industrial, technological, or educational policy that led to comparative advantage in industry based on skills, rather than on cheap labor.

Migration

Many workers who cannot find jobs at home migrate from rural areas to cities, or between cities, in Mexico. Many Mexicans, and others passing through Mexico, migrate to the United States: A de facto common market with Mexico largely exists, mainly legally for the exchange of goods, services, and capital, but often illegally for the movement of labor. Mexico has lost more than 10 percent of its prime-working-age labor force in the last few decades. In 2003, $13.3 billion was transferred by migrants in the United States to Mexico; 48 percent went to rural areas. These money transfers are the country's second source of income after oil exports.

Migration from Mexico brings many benefits to the United States. The costs associated with migrants are borne mostly by the localities and states where they live. Considerable numbers of U.S. voters opposed continuing migration, yet the

Mexican government would like to arrange improved legal conditions for its migrant workers. In 2004, the Bush administration was concerned with reelection at home and terror abroad. In 2005, change in U.S. migration policy in the near future seemed unlikely.

Transformation of Political Institutions and Policies

The presidential victory of Vicente Fox of the PAN (Partido de Acción Nacional (National Action Party) in 2000 ended one-party domination of the Mexican presidency. The victory was made possible by increasing democratization both in presidential elections and in the internal organization of political parties. Political reforms made possible the establishment of new political parties and allowed for the electoral victory of parties other than the long-dominant Institutional Revolutionary Party (PRI—Partido Revolucionario Institucional) by removing the PRI from control of the authorities that supervised elections during the 1990s. The Federal Electoral Institute has increased the transparency of elections by involving ordinary citizens in running the polling stations and by installing advanced information systems for rapid disclosure of the election results.

The resulting multiparty system, however, leads to difficulties in passing legislation. The political reform did not change the requirement of "no reelection" of government officials, so that a substantial amount of power remains in the hands of the presidency because each elected or appointed official must look for a new position every three or six years.

Additional difficulties stem from the shortage of federal government funds, an important share of which was used for payment on the external debt, which led to the shedding of many functions and responsibilities by the central government. These responsibilities were given to state and local governments that sometimes could not carry them out because they lacked adequate financial, physical, and human resources. A widespread acceptance of cheating and a stalemate in Congress on reform led to widespread calls for reforms of both the tax system and of the constitutional provisions regarding length of term and numbers of terms in legislative office.

To some extent, government action has been replaced by that of nongovernmental organizations; tax deductions are now possible for contributions to some of them. A particularly interesting development is the imposition of a state tax on payrolls, at the suggestion of businessmen in Chihuahua, to finance a trust fund for social objectives in that state. The success of nongovernmental organizations, however, can be viewed as undermining the scope and legitimacy of the present governmental structure: the combination of decentralization of political power, the increase of nongovernmental organizations, and the increase in democracy has had the result that as Mexico shifted away from a basically one-party system where power was concentrated in the presidency, it now has a multiparty system in which none of the three leading political parties enjoys a majority in the legislature; the resulting legislative stalemate has increased the government's use of pacts with interest groups since the late eighties. Thus, rapid resolution of conflict is sought by pact making outside the system of formal government; this has weakened the government.

This evaluation is notably consistent with a shift in Mexican political values from 1990 to 2000. Although in 2000 a larger share of Mexicans believed that politics was important in their lives, they were decreasingly interested in discussing politics, belonging to political parties, or joining in legal demonstrations. They increasingly took part in local community action groups on specific issues. The problem of how best to represent individuals and interest groups within the official political system has not yet been resolved because Mexico's new democracy has features such as no reelection of legislators that make it inefficient, and because legislators depend on political parties, not their constituents, for their next job. An attempt to limit purely political criteria for selection of policies and programs targeted to benefit specified beneficiaries is provided by Congress's requirements that external evaluations be made of all programs that receive fiscal resources starting with the 2001 fiscal year, and that in all federal programs, a highly visible statement must be included saying that the programs did not come from only one political party, but from the government as a whole.

The existence of nongovernmental organizations has been particularly important for the political participation of women, for human rights, and for protection of the environment. In 2000, 42 percent of Mexicans surveyed believed that men were better political leaders than women. Women often expressed their political views outside of formal political structures. Five percent of Mexican women belong to women's groups, compared to 2 percent who belong to political parties, while 5 percent belong to local community action groups and 7 percent to groups concerned with health. The integration of women into political processes often occurred in new political groups, such as the Zapatistas; the groups formed for aid after the 1985 earthquake in Mexico City; and the Partido de la Revolución Democrática (Democratic Revolution Party—PRD), formed in 1989. The PRD established and sometimes observed quotas of 30 percent of the candidacies for women, which were later extended to other political parties. Nonetheless, few women have important positions within the political system. To the extent that only women can represent women's needs, the failure to integrate women and other sectors into the political process casts doubt on the political system's capacity of representation.

This lack of representation affects workers. Unionized labor, business, and the state have interacted efficiently through pacts to control inflation, limit salary increases, and suppress strike activity, bypassing the legislature; therefore political parties do not play the significant role they play in other national contexts on matters related to labor. The negotiations to join NAFTA decreased union control of hiring and work conditions, and payment systems were adjusted to reflect changes in productivity by replacing hourly wages by piece rate systems in order to offer the best chance to companies in their struggle to be competitive in the international market.

During the Fox government, tenured employment, labor control of hiring and firing decisions, and the forty-eight-hour workweek, among others, were modified while new benefits, more associated with direct assistance to the poor and jobless, were included in the package to ensure cogency to the political alliance. The labor leadership appeared increasingly identified with the official neoliberal policy and with the managers of companies, and the leadership of the Mexican Labor Confederation has been losing positions in its representation in the Chamber of Deputies since 1988. However, there have not been any initiatives to establish collective bargaining between business and labor without state intervention. In early 2004, expectations for a stable labor climate were not optimistic.

Although the labor climate may not be stable, the extremely poor were benefited by special programs that were essential to counteract the disastrous fall in per capita gross domestic product and disposable income, and the increase in inequality of income distribution, which varied during the business cycle. Except for 1993–1995, from 1988 to 2004, per capita disposable personal income grew more rapidly and fell less rapidly than per capita gross domestic product. From 2000 to 2004, extreme poverty fell from 24.2 percent of the population to 20.3 percent, which meant that 3.1 million Mexicans had left the ranks of those living on less than US$1 per day. Those living in "moderate" poverty, or on about US$10 a day, fell from 53.7 percent to 51.7 percent.[4] Extreme poverty on average in Mexico increased from 21 percent of the population in 1994 to 37 percent in 1996, and then decreased to 20 percent in 2002. However, the reduction in moderate and extreme poverty in urban areas was not significant. Spending on programs specifically targeted to the poor now represents 1.3 percent of GDP, compared with 0.7 percent in 1990. Programs involving transfers have grown rapidly, reaching 7 percent of average income. Transfers are most important for the poorest, especially in rural areas. The recent amelioration of the condition of the rural poor may contribute to the high approval ratings of President Fox, while the limited improvement of conditions in urban areas is consistent with the paradoxically equally high backing in fall 2004 of the candidacy of his political opponent Manuel López Obrador for the 2006 presidential election.

The programs to alleviate poverty are directed more and more to increasing the productive capacity of the poor, rather than subsidizing the prices of basic goods or stimulating economic development. The National Solidarity Program (1988–1994) provided assistance to groups that helped build and maintain schools, pave streets, and construct houses. Benefits were channeled to areas in which the PRI hoped to regain votes lost to the PRD, but these expenditures did not significantly change votes in the presidential elections.

The National Solidarity Program was replaced by PROGRESA (Programa de Educación, Salud y Alimentación—Program for Education, Health, and Nourishment (1997–2001). Health benefits were decentralized; several programs were established to improve education. PROGRESA was renamed OPORTUNIDADES (OPPORTUNITIES) by the Fox administration and extended to semi-urban and urban areas. Voluntary group medical insurance was established, which is especially important because in 2004, according to its directors, the Instituto Mexicano del Seguro Social (IMSS), Mexico's social security administration, spends more on pensions for its staff than on medicine and other medical materials for its patients. In August 2004, Mexico's Congress passed legislation that reduced the IMSS pension benefits.

Similar pension reforms of pension systems for other government workers were expected. Union reform proposals that would have treated old and new workers similarly were not adopted.[5] The process of IMSS pension reform highlights the tension between providing adequate safety nets and benefits for the population, government budget limits, and government workers' desire to safeguard their conditions of employment.

The government's poverty alleviation programs are complemented by the work of nongovernmental organizations, including business foundations. Mexican businesses, in a nation where 7.1 percent of GDP was spent on public order and security, have sought to ameliorate these conditions and also to improve their image by including social awareness in their governance, marketing, and advertising. In some cases, state and federal governments provide economic resources, so that both direct spending and "tax expenditures"—in the sense of foregone tax receipts, which came to 0.0259 percent of GDP in 2002—are devoted to philanthropic causes.

These social causes are recognized as being in the public interest; consequently, the government would be required to develop them by authorizing incentives and inviting the nonprofit organizations to participate in public policy making. Some wish the nonprofit sector to have a greater role in decision making, on the grounds that nonprofits have more contact with the community and more knowledge of its needs and problems.

In 2001, there were more than 6,000 legally recognized "religious associations." The Catholic Church is a special kind of nongovernmental organization. Its opposition to the Revolution resulted in the 1917 Constitution, which affirmed that churches and religious organizations had no legal personality, with the result that they could not engage in any kind of legal claims or other demands. The Constitution was amended in 1992 to recognize the legal status of the churches.

Some 88 percent of Mexicans are Catholic. The election in 2000 of Vicente Fox, a practicing Catholic, changed the way in which religious belief and behavior is presented in Mexico. The acknowledged role of religion in individual behavior has increased along with a general increase in conservative values among younger Mexicans, while the direct role of the Catholic Church, now in competition with other religions, has decreased. On the other hand, two-thirds of nongovernmental organizations in Mexico have a religious origin or influence. However, only 54 percent of Mexicans believe that churches give adequate answers to social problems, reflecting the fact that a good deal of Mexican behavior differs from that recommended by the Catholic Church: 53 percent of rural women use contraceptives; 20 percent have had an abortion. The Fox administration's attempts to use administrative means to impose some church policies—as of mid-2004—have failed. Nonetheless, the state has defended freedom of conscience by ensuring civil and religious liberties.

Women's health has been impacted both by international agreements and political pressures, as well as budgetary policies. Despite Mexico's sound epidemiological surveillance systems, and international conferences and recommendations, HIV/AIDS and other sexually transmitted infections are reaching epidemic proportions because of a continuing lack of access to contraceptives and affordable high-quality reproductive health services, particularly for adolescents. The Bush administration in the United States and other conservative groups have had a powerful negative influence internationally on attitudes toward and the resources available for women's health and development. Recent government actions to improve these conditions include the establishment of the National Center for Gender Equity and Reproductive Health, and the Fox administration plans to ensure universal access to anti retro-virals and high-quality HIV/AIDS care for all Mexicans by 2006. There has also been liberalization of laws permitting abortion, and the inclusion of emergency contraception in the national norms so that public health and family planning clinics are now obliged to provide this method of contraception. Nonetheless, there is evidence of frequent gender bias in the health care of women for problems other than those related to reproductive health.

Gender bias also exists in education. One explanation for the lack of efficiency in education is the result of social attitudes that favor men and make it difficult for women to advance in their professions. Most principals of elementary schools are men, despite the fact that schools run by men are less effective than those run by women, who on the whole have higher credentials and greater educational experience than men, perhaps because women have fewer opportunities for employment outside of education. Yet the effectiveness of women as teachers is not universal: in schools where teachers have lower levels of education, and where minimal instructional conditions are sorely deficient, teacher gender cannot compensate for those deficits. At the root of this situation are patriarchal and corrupt politics that undermine the foundations of the Mexican public education system. The Teachers' Union (Sindicato Nacional de Trabajadores de la Educacion, SNTE) has long supported the dominant PRI. Together with educational administrators, the union controls appointments and other conditions of employment. The SNTE has sold jobs. One education official in a Northern state in Mexico reported that in order to become a principal, a teacher had to help the union by working evenings and on weekends, often meeting in cantinas; sometimes union leaders expect sexual favors from women in order to help them advance in their careers. Women are unlikely to be willing to accept these conditions.

The inefficiencies of gender bias and union monopoly control of education do not, however, imply that all aspects of Mexican education are poor. For example, a recent study[6] shows that the PRONALEES (The National Program for the Strengthening of Reading and Writing in Primary Education) reading program significantly improves Mexican student achievement in the fourth grade in public elementary schools, suggesting that technical factors can increase student achievement, although the existing problems described above lower it.

Mexico: One Nation or Three?

The erosion of the traditional symbols of national unity and the Zapatista uprising in southern Mexico led to a reopening of the question of whether Mexico is a single nation, with a common identity, or a nation whose citizens identified themselves with their town or region rather than with the nation. The increasing political importance of many indigenous groups along with movements for autonomy for indigenous groups and reserved seats for minorities in some Latin American nations are increasingly discussed. Nonetheless, young Mexicans identify themselves with the nation and the world. This broadening view reflects the fact that although there are differences in well-being in Mexico, ranging from the best in the North, middling in the Center, and lowest in the South, these differences are not statistically significant, because of the great variation in well-being among the states in these groups. (Table 1.2 indicates the definitions of regions according to different contributors to this book; Map 1.1 indicates the location of states and regions.) Differences among neighboring municipalities appear smaller than those among states.[7] This is consistent with the fact that election results indicate that regional differences in voting patterns are not great enough to determine with near certainty that one political party or another is going to win an election because it is relatively strong in a region, although in the 2003 elections for the Chamber of Deputies, PAN was strongly represented in the center and the PRI was strongest in the share of votes in the South. Thus, Mexicans are proud of their nationality, especially among the older-age groups, and also have many varying opinions and values according to age, gender, income, and education. These characteristics help to determine the activities and voting behavior of Mexicans.

A result of these complexities has been the adoption of a pragmatic approach to policy decisions and analysis: there is no single, simple grand scheme for Mexico. Moreover, such a scheme, if it were to exist, could not be implemented because of the overlapping political and administrative jurisdictions that are charged with implementing policy. These jurisdictions, moreover, do not correspond to the geography of the areas impacted by common problems. The adjustment of the political system to changes in the underlying structure of Mexico is the subject of continuing discussion. Miguel Basáñez's conclusion of his essay highlights several themes that recur throughout the book: "To get to the optimistic scenario, the

Table 1.2   **Definitions of Regions**

Tamayo		Graizbord		Delgado		Basáñez	
States	**Regions**	**States**	**Regions**	**States**	**Regions**	**States**	**Regions**
		Same as Tamayo Plus:		Same as Tamayo Plus:			
Federal District						Federal District	
Hidalgo	Central		Center		Center	Hidalgo	Center
México	CE		C		C	México	C
Morelos						Morelos	
Tlaxcala						Puebla	
Aguascalientes						Tlaxcala	
Colima						Aguascalientes	West
Guanajuato	Central-west					Colima	W
Jalisco	CW					Guanajuato	
Nayarit		Michoacán		Michoacán		Jalisco	
Querétaro		Puebla		Puebla		Michoacán	
						Nayarit	
San Luis Potosí		Veracruz				Querétaro	
Baja California			North		North	Baja Calif. Sur	North
Chihuahua		Same as Tamayo Plus:	N		N	Baja California	N
Coahuila	Northern border					Chihuahua	
Nuevo León	NB	Nayarit				Coahuila	
Sonora		San Luis Potosí				Durango	
Tamaulipas						Nuevo León	
Baja Calif. Sur						San Luis Potosí	
Durango	Central-north					Sinaloa	
	CN					Sonora	
Sinaloa						Tamaulipas	
Zacatecas						Zacatecas	
Campeche		Same as Tamayo Minus:	South		South	Campeche	South
Quintana Roo	South-east		S		S	Chiapas	S
Tabasco	SE	Michoacán				Guerrero	
Yucatán		Puebla				Oaxaca	
Veracruz		Veracruz				Quintana Roo	
Chiapas						Tabasco	
Guerrero	South					Veracruz	
Oaxaca	SO					Yucatán	
Michoacán							
Puebla							

key point is to find the way to reach a sustained economic growth rate of at least 5 percent annually for a long period. This goal requires, in turn, a full fiscal and legal overhaul, and the abolishing of monopolies, either business or political. These ideas clearly mean a redistribution of economic, social, and political power. The *culture* of the three branches of power, the strong political parties, the Catholic Church, the business community, and the powerful unions constitute the heart of the power structure and have not agreed on the form change should take." This underlies the continuing debate about the reform of the Constitution and, consequently, of the political system, the justice system, and human rights.

The Justice System and Human Rights

In 1990, only 53 percent of Mexicans had quite a lot of confidence in the justice system. There are thirty-three Mexican judiciaries: one federal, one from the federal district (D.F.), and thirty-one from the Mexican states. There also are many other "ancillary" institutions, such as the police corps, prosecutors, penitentiaries, human rights commissions, and even executive offices that have "administrative courts" controlled by the president. These courts are in charge of labor, agrarian, administrative (complaints against the state as a party for the services it is supposed to provide), and electoral areas. The federal Judiciary could review and alter decisions made by the local judiciaries. Judicial institutions had limited jurisdiction and excluded political questions: the existence of political rights became uncertain when there were no means for protecting them.

The 1994–1995 Judicial Reform reduced the executive's control of the Judiciary. Under the reform, the Supreme Court of Justice was reduced from twenty-six to eleven seats and its members were selected in the Senate with senators choosing each justice from three names that the president presented for its consideration. Each justice would have a single term of fifteen years. The reform also created a Judiciary Council that absorbed all the administrative tasks the Court used to handle.

In 1996, the Electoral Court, previously part of the executive branch, became part of the Federal Judiciary, and procedural means were created to demand the protection of federal courts against the violation of political rights, although the *amparo* constitutional writ designed to protect rights in some cases was misused to shield criminals from arrest.

The overall picture was promising: since the mid-1990s Mexico has had a federal judiciary with an acceptable degree of independence that fulfilled its duties on time, but sometimes fast proceedings produced erratic resolutions. Military courts, however, have a separate justice system that remains as the only exception from regular jurisdiction of civil justice.

Human rights in Mexico consist of both traditional civil liberties and social rights that particularly protect workers and peasants. Nonetheless, there was a formal recognition by the government that more rights existed than those established in its Constitution. This leads to the question of whether and how the Constitution should be amended: this is a particularly difficult matter because there is no majority in Congress,[8] and the Constitution of 1917 does not provide for other means of amendment. There necessarily is a continuing debate not only about the rearrangement of political institutions, but also about whether the Constitution should be restricted to general rights and obligations, or whether it should be used to make provisions for specific topics that in other nations are determined by legislation rather than by the Constitution. Thus, the anticipated Constitutional reform will determine the scope and adequacy of the political and justice systems and human rights in Mexico, key themes in the 2000 presidential election and in the changing structure of Mexico.

Notes

1. Statements in this book about values held by Mexicans are based on Ronald Inglehart, Miguel Basáñez, Jaime Díez-Medrano, Loek Halman, and Ruud Luijkx, *Human Beliefs and Values: A Cross-Cultural Sourcebook Based on the 1999–2002 Values Surveys* (Mexico, D.F.: Siglo XXI Editores, 2004).
2. Available at www.cnh.gob.mx/.
3. MEXICO Source: Global Views, 2004. *Comparing Mexican and American Public Opinion and Foreign Policy,* p. 26. Available at www.ccfr.org/globalviews2004/sub/pdf/ Global_Views_2004_US_Mexico.pdf. The three groups jointly publishing this book, downloaded from the Web, are: Centro de Investigación y Docencia Económicas, Consejo Mexicano de Asuntos Internacionales, and the Chicago Council on Foreign Relations.
4. World Bank, *Poverty in Mexico: An Assessment of Conditions, Trends and Government Strategy* (Washington, DC, July 2004). Downloaded from: www.bancomundial.org.mx/ pdf/estudiosporsector/povertyinmexico/1.pdf. For regional and municipal incidence of extreme poverty and poverty, see Figure 8. For the incidence of benefits of several government programs, see Figure 11.
5. For a critical analysis of the process of proposing the reform, the timing on the vote, and possible technical defects in the reform measure, see *Mexican Labor News & Analysis* 9, no. 8 (August 2004). It reports that the union's proposal would have increased the retirement requirements to sixty years of age, thirty-five years of service, a reduced-base wage, and an undefined contribution to the pension fund by both active and new workers of up to 10 percent of their wages.
6. Laura Randall, *Factors Affecting Learning and Cost-Effective Schooling: Primary Schools in Latin America* (Lewiston, NY: Edwin Mellen Press, 2005).
7. See note 4.
8. Article 135.(59). The present Constitution may be added to or amended. In order that the additions or amendments shall become a part thereof, it shall be required that the Congress of the Union, by a vote of two-thirds of the individuals present, agree to the amendments or additions and that they be approved by a majority of the legislatures of the States. The Congress of the Union or the Permanent Committee, as the case may be, shall count the votes of the legislatures and shall announce those additions or amendments that have been approved. Text translated from Constitución Política de los Estados Unidos Mexicanos, Trigésima Quinta Edición, 1967, Editorial Porrua S.A. Mexico, D.F. Originally Publisher by Pan American Union, General Secretariat, Organization of American Status, Washington, DC, 1968. Available at www.latinamericanstudies.org/mexico/ 1917_constitution.htm.

2

Miguel Basáñez

Ideologies and Values

Mexico is reinventing itself. Miguel Basáñez writes that it is changing from a traditional society that is Catholic, nationalist, and supportive of Mexico's revolution to a more tolerant, global, market-oriented, and democratic society. Traditionally, support of Mexico's revolution involved support of peasants, blue-collar workers, and lower urban classes. Nationalism involved anti-Spanish and anti-U.S. sentiments that have been modified as part of the modernization of Mexico, itself a by-product of (1) an increase of legal and illegal migration to and trade with the United States; (2) feminization of the labor force; and (3) explosion of the informal economy. The rapid change in new cultural values has resulted in a strong convergence of values between Mexico, Canada, and the United States. None of the three countries really led the change. It seems as if a new entity is in formation, as indicated by a preliminary review of the 2000 World Value Survey data, which suggest that "willingness to do away with the border and readiness to form one country" with the United States has increased in Mexico.

This willingness to form one country is consistent with a remarkable increase of Protestantism in Mexico, at all social levels, which is altering the deepest pillar of the old value system. As of today, Catholicism remains at the core of the Mexican value system, but the ideological constructions that validated the old regime—nationalism and revolution—are weakening by the day.

This shift in values is led by the younger generation of Mexicans, who are more tolerant, favor globalization, and want fewer children than their predecessor. Those favoring modernization live in larger cities and are likely to live in the Central or Northern regions and to be affiliated with small political parties or with the National Action Party (PAN).

Modernization is hampered by widespread acceptance by moderately educated Mexicans of cheating. Miguel Basáñez believes that "This feature may reflect an unfair fiscal system that rests mainly on the shoulders of the top third of the population. The Mexican government mistakenly exempts from tax payment (and hence alienates from a culture of responsibility) the lower two-thirds of the population."

Basáñez's conclusion of his essay highlights several themes that recur throughout the book: "To get to the optimistic scenario, the key point is to find the way to reach a sustained economic growth rate of at least 5 percent annually for a long period. This goal requires, in turn, a full fiscal and legal overhaul, and the abolishing of monopolies, either business or political. These ideas clearly mean a redistribution of economic, social, and political power. The culture of the three branches of power, the strong political parties, the Catholic Church, the business community, and the powerful unions constitute the heart of the power structure and have not agreed on the form change should take."

The process of constructing the current Mexican system of values—which transformed the pre-Hispanic indigenous culture—took four centuries, and its deconstruction is taking less than four decades. What were the traditional values that were formed so slowly, and what are the new ones that are changing so rapidly? The three cultural pillars of traditional Mexican values and ideology can be summarized as (1) Catholic, (2) nationalistic (anti-Spain and anti-United States), and (3) revolutionary. The new ones are still in formation. However, they seem to be moving toward a more tolerant, global, market-oriented, and democratic society.

Mexico went through a rapid modernization from 1933 to 1982, which led to a deep shift in values from *traditional* to *modern*. The stagnation of real GNP per capita since 1982 paradoxically propelled an acceleration of the trend toward modernization. The acceleration is a by-product of (1) an increase of legal and illegal migration to and trade with the United States, which brought an enormous economic influx of revenues; this development was incompatible with the old anti-U.S. ideology; (2) feminization of the labor force, which propelled gender equality and, in turn, pushed for changes in family structure and values; and (3) explosion of the informal economy. The rapid change in new cultural values has resulted in a strong convergence of values between Mexico, Canada, and the United States. The signing of the North American Free Trade Agreement (NAFTA) was framed in the above conditions.

Analyzing changes in values over time used to be very difficult due to the lack of consistent and reliable measures. The World Values Survey (WVS), conducted in four rounds between 1981 and 2000, now fills that void, and gives us a unique opportunity to track changes in values after 1980. In thirty-one out of the thirty-four WVS variables used to measure changes in values between Canada, Mexico, and the United States, the three countries converged during the 1980–1990 decade. Interestingly, none of the three countries really led the change. It seems as if a new entity is in formation (Inglehart, Nevitte, and Basáñez 1996).

A preliminary review of the 2000 WVS data suggests that the convergent trend continues. *Willingness to do away with the border* increased in Mexico from 22 percent in 1990 to 36 percent in 2000. In the United States, it grew from 37 to 42 percent in the same period in relation to the Canadian border. Unfortunately, we did not have a question in the United States about the Mexican border. Similarly, *readiness to form one country* with the United States increased in Mexico from 21 percent to 31 percent in the decade when the question was posed under a very unappealing condition—*adding one more state*. However, if the condition is posed under an appealing condition—*to improve quality of life*—the readiness to form one country goes up to 58 percent. For the United States with respect to Canada, the value is an impressive 76 percent (Basáñez and Reyes Heroles 2003).

Constructing and Deconstructing Ideologies and the Value System

Values are taken in this chapter as units, and ideologies are taken as constructions based on those units. Along these lines, ideologies are clusters of values that validate an economic, social, or political end. The ultimate construction is a value system that aims at being holistic. Value systems around the world are best encapsulated in religion, which deeply pervades all dimensions of life: economic, social, political, and private.

Mexico is above all historically structured around the pillar of Catholic value system that started with the Spanish colonization. The War of Independence of 1810 understandably aroused an anti-Spain ideology. The loss of half of Mexico's territory in 1848 to the United States produced an anti-U.S. ideology, further reinforced by many more grievances throughout the history of both countries. Those two *anti* sentiments have been at the core of Mexico's second pillar, *nationalism.* Finally, the Mexican Revolution of 1910 justified the pillar of *revolutionary* ideology that validated the government and its political parties, successively known as the PNR, the PRM, and the PRI (respectively, the National Revolutionary Party, Mexican Revolutionary Party, and the Institutional Revolutionary Party). These three cultural pillars of Catholicism, nationalism, and revolution deeply shaped the Mexicans' values, and they still are at the foundation of the belief system of many groups in Mexico.

It is important to notice that the old value system fits a *traditional* society well. Mexico in the 1930s was a traditional society. It was thinly populated, rural, employed in the agrarian sector, illiterate, had poor communications, and had little mobility. The country leadership that handled such a social, political, and economic structure was institutionalized into a set of laws and power coalitions that produced a network of monopolies in politics, business, and religion at all federal, state, and local levels. This institutional arrangement still remains and today constitutes the status quo, in which the conservative forces resist change.

However, in 1933 the country entered into a fifty-year accelerated modernization powered by an average 5.93 percent annual constant GDP growth, sometimes referred to as "the Mexican miracle" (INEGI 1986). The outcome of that growth was an 18.9-fold increase in Mexico's economic size and a 4.3-fold increase of income per capita (using 1932 as the base year). Thus, the country became highly populated, urban, employed in the service sector, literate, had good communications, and was very mobile—the opposite of what it had been fifty-one years earlier. The old system of values did not fit the new *modern* society well.

Some say that the deconstruction of the old value system started in the middle of the nineteenth century, when the Mexican government expropriated the Catholic Church, but this is not realistic. Despite the big liberal governments' efforts since the 1857 Constitution to establish laicism and counter-balance the influence of the Catholic Church, the impact on the values of the masses was negligible. The process of dismantling the traditional values really started in 1968 with the student movement protests, which ended with the Tlatelolco massacre (the Mexican Tianamen Square), in which troops sent by Miguel Nazar Haro, who was head of the National Security Agency (Policía Federal de Seguridad), fired on student demonstrators. Thirty-six people were killed and over 1,500 jailed. The bottom line is that this violent clash was the first open and extended challenge to the contradictory elements of the official revolutionary ideology. On that occasion, Nobel Prize winner Octavio Paz, then ambassador to India, and Carlos Fuentes, then ambassador to France, resigned in protest. However, references by government officials to *the revolution* continued for twenty years until President Carlos Salinas took office in 1988. The shift in values toward greater accountability of public officials since that time is shown by the fact that finally in 2003 orders for Nazar Haro's arrest were issued and as of January 2004 he was in hiding.

The contradictions within the revolutionary ideology and its distinction from nationalism are important. The Mexican Civil War was not between the North and the South, but between the masses and the elite. That's why it was referred to as a *revolution,* rather than as a war. Being *revolutionary* meant an open preference for peasants, blue collars, lower urban classes, and a detachment from businessmen. Nationalism was also an ingredient, but it was present since before the revolution. The contradictions were built into the 1917 Constitution, because of its origin in concern for the *masses* and its commitment to the rationality (not its agents or institutions) of capitalism. That explains why the Mexican government, trying to escape being labeled, used to say that the country was neither a capitalist nor a communist system, but a *mixed economic* system. The contradictions hidden in those two elements did not show up until the 1968 movement exploded. It highlighted new currents of thinking. The new *counter-intelligentsia* was born.

The weakening of the nationalist ideology started a decade after the Tlatelolco massacres, when Mexico reestablished relations with Spain in 1977 and the anti-Spain governmental rhetoric stopped. When President Miguel de la Madrid (1982–1988) came into power, the anti-U.S. rhetoric by the government decreased rapidly and disappeared as NAFTA negotiations advanced (1990–1994), although anti-U.S. rhetoric continued among union (but not peasant) leaders and some leftist opposition groups. It also continued among faculty and students of the national university (UNAM), but not among those of private universities.

A remarkable trend that is largely neglected in most analyses is the increase of Protestantism in Mexico, at all social levels, which is altering the deepest pillar of the old value system. It is introducing competition for adherents among religion, in addition to providing a beneficial influx of a different value system (Harrison and Huntington 2000). Despite the reestablishing of diplomatic relations with the

Vatican in 1992, Mexican Catholicism is in decline today. It has gone as low as 81 percent of the population (Inglehart et al. 2004), down from the almost totally Catholic society of a few decades earlier. As of today, Catholicism remains at the core of the Mexican value system, but the ideological constructions that validated the old regime—*nationalism* and *revolution*—are weakening by the day.

In summary, the shift in values implied in such a structural change explains why Mexican society started *boiling* increasingly powerfully since 1968. Demands for political, social, and economic change were an outcome of the modern values. However, the media, elections, and the intelligentsia that were supposed to transmit changes in society to the centers of power were severely controlled by the government. The *boiling* brought the country into a cycle crises (1968–1976–1982–1987–1994) centering around the excessive power of the president and his term in office (Basáñez 1993). The vicious cycle finally ended in the year 2000 with the democratic opening implied in President Vicente Fox's victory.

Tracking the Acceleration of Value Change in the Last Twenty Years

For the first time after five decades of sustained economic success, Mexico in 1982 showed a negative economic growth rate. The Mexican economy has receded since. Income per capita in 1981 was $3,486 in constant 1995 dollars; in 2003, it was $3,888 (World Bank 2002). Modernization as a source of structural change stopped in 1982. Nevertheless, economic stagnation in per capita terms became the new engine of structural change, and hence of a shift in values.

Values alone are not in general that relevant to understanding people's attitudes and behavior. Values have to be observed within the system to which they belong. However, some are very useful as they indicate a change in context. That is the case with tolerance, globalization, transparency, and ideal family size, the indicators under analysis below. These four items are taken from the values that show variations of more than 20 percent from 1980 to 2000 in Mexico's World Values Survey rounds (Basáñez and Moreno 2004). A fifth very important indicator that is also rapidly improving in Mexico is gender equality. The change in attitudes toward equal treatment of men and women can only be measured in the last five years, because a question about these attitudes was not included until the WVS round of 1995.

Survey researchers have found that *direct* questions are frequently not the best way to measure values, attitudes, opinions, or facts. Everybody around the world pays lip service to democracy, for instance. Indirect questions often better help us to get the information we need. In Mexico, a better measure of family income in surveys is to ask the number of light bulbs in a home rather than asking for salary levels.

The literature has found powerful predictors that can anticipate political, economic, or social change. That is the case of tolerance as an essential component of and a predictor for democracy. In turn, a highly sensitive item in measuring tolerance is *acceptance of homosexuality*. That explains why countries with high scores on democracy (as measured by the Freedom House Index on political rights and civil liberties) also show more approval of homosexuality. Tolerance of homosexuality shows a 0.804 correlation with democracy (Inglehart 2003). The *geographic group you belong to* serves as an indicator of openness to globalization as opposed to parochialism, which in turn may predict economic integration. Rejection of *cheating on taxes* indicates a shift from corrupt and dysfunctional business practices to a more transparent form of economic modernization. The notion of *ideal family size* is a powerful indicator of demographic trends, and could release social pressure by diminishing population growth. These four values have the potential to anticipate trends of structural change.

The topic of tolerance is measured in the 2000 World Values Survey with the following question, to be answered on a one-to-ten scale: *Please tell me for each of the following statements whether you think it can always be justified, never be justified, or something in between: homosexuality* (v208). On the scale where one means never and ten means always, 53 percent of Mexicans reply one (i.e., never justified). If the answers one to five are added, the disapproval increases to 74 percent. Only a minority approves: 11 percent replied ten (i.e., always justified), but 26 percent approve if the answers six to ten are added. The world scale variation on this question is very wide: from 100 percent disapproval (answer one) in Egypt, to 32 percent in the United States, and the lowest—7 percent—in the Netherlands. The increase in the average score on this question from 1980 to 2000 (2.7 to 3.8) is equivalent to 66 percent, the highest difference of all the 300 variables on the Mexican World Values Survey.

A person's identification with a geographic group is measured with the following question: *To which of these geographical groups would you say you belong first of all? (1) Locality or town where you live; (2) State or region of country where you live; (3) [Mexico] as a whole; (4) [Latin America]; (5) The world as a whole* (v214). Mexicans identified themselves as much with their town (35 percent) as with their country (35 percent); then with the world (16 percent); their state or region (11 percent); and finally Latin America (4 percent). The increase in the average score of this question from 1980 to 2000 (from 1.8 to 2.6) is equivalent to 46 percent, the second highest difference in the Mexican World Values Survey. It is interesting to note that in 1980 only 3 percent felt they belonged to the world as a whole.

The answers to this question can be supplemented by the responses to a question on migration in a poll on migration carried out in May 2003, which could indicate how long this self-identification will be maintained. When asked, *Would you like to migrate to the U.S.?* the answers were: "a lot," 19 percent; "somewhat," 57 percent; "little" 5 percent; "no" 14 percent; and "don't know," 5 percent. In other words, 81 percent said "yes" and 14 percent "no." The group that answered "no" is mainly composed of older people; those who are at the two ends of the educational spectrum, either the illiterate or the post-graduate; and those who live in the Northwest Mexican border states (Alduncin 2003).

The question about cheating on taxes is measured by asking: *Would you cheat on taxes if you have a chance?* On the scale where one means never and ten means always, 69 percent of Mexicans reply one (i.e., never). If the answers one to five are added, the disapproval of cheating increases to 90 percent. Only a tiny minority approves: 4 percent replied ten (i.e., always) and 10 percent approve if the answers six to ten are added. The increase in the mean score of this question in Mexico from 1980 to 2000 is equivalent to 31 percent, the third highest difference in the Mexican World Values Survey.

Finally, the number of children desired is measured in the 2000 World Values Survey with the following question: *What do you think is the ideal size of the family—how many children, if any?* Only 3 percent of Mexicans replied one, 43 percent said two, 35 percent three, but still 19 percent said four or more. However, the decrease on the mean score of this question in Mexico from 1980 to 2000 is equivalent to 23 percent, from 3.6 to 2.8 children per family.

Gender equality is another strong indicator that predicts change. The 2000 World Values Survey asks: *For each of the following statements I read out, tell me how much you agree with each. Do you agree strongly, agree, disagree, or disagree strongly? On the whole, men make better political leaders than women do.* In Mexico, 59 percent disagreed with the statement: 56 percent of men and 62 percent of women. When looked at on a world scale the variation on this question is very wide: from the highest 94 percent disagreement in Iceland, to the lowest 10 percent in Egypt. Religion seems to play an important role in the way women leaders are perceived: from a low 21 percent approval in Islamic countries, to 62 percent in Catholic countries, and the highest, 76 percent, in Protestant countries.

All of the above appears to be good news for Mexico's structural change prospects. Mexicans' tolerance of homosexuality has improved the most in the twenty-year period from 1980 to 2000, which is very positive for democracy. Mexicans' self-identification in a geographic group has clearly moved from local to global. Rejection of cheating on taxes is also a positive sign for business and the economy. Finally, thinking today that the ideal number of children is 2.8 is not that good in terms of overpopulation, but it is much better than thinking it is 3.6. However, values, attitudes, and opinions are not evenly distributed across society. Hence, it is important to look at which groups adhere to the positive trends.

Distribution of Values by Age, Party, Education, Region, and Town Size

Three of the independent variables used in this section (age, education, and town size) serve as predictors of future trends. Age does so because of the natural replacement of the older by the younger generations. Education also does so as long as improvements in educational levels continue. Town size does as well because of the flow of people from smaller to larger cities seeking better opportunities. Political parties and regions used as independent variables also help the analysis. However, for these two variables it is necessary to take into account the relative political

Table 2.1

Values by Age, Party, Education, Region, and Town Size, 2000

Category	v 208 Homosexuality acceptance	v 214 Geographic group	v 206 Cheat on tax	v 108 Ideal family size
Age group				
Under 25	4.6	2.7	2.6	2.5
25–34	3.8	2.5	2.4	2.6
35–44	3.4	2.6	2.5	3.0
45–54	3.0	2.6	2.0	3.0
55–64	3.0	2.5	2.0	3.1
Over 65	2.5	2.2	1.8	3.7
Party identification				
PRI	3.2	2.5	2.3	2.9
PAN	4.1	2.7	2.4	2.8
PRD	3.7	2.5	2.2	2.8
Other	4.8	2.5	2.9	2.7
None	3.5	2.6	2.2	2.9
Education				
Low	3.0	2.4	2.2	3.1
Medium	4.2	2.7	2.5	2.6
High	4.7	3.0	2.1	2.5
Region				
North	3.6	2.6	2.2	3.0
West	3.2	2.3	2.5	3.2
Central	4.0	2.8	2.4	2.7
South	3.1	2.3	2.2	2.8
Town size				
Under 2k	3.0	2.2	2.0	3.4
2k–100k	3.4	2.6	2.6	2.8
100k–500k	3.5	2.8	2.4	2.4
Over 500k	4.5	2.8	2.3	2.7
Total	3.6	2.6	2.3	2.8

Source: Inglehart and Basáñez, 2000 U.S. World Values Survey database, www.globalqr.net, 2000.

strength of the different parties as well as the relative economic size and growth of the regions, and each region's demographic weight.

Prospects for Democracy

The prospects for democracy in Mexico look promising, considering the disaggregation of the increase in tolerance as measured by approval of homosexuality. As Table 2.1, column v208, shows, the younger age group (4.6 mean score) is much more tolerant than the older (2.5 mean score). The way in which tolerance diminishes as people age could lead us to think of an age effect that would neutralize the positive impact of tolerance. However, cohort analysis shows that it is a generational, not an age, effect (Inglehart 1997). The younger generations are becoming consistently more tolerant than the older. The picture is similar with regard to education: higher education (i.e., above high school) predicts higher tolerance (4.7) as compared to lower levels of education (below 9th grade) (3.0). Larger town size, as expected, increases tolerance, which rises from 3.0 in towns with fewer than 2,000 inhabitants to 4.5 in cities of over 500,000. By region (see Table 1.2), the ranking from more to less tolerant is Center (4.0), North (3.6), West (3.2), and South (3.1). The Central region is more cosmopolitan and full of contrasts and the Northern region is more progressive and closer to the United States. On the other end of the ranking, the Western region is more traditional and conservative and the Southern more agricultural, rural, and poor.

When looking at tolerance by political party, it is not surprising that the PRI partisans are the less tolerant (mean score 3.2). The PRI monopoly ruled the country for seventy-two years until losing the national presidency in 2000 to PAN. Its partisans were not really used to competition among political parties. Hence, it is understandable that tolerance was not among the values and attitudes that were relevant for them (Moreno 2003). The second least tolerant political partisans are those that reply *none* to the question about which political party they favor. They are referred to as "NONE" in this chapter. Their score for tolerance was (3.5). The next group is the partisans of PRD (Partido de la Revolución Democrática— Democratic Revolution Party) (3.7), the left-of-center party born after the 1987 PRI split. PAN partisans show a better score (4.0) than most parties, except for the recent and small *other* parties (4.8), which are at the top. Clearly, the small parties appeal to those portions of the electorate that are not attracted by the traditional parties. That part of the electorate unfortunately is still small and divided.

The prospects for democracy do not look very promising when we look at the poor performance in Congress of the party leaders. In particular, the PRI did not take control of its own congressmen during the last weeks of December 2003, and the outcome of their quarrels was a split of the PRI congressmen into two factions and a deadlock that made it impossible to consider or act on the important initiatives they were supposed to discuss before the end of the year. All this illustrates that they are far behind society in their values and actions. In return, public opinion polls show only a 17 percent approval rate for congressmen (Parametría 2003).

Prospects for Economic Integration

The prospects for economic integration in Mexico look promising, considering the disaggregation of the increase in globalization and cosmopolitanism as measured by self-identification with respect to geography. However, prospects do not look promising if attention is paid to political parties and political debates. As

Table 2.1, column v214, shows, the younger age group (2.7 mean score) is more prone to favor globalization than the older (2.2). By education, the picture is similar. Higher education (3.0) predicts higher globalization as compared to lower education (2.4). By town size, responses were that the tendency toward favoring globalization increases from 2.2 in towns with fewer than 2,000 inhabitants to 2.8 in cities of over 500,000. By region, the ranking from more to less support for globalization is Central (2.8), North (2.6), and equal for West and South (2.3). The contrasts in this area are smaller to those in tolerance, but all are consistent and point in the same direction as tolerance.

When looking at attitude toward globalization by political party, the variations are minor. PRI, PRD, and the *other* small parties are all at 2.5. Those that identified with NONE are at 2.6 and PAN partisans at 2.7. This minor variation may signal the lack of attention that political parties pay to economic integration or the fact that political leadership is frankly lukewarm in this respect. It seems as if political leaders are afraid to upset their partisans with the topic because anti-U.S. sentiment is still present in large pockets of population. However, the numbers reviewed in the paragraph above show the need to inform the population and educate them about their opinions as indicated by the survey. The outcry in the Mexican printed press and television and radio news in the first days of 2004 on occasion of the US-VISIT program (which requires providing photographs and fingerprints as you enter the United States) and the tightening of security regulations for air passengers (which requires placing armed police agents on planes to and from Mexico) illustrates the point. Complaints about a violation of Mexico's sovereignty were constantly repeated for many days.

Prospects for Economic Modernization

The prospects for economic modernization in Mexico look contradictory, considering the disaggregation of *transparency* as measured by the decreased acceptance of tax cheating. As Table 2.1, column v206 shows the groups under forty-five years of age (2.5 mean score) accept cheating on taxes more than the older groups (2.0). By education, the picture is better. People with higher and lower levels of education (2.1 and 2.2) accept cheating on taxes less than those who have a medium level of education (between ninth and twelfth grades) (2.5). This trend may reflect an extended culture of cheating of cheating among the middle educated (representatives of the informal economy?). This feature may reflect an unfair fiscal system that rests mainly on the shoulders of the top one-third of the population. The Mexican government mistakenly exempts from tax payment (and hence alienates from a culture of responsibility) the lower two-thirds of the population (see Elizondo chapter in this book). Analysis of attitudes toward cheating on taxes according to town size is similar to analysis by education: acceptance of cheating is less in towns under 2,000 inhabitants (2.0) than in small cities from 2,000 to 100,000 (2.6). However, in middle-size cities transparency improves to 2.4 to further improve to 2.3 in cities over 500,000. By region, the ranking from less to more transparent is similar to what was found in the two topics above. The traditional West (2.5) is less transparent, followed by the powerful Center region (2.4), and equally transparent for the entrepreneurial North and the poor South (2.2). However, the differences on this topic are even smaller than on globalization. Nonetheless, it seems to show that being poor and less educated do not make them more willing to accept cheating on taxes.

When looking at acceptance of cheating on taxes by political party, the variations are minor, except among partisans of *other* small parties (2.9), probably made up of millions living and working in the informal economy. PRD, NONE, PRI, and even PAN partisans are all between 2.2 and 2.4. This ranking may again signal both the lack of attention that political parties pay to fiscal policy and the need to share the expenses of the nation among the whole population. It seems as if political leaders are afraid to upset their partisans with this topic. Yet there is no truth in such a fear. The fear may instead more clearly relate to the loss of economic and possibly illegitimate benefits of the leadership itself.

Prospects for Social Structure Change

The prospects for reducing demographic growth in Mexico look promising, considering the disaggregation of the decrease in population as measured by opinions on ideal family size. As Table 2.1, column v108 shows, the younger age group (preferring 2.5 children) is more aware of family planning than the older age group (3.7 children). The increase in the initial number of children by age is not again an age, but a generational, effect, as described above in the analysis of democracy. The younger generations are decreasing the number of people in their concept of ideal family size. People with higher education (2.5 children) are associated with a lower number of children desired as opposed people with a lower education (3.1). The relation of town size to the size of family desired is that ideal family size decreases from 3.4 children in towns fewer than 2,000 inhabitants to 2.7 in cities over 500,000. However, middle-sized cities of 100,000 to 500,000 show a better score of 2.4. By region, the ranking of preference from smaller to larger families begins in the sophisticated Center region (2.7), then goes to the poor South (2.8), the prosperous North (3.0), and the traditional West (3.2). Unless the scores of South and North regions are a function of economic success, the meaning of their order is not clear. However, the number of children desired in the Central and West regions is consistent with the characteristics of these regions.

When looking at ideal family size by political partisanship, the variations are minor. PAN and PRD are at the 2.8 average score. PRI and NONE partisans are slightly above at 2.9. The *other* partisans are slightly below at 2.7. This may signal the lack of attention political parties pay to the topic, or may be due to clear improvements in the reduction of demographic growth since the mid-1970s.

Final Remarks

Which values are most likely to predominate and influence the changing structure of Mexico? In the *long run* (twenty to thirty years), the trends reviewed above—democratization, economic modernization and integration, and social improvements—are likely to prevail. However, the question now is how to be there in the *short run* and avoid the pain and suffering of another quarter-century of hard times in the current generation. One approach is to explore which values the current political parties promote. As seen above, PRI partisans are less tolerant, more parochial, have an average rejection of cheating, and are more prone to favor larger families. They form a strong *traditional* party. PRD partisans are slightly more open and modern than those of PRI. PAN partisans are more inclined to modern values, but not as much as the partisans of the *other* small parties.

A way to see the balance of power among parties is to look at how many governorships, state legislatures, and city government offices they hold. In those terms the PRI still is dominant, which was confirmed by the mid-term congressional election of July 2003. This balance will probably change as the gubernatorial elections in the next two years take place. However, the most important office is still the national presidency. Therefore, it is relevant to ask how the 2006 presidential election might influence future trends. According to the analysis of values, a victory of the small parties would be the most promising for the modernization of Mexico, but the probability of their victory is tiny.

Next, a PAN victory would also be very promising, according to the analysis of values. It is worth noticing that although President Fox has faced the opposition of Congress throughout his term, which makes it almost impossible to obtain structural legislation changes, he nevertheless enjoys high approval rates: 59 percent approve of his performance (Moreno and Mancillas 2005, 1). His government's performance also receives positive ratings for honesty, fighting poverty, the economy, and U.S.–Mexico relations, but does not receive high ratings for creating employment and fighting corruption.

Up to now, the most popular countrywide potential candidate for president is the former PRD president and current Mexico City mayor, Manuel López Obrador, who enjoys an approval rate of 56 percent (Moreno and Gutiérrez 2005, 6A), far above that of any other potential competitor. The election is still far away (July 2006), but the PRD cannot be disregarded despite its low penetration in many states, its small proportion in Congress, and the current impeachment proceedings against López Obrador. Finally, the PRI is a party with a wide and good menu of candidates, but the network of alliances at the national leadership level, as well as the preference of their partisans, are not promising for modernization.

What then, are the prospects for Mexico's future? An optimistic scenario would be one in which (1) employment and salaries improve, (2) economic and business growth resumes, and (3) democratization accelerates. A "tendency" scenario maintains current levels in these variables. A pessimistic scenario would have all three dimensions worsening. The most probable to happen is the tendency scenario. The other two scenarios seem equally improbable.

To get to the optimistic scenario, the key point is to find the way to reach a sustained economic growth rate of at least 5 percent annually for a long period. This goal requires in turn of a full fiscal and legal overhaul, and the abolishment of monopolies, either business or political. These ideas clearly mean a redistribution of economic, social, and political power. It is not enough that this would be the rational course of action, or a demand by large sectors of the Mexican population for action. Powerful forces with much at stake are affected and hence oppose change. The *culture* of the executive, legislative, and judicial branches of government, the strong political parties, the Catholic Church, the business community, and the powerful unions constitute the heart of the power structure and have not agreed on the form change should take.

References

Alduncin, Enrique. 2003. *Encuesta de Migración*. México: Alduncin y Asociados. May.
Basáñez, Miguel.1993. "Is Mexico Headed Toward Its Fifth Crisis?" In *Political and Economic Liberalization in Mexico: At a Critical Juncture?*, ed. Riordan Roett. Boulder, CO: Lynne Rienner.
Basáñez, Miguel, and Alejandro Moreno. 2004. "Changes in Values in Mexico, 1980–2000: Evidence from the World Values Survey." In *The 2000 World Values Survey Report*, ed. Ronald Inglehart et al., unpublished.
Basáñez, Miguel, and Federico Reyes Heroles. 2003. "Actualización del nacionalismo mexicano." In *En la frontera del imperio*, ed. Rafael Fernández de Castro. Mexico: Ariel.
Harrison, Lawrence, and Samuel Huntington, eds. 2000. *Culture Matters: How Values Shape Human Progress*. New York: Basic Books.
INEGI (Instituto Nacional de Estadística, Geografía e informática). 1986. *Estadísticas históricas de México*. Vol. 1. Mexico: INEGI.
Inglehart, Ronald. 1997. *Modernization and Postmodernization*. Princeton, NJ: Princeton University Press.
———. 2003. "How Solid Is Mass Support for Democracy—and How Can We Measure It?" *PS: Political Science and Politics* 35, no. 1 (January).
Inglehart, Ronald, Miguel Basáñez, Jaime Díez-Medrano, Loek Hallman, and Ruud Luijkx, eds. 2004. *Human Beliefs and Values: A Cross-Cultural Sourcebook Based on the 1999–2002 Values Surveys*. Mexico, D.F.: Siglo XXI.
Inglehart, Ronald, Neil Nevitte, and Miguel Basáñez. 1996. *The North American Trajectory: Cultural, Economic, and Political Ties Among the United States, Canada, and Mexico*. New York: Aldyne de Gruyter.
Moreno, Alejandro. 2003. *El votante mexicano: Democracia, actitudes políticas y conducta electoral*. México: Fondo de Cultura Económica.
Moreno, Alejandro, and Roberto Gutiérrez. 2005. "Dividen votos por regiones," *Reforma*, February 28.
Moreno, Alejandro, and María Mancillas. 2005. "Abre aprobación brecha regional," *Reforma*, March 1.
Parametría. 2003. *Carta Paramétrica*. November 29. México.
Reforma. 2003. December 1.
———. Enfoque. 2003. November 30.
World Bank. 2002. *World Development Indicators*. CD-ROM. World Bank.
World Values Survey. 2000. Available at www.worldvaluessurvey.org.

3

SOLEDAD LOAEZA

Problems of Political
Consolidation in Mexico

Ideally, governments should have democratic electoral processes and efficient administration. Mexico's reforms have opened its economic and political processes. When speedy resolution of conflict is needed, however, the government often has not used formal political procedures but instead, has relied on making pacts among interested parties to design and administer policies to resolve problems, instead of using the legislature to do so. The best-known example is the government sponsored Economic Solidarity Pact of 1987 in which agreement on measures to reduce inflation was reached by unions and business organizations.

Soledad Loaeza argues that continued use of this process has weakened the Mexican government, and that its current problems are a result of this weakness and are not derived from the composition of Congress or the lack of experience of new officials. Pact making and the multiparty system perpetuate both the weakness of the state and the fragmentation of interests that dismantled the earlier more authoritarian political system.

This evaluation is notably consistent with a shift in Mexican political values from 1990 to 2000. Although in 2000 a larger share of Mexicans believed that politics was important in their lives, they were decreasingly interested in discussing politics, belonging to political parties, or joining in legal demonstrations. They increasingly thought new ideas were better than old, and took part in local community action groups on specific issues. The problem of how best to represent individuals and interest groups within the official political system has not yet been resolved.

During the last third of the twentieth century, Mexican economic and political institutions underwent profound transformations. In this period, the last three governments of the hegemonic political party, the Partido Revolucionario Institucional (PRI), in power since 1946,[1] introduced structural reforms that resulted in the opening of the economy and liberalization of markets. In this context, open processes of government decision making were installed and a multiparty system was formed that has limited the dominance of the presidency over the other branches of government. Political pluralism has favored the formation of new forces, some of which have integrated into formal political institutions; a multiparty system has also contributed to the emergence of new political elites.

Today the Mexican economy is one of the most open in the world; moreover, since the middle of the 1990s, the political diversity of Mexican society has been institutionalized in government. In this perspective, the victory of the candidate of the Partido Acción Nacional (PAN), Vicente Fox, in the presidential election of July 2000 was not the beginning of the Mexican transition, but the culmination of the construction of a new regime whose bases had been established by the preceding governments. These economic and political changes were the result of a gradual process that, while lacking the drama that accompanied the end of authoritarian regimes in other Latin American nations, bears a significance that should not be underestimated.

The national and the international contexts favored reform in Mexico. At the beginning of the 1980s the Mexican state faced an unprecedented economic crisis that led to widespread political discontent and the weakening of its traditional bases of support. Stabilization and economic adjustment programs, established in accordance with International Monetary Fund (IMF) guidelines, did not restore solid foundations for economic growth. The Mexican state had not recovered from the crisis when two different international phenomena concurred to increase pressures toward reform: globalization—that is, the transnationalization of economic decisions—and the third wave of democratization that in the nineties swept authoritarian regimes in southern Europe, Latin America, and the former socialist bloc. The Mexican traditional regime was engulfed by both phenomena.

In contrast to the relative support for reform mobilized by the successive Mexican governments of the late twentieth century (Miguel de la Madrid, 1982–1988; Carlos Salinas de Gortari, 1988–1994; Ernesto Zedillo, 1994–2000), Vicente Fox (2000–2006) has met with powerful resistance to his proposed reforms. The democratic legitimacy of President Fox was broadly acknowledged after he was elected in the first widely recognized clean and fair election in contemporary Mexico; paradoxically, this administration has been unable to build the consensus and legislative majorities needed to implement its decisions.

Fox's difficulties have been attributed to the situation of divided government he has faced since the beginning of his term. It is true that the lack of a clear majority for the president's party—the *Partido Acción Nacional,* PAN—in Congress has been a major obstacle to a more fluid decision-making process and for an appropriate implementation of governmental policies. Yet however important the congressional opposition to government policies may be, the weakness of the Mexican state seems a much more powerful obstacle to the success of the Fox administration.

This weakness is the outcome of almost fifteen years of reforms aimed at the reduction of state intervention. President Salinas's main argument in support of the liberal reforms was that a smaller state would be stronger; according to him, the reduction of state economic intervention would increase the state's efficiency and redistributive capacities by concentrating its resources and actions in targeted areas and social groups. His successor, President Zedillo, maintained the continuity of structural reforms; nevertheless, Salinas's argument about the eventual strengthening of the state was replaced by a strong defense of the virtues of the free market that was the hallmark of Zedillo's policies. The strengthening of the private sector has been a priority for Vicente Fox, a line of policy that fits well into the anti-statist traditions of PAN.

In addition to public policies, the erosion of authoritarian institutions fostered the creation and growth of autonomous associations and organizations representing the vast diversity of Mexican society and questioning PRI claims to electoral hegemony. This process of pluralization provided a firm basis for the development of the multiparty system and of a very complex network of nongovernmental associations. However desirable this process may be in terms of democratization, it has also meant a significant rise in the number of political actors that claim to represent legitimate interests seeking to influence decision-making processes. The increase of organized interests has multiplied sources of conflict. This situation challenges the state's abilities to identify the public interest and to represent it in the face of particular interests. To respond to these changes in the political system, since the end of the eighties successive governments have resorted to pact making —*pactismo* in Spanish—among interested parties to design and administer policy in specific areas in order to resolve problems, instead of using the legislature or following established administrative procedures to do so. Although in many cases this has speeded the resolution of conflicts, the use of this process has weakened the Mexican state.

In this chapter it is argued that the weakness of the Mexican state has become a feature of the prevailing institutional arrangement. In the new regime the state does not have the instruments to balance contradictory interests, some of which are better organized and more coherent than the state itself. The internationalization of the economy and the open polity aggravate a situation characterized by fragmented interests and power dispersion.

The Mexican State at the End of the Twentieth Century: From One Weakness to Another, 1982–2000

Until the 1980s, the Mexican state was at the center of an authoritarian institutional arrangement in which government functions were carried out by a highly centralized executive power and a public administration in which decision-making processes were concentrated.

Historically in Mexico, the state was the principal agent of modernization. Within the mixed economic growth model, public investment was greater than private investment only in exceptional circumstances. However, the state designed the model of development and assumed central responsibilities in the promotion and implementation of this model: it constructed the infrastructure needed for industrialization, it was the central protagonist of industrial and agrarian economic policies, government spending was a central component of economic activity, and price and tariff policies were a preferred method for encouraging industrial development. Moreover, since the beginning of industrialization during the 1930s, the state wanted to create a national industrial sector and consequently it assumed the responsibility of aiding it by means of subsidies and protectionist tariffs. Interventionism also signified that it was the responsibility of the state, at least indirectly, to create jobs for a population that almost tripled between 1950 and 2000, growing from less than 40 million to more than 100 million people.

The modernizing action of the state was not limited to the economic sphere, but extended as well to political development, even though its action in this area was relatively limited because it had few available instruments to regulate political representation and participation. These instruments were the electoral process, legislation about this topic, and the hegemonic party.

The formation of the PRI (Partido Revolucionario Internacional) in 1946 was inspired by a concept of democracy that was common enough in the immediate post–World War II period, and that understood this type of regime as a final stage in a gradual evolution that led to political modernization. The electoral hegemony of the official party was a way of negating the political diversity of Mexican society, but it also was a formula for achieving the stabilization and centralization of power that were seen as necessary conditions for successful economic development. From 1940 and until the end of the 1960s, an annual 6.5 percent growth rate of gross domestic product and a rate of inflation that consistently remained under 5 percent were strong evidence of the success of the Mexican system.

The PRI was also an instrument of political modernization that carried out functions of socialization by, in principle, encouraging political attitudes and democratic values among broad groups of the population by means of their integration into formal politics, within a scheme of controlled representation and participation. The hegemonic party was a privileged instrument in the recruitment of bureaucratic and civilian elites. However, the PRI's dependency on the state arrested its institutional development as an independent organization. By the 1970s the PRI was essentially an electoral machine whose basic function was to maintain under control a quasi monopoly of elective offices at the municipal, local, and federal levels. In this system, opposition parties were condemned to be permanent minorities. By virtue of the subordination of the PRI to the state's authority—as incarnated in the president—and of the political irrelevance of the opposition parties (until the mid-seventies there were never more than four), the party system did not represent political cleavages as it does in a democracy, and it played an increasingly minor role in the resolution of political conflict. By contrast, the state remained as the supreme arbiter of political conflict. From this position it exercised a privileged authority in the sphere of political participation and representation. As a result, the crisis of the state had greater consequences for the transformation of the political system than the successive defeats of the PRI.

The Crisis of the Authoritarian State

In 1982 the Mexican state faced a severe financial and political crisis whose effects definitively undermined the legitimacy of state intervention. On September 1 of this year, President José López Portillo (1976–1982) surprisingly announced the expropriation of commercial banks. This decision was a desperate response to a critical financial situation precipitated by the loss of confidence of international credit agencies and of Mexican investors in a government that had incurred an unprecedented amount of international debt based on the euphoria of the oil boom. Despite the fact that this decision to expropriate commercial banks could be inscribed in the authoritarian tradition of the postrevolutionary state, it was also a measure of weakness. In August 1982, Mexico declared a temporary suspension of payments; it was also forced to request an emergency loan from the U.S. government.

The expropriation decision neither aided economic recovery, nor—contrary to appearances—strengthened the state, but instead led to the recognition that the Mexican development model was no longer functional. Four months after taking office, the government of Miguel de la Madrid (1982–1988) had to admit that a restoration of the past was impossible. In December 1982, when he took office, the economic situation of Mexico was chaotic. The budget and the balance of payments registered severe disequilibria, foreign credit was suspended, the terms of trade had deteriorated, and the exchange rate had collapsed. All of this was a prelude to the worst economic crisis that had occurred in Mexico in fifty years: two unprecedented phenomena were combined in a stagflation, in which inflation increased and the economy stagnated. In 1982 the Mexican economy registered a negative growth rate, –0.6 percent, and the rate of inflation was 99 percent; in 1983 economic growth had a catastrophic level, –5.2 percent.

In these very restrictive conditions, the state could not continue to function as an agent of economic and social change as it had during the long period of authoritarian regime, which had sustained the idea that the state was a key democratizing agent. The corollary of this idea had been "more state, more democracy." The expropriation decision of September 1, 1982, brutally overturned this assumption. In the eyes of many Mexicans, the decision to expropriate and its authoritarian imposition on economic agents was evidence that the state was the main obstacle to achieving democracy. An anti-statist current of opinion emerged that acquired momentum in the following decade. This movement was one of the strongest bases of support for the Partido Acción Nacional, which, starting in 1985, began to accumulate local electoral victories, particularly in the most developed states. This was the beginning of a powerful process of political decentralization by which local elites undertook an electoral offensive aimed at the dismantling of PRI hegemony and in defense of municipal autonomy and of the federal states' sovereignty against imposition from Mexico City.

Fragmentation of Interests, Pact Making, and the Multiparty System

The economic weakness of the authoritarian state also reduced its capacity for political leadership; thus decentralization of power began in the 1980s. The result was a process of pluralization that uncovered the diversity of interests of a society whose complexity manifested itself in an authentic explosion of independent organizations and participation.

The first real step in transforming the political functions of the state took place in the process of decision making. Between 1983 and 1987 the de la Madrid government had scrupulously complied with the stabilization strategy dictated by the International Monetary Fund. A drastic reduction in public spending and an increase in public sector prices and rates were unilaterally adopted by the government because these matters were under its exclusive responsibility and did not have to be negotiated with economic agents. In 1983, public spending fell by 17 percent. However, at the end of four years of fruitless efforts at controlling a rate of inflation that in 1987 reached 106 percent in the midst of a severe economic recession, and faced with the growing deterioration that equally damaged businesses and salaries, the government reverted to a heterodox stabilization plan that proposed the coordination between government and nongovernment economic actors: the Economic Solidarity Pact (Pacto de Solidaridad Económica, PSE). By adopting this mechanism the government acknowledged implicitly that state autonomy was not sustainable in conditions of financial bankruptcy; it also recognized that the state did not have the power nor the ability to impose unilateral decisions, such as the expropriation of banks. From then on policy making and policy implementation would have to be negotiated and agreed between State and non-State actors.

The main purpose of the PSE was to build a consensus between economic actors—unions and business organizations—regarding increases in salaries and prices, with the ultimate aim of controlling inflation. Although originally it was an emergency formula, soon the Pacto was institutionalized: an administrative commission was created (Comisión de Seguimiento) to supervise the compliance with the agreements that were revised for adjustment every three months. Until 1992, when the pact ended, the commission met thirty-two times. The Pacto was almost immediately successful: in less than six months inflation fell by 80 percent. Even more, in the meetings of the Pacto, the participants did not limit themselves to revising the behavior of prices and salaries, but extended their discussions to suggestions related to structural reforms.

The new formula of cooperation rested on the implicit recognition that none of the economic actors, not even the state, could impose its decisions on the others, and neither could any of these actors make them effective by themselves. Consensus building among the economic actors was based on their respective weakness. The principle of cooperation or coordination on which the PSE rested was the basis of negotiations, of adjustment of conflicting interests, and of concessions among distinct groups, and therefore, it was very far from the unilateralism that had been characteristic of the authoritarianism of the past. The pact-making formula was also a mechanism of responding to the fragmentation that was occasioned by the dismantling of the authoritarian state. For example, for unions who traditionally had been represented by the PRI, pact making was an efficient alternative in the face of the loss of legitimacy of the hegemonic party.

The experience gained by the PSE opened the doors to public debate and the redefinition of the borders between the public and the private, as well as to the discussion of the responsibility of the state and of the participation of nongovernmental actors in the processes of the definition and decision making of government policies. The consultations between the government and the private sector, which now no longer were uniquely with entrepreneurs but with numerous private interest groups, were intense and consistent during the 1990s. Thus relative horizontality was instilled in the relationships between the state and the new actors, and short-term alliances were constructed between groups that shared common interests.

The principles and mechanisms of the PSE were a model for the negotiations that President Carlos Salinas engaged in with relevant economic and political actors to generate consensus about structural reforms in the 1990s. The pact-making experience became a standard for the negotiation of constitutional amendments referring to land ownership, the legal status of religious denominations, and to privatization and trade liberalization policies. For example, the North American Free Trade Agreement (NAFTA) was a matter of intense lobbying, negotiations, debates, and consultations among export businesses, workers' organizations, businessmen, academics, journalists, and opinion makers, among others.

Pact making, or *pactismo,* is a compelling formula of cooperation that deactivates conflict and encourages negotiations among political or economic actors; it facilitates agreement by liberating the negotiating parties from the constraints of party or parliamentary rules and mechanisms. It is a flexible mechanism that lends itself to pragmatic solutions that temporarily stabilize emergency situations.

The formula of cooperation and negotiation of the PSE also was appropriate to deal with the multiplication and diversification of political actors that eroded the PRI hegemony. The official party encountered the first serious electoral challenges to its dominance over elective offices at the local level in December 1982; in the following years this type of challenge was extended to broad regions where opposition parties, especially PAN, were gaining influence.

Parallel to the strengthening of party opposition, the eighties witnessed a powerful social mobilization that gave rise to a multitude of associations that threatened the development of political parties and electoral processes. The origin of these movements can be traced to the traumatic earthquakes that destroyed large zones of Mexico City in September 1985. To respond to the emergency situation the residents of the devastated areas of Mexico City organized themselves, independently from the government or PRI-led organizations, to aid the victims, compensating for the inability of the government to react promptly to the tragedy.

It is noteworthy that from this time forward, these new political actors avoided going through the PRI, because, among other reasons, the economic crisis and the reduction of public expenditure had significantly and inevitably diminished the resources the party needed to maintain its clientelistic networks. In fact, in order to attend to the requirements of aid for the victims of the earthquake, the representatives of the de la Madrid government met with the leaders of the organizations that had been formed by families and residents to define programs of reconstruction and compensation in a scheme that could be seen as a precedent for the PSE. What is important is that the experience of independent organization of the inhabitants of Mexico City encouraged the growth of similar mobilizations in the rest of the country.

Thus, between 1980 and 2000, the Mexican political universe expanded into a myriad of particular interest groups, private organizations, and nongovernmental organizations that, at the margin of the political parties, required government attention, claiming to represent social groups and the right to participate in making decisions that affected their interests. The political reforms were concentrated in the electoral and party areas; they only indirectly referred to this variegated constellation of political actors of different sizes and capacities to influence decisions.

From the 1980s, pactismo became a central resource for conflict resolution, mostly when nongovernmental, nonparty organizations were involved. Many of these groups have resisted integration into formal political processes by instead using the traditions of popular mobilization and direct democracy, and also because they have verified that ad hoc negotiations are more expeditious and effective than normal legislative or administrative processes.

In many cases the same negotiating mechanisms have justified noncompliance with the law; this has repeatedly been the case in postelectoral conflicts that have been resolved by means of political negotiations, to the detriment of legal methods. This occurred in Guanajuato and in San Luis Potosí in 1991, where the electoral victories of PRI were questioned by PAN, but instead of submitting the controversy to the legally constituted authorities, a solution was negotiated by President Salinas and the leaders of the opposition. In both cases, the PRI candidate who had been declared the winner was forced to renounce his victory.

These and other similar experiences explain the reluctance of the Zapatista National Liberation Army (Ejército Zapatista de Liberación Nacional—EZLN), which became known to the public on January 1, 1994, to integrate itself into formal political processes. The EZLN has maintained its capacity to influence politics for a decade because it has insisted that its demands be attended to in extra-constitutional and extra-parliamentary negotiations. It is clear that these have not yielded results; however, it is also clear that none of the three presidents who have been faced with this problem (Salinas, Zedillo, and Fox) have been able to convince the Zapatistas to openly integrate themselves into the institutional framework.

The government of President Vicente Fox has been very vulnerable to pressures from nongovernmental actors who resort to informal mechanisms to protest against certain decisions, and have thereby been able to modify them even if they are not able to reverse them. For example, in the spring of 2002, after years of planning and in order to respond to the increasing limitations of the Mexico City airport, construction began on an alternate international airport, in San Salvador Atenco in the state of Mexico. Work was suspended a few days after it had begun, because of pressure by a group of farmers who organized to reject the initial offer by the government for the purchase of their land. The decision to construct the airport was reversed in negotiations between the government and representatives of the protesting organizations in spite of prior commitments to investors and construction firms, and in spite of the loss that this decision signified for the government. As a result, instead of strengthening the regulatory functions of the state, as the sole actor responsible for the maintenance of legal order, pact making has undermined its institutional authority. Even worse, it generates a permanent tension with the party system, because it has become a rival to this system for the organization and representation of citizens. The inability of government authorities to assure the rule of law is a major manifestation of the weakness of the state.

The multiparty system has also eroded the political leadership of the state and its capacity to administer and resolve conflicts. True, its development has been the most palpable achievement of democratization. In 1997, Mexican political pluralism was a reality that was expressed in the diversity of local governments and of congressional representation: in this year the PAN and PRD (Partido de la Revolución Democrática) held altogether more than 50 percent of the seats in the Chamber of Deputies, and half of Mexicans were living in communities governed by a party other than the PRI. Until now the Mexican electorate has tended to concentrate its votes in three large parties: PRI, PAN, and PRD. Smaller organizations, such as the Partido del Trabajo (PT), the Partido Verde Ecologista de México (PVEM), and the Partido de Convergencia Democrática (PCD) are also represented in Congress. These parties are eligible to receive public funding and to be placed on the national ballot on the basis of their share of at least 2.5 percent of the national vote.

Today in Mexico political parties are the object of bitter criticism as in all parts of the world. Observers and analysts allege that political parties are the main obstacle to the efficient implementation of the policies of the Fox government, as neither the president nor his party have been able to build a congressional majority and reach agreements on proposed reforms, even when their urgency is widely recognized. President Fox himself has reproached the political parties for the paralysis of the government and the blocking of decision implementation.

In the nineties, political parties in Mexico became the central players of the politi-

cal game, performing the functions of organization and control of political representation and participation that in the past were monopolized by the state. Political
parties have absorbed many of the shocks of the economic reforms, and they have
checked presidential power; they have also stabilized political relations and have
been effective agents of cooperation and negotiation. The political importance of the
parties was consolidated in 2000, with the success of the presidential election. Even
though they did not receive any credit for the crucial role that they played in the
organization of the electorate and of the competition among the candidates for Congress and for the presidency, it is unquestionable that political parties fulfilled a
stabilizing function that was crucial to the success of the election.

The developments in the political system associated with the consolidation of
political pluralism were desirable and are a democratic characteristic of the new
political regime. Nevertheless, the participation of these parties in decision making has suffered from the dispersion that is inherent in the existence of multiple
political actors; their increased participation in policy making may explain the
instability of agreements. For example, the implementation of the legislative reforms concerning indigenous communities has been blocked by the PRD, which
refuses to recognize them as long as Congress refuses to grant these communities
full autonomy with respect to the federal state.

*Internationalization: An Obstacle for the Consolidation of
the New Regime*

One of the outstanding characteristics of the end of the twentieth century was the
growing imprecision of the borders between the international and local systems.
Thus, democracies of the fourth wave of democratization are polities open to the
influence of international actors. This is one of the most powerful challenges that
these regimes confront today. At the beginning of the democratization process the
international context had a positive impact on the dismantling authoritarianism;
however, twenty years later, internationalization limits the options of a weakened
national state that has a tenuous control over many of the variables that impact
consolidation, such as interest fragmentation and power dispersion.

In 1985 Mexico became a signatory of the General Agreement on Tariffs and
Trade (GATT). This was an important step toward the building of an export-oriented
economy. Since then every government has sustained the continuity of this trade
liberalization policy. In 1991 it was furthered by the signing of the North American Free Trade Agreement with Canada and the United States, NAFTA. Also, financial markets were liberalized. After 1995, foreign direct investment, FDI, became
dominant in the banking system.

In 2000, the government of Ernesto Zedillo, the last president elected as a candidate of the PRI, concluded its term of office with self-congratulatory announce-
ments that in Mexico free trade was the "key factor of economic growth." Until
then, in addition to NAFTA, Mexico had signed free trade treaties with Bolivia,

Colombia, Venezuela, Costa Rica, Nicaragua, the European Union, El Salvador, Guatemala, and Honduras. According to official figures, between 1989 and 1999 Mexican exports quadrupled, while imports increased by 300 percent. President Zedillo considered that the amount of FDI was a measure of the success of his economic policy, and believed that exports were a fundamental pillar of economic growth and of job creation.

The internationalization of the Mexican economy inevitably has affected the position and power of internal actors. For example, if economic growth depends on FDI, the foreign investors' ability to influence the definition of investment or financial policy increases considerably, just as the importance of foreign trade in the behavior of the economy has strengthened the position of exporters in the process of making economic decisions. Contrastingly, the state does not yet have many of the instruments that it used in the past to define the general lines of industrial or regional development (see chapters 7 and 17). Moreover, one of the basic characteristics of the new development model is that state authority is secondary in some of the areas of decision making that in the past were considered its exclusive responsibility—for example, those decisions relating to the rules of foreign trade, production for export, or the emission of money.

The internationalization of the economy does not uniquely refer to trade policy and it did not begin with Mexico's adhesion to the GATT. In the 1980s, the rescue and stabilization programs and the reforms promoted by the IMF (International Monetary Fund) and the World Bank favored the transfer abroad of the decision-making processes that were related to decentralization, regional autonomy, the privatization of government firms and services, and the deregulation of the financial sector. These reforms were not seeking to restore the federal government's decision-making power. Thus, the present situation of the Mexican state could be seen as a success of these policies.

The internationalization of the political system began in 1977 when the government of President López Portillo introduced a political reform whose basic objective was the promotion of a multiparty system in Mexico. For the first time in the twentieth century, the model that would guide political development was not inspired by the Mexican Revolution, but by the Spanish Law of Political Associations of 1976 that was voted by the Spanish Cortes after the death of Francisco Franco. Similar to the conditions that ruled in Spain at that time, where the new law was designed in conformity with the juridical regime of the Franco government that was still in effect, the Mexican government proposed to develop a multiparty system within the framework of the authoritarian regime in place. The goals of the new Mexican electoral law—the Ley Federal de Organizaciones, Procesos y Participación Electorales, LOPPE—were seemingly limited, since it proposed to support the founding and development of opposition parties. However, the new legislation was very ambitious in that it pursued the transformation of radical political ideas and strategies of guerrilla movements that had appeared throughout Mexico in the seventies, in order to integrate them into the institutional framework.

The opening of the political system to foreign influence was also a gradual process that began in the mid-eighties when PAN, the main opposition party at the time, took advantage of the weakness of the de la Madrid government in the face of international pressures to advance its own cause. In 1986, based on a post-electoral conflict regarding the election of the governor of Chihuahua, the members of PAN defended their claims of victory by mobilizing support from the Organization of American States (OAS), as well as from the U.S. Embassy, the Republican party, and the international media. From then on, the change of political regime, which historically had been by definition a national process, was open to the participation of a broad constellation of political actors that included foreign governments, nongovernmental organizations and agencies, and the media. In the midst of the fourth wave of democratization, the participation of international actors in local processes was deemed a factor of democratization that could not be rejected by national governments. This truism of the late twentieth century was particularly important for the Mexican government, for which a good image abroad was indispensable for Mexico's insertion into the process of globalization.

When the liberalizing reforms were first launched, it was believed that the close interaction between the international system and economic and political national regimes would guarantee the continuity of the new regimes and of liberal policies. However, the political problems that have recently erupted in Argentina, Bolivia, Haiti, and Venezuela are symptomatic of the weakness that afflicts institutions and policies identified with external influences.

The increasing discontent with foreign influence in processes that in the past were seen as pertaining to the exclusive realm of national sovereignty is a growing threat to the democratic experience in Latin America. In the spring of 2004, the United Nations released a report that analyzes the future of democracy in the region. Similarly to other Latin American nations, in Mexico regime change has occurred in the context of social deterioration that is a menace for the continuity of the new regime. The same report pointed out that the region's persistant poverty and the highest levels in the world of inequality in the distribution of income contradict the claims of success of the liberalizing reforms, and suggest that dissatisfaction in Latin America is not directly related to the performance of democratic institutions, but instead to the unfulfilled promises of economic reform. This is an important differentiation. It indicates that the democratic ideals and attitudes have survived the frustration that, on the other hand, inspires the economic reforms that have not resulted in better long-term economic performance nor have reduced the Latin American propensity for recurring economic and financial crises.

Diverse findings of the report suggest that in the eyes of a large percentage of Latin Americans, many of the economic ills of the region are associated with international actors more than with the democratic institutions themselves. In recent times a powerful anti-U.S. sentiment has led to reactions opposing internationalization. In a recent article in *Current History*, Michael Shifter indicated that the lack of confidence in and resentment toward the United States dominated Latin

American attitudes. A survey by Zogby International in 2003 revealed that 87 percent of opinion makers in six Latin American nations had a poor opinion of President George W. Bush. In Shifter's interpretation, the war in Iraq is the basis of the growing anti-U.S. sentiment in the region. However, there are more indicators that the association of Washington with the economic reforms that it energetically promoted in the region increases the Latin American resentment against the United States. Thus, the United States has become once again associated with poverty, exploitation, and policies that hurt the people.

These attitudes are also present in Mexico. The leftists organized in the PRD have recently gained ground following a strategy of rejection of liberal reforms, the so-called Washington Consensus, and the politics of privatization and opening of markets that, according to this party, have been a source of corruption, concentration of, and aggravation of social inequalities. All of these themes are topics of a populist discourse that could take anti-imperialist paths, as occurred in Bolivia and Venezuela. This discourse could encourage a nationalist reaction that would reanimate the populist authoritarianism of the past.

Conclusion

The importance of understanding the origin of the difficulties of the Fox government lies in the fact that its success—or failure—will determine the future of the liberal and pluralist regime that was constructed at the end of the twentieth century.

It has been argued here that President Fox's problems do not derive from temporary circumstances such as the composition of Congress or the lack of experience of new officials; the government's difficulties derive from the weakness of the Mexican state. This weakness is a stable condition of the new institutional arrangement and not a more or less transitory situation. It is the outcome of more than fifteen years of anti-statist policies and of the emergence of a powerful current of independent organization and mobilization. In this sense it is argued that pact making and the multiparty system increase the fragility of new institutions because they perpetuate the weakness of the state, as well the fragmentation of interests.

The recent Mexican experience suggests that neither the market nor the political parties have been able to supply the essential functions that the state carried out in the past in regard to redistribution and in the orientation of economic and political processes. Nor has the state developed the capacity to identify and defend the public interest in a context of growing influence of particular interests. In these conditions, fragmentation is an obstacle for the stabilization of predictable and consistent decision-making processes.

Finally, the growing criticism by broad sectors of public opinion of the results of the reforms should be a reminder of the fragility of institutions and policies of an open polity. For Mexico the main challenge of the future lies in the need to overcome the fragility that weighs upon the consolidation of the changes that have led to democratization of policy making, namely, political pluralism and administrative decentralization. However, this undertaking would not be free of contradiction and conflict. Liberal reforms were politically divisive. Strategies of consolidation can be equally disruptive, even more so when bringing the state back in is a likely strategy for all of those who believe that the state is the only institution that has the potential to develop the political and social authority needed to protect the open polity.

Notes

This article was written while the author was Radcliffe Fellow at Harvard University in the academic year 2003–2004. For more extensive treatment of this topic, see the author's forthcoming "La transition de l'etat mexicain. D'une faiblesse à l'autre" in *La Gouvernance*, ed. Guy Hermet and Jean Francois Prud'homme (Paris: Editions Karthala, 2004).
    1. The PRI was established in January 1946. It succeeded earlier versions of the same political party: in March 1929, the Partido Nacional Revolucionario (PNR), and in 1938 the Partido de la Revolución Mexicana (PRM) had been founded. The three formulations had a common dependency on the state; however, they are distinguished by important differences in function, ideology, and organization. Partido Acción Nacional (PAN), was founded in 1939. During the PRI hegemony, PAN was perceived as the only independent party, whereas Partido Popular Socialista (PPS), founded in 1948, and Partido Auténtico de la Revolución Mexicana (PARM), founded in 1954, were always seen as subordinate to the PRI. Neither of these two parties survived the political reforms of the late seventies. The Communist Party, founded in 1920, participated for the first time in an electoral process in 1979. In 1982 it became the Partido Socialista Unificado de Mexico (PSUM); in 1986 this organization became the Partido Mexicano Socialista (PMS); this in turn provided the basis for the Partido de la Revolución Democrática (PRD), in 1989. The Partido del Trabajo (PT), 1990, the Partido Verde Ecologista de México (PVEM), 1986, and the Partido de Convergencia Democrática (PCD), 1997, were organized within the framework of democratization.

References

Alba, Carlos. 2002. "México después del TLCAN. El impacto económico y sus consecuencias políticas y sociales." *Foro Internacional* 43, no. 1.
Armijo, Leslie Elliott, and Philippe Faucher. 2002. "'We Have a Consensus': Explaining Political Support for Market Reforms in Latin America." *Latin American Politics and Society* 44, no. 2 (Summer).
Aspe, Pedro. 1993. *Economic Transformation the Mexican Way*. Cambridge: MIT Press.
Baer, M. Delal, and Sidney Weintraub, eds.1994. *The Nafta Debate: Grappling with Unconventional Trade Issues*. Boulder and London: Lynne Rienner.
de la Madrid H., Miguel, with Alejandra Lajous. 2004. *Cambio de rumbo*. México, D.F.: Fondo de Cultura Económica.
Heredia, Blanca. 1996. "State–Business Relations in Contemporary Mexico." In *Rebuilding the State: Mexico after Salinas,* ed. Mónica Serrano and Victor Bulmer-Thomas. London: Institute of Latin American Studies, London University.
Hojman, David E. 1994, "The Political Economy of Recent Conversions to Market Economics in Latin America." *Journal of Latin American Studies* 26, no. 1.

Kessler, Timothy P. 1999. "Capital político: política financiera mexicana durante el gobierno de Salinas." *Foro Internacional* 39, nos. 2–3.

Loaeza, Soledad. 1999. *El Partido Acción Nacional, la larga marcha, 1939–1994: Oposición leal y partido de protesta.* México, D.F.: Fondo de Cultura Económica.

Lustig, Nora. 1998. *Mexico. The Remaking of an Economy.* Washington, DC: Brookings Institution Press.

Middlebrook, Kevin J. 1989. "The Sounds of Silence: Organised Labour's Response to Economic Crisis in Mexico." *Journal of Latin American Studies* 21, no. 2.

Roxborough, Ian. 1992, "Inflation and Social Pacts in Brazil and Mexico." *Journal of Latin American Studies* 24, no. 3.

Shifter, Michael. 2004. "The U.S. and Latin America Through the Lens of Empire." *Current History* 103 (February).

II

Current Policy Issues

4

PAMELA K. STARR

Mexican Foreign Policy

Mexico's foreign policy reflects a basic change in its citizens' attitudes and the nation's integration into a new world order. Traditionally, many Mexicans identified with their locality rather than the nation. The number of Mexicans who identified themselves as first belonging to the world rather than to a smaller unit increased from 12.3 percent in 1980 to 18 percent in 1990 and 19 percent in 2000. This coincides with Mexico's opening to greater world trade and investment, and to the surprising fact that although in 1990, 28 percent of Mexicans had a lot of confidence in their government, in 2000 while 37 percent had a great deal of confidence in the government, some 46 percent had a great deal of confidence in the United Nations, as indicated in their answers to the Human Beliefs and Values Survey.

This shift in attitudes is consistent with shifts in Mexican foreign policy from its pre-1985s focus on the United States and its support of revolutionary regimes to its mid-1980s low-key foreign policy that would not threaten U.S. willingness to help minimize the costs of Mexico's 1982 economic crisis. Mexico's increasing opening to trade and investment was accompanied by the strengthening of its alliances with other Latin American nations in forming the Contadora Group to demand a negotiated solution to Central America's civil wars, signing several free trade treaties in the 1990s, as well as in sponsoring regional representation in international forums.

The decline of the Partido Revolucionario Institucional (PRI) and the U.S. preoccupation with terrorism between 1995 and 2003 made it difficult to define and implement Mexican foreign policy. Mexico's new democracy reinforced its support for human rights and democracy in Latin America while proposing the broadening of NAFTA (North American Free Trade Agreement) to an arrangement similar to the European Union, with a bilateral migration agreement as the first step toward this goal.

Pamela K. Starr writes that the Fox administration overestimated the extent to which democratization in Mexico would create shared interests with the United States, and that "Mexico's deep and asymmetrical economic dependence on the United States combined with a deep-seated national mistrust of the United States guarantees that Mexico will continue its efforts to diversify its foreign interactions."

The history of Mexican foreign policy is that of a poor country with limited international interests and living on the border of a great power with a demonstrated predilection for intervening in Mexican affairs. The United States absorbed half of Mexican territory following the Mexican-American War (1846–1848) and serious U.S. politicians later proposed annexing even more. In the twentieth century, the United States occupied Mexico's principal port of Veracruz, unilaterally ordered its army onto Mexican soil in search of a Mexican rebel leader (Francisco "Pancho" Villa), and repeatedly exploited its superior economic and military might to pressure the Mexican government to adopt policies favorable to U.S. interests. The United States ceased this direct intervention in Mexico at the outset of World War II, but the scar it left on the bilateral relationship and its resulting impact on Mexican foreign policy remains to this day.

This reality shaped the core characteristics of Mexican foreign policy: legalistic, concentrated on the United States in fact, but rhetorically diversified. The way in which these three drivers of Mexico's international affairs have been translated into policy positions, however, has varied significantly during the past two generations: from an activist foreign policy to a more passive approach and back again; from the support of revolution abroad to support for human rights and democracy; and from keeping the "Colossus of the North" at arm's length to a much closer relationship with the United States. This chapter will explain both the core continuity and the evident policy change in Mexican foreign policy during the past two generations.

The Foundations of Mexican Foreign Policy

The historically sharp power differential between Mexico and its northern neighbor has profoundly influenced Mexican foreign policy (Domínguez and Fernández de Castro 2001). Unable to corral the United States by force, Mexico has relied on a set of moral principles that, when respected, would help restrain the behavior of the United States. Gradually these principles—self-determination, nonintervention, and the peaceful resolution of disputes—became enshrined as the rules of behavior governing the members of international institutions such as the United Nations and the Organization of American States. The result has been a moral and legal pressure that on occasion has limited the U.S. freedom of foreign policy action and thereby advanced Mexican national interests.

Alongside this principled foreign policy, Mexican geographic reality has also dictated a cooperative relationship, albeit one often hidden behind a more conflictive public stance, with its northern neighbor on a wide variety of issues of bilateral importance—from managing migration, to border security, water disputes, and economic integration. Given Mexico's deep economic dependence on the United States and the inevitable appearance of bilateral problems between two countries with a 3,000-mile border, working pragmatically with the United States has always been essential.

Finally, Mexico's weak and vulnerable position relative to the United States has informed a persistent Mexican effort to diversify its economic and political interactions away from the United States. This strategy of "diversification" has traditionally focused on Europe and Latin America, although it recently has incorporated some Asian countries a well, and it has relied on the United Nations, trade treaties, and ad hoc regional organizations for its implementation. At the end of the day, diversification has been uniformly unsuccessful in real terms—Mexico's international interactions remain as concentrated with the United States as ever— but highly successful psychologically—Mexico is eternally hopeful that this dependence can and will fade.

Foreign Policy Activism

Mexico's traditionally passive and defensive foreign policy during the post–World War II period underwent a marked change beginning in the 1960s. From the 1960s through the mid-1980s, Mexican foreign policy was characterized by two overlapping objectives—supporting revolutionary regimes during the Cold War and keeping the United States at a very long arm's distance—pursued in an increasing activist manner over time. This strategy was informed and enabled by the economic and political context, both within Mexico and in the world, in which it developed. When these circumstances changed, the supporting framework for this policy approach crumbled, and Mexico was forced to rethink its foreign policy goals.

Three economic factors helped to shape Mexican foreign policy from 1960 to 1985: the absence of globalization in the world economy, Mexico's inward-oriented economic model, and beginning in the 1970s, Mexico's newfound oil wealth. A world economy lacking significant movement of goods internationally provided few incentives for developing countries to embrace the world economy as the motor of economic growth (the amount of world production that is traded increased from 25 percent in 1960 to nearly 40 percent in 1980). Mexico, like other developing nations, chose to make the domestic market the axis of economic development and to restrict its integration with the world economy. Mexico's resulting relative economic independence from world markets (although the Mexican economy did not depend on trade, it did rely on foreign direct investment) made it much easier to ignore investor concerns in the formation of foreign policy and thus to pursue more revolutionary objectives. The discovery of huge oil reserves and the international lending it enticed during the 1970s reinforced Mexico's economic independence and provided the resources needed to underwrite an activist foreign policy. Not only did oil wealth increase Mexico's independence from the United States, for the first time in Mexican history it gave the country the capacity to support its allies with economic assistance.

Alongside this economic context enabling "revolutionary autonomy" in Mexican foreign policy, Mexico's ruling party (PRI) created the political incentive to pursue this policy; as an authoritarian government (the PRI governed Mexico continually from 1929–2000) the PRI could derive only a limited degree of legitimacy in the eyes of the Mexican population through Mexico's regularly held but often rigged elections. As the descendent of the forces that won the Mexican Revolution of 1913–1917, the PRI could legitimate its rule by living up to the ideals of a revolution fought against the Mexican economic elite that had close ties to the United States. Supporting revolution abroad and demonstrating Mexico's independence from the United States were extremely useful instruments for legitimating one-party rule in Mexico, especially as economic problems began to mount during the 1960s.

The Cold War and U.S. toleration created the means by which Mexico could pursue a foreign policy defined by "revolutionary autonomy" without damaging its all-important bilateral relationship with the United States. The Cold War created a predictable framework within which Mexico could stake out a position independent of the United States but never at odds with its neighbor's core security needs. For example, Mexico commonly defied the United States on individual policy issues but it never crossed the line between irritant and strategic threat by formally declaring its neutrality in the Cold War. The United States was willing to tolerate this behavior for three reasons: (1) the recognized importance of an independent, revolutionary foreign policy to the legitimacy of the PRI and hence to political stability in Mexico; (2) the need for political stability on the U.S. frontier during the Cold War; and (3) the predictable limits of Mexican "disloyalty" to the United States.

The opportunities and incentives inherent in this political-economic context shaped the manner in which Mexico advanced the three driving principles of its foreign policy. For twenty-five years, Mexican foreign policy was defined by an increasingly activist support of revolutionary regimes abroad and rhetorical distancing from the United States. At the heart of this policy was Mexico's support of revolutionary Cuba. Mexico was the only Latin American country to oppose the economic embargo against Cuba and Cuba's expulsion from the Organization of American States (OAS), and to maintain diplomatic relations with the Castro regime throughout the 1960s.

As the PRI's need to use foreign policy to maintain its legitimacy as well as its oil wealth grew during the 1970s, Mexico's pursuit of "revolutionary autonomy" became increasingly activist. During the 1970s, Mexico adopted a series of positions that directly challenged U.S. policy. It took up the leadership of developing country efforts to require rich countries to transfer more economic resources to poor countries. This effort culminated in the 1974 approval by the United Nations General Assembly of the "Charter of Economic Rights and Duties of States," which established rules of international economic behavior that were supposed to lead to increased transfers of wealth from rich countries to poor ones (Grayson 1988; Shapira 1978).

In 1975, Mexico led the charge in the Organization of American States to lift the economic and diplomatic embargo against Cuba and strongly supported revolutionary regimes wherever they came to power in Latin America. Mexico supported the government of Salvador Allende in Chile and gave asylum to its supporters following the 1973 coup that overthrew it. Mexico backed the Sandinista rebels in Nicaragua during the late 1970s, immediately recognized their new government in July 1979, helped them with sharply discounted sales of petroleum, and strongly opposed U.S. efforts to overthrow the Sandinistas during the 1980s. Mexico also worked with France to find a negotiated solution to the civil war in El Salvador, in direct opposition to the U.S. preference for a military victory by the Salvadorian government in its war against leftist rebels.

At this moment, at the height of Mexico's activist pursuit of "revolutionary autonomy," one of the key economic supports for this policy buckled—Mexico's oil-based economic independence. Collapsing oil prices and rising international interest rates erased Mexico's economic surplus and forced an effective default on its foreign debt in 1982. Mexico now lacked the economic resources to finance an activist foreign policy. Worse, Mexico needed the active support of the United States to minimize the economic costs of default. As Mexico lost the economic freedom with which it might "tweak the Empire's nose," however, the country's economic crisis magnified the domestic legitimation needs of the PRI. The shifts in Mexican foreign policy toward Central America during the mid-1980s reflected this new political-economic context.

Economically unable to sustain its activist policy in Central America, yet politically unable to abandon it, Mexico needed to find a more nuanced means to advance its interest in a peaceful solution to the expanding conflicts on its southern border. The solution was the formation of the Contadora Group, an alliance of Latin American nations that supported Mexico's demand for a negotiated solution to Central America's civil wars. The alliance enabled Mexico to lower its profile and thereby reduce the risk of angering the United States without sacrificing either its core foreign policy interests or the legitimation needs of the PRI.

Transitioning to a New Foreign Policy

As the 1980s progressed, it gradually became apparent that globalization had changed the calculus for economic development and that Mexico's inward-oriented economic model was no longer viable. With the end of the Cold War at the close of the 1980s, four of the six political-economic supports for "revolutionary autonomy" in Mexican foreign policy had disappeared, leaving only the PRI's legitimation needs and the U.S. toleration of Mexican foreign policy autonomy in force. It is not surprising, therefore, that the content of Mexican foreign policy began to change as well.

The opening of the world economy to an increased flow of goods and services made it increasingly costly for developing countries to sustain their protectionist approach to development. For Mexico, these costs were demonstrated by the economic crisis of the 1980s (1982–1989 annual growth averaged less than one percent) while the benefits of relying on the world market to drive development seemed evident in the economic success of South Korea, Taiwan, and Chile. Mexico began a process of economic reform that included the 1986 decision to open its economy to world trade (Sepúlveda 1994). This decision made increased economic integration with the United States, the world's largest trading economy and Mexico's dominant economic partner, virtually inevitable.

In 1990 Mexico proposed a free trade agreement with the United States to improve its access to the U.S. market and to lock in associated economic reforms. NAFTA also incorporated Canada and took effect in 1994. This striking change in Mexican foreign policy—from keeping the United States at arm's length for generations to embracing it, and from minimizing Mexican economic dependence on the United States to dramatically deepening it—was a direct consequence of the changed economic context, both domestic and international, within which Mexico now operated. Yet Mexico was still governed by the PRI and populated by a citizenry that had been raised on the logic of "revolutionary autonomy." Mexico thus needed to find a way to mitigate the domestic political costs of its foreign policy about-face. It did so in two ways—by reaching out to Latin America and by sustaining its strong support for Castro's Cuba.

In the decade between 1985 and 1995, Mexico did not abandon foreign policy activism but redirected it. In a conscious effort to balance its closer relationship with the United States, Mexico actively sought to diversify its foreign relations throughout the world, but it had success only in Latin America (Chabat 1993). Under the presidency of Carlos Salinas (1988–1994), Mexico actively participated in the Rio Group of Latin American countries organized to promote regional dialogue, economic integration, and regional representation in international forums. Mexico also signed a large number of free trade treaties throughout the region during the early 1990s and sponsored the first Iberoamerica Summit between Latin America, Spain, and Portugal.

Mexico strongly sustained its historic support for nonintervention in the internal affairs of regional states during this ten-year period. It opposed the U.S. invasion of Panama in 1989 and the 1991 OAS decision to intervene militarily in Haiti to reestablish an ousted democratic government. Mexico also continued to support Cuba against regional and international criticism of its record on human rights and democracy, but its rationale for doing so had changed. A country that increasingly relied on the perceptions of international capitalist markets for its economic well-being no longer supported the Cuban Revolution, but did support the international legal principle of nonintervention.

The end of the Cold War reinforced the effectiveness of this revised version of Mexican foreign policy activism. The end of East–West tensions changed the tenor of the conflicts in Central America. No longer perceived by the United States as proxy wars in the East–West struggle, they became more amenable to the peaceful solution Mexico had been promoting since the early 1980s. El Salvador's former combatants recognized this victory for Mexican foreign policy when they signed their peace agreement in Mexico City in early 1992.

Mexico's New Foreign Policy

Between 1995 and 2003, Mexico was forced to adapt to two further changes in the political-economic context—the decline of the PRI and the emergence of a new, global strategic threat to the United States. Mexico alternated between foreign policy passivity and activism as it struggled to adjust to these new circumstances and to define the final details of its new foreign policy. The result finalized Mexico's shift away from "revolutionary autonomy" and its open embrace of the United States, but without abandoning the principles of self-determination, nonintervention, and the peaceful resolution of disputes or Mexico's historic mistrust of the United States.

As 1995 dawned, Mexico found itself in the midst of another financial crisis and governed by a new president unconcerned about the political needs of the PRI and devoted to the success of NAFTA and the economic model it supported. Lacking the economic resources and the political incentive to continue Salinas's active policy of diversification, President Ernesto Zedillo (1994–2000) oversaw a more restrained foreign policy concentrated on economic matters and on solidifying Mexico's new economic relationship with the United States. Although Mexico would still participate in the Rio Group and the Iberoamerican Summits, it would no longer be a leader. Instead, it would become the regional leader for free trade, strongly supporting a hemisphere-wide free trade area, signing additional bilateral trade agreements, and negotiating a free trade agreement with the European Union.

President Zedillo's preference for a "healthy distance" between himself and the PRI, and his implementation of democratic reforms that deprived the PRI of a congressional majority for the first time in nearly seventy years, help to explain an important shift in Mexico's Cuba policy. Although Mexico would continue to support Cuba's sovereign right to determine its own internal affairs, Mexico also increased its indirect criticism of the lack of democracy and human rights in Cuba, leading to a bilateral dispute in late 2000 (Covarrubias Velasco 2003).

The inauguration of President Vicente Fox on December 1, 2000, finalized Mexico's transition away from PRI authoritarianism. Intoxicated by the possibilities inherent in leading Mexico's first democratic government in nearly a century, the Fox administration opted to push recent changes in Mexican foreign policy to their logical limit. Mexico further distanced itself from Castro's Cuba, vigorously pursued a policy of diversification in Latin America and beyond, and actively pursued a very close relationship with the United States. Although the Fox team would ultimately tone down the activism evident in its early approach to Latin America and the United States, this process confirmed the shape of Mexico's new foreign policy.

Mexico's new democracy reinforced its support for human rights and democracy in Latin America. Nor did Mexico relent when this policy immediately led to a direct and growing conflict with Cuba. In 2001 Cuba accused Mexico of being Washington's puppet, and in 2002 Mexico voted against Cuba in the UN's Human Rights Commission for the first time ever. Without Cuba to balance Mexico's active embrace of the United States, Mexico turned south and global. President Fox pointedly made his first foreign trip as president-elect to Latin America, his administration offered to mediate between the Colombian government and rebel groups, and Mexico tried to position itself as a bridge between Washington and Latin America. On the global stage, Mexico pressed for and obtained the rotating Latin American seat on the United Nations Security Council, only the second time in history that Mexico had occupied this seat and the first time that Mexico had requested it. On this foundation of policy diversification, Mexico openly and actively engaged the United States as never before (Starr 2004; Starr and Ayón 2003). It proposed something previously unimaginable, the deepening and widening of NAFTA into an arrangement like the European Union and a bilateral migration agreement as the first step toward this broader goal.

Unfortunately, this newly activist Mexican foreign policy was at odds with the political-economic context within which it was implemented. The Fox government overestimated the extent to which democratization in Mexico would create shared interests between itself and the United States, and it mistakenly believed that Mexico's historic respect for international law and its mistrust of the United States were based only on the legitimation needs of the PRI rather than the balance of power between Mexico and the United States. Making matters worse, the U.S. foreign policy calculus changed dramatically in September 2001, creating a new policy context with which Mexico had absolutely no experience.

The terrorist attacks of September 11, 2001, and the U.S. decision to go to war in Iraq eighteen months later brought Mexican foreign policy back to earth. These events created a direct conflict between Mexico's recent efforts to become a reliable partner of the United States, and its historic interest in guaranteeing self-determination, nonintervention, and the peaceful resolution of disputes as well as the deep-seated mistrust of the United States in Mexican public opinion. In its struggle to balance these conflicting preferences, Mexico had to estimate how much policy independence the United States would tolerate without a clear strategic framework (such as the Cold War in the past). It is not surprising, therefore, that U.S.—Mexican relations suffered a serious setback in 2002–2003 as a result of Mexico "stepping over the line" by refusing to support the war in Iraq. Nor is it surprising that the relationship later got back on track, but with Mexico as a less active and enthusiastic partner. After months of rebuffing President Fox's entreaties for a meeting to work through their disagreements, U.S. president George W. Bush finally agreed to meet with Fox during an international gathering in late 2003 followed by a weekend meeting at the Bush ranch in early 2004. Unlike 2001, when Mexico set the agenda for the bilateral relationship, however, Mexico now allowed the United States to take the lead even though this meant that the agenda was defined by U.S. rather than Mexican national interests.

Conclusion

Over the past twenty years, Mexican foreign policy has undergone a dramatic shift in response to the changing context in which it must operate. The adjustment has not always been easy or smooth, but by the early twenty-first century a new Mexican foreign policy seems to have emerged. Mexico's relationship with the United States will be closer and more institutionalized than in the past as a result of economic globalization and geographic reality. As a weak country on the border of a superpower, however, Mexico will also hold fast to its support of the peaceful resolution of disputes, self-determination, and nonintervention (with the sole exception of promoting democracy and human rights). Mexico's deep and asymmetrical economic dependence on the United States combined with a deep-seated national mistrust of the United States guarantees that Mexico will continue its efforts to diversify its foreign interactions. And Mexico's geostrategic importance to the United States ensures that U.S. tolerance of Mexico's need for foreign policy independence will persist, although the road may be bumpy for a time as Mexico struggles to find the balance between autonomy and loyalty that fits both its own national interests and the new framework for U.S. foreign policy.

References

Chabat, Jorge. 1993. "Mexico: So Close to the United States, So Far from Latin America." *Current History* 571 (February).

Covarrubias Velasco, Ana. 2003. "La política mexicana hacia Cuba." *Foro Internacional* 43, no. 1 (July–September).

Domínguez, Jorge I., and Rafael Fernández de Castro, eds., 2001. *The United States and Mexico: Between Partnership and Conflict.* New York: Routledge.

Grayson, George W. 1988. *Oil and Mexican Foreign Policy.* Pittsburgh, PA: University of Pittsburgh Press.

Sepúlveda, Cesar. 1994. *La política internacional de México en el decenio de 1980.* Mexico City: Fondo de Cultura Económica.

Shapira, Yoram. 1978. *Mexican Foreign Policy Under Echeverría.* Beverly Hills, CA: Sage Publications.

Starr, Pamela K. 2004. "U.S.–Mexico Relations." *Hemisphere Focus* 12, no. 2 (January). Center for Strategic and International Sudies (CSIS), www.csis.org.

Starr, Pamela K., and David R. Ayón. 2003. "El interludio Castañeda y el sueño de América del Norte." *En la frontera del imperio: México en el mundo 2003,* ed. Rafael Fernández de Castro. Mexico City: Planeta.

5

SIDNEY WEINTRAUB

Mexico's Foreign Economic Policy

How much does free trade matter? Directly, it influences the share of trade and foreign investment in total supply and investment in the Mexican economy. Indirectly, the competition that comes from trade could increase the efficiency of Mexican producers, while foreign investment that was facilitated under the North American Free Trade Agreement (NAFTA) could increase net investment.

The creation of NAFTA was part of a policy of continuing the opening of Mexico to trade that began with Mexico's joining the General Agreement on Tariffs and Trade (GATT) in 1986. In 2002, intra-NAFTA trade accounted for 45 percent of the total trade of Canada, Mexico, and the United States. Although some attempts have been made to broaden the NAFTA agreement, the future impact of NAFTA may decline when more nations enjoy free trade with the NAFTA partners. Moreover, Mexico's benefits from NAFTA are lower than Mexicans had hoped because of Mexico's diminishing competitiveness in manufactures, although there recently have been new attempts by the Science and Technology Council to increase the technological content of Mexican production. This analysis reinforces the view that Mexico's ability to carry out a successful foreign economic policy depends on the nation's economic competitiveness.

Sidney Weintraub emphasizes the fact that Mexico's competitiveness depends on the nation's productive capacity as well as on macroeconomic policy. Thus, the fact that Mexico grew at only around 1 percent per capita in real terms since NAFTA began is not the result of the almost tripling of Mexican exports during this period. Instead, it reflects the political stalemate that has impeded structural reforms, especially those of educational and fiscal policy. From this point of view, the evaluation of Mexico's foreign economic policy depends on what an observer believes could have happened to Mexican economic growth either without NAFTA or if a different economic policy had been carried out.

The free trade agreement between Canada, Mexico, and the United States has been at the heart of Mexico's foreign economic policy for the past ten years. During this period, Mexico's merchandise exports to the United States and Canada increased from 85 percent of total exports in 1993 to 90 percent in 2002. The nominal value of trade within NAFTA increased by $322 billion over this period. In 2002, intra-NAFTA trade accounted for 45 percent of the total trade of the three countries. Despite this large increase in trade, official and public interest in NAFTA has waned, and ideas for deepening the agreement have atrophied. The viewpoint taken here is that an economic integration relationship must evolve with the times if it is to retain its dynamism.

It is informative that the professional literature is giving as much attention to altering the administrative features of the agreement as opposed to its substantive aspects as the way to revive its vitality (Pastor 2001). When all else fails, reorganize.

The negotiation of NAFTA was made possible by economic actions taken by Mexico following the collapse of its economy in 1982. These measures included a substantial devaluation of the peso, joining and accepting the discipline of the GATT in 1986, unilaterally reducing import impediments in order to make nonoil exports more competitive, and seeking out rather than reluctantly tolerating foreign direct investment (FDI). The immediate impetus for proposing a free trade agreement with the United States was the realization by President Carlos Salinas de Gortari that the necessary level of capital flows would not be forthcoming from Europe in light of its preoccupation with Russia and Eastern Europe after the Berlin Wall came down in 1989 (Salinas de Gortari 2000). Mexico, Salinas concluded, had no choice but to knock at President George H.W. Bush's door in the Oval Office. President Bush (father) responded positively.

Once NAFTA was assured, Mexico embarked on a frenzied pace of concluding other free trade agreements (FTAs), largely in Latin America (de Mateo V. 2003), but including as well an FTA with the European Union. The main motive for these FTAs was to diversify export markets. The absolute value of exports to non-U.S. destinations has indeed risen, but so had the reliance on the U.S. market as a proportion of total exports. Exports of goods and services today to the United States represent more than 30 percent of Mexico's gross domestic product (GDP).

The rest of this chapter will focus on Mexico's current foreign economic policy and the problems that exist, and on suggestions for the future. Many of the present foreign economic problems are rooted in domestic politics, and many foreign economic problems have their origin in internal economic policy. Both of these aspects will be brought out in what follows.

The Current Policy Configuration

When Vicente Fox became president of Mexico in December of 2000, he and his then foreign secretary, Jorge Castañeda, vigorously pushed what they called "NAFTA plus." This consisted essentially of adding migration to the agreement or in addition to the agreement. Even when NAFTA was under negotiation, many intellectuals in Mexico argued that if other factors of production—capital flows in particular—were to be freed under the economic integration, so, too, should labor movements. Castañeda said that what Mexico wanted was the "whole enchilada," which meant the legalization (or regularization) of the estimated 5 to 6 million Mexicans in the United States without papers, some form of guest worker program, and, eventually, when economic differentials were reduced, a single labor market (Fernández de Castro and Rosental 2003). Some progress was apparently made in pre-9/11 discussions, although we do not know how much. In any event, the conversation shifted sharply after 9/11 when U.S. attention shifted to security. A former U.S. ambassador to Mexico, Jeffrey Davidow, commented that just as it had been a mistake for the United States to have *narcotized* the relationship, so was it an error for Mexico to *migratize* it (Davidow 2003). In any event, neither Mexico nor the United States gave much attention to how to deepen the agreement in other respects.

In early 2004, President Bush did make an immigration proposal. The proposal was sketchy, but it contained two key elements. The first was to give legal status for three years, renewable for another three, to the 10 million or more undocumented or illegal immigrants currently in the United States (about half of these are Mexican) if they came forward and registered. The immigrants could simultaneously apply for green cards to remain in the United States, but would not be given preference over other applicants. The president was specific that he was not proposing an amnesty. Most Latino organizations argued that few undocumented immigrants would come forth under these conditions.

The second element was to institute a new temporary worker program to match willing workers with willing employers. The support for this program came primarily from a group of employers who called themselves the Essential Workers Immigration Coalition, which includes companies and associations in businesses such as restaurants, hotels, health care, construction, and tourism; the coalition includes the U.S. Chamber of Commerce. Agricultural groups have a separate coalition favoring the importation of temporary workers.

The proposal is controversial and not supported by the general public (based on opinion polls) and it is too early to predict the path the initiative will take because of the higher priority placed by President Bush in his second term on other time-consuming and controversial issues such as social security reform.

One hears much today in Mexico that NAFTA not only was of little benefit to the country, but in fact worsened the economic and social situation. Recent public opinion surveys show that about half of those polled believe NAFTA benefited Mexico and the other half believe it did not. Given the phenomenal rise in Mexican exports to the United States, the diverse character of these exports, and the dramatic increase in annual inflows of FDI, one has to ask why this denigration of NAFTA has occurred.

The main reasons are clear enough. Real per capita income in Mexico has not risen much after NAFTA came into effect. Mexico, in 1995, suffered a dramatic decline in GDP of 6.1 percent. The benefits of NAFTA went to the northern states and the states in the valley of Mexico, and hardly reached the much poorer southern states. Consequently, regional economic disparities grew. Real wages have remained stagnant in most of the economy. The poverty level is about where it was ten years ago, and so is income inequality. Rather than declining, clandestine migration from Mexico to the United States has risen.

This can be put differently, of course: all the problems that antedated NAFTA are still there ten years later, except that Mexico is now a major world exporter and major destination for foreign direct investment. The broad figures that economists like me cite are abstractions to the average Mexican. He or she sees no change in living standards. All of this coincided with NAFTA. Hence, NAFTA must be at fault. (Because all of these realities preceded NAFTA, it is not clear what those who berate NAFTA want to return to.) This judgment is based in part on the fact that NAFTA was sold to the Mexican population as a panacea, and it evidently is not.

This is the essential argument in a series of papers edited by John Audley under the imprimatur of the Carnegie Endowment for International Peace—that NAFTA is a failure because the economic lot of most Mexicans remains dismal (Audley 2003). The failure in this kind of analysis is the inability to disentangle trade policy— and this is what NAFTA, at its core, deals with—from macroeconomic policy. The financial collapse at the end of 1994 and the ensuing economic depression in 1995 was not occasioned by NAFTA—NAFTA had been in existence for less than one year by then—but by faulty fiscal and monetary policy (Weintraub 2000). The economic stagnation that has beset Mexico during the past three years stems from a number of causes, such as an overvalued exchange rate for much of this period and the slowdown in the U.S. economy, which led to declines in Mexican exports—but mainly from the political inability of President Fox to reach legislative and structural agreements with a Congress dominated by opposition parties.

No critic of NAFTA has gone so far as to state that Mexico would be better off today if its exports to the United States had remained stagnant during the past ten years. Yet, that is the logical conclusion of the assertion that NAFTA has failed. Even the argument that a more generous migration agreement would have corrected Mexico's internal problems omits the fact that outmigration increased substantially in any event. The migrants themselves would have been better off if they had legal status, and they might have been able to send more remittances back to Mexico,[1] but this strays from the need for Mexico to grow economically and be able to keep its nationals at home. Those who argue that Mexico must look internally for growth are correct, but their simplification is that this is not enough for a country with limited internal demand. It is not either grow via the internal market or grow because of exports—the policy structure must include both.

NAFTA is a bifurcated agreement in agriculture. The sector was included in the transition to zero duties for most products traded between Mexico and the United States, but not between these two countries and Canada. Agriculture is politically sensitive in most countries and the transition time to zero tariffs as between Mexico and the United States was set at ten years for many products, and fifteen years for the most contentious. In retrospect, the time was too short in that GDP growth rates of 6 percent or more per year in Mexico, on which the transition time was premised, did not materialize. The hope was that GDP growth would be sufficient to create enough nonagricultural jobs to permit impoverished rural residents to find an alternative to staying put in the countryside, largely forlorn of any hope of a decent future for themselves and their families. I will return to the situation in rural Mexico because it is a theme ripe for political demagoguery that offers no solution—which is as true in the United States as it is in Mexico.

As the time approached for the move to zero import duties for many farm products under the ten-year transition at the end of 2003, a clamor arose over the allegedly unfair provisions in NAFTA. Some 90 percent of farm products that were allowed into Mexico had duties that were scheduled to decline to zero from between 1 and 2 percent as of January 1, 2004. Pork had a low tariff, but within a quota. So did poultry products. The most sensitive products, like corn, beans, and powdered milk, had until 2008 (a fifteen-year transition under NAFTA) before tariffs were completely removed. In the case of corn, Mexico has a tariff-rate quota under which in-quota imports are duty free, but the out-of-quota duty was more than 100 percent to be gradually reduced to zero by 2008. Beans are treated similarly. During most years after NAFTA was signed, Mexico allowed over-quota corn imports because of a domestic shortage stemming from drought.[2] The point being made here is that it was known to the Mexican government and producers when NAFTA was negotiated in 1993 that agricultural tariffs would decline gradually to zero over ten years for some products, and over fifteen years for others. Why did it take ten years for this reality to sink in?

The demand from many politicians in Mexico, including cabinet officials, was for a renegotiation of the agricultural provisions of NAFTA. This action has about zero percent possibility of being taken, unless the purpose is to destroy NAFTA. Many Mexican producers, those of fruits and vegetables, would not want this because their exports to the United States have increased. Taking agriculture and processed foods together, Mexico's exports within NAFTA rose by 9.4 percent a year between 1994 and 2001, and agro-food imports within NAFTA rose by 6.9 percent a year (Sarmiento 2003).

Before leaving the theme of Mexican trade and its problems, I wish to touch on the situation of the maquiladora production and exports because this has been much in the news. Agricultural exports in 2002 were 2.5 percent of total merchandise exports; manufactured goods, by contrast, comprised 89 percent of the total, of which maquiladora plants accounted for half. Maquiladora production and employment, after growing rapidly in the 1990s and before, started to decline in October 2000. In 2002, production declined by about 20 percent—by more in some industries—and employment fell by nearly 290,000 jobs (U.S. General Accounting Office 2003). The decline was due in part to the U.S. economic slowdown in 2000, but in larger measure because of relocation to lower-wage areas like

China and Central America. Mexico also worsened the tax treatment of maquiladoras, and this encouraged many companies to leave. What this means is that the co-production with the United States, which is what the maquiladora plants represent, can no longer be based solely on low wages in Mexico. I will return to this theme in the final section because it points up an issue that Mexico must face in the future if its foreign economic policy is to prosper.

Another development that will have repercussions for Mexico's access to the U.S. market is that Mexico will have to share its preferential advantage, making the need for increased competitiveness all the more urgent. Under NAFTA, Mexico became the largest foreign supplier of textiles and apparel to the U.S. market after 1994. In 2005, when the worldwide textile agreement limiting exports of textile products is scheduled to end, U.S. and other import quotas under that agreement will terminate and Mexico will surely lose most of the U.S. market in these products to other countries, such as China. Looking at all products, Chile now has preferential access to the U.S. market under its recent FTA, and the five Central American countries will likely soon enjoy this treatment when the Central America Free Trade Agreement (CAFTA) approved by the Congress enters into force. CAFTA is particularly germane because many of the region's nonagricultural exports compete with products produced by Mexican maquiladora plants. The future of the Free Trade Area of the Americas (FTAA) is uncertain, but if this agreement comes into existence, Mexico will share its preferences in the U.S. market with the entire hemisphere. If the FTAA does not prosper, new U.S. bilateral FTAs with hemispheric countries (Colombia, Peru, Panama, the Dominican Republic, Ecuador, and perhaps others) will bring about a similar sharing of preferences.

Looking Ahead

The two developments cited in the last section—the loss of maquiladora competitiveness to lower-wage countries and the sharing of preferential access to the U.S. market—highlight the need for Mexico to pay attention to its diminishing competitiveness in manufactured goods. Mexico's science and technology council (CONACYT in its Spanish abbreviation) is focusing on this problem, namely, the need to augment the technological content of Mexico's production and reduce the extent of the reliance on low wages to achieve competitiveness (CONACYT n.d.). This, in turn, demands greater attention to upgrading Mexico's educational structure at all levels. Mexico ranks last among the thirty nations of the Organization for Economic Cooperation and Development (OECD) in the reading skills of people aged twenty-five to thirty-four. Some 300,000 Mexican children leave school by age fourteen.[3] Even if the will is there, and funds are provided to deal with the education problem, this cannot be corrected in the short term—but a start can be made.

If Mexico hopes to emerge from its status as a developing country, this combination of educational upgrading and technological improvement has to be public requirement number one. Making a start on rectifying this dual problem also requires sustained higher growth in GDP than Mexico has achieved during the past twenty-plus years. Failing this, the funds for educational upgrading are unlikely to be available. This is a chicken-and-egg issue in that economic growth is necessary to generate the needed budgetary funds, and this growth requires a more educated population. This is why the tax/fiscal reform under discussion in Mexico for the past several years is so critical. Mexico's level of tax collection is only 11.5 percent of GDP; the comparable figure for the United States is 34 percent of GDP, and for Brazil it is 37 percent. Economists refer to this as structural reform, a bland term for something as important as providing the wherewithal to meet a social need as important as education.

More broadly, the criticism that trade policy has not solved basic economic and social problems—which is heard regularly in Mexico when the shortcomings of NAFTA are cited—distracts from the real needs. These deal with macroeconomic and structural policies, of which fiscal reform is only one.

The internal debate in Mexico about the fairness of the agricultural provisions of NAFTA may have some validity at the margin, but in the main is also a distraction. If the 25 percent of Mexico's population that lives in rural areas is able to generate only 6 percent of the country's GDP, the basis for rural poverty is evident. If all the corrections that particular agricultural interests seek are granted—for corn, beans, poultry, pork, sugar, apples, and other commodities—the reality of rural poverty would hardly be altered, particularly in the nonirrigated areas of the country. Much of the rural population will have to emigrate over time, and, in order to do so, jobs must be available in urban centers. This brings us back to the imperative of sustained higher GDP growth. In the interim, the problem is probably best dealt with by federal subsidies in rural areas; in this respect, policy in Mexico merits much praise for a program called Oportunidades (formerly Progresa) focused on giving direct benefits in such fields as education, health care, and food to 20 million people living in poverty.

A large proportion of Mexico's manufactured exports to the United States takes place in intermediate products that later are incorporated in final products. Much of this trade is between related firms, such as a parent and a subsidiary, or where there are cooperative agreements. This is similar to Canada–U.S. trade, although Canada's exports of manufactures tend to be more technologically sophisticated. Beyond this, much of the shipment of intermediate products from Canada to the United States, especially in the automotive industry, is based on a just-in-time (JIT) production process in order to reduce inventory costs. The use of JIT is far less advanced between Mexico and the United States. The upgrading of a JIT system is one way for Mexico to benefit from its locational advantage of proximity to its dominant market.

Many other substantive improvements can be made in the operations of Mexico–U.S. relations. Luis de la Calle Pardo has listed some of these, beyond the JIT co-production technique: improved infrastructure (roads, bridges, ports, airports) in both countries; the possibility of maritime cabotage for the North American region as a whole; better customs services to speed the movement of goods; more scholarships for attendance by Mexican students in U.S. community colleges; technical assistance from the United States in agriculture; more assistance to Mexico for the transfer of technology; eliminating antidumping safeguards in intra-NAFTA trade; and others (de la Calle Pardo 2003).

The main point that this chapter wishes to leave with the reader is that Mexico's foreign economic policy is not independent of its domestic economic policy. Indeed, the latter is dominant in determining Mexico's ability to conduct foreign policy. The second point that deserves stress to a noneconomist audience is that trade policy, although an important part of total economic policy, is no substitute for effective macroeconomic policy. And, finally, if Mexico is to succeed in upgrading its foreign economic policy and its competitive position in the world, a number of structural reforms will be necessary. This chapter focused on just two of these, educational and fiscal reform.

Notes

1. Remittances to Mexico in 2003 were apparently $12 billion, an astoundingly high figure.
2. The data in this paragraph come from Sergio Sarmiento (2003).
3. An article in the *Washington Post* by Kevin Sullivan and Mary Jordan (2003, A1) provides a vivid picture of this problem for primary education.

References

Audley, John J. 2003. "Introduction" to "NAFTA's Promise and Reality: Lessons from Mexico for the Hemisphere." Carnegie Endowment for International Peace.
Consejo Nacional de Ciencia y Tecnología (CONACYT). n.d. *Plan Nacional de Desarrollo 2001–2006.* See also www.conacyt.mx/dap/pecyt/index.html.
Davidow, Jeffrey. 2003. *El oso y el puercoespín. Testimonio de un embajador de Estados Unidos en México.* México, D.F.: Grijalbo.
de la Calle Pardo, Luis. 2003. "10 años del TLCAN: El fin del acceso preferencial?" In *En la frontera del imperio,* ed. Rafael Fernández de Castro México, D.F.: Planeta.
de Mateo V., Fernando. 2003. "La política comercial de México con América Latina." In *En la frontera del imperio,* ed. Rafael Fernández de Castro. México, D.F.: Planeta.
Fernández de Castro, Rafael, and Andrés Rosental. 2003. "El amor, la decepción y cómo aprovechar la realidad: La relación México–Estados Unidos 2000–2003." In *En la frontera del imperio,* ed. Rafael Fernández de Castro. México, D.F.: Planeta.
Pastor, Robert. 2001. *Toward a North American Community: Lessons from the Old World for the New.* Washington, DC: Institute for International Economics.
Salinas de Gortari, Carlos. 2000. *México: Un paso difícil a la modernidad.* Barcelona: Plaza & Janés Editores.
Sarmiento, Sergio. 2003. "NAFTA and Mexico's Agricultura." *Hemisphere Focus,* Center for Strategic and International Studies, March 4.
Sullivan, Kevin, and Mary Jordan. 2003. "Mexico's Dropout Economy." *Washington Post,* November 24.

U.S. General Accounting Office. 2003. "International Trade: Mexico's Maquiladora Decline Affects U.S.–Mexico Border Communities and Trade; Recovery Depends in Part on Mexico's Actions." July 25, GAO-03-891.

Weintraub, Sidney. 2000. *Financial Decision-Making in Mexico: To Bet a Nation.* Pittsburgh, PA: University of Pittsburgh Press.

6

ALEJANDRO M. WERNER,
RODRIGO BARROS, AND JOSÉ F. URSÚA

The Mexican Economy

Transformation and Challenges

The Mexican economy went through a significant transformation during the last two decades by which the economic policy framework and the structure of economic activity were reshaped in many important respects. To understand the factors that led to this transformation and its implications on the more recent economic developments in Mexico, Werner, Ursúa and Barros, begin by reviewing the evolution of the economy since the early 1980s in two fronts: macroeconomic stabilization and structural change. With respect to the first one, they identify four features that broadly characterized the shift in economic policy: (1) strengthening public finances, (2) reducing inflation, (3) transforming a closed into an open economy actively integrated to global trade and finance, and (4) deregulating the economy and opening several areas to the private sector. The authors discuss how these guidelines were implemented with various degrees of intensity and success during three phases that correspond to the administrations of Miguel De la Madrid, Carlos Salinas and Ernesto Zedillo. With respect to the second front, they explain the role of trade liberalization as a catalyst of the structural transformation, which reoriented the production structure toward industrial activities closely related to the exporting sector. The other large structural transformation aimed at the financial system. Although it had begun since the early 1990s, the direction of the reforms was ultimately defined by valuable lessons that were drawn from the 1994–1995 crisis.

The second section of the chapter describes the results of this large-scale transformation of the Mexican economy. There are substantial achievements that can be highlighted in the area of macroeconomic stabilization, which are related to the efficacy of the fiscal and monetary policy schemes that were implemented by the successive reforms outlined above. Moreover, the structural change has been reflected in a higher synchronization of the Mexican and U.S. economic cycles, especially in more recent periods. Overall, economic growth was higher during the 1990s than during the 1980s (3.4 percent and 1.9 percent, respectively), which also indicates a favorable impact of the reforms. Nevertheless, in the last section of the chapter, the authors also argue that in order to reach higher levels of economic development there are key challenges that must be addressed in the near future: flaws in the institutional framework, structural weaknesses that remain in public finances, and the inadequate stock of human and physical capital. Overcoming these challenges would foster productivity increases and the competitiveness of the economy, thereby consolidating the gains of reforms that have already been undertaken and promoting economic growth.

The Evolution of the Mexican Economy: An Overview

During the last two decades the Mexican economy went through a significant transformation. Throughout these two decades, economic policy has focused on four main areas: (1) strengthening public finances, (2) reducing inflation, (3) transforming a closed economy into an open one actively integrated into global trade and finance, and (4) deregulating the economy and opening several areas to the private sector. In the following pages, the main changes in these areas will be described.

Macroeconomic Stabilization

An important part of Mexico's economic transformation consisted of a major macroeconomic stabilization effort. This accomplishment followed three phases that are associated with the three administrations that followed the 1982 crisis. President de la Madrid's administration (1982–1988) faced the debt crisis by implementing an important fiscal adjustment through government spending reduction, debt control, and a first phase of privatizations. However, natural disasters, a severe reduction in oil prices, and the 1987 U.S. stock market crash pushed the economy into a new crisis in 1987. The Salinas administration (1988–1994) continued with the fiscal adjustment effort, and it extended the stabilization program into an exchange rate–based inflation stabilization with additional elements of coordination among major economic agents (which allowed a reduction of inflation by using a semi-fixed exchange rate as a nominal anchor). Other changes were then put in practice, especially in regards to the opening of the economy to international trade, deregulating the economy, increasing the privatization of government firms, and renegotiating the foreign debt. President Zedillo's administration (1994–2000) put in place a large fiscal correction in response to the 1994 crisis and adopted a floating exchange rate regime. Also, in order to avoid major fiscal pressures associated with the pension system, a reform was approved in which a scheme of individual accounts and defined contributions replaced a pay-as-you-go system. During Zedillo's administration the degree of synchronization of Mexican economic activity with the U.S. economy increased markedly and important political reforms were made.

Figure 6.1 **Public Sector Primary Balance, 1980–2003**

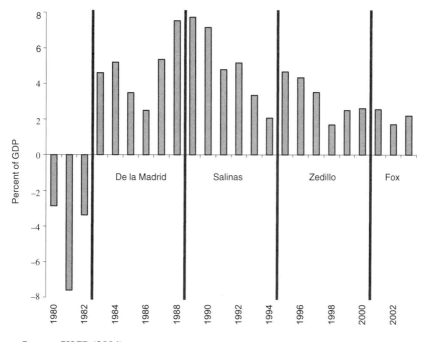

Source: SHCP (2004).

Public Finances

Public finances have undergone major changes since the early 1980s. After reaching a deficit of close to 8 percent of gross domestic product (GDP) in 1982, the public sector primary balance[1] was turned into a surplus larger than 5 percent of GDP by 1984, due to a program implemented by the administration of Miguel de la Madrid, which consisted in large cuts of public spending (primarily public investment). Although unexpected shocks, such as the dramatic fall in international oil prices and the 1985 earthquake, induced a temporary reduction of the surplus, the commitment of that administration to sound public finances proved to be crucial for long-term stability. Ever since, the primary balance has been consistently positive (see Figure 6.1), and programmable government spending (which also excludes interest payments and is destined to specific programs and government operation) was permanently reduced from levels between 20 and 25 percent of GDP to levels between 15 and 20 percent of GDP (see Figure 6.2). After the huge adjustment of President de la Madrid's administration, other fiscal adjustments followed the crises that ensued in 1986–1987 and 1994, and are reflected in spending reductions and increases in the public sector primary balance.

Figure 6.2   **Programmable Spending, 1980–2003**

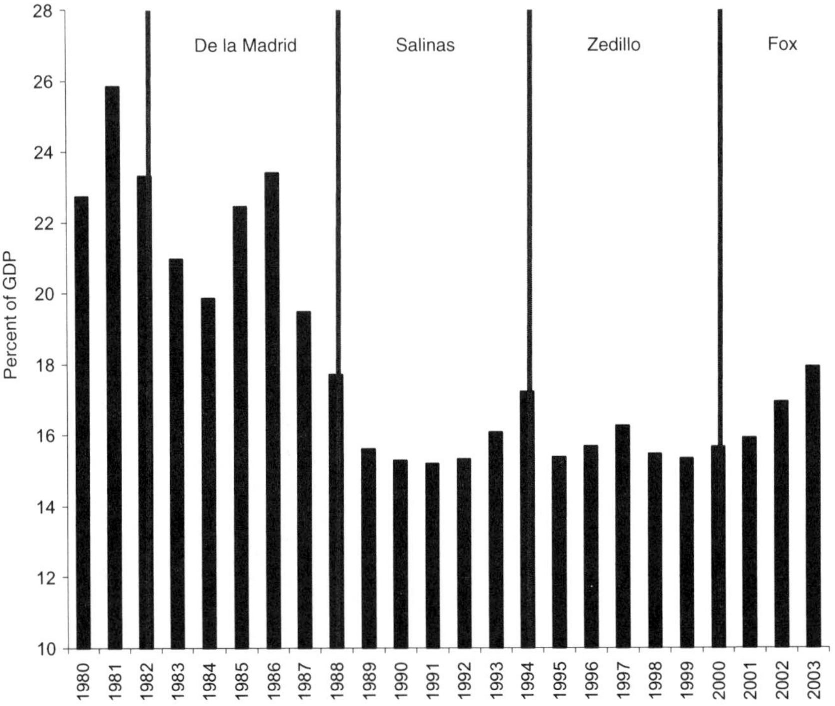

Source: SHCP (2004).

Public Debt

As a result of the important fiscal effort described in the previous section, the debt-to-GDP ratio fell from 90 percent in 1986 to 26 percent in 2003. The debt crisis of the 1980s was addressed in 1989 through the Brady Plan, which started by recognizing that the problem was not one of liquidity but of solvency (the former consisting of the ability to obtain resources in the short term and the latter of a capability to repay). Thus, the solution consisted of allowing certain eligible countries to renegotiate the amount and service of their debt with international creditors. In exchange for this relief, creditors would be granted stronger collaterals and more tradable restructured debt, as well as the promise of the countries involved to engage in economic reforms (Berthélemy and Lensink 1992; Dijkstra and Hermes 2001). Mexico became the first country to resettle its debt under the plan.

Recently, Mexican public debt reached its lowest level in two decades. During the last few years, a key element of the debt management policy has been the gradual reduction of the reliance on external debt and the increasing importance of

Figure 6.3 **Traditional Net Public Debt, 1980–2003**

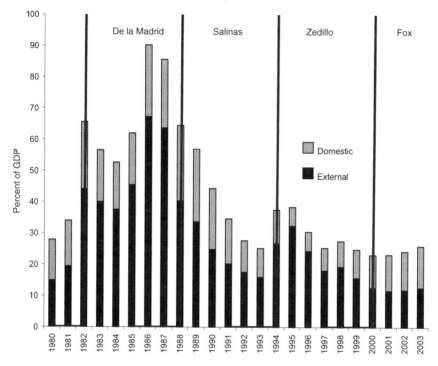

Source: SHCP (2004).

domestic debt denominated in local currency, which makes the economy less vulnerable to sudden changes in international financial markets. As a result of this effort, Mexican domestic debt in 2003 represented more than 50 percent of the total public debt, while in 1986 it represented only 25 percent of total debt (see Figure 6.3). In addition, broad public debt (which includes all the public sector's liabilities) has been held relatively constant as percentage of GDP (see Figure 6.4). Altogether, broad debt levels in Mexico are compared favorably to those of other countries with similar economic conditions.[2]

The result of this change in the situation of the public debt has been an improvement of the conditions in which private agents and the government have access to international financial markets, as is shown by the fact that the indicators of country risk for Mexico have steadily fallen over the last years. Moreover, the overall reduction and restructuring of public debt has been complemented by a large increase of its average maturity. The latter figure for public domestic bonds has grown from 3 months in 1990, to 15 in 1998, and to 30 in 2004 (see Figure 6.5). During the last three years, government bonds in local currency have been issued with maturities as high as twenty years, a historical achievement for a Latin American country.

Figure 6.4   **Broad Net Public Debt, 1980–2003**

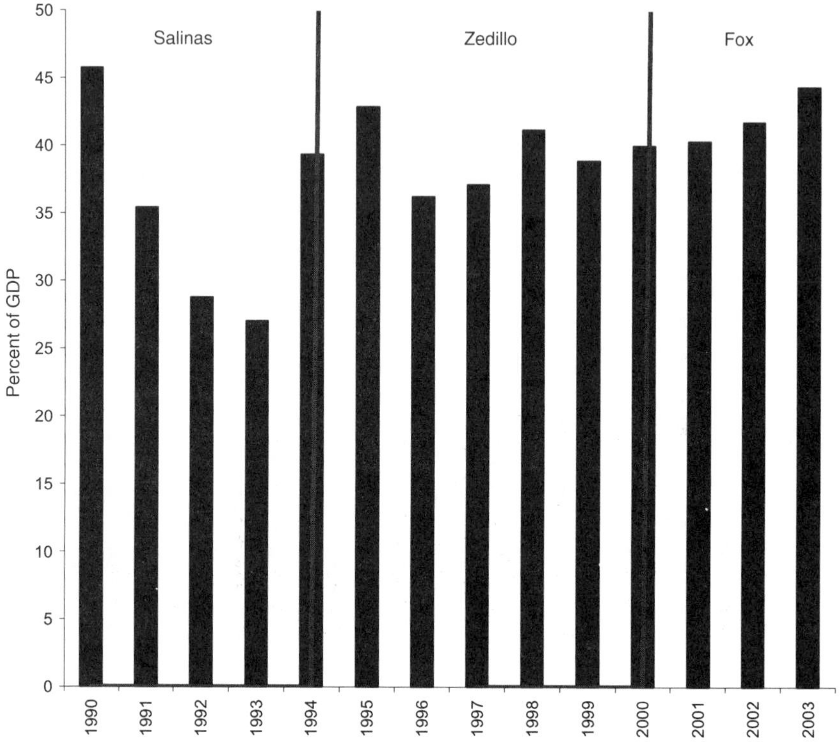

Source: SHCP (2004).

Privatizations

The reduction of the public sector also included the sale of several enterprises previously owned and run by the state. There were several reasons to promote a large-scale privatization strategy. First of all, there was no reason for the government to own and run most of these enterprises, as they could work properly under a competitive market setting. Second, the privatization was aimed at increasing public revenues, redirecting public investment, and regaining the trust of the private sector in the government. The privatization impulse began in 1983 as a corrective policy that followed the 1982 crisis, but it was deepened during the early 1990s. The government began by selling an important number of small enterprises, and later sold firms that had a higher relative importance (see Table 6.1). These companies belonged to several sectors, among others: automobiles and trucks (e.g., Renault México, DINA), aviation (e.g., Mexicana, Aeroméxico), sugar refineries, mining (e.g., Cananea), railroads (e.g., Concarril), food and beverages (e.g., Conasupo plants), telecommunications (e.g., Telmex) and most noticeably

Figure 6.5 **Average Maturity of Public Domestic Bonds, 1990–2004**

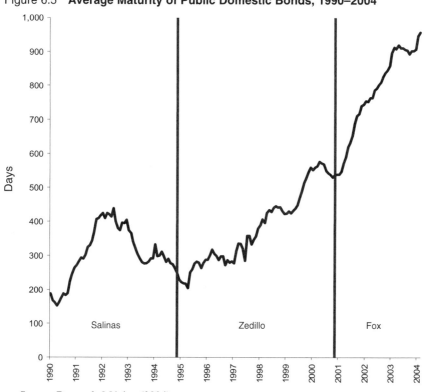

Source: Banco de México (2004).

banking (e.g., Banamex, Bancomer). State-owned banks were sold in the last phase of the privatization process, but undoubtedly constituted one of the most important operations, both because of the confirmation to the private sector of the commitment of the administration to structural reform and because of the resources that were obtained through the operation (Rogozinski 1993; Teichman 1995).

Monetary Policy and Exchange Rate Regime

Monetary policy has also gone through considerable changes. The two most important ones are the establishment of the central bank's independence and the adoption of a floating exchange rate regime. These constitute the foundations of the current independent monetary policy framework, the first by providing the legal arrangement for an independent monetary authority, and the second by allowing the Central Bank to operate monetary policy free from exchange rate commitments. As a result of these changes and the fiscal and financial efforts, inflation was reduced to a level below 4 percent in 2003, and is targeted to reach 3 percent in the years to come.

Table 6.1

Public Sector Enterprises and Entities Figures, 1983–1992

	1983	1984	1985	1986	1987	1988	1989	1990	1991	1992
Total public sector enterprises and entities (number of)	1,074	1,049	941	737	617	412	379	280	241	217
Public enterprise investment (as percent of total public sector expenditure)	14.7	15.1	13.0	11.5	10.2	10.1	10.6	10.8	12.6	12.9
Public enterprise investment (as percent of GDP)	6.0	5.9	4.9	4.8	4.5	4.0	2.9	2.1	2.0	3.1

Source: Yearly presidential address to the nation.

Figure 6.6 **Annual CPI Inflation, 1980–2004**

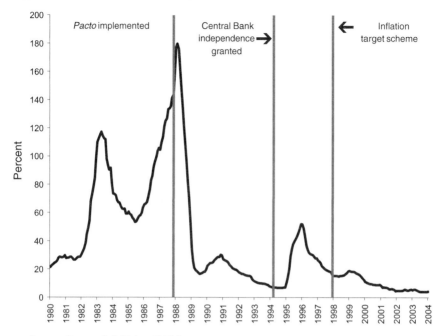

Source: Banco de México (2004).

In broad terms, the reduction of inflation went through three major episodes. The first of these dates back to 1987. As a result of an upward trend throughout the first half of the decade, inflation surpassed 150 percent that year. Then, in September of 1987 the government reached an agreement (known as the Economic Stability Pact, or *Pacto* in Spanish) with large producers and labor unions. Thereby the government committed itself to reduce its expenditure, push forward the privatization agenda, fix public sector prices in accordance to budgetary targets, and apply a restrictive monetary policy within the framework of a crawling exchange rate regime. Producers committed themselves not to raise prices above agreed-upon growth rates, and labor unions committed themselves to moderate wage increases. Although inflation still maintained its increasing path for a couple of months, this framework proved to be extremely successful: by early 1989 inflation had reached levels below 20 percent, and by the end of the Salinas administration it was well below 10 percent (see Figure 6.6).

The Salinas administration complemented the pacto with an exchange rate–based stabilization. At the very beginning, the exchange rate was fixed at a level that supported the effort of reducing inflation. Starting in 1989, the peso was gradually depreciated by a predetermined small amount on a daily basis. This amount was reduced over the months, and by 1992 the peso was allowed to fluctuate within

Figure 6.7   **Exchange Rate, 1980–2004**

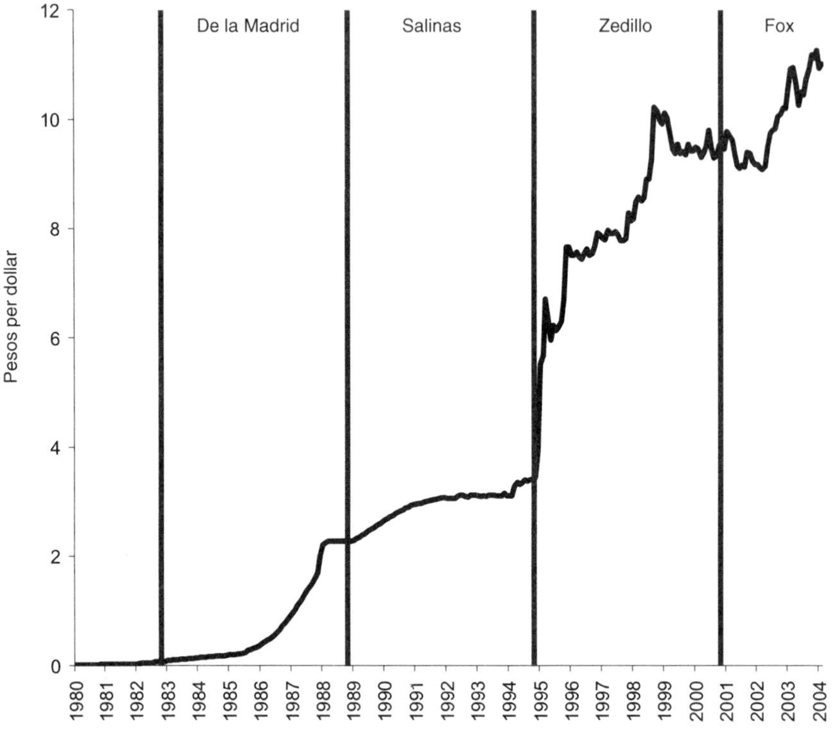

Source: Banco de México (2004).

a mobile narrow band (Aspe 1993). However, the movement of the band was not large enough to compensate for the size of the economy's imbalances over the long term. This crawling peg scheme collapsed abruptly after the 1994 crisis, when the peso was devalued by approximately 40 percent over one month (see Figure 6.7). The entering Zedillo administration had to adopt a free-floating exchange rate regime due to the depletion of international reserves (Carstens and Werner 1999). Afterward, the monetary policy framework started a gradual convergence toward inflation targeting. This framework is characterized by an explicit recognition of price stability as the Central Bank's main objective, the adoption of explicit inflation targets, and the implementation of a strategy to enhance communication with the public (Martínez, Sanchez, and Werner 2001). Subsequently, inflation was targeted to reach a long-term level of 3 percent by 2003 within a tolerance band of +/–1 percent. The new policy scheme proved to be very effective: in 2003 annual inflation reached its lowest level in more than thirty years. As time went by and reserves were replenished, the flexible exchange rate regime gained popularity as the best choice for the monetary policy framework.

A floating exchange rate regime has a number of advantages. First, a flexible regime allows for facing external shocks with greater adjustment capacity than a fixed regime because it allows for the distribution of the adjustment among several financial variables. Second, a free-floating scheme allows the Central Bank to focus its actions on anti-inflationary tasks instead of having to deal with both inflation and the fixed exchange rate with only one instrument. Third, under a flexible regime risks are more efficiently distributed, since agents internalize risk and have greater incentives to cover their positions, thereby reducing moral hazard.[3] Altogether, this framework allows for the reduction of financial vulnerability to external adverse shocks, mainly through the decline in speculative short-run capital flows and the avoidance of currency mismatches, which are less likely to occur in this setting (Martínez and Werner 2002).

Structural Change

During the last twenty years the Mexican economy has gone through deep changes. The principal catalyst for these changes was the opening to international trade, which caused a shift in the production structure as well as a radical increase in the volume of trade with the rest of the world.

International Trade

The most important determinant of the structural transformation experienced by the Mexican economy during the last two decades was the liberalization of trade. Its origin can be traced back to 1986, when the country entered the GATT (General Agreement on Tariffs and Trade). The value of imports subject to permits as a percentage of the total fell from 83 percent at the beginning of 1985 to 28 percent by the end of 1986. From then on, especially during the 1990s, trade barriers were progressively eliminated: from an average tax on imports of 9.7 percent in 1990, to 3.7 percent in 1995, and 2.2 percent in 2003.[4]

Moreover, since the early 1990s the government undertook a proactive trade liberalization strategy, and as a result a number of free trade agreements were signed with different countries (see Table 6.2). Among them, the North American Free Trade Agreement (NAFTA) stands out because of its significance and the effects it had on the economic transformation. On the one hand, NAFTA institutionalized the liberalization of the economy by clearly establishing the commercial strategy through which the country would definitely open itself to trade. It promoted foreign and domestic investment in a new business environment, which was characterized by greater certainty in the policy direction and the safety net of a binding economic link with the United States and Canada. On the other hand, NAFTA gave a valuable impulse to the manufacturing sector of the economy, which became an important growth engine through its exports.

Table 6.2

Free Trade Agreements in Which Mexico Takes Part, 1994–2005

Countries involved	Date of enactment
Canada, United States	Jan-94
Costa Rica	Jan-95
Colombia, Venezuela	Jan-95
Bolivia	Jan-95
Nicaragua	Jul-98
Chile	Aug-99
Austria, Belgium-Luxembourg, Denmark, Finland, France, Germany, Greece, Ireland, Italy, Netherlands, Portugal, Spain, Sweden, United Kingdom	Jul-00
Israel	Jul-00
El Salvador, Guatemala, Honduras[a]	Mar-01
Iceland, Liechtenstein, Norway, Switzerland	Jul-01
Uruguay	Jul-04
Japan[b]	Apr-05

Source: Secretaría de Hacienda y Crédito Público, SHCP (2004).
[a]Aggreement with Honduras was enacted on June 2001.
[b]Economic Association Agreement.

This policy had deep consequences for the structure of the Mexican economy. The volume of trade (exports plus imports) as a share of GDP went from 20 percent in 1980 to 40 percent in 1994 and 70 percent in 2003.[5] Mexico became the eighth largest exporting economy in the world and its export sector evolved into the primary growth engine in the economy. Moreover, the liberalization also brought about a substantial increase of foreign direct investment flows directed toward the country, from levels of around 1 percent of GDP by 1980 to 2.6 percent in 1994 and more than 4 percent by 2001.[6] Foreign direct investment complements domestic savings in the formation of infrastructure and implies a direct transfer of technology, which can in turn increase productivity.

Trade liberalization also made the economy less vulnerable to external shocks by reducing its dependence on oil. While in 1980 oil exports represented more than two-thirds of the value of the country's total exports, by 2003 the corresponding figure was below 10 percent. Just as the importance of oil on Mexican exports decreased, the importance of manufacturing activities increased. Between 1980 and 2003 the participation of manufacturing exports in total exports went from less than 25 percent to more than 85 percent.[7]

The Restructuring of the Financial System

In 1982, the fundamental macroeconomic imbalances that had been created by the economic policies of the previous twelve years found an adverse external environment that made them unsustainable. This led to a serious balance-of-payments and debt crisis to which the government at the time responded with, among other policies, the expropriation of all privately owned domestic banks. A few months later, President de la Madrid's administration took office, facing the difficult task of rearranging a disordered economy (Lustig 1994). Many of the corrective measures that were undertaken were aimed at reversing the policy heritage of the previous governments, but the reversal of the nationalization of the banking system had to wait for better macroeconomic conditions. In the meantime, nationalized banks performed poorly: surveillance was weak, employees were often unqualified, and credit was restricted to government handpicked strategic sectors. By 1990, as part of other market-oriented reforms, the Salinas administration pushed forward the approval of the constitutional amendments needed to privatize the banks owned by the state. The process was finished by mid-1992: eighteen banks were assigned to the winning bidders for approximately 12 billion dollars. Financing to the private sector, which had begun to grow a couple of years before, saw a great increase, reaching 43 percent of GDP by 1994 (see Figure 6.8).

During the years that followed the privatization process, the banking system grew more competitive and operational earnings were obtained. The general economic conditions of the country had improved, but there were also weaknesses, especially regarding a rapidly growing current account deficit financed with short-term debt, which coexisted with the commitment to maintain the exchange rate within a relatively tight band. At the same time, the credit expansion (to which development banks also contributed) happened too fast and often without the proper risk screening, partly because of the inexperience of bankers, but also because of the weak supervision capacity of the government. All of these factors, in conjunction with domestic political commotion and rising interest rates in the United States, eventually triggered the 1994 crisis (Gil Díaz 1998).

The crisis unfolded quickly. After the exchange rate devaluation in December of 1994, inflation and interest rates rose sharply, while banks' capitalization levels fell and their balance sheets deteriorated due to the outburst of nonperforming loans. Three basic problems emerged with regard to the banking crisis: illiquidity, lack of capitalization, and the risk of a bank run. Besides the adoption of a floating exchange rate regime, the immediate response of the Zedillo administration consisted of several programs: a dollar-selling scheme to provide liquidity, the issuance of debt to recapitalize the banks, and the government intervention in banks that had performed irregular operations. Solvent banks were allowed to sell their poorly per-

Figure 6.8 **Direct Financing to the Nonbanking Private Sector, 1980–2003**

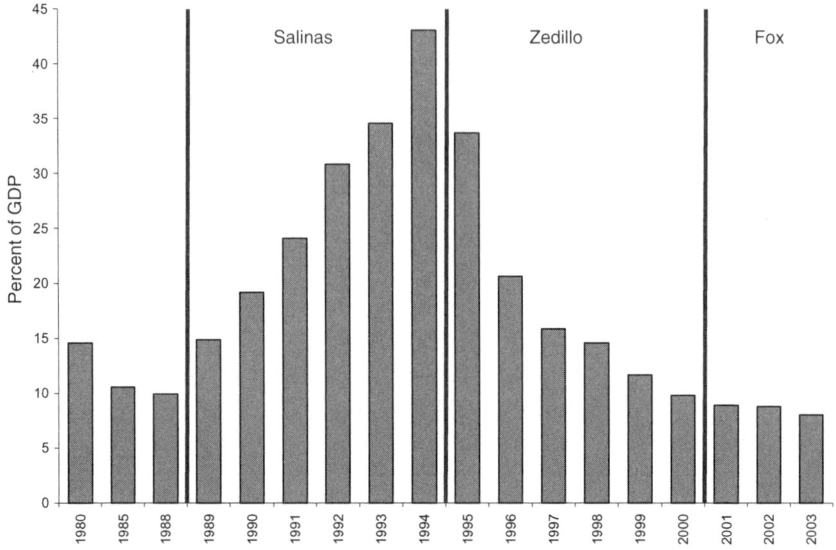

Source: Banco de México (2004).

forming credit portfolios to a government trust; in exchange they would make further additions to their capital to comply with new capitalization requirements. Finally, programs aimed at helping debtors were developed, mainly through the indexation of their debt to inflation and the negotiation of credit discounts. In the end, although the cost of these measures reached almost 20 percent of GDP, a bank run was avoided, the banking system was rescued, and all savings were protected.

The years that followed the crisis saw important changes in banking regulation and operation. The opening of the banking system to foreign investment was accelerated through the reduction of the limits on foreign capital's investment and ownership in the banking system originally established in NAFTA. The process finished in 1998, when all restrictions on foreign capital were eliminated, which allowed for the acquisitions of Mexican banks by world-size financial groups that followed in the next few years (Murillo 2003). This opening brought remarkable changes in the structure of foreign ownership and control in the banking system, whose capital represented almost 80 percent of the total in 2003 (in more detailed figures, the composition of the banking sector's capital by origin was the following: Spain, 39.0 percent; United States, 29.9 percent; United Kingdom, 5.5 percent; Canada, 3.5 percent; other foreign, 3.1 percent).[8]

The crisis taught important lessons, above all that an exchange rate commitment combined with unlimited deposit insurance and undue credit expansion creates a moral hazard that may easily crumble liquid financial markets (Gil Díaz

2000). It also showed that banks' accountability and regulation were indispensable to build a healthy financial system. After the outburst of the crisis, those lessons were turned into a series of economic reforms aimed at reshaping the banking system. A first group of reforms was aimed at reordering the system in the short run; a second group was designed to correct the deficiencies that led to the crisis, in order to avoid similar episodes in the future; and a third group was directed to reactivating the credit market in an orderly manner. Several laws were approved in order to improve surveillance by authorities and credit bureaus, and establish new capitalization requirements and accountability procedures, so as to speed up the execution of guarantees and collaterals. Other reforms undertaken were directed toward the protection of minority shareholders, increasing popular savings, and redesigning deposit insurance.

Finally, a review of the restructuring of the financial system must inevitably mention the impact of the pension system reform approved in 1995–1996 in increasing the availability of resources. Prior to the reform, the system was based upon a pay-as-you-go scheme, in which contributions from current workers were used to pay current pensions. The reform established a defined contributions system, in which contributions from each worker go into an individual account from which pension payments are made once the worker retires. The individual accounts are managed by specialized private firms. Beginning in September 1997, contributions to the new system became compulsory for all private sector workers. The retirement funds stock has been growing rapidly ever since; as a percentage of GDP it went from 0.2 percent in 1997, to 4.2 percent in 2001, and reached almost 6 percent in 2003.[9]

Results of an Economic Transformation

Economic Growth in the Last Two Decades

Mexican economic growth in the last two decades can be separated in four episodes. The first one comprises the adjustment period from 1983 to 1988 (covering President de la Madrid's administration), in which GDP growth averaged 0.3 percent. This disappointing figure was to a great extent a result of imbalances that had been created during the 1970s and early 1980s through a growth policy based on oil exports, government spending, and an overvalued exchange rate. After six years of intensive economic correction under de la Madrid, the Salinas administration was able to carry out important reforms and to generate more vigorous growth. In this second period, from 1989 to 1994, average GDP growth was 3.9 percent. This was made possible by the agreements reached in the Economic Stability Pact, increased levels of foreign capital inflows, credit expansion, privatization and deregulation policies, and, most important, the opening of the Mexican economy to international trade.

The 1994 crisis had terrible consequences for economic growth, which in 1995

Figure 6.9   **GDP Real Growth Rate, 1981–2003** (in percent)

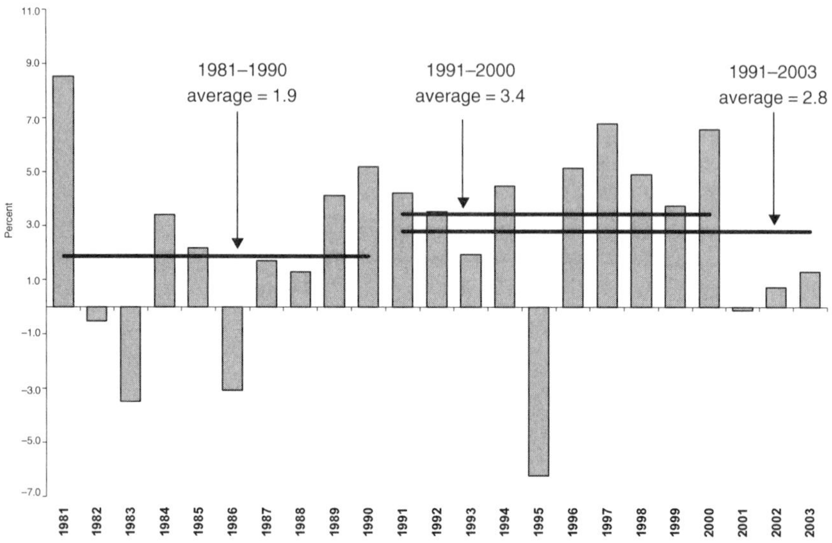

Source: INEGI (2004).

fell to –6.2 percent (see Figure 6.9). Notwithstanding the magnitude of the crisis, the following years showed the highest growth rates in the decade, averaging 5.4 percent from 1996 to 2000. The economic recovery was greatly favored by an expansionary cycle of the U.S. economy. This was made possible because of the consolidation of the exporting sector in the full operation of NAFTA. Overall, economic growth during the 1990s was higher than that registered during the 1980s, which highlights the favorable impact of the economic transformation that was implemented. However, it must also be recognized that even the higher GDP growth rates attained during the 1990s are still below a fully satisfactory level.

Finally, it is precisely the synchronization with the U.S. economy that lies beneath the slim GDP growth that has been achieved in the fourth episode, beginning in 2001. Although other internal factors have played a role, the economic slowdown in the United States during the last three years has undoubtedly been an important factor in explaining why the Mexican economy has staggered. These last issues are developed in more detail in the following section.

A Synchronized Economy

One of the most important structural changes that the Mexican economy has undergone is the opening to international trade. A direct consequence of this transformation is the synchronization of Mexico's economy to that of its main commercial partners, and most noticeably to that of the United States. Accord-

Figure 6.10   **Mexico's Exports and U.S. Imports, 1990–2004**
(nonoil, seasonally adjusted data)

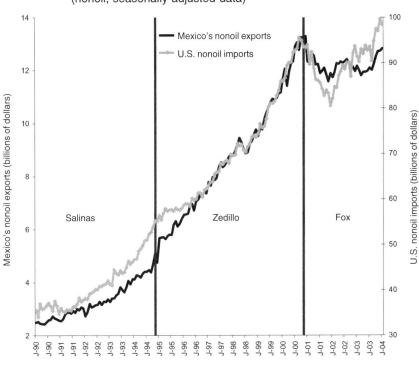

Source: INEGI (2004), U.S. Census Bureau (2004).

ingly, trade has become the natural synchronization channel, as it is shown by the co-movements displayed by Mexican nonoil exports and U.S. nonoil imports (see Figure 6.10). The synchronization phenomenon is clearly appreciated in the connection of economic growth trends, economic cycles, industrial production, and economic activity in general. These relationships are described next.

The full operation of NAFTA generated a high correlation of U.S. and Mexican economic cycles. In the early 1980s the correlation was null and even negative, which was reversed with the reforms implemented in the last years of that decade and the early 1990s. In more recent periods, especially since 1998, the cycles have moved remarkably close. In terms of industrial production, the synchronization of the United States and Mexico is surprising. Again, before the 1994 crisis there were some movements in the same direction of both indices' growth trends, but afterward the correlation became almost perfect (see Figure 6.11). This strong link is due to the large part of the trade volume that is concentrated in the industrial sector. The manufacturing branch, which accounts for approximately 70 percent of Mexico's total industrial production, in 2003 represented more than 85 percent

Figure 6.11   **Total Industrial Production, 1988–2003**
(SA indexes, mom percent change, 6mma)

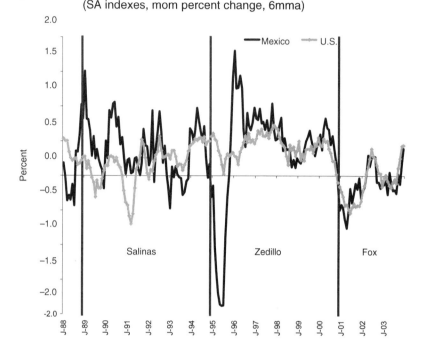

Source: INEGI (2004), Federal Reserve Bank of St. Louis (2004).

of total exports and 94 percent of total imports (see Figure 6.12). Both levels are much higher than they were in previous decades, which reflects the structural transformation of the economy and explains the close industrial association with the United States through trade (Cuevas, Messmacher, and Werner 2003).

Recent Economic Performance

The turn of the century coincided with a worsening of Mexican economic performance. The GDP growth rate averaged 0.4 percent during the last three years and industrial production fell by 1.5 percent on average. The same figures for the United States are not encouraging either: 1.9 percent for average GDP variation and –1.2 in the case of industrial production. Considering the high degree of synchronization of the two economies, it is not surprising that Mexico's economy stagnated in the period 2001–2003.

Another factor that affected Mexico in recent years is the loss of penetration of its exports in the U.S. market (see Figure 6.13). During the period 2001–2003, Mexico's share of U.S. imports fell by approximately 0.5 percent, while China increased its share by 3 percentage points. China's vigorous commercial activity

Figure 6.12 **Manufacturing Sector's Exports and Imports as Percentage of the Total, 1980–2003**

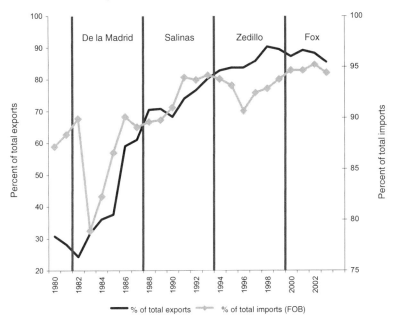

Source: INEGI (2004).

represents an important challenge for other manufacturing countries; therefore in the years to come, Mexico must improve its export sector's competitiveness to face that challenge.

The unfavorable external environment that the Mexican economy faced during the early 2000s raised awareness of the need to strengthen inner sources of growth. More specifically, lack of productivity growth and general competitiveness were pointed to as possible reasons why, in conjunction with the U.S. slowdown, Mexico's economic performance in these years was disappointing. Although the economy started to recover by the end of 2003, those and many other challenges persist.

The large degree of synchronization also caused a generalized amelioration of economic conditions in Mexico over the last months of 2003 and the first months of 2004, in line with the cyclical upturn that the U.S. economy experienced during this period. Signs of this recent amelioration of economic activity in Mexico are numerous. For example, during the last quarter of 2003, the quarterly growth of GDP in seasonally adjusted terms was 1.2 percent. This is by far the largest figure for the last three years. The external sector has also taken part in the economic recovery. Manufacturing exports started to grow in seasonally adjusted terms beginning in the first months of 2003, after experiencing a sharp decline in the sec-

Figure 6.13   **Participation in U.S. Total Nonoil Imports, 1996–2004**
(seasonally adjusted data, percent)

Source: Author's calculations with data from INEGI (2004) and U.S. Census Bureau (2004).

ond half of 2002. Moreover, they steadily increased in the first months of 2004 as well, reaching their highest level in three years.[10]

A development that is worth highlighting is that, for the first time in more than twenty years, the Mexican economy experienced a cyclical downturn rather than a crisis. This is a markedly positive development, given the large costs associated with crisis episodes. Moreover, as a direct consequence of it, the Mexican economy is entering the expansionary phase of the cycle with a solid macroeconomic background characterized by low inflation and interest rates, low private sector indebtedness levels, a sound financial sector, and solid public finances. All of these factors should allow the economy to continue its expansion in the upcoming months.

Future Challenges

The Mexican economy faces a large number of important challenges that need to be addressed in the near future in order to promote a greater degree of economic development. Although the number of fronts on which progress could be achieved is overwhelming, in this section only the most urgent ones will be briefly mentioned: the flaws of the institutional framework, the structural weakness of public finances, and the inadequate stock of human and physical capital.

Although it is difficult to find an unambiguous measure of the extent to which the institutional setup of a particular country is conducive to economic growth, practically all the measures we have indicate that the Mexican institutional framework does not provide the appropriate framework for its economy to operate efficiently.

One of the most evident manifestations of the inadequacy of the Mexican institutional setup is the lack of a reliable justice system that guarantees respect of contracts. A basic prerequisite for market economies is certainty regarding property rights. However, judicial processes in Mexico are long, expensive, and unpredictable (Marín 2003). Existing measures of the effectiveness of justice systems across different countries clearly show this: according to a Rule of Law Index, which assesses the law-and-order tradition in a country, Mexico performs poorly even when compared to other Latin American countries with similar levels of development, such as Brazil and Chile. On a scale of 1 to 10, where 10 is the highest score, Mexico's score is 5.4, while the latter countries' scores are 7 and 6.3, respectively (La Porta et al. 1997).

Another way to verify whether the institutional framework provides the appropriate environment for individual initiative is to look at the barriers faced by individuals who want to start an enterprise. Mexico also performs poorly with respect to this issue: on average, sixty-seven business days are needed to obtain legal status to operate a firm, compared to an average of sixty for other Latin American countries and twenty-seven for developed countries (Djankov et al. 2001).

Therefore, probably the major challenge that Mexico faces at present is the need to establish a reliable and accessible justice system that guarantees respect for property rights within reasonable periods. Moreover, rules regulating firms must be modernized and simplified in order to promote individual initiative.

Another area in which immediate action is urgent is that of public finances. At present, the Mexican public revenue system is flawed in at least two ways (World Bank 2001). First of all, it fails to provide the government the resources needed to promote a greater degree of competitiveness through investment in human and physical capital, and to guarantee long-term macroeconomic stability. In second place, it relies heavily on oil-related income, which is highly volatile.

This is largely a consequence of a dysfunctional tax system. At present, the Mexican tax system is extremely complicated, contains a lot of exemptions and exceptional regimes, and places all the collection effort on the Central Government. As a result, tax evasion is rampant and public sector revenues are considerably low: for 2000 they represented approximately 15 percent of GDP, while the average figure for Latin American countries was 21 percent, and that for Organization for Economic Cooperation and Development (OECD) countries was 32 percent (World Bank 2003).

In line with this low level of public revenues, the Mexican government has a limited capacity, when compared to other countries, to attend to basic social needs: while in 2000 central government expenditure was 16 percent of GDP in Mexico, it was 24 percent for the average of Latin American countries, and it was 33 percent for the average of OECD countries (World Bank 2003). Besides, as a consequence of the structure of the public revenue system, fiscal adjustments rely largely on cuts in government spending (OECD 2002), preventing socially profitable investment from being made.

Therefore, a prerequisite for further economic progress in the near future is an integral reform of the tax system, which provides the resources needed to increase the human and physical capital stock, and guarantees the long-term viability of public finances.

Mexico also faces important challenges regarding the existing stocks of human and physical capital. They are both too low at present, and they have been recognized as important determinants of economic growth by economic theory. The importance of human capital, particularly education, as a promoter of economic growth has long been recognized (OECD 2003). However, Mexico performs poorly regarding educational outputs when compared to other countries in the OECD. This is shown by the fact that Mexico has the lowest percentage of secondary education attainment in the 25–34 years age group: 25 percent, while the average for OECD countries is 75 percent. Moreover, Mexico also has one of the lowest percentages of secondary education attainment for the 45–54 years age group: 17 percent, while the average for OECD countries is 62 percent. This indicates that the country was lagging behind the rest of the OECD countries some decades ago and that it has failed to close the gap.

Mexico's stock of physical capital is also deficient. This is a result both of the large public sector investment cuts implemented during periods of crisis and of a defective regulatory setup in many strategic sectors, such as electricity and oil and gas production. One of the indicators of this are energy production costs, which are considerably higher than for most developing countries: in 1998 they reached an estimate of 10.1 U.S. dollars per kilowatt hour, compared to 6.4 U.S. dollars in average costs for the group of Chile, Argentina, Venezuela, Colombia, and Brazil (IMD 1999). Significant changes in the regulatory framework of strategic energy sectors need to be implemented in the future in order to provide agents with the appropriate incentives to direct resources toward them.

Summing up, during the last decades the Mexican economy has gone through a deep transformation, which affected both the economic policy framework and the structure of economic activity. The transformation has been mostly beneficial. As a result of it, the Mexican economy greatly reduced its vulnerability to crisis, and experienced periods of intense economic growth. However, as the recent economic performance shows, there is still much work to be done. Mexico has to undergo important changes in order to consolidate the gains of reforms already undertaken, and to significantly increase the welfare of its population.

Notes

Alejandro M. Werner is director of Economic Policy at Mexico's Ministry of Finance. Rodrigo Barros and José F. Ursúa work in the Fiscal Policy Division of the same office. The views expressed here are those of the authors and do not necessarily reflect those of the Ministry of Finance.
  1. The primary balance reflects the actual effort undertaken by the government, since it excludes interest payments.
  2. See IMF (2004).
  3. Moral hazard problems arise when a party takes actions that it would otherwise avoid if there did not exist the possibility of sharing their costs with another party that implicitly or explicitly insures them.
  4. Data from Secretaría de Hacienda y Crédito Público, SHCP (2004).
  5. Data from Instituto Nacional de Estadística, Geografía e Informática, INEGI (2004).
  6. Data from Banco de México (2004).
  7. Data from Instituto Nacional de Estadística, Geografía e Informática, INEGI (2004).
  8. Data from Comisión Nacional Bancaria y de Valores, CNBV (2004).
  9. Data from Comisión Nacional del Sistema de Ahorro para el Retiro, CONSAR (2004).
  10. Figures can be found in Instituto Nacional de Estadística, Geografía e Informática, INEGI (2004).

References

Aspe, P. 1993. *El camino mexicano de la transformación económica.* México, D.F.: Fondo de Cultura Económica.
Banco de México. 2004. "Indicadores económicos y financieros." Available at www.banxico.org.mx, Información Económica y Financiera.
Berthélemy, J., and R. Lensink. 1992. "An Assessment of the Brady Plan Agreements." *Technical papers No. 67,* Paris, France: OECD.
Carstens, A., and A. Werner. 1999. "Mexico's Monetary Policy Framework Under a Floating Exchange Rate Regime." Dirección General de Investigación Económica, Banco de México. México, D.F.: *Documento de investigación 1999–05.*
CNBV. 2004. "Información estadística de Banca Múltiple." Available at www.cnbv.gob.mx. Comisión Nacional Bancaria y de Valores.
CONSAR. 2004. "Estadísticas históricas." Available at www.consar.gob.mx. Comisión Nacional del Sistema de Ahorro para el Retiro.
Cuevas, Alfredo, Miguel Messmacher, and Alejandro Werner. 2003. "Sincronización macroeconómica entre México y sus socios comerciales del TLCAN." *Documento de investigación 2003–01,* México, D.F.: Dirección General de Investigación Económica, Banco de México.
Dijkstra, G., and N. Hermes. 2001. "Debt Relief and Economic Recovery in Latin America: Lessons for HIPCs." Paper presented at the XXIII International Congress of the Latin American Studies Association (LASA), Washington, DC.
Djankov, Simeon, Rafael La Porta, Florencio López de Silanes, and Andrei Shleifer. 2001. "The Regulation of Entry." Third draft, mimeo.
Federal Reserve Bank of St. Louis. 2004. "Economic Data—FRED II." Available at http://research.stlouisfed.org/fred2/Business/Fiscal.
Gil Díaz, F. 1998. "The Origin of Mexico's 1994 Financial Crisis." *The Cato Journal* 17, no. 3 (Winter).

————. 2000. "The China Sindrome or the Tequila Crisis." Paper presented at Conference on Fiscal and Financial Reforms in Latin America, November 9–11, 2000, Stanford, California.

————. 2003. "Don't Blame Our Failures on Reforms that Have Not Taken Place." *Fraser Forum* (June), Vancouver, Canada.

IMD (International Institute for Management Development). 1999. *World Competitiveness Yearbook 1998.* Lausanne, Switzerland: IMD.

IMF (International Monetary Fund). 2004. "International Financial Statistics." Available at http://ifs.apdi.net/imf/logon.aspx.

INEGI (Instituto Nacional de Estadística, Geografía e Informática). 2004. *Banco de información económica.* Available at www.inegi.gob.mx.

La Porta, R., Florencio López de Silance, Andrei Schleifer, and Robert Vishny. 1997. "Legal Determinants of External Finance." *NBER Working Paper 5879,* Cambridge, MA: National Bureau of Economic Research.

Lustig, N. 1994. *México: Hacia la reconstrucción de una economía.* El Colegio de México, Fondo de Cultura Económica, México, D.F.

Marín, J. 2003. "Desafíos de la justicia civil en México," *Cambio Institucional: Agenda Pendiente para las Políticas Públicas en México.* México, D.F.: Gaceta de Economía.

Martínez, L., and A. Werner. 2002. "The Exchange Rate Regime and the Currency Composition of Corporate Debt: The Mexican Experience." *Journal of Development Economics* (December).

Martínez, Lorenza, Oscar Sánchez, and Alejandro Werner. 2001. "Consideraciones sobre la conducción de la política monetaria y el mecanismo de transmisión en México." *Documento de investigación 2001–02.* México, D.F.: Dirección General de Investigación Económica, Banco de México.

Murillo, J. 2003. "La banca en México después de la privatización: Auge crisis y reordenamiento." Mimeo, México, D.F.

OECD (Organization for Economic Cooperation and Development). 2002. *Estudios económicos de la OCDE: México.* México, D.F.: Gaceta de Economía.

————. 2003. *Education at a Glance, OECD Economic Indicators 2003.* Paris, France: OECD.

México. Presidencia de la República. Various years. *Informe de Gobierno.*

Rogozinski, J. 1993. *La privatización de empresas paraestatales.* México, D.F.: Fondo de Cultura Económica.

SHCP (Secretaría de Hacienda y Crédito Público). 2004. "Estadísticas oportunas de finanzas públicas y deuda pública." Available at www.shcp.gob.mx, *Información Económica, Datos Económicos y Financieros.*

Teichman, J. 1995. *Privatization and Political Change in Mexico.* Pittsburgh, PA: Pitt Latin American Series, University of Pittsburgh Press.

U.S. Census Bureau. 2001. "Historical Series." Available at www.census.gov.gov, Statistics, Foreign Trade.

World Bank. 2001. *Mexico: A Comprehensive Development Agenda for the New Era.* Washington, DC: The World Bank.

————. 2003. *World Development Indicators.* Washington, DC: The World Bank.

7

BORIS GRAIZBORD AND ADRIÁN GUILLERMO AGUILAR

Regional Differences and the Economic and Social Geography of Mexico at the Beginning of the Twenty-first Century

The differences between rich and poor in Mexico were roughly constant from 1994 to 2002, when the richest 10 percent had an average income 23 to 24 times greater than that of the poorest 10 percent. Graizbord and Aguilar report that the gap between the Center and the North is narrowing, because although the North had a higher per capita income than the Center, it grew more slowly. The poorest region in Mexico, the South, grew very slowly. (For definitions of regions, see Map 1.1 and Table 1.2).

The disparate growth rates reflect the high foreign direct investment as well as the location of large corporate headquarters and high-end financial and communication services in the Federal District.

Activities leading to local growth were oil in Campeche and tourism in Cancún in the state of Quintana Roo. Unlike activities that have little impact on other sectors of the economy, industrial growth in the North induced growth in activities supplying industry and using its products.

Some amelioration of this polarizing trend can be expected because investment in schools and hospitals, which makes regions attractive for investment, was more evenly spread across Mexico than investment in economic overhead capital. Nonetheless, Mexico does not have an overall implemented development plan; unification of various government plans and coordination among the several government bureaucracies is needed for government activities to have a unified impact on regional development.

Introduction: The National Context

Throughout its history, Mexico has been characterized by strikingly different conditions between rich and poor, urban and rural, and among its regions (Graizbord and Ruiz 1996). The economic crisis of the early 1990s was accompanied by increasing inequality in income distribution, as well as by a decline in the level of living of much of the population. In 1994, the buying power of the minimum wage in Mexico was 40 percent of what it had been in 1982. The number of poor people was 39.8 million in 1990, with more than 15 million in extreme poverty[1] (seven out of ten of whom lived in rural areas). In 1999, these figures increased to 46 million and 18 million respectively. By 2004, it was estimated that both the share and absolute number of the Mexican population living in poverty and in extreme poverty had decreased from 1999 levels, as shown in Table 7.1, which indicates that the share of indigent and poor fell from 65.4 to 56.3 percent of the population during this period.

Despite this improvement, the average income of those households in the richest 10 percent was almost twenty-three times that of the lowest decile in 2000, compared to fourteen in 1984 and twenty-four times in 1994. The total household income share of the richest 10 percent was 42.7 percent in 2000 compared to the middle strata (deciles IV to VII), which together participated with 24.2 percent, and was 2.4 times the average income of those in the next decile just below them (only 1.8 times in 1984). As Table 7.2a shows, the Gini coefficient (a measure of inequality) increased from 0.477 in 1984 to 0.518 in 1989 and stabilized around this mark throughout the next decade, reaching its highest value of 0.538 in 1994. Also, the average number of household members who became recipients of monetary income increased from 1.58 in 1984 to 1.67 in 1989 and to almost two (1.92) in 2000 (Table 7.2b).

The Regional Context

Mexico is a federal republic. It is administratively and politically divided into thirty-two states (including a Federal District, which is now in a transition toward becoming the thirty-second state with full rights and obligations),[2] and more than 2,400 municipalities.

Changes in the distribution of per capita income in Mexico's states are indicated in Table 7.3, and its current level of well-being is shown in Map 7.1. The highest income per capita, according to the state in which it was received, reflected the administrative role of the Federal District (whose income was 2.6 times that of the national average in 2002), and the influence of oil (Campeche), tourism (Cancún in Quintana Roo), and industrial growth (Nuevo León).

From 1993 to 2002, the highest average growth rate, of more than 4 percent, occurred basically due to industrial growth and in particular the arrival of transnational corporation plants and subsidiaries in Aguascalientes, Querétaro, and Guanajuato, while political unrest in Chiapas and Oaxaca was at least in part the result of these areas having a per capita income only one-sixth that of the Federal District (2 thousand versus 13 thousand U.S. dollars) during these years (see Table 7.3). States in the Central and Northern regions show, with exceptions (Morelos, Hidalgo, México,

Table 7.1

Poverty Indicators for Mexico, 1980–2004

| | 1980 | | | 1990 | | | 1999 | | | 2004[a] | |
| | Households | Population | | Households | Population | | Households | Population | | Population | |
	%	Million	%	%	Million	%	%	Million	%	Million	%
Poverty[b]	34	28.7	42.5	39.3	39.8	47.8	38	45.7	46.9	41.1	41.1
Indigence[c]	11	10.6	15.7	14.1	15.6	18.8	13	18	18.5	15.2	15.2

Source: UTAL, América Latina: hogares y población bajo las líneas de la pobreza y de indigencia. Available at www.utal.org/hogaresypoblacion2.htm. Also, NOTIMEX, Santiago de Chile, April 5, 2004.

[a]Estimated.

[b]Considered in "patrimonial poverty." This category refers, according to SEDESOL's Technical Committee for the Measurement of Poverty, to all those households whose daily income was less than $41.80 Mexican pesos (approx. US$4.50) in 2000. Being this to all those households whose daily income was less than $41.80 Mexican pesos (approx. US$4.50) in 2000. This amount is the minimum estimated family income to satisfy the needs for food, health, education, transport, and other goods and services considered basic for human beings.

[c]Not enough to provide for minimum food requirements.

94

Table 7.2a

Mexico: Percentage Distribution of Household Monetary Income by Decile, 1984–2000

Decile	1984	1989	1992	1994	1996	1998	2000
I	1.4	1.1	1.0	1.0	1.1	0.9	1.1
II	2.5	2.3	2.1	2.1	2.3	2.0	2.1
III	3.6	3.3	3.1	3.0	3.2	3.0	3.1
IV	4.6	4.4	4.0	3.9	4.1	4.0	4.1
V	5.8	5.5	5.1	4.9	5.2	5.2	5.2
VI	7.3	6.7	6.3	6.2	6.5	6.5	6.6
VII	9.2	8.5	8.1	8.0	8.2	8.2	8.3
VIII	12.0	11.0	10.8	10.5	10.9	10.9	10.8
IX	16.8	15.6	15.9	15.6	15.6	16.0	15.9
X	36.8	41.6	43.6	44.7	42.8	43.3	42.7
Total	100.0	100.0	100.0	100.0	100.0	100.0	100.0
Gini[a]	0.477	0.518	0.532	0.538	0.521	0.534	0.523

Source: Cortés (2003 Table 2).
[a]A measure of inequality of a distribution, usually income. In the Gini coefficient a maximum value of 1 means absolute inequality, and minimum values of 0 absolute equality.

Table 7.2b

Mexico: Average Household Monetary Income by Decile, 1984–2000
(in 2001 Mexican pesos[a])

Decile	1984	1989	1992	1994	1996	1998	2000
I	1,031.7	978.0	799.6	923.5	793.8	621.3	910.6
II	1,777.5	1,896.5	1,758.2	1,814.1	1,524.6	1,444.4	1,732.4
III	2,436.7	2,537.0	2,581.4	2,547.0	1,980.3	1,965.2	2,346.4
IV	2,978.3	3,137.4	3,087.9	3,206.1	2,481.8	2,565.6	2,938.9
V	3,645.3	3,796.5	3,745.6	3,881.0	2,867.3	3,017.0	3,562.2
VI	4,401.9	4,530.1	4,390.4	4,489.3	3,557.2	3,739.9	4,240.0
VII	5,251.6	5,255.9	5,265.9	5,396.3	4,077.3	4,391.2	5,291.0
VIII	6,489.7	6,490.4	6,407.3	6,780.5	5,028.1	5,564.7	6,584.9
IX	7,959.1	8,244.3	8,869.0	9,221.5	6,828.5	7,552.9	8,484.3
X	14,422.2	18,847.8	21,344.6	22,517.5	15,464.7	17,522.4	20,639.6
Total	5,791.1	6,481.1	6,777.0	7,115.1	5,246.6	5,628.5	6,258.3
recipients per household	1.58	1.67	1.69	1.73	1.77	1.80	1.92

Source: Cortés (2003 Table 1).
[a]US$1.00 = $9.34 Mexican pesos in 2001.

Table 7.3

Mexican States by Region and Income per Capita (GDPpc$_i$), 1993 and 2002

Mexican states	GDPpc 1993[a]	GDPpc 2002 [b]	(GDPpc$_i$/ GDP pc$_n$) 100 in 1993c	(GDPpc$_i$/ GDP pc$_n$) 100 in 2002c	Growth rate 1993–2002
Mexico	4,101.08	5,164.65	100.00	100.00	2.60
Center	4,264.11	5,333.37	103.98	103.27	2.52
Aguascalientes	4,460.79	6,626.44	108.8	128.30	4.50
Colima	4,169.57	5,117.14	101.6	99.08	2.30
Distrito Federal	10,099.53	13,312.96	246.2	257.77	3.12
Guanajuato	2,829.36	4,034.87	68.9	78.12	4.02
Hidalgo	2,715.46	3,135.93	66.2	60.72	1.61
Jalisco	4,131.85	5,173.66	100.7	100.17	2.53
México	3,329.93	3,979.92	81.1	77.06	2.00
Michoacán	2,237.61	2,906.31	54.5	56.27	2.95
Morelos	3,869.71	4,442.23	94.3	86.01	1.54
Puebla	2,584.65	3,426.98	63.0	66.35	3.18
Querétaro	4,245.08	6,211.44	103.4	120.27	4.32
Tlaxcala	2,202.59	2,813.03	53.7	54.47	2.76
Veracruz	2,505.42	2,998.91	61.0	58.07	2.02
North	4,676.06	5,997.48	114.02	116.13	2.80
Baja California	6,085.52	6,244.34	148.4	120.91	0.29
Baja California Sur	5,588.16	6,446.28	136.2	124.82	1.60
Chihuahua	5,431.89	7,112.04	132.4	137.71	3.04
Coahuila	5,151.97	7,287.97	125.6	141.11	3.93
Durango	3,367.81	4,427.49	82.1	85.73	3.09
Nayarit	2,732.94	3,059.42	66.6	59.24	1.26
Nuevo León	6,948.08	9,335.04	169.3	180.75	3.34
San Luis Potosí	3,060.24	3,878.79	74.6	75.10	2.67
Sinaloa	3,526.64	4,074.37	86.0	78.89	1.62
Sonora	4,882.88	6,014.06	119.0	116.45	2.34
Tamaulipas	4,186.13	5,415.90	102.0	104.86	2.90
Zacatecas	2,298.87	3,188.48	56.0	61.74	3.70
South	2,681.75	3,187.47	65.39	61.72	1.94
Campeche	7,226.31	8,174.48	176.1	158.28	1.38
Chiapas	1,853.86	2,230.27	45.2	43.18	2.08
Guerrero	2,335.03	2,671.13	56.9	51.72	1.51
Oaxaca	1,871.18	2,148.82	45.6	41.61	1.55
Quintana Roo	7,171.17	7,671.53	174.8	148.54	0.75
Tabasco	2,769.61	3,064.64	67.5	59.34	1.13
Yucatán	3,187.09	4,160.17	77.7	80.55	3.00

Source: Proyecciones de población y principales características por entidad federativa, CONAPO, available at www.conapo.gob.mx/micros/informe/anexo04.xls; data on GDP (gross domestic product) in Producto Interno Bruto por Entidad Federativa, BIE, INEGI, available at http://dgcnesyp.inegi.gob.mx/bdine/m15/m1501109.htm.
[a]In current dollars of 1993. 1 dollar = 3.1152 current pesos of 1993.
[b]In current dollars of 2002. 1 dollar = 9.6560 current pesos of 2002.
[c]Compares the state value against the national value in 1993 and 2002.

Map 7.1 **Mexico: Social Well-Being Levels,* 1995**

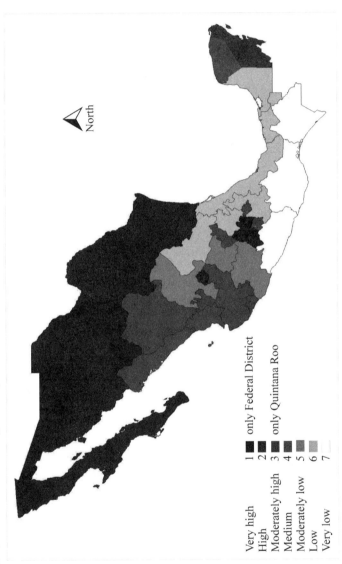

Very high	1	only Federal District
High	2	
Moderately high	3	only Quintana Roo
Medium	4	
Moderately low	5	
Low	6	
Very low	7	

Source: INEGI, 1996, Sistema Nacional Estadístico y de Información Geográfica, www.inegi.gob.mx/prod_serv/contenidos/espanol/niveles/prod_serv96.asp?c=96

*Social well-being levels in Mexico are measured by INEGI considering thirty-five census variables. These include basically indicators related to (i) age structure of the population; (ii) schooling; (iii) working population; and (iv) housing conditions variables.

A cluster analysis was used to find groups with similar values in the standardized variables included in a K dimensional statistical space. The resulting seven groups go from "very high" (1) to "very low" (7).

Veracruz, Baja California, Baja California Sur, Nayarit, Sinaloa), a higher or similar growth rate than the country as a whole. On the other hand, per capita income growth in the Southern states was below the country's average, with the exception of Yucatán. There are many ways to subdivide (regionalize) the vast 2 million square kilometers of Mexico's land surface. The country's territory has been conventionally divided into nine geoeconomic regions (Graizbord and Ruiz 1996), and intermittently perceived as divided in three "great" regions: North, Center, and South (Alba 1976; Durand 1998; Graizbord and León 2002).

Some of the states within a great region have very different levels of "well-being" classifications from the others. The Mexican statistical institute (Instituto Nacional de Estadistíca, Geografia e Informática) measures well-being in each state by assessing the age structure of its population, years of school of its working population, and housing conditions (see note in Map 7.1), creating an index that ranges from 1 (highest) to 7 (lowest). In general it is not difficult to see that the majority of the states in the North are classified with a well-being index of 2, with some exceptions, and those in the South with a 6 or 7, while the Center is more heterogeneous. Of course, none of these regions are homogeneous. The reader should be aware that the larger the region, or subnational territorial unit, the greater the internal variation among its constituent states. Consequently, we note that the average well-being index for Mexico in 1995 was moderately high, indicated by a score of 3, and also that the variations in well-being within regions were so great that the differences in well-being among the regions was not statistically significant.[3]

Nevertheless, these huge territorial entities (North, Center, and South regions) seem to correspond to different ecological conditions, natural endowments, historical development, cultural traits, and political preferences.[4] Until recently, the South was an underdeveloped region with abundant water resources,[5] and not inclined yet to any political party in the national ideological left-right spectrum; the developed industrial North with limited water resources, but irrigated agriculture, has been historically inclined to center-right politics; and the traditionally congested Center of the country, where water resources are mined and polluted, with a mixture of migrants from all over the country and a cosmopolitan and sophisticated population, shows preferences for left-center ideologies, and has been the leading economic, political, and cultural engine in Mexico's development.

The economic development of these regions is often tied to their economic conditions and to factors such as policy, weather, political conditions, and so forth. In the following pages, we first summarize some economic growth theories and then indicate the regional distribution of public investment (overhead capital investment: OC); both economic and social overhead capital (EOC and SOC); private investment (PI); gross domestic capital formation (GKF); and foreign direct investment (FDI). The level and distribution of these variables has led to reducing regional differences, called "convergence," in social and economic conditions among these regions, despite the fact that, according to our current research findings,[6] there are opposing trends in per capita wages and salaries and labor produc-

Table 7.4

Mexican States by Region: Population and Levels of Well-Being, 1995

Region and states	Population (thousands)	Level of well-being
Center[a]	52,867.2	4
Aguascalientes	862.7	2
Colima	488.0	4
Distrito Federal	8,489.0	1
Guanajuato	4,406.5	7
Hidalgo	2,112.4	4
Jalisco	5,991.1	2
México	11,707.9	5
Michoacán	3,870.6	4
Morelos	1,442.6	
Puebla	4,624.3	6
Querétaro	1,250.4	4
Tlaxcala	883.9	4
Veracruz	6,737.3	6
North[a]	23,909.3	3
Baja California	2112.1	2
Baja California Sur	375.4	
Chihuahua	2,793.5	2
Coahuila	2,173.7	2
Durango	1,431.7	4
Nayarit	896.7	4
Nuevo León	3,550.1	2
San Luis Potosí	2,200.7	6
Sinaloa	2,425.6	2
Sonora	2,085.5	2
Tamaulipas	2,527.3	2
Zacatecas	1,336.4	4
South[a]	14,161.5	6
Campeche	642.5	6
Chiapas	3,584.7	7
Guerrero	2,916.5	6
Oaxaca	3,228.8	7
Quintana Roo	703.5	3
Tabasco	1,748.7	6
Yucatán	1,336.4	4

Source: Author's classification for North, Center, and South; for well-being level see note in Map 7.1.

[a]Author's classification for North, Center, and South Great Regions: we have included in those great regions states which belong to recognized geoeconomic regions, with one exception being the five Center-North states, of which Zacatecas and San Luis Potosí have been assigned to the North Great Region and Aguascalientes, Guanajuato, and Querétaro to the Center Great Region. These last three are part of the Bajío natural region that also includes part of Jalisco and part of Michoacán. For geoeconomic regions see Graizbord and Ruiz 1996. Well-being level for each region was estimated by multiplying the 1995 well-being level for each state by its 1995 population, and then summing the total for a region and dividing by the population for the region.

tivity. We conclude our chapter by discussing regional policy and the social impacts of economic integration.

Growth Theories

The neoclassical model identifies three sources of output growth: capital stock, the labor force, and technology. The Solow (1979 [1956]) growth model argues that the growth in output per capita is driven by the rate of technological progress that occurs because entrepreneurs are looking for ways to make a profit and one way of doing this is to produce new ideas (Armstrong and Taylor 2000). More recently, analytical models have been developed by Romer (1986) in which it is implied that marginal productivity of knowledge increases while marginal productivity of physical capital decreases—thus the importance of education,[7] social capital,[8] and institutional development,[9] as well as arguments about increasing economies of small-scale production (Piore and Sabel 1984). A study by Harris and Trainor (1997, cited in Armstrong and Taylor 2000) found that the determinant factors of regional disparities in the United Kingdom were: the skill level of a region's working force; its flexibility; the proportion of small plants in a region (since scale economies have become less important due to recent changes in production techniques); and better industrial relations compared to years previous to 1980.

Economic growth, however, does not occur evenly throughout a nation. According to Perroux (1950), Myrdal (1959), and Hirschman (1958), national or regional economic growth will occur differentially in space and time. Geographical association of a large population and numerous economic activities give rise to localization and urbanization economies, external to firms. Development of these agglomeration economies or "growth poles" will create regional disparities that tend to disappear once new opportunities emerge. The additional income in the newly favored areas will lead to "convergence," as factors of production adjust by migrating or moving to regions or sectors where jobs are being created.

The speed at which a region's output per capita grows, as argued by Kaldor (1970, cited in Armstrong and Taylor 2000), is determined by the extent to which the region is able to exploit scale economies and to reap the benefits that accrue from greater specialization. These benefits vary according to the type of productive activity in which a region specializes. In particular, the manufacturing sector is able to reap substantially greater benefits from growth than accrue from land-based activities like mining and agriculture.

Another way of looking at regional differences in growth is that technical progress diffuses across the world so that even small economies can benefit without having to rely on knowledge created within their own boundaries. A rapid transfer of technological knowledge across regions means that there is less reason to expect spatial disparities in growth rate, and that spatial disparities in per capita incomes should converge over the long run (Armstrong and Taylor 2000).

The question is, why are there spatial disparities in growth rates? The answer is because different economies have different incentives to invest and to use existing technical knowledge due to more or less favorable economic and social infrastructure, more or less developed legal and political institutions, and more or less stable social and political environment (Armstrong and Taylor 2000).

Public Investment

Regional inequalities reflect differences in physical and social infrastructure (Fuentes 2003).[10] Economists call additions to capital "investment." The sum of investment or gross domestic capital formation (GKF) includes public investment (OC), private investment (PI), and foreign direct investment (FDI), which can be carried out by private domestic and foreign units with some restrictions on activities in which they are permitted, and by national government entities. In recent years, public investment in Mexico has been directed to infrastructure, rather than to directly productive activities, as was the case before the explicit adoption of the neoliberal and open market model during the Salinas administration in the early nineties. Public investment in infrastructure is divided into economic overhead capital (EOC)—composed of physical infrastructure such as airports, highways, railroads, ports, electricity, telecommunications—and social overhead capital (SOC) —composed of schools and hospitals (Hirschman 1958; Hansen 1965; Fuentes 2003).

The investment of public capital is more productive in low-income regions of Mexico because of diminishing returns to scale. According to Hansen (1965, cited in Fuentes 2003), EOC explains disparities in gross domestic product per capita (GDPpc) in the moderately developed states, those with a GDPpc around the national value, and SOC explains it in the less developed states, those with lower than the national GDPpc. Proportionately there is more SOC than EOC investment, and the first social overhead capital is more evenly spread among the states, which is consistent with an increasing emphasis on investment in "human capital."[11]

There is an apparent rationality in the EOC and SOC mix by state. Table 7.5 shows the highest EOC index values in the higher-income states (GDPpc > 38.8, measured as an index where the GDPpc of the Federal District is equal to 100, and well-being levels 1 and 2), and the highest SOC index values in the lower-income states (GDPpc < 38.8, and well-being levels 6 and 7). Exceptions are the state of Mexico, a rich state economy with wide socioeconomic differences but a high well-being level and a low income per capita and, consequently, a high SOC index, and Veracruz, a relatively large state economy, with a low well-being level and the highest SOC index.

Private Investment

Private investment (PI) takes place each year. The sum of private investment was obtained as a residual, as information is not available. This residual is obtained by

Table 7.5

Mexican States: Disparities in Public Infrastructure by GDP per Capita and Level of Well-Being, 1998

Mexican states	EOC[a]	SOC[b]	OC[c]	GDP[d]	GDPpc[e]	Well-being level[f]
Mexico	33.37	55.95	61.42	—	38.80	
Richest						
1 Distrito Federal	100.00[g]	45.42	100.00[g]	100.00[g]	100.00[g]	1
2 Nuevo León	45.09	48.15	64.11	29.74	70.11	2
3 Coahuila	31.75	43.33	51.63	14.20	54.73	2
4 Chihuahua	27.25	56.14	57.34	18.68	53.41	2
5 Aguascalientes	31.91	28.19	41.33	4.92	49.77	2
6 Baja California Sur	52.45	37.61	61.93	2.42	48.42	2
7 Baja California	50.37	27.65	53.65	13.70	46.88	2
8 Sonora	46.95	44.63	62.98	12.22	45.16	2
9 Tamaulipas	35.83	52.39	60.67	13.10	40.69	2
10 Estado de México	36.73	66.24	70.80	47.01	29.88	2
Moderate						
11 Qintana Roo	54.76	34.40	61.31	6.20	57.62	3
12 Sinaloa	36.78	60.44	66.86	9.25	30.60	4
13 Durango	17.87	73.52	62.84	5.89	33.26	4
14 Nayarit	23.56	55.73	54.52	2.59	22.98	4
15 Jalisco	36.80	69.45	73.06	28.25	38.86	4
16 Colima	45.70	39.14	58.34	2.50	38.44	4
17 Queretaro	32.80	41.50	51.09	7.49	46.66	4
18 Tlaxcala	31.22	31.37	43.03	2.40	21.13	4
19 Morelos	38.93	32.60	49.19	6.04	33.37	4
20 Yucatán	38.94	39.12	53.67	5.85	31.25	4
21 Guanajuato	24.43	53.87	53.84	14.81	30.31	5
22 Michoacán	21.62	75.86	67.03	10.91	21.83	5
23 Zacatecas	13.61	64.28	53.56	3.59	23.95	5

(Continued)

Table 7.5 (continued)

Mexican states	EOC[a]	SOC[b]	OC[c]	GDP[d]	GDPpc[e]	Well-being level[f]
Mexico		33.37	55.95	61.42	—	38.80
Richest						
Poorest						
24 Campeche	24.83	28.19	41.33	4.92	61.38	6
25 San Luis Potosí	19.70	66.75	59.45	7.64	29.13	6
26 Puebla	19.31	63.95	57.26	15.08	25.73	6
27 Hidalgo	20.36	67.69	60.55	6.61	23.55	6
28 Tabasco	21.08	56.98	53.68	5.44	23.01	6
29 Veracruz	38.22	100.00[g]	95.04	19.51	22.53	6
30 Guerrero	23.92	84.13	74.30	7.52	20.07	7
31 Chiapas	8.97	95.79	72.04	7.89	16.76	7
32 Oaxaca	15.97	84.69	69.22	6.71	16.14	7

Source: For EOC, SOC, and OC, see Fuentes 2003, cuadro 2; Table 3 for GDP per capita; for level of well-being see note in Map 7.1.
[a]EOC = Economic Overhead Capital investment, includes public investment in airports, highways, railroads, ports, electricity, telecommunications.
[b]SOC = Social Overhead Capital investment, includes education and health facilities.
[c]OC = Sum of EOC and SOC.
[d]GDP = Gross Domestic Product, which in this case indicates the relative size of the state's economy, compared with that of the largest state economy (Distrito Federal = 100.00).
[e]GDPpc = Gross Domestic Product/state population for 2002 as percentage from highest (Distrito Federal = 100.00).
[f]See note in Map 7.1.
[g]Values are percentage of, not highest.

subtracting foreign investment, from gross capital formation (GKF) to obtain total national or domestic investment; public investment (OC) is deducted from this figure to obtain private investment. In Mexico, GKF has grown by a yearly rate of around 5 percent between 1995 and 2001. As a percentage of the country's GDP in 1995 it reached more than 18 percent while in 2001 it reached almost 23 percent of that year's GDP. On the other hand private investment was 66.3 percent of GKF in 1995 and 65.4 percent in 2001. These proportions represent close to 12 percent and 15 percent of the country's GDP in 1995 and 2001, respectively.

In aggregated terms, private investment in the Northern states in 2001 reached 16.3 percent of gross regional product, from 10.1 percent in 1995, while the Southern states increased from 9.2 percent in 1995 to 42.1 percent in 2001 of the region's share in the country's GDP. These regional differences show the contradictory impacts of the North American Free Trade Agreement (NAFTA), as the Southern states took advantage of a decentralizing trend. In particular, private investment was directed mainly to tourism (Oaxaca and Guerrero) but also to oil associated activities (Tabasco) in the South. The private investment share in the Central Region fell from 13.4 percent of the 1995 Gross Regional Product to 9.8 in 2001, as a result of the absolute and relative decline in private investment in the Federal District from US$1.4 billion and a relatively low 2.4 percent of the GDP total in 1995 to a disinvestment of US$10.1 billion in 2001. A partial reason for this negative figure of disinvestment in the Federal District was probably the decentralization of manufacturing activities as well as of population to the neighboring states (Estado de México, Querétaro, Puebla, etc.) and the rest of the country.

In 1995 the state of Mexico received the highest share of PI in the Central Region up to US$6.4 billion or 31 percent of this region's total. This amount represented 20.7 percent of total private investment in the country in 1995. In 2001, PI in the state of Mexico amounted to US$11.8 billion representing again the highest share in the Central Region (38 percent) and in the country as a whole (14.8 percent). Coahuila in the North was the destination of the highest regional flow in regional PI, representing US$2.1 billion or 27.2 percent of the regional total. And in the South, PI in Guerrero amounted to US$1.4 billion or more than half (57.5 percent) in that region.

The reader should be aware that, in general, for the country as a whole, around 15 percent of total GKF figures correspond to public investment and 65 percent to private investment. The remaining 20 percent is direct foreign investment . These proportions vary within the three great regions. In the Center private investment reached almost 70 percent in 1995 and only 50 percent in 2001 of total investment while public investment maintained its share of 13 percent of GKF in both years, while FDI represented 35 percent in 2001 against only 18 percent in 1995. Private investment in the North showed similar proportion of GKF in 1995 but a lower 51 percent in 2001. An opposite tendency was experienced in the South: while private investment's share of GKF was 55 percent in 1995 by 2001 it reached

Table7. 6a

Mexican States by Region: GDP, GKF, FDI, OC, and PI, 1995 and 2001
(in millions of current dollars)[a]

Mexican States	Gross domestic product (GDP)		Gross capital formation (GKF)		Foreign direct investment (FDI)		Public investment (OC)		Private investment (PI)[b]	
	1995	2001	1995	2001	1995	2001	1995	2001	1995	2001
Mexico	256,299.1	529,874.6	46,269.7	121,636.6	8,332.9	26,569.2	7,265.9	15,525.2	30,670.9	79,542.2
Center	153,410.7	315,313.7	29,952.8	61,191.4	5,506.1	21,921.3	3,902.0	8,272.2	20,544.6	30,997.9
Aguascalientes	2,683.4	6,466.9	832.0	1,990.0	27.1	90.1	56.3	92.3	748.6	1,809.1
Colima	1,453.9	2,838.2	323.6	870.6	3.0	2.7	41.9	93.3	278.7	775.7
Distrito Federal	59,071.2	116,392.3	7,858.0	12,934.8	4,476.9	19,521.5	1,970.4	3,501.0	1,410.6	−10,087.7
Guanajuato	8,870.5	19,076.8	1,664.0	5,348.0	6.3	217.0	179.0	391.0	1,478.7	4,740.0
Hidalgo	3,600.0	7,359.3	1,063.1	2,363.1	48.3	76.5	120.9	339.1	894.0	1,947.5
Jalisco	16,362.9	34,273.7	1,109.4	3,979.9	114.4	444.0	158.8	489.9	836.2	3,046.1
México	25,738.2	56,450.4	7,442.0	13,432.3	606.2	746.0	468.6	864.6	6,367.1	11,821.7
Michoacán	6,372.5	12,282.9	1,294.3	5,348.0	48.8	5.8	106.0	375.9	1,139.5	4,966.3
Morelos	3,593.6	7,534.3	1,664.0	1,368.1	67.6	18.5	62.0	135.0	1,534.4	1,214.6
Puebla	8,154.1	18,843.5	2,403.6	4,726.2	25.3	488.5	96.9	459.2	2,281.4	3,778.5
Querétaro	3,852.5	9,123.1	1,340.5	2,363.1	42.0	177.4	65.9	156.0	1,232.6	2,029.7
Tlaxcala	1,338.6	2,948.0	92.4	870.6	11.2	13.2	57.4	82.5	23.8	775.0
Veracruz	12,319.3	21,724.5	2,865.9	5,596.8	29.0	120.1	517.9	1,295.1	2,318.9	4,181.6
North	75,588.0	161,761.3	11,740.8	33,953.8	2,741.6	4,430.6	1,388.6	3,229.6	7,610.6	26,293.5
Baja California	7,413.5	17,282.8	878.2	2,363.1	538.1	813.6	75.9	247.8	264.2	1,301.7
Baja California Sur	1,432.4	2,980.0	92.4	995.0	20.9	136.1	45.6	92.5	26.0	766.3
Chihuahua	10,143.1	23,068.4	924.5	5,472.4	528.7	742.1	162.8	307.9	232.9	4,422.4
Coahuila	7,852.5	16,985.0	2,311.2	3,606.8	120.4	160.6	116.9	189.7	2,073.9	3,256.5
Durango	3,419.2	6,691.3	184.9	1,741.2	40.5	9.9	71.0	191.5	73.4	1,539.9
Nayarit	1,586.2	3,069.8	277.3	1,741.2	2.0	33.2	68.0	116.4	207.3	1,591.6
Nuevo León	16,556.6	36,552.3	1,941.4	4,850.5	704.1	1,751.0	198.8	493.9	1,038.5	2,605.7

San Luis Potosí	4,404.8	9,124.9	277.3	2,363.1	131.5	207.1	65.6	226.9	80.2	1,929.1
Sinaloa	5,931.3	11,154.0	785.8	995.0	94.1	59.8	216.5	255.1	475.2	680.0
Sonora	7,194.6	15,010.4	1,756.5	2,984.9	155.4	175.7	140.4	320.4	1,460.7	2,488.8
Tamaulipas	7,406.2	15,711.9	2,080.1	5,223.7	393.7	336.0	193.3	607.5	1,493.0	4,280.1
Zacatecas	2,247.7	4,130.3	231.1	1,616.8	12.2	5.5	33.6	180.0	185.3	1,431.4
South	27,300.4	52,799.7	4,576.1	26,491.4	85.2	217.3	1,975.3	4,023.4	2,515.7	22,250.7
Campeche	3,096.6	5,972.3	277.3	2,363.1	0.5	-21.4	404.6	901.6	-127.8	1,482.8
Chiapas	4,851.6	9,189.1	1,155.6	5,845.5	0.4	-0.9	361.6	747.9	793.5	5,098.5
Guerrero	4,845.1	8,733.7	1,664.0	4,974.9	45.2	20.7	171.1	411.3	1,447.7	4,542.9
Oaxaca	4,302.8	7,963.8	647.1	4,104.3	-2.1	-1.7	188.4	564.5	460.8	3,541.5
Quintana Roo	3,347.1	7,433.6	138.7	1,616.8	20.5	78.0	54.2	120.9	64.0	1,417.9
Tabasco	3,467.5	6,259.5	416.0	6,218.6	1.2	4.1	737.4	1,049.2	-322.5	5,165.4
Yucatán	3,389.6	7,247.6	277.3	1,368.1	19.5	138.5	58.0	227.9	199.9	1,001.7

Source: Estimates based on INEGI for GKF: http://dgcnesyp.inegi.gob.mx/BDINE/M10/M1000062.htm; and www.inegi.gob.mx/est/contenidos/espanol/tematicos/mediano/med.asp?t=goes018&c=1697; for GDP: http://dgcnesyp.inegi.gob.mx/BDINE/M15/M1500002.htm; and for FDI: http://dgcnesyp.inegi.gob.mx/BDINE/K10/K1000005.htm; and for OC: Presidencia de la República, Anexo Estadístico del Segundo Informe de Gobierno (Ernesto Zedillo Poncede León), 1996:285, and Anexo Estadístico del Segundo Informe de Gobierno (Vicente Fox Quezada), 2002:459.

[a]US$1 = 6.419 current pesos of 1995 and = 9.3425 current pesos of 2001.

[b]PI = GKF – (FDI + OC).

Table7.6b

Mexican States by Region: GDP, GKF, FDI, OC, and PI, 1995 and 2001 (percentages)

Mexican States	1995					2001				
	GDP	GKF	FDI	OC	PI	GDP	GKF	FDI	OC	PI
Mexico	100.0	18.1	3.3	2.8	12.0	100.0	23.0	5.0	2.9	15.0
Center	100.0	19.5	3.6	2.5	13.4	100.0	19.4	7.0	2.6	9.8
Aguascalientes	100.0	31.0	1.0	2.1	27.9	100.0	30.8	1.4	1.4	28.0
Colima	100.0	22.3	0.2	2.9	19.2	100.0	30.7	0.1	3.3	27.3
Distrito Federal	100.0	13.3	7.6	3.3	2.4	100.0	11.1	16.8	3.0	-8.7
Guanajuato	100.0	18.8	0.1	2.0	16.7	100.0	28.0	1.1	2.0	24.8
Hidalgo	100.0	29.5	1.3	3.4	24.8	100.0	32.1	1.0	4.6	26.5
Jalisco	100.0	6.8	0.7	1.0	5.1	100.0	11.6	1.3	1.4	8.9
México	100.0	28.9	2.4	1.8	24.7	100.0	23.8	1.3	1.5	20.9
Michoacán	100.0	20.3	0.8	1.7	17.9	100.0	43.5	0.0	3.1	40.4
Morelos	100.0	46.3	1.9	1.7	42.7	100.0	18.2	0.2	1.8	16.1
Puebla	100.0	29.5	0.3	1.2	28.0	100.0	25.1	2.6	2.4	20.1
Querétaro	100.0	34.8	1.1	1.7	32.0	100.0	25.9	1.9	1.7	22.2
Tlaxcala	100.0	6.9	0.8	4.3	1.8	100.0	29.5	0.4	2.8	26.3
Veracruz	100.0	23.3	0.2	4.2	18.8	100.0	25.8	0.6	6.0	19.2
North	100.0	15.5	3.6	1.8	10.1	100.0	21.0	2.7	2.0	16.3
Baja California	100.0	11.8	7.3	1.0	3.6	100.0	13.7	4.7	1.4	7.5
Baja California Sur	100.0	6.5	1.5	3.2	1.8	100.0	33.4	4.6	3.1	25.7
Chihuahua	100.0	9.1	5.2	1.6	2.3	100.0	23.7	3.2	1.3	19.2
Coahuila	100.0	29.4	1.5	1.5	26.4	100.0	21.2	0.9	1.1	19.2
Durango	100.0	5.4	1.2	2.1	2.1	100.0	26.0	0.1	2.9	23.0

Nayarit	100.0	17.5	0.1	4.3	13.1	100.0	56.7	1.1	3.8	51.8
Nuevo León	100.0	11.7	4.3	1.2	6.3	100.0	13.3	4.8	1.4	7.1
San Luis Potosí	100.0	6.3	3.0	1.5	1.8	100.0	25.9	2.3	2.5	21.1
Sinaloa	100.0	13.2	1.6	3.7	8.0	100.0	8.9	0.5	2.3	6.1
Sonora	100.0	24.4	2.2	2.0	20.3	100.0	19.9	1.2	2.1	16.6
Tamaulipas	100.0	28.1	5.3	2.6	20.2	100.0	33.2	2.1	3.9	27.2
Zacatecas	100.0	10.3	0.5	1.5	8.2	100.0	39.1	0.1	4.4	34.7
South	100.0	16.8	0.3	7.2	9.2	100.0	50.2	0.4	7.6	42.1
Campeche	100.0	9.0	0.0	13.1	-4.1	100.0	39.6	-0.4	15.1	24.8
Chiapas	100.0	23.8	0.0	7.5	16.4	100.0	63.6	0.0	8.1	55.5
Guerrero	100.0	34.3	0.9	3.5	29.9	100.0	57.0	0.2	4.7	52.0
Oaxaca	100.0	15.0	0.0	4.4	10.7	100.0	51.5	0.0	7.1	44.5
Quintana Roo	100.0	4.1	0.6	1.6	1.9	100.0	21.8	1.0	1.6	19.1
Tabasco	100.0	12.0	0.0	21.3	-9.3	100.0	99.3	0.1	16.8	82.5
Yucatán	100.0	8.2	0.6	1.7	5.9	100.0	18.9	1.9	3.1	13.8

Source: Table 7.6a.

Table 7.7a

Regional Distribution of GDP, GKF, OC, PI, 1995 and 2001 (percentage)

Great Region	Gross domestic product (GDP)		Gross capital formation (GKF)		Foreign direct investment (FDI)		Public investment (OC)		Private investment (PI)	
	1995	2001	1995	2001	1995	2001	1995	2001	1995	2001
Mexico	100.0	100.0	100.0	100.0	100.0	100.0	100.0	100.0	100.0	100.0
Center	59.9	59.5	64.7	50.3	66.1	82.5	53.7	53.3	67.0	39.0
North	29.5	30.5	25.4	27.9	32.9	16.7	19.1	20.8	24.8	33.1
South	10.7	10.0	9.9	21.8	1.0	0.8	27.2	25.9	8.2	28.0

Source: Table 7.6a.

Table 7.7b

Mexico Great Regions: Distribution of Investment by Source, 1995 and 2001 (percentage)

Great Region	Gross capital formation (GKF)		Foreign direct investment (FDI)		Public investment (OC)		Private investment (PI)	
	1995	2001	1995	2001	1995	2001	1995	2001
Mexico	100.0	100.0	18.0	21.8	15.7	12.8	66.3	65.4
Center	100.0	100.0	18.4	35.8	13.0	13.5	68.6	50.7
North	100.0	100.0	23.4	13.0	11.8	9.5	64.8	77.4
South	100.0	100.0	1.9	0.8	43.2	15.2	55.0	84.0

Source: Table 7.6a.

84 percent. On the other hand, public investment in the South represented 43 percent of GKF in 1995 but was reduced to only 15.2 percent in 2001 (Tables 7.7a and 7.7b).

Foreign Investment and Trade

NAFTA was expected to lead to a substantial amount of FDI and to provide Mexico with greater access to the huge markets of its main trading partner. There is no doubt that NAFTA triggered a massive inflow of foreign investment during the 1990s. In fact, this increasing trend was maintained up to 2001, when the country still received US$26.5 billions of FDI. However, in 2002 the country received only US$13.1 billion and in 2003 till September almost US$10 billion, showing a declining trend in FDI. Of course, these changing trends are clearly shown by subperiods (Table 7.8).

Table 7.8

Mexican States by Region: Foreign Direct Investment (FDI),[a] 1999–2003 (millions of current dollars)

Mexican states	Investment				Percent distribution	
				Accumulated[b]		
	1999	2001	2003	1999–2003	2003	Accumulated
Mexico	13,153.1	26,536.6	9,738.5	76,286.5	100.00	100.0
Center	8,534.7	21,939.5	6,752.2	55,244.8	69.34	72.42
Aguascalientes	72.2	89.8	23.4	268.5	0.2	0.4
Colima	4.2	2.7	11.5	30.8	0.1	0.0
Distrito Federal	5,960.8	19,556.3	5,641.6	45,359.5	57.9	59.5
Guanajuato	136.8	217.0	183.5	734.2	1.9	1.0
Hidalgo	0.7	76.5	0.5	86.6	0.0	0.1
Jalisco	522.1	433.2	200.5	2,402.9	2.1	3.1
México	1,375.6	743.5	324.6	3,373.0	3.3	4.4
Michoacán	6.3	2.9	5.8	43.6	0.0	0.1
Morelos	146.0	18.4	47.1	242.7	0.5	0.3
Puebla	199.7	488.5	246.8	1,946.3	2.5	2.6
Querétaro	138.9	177.4	36.3	568.9	0.4	0.7
Tlaxcala	44.5	13.2	2.5	39.4	0.0	0.1
Veracruz	−73.1	120.1	28.1	148.4	0.3	0.2
North	4,389.3	4,385.3	2,891.3	20,287.3	29.69	26.59
Baja California	1,165.9	813.6	658.0	4,331.3	6.7	5.7
Baja California Sur	97.7	127.9	74.0	545.8	0.8	0.7
Chihuahua	602.4	733.4	666.5	3,419.9	6.8	4.5
Coahuila	206.9	163.8	110.9	913.0	1.1	1.2
Durango	7.1	8.2	8.5	120.2	0.1	0.2
Nayarit	15.2	33.2	57.2	137.6	0.6	0.2
Nuevo León	1,367.2	1,724.3	870.5	7,054.6	8.9	9.2
San Luis Potosí	209.9	207.1	10.3	738.2	0.1	1.0
Sinaloa	40.9	59.5	15.7	130.7	0.2	0.2

(Continued)

Table 7.8 (continued)

Mexican states	Investment			Accumulated[b]	Percent distribution	
	1999	2001	2003	1999–2003	2003	Accumulated
Sonora	203.1	175.7	119.9	1,035.7	1.2	1.4
Tamaulipas	461.7	333.0	298.6	1,825.2	3.1	2.4
Zacatecas	11.1	5.5	1.2	35.1	0.0	0.0
South	229.1	211.8	96	754.5	0.99	0.99
Campeche	4.6	−21.4	11.1	15.9	0.1	0.0
Chiapas	3.3	−0.9	−0.1	4.7	0.0	0.0
Guerrero	34.3	20.7	13.5	87.9	0.1	0.1
Oaxaca	1.1	−1.7	0.2	−0.3	0.0	0.0
Quintana Roo	91.7	77.8	54.7	302.3	0.6	0.4
Tabasco	52.8	4.1	0.0	97.1	0.0	0.1
Yucatán	41.3	133.2	16.6	246.9	0.2	0.3

Source: Secretaría de Economía. Dirección General de Inversión Extranjera, México, 2003.
[a]FDI includes investment, benefits reinvested, plus fixed assets imported by in-bond plants.
[b]Till September 30, 2003.

Mexico, the United States, and Canada were expected to become more closely integrated as a result of NAFTA. The regions of each nation that were most closely integrated in part depended on the regional distribution of investment that we indicated above and reflects a diverging trend observed between the southern and northern Mexican states from the beginning of NAFTA. The southern states obtained only 1 percent of FDI during 1999–2003, despite the relative importance of public and private investment in this region.

On the other hand, the ability of northern states and localities to attract a good deal of that foreign investment because of their proximity to the United States is indicated by the growth of assembly plants (maquiladoras) along the northern border in cities such as Tijuana, Ciudad Juárez, Nuevo Laredo, and Reynosa. In the same period, the six northern states (Baja California, Sonora, Chihuahua, Coahuila, Nuevo León, and Tamaulipas) obtained 24.4 percent of the total FDI in the country. But the real beneficiary of economic integration, in terms of absolute FDI, has been the Central Region. The Federal District and the states of México and Puebla received 66.5 percent of the total FDI in the country. The highest proportion is concentrated in the Federal District because, despite decentralization, the Mexican capital city, or rather Mexico City Metropolitan Area,[12] provides attractive opportunities due to agglomeration economies as it is the host of the federal government and concentrates the location of most of the large corporate headquarters of new tertiary activities such as the Stock Exchange and other financial services, law, audit and accounting international firms, and multinational corporations' headquarters. It also serves as the main hub in the communications network at the national level. Big cities exert a strong pull in the economic integration process, as can be confirmed by FDI in Jalisco, Nuevo León, Baja California, and Chihuahua, where the metropolitan areas of Guadalajara, Monterrey, Tijuana, and Ciudad Juárez are situated.

In fact, those regions with competitive advantages capture a larger share of the aggregated NAFTA gains: FDI flows; export capacity develops; technology transfers through partnerships; and strategic alliances consolidate with foreign firms. To the extent that such clusters are closer to the potential markets (United States), and are located in large urban-industrial concentrations, the integration process may result in an intensification of regional economic disparities and polarization tendencies with a detrimental effect for poor and backward regions. We can therefore conclude that so far NAFTA has tended to stretch the gap between the southern and the northern states and regions in Mexico. The implementation of NAFTA by itself does not completely explain disparities among Mexico's regions. Ocegueda (2003) states that there is empirical support for the hypothesis that growth in the manufacturing sector induced growth in the other sectors of the Mexican economy, which could be interpreted as indicating that Mexico's polarized regional development is associated with processes of economic specialization. (See chapter 8 by Tamayo-Flores for FDI growth rates by sector and region.) With this in mind, we next highlight the limits of regional policy in Mexico.

Concluding Remarks: The Absence of a Comprehensive Regional Policy

Economic integration in Mexico has not yet been accompanied by comprehensive policies for regional development in a systematic fashion. Generally speaking, topics of national economic growth are given priority over those related to inter-regional equality in a context of marked social and regional disparities. Most of the federal policies with a significant regional impact in the country are originally directed to specific sectors; therefore an analysis of regional policies in Mexico can be done with reference to industrial policies, social policies, and so forth, that normally do not have a broad regional aim, although they may be directed for political reasons to specific areas and, therefore, along with sectoral policies, may have significant regional impacts. Particularly since the mid-1980s, when the economic strategy dismissed the role of the state while promoting the competitiveness of the private sector, this has been the hallmark of regional policy in Mexico.

Industrial Policy

Since the Salinas administration (1988–1994) it was clear that, despite the creation in 1988 of a Secretaría de Fomento Industrial (Ministry for Industrial Promotion), there was no central body responsible for industrial development in Mexico's underdeveloped regions, nor a way to stimulate economic progress by making a distinction among regions for government subsidies for employment and investment. For decades, the public industrial sector (oil, petrochemicals, electricity, mining, and manufacturing) was an important mechanism for regional development but it was not often considered as a basis for a regional policy. With economic integration and liberalization, the possibility of a regional development policy has been drastically reduced.

Furthermore, until the beginning of the 1980s the federal government introduced measures to limit industrial growth in Mexico City, but this strategy was abandoned in the second half of the 1980s in a neoliberal context; as a result, industrial dynamism was recovered by the capital city. Similarly, a conventional industrial policy to induce development in the lagged regions has had very few possibilities of being successful, being also very costly. Another important factor that reduces potential decentralization and regional development is the very small variation in official minimum wages among states, prevalent in formal economic activities, depriving backward or less developed regions of a potential comparative advantage (OECD 1998, 60). In fact, given the abundant cheap labor, not everyone who ought to receive the official minimum wage received it.

Social Policy

The social sector was given a high priority during the 1990s, a fact that was apparent in the federal budget. For example, in 1997, federal government expenditure in social development represented 9 percent of GDP, and it reached 10.4 percent in 2003.[13] During President Salinas's administration, the main program for social development was PRONASOL (National Solidarity Program—Programa Nacional de Solidaridad). This outstanding program, in a context of a withdrawal of all subsidies, was designed to aid local settlements with high levels of poverty. It is estimated that PRONASOL benefited 9 million people in eleven different states and 375 urban centers between 1989 and 1992. Each project had three main components: agricultural production, protection of natural resources, and social well-being (OECD 1998). PRONASOL's actions included the construction of roads, schools, and health centers; financial and technical support to peasants; community development, and programs to foster women's qualifications, among others. In fact, the central objective in rural and urban projects was to alleviate poverty (see chapter 29 by Gordon).

Additionally, from 1995 onward the Secretaría of Social Development (SEDESOL) formulated a strategy to assist marginal microregions. A total of ninety-one such regions were identified, which included municipalities characterized by the most severe indices of marginalization (at least 60 percent of the active population with no income, a high proportion of indigenous population, and only about 20 percent of the economically active population earning more than one minimum salary). SEDESOL's main actions concentrated on improving education and nutrition, distributing basic products, providing temporary employment, and building basic social infrastructure (SOC).

Social policy cannot be considered an explicit regional policy. All of the programs under the heading of regional and urban development, including alleviation of poverty, may have had an important impact at the local level but they represented a very small proportion of the federal budget (less than 1 percent of GDP) and therefore not important as a regional incentive. Furthermore, the financial resources for the projects were partially or even totally decentralized, which meant that municipalities were free to allocate resources to specific ends or projects (OECD 1998). These projects were not aimed at solving regional or state inequalities but were local in nature, and ameliorative actions did not dramatically change the existing gaps in the provision of education, health, employment, nor the effects of macroeconomic policies.

President Fox's administration (2000–2006) seems committed to bringing regional development to the forefront of the public agenda and to giving greater weight to spatially based policies vis-à-vis the traditional sectorial approach. The Fox administration's actions include: the incorporation of regional development policies in the National Development Plan; the appointment, within the Executive Office of the President, of an officer for strategic planning and regional development; and the presentation of a National Program for Urban Development and Territorial Planning (PNDU-OT). The Office for Strategic Planning tried to implement a model of regional development that would take into consideration a new political reality of increasing democratization, which means that a greater emphasis was given to what has been called in Mexico a new federalism, accompanied by a correlative decentralization of functions and responsibilities to the subnational (state) level reaching the municipalities, with a greater emphasis in local planning. This model tries to promote regional development by mobilizing political will and resources in areas that have been denominated as "meso-regions," in a scheme that allows individual states to participate in more than one of those (OECD 2003). The PNDU-OT sees spatial planning as the process "through which to orient the spatial evolution of economy and society, and that promotes the establishment of new functional relationships between regions, towns and cities, as well as between the urban and rural spaces" (SEDESOL 2001). And, although its goal is to achieve complementarities between local and regional objectives and national ones, there seems to be an important emphasis on urban questions such as the consolidation of the National Urban System (all localities with 15,000 inhabitants and more, including metropolitan areas), a National Land and Territorial Reserve Policy (to incorporate available urban land in the development process), and the Habitat Housing Program (to promote investment and employment, as well as a better quality of life in the poorer city neighborhoods).

Despite these efforts, a good example of how regional policy has weakened in the present administration, and faces several implementation difficulties, is the case of the Plan Puebla-Panamá (PPP). Its primary objective is to correct the structural conditions that have obstructed the development of the Southern region of Mexico (Veracruz, Guerrero, Oaxaca, Chiapas, Tabasco, Campeche, Yucatán, and Quintana Roo), including Puebla, while promoting development in the Central American region of actors from both the public sphere and civil society in areas such as human development, poverty alleviation, strategic infrastructure investment, and environmental sustainability. However, at the moment some difficulties can be identified: First, the PPP started in the president's Executive Office, but responsibilities were transferred to the Secretary of Foreign Affairs (SRE), which clearly weakens the whole strategy. Second, much of the progress so far has been achieved in the area of transport and communication infrastructure, but not yet in the productive sector; while infrastructure is needed to promote productive activity, there are urgent needs in actively promoting productive projects in the poorer areas. Third, the institutional capacity to catalyze support from all levels of government toward such strategy is not equally shared by all participants, from both Mexican institutions and the seven Central American countries' governments. Fourth, there is no precise delimitation of responsibilities between the PPP and other elements of the territorial development strategy, and it is not clear where its place is within the Mexican public administration structure (OECD 2003).

Finally, we believe that a regional strategy must be based on horizontal cooperation among the federal government ministries and decentralized agencies and should be clearly structured and mandated; the allocation of responsibilities and resources among sectors and levels of governments should be accompanied by a definition of commitments. A close collaboration between SEDESOL and the presidency is necessary for the planning and implementation of spatial focused plans at the micro and meso levels, and an overlapping between the two bodies should be avoided.

The vision that sustains this regional approach should be more comprehensive. So far, the meso-region proposal is applied in the PPP and to some extent in the Northern border, while the micro-regional approach is currently utilized in the context of poverty alleviation at the local level; but these proposals should be extended to all regions, incorporating a larger number of economic development concerns and simultaneously improving, at the macro, meso, and micro levels, the conditions of social groups that have the lowest levels of well-being.

Notes

The authors would like to thank Marlon Santillán and Irma Escamilla for their participation in the research and construction of tables. Thanks also to José Romero for his advice on investment analysis.

1. Meaning not enough income for a basic diet.

2. In 1928 the Federal District was removed from the municipal system, a change that is now being reversed thanks to the efforts of the country's political institutions, which have achieved significant political and democratic improvements in the capital. The fact that it now has its own legislative body and citizens can elect their own head of government and local delegates reflects these advances. The first reform to allow these changes to take place was passed in 1996, modifying Article 122 of the Constitution. The idea was to give back to citizens the right to vote for the most important authorities without actually changing the nature of the Federal District's judicial system. The second reform, passed on December 4, 1999, focused on electoral law in the capital, creating the Electoral Tribunal of the Federal District, an autonomous body to regulate elections in the capital. Although these changes have opened-up possibilities for the capital's citizens, they do not alter the legal status of the Federal District and still allow federal law to interfere in the actions of the capital's government.

3. The statement about lack of significant difference in well-being indicators among the three regions is based on t tests. The t test on the difference in well-being between the Center and the North indicates $t = .61$; between Center and South, $t = .74$; and between North and South $t = .689$.

4. Ortega (2001) argues that the critical realignment of political party affiliation according to region that occurred in the presidential election in 2000, and was modified in the election for the Chamber of Deputies in 2003, strengthened a pluralistic system (with three relevant parties) that presents itself on the state level as a bi- or tri-party system with clear regional overtones.

5. The underdevelopment led to conflicts on social, economic, and environmental issues. See Graizbord and Arroyo 2004.

6. Regional convergence in per capita income (GDPpc) has been analyzed for Mexico by Esquivel (1999) and more recently by Ocegueda (2003). For a technical study of regional convergence of productivity per capita and salaries in Mexico, please contact graizbord@lead.colmex.mx.

7. That education level is permanently related to wages and labor income has been proved empirically through the application of different models by Becker (1964) and later by Mincer (1974).

8. While geographers have signaled the importance of social processes and associative behavior to the performance of firms in industrial districts, it was Putnam (1993, cited in Johnston et al. 2000, 746–747) who encapsulated in the term *social capital* "those charac-

teristics of social structure or social relations that facilitate collaborative action and, as a result, enhance economic performance."

9. Ideas by North (1991) on the role of national social institutions can be recognized as the background for a literature that augmented and refined regional microeconomic analysis. North's *institutional development* and Porter's (1990) *competitive advantages* revived the interest in the impact of civil institutions in regional economic performance and were, as far as we see it, the recent building blocks for proposals of endogenous growth. See Barro (1990), Mankiw, Romer, and Weil (1992), and Romer (1994), among others.

10. Fuentes (2003) refers to a study by Looney and Frederiksen (1981) for Mexico in the seventies in which these authors found that infrastructure affected GDP according to type of investment and type of region (intermediate or depressed). These authors use Hansen's (1965) regional typology, in which he proposes three categories: congested (relatively developed, corresponding to primate cities or large agglomeration regions), lagging or depressed (underdeveloped poor rural areas, having few attributes that would tend to attract new economic activity), and intermediate (regions offering significant advantages to businesses but not yet generating external diseconomies of agglomeration).

11. Investments are made in human resources so as to improve their productivity. Costs are incurred in the expectation of future benefits; hence, the term "investment in human resources" (Pearce 1995, 188).

12. There is a methodological question in the way FDI is registered; surely there is a bias in favor of Mexico City because a high proportion of multinational corporate headquarters are located in the capital city, while their productive units might be located in other regions of the country.

13. This year the federal government expenditure in social development was 681,956 millions of current pesos of which 85 percent was directed to education, health, and social security, and the remaining 15 percent to housing and community development (President Fox's *Tercer Informe de Gobierno,* see México 2003). The reader should be aware that the current year's *Informe* refers to programmed investment for that year, which is being adjusted for actual investment.

References

Alba, F. 1976. "Éxodo silencioso: La migración de trabajadores mexicanos a Estados Unidos." *Foro Internacional* 17 (October–December).

Armstrong, H., and J. Taylor. 2000. *Regional Economics and Policy.* 3d ed. Oxford: Blackwell.

Barro, R. 1990. "Government Spending in a Simple Model of Endogenous Growth." *Journal of Political Economy* 98 (supplement).

Becker, G. 1964. *Human Capital: A Theoretical and Empirical Analysis with Special Reference to Education.* New York: National Bureau of Economic Research.

Consejo Nacional de Población (CONAPO). 2000. *Serie histórica basada en la conciliación demográfica a partir del XII Censo General de Población y Vivienda de 2000.* December. Available at www.conapo.gob.mx/micros/informe/anex004.xls.

Cortés, F. 2003. "El ingreso y la desigualdad en su distribución. México: 1977–2000," *Papeles de Población* 9, no. 35.

Durand, J. 1998. "¿Nuevas regiones migratorias?" In *Población, Desarrollo y Globalización,* ed. R.M. Zenteno. México: SOMEDE and El Colegio de la Frontera Norte.

Esquivel, G. 1999. "Convergencia regional en México, 1940–1995." *El Trimestre Económico* 66(4), no. 264.

Fuentes, N.A. 2003. "Desigualdades regionales en México: Los efectos de la infraestructura." *Comercio Exterior* 53, no. 11.

Graizbord, B., and J. Arroyo, ed. 2004. *El futuro del agua en México.* México: El Colegio de México, Universidad de Guadalajara. UCLA program on Mexico (PROFMEX) and Casa Juan Pablos.

Graizbord, B., and C. Ruiz. 1996. "Recent Changes in the Economic and Social Structure of Mexico's Regions." In *Changing Structure of Mexico,* ed. L. Randall. *Political, Social, and Economic Prospects.* Armonk, NY: M.E. Sharpe.

Graizbord, B., and C. León. 2002. "Cambios regionales en la geografía mexicana." In *El siglo XX mexicano,* vol. 5, *Gran historia de México ilustrada,* ed. S. Loaeza. México: Planeta, CONACULTA, INAH.

Hansen, N. 1965. "Unbalanced Growth and Regional Development." *Western Economic Journal* 4, no. 1.

Harris, R., and M. Trainor. 1997. "Productivity Growth in the UK Regions, 1968–91." *Oxford Bulletin of Economics and Statistics* 59, no. 4.

Hirschman, A. 1958. *The Strategy of Economic Development.* New Haven, CT: Yale University Press.

INEGI. 1996. *Sistema nacional estadístico y de información geográfica.* México: Instituto Nacional de Estadística, Geografía e Informática. Available at www.inegi.gob.mx/prod_serv/contenidos.

———. 2002. *Sistema de cuentas nacionales de México.* México: Instituto Nacional de Estadística, Geografía e Informática. Available at www.inegi.gob.mx/est.

———. n.d. www.dgcnesyp.inegi.gob.mx/bdine/m15/m1501109.htm.

Johnston, R., D. Gregory, G. Pratt, and M. Watts, eds. 2000. *The Dictionary of Human Geography.* Oxford: Blackwell.

Kaldor, N. 1970. "The Case for Regional Policy." *Scottish Journal of Political Economy* 18, no. 3.

Looney R., and P. Frederiksen. 1981. "The Regional Impact of Infrastructure in Mexico." *Regional Studies* 15, no. 4.

Mankiw, G., D. Romer, and D. Weil. 1992. "A Contribution to the Empirics of Economic Growth." *Quarterly Journal of Economics* 107, no. 2.

México. 2003. *Tercer Informe de Gobierno.*

Mincer J. 1974. *Schooling, Experience and Earnings.* New York: National Bureau of Economic Research.

Myrdal, G. 1959. *Teoría económica y regiones subdesarrolladas.* México: Fondo de Cultura Económica.

North, D. 1991. *Institutions, Institutional Change and Economic Performance.* Cambridge, UK: Cambridge University Press.

NOTIMEX. 2004. Santiago de Chile, April.

Ocegueda, J.M. 2003. "Análisis kaldoriano del crecimiento económico de los estados de México, 1980–2000." *Comercio Exterior* 53, no. 11.

OECD (Organization for Economic Cooperation and Development). 1998. *Desarrollo Regional y Política Estructural en México.* Paris, France: OECD (Organisation de Coopération et de Développement Économiques).

OECD. 2003. *Territorial Reviews. Mexico.* Paris, France: OECD.

Ortega, R. ed. 2001. *Caminos a la democracia.* México: El Colegio de México.

Pearce, D. ed. 1995. *The MIT Dictionary of Modern Economics. Fourth Edition.* Cambridge, Massachusetts: The MIT Press.

Perroux, F. 1950. "Economic Space: Theory and Applications." *Quarterly Journal of Economics* 65.

Piore, M., and C. Sabel. 1984. *The Second Industrial Divide: Possibilities for Prosperity.* New York: Basic Books.

Porter, M. 1990. *The Competitive Advantage of Nations.* New York: The Free Press.

Putnam, R. 1993. *Making Democracy Work*. Princeton, NJ: Princeton University Press.
Romer, P. 1986, "Increasing Returns and Long Run Growth." *Journal of Political Economy* 94, no. 5.
———. 1994. "The Origins of Endogenous Growth." *Journal of Economic Perspectives* 8, no. 1.
SEDESOL (Secretaría of Social Development) 2001. *Programa Nacional de Desarrollo Urbano y Ordenación del Territorio, 2001–2006*. México: Secretaría de Desarrollo Social.
Solow, R. 1979 (1956). "Un modelo de crecimiento." Reedited in *Economía del crecimiento*, ed. A. Sen. México: Fondo de Cultura Económica.
———. 1957. "Technical Progress and the Aggregate Production Function," *Review of Economics and Statistics* 39, no. 3.
Universidad de los Trabajadores de América Latina "Emilio Máspero." (UTAL). n.d. *América Latina: Hogares y población bajo las líneas de la pobreza y de indigencia*. Available at www.utal.org/hogaresypoblacion2.htm.

8

RAFAEL TAMAYO-FLORES

NAFTA-Driven Changes in the Regional Pattern of Economic Growth in Mexico

Profile and Determinants

Rafael Tamayo-Flores examines in detail the impact of the North American Free Trade Agreement (NAFTA) on the regional distribution of economic growth in Mexico. NAFTA is not a common market, and lacks legal free movement of labor as well as a coordinated policy among its members.

The removal of barriers to trade has an impact similar to that of a reduction in transport costs. Industries with strong existing export potential flourish; other industries may be harmed by imports. The reduction in barriers to trade also lessens the need for self-reliance in production. Specialization in production by regions becomes efficient. The ability of firms to adjust is more important than initial industrial conditions for regional development. Thus, during the NAFTA era, the regional pattern of industry has shifted from large agglomerations in the Center to specialized centers, especially in the North. Manufacturing growth was highest in regions that produced inputs for their industries and had industrial customers for their products; manufacturing growth did not depend on how many diverse industries existed in a region.

During the last decade, growth in Mexico, except for the South, has increasingly depended on growth in the Pacific region of the United States. The expansion of the domestic and foreign market for Mexican goods and the increased openness of the Mexican economy, largely because of NAFTA, together may have increased foreign direct investment in Mexico by about 70 percent.

The NAFTA-related growth has increased inequality among regions. For example, in the apparel industry, the highest value-added activities remained in the United States; the next most valuable activities are in the North of Mexico; and the simplest activities with the lowest value added are in the South of Mexico.

NAFTA had an important impact on the regional distribution of economic growth. Tamayo-Flores's analysis implies that in the future, the reduction in costs of transportation and communication may increase the speed with which economic conditions in the United States influence the Mexican economy and the consequent distribution of economic growth at the same time that the increasing number of nations effectively incorporated into world trade and investment decrease the relative impact of NAFTA on Mexico.

NAFTA came into effect on January 1, 1994. It represents the consolidation of Mexico's shift toward an export-led development strategy. A far-reaching unilateral opening of the Mexican economy had been under way since the mid-1980s. Trade between Mexico and the United States was already fairly open, but significant U.S. nontariff barriers, managed on a discretionary basis, remained. For Mexico, the main expected gains from NAFTA concentrated on the attraction of foreign direct investment (FDI) mainly from United States, but also from third-country transnational corporations, as Mexico would have a guaranteed stable access to the U.S. and Canadian markets. During its first decade, NAFTA was largely responsible for the exploding growth of nonoil exports and the unprecedented influx of FDI experienced by Mexico since the mid-1990s. During the NAFTA era, the number of maquiladora plants,[1] which account for most Mexican nonoil exports and FDI in manufactures, not only have increased quite rapidly, but also have undergone a qualitative change upgrading Mexico's role in global production chains.

Certainly, NAFTA has significantly improved Mexico's attractiveness for international investment, and has notably strengthened Mexico's export capacity. However, as expected, the NAFTA-related benefits have not been evenly distributed across Mexican regions. The ability to take advantage of the opportunities opened or to cope with the challenges imposed by free trade varies across subnational regions. The objective of this chapter is precisely to provide a further understanding of how NAFTA has influenced and changed the regional pattern of economic growth in Mexico, by providing a careful definition of the main changes in the pattern of regional growth during the NAFTA era, and then proceeding with a discussion of the NAFTA-related factors behind these changes. Special emphasis is thus placed on the impact of NAFTA on economic growth across regions.

NAFTA involves the elimination of barriers to trade and investment between Mexico, the United States, and Canada. Unlike a common market, NAFTA does not include legal free movement of labor nor policy coordination among the three nations. Unlike the European Union, NAFTA does not incorporate any recognition of the marked differences in level of development among its members.

A Brief Analytical Framework

The formation of free trade areas (FTAs) can be justified on welfare grounds. If trade creation is large enough relative to trade diversion,[2] then FTAs improve world economic welfare. If trade creation is small, the FTA is likely to reduce welfare. It has been shown that trade diversion is minimized when the FTA is formed by countries that are located close together (Helpman 1987; Helpman and Krugman

1985),[3] but even in that case welfare can be reduced if transport costs are low and the reduction of tariffs and nontariff barriers are high (Frankel 1997). So, the recommendation is that FTAs among neighbors should be extended to the rest of the geographical region and trade preferences should be kept as low as possible.

But the relevant issue here is how the formation of an FTA in a single geographical area can cause shifts in economic growth across the regions of each member country. Conventionally, it is expected that economically small and backward regions would suffer a setback, whereas those with a prominent and/or highly dynamic economic base would be further promoted. Thus, a further regional income inequality and concentration of economic activity is the anticipated outcome.

The model of cumulative causation (Myrdal 1957; Hirschman 1958) provides a framework to explain how the dynamics of regional polarization work. The argument is that on the road to national development, those regions with an initial advantage (e.g., natural resource endowments, a sizable market, a nodal location in the transport network) experience well-above-average economic growth. The progressive concentration of production in the dynamic regions, compounded by the provision of infrastructure, allows for significant cost savings for firms and industries. For instance, the development of tight inter-industry (and inter-firm) linkages allow for economies of scale.[4] Also, assembly and distribution costs are reduced when activities with forward and backward linkages are located in a small area. Similarly, firms and industries benefit from the availability of a trained labor force residing within a small area. The clustering of firms in a small area also facilitates the exchange of information and knowledge among them. It turns out that these regions naturally play the role of "growth poles" for the national economy.

The recently developed New Economic Geography (NEG) models (Krugman and Venables 1995; Venables 1996) are very helpful in establishing how the regional pattern of growth and competitive advantage can change over time as transport costs fall. When transport costs are high, the volume of interregional trade remains at very low levels. Each region produces its own intermediate industrial inputs (used to produce final consumption goods), even in industries with strong economies of scale. Hence, the production of each industry is distributed among different regions—it exhibits a de-concentrated pattern. However, as transport costs fall it becomes feasible to concentrate production in some regions and a process of increasing industrial concentration starts. Concentration takes place in those regions with a head start (for example, population centers, transportation nodes), which are the so-called "growth poles." As production of intermediate inputs gravitates to those regions, tight input–output linkages develop, allowing for cost reductions as predicted in Hirschman's cumulative causation model. Firms in these regions are thus able to supply the national market (export).

Nevertheless, in subsequent stages of economic development the pattern of industrial concentration starts to be reversed as transport costs continue falling and the economic advantages of the "growth poles" erode. Other regions are better able to compete. Here, it is very important to note that reductions of tariff and nontariff trade barriers have the same effects as a fall in transport costs, which improve the access to export markets. In the case of Mexico, NAFTA, together with the structural reforms introduced before 1993 that promoted a sizable expansion of the transport and communications sector, led to a process of territorial de-concentration of industrial growth away from the most prominent "growth pole," the Metropolitan Area of Mexico City (MAMC).[5] Northern Mexican mid-sized cities became more attractive for investment and production to foreign and national firms because they are closer to the U.S. market. Over time, industry-specific clusters with significant forward and backward inter-firm linkages have developed in these northern sites, which give them an additional competitive advantage.

In the short run the regional *industrial mix,* or specialization, also can influence growth prospects. Those regions specializing in industries with high export-growth potential (important foreign markets) would be expected to flourish, whereas those with a high share in industries where competing imports are likely to make substantial inroads would be expected to suffer. Regional growth will also depend on the ability of local firms to undertake survival measures other than relocation (e.g., technology improvements, organizational restructuring, product innovation and specialization, and market reorientation). Thus, within a given region it is possible that expansion of existing firms and new entries more than offset casualties, even in those industries that are declining at the national level. While the initial industrial mix affects local growth performance in the short run, it is the ability of local firms and industries to adjust that matters at the end.

In order to analyze the changes in Mexico's regional pattern of growth during the NAFTA era, the regional division presented in Table 8.1 is adopted.[6] Table 8.1 also shows the main economic sectors in each Mexican region and the share of each region in these sectors at the national level. There are large size differences between the highly prominent Central region, wherein the MAMC is located, and the relatively small economies of the Central-North, Southeast, and South at the beginning of NAFTA. It is also noticeable that the manufacturing sector is important only in the three largest regions.

The Regional Pattern of Economic Growth Under NAFTA

In the decade before NAFTA (1984–1993), the Mexican economy, as measured by gross domestic product (GDP), grew at an annual rate of 2.52 percent. Mexico had already embarked on a far-reaching process of trade and investment liberalization, which started with its accession to the General Agreement on Tariffs and Trade in 1986. A spatial shift of production toward the Northern Border (NB) and the Central-West (CW) regions had been observed since then. The NB benefited chiefly from Mexico's export-oriented growth strategy and, in particular, from the maquiladora regime, which attracted large FDI to that region and promoted exports. Different mid-sized cities in the NB, but mostly those bordering the United States, had been improving their competitive advantages and started to function as regional growth enclaves.

Table 8.1

Definition and Main Activities of Major Regions

State	Region	Main regional activities	Activity share[a] Of regional GDP	Of sectoral national GDP
Federal District		Community, social,	25.6	44.8
Hidalgo	Central	and personal service		
México	(CE)	Manufactures	20.9	43.2
Morelos		Trade-restaurants-	20.5	37.1
Tlaxcala		lodging		
Aguascalientes		Trade-restaurants-	21.6	15.5
Colima		lodging		
		Manufactures		
Guanajuato	Central-West	Community, social,	20.2	16.6
Jalisco	(CW)	and personal service	18.8	12.9
Nayarit				
Querétaro				
San Luis Potosí				
Baja California		Trade-restaurants-	22.1	22.4
Chihuahua		lodging		
Coahuila	Northern	Manufactures	21.4	24.9
Nuevo León	Border	Community, social,	20	19.2
Sonora	(NB)	and personal service		
Tamaulipas				
Baja Calif. Sur		Community, social,	20.9	4.7
Durango	Central-North	and personal service		
Sinaloa	(CN)	Agriculture-cattle-fishery	19.2	15.6
Zacatecas		Trade-restaurants-	18.8	4.4
		lodging		
Campeche		Trade-restaurants-	23.4	10.5
Quintana Roo	Southeast	lodging		
Tabasco	(SE)	Community, social,	19.2	8.2
Yucatán		and personal service		
Veracruz		Banking-insurance	14.7	9.1
		-real estate		
Chiapas		Community, social,	21.1	10.2
Guerrero	South	and personal service		
Oaxaca	(SO)	Trade-restaurants-	20	10.2
Michoacán		lodging		
Puebla		Banking-insurance	18	12.5
		-real estate		

Source: Based on data from INEGI.
[a]Percentage of gross domestic product in 1993.

Table 8.2

Regional Economic Growth in the NAFTA Era, 1993–2002

Region	GDP per capita[a]		GDP share				GDP average annual growth
	1993	1980	1985	1993	1998	2002	1993–2002
Central (CE)	18.58	39.3	35.4	37.8	36.6	35.9	2.35
Central-West (CW)	11.49	13.8	14.8	15.3	15.5	15.8	3.21
Northern Border (NB)	17.21	19.1	19.4	21.4	22.9	23.6	3.97
Central-North (CN)	10.63	4.6	5.0	5.0	4.8	4.6	1.66
Southeast (SE)	10.23	11.8	14.0	9.6	9.4	9.4	2.58
South (SO)	7.18	11.4	11.4	10.9	10.8	10.7	2.66
Nation	13.27	100.0	100.0	100.0	100.0	100.0	2.76

Source: Based on data from INEGI.
Note: The data for GDP by state still are not available for 2003.
[a]Real GDP. Thousand pesos.

During the first nine years of the NAFTA period (1994–2002), Mexico's GDP grew at an average annual rate of 2.75 percent,[7] despite the fact that growth was negative in 1995 and nil in 2001 and 2002 (see Table 8.2). The decline of 1995 was provoked by the crisis ignited by the major peso devaluation at the end of 1994, whereas the drastic abatement of 2001 and 2002 was caused largely by the U.S. recession. It should be noted, though, that between 1995 and 2000 Mexico's GDP had experienced a stable, strong growth averaging 5.4 percent. Economic growth, however, has not been homogeneous across regions. In that period, the NB performed well above average (3.97) and the CW also recorded an above-average growth (3.21), whereas the other four major regions underperformed, including the prominent Central region (CE), which grew at an average rate of 2.35 percent. The growth rates of the lagging Southeast (SE), South (SO), and Central-North (CN) were 2.58, 2.66, and 1.66 (Table 8.2, last column). Hence, between 1994 and 2002 the NB share of GDP rose steadily from 21.4 to 23.6 percent. Likewise, the share of the CW increased slightly from 15.3 to 15.8 percent. In contrast, the contribution to GDP of the economically large CE experienced a decline from 37.8 to 35.9 percent. Similarly, the share of the other three economically backward regions alike experienced a small decline (Table 8.2).

In short, during the NAFTA era the territorial de-concentration of economic activity from the rich and still economically prominent CE toward the dynamic NB and CW continued. The relative gains of these two dynamic regions, however, were also at the expense of the traditionally poor, backward SE, SO, and CN. Thus, the NAFTA era has also been characterized by a trend of regional polarization. As shown in Table 8.2, just before NAFTA (1993) the NB—the winning region—had a per capita GDP almost as high as that of the CE, whereas the CN, SE, and SO—the losing regions—had the lowest per capita GDP (Table 8.2, column 2).

While adversely affecting the growth performance of every region, the slowdown of the U.S. economy also offset to some extent the northward shift of production. The NB experienced nil average growth in 2001–2002 (it was actually negative in 2001), whereas it had achieved the highest average growth of all regions between 1996 and 2000 (6.91). In contrast, the economically backward southern regions (SO and SE) experienced an above-average growth amid the U.S. recession. In fact, the SE had the highest average growth of all regions in these years (2.31). Unlike the NB, the CW, which is also a dynamic region, was able to grow despite the slowdown of the U.S. economy (its growth in 2001–2002 averaged 1.34). The still prominent CE was the only region that suffered negative growth in 2001 and 2002.

Overall, the regional output growth trends during the NAFTA era allow us to distinguish two types of regions. On one hand, there are regions with a seemingly high sensitivity to U.S. growth, such as the NB and the CW, which suggests a high degree of integration, even though the CW somehow was able to keep growing amid the U.S. recession. On the other hand, there are regions that are insensitive to U.S. growth, such as the SO, SE, and CN, even though the CN has been particularly hard hit by the U.S. recession. Growth in the prominent CE has been restricted by the U.S. recession, but this region also had experienced a slightly below-average growth performance between 1993 and 2000 (see chapter 6 in this book).

In general, during the NAFTA era, economic growth in most Mexican regions— as measured by employment—has become more sensitive to growth in the United States and particularly in the U.S. Pacific region. The only unambiguous exception has been the SO, although the sensitivity of the SE has decreased lately. The growth in output and employment in the NB is definitely the most sensitive to U.S. developments. Nevertheless, the sensitivity of the other three regions (CW, CE, and CN) has increased more than that of the NB since 1997. The reason is that the NB was already so highly integrated that there was little room for additional integration to the U.S. economy (Cuevas, Messmacher, and Werner 2002). In short, NAFTA has consolidated previous important linkages between Mexico's NB region and the U.S. economy and also has reinforced those of other Mexican regions. Nevertheless, idiosyncratic shocks related to domestic investment and consumption still are quite relevant for growth performance in all Mexican regions. Some more detailed and illustrative elements of the degree of integration of Mexican regions to U.S. developments during the NAFTA era are outlined in Box 8.1.

The Linkage Between Foreign Direct Investment and Export Growth

At the regional level, the pattern of growth during the NAFTA era, described above, coincides to a large degree with the allocation of FDI and the pattern of export growth. This suggests a strong connection between FDI inflows and export growth in manufactures, which in turn might be associated with economic growth at both the national and regional levels. Arguably, international trade and FDI might lead to increases

---

Box 8.1

Synchronization of Employment Growth Across Mexican and U.S. Regions, 1992–2001

- The correlation of employment growth trends between each Mexican region and the United States increased during 1997–2001 (as compared with the period 1993–1996) to become moderate and moderately high. (The only exception is the SO, wherein the already low degree of correlation with U.S. growth dropped even more.)
- The correlations between each Mexican region and the U.S. Pacific region were already high during 1993–1996, and increased even more during 1997–2001. (Again the exception was the SO, whose correlation with growth in the U.S. Pacific region reached only a low-to-moderate level during 1997–2001.)
- The lowest correlation increase in the period 1997–2001 occurred in the NB, which suggest that a good deal of the integration of the NB with the United States had happened before NAFTA.
- During the whole 1993–2001 period the correlations between growth in the U.S. Pacific and growth in the Mexican regions were higher than some correlations among Mexican regions and also higher (with the exception of the SO) than that between the U.S. Pacific and total U.S. growth.
- The correlations between growth in each Mexican region and national growth were also high and remained stable throughout the period 1993–2001. (The SO exhibits the lowest correlation with national growth and it is only moderate.)
- The correlation of growth between each Mexican region and national growth is much higher in all cases than with respect to U.S. growth.

---

in factor accumulation and efficiency, which in turn promote economic growth.[8] Also, the exporting sector creates positive externalities for nonexporting activities and the economy at large. Moreover, export activities usually have a higher productivity than the rest of manufacturing. Thus, in the long run those regions better integrated to global markets can be expected to achieve higher growth rates.

The Influx of Foreign Direct Investment

Certainly, NAFTA triggered FDI inflows into Mexico, mainly from the United States, which improved growth prospects for the economy as a whole. A rough estimation of the impact of NAFTA on FDI inflows to Mexico reports an addition of around 40 percent, the bulk of which is driven by the extended market size. If the effect of a further openness of the Mexican economy implied by NAFTA is added, the estimates reach a high 70 percent of additional FDI (Lederman, Maloney, and Serven 2003). During 1994–2003, the FDI received by Mexico reached $127.2 billion, an average annual inflow of $12.7 billion (see Table 8.3, last row). In contrast, between 1986 and 1993—before the NAFTA era—Mexico received an influx of FDI amounting to $27.3 billion, a yearly average of $3.4 billion. Thus, there was nearly a fourfold increase after NAFTA. Global manufacturing firms based in non-NAFTA countries indeed took into consideration the strategic value of having guaranteed access to the U.S. and Canadian markets, while many U.S.-based firms still regard Mexico as a relevant location alternative to remain competitive in the NAFTA market, given its geographical proximity and adequate labor supply. This was reflected in an exploding growth of the maquiladoras—most of which are foreign owned—whose number (monthly average) increased steadily from 2,114 to 3,630 between 1993 and 2000 (in 1990 there were 1,703 plants).

However, massive closings in 2002 and 2003 resulted in a net decline of around 800 maquiladora plants, mainly because of the U.S. recession, but also due to relocations from Mexico to China; this is especially true of production lines in the garments industry. In 2003 the number of maquiladoras had dropped to 2,860 (the regional shifts of the export maquiladoras during the NAFTA era are described below). Certainly, China's accession to the World Trade Organization (WTO) has been offsetting many of Mexico's NAFTA-related trade advantages, particularly in garments and other labor-intensive industries. In addition, much lower labor costs and environmental standards as well as a reasonably educated labor force in China are also the causes behind these recent notorious relocations. Another important factor is the continuing reduction of transport costs.

It should be pointed out that, beyond manufacturing, foreign firms have also sought to exploit important Mexican markets in nontradables such as financial services and telecommunications. This has been conducted primarily through mergers and acquisitions of large Mexican firms, which were encouraged by the asset depreciation derived from the sharp peso devaluation of 1994, and by more general factors such as the bold relaxation of the legal framework that regulates foreign investment in 1993, the privatization of formerly state-owned firms, and the favorable business environment provided by NAFTA.[9] Hence, while almost one-half (49.3 percent) of the $127.2 billion of FDI entering Mexico between 1994 and 2003 was allocated in manufactures, financial services also accounted for a high 24.5 percent; trade accounted for 10.5 percent during the same period. This distribution across sectors shows that FDI aimed at exporting production back to the source country or to third countries (manufactures) has been the most sizable; nevertheless, FDI aimed at serving Mexican markets with high potential (financial services and trade) has also been quite important.

In regards to the regional allocation of FDI in Mexico, in general it shows a quite marked pattern of concentration. Table 8.3 shows that almost two-thirds of the $127.2 billion that arrived during 1994–2003 was allocated in the CE. The NB received 24.7 percent. Hence, these two regions together concentrated 90 percent of the total influx. In contrast, the CW shared only 5.2 percent, and the three most

Table 8. 3

Foreign Direct Investment by Regions and Main Sectors in the NAFTA Era, 1994–2003

			Sectoral share, 1999–2003[a]	
Region	FDI share (1994–2003)	Main sectors receiving FDI (1999–2003)[a]	Of FDI allocated in the region	Of FDI allocated in the sector nationally
Central (CE)	65.7	Financial services	48.20	91.80
		Manufactures	25.30	40.20
		Trade	11.40	83.70
Central-West (CW)	5.2	Manufactures	80.30	11.10
		Other services	9.20	7.10
		Trade	6.80	4.30
Northern Border (NB)	24.7	Manufactures	77.80	43.20
		Financial services	12.00	8.00
		Trade	3.80	9.70
Central-North (CN)	1.1	Other services	58.50	8.10
		Manufactures	16.90	0.30
		Mining	10.80	17.00
Southeast (SE)	1.2	Other services	41.40	6.40
		Manufactures	26.40	0.70
		Construction	14.80	23.30
South (SO)	2.1	Manufactures	75.80	4.50
		Other services	19.20	6.40
		Trade	3.90	1.10
Nation	100	Manufactures	41.20	
		Financial services	34.80	
		Trade	9.10	
FDI (U.S.$ bil.)	127.2		87.40	

Source: Based on data from Secretaría de Economía.
[a]FDI recorded as of March 2004. Records include new investment, reinvestment of earnings (starting in 1999) and importation of fixed assets by the maquiladoras. FDI is assigned to the state where the firms' headquarters are located, which in some cases does not coincide with the state where the investment actually takes place.

laggardly regions shared the remaining 4.4 percent altogether (second column). For all six regions, the largest or second largest amount of FDI, during 1999–2003, has been allocated in manufactures (fourth column). However, 43.4 percent of FDI in manufactures has been concentrated in the NB alone, 40.2 percent in the CE, and 11.1 percent in the CW (fifth column). This leaves the three most laggardly regions with a share of 5.5 percent. The concentration of FDI in financial services is even higher. The CE alone has received 91.8 percent of it, and another 8 percent has been allocated in the NB in the same period.

Traditionally, most FDI inflows to Mexico come from the United States. During the period 1994–2003, 64.4 percent was accounted for by U.S. sources. The European Union altogether accounted for 22.1 percent, notably the Netherlands (8.8), Spain (5.0), United Kingdom (4.0), and Germany (2.8).[10] Japan accounted for 2.7 percent and Canada 3.6 percent in that period. It should be noted that while Mexico's share in worldwide U.S.-based investment remained remarkably constant within a range of 4–6 percent throughout the 1990s, the share of the rest of Latin America in U.S. investment declined sharply. Thus, NAFTA might have prevented a decline of Mexico's share. (In 2001 there was a big jump, reflecting the purchase of Banamex by Citigroup.)

The Dynamics of Export Growth

In the period 1986–1993, Mexico's annual export value rose from $22 to 52 billion. Export value averaged $37.2 billion per year and experienced an average annual growth of 13 percent. During the NAFTA period, 1994–2003, export value grew at a yearly rate of 12.6 percent, but it averaged $125.1 billion per year, an amount more than three times higher than that between 1986 and 1993.[11] It peaked at $166.5 billion in 2000. Moreover, between 1994 and 2000—before the U.S. recession—it grew at an average yearly rate of 18.9 percent. As the U.S. recession took place, the absolute amount decreased, but not significantly. It declined to $158.4 billion in 2001, but then it went up right away to $ 160.7 billion in 2002 and to $164.9 billion in 2003. The export growth rate was much greater than Mexico's 2.76 percent annual GDP growth during 1993–2002. Thus, the ratio of exports to GDP had a big jump in 1995 that has been sustained so far (during 1986–1994 it oscillated between 15 and 19 percent, whereas during 1995–2000 it was always higher than 30 percent). This strongly suggests that manufacturing exports, largely produced in the NB, have become Mexico's engine of economic growth.

A high 95–97 percent of total nonoil export value is accounted for by manufacturing exports, and 50–55 percent of manufacturing export value is conducted through the maquiladora sector.[12] The United States has been by far the main export market for Mexico—during the last decade 85–88 percent of Mexican exports were shipped to U.S. destinations. Mexico's share in U.S. imports rose continuously from 1990 to 2002, particularly since 1994: it reached 6.1 percent in 1990, 7.5 in 1994, and 11.7 in 2002. In 2001 Mexico overcame Japan as the second largest exporter to the United States, just after Canada.

Traditionally, Mexico's exports had been highly concentrated in the NB as well as in the CE. As shown in Table 8.4,[13] the exceptional export growth shown by the SO is completely determined by the state of Puebla and specifically by the automobile and garment industries located there. It can be seen that Mexico's export growth dwindled during the years of the U.S. recession, bringing a decline of the export dynamism in the NB. In contrast, the CE's poor performance improved and the CW was able to achieve an even higher growth rate of exports. The lagging regions showed mixed results. In the CN export growth became negative, in the

Table 8.4

Regional Export-Value Growth in the NAFTA Era, 1996–2002[a]

	Share			Average annual growth			Value (U.S.$ bil.)
Region	1996	1998	2002	1996–2002	1996–1999	1996–2002	1996–2002
Central (CE)	41.1	34.4	41.7	38.3	−4.28	0.93	239.5
Central-West (CW)	5.2	5.5	7.1	5.9	3.54	6.01	36.9
Northern Border (NB)	45	50	42.3	46.3	5.73	−0.79	289.8
Central-North (CN)	1.6	1.8	1.2	1.4	0.02	−4.89	8.8
Southeast (SE)	2	1.5	1.3	1.5	−12.69	−5.52	9.1
South (SO)	5.1	6.7	6.4	6.6	19.73	4.92	41.3
Nation					2.09	0.15	625.4

Source: Based on data from BANCOMEXT.
Note: The data for exports by states are available only from 1996 and are still not available for 2003.
[a]Includes only exports for which a place (state) of origin has been identified. On average, that portion amounts to 70 percent of total exports during the period.

SO it slowed down even though it still was above average, and the negative trend of the SE was ameliorated (see Table 8.4).

Overall, during the NAFTA era the traditional pattern of high export concentration has not been modified significantly. Invariably, the NB and the CE together accounted for almost 85 percent of national exports during 1996–2002. The shares of the CW and SO (Puebla mainly) still are much lower, despite their above average export growth during the NAFTA era.

The Export Maquiladoras

Traditionally, export growth in Mexico has been closely tied to the maquiladora sector, which accounts for approximately one-half of total exports and for 55–60 percent of manufacturing exports. As can be seen from Table 8.5, the growth in the number of these plants has been adversely affected by the U.S. economic slowdown. The average growth of the number (monthly average) of maquiladoras in the period 1990–1994 is higher than in the first decade of the NAFTA era (1994–2003) (5.33 vs. 4.03), but much lower—almost by one-half—than in the period 1994–2000 (9.54) (last row). This reflects the massive closings that occurred between 2001 and 2003 because of the U.S. recession and to a less extent the increased attractiveness of China, described above.

Nevertheless, it seems that the downward trend reversed early in 2004; there are reports of significant new investments that have arrived and are planned for the near future. After three years of sluggish or negative export growth, during the first

Table 8. 5

The Growth of Maquiladora Plants Across Regions, 1990–2003

Region	Share[a]			Average annual growth NAFTA periods			
	1993	1998	2003	1990– 1994	1994– 2003	1994– 2000	2000– 2003
Central (CE)	1.2[b]	2.4[c]	2.2[c]	13.62	8.98	18.54	−10.14
Central-West (CW)	1.9[d]	6.8[e]	8.1[e]	2.38	25.40	41.55	−6.99
Northern Border (NB)	87.4	79.3	78.6	4.31	2.87	7.46	−6.30
Central-North (CN)	2.8[f]	4.0	2.6	0.70	4.08	14.78	−17.31
Southeast (SE)	1.2[g]	2.2[g]	3.1[g]	20.96	15.70	28.75	−10.42
South (SO)	0.0	2.2[h]	2.8[h]	—	—	—	−9.89
Nation				5.33	4.03	9.54	−7.00

Source: Based on data from INEGI.
[a]The sum of the percentages does not add to 100 because some plants are assigned to an "other states" category; [b]State of México; [c]State of Méxicoand Federal District; [d]Jalisco; [e]Jalisco, Guanajuato and Aguascalientes; [f]Baja California Sur and Durango; [g]Yucatán; [h]Puebla.

seven months of 2004, maquiladora exports and nonoil exports report a 12.7 and 12.8 percent growth, respectively, compared to the corresponding exports during the same period of the preceding year.

However, the recovery is not homogeneous across industries. Investment and export growth is being led by the automotive and electronic industries, whereas the performance in textile and garments is still depressed. The impending end of textile quotas on January 1, 2005, stands as the initiation of a devastating competition from China. It might be that Mexico will not be able to meet the challenge of competing successfully in the U.S. market, despite its NAFTA preferences.[14]

As is well known, maquiladora plants have been heavily concentrated in NB cities. Nevertheless, throughout the period 1990–2003 there was a continuous shift toward nonborder regions. The number of maquiladoras has grown faster in every nonborder region, as shown in Table 8.5. The U.S. slowdown (2000–2003) resulted in a decline in the number of plants in every region. While the relative decline in the NB was lower than that in any other region, which increased its share of the total, a high 70 percent of the plants closures and/or relocations occurred in that region.

Overall, between 1993 and 2003 the share of the NB declined significantly from 87.4 to 78.6 percent, whereas constant increases throughout the period occurred in the dynamic CW, whose share rose from 1.9 to 8.1 percent, as well as in the lagging SE (mainly in the state of Yucatán) and SO (mainly in the state of Puebla), which together accounted for almost 6 percent.[15] Between 1993 and 2000 maquiladora employment tripled, adding around 900,000 jobs during this period.

In 2000, when the number of plants reached a peak, maquiladoras accounted for 20 percent of manufacturing employment.

The Factors Behind Regional Manufacturing Change in the NAFTA Era

For most of the 1990s, interregional differences in sectoral structure (specialization) have been responsible for a high proportion of the interregional differences in economic growth. Those regions specialized in fast-growing sectors such as manufactures and transport and communications tended to experience faster economic growth. Likewise, those regions with a growing specialization in metallic products, machinery, and equipment, and in basic metals, by far the most dynamic manufacturing industries in the NAFTA era and accounting for a large part of export growth, have recorded well-above-average economic growth (Messmacher 2000).[16] Nevertheless, during 1993–1998 most states in the NB and CW grew faster than what would be expected from their economic specialization. This suggests the existence of other region-specific factors boosting growth beyond the contribution of a favorable economic specialization. In contrast, in the SO, SE, and CE there were and still are regional factors that obstructed growth (Messmacher 2000).

The lagging southern regions not only lack these growth-promoting elements, but also have been adversely affected by their remoteness and poor connection to the United States and by the existence of institutional obstacles—for example, local civil organizations that systematically oppose infrastructure projects and groups of local prominent businessmen and politicians that have long obstructed private investments, mostly in wholesale and retail trade as well as in distribution networks in order to keep control of such activities in the region.

During the NAFTA era, there has been a shift away from large industrial agglomerations in central Mexico toward broadly specialized industrial centers in northern Mexico and other regions of the country (Hanson 1998). Manufacturing growth has tended to be higher in regions with relatively strong backward-forward industry linkages (vertically integrated sectoral clusters), but insensitive to the existence of industrial diversity and large agglomerations. Growth has also been higher in regions that are relatively well connected to the United States. Thus, Mexico's shift toward an outward-oriented growth strategy has been accompanied by the emergence, mostly in the NB and CW, of export-oriented industrial clusters in automobiles, electronics, and garments that have boosted regional industrial growth.

More than 50 percent of manufacturing exports is conducted by wholly or majority foreign-owned export maquiladoras. Most export maquiladoras are located in the NB and many have been leading the development of dynamic vertically integrated clusters. Thus, the growth of the export-maquiladora sector is very symptomatic of that connection between export orientation, formation of clusters, and regional economic growth. It has been reported recently that 88.9 and 57.1 percent of the maquiladora plants in electronics and automobiles located in the border cities of Tijuana, Mexicali, and Juárez are majority foreign owned and majority U.S. owned, respectively (COLEF 2002). Also, a small group of about 300 large firms with participation of foreign capital (some of which are registered as maquiladoras) have accounted for at least 50 percent of total exports since 1994. About 25 percent of these firms are majority foreign owned.

In some industrial clusters, NAFTA has brought about a qualitative change in the way local firms are connected to export markets. For instance, in the garment cluster of Torreón (north), the traditional, pure assembly subcontracting network has been largely transformed into a network that allows for the addition of more value locally (Bair and Gereffi 2001). Before NAFTA, a few large apparel manufacturers located in the United States used to dominate the region's export-oriented apparel production. These manufacturers' sourcing needs from Mexico were limited to assembly operations. With NAFTA, garment production can access the U.S. market carrying a duty-free status for North American components, which has induced the relocation of important manufacturers from East Asia to Mexico. These relocations have entailed the conduction of a larger part of the apparel commodity chain including fabric procurement, cutting, sewing, washing, and finishing, and even distributing in northern Mexico, although the highest-value activities such as design and product development, marketing, and retail remain in the United States. Moreover, the manufacturers are not only U.S. subsidiaries, but also joint ventures and large Mexican-owned firms, all of which keep subcontracting assembly operations locally. The insertion of Mexican firms into subcontracting networks varies widely depending on foreign firms' competitive strategy, type of product, and process or technological confidentiality, but in general remains quite limited.

This transformation had thus upgraded the role of Torreón's garment clusters in the global production chain. It had also led to an exploding growth in export value as well as an exceptional creation of local employment. However, the slowdown of the U.S. economy and the relocation of firms to China have affected the local performance of this industry. Plant closings have reportedly been massive, as have lay offs. Local estimates indicate that 30,000 jobs were lost in the export sector in 2001 and 2002, most in the garment industry (van Dooren and Zárate-Hoyos 2003).

Analyses of location decisions of plants in the most dynamic sectors also have provided valuable insights into the location of important clusters. For instance, the single most important factor in the decision to locate an auto plant in northern Mexico is the existence of conditions that make it possible to implant just-in-time (JIT) production systems.[17] Thus, the observed northward shift of automotive assemblers (the most dynamic industry of the economy at large) and the development of automotive clusters in northern Mexico are related to the availability in northern locations of a compliant, malleable labor force willing to learn different skills and perform multiple functions on the shop-floor, as that is an important condition for implanting JIT systems in the electronics and, to a lesser extent, the garment and automobile industries. The advantages conferred by northern locations in terms of access to the U.S and Mexican markets and coordination with parent firms in the United States is another decisive location factor (Ramírez 1995; Shaiken 1994).

Other studies of other export-oriented clusters focus on different aspects of firms' behavior, such as cooperation among firms in a footwear cluster in Guadalajara (Rabellotti 1999) or the exchange of information and knowledge in the automobile and electronic clusters of Aguascalientes (Abdel 2000). Overall, the most economically dynamic states/regions during the last decade are those in which important export-oriented industrial clusters have developed. It is also very symptomatic that there are no industrial clusters in the Southeast and South (OECD 2003). Thus, it is reasonable to assert that clusters are largely responsible for the observed shift of industrial growth toward the NB and CW states, insofar as such place-bounded form of organization allows firms to operate at higher levels of efficiency.

It has been observed that maquiladoras in the garment industry are being attracted recently to rural areas. This phenomenon has been notable in the state of Yucatan (SE) and in La Laguna—a zone at the border of the states of Coahuila (NB) and Durango (CN)—where dynamic garment clusters exhibiting an important export growth have developed. The garment industry suddenly has become the most important source of employment and income in these rural settings, in the context of declining agricultural production.[18] In the case of La Laguna, tight urban labor markets in the city of Torreón (the capital of the state of Coahuila), which have driven up wages and other benefits, and have increased training costs due to high turnover and absenteeism rates, are largely responsible for location or relocation of firms to rural areas. In the case of Yucatán, turnover ratios and labor shortages in the city of Mérida (the state capital) are the main factors underlying the preference for rural locations, compounded by important infrastructure improvements related to the supply of energy and equipped sites (van Dooren and Zárate-Hoyos 2003).

In La Laguna, industry traditionally consisted of locally owned companies, but during the NAFTA era these have been joined by a considerable number of foreign-owned firms. While foreign firms have tended to locate in main rural towns on the outskirts of urban areas, the location of locally owned firms spreads further away to include smaller villages. Moreover, locally owned firms have established facilities in association with *ejidatarios* (rural garment cooperatives) to produce the most standardized and simple components. These are located in rural *ejido* land. In the state of Yucatan, foreign-owned maquiladoras grew from 28 to 130 between 1994 and 2001. In 1999, 41 of 111 maquiladoras were located in 24 rural municipalities of the Henequen Zone. Thirty-three of the 41 rural plants were in garment production and accounted for 93 percent of maquiladora employment in the Henequen Zone and half of statewide employment in garment maquiladoras (van Dooren and Zárate-Hoyos 2003).

However, garment plants in these rural areas have no local linkages other than creating low-skilled employment. Training by clients is minimal and technology transfer nil. Reportedly, maquiladora closures were massive during the years of the U.S. recession, particularly in garments, and unemployment soared.[19] Rural factories were among the first victims, and there are no local employment alternatives for former garment workers. Thus, the future of traditional maquiladoras as a source of rural employment and income remains largely uncertain.

Finally, NAFTA has had an important effect on regional growth through its impact on wage income. The relative demand for high-skilled workers has been higher in those areas where the bulk of maquiladora plants are concentrated—the NB states. During the late 1980s and early 1990s, over 50 percent of the increase in the skilled labor wage in that region was accounted for by the growth of maquiladora activity (Feenstra and Hanson 1997). Wage growth throughout the 1990s was higher in those regions with a relatively high share of FDI and with high migration rates (Hanson 2002). The former reflects a higher labor demand, whereas the latter reflects a greater integration of labor markets or the role of international remittances in starting businesses. In short, the high shares of trade, FDI, and maquila operations in the GDP of the North are key elements in the process of industrial reallocation, which in turn is partially driven by the spatial distribution of wages. In general, relative wages decrease with distance from Mexico City and from the Mexico–U.S. border, but after trade reform the relationship weakens in the former case whereas it becomes stronger in the latter (Lederman, Maloney, and Serven 2003). Overall, those regions better integrated with foreign markets have experienced greater labor demand, which in turn is manifested in reduced unemployment and higher wages. Since this happened during a time of great U.S. restrictions on migration from Mexico, it is more likely to be due to trade and investment liberalization.

Conclusion

NAFTA has led to an increasing economic integration between most Mexican regions and the U.S. economy, particularly the U.S. Pacific region. The only unambiguous exception is the Mexican South, which remains largely isolated not only from U.S. developments, but also from national growth trends. While, the Northern Border region seems to be the most integrated into the U.S. economy, every other region but the South has deepened its process of integration. Moreover, the dynamic Mexican regions, in general, seem to have a higher degree of integration with the U.S. Pacific region than with the Mexican South or Southeast, as indicated by the degree of synchronization of growth trends.

A good part of the observed shift of economic growth toward the Northern Border and Central-West can be attributed to regional specialization or industry mix. Indeed, those two major regions have specialized in fast-growth sectors such as manufactures, as well as in the most dynamic highly export-oriented manufacturing industries such as metallic products, machinery, and equipment, in which the production of automobiles is comprised. Nevertheless, NAFTA has boosted growth in these two regions by enhancing their competitive advantages. First of all, NAFTA has lowered the costs of accessing the U.S. market, particularly for the NB and CW, which are close and well connected to the United States. Hence, large amounts of FDI aimed at exporting to the United States has been attracted to these regions. Second, local content requirements have led to the establishment of operations well beyond assembling, which allow for the addition of more value locally. Third, the interaction between access to the U.S. market and technological decisions has led to the development of vertically integrated clusters in dynamic export-oriented industries, particularly automobiles, electronics, and garments, which allow firms to reduce production and distribution costs, thus contributing to regional growth.

In short, the location decision of clusters has been largely a compromise between meeting conditions for the implantation of new technologies and preserving good access to the U.S. market. Hence, the clusters have developed mostly within the Northern Border and Central-West regions, but not necessarily within the traditional sites of pure assembly maquiladoras. Thus, NAFTA has induced the emergence of a more dispersed pattern of location within the NB region well beyond the cities bordering the United States. The same effect has been observed within the Central-West. Finally, the higher integration of the NB and CW to foreign markets through trade, FDI, maquiladoras, or migration has led to greater labor demand, which in turn is manifested in reduced unemployment and higher wages.

A general outcome of this process of economic integration has been a deepening of regional polarization, which in fact was anticipated. Attempts have been made to address growing regional divergences through the implementation of sectoral and regional policies aimed at compensating for the damage caused by increasing competition or for the inability to capture the opportunities opened by NAFTA. These policies are discussed in the chapters 7, 13, and 29 in this book.

Notes

This research was awarded financial support from Mexico's National Council of Science and Technology (CONACYT) under the project 37932-D coordinated by the author, as well as from the program Cátedras de Investigación of the Tecnológico de Monterrey. For any information or comment regarding the content of this document, write to rtamayo@itesm.mx.

1. The maquiladoras are offshore assembly plants that operate under a special tax regime. Mexico allows for temporary imports of components and supplies without duties; taxes are paid only on value added. The production has to be reexported to the United States under a duty-free status. Hence, these plants traditionally have performed assembly operations with a quite low local content.

2. *Trade creation* occurs in international trade when high-cost sources (a third country) are replaced by lower-cost sources (a member of the FTA) as the result of a change in tariffs, quotas, or other trade barriers on a geographical basis (e.g., the formation of a FTA). *Trade diversion* occurs when such changes lead to the replacement of a more efficient source (a third country) by a less efficient source (a member of the FTA).

3. For instance, because of transport costs, the U.S.–Israel trade agreement is more likely to create trade diversion and reduce world economic welfare than NAFTA or MERCOSUR, assuming that there is no product differentiation.

4. *Forward linkages* are described by the relationship between an industry or firm and the clients that buy its output and use it as an input. *Backward linkages* are defined by the relationship between an industry or firm and the suppliers of its inputs. The *economies of scale* are reductions in the average cost of a product resulting from an increase in the level of output. There are internal economies of scale, which arise from the expansion of the individual firm, and external economies of scale, which arise from the expansion of an industry (the expansion of the industry makes possible the specialization of suppliers and, thus, the reduction of costs of all firms in the industry).

5. The MAMC is defined as the built-up area including the Federal District plus thirty-four adjacent or nearby urban municipalities of the state of Mexico. It accounts for 0.8 percent of the national territory and for 18 percent of the national population. There are over 19 million inhabitants.

6. Definitions of regions are given in Table 1.2 in chapter 1 of this book.

7. It should be noted that between 1995 and 2000 the Mexican economy exhibited a quite strong GDP average growth of 5.43 percent.

8. International trade and FDI might affect economic growth through various channels. They potentially have positive effects on factor accumulation and efficiency. Factor accumulation can increase if, as expected, the price of capital or investment goods falls and because of the market for exports increases. Efficiency gains can result from reallocation of factors across firms and industries or from the exit of inefficient firms as competition intensifies (these are once-and-for-all static welfare gains). Trade-induced efficiency gains can also arise from technological spillovers or learning (dynamic), which entails the transmission of knowledge regarding production processes via the importation of foreign final and intermediate capital goods. Also, there are learning-by-exporting effects, whereby exporting firms learn about production (or management) processes from their competitors in foreign markets.

9. The probable impact of NAFTA is lessened by the fact that the steady increase in FDI to Mexico was part of a global rise in FDI flows to developing countries during the 1990s. Other countries in Latin America such as Brazil and Argentina attracted similarly large or even larger absolute and relative volumes. Actually, Mexico's share of global FDI flows to developing countries peaked to an average of 8–9 percent in the early 1990s, and then fell in the late 1990s to an average of 6 percent (Lederman, Maloney, and Serven 2003).

10. The Free Trade Agreement between the European Union (EU) and Mexico was enacted on July 1, 2000. It is the first trade agreement between the EU and a Latin American country. This agreement eliminates barriers to 95 percent of the goods traded between Mexico and the EU over a ten-year period. It includes the liberalization of services and government purchases. The EU will liberalize industrial goods faster than Mexico. Only 62 percent of the agricultural goods will be liberalized.

11. This information on exports does not coincide with the data presented in Table 8.4 because the latter considers only exports for which it has been possible to determine place (state) of origin. This database is the only source of information on exports available by states. It has been built by the Mexican Bank of Foreign Trade (BANCOMEXT), which is still working on methodological refinements. The information included in the database initiates in 1996. In some years, the proportion of exports whose place of origin has not been yet determined still is substantial.

12. The exports of maquiladoras are recorded as exports of manufactured goods. The figures on export value thus include the complete value of these goods and not only the value added in Mexico, which remains in general at very low levels.

13. This analysis is based on exports for which a state of origin has been identified. These exports account approximately for 70–75 percent of national exports. Hence, the resulting regional trends should be taken with caution.

14. While the textile and apparel sector enjoys the highest preferential treatment under NAFTA, only about 62 percent of Mexican exports of textile and apparel enter the U.S. market under NAFTA preferences. This low utilization rate of NAFTA preferences is explained by two factors. First is that such preferences have been diluted by the Caribbean Basin Economic Recovery Act (2000), which allowed exports of apparel from the Caribbean and Central American countries to enter duty-free the U.S. market as long as the yarn used originates in the United States. Second is Mexico's lack of comparative advantage in textiles (it is a large net importer), the main input in garment production, compounded by NAFTA rules of origin that require Mexico to import textiles from the United States (which is not Mexico's low-cost source of textiles), in order for its garment producers to export to the United States under NAFTA preferences.

15. These percentages exclude a small number of plants for which the state where they are located is not revealed. These plants are aggregated into a category called "all other states." The fact that none of these states borders the United States causes an overestimation, however minimal, of the share of the Northern Border and an underestimation for the other regions (see footnote in Table 8.5).

16. The level of aggregation of these industries prevents us from distinguishing between intermediate industrial inputs and final consumption goods. Both of them are considered together. For instance, the metallic products, machinery, and equipment industry includes automobile production, which in turn includes a high variety of auto parts.

17. Just-in-time systems imply a vertically integrated production organization with extensive subcontracting practices and a tight interdependency among plants. Based on technology (equipment) and a labor force that allow for rapid changes of product characteristics and/or the mix of products, JIT systems allow firms to react promptly to sudden changes in demand. In short, the production schedule can be modified quickly and with it the allocation of workers across different tasks. The system thus requires highly cooperative labor relations and fluid interaction between workers, technicians, and managers. Proximity between the leading plant and its suppliers down the productive chain becomes critical in order to keep timely coordination in the flow of inputs and to receive advice from customer firms. The network as a whole is known as a flexible production system.

18. Natural factors impose severe constraints on agricultural production in La Laguna. Only a little over 5 percent of the region's land can be effectively used for agricultural purposes. In addition, a prolonged drought has affected the region throughout most of the last decade. The main crop, cotton, has been affected by low and declining international prices. Thus, during the second half of the 1990s, agricultural employment decreased by 12 percent. Agriculture is now surpassed by industry as a source of income and employment. In the state of Yucatan, henequen cultivation has been the most important activity for more than a century. However, natural fibers had been long subjected to adverse international market conditions due to the introduction of synthetic fibers. The collapse of the natural textile fibers in Yucatan was imminent by the late 1970s, releasing labor force in important quantities.

19. Official sources report a decline in the number of plants from 130 to 89 in Yucatan and from 279 to 219 in Coahuila during 2002 and 2003.

References

Bair, Jennifer, and G. Gereffi. 2001. "Local Clusters in Global Chains: The Causes and Consequences of Export Dynamism in Torreon's Blue Jeans Industry." *World Development* 29, no. 11.

COLEF (Colegio de la Frontera Norte). 2002. *Encuesta: Aprendizaje tecnológico y escalamiento industrial en plantas maquiladoras.* Tijuana: Departamento de Estudios Sociales, COLEF.

Cuevas, Alfredo, M. Messmacher, and A. Werner. 2002. *Macroeconomic Synchronization Between Mexico and Its NAFTA Partners.* Mexico City: Banco de México.

Frankel, Jeffrey A. 1997. *Regional Trading Blocks in the World Economic System.* Washington, DC: Institute for International Economics.

Feenstra, R.C., and G.H. Hanson. 1997. "Foreign Direct Investment and Relative Wages: Evidence from Mexico's Maquiladoras." *Journal of International Economics* 42, no. 3.

Hanson, Gordon H. 1998. "Regional Adjustment to Trade Liberalization." *Regional Science and Urban Economics* 28, no. 4.

Hanson, Gordon H. 2002. "What Has Happened to Wages in Mexico Since NAFTA?" Mimeo, The World Bank.

Helpman, Elhanan. 1987. "Imperfect Competition and International Trade: Evidence from Fourteen Industrial Countries." *Journal of the Japanese and International Economies* 1 (March).

Helpman, Elhanan, and P. Krugman. 1985. *Market Structure and Foreign Trade.* Cambridge, MA: MIT Press.

Hirschman, Albert O. 1958. *The Strategy of Economic Development.* New Haven, CT: Yale University Press.

Krugman, Paul, and A. Venables. 1995. "Globalization and the Inequality of Nations." *Quarterly Journal of Economics,* 110, no. 4.

Lederman, Daniel, W.F. Maloney, and L. Serven. 2003. *Lessons from NAFTA for Latin American and Caribbean Countries.* The World Bank.

Messmacher, Miguel. 2000. "Desigualdad regional en México. El efecto del TLCAN y otras reformas estructurales." *Documento de Investigación No. 2000–4,* Banco de México.

Myrdal, Gunnar. 1957. *Economic Theory and Underdeveloped Regions.* London: Duckworth.

OECD (Organization for Economic Cooperation and Development). 2003. *OECD Territorial Reviews—Mexico.* Paris: OECD.

Rabellotti, Roberta.1999. "Recovery of a Mexican Cluster: Devaluation Bonanza or Collective Efficiency?" *World Development* 27, no. 9.

Ramírez, José C. 1995. "La Organización justo a tiempo en la industria automotriz del norte de México. Nuevos patrones de localización y eficiencia." *Documento de Trabajo E-33,* Centro de Investigación y Docencia Económicas, México, D.F.

Shaiken, Harvey. 1994. "Advanced Manufacturing and Mexico: A New International Division of Labor." *Latin American Research Review* 29, no. 2.

van Dooren, Robine, and G. Zárate-Hoyos. 2003. "The Insertion of Rural Areas into Global Markets: A Comparison of Garment Production in Yucatan and La Laguna, México." *Journal of Latin American Studies* 35, no. 3.

Venables, A.J. 1996. "Equilibrium Location with Vertically-linked Industries." *International Economic Review* 37, no. 2.

9

CARLOS ELIZONDO MAYER-SERRA

Changes in Determinants of Tax Policy

Mexico has a remarkably low tax burden. Tax collections are low both because individuals do not always pay their taxes and because it has not yet been possible to reform Mexico's tax structure.

The reasons that people do not always pay their taxes are not unique to Mexico. For example, many people in the world believe that they are responsible for their own welfare and that the government cannot be relied on to aid them. In order to protect its income and assets, a family might hide its income and/or send its money abroad, and not pay taxes. The outlook for future tax collection is mixed: the World Values Survey reports that although there has been a more than 50 percent increase in the percentage of Mexicans who disapprove of claiming benefits to which they have no right, of cheating on taxes, or of accepting a bribe, this disapproval is weakest in the sixteen to twenty-nine years age group, either because younger people are more likely to engage in risky behavior or because they grew up in a world in which rich corporations with dishonest practices were bailed out by the government and, until recently, politicians and their close relatives were not subject to legal sanctions. The more educated Mexicans disapprove of many dishonest behaviors less than do other Mexicans.

Carlos Elizondo writes that total collections of value added tax (VAT) as a percentage of gross domestic product (GDP) are difficult to measure. However, tax evasion estimated as equal to at least 2 percent of gross domestic product, exemptions from taxes, and special tax treatments make tax administration complex, distort the economy, imply a loss of income (defined as tax expenditures) of more than 5 percent of gross domestic product, and indicate that important groups of the population are outside of the tax system.

The resulting limited resources of the federal government are shared with municipal and state governments, and are also used to pay interest and amortization on Mexico's large public debt. The government has cut its expenditures, but the political parties have not yet agreed on tax reform at the municipal, state, or federal level that would increase the share of gross domestic product that is collected in taxes and facilitate the greatly needed increase in social expenditure and spending on public goods.

Among the thirty member nations of the Organization for Economic Cooperation and Development (OECD), Mexico has the lowest tax revenue of all (OECD 2002). Compared to other Latin American upper-middle-income countries, Mexico's tax collection is one of the lowest, behind Brazil, Argentina, Chile, and Uruguay (Ortiz 2003). Excluding the income of state owned firms and social security contributions, the total income of the federal government in 2000 was 15.4 percent of GDP. This includes tax and nontax revenue, the latter mainly royalties paid by PEMEX (Mexican national oil company).

The federal government's income has remained virtually unchanged in the past twenty years, in spite of a change in the development model and the need to adjust public finances to meet the expenditure excesses of the 1970s and early 1980s that led to a high and unsustainable public debt, which reached 86.5 percent of GDP in 1983 and 217 percent in 1987. To confront this high debt, the main policy instrument was contracting expenditure, not raising resources.

After the budgetary discipline that started in the mid-1980s, even after the 1994 crisis, public debt was stabilized at a manageable ratio. In 2003 it was 26.5 percent of GDP, including US$76 billion of foreign debt, equal to 13.4 percent of GDP. However, if all financial obligations of the federal government are included, such as those arising from the financial rescue of 1995 and private infrastructure investment in the energy sector backed by public resources, total debt was nearly 46 percent of GDP by the end of 2003. This does not include the resources needed to fund pensions of workers in the government or in state-owned firms. During the turbulent 1980s and a few years after the 1994 crisis, inflation was the tax of last resort, although it also implied high real interest rates for long periods, with a high budgetary cost. Currently inflation is low, around 4 percent.

The structure of tax revenues has not changed much either in the last twenty years since the mid-1980s. It still relies on income tax and VAT. The number of excise taxes was diminished in the early nineties, but the most relevant excise tax, that on gasoline and diesel, has been maintained (see Table 9.1). Due to the opening of the economy the importance of import taxes diminished from 4.2 percent of federal revenues in 1980–1982 to 0.5 percent in 2000–2002.

During these twenty years, public finances have depended enormously on oil income. This dependence has fluctuated, following the price of oil (see Figure 9.1) and the value of the peso, grossly undervalued in the mid-1980s as a result of capital flight and the need to pay the debt, much stronger from 1990 to 1994 and from 1999 onwards (Figure 9.2), once inflation was controlled. These instabilities have had a severe impact on the government's ability to project its revenues and expenditures, in particular to invest in infrastructure, and have affected the capacity of the oil industry to invest to maintain reserve levels.

Matters are made worse by tax evasion and special exemptions from taxes. VAT evasion has been calculated at 2.28 percent of GDP, compared to a VAT income of 3.5 percent of GDP.[1] In addition to tax evasion there are many exemptions from taxes and special tax treatments that makes tax administration complex, distorts

Table 9.1

Federal Government Budget Revenue, 1985–2003 (total percentage)

Concept	1985	1986	1987	1988	1989	1990	1991	1992	1993	1994	1995	1996	1997	1998	1999	2000	2001	2002[b]	2003 p/
Total	100.0	100.0	100.0	100.0	100.0	100.0	100.0	100.0	100.0	100.0	100.0	100.0	100.0	100.0	100.0	100.0	100.0	100.0	100.0
Oil sector	45.0	38.3	43.3	35.0	31.8	29.5	28.8	28.3	27.1	27.2	35.3	37.6	36.0	31.4	31.1	25.1	23.7	29.8	23.5
—PEMEX rights[a]	34.3	23.5	30.8	20.5	19.9	22.2	21.2	19.1	18.0	14.5	25.7	28.8	25.8	16.5	14.5	17.2	16.2	na	na
—Gas and other fuel taxes	8.5	11.8	9.9	11.1	8.9	4.4	4.7	7.0	6.9	10.1	6.2	5.2	6.8	11.3	13.0	5.2	4.9	na	na
—PEMEX gross VAT	2.2	3.0	2.6	3.3	3.0	3.0	2.9	2.2	2.2	2.7	3.4	3.6	3.4	3.6	3.6	2.7	2.5	na	na
Nonoil sector	55.0	61.7	56.7	65.0	68.2	70.5	71.2	71.7	72.9	72.8	64.7	62.4	64.0	68.6	68.9	74.9	76.3	70.1	76.5
—Fiscal	49.8	55.6	50.4	57.8	55.7	59.9	62.5	61.0	64.3	61.6	51.1	48.7	51.7	59.2	60.7	67.0	69.8	na	na
—Nonfiscal	5.2	6.1	6.3	7.2	12.6	10.6	8.6	10.7	8.6	11.1	13.4	13.7	12.3	9.5	8.2	7.9	6.5	na	na

Source: INEGI n.d.; INEGI 1992.
Note: Totals may not match because amounts were rounded up.
p/ = preliminary amounts.
[a]Includes hydrocarbon rights and use of surplus products.
[b]data for 2002 were taken from Presidencia de la República (2003, 243).

Figure 9.1 **Oil Prices, 1970–2002** (U.S. dollars in 2002)

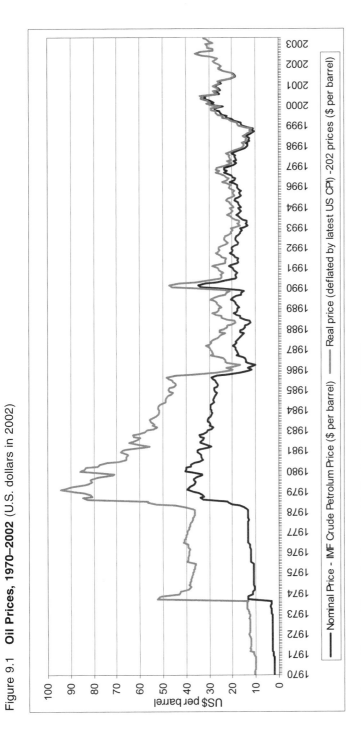

Source: Extracted from a database provided by the *Financial Times* (2001).

Figure 9.2 **Real Exchange Rate, Pesos per U.S. Dollar, 1980–2003** (August 2003 prices)

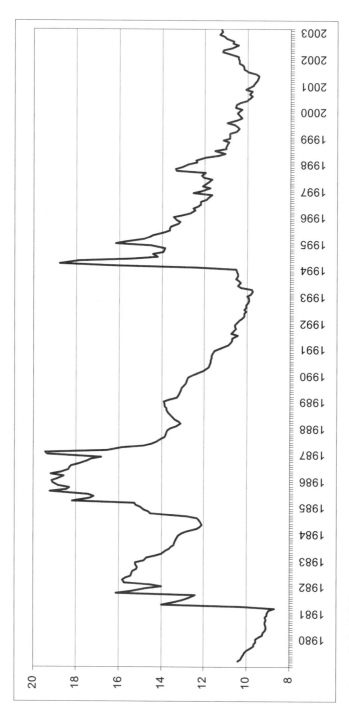

Source: Feliz (2003).

Table 9.2

Social Effects of Education Expenditure, Chile and Mexico

Quintile	Education expenditure (percent)			
	Total	Elementary	Secondary	Postsecondary
Mexico, 1996				
1	18.4	30.6	12.2	0.7
2	19.6	25.0	22.9	6.0
3	20.1	20.5	24.8	10.5
4	20.5	15.3	25.0	25.0
5	21.4	8.6	15.1	57.9
Chile, 1990				
1	34	36	24	23
2	27	27	26	16
3	19	18	22	22
4	13	13	17	20
5	8	7	10	20

Source: Scott (2002).
Note: Quintile 1 represents the poorest 20 percent, while quintile 5 the 20 percent richest.

the economy, and implies a loss of income, defined as tax expenditure, of nearly 5.32 percent of GDP (see Appendix Table 9.5).

Tax collection difficulties in Mexico are not limited to the federal government. The Constitution gives states and local governments fiscal faculties. However, these have only been minimally used, basically as a result of a political agreement reached in the early seventies between the federal and state governments that has given most tax responsibilities to the federal government. The collection of the most relevant tax still under the responsibility of local governments, the property tax, is very low compared to other countries.

As a result of low collection capacity and numerous expenditure commitments acquired in the past, reflected in high debt payments and underfunded pension responsibilities that are increasingly a budgetary cost, many social demands have been left unattended. Perhaps the most serious of these is the increasing inequality in the access to education and health services. In Mexico, taxation is quite progressive and social expenditure is fairly neutral, far less progressive than in other Latin American countries (Scott 2004). For example, in the 1990s, Mexican government spending on education was more favorable to those in the richest quintile of income recipients, while Chilean government spending on education favored those in the lowest quintile of income recipients. Although spending on primary education favored the worst off in both countries, spending on higher education in Mexico benefited almost exclusively the richest quintile (see Table 9.2).

An Explanation of Mexican Tax Administration

Why has the Mexican government been such an inefficient tax collector? There is no single answer. Economic crises every six years, linked between 1976 and 1994 to the change of president, have kept the GDP per capita without a substantial increase since 1981. Without an increase in income, raising taxes is always more difficult. Two structural conditions, however, are critical in explaining this fragility.

First, governments, independent of their ideology, face strong resistance when promoting a profound tax reform. Both financial and human capital is highly volatile, and tax evasion is greater at high tax rates. This limits the tax collecting pretensions of any government.

Globalization also enhances peoples' mobility. Those with few skills move illegally, and those with more financial or human capital can move legally, to countries with better public services. Emigration from Mexico to the United States weakens Mexico's tax base. The border limits Mexico's capacity to increase the rate of consumption taxes, as they cannot be much higher than those of its neighbor. The United States has a very low tax rate for consumption goods compared to other developed countries. This has led to the imposition of a 10 percent VAT in the northern border, lower than in the rest of the country,[2] and to a lower effective VAT rate than most Latin American countries. Argentina has a VAT rate of 21 percent, Brazil 20.5 percent, Chile 18 percent, and Mexico 15 percent. Argentina raises 4.41 points of GDP through VAT, Brazil 9.21, Chile 8.64, and Mexico 3.45 (Ortiz 2003). But the border, by itself, does not determine Mexico's low rate of tax collection. The other United States neighbor, Canada, has been able to uphold superior tax collection compared to that of Mexico and even to that of the United States (see Table 9.3).

Second, due to the high concentration in income, the cost of increasing taxes will tend to affect a small group of taxpayers. For instance, even with all the exemptions that favor them, 10 percent of people with the highest income levels pay 37.18 percent of the total of consumption taxes collected (IVA), while the poorest 10 percent only pay 1.71 percent (Hernández, Scott, and Zamudio 2001). Income tax is even more concentrated in the richest 10 percent.

The minority of Mexicans, those with high levels of income and wealth, are able to either oppose increases in taxes or to take their capital out of the country (Przeworksi 1998). These affluent Mexicans confront a very weak tax administration that can be defeated through good legal advice in most cases. The potential recipients of tax increments, those who would benefit from government spending, are, on the contrary, much more dispersed; for that reason, it is more difficult to mobilize this group to support tax reform. The tension between the active rich minority and the dispersed majority has been resolved in the past through low tax revenue as a percentage of GDP and low public expenditure. Only in the happy period that started in 1972 and ended with the 1982 crisis could very large deficits fund more public spending.

Table 9.3

Government Tax Revenue, Canada, United States, Mexico, Brazil, and Chile, 1980–2000 (GDP percentage)

	Total	Direct	Indirect	Social Security
Canada				
1980	31.6	17.8	10.4	3.4
1985	32.7	17.7	10.5	4.5
1990	35.6	21.1	9.3	5.2
1995	35.5	20.6	9.0	5.9
2000	36.4	NA	NA	NA
United States				
1980	26.9	16.3	4.7	5.9
1985	26.1	14.6	4.9	6.6
1990	26.6	15.1	4.6	6.9
1995	27.9	15.9	5.0	7.0
2000	28.3	NA	NA	NA
Mexico				
1980	15.9	5.3	8.3	2.3
1985	17.0	4.1	11.0	1.9
1990	17.1	5.2	9.6	2.3
1995	16.3	4.6	9.0	2.7
2000	16.1	NA	NA	NA
Brazil				
1988	15.70	10.61	5.07	NA
1991	15.90	10.95	4.91	NA
1994	18.40	13.11	5.28	NA
1997	19.21	NA	NA	NA
2000	29.30	NA	NA	NA
Chile				
1988	18.1	6.0	12.2	NA
1991	17.6	5.2	12.3	NA
1994	17.7	4.8	12.9	NA
1997	18.0	4.1	13.9	NA
2000	19.1	NA	NA	NA

Source: OECD (2002); UNPAN, n.d. Statistical Database, available at www.unpan.org/statistical_database-publicsector.asp

Notes: Direct income accounts for capital income and profit taxes, and indirect income for salary, property, goods and services taxes.

For Brazil 2000 average only 1997 and 1998 were used because of data availability.

Data are not comparable with that of other sources.

NA = data not available.

It seems easier to collect taxes from a small group than from dispersed taxpayers, but in Mexico, the regressive distribution of income becomes a political challenge when extending the tax base is attempted. Yet this is not an insurmountable obstacle. The distribution of income in Chile and Brazil is more unequal than in Mexico, yet these nations' taxes as a share of GDP are notably higher than Mexican taxes as a share of GDP (see Table 9.3).

Mexico's proximity to the United States, and its historical inequalities, increases the costs of collecting taxes; however, the main reason behind the Mexican tax fragility is found in the corporative political regime created after the Revolution of 1910. Four key elements of this system seem to have gravitated against a stronger tax capacity. These elements are: (1) A corporative agreement based on discretionary privileges that reduced the tax base; (2) the low legitimacy of the government; (3) the absence of a relatively stable professional bureaucracy resistant to political pressure that would be able to implement tax policies correctly; and (4) the centralization of public spending and public revenues that hinder the local authorities' capacity to collect taxes.

Other Latin American countries that have had extended periods of nondemocratic governments with corporative characteristics share some of these aspects. Nevertheless, because Mexico's corporatist government lasted longer than comparable regimes in Latin America, it had greater difficulty in improving its collection of taxes.

The Corporative Logic

A critical element in Mexico's institutions has been the president's discretionary powers, which enable him to distribute privileges among groups, sectors, and even individuals. They were incorporated into the development model that was based on protectionism and subsidies. The tax system was no exception.

Some of these taxation privileges were justified at the beginning, in order to encourage investment. They were granted directly by the secretary of Treasury or even by public servants at lower levels. Defended for economic reasons, this discretionary power facilitated the construction of patronage webs that went beyond the initial economic rationality. Once these privileges were conferred, it was very difficult to remove them.

Due to the importance of entrepreneurs in the development model, authorities were unwilling to harm one of the bases of the "alliances for profits": high profits with low tax rates (Reynolds 1970). The fear of either capital flight or of a decrease in private investment prevented a thorough tax reform (Elizondo 1994). Similarly, the administration's fragility allowed the creation of an underground economy that grew with every new crisis, leaving important segments of the population outside of the tax system (OECD 1998).

Many other groups were given special tax conditions. After decades of reforms aimed at diminishing all these privileges, taxes not collected due to these exemptions and special treatments account for nearly 5.32 percent of GDP. These special treatments were given to groups ranging from transport firms critical for mobilizing political supporters to intellectuals who could be seduced into being less critical of the government in exchange for tax exemptions in income derived from intellectual property and zero VAT on books, newspapers, and magazines. Other examples of special treatment are more general, such as exemptions to wage earners from a variety of income categories that favor those workers in powerful trade unions. Many groups gained from the government's fragility. It was easier to contract expenditure than to eliminate these tax privileges.

Legitimacy

Taxes reflect the relation between society and the state. Adequate compliance requires a certain perception of justice in the tax system and in how resources are used (Levy 1988). Prior to 1997, Mexico had a nondemocratic government. The Mexican authoritarian regime relied on discretionality; public spending was not transparent. Corruption was perceived as extended and generalized. As a result, spending is hardly seen as a public service that could generate greater social benefits than those offered by private spending sacrificed by taxes.

To the degree that an increasingly poor and ineffective government provides fewer or very low quality public services, citizens with resources begin to pay for goods and services usually provided by the government in other societies. As they receive few public services, the legitimacy of paying taxes is low.[3]

As the government is under pressure to increase revenues, there is a continuous search for new ways of imposing taxes. So many changes cause great difficulties when the citizens try to understand the new rules of the game. This forces taxpayers to consult a specialist to fill in tax forms. The common perception is that tax legislation in Mexico is more complicated than in other countries. This situation helps to justify tax evasion by more affluent Mexicans who have to file a tax return, just a minority of taxpayers.

The debt crisis in 1982 and the banking crisis in 1995 led to large public debts. Consequently, all administrations after this crisis have had to generate a fiscal surplus in order to pay the interest and amortization of these debts that in many cases were not invested in such a way that society gets more or better quality public goods. These payments were equal on average from 2000–2004, 14.1 percent of the federal budget (Presidencia de la República 2003), which limits the capacity of the government to make taxes visible to taxpayers.

In order to increase the acceptability of an increase in taxes, there is a continuous search for new ways of imposing them. The resulting changes cause great difficulty when the citizens try to understand the new rules of the game. This forces taxpayers to consult a specialist to fill in tax forms. The common perception is that tax legislation in Mexico is more complicated than in other countries, and that this situation helps to justify tax evasion.

Administrative Fragility

In order to maintain political stability, the Mexican president has traditionally redistributed thousands of public positions among his party and sympathizers. The distinction between the professional bureaucracy and the political class did not evolve properly, which resulted in the persistence of weak bureaucratic bodies that rarely were able to implement complex policy. President José López Portillo expropriated the banks in 1982, yet the government could not manage the daily and boring duty of collecting taxes (Elizondo 2001a, chap. 3).

There is high quality at the top levels of bureaucracy with the ability to design tax policies (OECD 2002). However, this professional bureaucracy is too small to be able to adequately implement fiscal reforms. Relatively low salaries and job insecurity in the Finance Ministry make it difficult to retain the best civil servants, who can achieve a more successful career in the private sector. Corruption undermines the capacity to audit properly.

Compared to Chile and Argentina, Mexico has a more clumsy and expensive tax administration: it costs US$1.10 to collect $100, compared to $0.40 in Chile. In addition, Mexico uses 1,962 employees per point of GDP collected, compared to 876 in Argentina and 146 in Chile (Bergman 2002).

When the government finally locates a citizen who has not paid his or her taxes, it is highly possible that it will lose its case in court as a result of poorly devised legislation, the public prosecutor's lack of resources, and judges' interpretation of the law in favor of the taxpayer. Corruption is likely to undermine the whole process. According to judicial statistics in 2001, just 802 presumed tax law violations were registered that year, from which 545 offenders were sentenced (INEGI 2002).

The Federal Agreement

The Federal Constitution of 1917 gave the states ample rights to impose taxes, while sharing them with the federal government. However, the federal government, through the Fiscal Coordination Law (Orrantía Arellano 1998), is responsible for most tax and spending responsibilities. This has allowed the federal executive to strengthen its power over local politicians—both state governors and municipal presidents—building a paternalistic relationship with local governors who neither paid the price of collecting taxes nor were able to spend freely.

With the victory of the opposition in the mid-term elections of 1997, and more clearly after 2000, state and municipal governments became quite successful in demanding that the federal government provide more resources, as they considered it was politically less expensive than collecting taxes locally or demanding more tax responsibilities. The concentration of resources in the federation has diminished over the last years, as Table 9.4 shows. However, tax responsibilities have not been modified substantially. Neither has one of its worst flaws varied: the low incentives for local authorities to collect taxes (Raich 2001). The evidence available for some municipalities shows that due to increased resources, income—the only important tax municipalities have—has actually decreased from 0.28 percent GDP in 1994 to 0.24 percent in 2002 (Primera Convención Nacional Hacendaria 2003).

Table 9.4

Tax Relationship Between State and Local Governments and the Federal Government, 1998–2004 (as percentage of GDP)

	Federal revenue[a]		Federalized expenditure[b]			
	Total	Tax collection	Total	Federal shares[c]	Federal transfers[d]	Others
1998	14.2	10.5	6.47	2.95	2.98	0.54
1999	14.7	11.4	7.04	3.06	3.31	0.67
2000	15.8	10.6	7.36	3.25	3.31	0.80
2001	16.1	11.2	7.98	3.41	3.63	0.94
2002	16.1	11.8	8.18	3.49	3.67	1.02
2003	17.2	11.6	8.06	3.44	3.56	1.06
2004[e]	17.1	12.0	7.86	3.38	3.54	0.94

Source: Presidencia de la República, (2001); SHCP, www.shcp.gob.mx; Reyes Tépach, (2003).
[a]Includes tax revenues and nontax revenues.
[b]Includes federal shares, contributions, and federal provisions to states and local governments as well as decentralized agreements.
[c]Federal shares refer to resources given to state and local governments to spend without restraint. Includes share general fund, complementary financial fund, emergency reserve, local development fund, urban commerce reordering fund, tenure, foreign commerce, economic incentives, joint taxation, tobacco, beer and alcohol, and new cars.
[d]Federal transfers account for categorized resources determined by the federal government.
[e]Data for 2004 are a projection taken from General Criteria of Economic Policy.

Changes After the Defeat of the PRI

Difficulties of tax collection, I have argued, are basically the result of the nature of Mexico's political system. With the defeat of the Partido Revolucionario Institucional (PRI) in the presidential elections of July 2, 2000, Mexico became unambiguously democratic. A new relationship between citizens and their government is developing. Political power is less concentrated and the media are more open and critical. Mexican citizens now demand more and better public services. A new law has made public expenditure more transparent, and citizens can demand specific information on how public resources are being used. For probably the first time in our history there is no important dispute with respect to the right of those in power to govern.

These conditions should make it easier to raise tax revenue to the level needed to finance the public goods a democratic society demands. Although the academic literature shows that democracies do not tax more than authoritarian systems (Przeworski et al. 2000), in the transition to a democracy an increase in tax capacity has been found to be statistically significant (Cheibub 1998). Spain is a clear example of a country in which a significant increase of the taxing capacity of the government came after it became democratic, although this acquired momentum with the government of Felipe González, which started seven years after the death of Francisco Franco. This increased taxation, plus the funds transferred by the European Community, helped the democratic government of Spain finance the public goods society demanded.

Tax revenue, and more importantly the tax structure, did not change significantly in the first three years of the government of Vicente Fox. The two most relevant changes were an improvement in the administration of the income tax law and some changes in the income tax law enacted in 2001, which allowed the government to better monitor income through the banking system by obliging all taxpayers to declare income derived from financial investments and making the banks responsible for providing that figure to the taxpayer and to the tax collector if so demanded. The result was an increase in tax revenues of nearly one percentage point of GDP (see Table 9.4). This took place in spite of very low economic growth. Data for the first months of 2004, where growth picked up, show this trend continued even further, reaching nearly 1.5 percent of GDP in extra tax revenue.

A more profound change that would allow Mexico's tax revenue to get closer to those of countries with similar level of development and become less dependent on oil revenue has not taken place, however. The government pursued a profound tax reform based on the principle of eliminating most exemptions and privileged treatments on two occasions, in the years 2001 and in 2003, without success. The main reform, a general VAT, or at least a special rate for medicines and food as was proposed in 2003, was twice rejected by Congress.

The Partido Acción Nacional, National Action Party (PAN), the president's party, has no majority in either of the chambers. It needs the support of the PRI, the former ruling party, or of the PRD (Partido de la Revolución Democrática, democratic revolution party), a left-wing party, which opposed from its origins after the contested 1988 election any VAT on food, medicine, and printed material, and has traditionally opposed economic reform. To make things more difficult for the government, in the midterm election of 2003 when the Chamber of Deputies was fully replaced, the PAN went from having 41.4 percent of the seats to 30.3, in some degree as a result of its efforts to raise taxes, which were widely publicized by the PRI during the campaign. The PRI is now closer to having a majority in this chamber, and in the Senate it has a majority with the help of the PVEM (Partido Verde Ecologista de México), the green party, originally a supporter of the coalition that made Fox's victory possible.

Both in 2001 and 2003 the government tried to strike a deal with the PRI. A significant proportion of the new resources would be allocated to the state governments, where the PRI still controls seventeen of thirty-one governorships. The PRI, when in power, had defended most of the reforms now proposed by a PAN administration. However, even though some segments of the PRI wanted to cooperate with the government, the reform efforts failed. In 2001, the election of a new

PRI leadership led to a polarization within the PRI, as no group wanted to face an internal election having supported the cornerstone of the proposed reform, which was a unified 15 percent VAT that would imply taxing food, drugs, and printed material. Instead the Congress opted for a tax reform based on special taxes that did not raise the revenue expected because the reforms were based on optimistic assumptions such as a surtax on luxury goods, and some of the changes were determined to be unconstitutional by the Supreme Court.

In 2003, the PRI leader of the chamber of deputies and even the president of the PRI, Roberto Madrazo, initially favored some kind of tax reform along the lines proposed by the government. However, those in the PRI opposed to any tax on medicine and foodstuffs prevailed, forcing the resignation of the PRI leader in the Chamber of Deputies and a change of position of Madrazo, who stopped backing the cornerstone of the reform, which was some kind of tax on food stuffs and medicines. PRI members now have to fight for candidacies in very competitive internal elections, and few wanted to pay the cost of having supported a tax reform. The PRI president did not have the strength or will to discipline his party.

Fiscal discipline has been maintained, in spite of demands of several actors for an increase in public spending. Some resources have been allocated in favor of local governments, but an overall deficit has been kept at bay. The cost of former deficits is still remembered by all political actors, and the independence of the Central Bank does not allow for a lax monetary policy. Higher oil prices have helped to accommodate some of these pressures.

All political parties agree that the fiscal resources are insufficient. Even businessmen applauded the specific strategy proposed by the government to raise more resources in 2001 and 2003. Yet polls show that the younger generation rejects cheating on taxes less than their elders (see Basáñez, chapter 2 in this volume). Far from moving into a society more concerned about funding public expenditure through taxation, a very large proportion of Mexicans are against more taxes. In this sense, opposition political parties have represented social preferences in opposing tax reform, at least from a short-term perspective.

Although the government of President Fox is perceived to have won in a legitimate way, public expenditure is considered inefficient and probably corrupt. It is believed by public opinion that the government has more than enough resources, and although there is clear demand for better services, there is no recognition that this demand requires more tax resources (see Figure 9.3 and Figure 9.4). The government, although enacting a transparency law, did not make significant and visible changes in the way resources are used, which could have modified the perception that the government is corrupt, inefficient, and does not need more resources.

In the three years since Fox's inauguration the tax structure has remained virtually unchanged. Although tax administration has improved, Mexico is still collecting few taxes and is greatly dependant on oil revenues that, fortunately for the country, have been higher than expected due to exceptionally high prices. However, some mandatory expenditure (such as for pensions) has increased, thus leav-

Figure 9.3   *Reforma* **Fiscal Reform Opinion Poll, 2003**

Do you think that trying to impose a tax on food and medicines is a good idea or a mistake from President Fox?

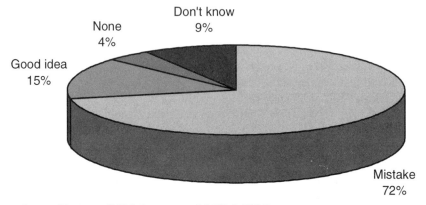

Source: "Daña credibilidad propuesta del IVA," (2003).

Figure 9.4   *Bimsa* **Fiscal Reform Opinion Poll, 2003**

The government requires resources in order to pay for the services it provides the population, such as education, health, security, pensions, and water. With what you know, do you think the government has more money than it actually requires, exactly the amount it requires, or less money than it actually requires?

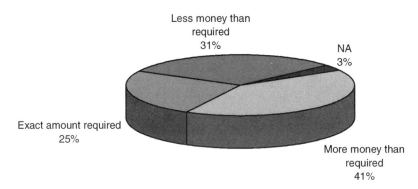

Source: "Imagen del Congreso," (2003).

ing few resources for expanding social transfers and investing in basic public goods such as infrastructure. Without well-targeted social transfers, it is impossible to move toward a more equal society in the short run. And without better and more widely available public goods, it is very difficult to compete in a global economy, the only way to increase the income of a population on a stable basis.

Appendix Table 9.5

Tax Expenditures, 2002

Concept	Millions of pesos	GDP (percent)
Income tax (IT)	167,631.00	2.7107
Corporate income tax	52,418.80	0.8434
Special treatments	11,631.40	-0.1881
Fiscal consolidation regime	-643.2	-0.0104
Taxpayers that work in agriculture	11,835.60	0.1914
50 percent reduction of income tax (IT)	9,856.80	0.1594
20 minimum wages per year (SMA) exemption for each member or partner	1,978.80	0.032
Book editors: 40 percent reduction on IT	439	0.0071
Authorized deductions	30,446.40	0.4924
Authorized purchases	13,492.80	0.2182
Retirement funds	4,687.20	0.0758
50 percent restaurant consumption	7,197.80	0.1164
Cars below $200,000	2,362.50	0.0382
IMSS worker's fee paid by employers	1,104.50	0.0179
Nonprofit donations to authorized agencies	1,604.60	0.0259
Loans over salary credit	10,071.00	0.1629
Income tax on persons	115,482.20	1.8673
Special treatments	1,663.40	0.0269
20 SMA exemption	1,181.10	0.0191
1 percent rate on prizes	482.3	0.0078
IT on salaries	67,910.00	1.0982
Raise of fiscal subsidy when excluding fees from social security (IMSS), housing program (Infonavit), and special retirement fund (SAR)	15,000.00	0.2426
Fiscal subsidy (a tax credit given for any person employed)	52,910.00	0.8556
Salary exemptions	38,946.00	0.6296
Extra hours	3,657.00	0.0591
Sunday extra bonus	473	0.0076
Savings funds	12,010.00	0.1942
Worker's social security paid by employers	972	0.0157
Seniority, severance payment and retirement bonus	1,294.00	0.0209
Annual gratification (2 weeks pay at end of year)	4,078.00	0.0659
Vacation bonus	1,292.00	0.0209
Worker's shares of business profits	869	0.0141
Social prevention and services such as daycare allowances.	13,680.00	0.2212
Income derived from retirement allowances and pensions	464	0.0075
Reimbursements of medical, dental, hospital, and funeral expenses that can be deducted from income tax	157	0.0025
Authorized personal deductions	6,962.80	0.01126
Value added tax (VAT)	104,875.80	1.696
Zero rate	82,799.80	1.339
Food	70,061.30	1.133

(continued)

Appendix Table 9.5 *(continued)*

Concept	Millions of pesos	GDP (percent)
Medicines	6,183.70	0.1
Books, newspapers, and magazines	5,318.00	0.086
Other products	1,236.00	0.02
Exemptions	14,408.00	0.233
Medical services	1,360.40	0.0202
Teaching services	6,369.00	0.103
Terrestrial public transport services	5,503.50	0.089
Water for household use provided services	742	0.012
Others	432	0.007
10 percent rate for border region	7,667.80	0.124
Special taxes	54,989.30	0.8892
Production and services special tax (IEPS)	54,752.80	0.8854
Hand made tobacco. Lower rate than other tobaccos	889.8	0.0144
Telephone exemption (all modalities)	11,254.30	0.182
IEPS exemption on sodas as they no longer pay any special tax paid by alcoholic beverages	12,170.40	0.1968
60 to 50 percent IEPS reduction on alcoholic drinks	902.8	0.0146
No tax on petroleum liquid gas primarily used by households		
All other fuels derived from oil are taxed	29,535.50	0.4776
New vehicles' tax	236.5	0.00382
Exemption on popular vehicles defined on a prize basis	235	0.0038
Exemption on diplomatic franchised import vehicles	1.5	0.00002
Fiscal stimulus	1,949.60	0.0315
Maritime and air transportation	113.8	0.00184
Air transportation	92.8	0.0015
Sea transportation	21	0.00034
Deposit warehouse	8	0.00013
IEPS warranty on special sea diesel (merchant marine)	817.8	0.00034
Stimulus for buying agave	477.5	0.0077
Technology investigation and development	500	0.0081
Total	329,445.70	5.3274

Source: Secretaría de Hacienda y Crédito Público.
Note: Some of the fiscal expenditures described in this table can pursue valuable social objectives, such as increasing the income of workers or stimulating the production of books. What this annex portrays is the loss of tax income derived from so many special tax treatments.

Notes

A more detailed version of the first part of this text is found in Elizondo (2001b).
1. Data were calculated by the Tributary Administration Service (SAT) and quoted in Díaz 2004.
2. The northern border, relatively richer than the rest of the country, pays lower VAT. For this same reason it is not easy to increase such an efficient tax as the tax on gasoline, as gasoline taxes in the United States are the lowest in any developed country.
3. Therefore the effective tax burden of those citizens that pay for most of their goods and services is much higher than in societies where they are provided by the government.

References

Bergman, Marcelo. 2002. "La capacidad de recaudar impuestos del gobierno Mexicano: ¿El tema previo a la reforma fiscal." México, D.F.: CIDE (Centro de Investigación y Docencia Económicas), Programa de Presupuesto Público.

Cheibub, José Antonio. 1998. "Political Regimes and the Extractive Capacity of Governments: Taxation in Democracies and Dictatorships." *World Politics,* April.

Díaz, Alicia. 2004. "Calcula el SAT evasión del IVA." *Reforma,* February 20.

"Daña credibilidad propuesta del IVA." 2003. *Reforma,* December 1. Available at www.reforma.com/encuestas.

Elizondo, Carlos. 1994. "In Search of Revenue: Tax Reform in Mexico Under the Administration of Echeverría and Salinas." *Journal of Latin American Studies* 26, no. 1.

———. 2001a. *La importancia de las reglas. Gobierno y empresario después de la nacionalización bancaria.* México, D.F.: Fondo de Cultura Económica.

———. 2001b. *Impuestos, democracia y transparencia,* Mexico, Cámara de Diputados.

Feliz, Raúl. 2003. "Entorno macroeconómico México 2003." México, D.F.: CIDE.

Financial Times. 2001. Database.

Hernández, Fausto, John Scott, and Andrés Zamudio 2001. "La reforma hacendaria integral: Algunos retos." *Este País,* no. 119, February.

"Imagen del Congreso. Agenda legislativa: Reforma eléctrica y fiscal." 2003. *Bimsa,* September. Available at www.bimsa.com.mx.

INEGI (Instituto Nacional de Estadística). 1992. *Anuario estadístico de los Estados Unidos Mexicanos.* México, D.F.: INEGI.

———. n.d. *Banco de información económica.* Web page INEGI. Available at www .inegi.gob.mx/inegi/

———. 2002. *Cuaderno de Estadísticas Judiciales,* num. 10. México, D.F.: INEGI.

Levy, Margaret. 1988. *Of Rule and Revenue.* Los Angeles: University of California Press.

OECD (Organization for Economic Cooperation and Development). 1998. *Harmful Tax Competition. An Emerging Global Issue.* Paris: OECD.

———. 2002. *Revenue Statistics 1965–2001.* Paris: OECD.

Orrantía Arellano, Fernando A. 1998. *Las facultades del Congreso Federal en materia fiscal,* México, D.F.: Porrua.

Ortiz, Guillermo. 2003. "Un comparativo internacional de la recaudación tributaria." México, D.F.: Banco de México, May.

Presidencia de la República. 2003. "Anexo estadístico." *Tercer Informe de Gobierno.* México, D.F.: Presidencia de la República.

Primera Convención Nacional Hacendaria. 2003. "Trabajos preparatorios," Mexico, Coordinación Técnica (SCHP, CFF, INDETEC), February–July.

Przeworski, Adam. 1998. "El estado y el ciudadano." *Política y Gobierno* 5, no. 1 (Spring), CIDE.

Przeworski, Adam, Michael E. Alvarez, José Antonio Cheibob, and Fernando Limougí. 2000. *Democracy and Development. Political Institutions and Well-Being in the World, 1950–1990.* Cambridge Studies in the Theory of Democracy. Cambridge, UK: Cambridge University Press.

Raich, Uri. 2001. "Impacts of Expenditure Decentralization on Mexican Local Governments." División de Administración Pública, *Documento de Trabajo #102.* México, D.F.: CIDE.

Reynolds, Clark. 1970. *The Mexican Economy: Twentieth Century Structure and Growth.* New Haven, CT: Yale University Press.

Scott. John. 2002. "High Inequality, Low Revenue: Redistributive Efficiency of Latin American Fiscal Policy in Comparative Perspective," CIDE Working Paper DE-236.

————. 2005. "Desigualdad de oportunidades y políticas públicas en México." In *México en la perspectiva de la modernización,* ed. Héctor Aguilar Camín and Enrique Flores Cano. México, D.F.: Fondo de Cultura Económica.

Secretaría de Hacienda y Crédito Público (SHCP). *Sistema de Finanzas públicas y deuda pública.* Available at www.shcp.gob.mx.

Tépach, Reyes. 2003. "El gasto federalizado y las aportaciones para los estados y municipios en México 1988–2004." Cámara de Diputados, Servicios de Investigación y Análisis, November.

UNPAN (United Nations Online Network in Public Administration and Finance). n.d. *Statistical Database.* Available at www.unpan.org/statistical_database-publicsector.asp.

10

Eugenia Correa

Changing Constraints of Monetary Policy

Distortions and Resolutions in Mexico's Financial System

Money is a veil that often hides what is taking place in an economy. The changing purchasing power of local currency either for domestic goods or for foreign exchange leads many policymakers to mistakenly believe that controlling inflation and the exchange rate are policies that are sufficient to attain economic objectives. Mexico's ability to produce goods efficiently and its ability to attract (or lose) foreign exchange based on its long-term growth prospects limit the impact of monetary policy—in isolation from other economic policies and world economic conditions—to have a consistently predictable and significant impact on Mexico's economic achievements.

Eugenia Correa traces in detail the steps that were intended to limit inflation, grant autonomy of the central bank—which was no longer required to finance the government deficit—deregulate the stock market, and expand foreign ownership of banks. The mid-1990s economic crisis led many banks into technical bankruptcy. The bailout of these banks through increased lending by the central bank and the assumption of the bad loans of commercial banks by the institutions designed to maintain bank solvency and protect depositors, FOBAPROA (Fondo Bancario de Protección al Ahorro or Bank Savings Protection Fund) and its successor IPAB (Institute for the Protection of Bank Savings, or Instituto de Protección al Ahorro Bancario), cost well over $100 billion, to be paid over several years. Congress has not yet passed legislation to improve bank-lending practices or to increase the cost to debtors of default.

The private banking sector is profitable. The rest of the economy has not grown adequately. Monetary policy has succeeded in stabilizing prices, through high foreign-reserve accumulation and the flexible exchange rate, which is supported by high interest rates on government securities held by foreign banks and other investors. But this policy has brought about a contraction of domestic investment and led to government over-indebtedness in domestic currency, which, in turn, has translated into a serious shortage of public revenues and rising financial commitments to pay internal and foreign debts.

In a global and open economy, monetary policy is highly dependent on foreign currency inflows and outflows, especially in emerging economies with a low level of foreign trade surplus that can be used to provide (1) a stable value of currency, indicated by a low inflation rate, and (2) a stable price in foreign exchange of domestic currency, indicated by a stable exchange rate. Years ago, in a so called "closed economy" monetary policy could impact the changes in price level and even in economic growth, providing sufficient credit to commercial banks to facilitate their making enough loans to create economic growth without inflation. Nowadays, in a global economy, enabling commercial banks to make loans for economic growth does not ensure that they will do so because growing money and credit in the market could mean capital outflows, falling international reserves, and the consequent currency devaluation and local inflation. Monetary policy may prevent banks from making loans, and consequently reduce growth and even contract the economy. For these reasons, government spending and policies other than monetary policy are considered crucial for economic growth.

Monetary policy therefore may focus on either preventing inflation or maintaining a stable exchange rate or both. A stable exchange rate reflects the supply of and the demand for Mexican currency, and is the product of inflows and outflows of currency as a result of trade, investment, and borrowing. It cannot be controlled by monetary policy alone.

The rate of inflation is measured by the ratio of domestic currency to gross domestic product (GDP). Inflation at first glance would seem likely to be controlled by monetary authorities, and control of inflation the preferred goal of monetary policy. However, Mexicans often are able to limit the amount of pesos that they hold by purchasing dollars, and thus some argue that this forces the government to finance its various activities either by borrowing or by creating even more pesos. Some approaches blame the government deficit for inflation and the instability of the exchange rate, because the central bank could create money in order to finance this deficit. This is not appropriate in Mexico, because in the late 1980s the public sector's balance sheet before financial costs showed a surplus rather than a deficit, and starting in 1987 the central bank stopped lending to the federal government. Since 1992 the government has achieved a primary budget surpluses (before financial costs) of above 2.5 percent of GDP.[1]

The constraint on Mexican monetary policy therefore is not lending to the central government to finance the budget deficit; in fact, the government made deposits in the central bank.[2] Instead, the Mexican government's ability to use monetary policy to limit the rate of inflation is constrained by the ability of Mexican and foreign savers and investors to switch from pesos to dollars and other foreign currencies. The more pesos are offered to purchase dollars, the lower the price of the peso and the more the cost in pesos of imports, which can give rise to inflation. Switching between currencies depends, among other things, on the foreign exchange rate—the number of pesos offered per dollar—which reflects the demand for and supply of foreign exchange. In order to counteract adverse changes in Mexico's economy that could arise from the switching of currencies, the Mexican government has intervened in the market for foreign exchange. The form of government intervention in the market for foreign exchange shifted over time: it maintained a fixed rate from 1954 through 1976, and it set an adjustable rate of foreign exchange from 1976 to 1982. The government tried to take into account the demand and supply of foreign exchange when it set the form and amount of intervention (Mantey 2002; Martínez, Sánchez, and Werner 2001).

The demand for foreign exchange arose (1) from the search by major Mexican savers (wealthy households and corporations) who switched from pesos to dollars when they expected an abrupt devaluation of the peso and wanted safety for and high returns on their deposits in the banking system; (2) from foreign investors (either corporations or investors in financial securities) who bought dollars in order to take out their financial yield or investment profits; and (3) local debtors (federal government, public and private corporations, and banks) who bought dollars for their payments of interest and amortization of their debt.

The supply of foreign exchange came from (1) the surplus on foreign trade (when there was any); (2) foreign direct investment (FDI) and investment in financial securities; (3) receipts from the sale of public and private bonds; and (4) remittances from Mexicans who work abroad. As a result of the link between foreign exchange and monetary policy, the periodization of monetary policy reflects the government's exchange rate policy, which has been an indicator of the result of both the factors shown above and the institutional changes in monetary and financial markets during the last thirty years. The six stages in domestic and foreign macroeconomic conditions and policies are shown in Table 10.1 and Table 10.2 (see page 164) , respectively. The reader is asked to refer to them while reading the analysis of monetary policy.

This overview indicates the context in which we place Mexico's monetary policy and its principal effects on the financial system. The first section of this chapter examines deregulation and foreign-debt flows in the 1970s as well as the 1982 crisis. The second section analyzes the financial reform that led to the banking crisis two years later during the negotiations on Chapter 14 of the North American Free Trade Agreement (NAFTA), which deals with financial services and the then-imminent opening of domestic market. The third section analyzes monetary and financial policy within the framework of the banking crisis and the costs for public finances of the bailout through FOBAPROA. Finally, this chapter will review monetary policy within the context of the new market position of foreign banks' affiliates and the consequences for government and private firms' access to credit in a banking system in which a main debtor again is the government—as it was in the sixties and seventies—in spite of all of the market policies that have been implemented.

Table 10.1

Mexico: Main Indicators. Inflows and Outflows by Presidential Period, 1977–2003 (annual average)

	1977–1982	1983–1988	1989–1994	1995–2000	2001–2003
Percentage					
1. Economic growth (per capita)	3.74	−1.23	1.86	1.59[a]	0.63
2. Inflation rate	29.2	62.7	14.7	19.8	4.6
3. Real interest rate	−4.5[b]	−23.9	7.27	5.69	3.41
4. Peso devaluation	27.9	68.2	14.9	9.04	5.13
Billion dollars					
5. Debt inflows	7.4	0.68	3.8	−0.6	−1.57
6. Portfolio inflows	0.57	−0.35	12.01	3.5	2.4
7. FDI inflows	1.6	2.3	5.05	12.2	17.2
8. Family transfers	na	na	na	4.99	10.4
9. Trade balance	−1.1	8.7	−9.2	−1.2	−7.9
10. Interest for private and public debt	6.01	9.5	10.01	13.08	12.16
11. FDI revenues	0.4	0.4	1.2	1.74	1.46

Sources: For 1977–1982, lines 1 and 8, Nacional Financiera (1988); Banco de México (n.d.), www.banxico.org.mx.
[a] 1994–2000
[b] 1978–1982

Deregulation and Capital Flows

Economic and financial liberalization, with their different paces and intensities, are worldwide phenomena resulting from the breakdown of the Bretton Woods monetary and financial order. Financial deregulation and innovation present since the 1970s expanded international banking credit amid a strong inflationary process in the developed countries. This growing international credit implied quick enlargement of commercial banks' overseas operations and those of other financial intermediaries such as insurance companies, investment banks, or institutional investors. Gradual financial deregulation limited the central bank's capacity to carry out monetary policy (Wray 1998; Mantey 2000). These phenomena have partially determined global economic performance, particularly that of developing nations. In Mexico, as in other Latin American countries, the processes of deregulation and financial opening have taken place amid doubts and vicissitudes, more or less acknowledged conflicts, alternating demands for a smaller role of government and urgent calls for intervention, and, lastly, successive financial crises.

Mexico's monetary and financial market changed within these international transformations, going from a fixed exchange rate to different forms of adjustable rate, from a stable to a growing inflation rate, from a fixed low and stable to a high real interest rate, from specialized to universal banks, and from a mixed (public and private) to a large private banking system.

During the years of growth with price stability (the 1950s, 1960s until the first years of the 1970s) the state's provision of resources for production was fundamental, through direct public investment in infrastructure, and, particularly, through the channeling of resources by the public development banks, for example, by NAFIN (Nacional Financiera), BANOBRAS (Banco Nacional de Obras Públicas), and BANCOMEXT (Banco Nacional de Comercio Exterior), and so forth (Correa 2001).

Monetary policy was directly linked to financing the government budget. The Central Bank provided funding of the state-owned development banks. Commercial banks were required to maintain obligatory deposits in the central bank (these functioned as reserve requirements) that earned yields above the interest rate paid by the commercial banks to their own customers. The commercial banks were then able to increase their operations by (1) creating nonrisk deposits in the central bank because the central bank paid the yields of the obligatory deposits; and (2) by generating yields with very small costs. The obligatory deposits in the central bank system allowed an expansion of the banking system in the Mexican economy that otherwise would have been limited because Mexico's highly unequal distribution of income. Finally, the obligatory deposit requirement was removed in 1988, so the commercial banks lost an important source of profits.

Public foreign debt was a source of foreign currency relatively stable with low cost, since it was sold principally to international agencies such as the World Bank. When the terms for repaying loans shortened (since 1973) and external interest rates rose (1978), the government suddenly found itself unable to continue to participate in productive investment because it had to obtain foreign currency to pay interest on public and private foreign-denominated liabilities. As a consequence, whereas in the 1950s and 1960s trade deficits were financed with foreign debt at stable interest rates, in the 1970s rising interest payments and shortening loan maturities created a vicious circle in which high current-account deficits increased the foreign debt (Girón 1991).

In 1979 the country's foreign debt had to be completely refinanced; hence, new loans were completely eaten up by debt servicing. The Central Bank authorized dollar deposits in the local market—with a high-required reserve on deposit—to prevent an outflow of capital and to continue the fixed-exchange-rate policy. The huge growth of dollar deposits quickly led to a dollarization of all bank operations, reflecting the firms' and households' growing savings in dollars. Thus, the fixed-exchange-rate regime broke in February 1982 and precipitated, in addition to a moratorium on foreign public debt, a shortfall of foreign exchange among commercial private banks that created a currency mismatch in banks' balance sheets, because they had dollar deposits and peso loans. The government guaranteed the payment of dollar deposits at a 50 : 1 (peso–dollar) fixed exchange rate in September, although it had been 25 : 1 in February and fell to 100 : 1 in December. After the López Portillo government nationalized the private commercial banks on Sep-

Table 10.2

Stages in Macrofinance Monetary Policy Constraints, 1979–2003

Years/president	Economic performance	Capital inflows/outflows	Foreign debt	Monetary policy	Exchange rate	Inflation rates	Ending shock
I. 1979 to 1982 López Portillo (last four years)	High economic growth	Huge inflows because of oil exports and high oil prices	Growing public and private foreign debt	Expansive monetary policy Foreign currency demand was made in local dollar denomination deposits because of Central Bank reform	Fixed real overvaluation	Increasing	Inflows stopped because the downturn in oil prices (1981) and smaller credit supply by U.S. banks with the increasing Federal Reserve interest rate since 1979
II. 1982 to 1988 de la Madrid	Strong economic downturn	Capital control and huge outflows	High outflows by debt service (interest and principal)	Restrictive monetary policy and bank credit	Ajustable real and nominal huge devaluation	Increasing 1987–88 hyper inflationary crisis	Foreign debt restructuring Stabilization program with foreign exchange rate anchor
III. 1989 to 1994 Salinas de Gortari	Poor economic growth	Huge inflows in portfolio investments	Growing private foreign debt	Expansive monetary policy and credit bank bubble, with growing dollar liabilities	Ajustable real and nominal overvaluation	Decreasing	Financial and banking crisis. FED federal funds rate increased (February 1994)

IV. 1995 to 1996 Zedillo	Strong economic downturn	Huge outflows	High outflows by debt service (interest and principal)	Restrictive monetary policy and shrinking bank credit	Adjustable real and nominal huge devaluation	Quick increase and decrease	Began new wave privatization and foreign capital acquisitions
V. 1997 to 2000 Zedillo	Economic growth in ascent	Growing FDI inflows	High outflows because of debt service (interest and principal)	Restrictive monetary policy and shrinking bank credit	Adjustable Nominal devaluation	Decreasing	U.S. stock bubble deflation and financial turbulence
VI. 2001 to 2003 Fox	Weak economic growth	Descending FDI inflows	Small descent in interest payments	Restrictive monetary policy and shrinking bank credit	Adjustable real overvaluation	Decreasing	Public expediture contraction. Growing peso-denominated public debt

tember 1, 1982, the new de la Madrid government negotiated compensatory payments to them in 1983. The commercial banks were publicly owned from September 1982 up to 1990–1991 when they were again sold to private investors. The 1982 crisis was triggered by the scarcity of resources in external financial markets that was a result of the U.S. Federal Reserve's hiking of interest rates. Mexico's foreign public debt had skyrocketed from US$26 billion in 1978 to US$59 billion in 1982. The Mexican economy was highly dollarized and indebted.

The restructuring of foreign debt and the partial "pesification" (a return to the use of pesos instead of dollars) of the domestic economy took nearly eight years (from 1982 to 1989). In the context of the managed floating of the exchange rate, and net outflows of US$69 billion, the growing inflation rate became hyperinflation between 1987 and 1988, ending up at higher than 150 percent. Monetary policy was characterized by increasingly tight restrictions on financing of the federal government budget by the central bank. Instead, the government obtained funds by issuing peso-denominated securities (see chapter 11 by Graciana del Castillo in this book).

At the beginning of the 1990s private and public companies and the government, on the debtors' side, and investment funds and banks, on the creditors' side, as well as rating agencies (like Standard & Poor's and Moody's), changed the direction of net flows in international markets. In order to improve their balance-sheet positions in the 1980s, creditors transformed their loans into bonds. The bonds were sold to investment funds, such as mutual and hedge funds, which served as underwriters of the loans. In this way the foreign creditor banks enlarged their available resources, because they did not have to keep reserves against bonds; in contrast, they would have had to keep reserves against loans.

The deregulation of the U.S. securities market and the privatization process in Mexico in the 1990s led both to the unprecedented boom in foreign financial placements in the Mexican market and to the purchase of securities by Mexican issuers in foreign markets (Vidal 1999). When the rating agencies improved the "country assessment" of Mexico, it became possible for institutional investors to increase their demand for Mexican securities in order to improve their returns on investment and to adjust the composition of their investment in foreign securities to the rules that each country has; these rules can be changed by their financial regulation authorities (Correa 2004).

Foreign portfolio investment grew spectacularly for nearly five years from 1990 to 1994, climaxing in 1993 when the net inflow rose to US$17 billion. Despite this dynamic growth, foreign portfolio investment was highly volatile and generated a process of overvaluing the peso that made it inexpensive to import and therefore turned the trade surplus into a trade deficit from 1990, which rose to US$18 billion by 1994. Table 10.1 shows the main economic trends and capital inflows and outflows during five six-year presidential periods, from 1977 to 2003. The capital inflows from 1990 to 1994 ended with a financial crisis and outflows of foreign exchange linked to public or private debt and its servicing, as well as to withdrawals of funds by institutional investors in public bonds or in private stocks. The capital inflows and outflows and their performance again were present in determining the Mexican exchange and inflation rates and monetary policy.

Financial Reform and NAFTA

During the years 1989 to 1994 Mexico had the most significant financial reform of its history. It took place as part of the policy package of the last renegotiation of the foreign public debt. These measures were essential for achieving full private control of lending and for initiating NAFTA negotiations; they were undertaken in order to attract foreign direct investment that was viewed as an essential component of economic growth (Correa 1995).

This financial reform began with the elimination of the mechanisms of direct control over interest rates in 1989 as well as of the selective-credit and obligatory-deposit requirements; this was followed by the Mexican bank reprivatization that was carried out over a period of eighteen months from 1990 to 1991. It was accompanied by a new monetary and financial policy that was based on: (1) an elimination of net credit from the central bank to the federal government and to the commercial banks; (2) an anti-inflationary policy with an "exchange-rate anchor," (meaning a stable predictable exchange rate that is used to control inflation) (Carstens and Reynoso 1997); (3) an attractive interest rate on domestic bonds for a broad promotion of portfolio investment; and (4) a deregulation of the stock market that allowed a new equities issue by large private firms and public firms in a process of stock market privatization. Finally, this financial reform process was accompanied by granting the central bank autonomy (which means that by law the central bank is not obligated to finance the government deficit) in 1993 (Mantey 2002) and by the NAFTA negotiation and its implementation in January of 1994 (Correa 1994).

The fundamental policies that impacted the banking sector were initiated as a result of the hyperinflationary crisis of 1987–1988. First, obligatory deposits in the central bank were quickly raised, finally reaching 100 percent of all inflows in 1988. Then, in a period of few months, starting in 1989 to 1991, obligatory deposits in Central Bank plummeted from 100 percent to zero; from then on, increased lending did not translate into risk-free returns. Lending grew quickly as a result of the growing volume of capital inflows, privatizations, and the refinancing of liabilities with high real-interest rates and higher bank margins. The lending boom (1990–1994) became unmanageable when debt-carrying capacity was limited by high concentration of ownership in some economic sectors as well as concentration of income, in addition to sluggish economic growth. The high ownership and income concentration put a very short limit to the banks' market expansion, because they have too few customers to secure a healthy financial position in order to fulfill their financial commitments. The elimination of obligatory deposits alone quickly created the conditions for a banking crisis, as had occurred in Chile in the early 1980s.

Second, in just the eighteen months from June 1991 to October 1992 the headlong bank privatization transferred banks' balance sheets to various business groups with varying interests and rates of growth, prompting a rapid change in the composition of borrowers that was not necessarily compatible with the volume and growth rate of assets of the newly privatized banks. The process by which each one of the different banks repositioned itself in the financial market increased inter-bank transactions and, therefore, funding costs and bank margins. All this contributed to higher lending rates that could cause bank failures when the market came under pressure as a result of the entry of new banks, because new loans went to more risky borrowers. In addition, the high margins due to "self-loans" and loans to insiders and bank shareholders also had an impact.

Third, an anti-inflationary policy with an exchange-rate anchor led to very high interest rates on government securities, because the market sets these rates so as to ensure that domestic investors continue to invest in pesos and to attract foreign investors. Higher capital inflows were necessary to finance the current-account-balance deficit because of the peso overvaluation, which was sustained by offering attractive interest rates to foreign capital. These high domestic interest rates in real terms (see Table 10.2) made funding in Mexican currency expensive, which, in turn, encouraged a rapid growth of bank liabilities denominated in foreign currency. Then banks accumulated liabilities in dollars and assets in pesos. The currency disequilibrium in the banks balance sheets was also a component of higher margins, because although the margin (difference between deposit and loans rates) should have included exchange rate, subsequently, with the 1994 peso devaluation, this currency disequilibrium or mismatching led to bank failure.

Fourth, when Mexico agreed to open its domestic financial sector in the framework of Chapter 14 of NAFTA in June–September 1992, each of the recently privatized domestic banking groups came up with its own strategy for competing under the most favorable conditions possible, for maintaining market position, or for devising the most advantageous terms for entering into partnerships with foreign banks. Mexico's banks coordinated the terms of the financial opening under NAFTA and devised a strategy for allowing foreign banks to enter into partnerships with them and acquire up to 30 percent of their capital stock, according to the terms of the Law to Regulate the Financial Institutions of July 1990. Relative profits and share prices were very important for the success of partnerships and of new share issues. Increasing lending rates, streamlining by closing branches and layoffs, charging for services, and borrowing abroad because it was cheaper than borrowing at home were the mechanisms for increasing reported profits. Mexican banks were among the most profitable in the world by the end of 1993. Their positioning and partnership strategy for facing new competition under NAFTA also generated, in itself, high lending interest rates and margins that indicated increasing risks because households and firms' customers as well as the banks could declare bankruptcy.

Any one of the four fundamental elements of the financial reform could, in isolation, have created the scenario for a banking crisis. Together, during the course of a few years, they led to financial collapse in December 1994. The anti-inflationary monetary policy based on the exchange-rate anchor applied during those years was transformed into a peso overvaluation (too few pesos are paid per dollar); the costs of this anti-inflationary policy were transferred both to public accounts by increasing the real interest rate on public bonds (peso-denominated) and to the Mexican companies through the hike in real domestic lending interest rates in pesos that were far above the prevailing rate in the markets of Mexico's principal trading partners.

Banking Crisis and Monetary Policy

High borrowing rates plus high bank margins turned the lending boom into debt rollovers in 1993–1994 (see Table 10.1), because the borrowers needed growing amounts of credit merely for repayment of debt in pesos. More risky credit for overindebted customers meant raising margins and increasing the numbers of customers (firms or households) that were no longer able to pay the interest and principal. The loans, in banking language, were "nonperforming." This occurred at least in part because of the sharp increase in the interest rate on federal funds by the U.S. Federal Reserve in February 1994. It rose from 3 percent to 6 percent from February 1994 to February 1995, and once again created an environment of financial crisis in Mexico.

In 1994 foreign portfolio investors exchanged their Mexican positions in Cetes (peso-denominated government bonds) for Tesobonos (dollar-denominated bonds that served as a hedge against fluctuations in the exchange rate). By its issuing of Tesobonos, the Finance Ministry attempted to guarantee yields and preclude an abrupt exit from the domestic market. As in 1982, borrowers found it difficult to refinance their debts, and the strong dollarization of financing and of local savings further aggravated the crisis.

Foreign holders of Tesobonos doubted that the Mexican government could meet its obligations for repayment of Tesobonos in dollars, and they sold their Tesobonos. In order to contain this crisis, the U.S. financial authorities provided extraordinary funds to the Mexican government, because this sell-off was aggravated by short- and long-term foreign debt payment commitments both by Mexican companies and banks as well as by the public sector itself. Mexican firms and government used those extraordinary funds to pay their foreign creditors.

The banking crisis was characterized by the amount tied up in nonperforming loans (loans that did not make either interest or amortization payments, and whose terms could not be changed by the lenders)[3] being larger than banks' own capital; it broke out in tandem with the 1994–1995 financial crisis (abrupt outflows of capital, a peso devaluation, and a 7.5 percent current-account deficit of GDP). The peso devaluation in December of 1994 increased the peso value of local banks' foreign-denominated liabilities, leading to a shortfall of some US$30 billion of foreign exchange, and raised the value of nonperforming loans to US$6.6 billion, equal to 8.4 percent of the total Mexican bank loan portfolio.

The Central Bank had begun to increase lending to commercial banks months before the outbreak of the crisis, because (1) even before December the banks were going into undeclared technical bankruptcy, which could be viewed either as a short-term aspect of a business cycle, when the value of bank assets declines but the value of their liabilities does not, or as an indication of long-term insolvency if the interest rate does not fall quickly and in a sustained way; (2) the commercial banks were borrowing only to refinance the interest payments of the customers; and (3) some firms foreseeing the peso devaluation changed some of their liabilities in foreign currency to liabilities in pesos. This lending rose to levels as high as 50 percent of inter-bank deposits, while lending to the federal government and the private sector continued to contract. For a few months real interest rates rose to rates as high as 40 percent, and the economy shrank by 6.9 percent in 1995, bringing with it a 9 percent decrease in real per capita income.

All the conditions that had led the economy to overindebtedness resulting from an increase in funding costs far above the rate of economic growth once again emerged. The disparity between real interest rates and real rates of economic growth in Mexico became evident, just as had occurred in the 1980s, and the public and private sectors found themselves overindebted: they had to reduce other expenditures in order to finance their payment of interest and amortization of the debt (Correa 2001; Vidal 2002).

In 1995, the return to solvency by borrowers—whether they were large, medium, or small companies—along with the banks' survival would have required the government to reduce the spread between borrowing and lending interest rates, and reduce the level of floor rates on Cetes, as well as to increase government expenditures to create economic growth permitting repayment of loans. The monetary and fiscal policy that was carried out was, however, precisely the opposite. Financial stabilization policies that the new Mexican government followed depended on continuing to offer attractive yields to foreign capital in the financial market and on finding a market-based solution to the banking crisis in order to avoid a loss of confidence in Mexico by foreign investors.

Policy was determined by the negotiation of emergency funding to avoid a moratorium on the foreign debt, and an attempt was made to reduce the risk of a systemic collapse and prevent the bankruptcy of the largest banks like Banamex and Bancomer. To stem the outflow of capital and the deterioration of loan portfolios, rather than following the 1982 policies of implementing foreign-exchange controls and taking over the largest banks, the government chose to (1) raise interest rates; (2) selectively take over smaller banks; (3) exchange bad loans for government no-risk and high-yield bonds; and (4) make contributions to increase the banks' capital. However, this bank bailout has been one of the most expensive of the emerging markets crises during the nineties: the estimated cost was 21 percent of Mexican gross domestic product (GDP) in 1999; this cost will be paid over many years by taxpayers and by shrinking public social expenditure, programs against poverty, and so forth.

This policy hampered the ability of local medium and small borrowers to repay their loans, and led a large number of bank customers to default on their loans. Their credit records would remain negative for many years. The no-refunds bank loans (unpaid principal and interest) and bank's capitalization requirements (to maintain a capital-liability ratio) were exchanged between the banks and FOBAPROA, the bank savings protection fund created in 1990 in order to refund a bank that had problems but with insufficient funds to resolve a systemic crisis, for high-yield no-risk bonds. FOBAPROA was replaced by IPAB, funded in 1998. (See chapter 11 by Graciana del Castillo in this volume) and their liabilities were almost totally transferred to bonds issued by IPAB with federal government guaranty.

Ten years after the outbreak of the banking and financial crisis, the most acute level of overindebtedness had been overcome, but the federal budget every year since 1998 has included 4 or 5 billion dollars for interest payments of those bonds, a sum that could reach 6 billion dollars as a result of an agreement reached in July 2004 (described below), which increases the public debt held by the banks and the burden of their service on government expenditure.

In 2003, 12.4 percent of net public expenditures (included federal, state, and county government and public enterprises and other governmental institutions) were used to meet interest payments on the federal government's debt (central government), which represented 3.5 percent of GDP, including 1 percent of GDP to pay the interest of IPAB bonds.

The banks had been selling their past-due loans at 16 cents on the dollar, and 75 percent of these loans had been converted to IPAB obligations. In 2005 and 2006 some FOBAPROA notes that had not been exchanged for IPAB bonds, because of the probable links of these notes to questionable bank operations, would have matured. Some sectors, including political parties and congressmen, for several years had believed that some FOBAPROA notes were the result of fraud and illegal loans that should not be transferred to taxpayers by exchanging them for IPAB bonds. In July 2004, a new agreement was signed between the banks that held these notes in their assets and IPAB in order to resolve this controversy and to establish a mechanism for settlement, either by payment or refinancing. (Foreign banks that held them were Banamex-Citigroup, BBVA-Bancomer, and HSBC; the Mexican bank that held them was Banorte.) This agreement reduces the cost of the IPAB (FOBAPROA) notes by just over half and implies that both parties desist from the judicial procedures that had begun and whose resolution eventually would have forced the banks to undergo audits and assume the losses that would be incurred if illegal or fraudulent operations were found to be the basis of these FOBAPROA notes; alternatively, the IPAB would have been forced to accept and redeem these obligations.

The July 2004 agreement requires the banks to (1) accept a final review of the portfolio in question; (2) recognize losses under the concept of insider loans estimated at US$826 million (9.48 billion pesos) as a result of sales to the portfolio purchase and capitalization program; this recognition takes place despite the fact that these loans were not included in the agreement signed with FOBAPROA; and (3) accept the final review results from which new liabilities can be derived. The agreement requires the IPAB to recognize and accept US$13.9 billion of obligations that could be decreased to $9.3 billion. It should be noted that the term *review* is used rather than the term *audit* because the documents needed for a full audit are missing.

The government initially bailed out the banks at a cost of about US$100 billion. The exact cost of the new bailout is not yet known. IPAB notes pay a premium of about fifteen basis points compared to notes directly issued by the federal government, which has not been able to obtain congressional approval to sell bonds to replace about $70 billion in notes issued for the bank bailout. Problems remain because banks reportedly accept as capital items that do not meet international standards, and there is little cost to debtors if they default. As of August 2004, the Congress had not passed new legislation addressing these issues.

Foreign Banks and Financing

Against the backdrop of a dynamic process of mergers and acquisitions in the global financial sector and banking crises in emerging markets during the second half of the 1990s, Latin America has witnessed a gradual positioning, and in some cases even a majority presence, of foreign banks in its financial systems. Of the region's large economies, Mexico has the greatest foreign presence—80 percent of total bank assets is held by foreigners, whereas before the 1994 crisis, foreign banks accounted for only one percent of bank assets (ECLAC 2002).

NAFTA opened up the Mexican banking system to greater foreign participation, although initially domestic capital's majority ownership of commercial banks remained intact. In 1994, Citibank, which had been doing business in the country for more than sixty years, opened a subsidiary and Banco Santander Central Hispano (BSCH) established operations for the first time. In 1995, another thirteen U.S., European, and Japanese banks entered the market through a wide range of operations.

During the first months of the banking crisis, the legal framework was reformed to scale back the limits that the NAFTA agreement had placed on foreign ownership of banks; the reform authorized greater participation by foreign investors, who were allowed to purchase medium-sized commercial banks, that is, those with between 5 and 10 billion dollars in assets. The principal buyers were Banco Bilbao Vizcaya Argentaria (BBVA) in 1996 and BSCH in 1997. In addition, Citigroup expanded its presence with the purchase of Banco Confía in 1998. The reform that made possible the purchase of the three largest banks was approved in late 1998; it allowed up to 100 percent of bank capital to be foreign-owned and removed all the safeguards that had been negotiated in NAFTA. In May 2000, BSCH acquired Grupo Financiero Serfín, the country's third-largest bank; in August of the same year, BBVA acquired control of Bancomer, the second-largest bank; and in the second quarter of 2001, Citigroup announced the purchase of Accival-Banamex, the largest domestic financial group. At present, these three large banks together account for 62 percent of all bank assets and control an even larger percentage of financial services (Maya 2004).

The banking crisis in 1994–95 spurred reforms in the payments system (especially the mechanism of inter-bank settlements), the introduction of capital standards (Bank of International Settlements agreement), accounting standards, and asset valuation (fair value of almost all assets and convergence with international accounting practices of the International Accounting Standards Board, or IASB). However, total lending has diminished since 1995 despite institutional reforms, rapid capitalization of banks, the presence of large foreign banks, and the government's backing of an important portion of assets. The loans portfolio average annual decrease from 1995 to 2003 was 8.6 percent. Commercial bank lending fell from 49 percent to 15 percent over the same period. Even in the period with the greatest expansion of foreign banks (1998–2001), the average annual decrease was 4.3 percent. Alternative funding sources for companies have also been scarce, except for foreign debt contracted by the private sector, which has grown nearly 4 percent per year, while the total for all alternative sources increased by only 0.7 percent and bank financing by issuers listed on the Mexican stock exchange (Bolsa Mexicana de Valores, BMV) increased 0.2 percent per year over the same period.

An important portion of bank transactions consists of IPAB bonds, which represent an average of 56 percent of the leading banks' current portfolio, including those of Bancomer-BBVA and Banamex-Citigroup. In recent years income from net fees and securities and brokerage of derivatives has grown increasingly important. Hence, the ratio of profits to shareholders' equity is above 8 percent for all banks taken together, despite the contraction of lending and deposits. The state retirement savings system was changed to a private management retirement savings system in 1996; by this means an important new business field was created in assets management, mainly for foreign banks. In 2003 they managed more than 35 billion dollars in workers' savings for retirement, which generated through commissions a net profit of about 85 million dollars.

Monetary policy has succeeded in stabilizing prices through high foreign-reserve accumulation and the flexible exchange rate, which is supported by high interest rates on government securities held by foreign banks and other investors. But this policy has brought about a contraction of domestic investment and led to government overindebtedness in domestic currency, which, in turn, has translated into a serious shortage of public revenues and rising financial commitments to pay internal and foreign debts.

Summary and Conclusion

This chapter examined monetary policy in the framework of economic and financial liberalization, when internal price stability has been closely linked to the peso–dollar exchange rate. The waves of capital inflows and outflows and their main characteristics in the last thirty years were analyzed. It was concluded that the relative level of foreign currency supply is one of the most important constraints of monetary policy. During the first two stages (1977–1989; see Table 10.2), the wave in capital inflows (outflows) and expansion (restriction) in monetary policy that even went to hyperinflationary crisis (1987–1988) led to a large level of public debt and to the process of privatization. The third and fourth stages (1989–1996) repeated the wave of inflow and outflows, but with a very weak Central Bank position for management of the bankruptcy of private commercial banks, leading to a large level of public debt and government bonds denominated in pesos that were placed in the domestic market and held by foreign banks and pension funds.

During the sixth stage (since 2001), the central bank, whose priority once again is to ensure price stability, intervened to avoid interest-rate volatility through the placement of government securities, thereby increasing public indebtedness for the sake of monetary regulation and accumulating and sterilizing international reserves. However, at the same time the availability of public funds for purposes other than covering financial costs diminished, and the largest banks sought profits mainly in yields on government securities, while reducing lending to the nonbanking private sector.

The highly restrictive monetary policy carried out in recent years, although successful in curbing inflation, has not avoided a steep increase in the peso-denominated government debt in the hands of the largest affiliates of foreign banks and pension funds, or even a significant rise in the foreign debt of Mexico's most important stock firms and especially of the state-owned oil company PEMEX, which has 34 billion dollars of foreign debt (most of them in PIDIREGAS, Proyectos de Impacto Diferido en el Registro del Gasto, which provide long term arrangement for investment and repayment). Consequently, flows linked to public or private debt and debt service continue to be a determinant of the evolution of the exchange rate and the inflation rate.

Notes

1. Statistical information herein is taken from the Banco de México's online databases, available at www.banxico.org.mx, and from the statistical appendices to the third State-of-the-Union Address of President Fox, 2003: http://informe.presidencia.gob.mx/index.php.
2. The law established limits on loans that the central bank could make to federal government, but there was no limit placed on federal government deposits in the central bank.
3. In this banking crisis some of the nonperforming loans were not paid because of: (1) household/firm bankruptcy; and (2) corruption in the granting of the loans, on the part of either the lenders, the borrowers, or both.

References

Banco de México. n.d. www.banxico.org.mx.
Carstens, Agustín, and Alejandro Reynoso. 1997. "Alcances de la política monetaria: Marco

teórico y regularidades empíricas en la experiencia mexicana." *Gaceta de economía* (ITSEM) 3 (Fall).

Correa, Eugenia. 1994. "Reorganización de la intermediación financiera, 1989–1993." *Comercio Exterior (Mexico):* 44, no. 12.

———. 1995. "Los servicios financieros en el TLC." In *Más allá del TLC: Integración financiera y desarrollo,* ed. Alicia Girón, Edgar Ortiz, and Eugenia Correa. Mexico City: Siglo XXI.

———. 2001. "La economía mexicana y los mercados financieros internacionales." *Información comercial española.* Available at www.mcx.es/polcomer/estudios/ (December).

———. 2004. "Inversionistas institucionales." In *Economía financiera contemporánea,* vol. 2, ed. Eugenia Correa and Alicia Girón. Mexico City: Miguel Ángel Porrúa.

ECLAC (Economic Commision for Latin America and the Caribbean). 2002. *La inversión extranjera en América Latina y el Caribe.* Available at www.eclac.org/publicaciones/ DesarrolloProductivo/8/LCG2178P/lcg2178.pdf.

Girón, Alicia. 1991. *Cincuenta años de deuda externa.* Mexico City: IIEC-UNAM.

Mantey, Guadalupe. 2000. "Desregulación financiera en el sudeste de Asia y en América Latina: Crisis bancarias y vulnerabilidad a los programas del FMI," In *De la desregulación financiera a la crisis cambiaria: Experiencias en América Latina y el sudeste asiático,* ed., Guadalupe Mantey, and Noemí Levy. Mexico City: UNAM.

———. 2002. "Política monetaria con oligopolio bancario: El gobierno como emisor de última instancia y el sobreendeudamiento público en México." *Momento Económico* (IIEC-UNAM) 120 (March–April).

Martínez, Lorenza, Oscar Sánchez, and Alejandro Werner. 2001. "Consideraciones sobre la conducción de la política monetaria y el mecanismo de transmisión en México." *Documento de Investigación 2001–02,* Dirección General de Investigación Económica, Banco de México.

Maya, Claudia. 2004. "Banca extranjera en México." In *Economía financiera contemporánea,* vol. 4, ed. Eugenia Correa and Alicia Girón. Mexico City: Miguel Ángel Porrúa.

Nacional Financiera. 1988. *La economía mexicana en cifras.* Mexico City: NAFINSA.

Vidal, Gregorio. 1999. "Las transformaciones financieras de los mercados de capital y el desarrollo de la crisis." *Revista comercio exterior* 49, no. 2.

———. 2002. *Grandes empresas, economía y poder en México.* Mexico City: Plaza y Valdés–UAM–I.

Wray, Randall. 1998. *Understanding Modern Money.* New York: Edward Elgar.

11

GRACIANA DEL CASTILLO

Mexico's Public Sector Debt and Debt Management

Although many analysts believe that Mexico's debt problems are over, Graciana del Castillo argues that Mexico's public sector debt, broadly defined to include foreign and domestic debt of federal and local governments and public enterprises, as well as debt relating to off-budget transactions (the so-called "augmented public sector debt"), grew to over 50 percent of GDP in 2003 and remained at that level in 2004, which is a source of concern.

Despite progress in reducing financial vulnerabilities since the 1994 crisis, other vulnerabilities remain. First, despite the maturity extension, about 20 percent of the debt issued in the domestic market (Cetes) remains short term and an additional 35 percent (Bondes) bear interest rates linked to short-term Cetes rates. Second, the pace of fiscal consolidation has been disappointing, despite higher than anticipated oil exports. Progress in this area has been slower than envisaged by the government due to its inability to pass significant tax and other critical reforms through Congress.

Lack of fiscal consolidation has led to a contractionary bias in monetary policy with a negative effect on investment, competitiveness, and growth. With tremendous social and infrastructural needs, falling per capita income in 2000–2003, and low tax revenues, which are highly dependent on oil, there is a need to reinvigorate the still pending reform agenda to allow for higher spending or to open the energy sector to private investment.

Public sector debt above the 50 percent threshold of GDP has been associated with debt difficulties in other countries. Part of the increase was due to sluggish growth in GDP and a fall in its dollar value due to depreciation of the Mexican peso. On the positive side, however, although the level remained practically unchanged until the end of 2003, the composition has improved. The share of investments in the energy sector (PIDIREGAS) has doubled to 5.1 percent of GDP in 2003, while debt relating to the banking bailout program (IPAB) and other debtor support programs has remained unchanged, indicating a slow fall in the share of finance costs associated with the 1995 restructuring of the banking system. Although a detailed analysis for 2004 could not be done at the time of writing, recent data shows that the augmented public sector debt remained at about 50 percent of GDP (IMF 2004). This was despite favorable external conditions, including the high price of oil and the strengthening of the U.S. industrial production in 2004, which allowed the Mexican economy to grow at close to 4 percent, after three years of stagnation.

Since Mexico's independence in 1820, a combination of factors—macroeconomic mismanagement, high external borrowing, and unsustainable debt servicing—have often led to default, debt restructuring, and a new debt cycle. This has had dire economic and social consequences for the population in general, and the most vulnerable groups in particular.[1] Ten years after the 1994 exchange rate and banking crisis, however, Mexico is hailed by academics and practitioners alike as an example of macroeconomic stability and good debt management.

The objective of this chapter is to evaluate progress made over the last few years with respect to Mexico's public sector debt and to assess whether the debt problem is definitely over or important vulnerabilities remain. While the objective here is certainly not to review past debt crises, a cursory mention of them allows us to identify situations, issues, and weaknesses that were present then in order to allow for comparison to present-day conditions. (The data cited throughout this chapter are placed in Table 11.1 and Table 11.2 at the end of the text.)

A combination of factors has put downward pressure on real financial vulnerabilities since the 1994 crisis. These include Mexico's comprehensive reform of the financial sector, its leadership in public sector external debt management, specific policy decisions to control net foreign indebtedness, the issuance of fixed-rate domestic-currency instruments, and the extension of the maturity (yield curve) of both foreign and domestic debt. Perceived vulnerabilities have also been reduced by Mexico's proximity and growing integration with the U.S. economy. This combination of factors has increased the possibilities of financing for the private sector, deepened the domestic capital market, and reduced foreign exchange risk, as firms switched from foreign to domestic capital markets to meet their financing needs.

Despite government efforts at improving the fiscal accounts and reducing indebtedness, public sector debt in relation to GDP—broadly defined for international comparison purposes to include debt of federal and local governments and public enterprises, as well as debt relating to off-budget transactions—has grown since 2000. In 2003 it surpassed the 50 percent threshold of GDP, which has been associated with debt difficulties in other countries. Progress to decrease public sector external debt has been disappointing despite larger amortizations than new budgetary borrowings, with external debt increasing as a proportion of GDP to 18 percent in 2003, a level comparable to that of the pre-1994 crisis. The 18 percent represents an increase from 2000, when the ratio had fallen to 16.6 percent of GDP. The increase is due to sluggish growth in GDP and a fall in its dollar value due to depreciation of the Mexican peso, as well as off-budget investments in the energy sector. At the same time, domestic debt increased to 32 percent of GDP and its exposure to short-term interest rates remains high.

In addition to the growing stock of public sector debt, other vulnerabilities remain. First, despite the maturity extension, about 20 percent of the debt issued in the domestic market (Cetes) remains short-term and an additional 35 percent (Bondes) bear interest rates linked to short-term Cetes rates.

Second, the pace of fiscal consolidation has also been slower than envisaged by the government, notwithstanding higher than anticipated oil exports. As a result, the gross public sector borrowing requirements (PSBR) (Table 11.1), which includes off-budget transactions and is the best measure of the consolidated public sector deficit, remains large and practically unchanged since 2000.[2] This is despite the relatively balanced situation shown in the traditional budget sent to Congress (which excludes off-budget transactions). Progress in fiscal consolidation has been impaired by the inability of the government to pass significant tax and other critical reform through Congress.

Putting pressure on monetary policy, this policy mix has had a negative impact on investment, competitiveness, and growth. Furthermore, with tremendous social and infrastructural needs, falling income per capita levels during the last three years, and tax revenues highly dependent on oil, there is a pressing need for structural reform to increase and diversify tax revenue to allow for higher public spending or to open up the energy sector to private investment. There is an urge to adopt such reforms since the benign international environment of low interest rates and high oil prices could change in the not so distant future. Until these reforms are successfully implemented, Mexico remains vulnerable to a reversal in market sentiment.

Mexico at the Forefront of Debt Problems

Since independence days Mexico has run into debt difficulties at various times and during very different circumstances. Miscalculation on the part of investors about Mexico's ability to pay was often to blame. When Mexico defaulted in 1827, the *Times* reported that the shock of the Mexican default was one of the worst since it caught even some of the most cautious investors by surprise. While other countries in the region had already defaulted, there was the belief among investors and the press that Mexico's resources were so abundant and her government so aware of the importance of maintaining its public credit that default would not happen. When it did, the *Courier* (U.K.) reported that "Mexico's default was a severe blow at South American credit, generally" (Dawson 1990).

Over the years investors continued to overestimate Mexico's ability to pay. Other crises included those at times of civil strife (the Mexican Revolution) and at times of world recession when demand for Mexican exports plummeted (the Great Depression of 1930 and the 1982 crisis). Crises even occurred at times when Mexican oil prospects had greatly improved and the price of oil in international markets had risen (1976), and also at times of large capital inflows and better prospects for integration with the United States (1994).

The tremendous borrowing of the 1970s, particularly since the oil shock in 1973, took place at very low interest rates. Zedillo (1986) shows that public sector net borrowing, which had averaged around US$200 million a year throughout the previous two decades, increased to more than US$1.6 billion in 1973 alone, and grew rapidly thereafter. Thus, the stock of debt grew from US$6.8 billion at the end of 1972, to US$21 billion by the end of the Echeverría administration (1976). At that time, the peso was devalued for the first time since 1954, when it was fixed to the U.S. dollar at 8 cents.[3] By the time López Portillo left office in 1982 the debt had soared to US$58 billion (44 percent of GDP). Zedillo linked the two financial crises at the end of the respective administrations to the hike in the external debt and to large capital flight.

In both cases, as the debt increased, lending conditions tightened. Moreover, international conditions changed drastically when the restrictive monetary policy of the U.S. Federal Reserve Bank led to high real interest rates in the early 1980s. This, in turn, led to declining economic activity in industrial countries and plummeting commodity prices in emerging ones. Thus, a combination of factors—both internal and external—contributed to the inability of the Mexican government to comply with its debt servicing in August 1982. Other countries in the region, also unable to service their debt at contracted terms, soon followed Mexico's default path.[4]

The economic strategy of the early 1990s was based on traditional budgetary and monetary discipline and the use of an exchange-rate anchor as the basic anti-inflationary instrument. Following a number of failed attempts to restore sustainable growth in the context of stable inflation, everything seemed to indicate, until December 20, 1994, that Mexico's stabilization-cum-reform, which brought inflation down from over 150 percent at the end of 1987 to 7 percent in 1994, was, at last, a resounding success.

The December 1994 crisis took many by surprise despite the fact that Mexico had increasingly relied on volatile short-term capital flows to finance a large current account imbalance of over 7 percent of GDP, in the presence of an appreciating real exchange rate. Also, the government had increased issuance of *tesobonos,* government bonds issued in pesos but redeemed at the exchange rate at the time of maturity, which offered investors an option to cover their exchange risk exposure in exchange for a lower rate of interest.

Inconsistent policies led to a 70 percent devaluation of the peso in December of that year and, as a result, inflation jumped to 35 percent in 1995, from 7 percent the year before. At the same time, GDP sunk by 7 percent and did not recover its

1994 level until 1997. Mexico's access to international capital markets was once again seriously curtailed and its creditworthiness was impaired.[5]

A serious stabilization and structural reform package put in place by the Zedillo administration soon after it assumed power on December 1, in conjunction with an unprecedentedly large international rescue package of close to US$50 billion, helped avoid default. The International Monetary Fund (IMF) provided almost $18 billion (nearly 720 percent of Mexico's quota in the fund)—a record amount at the time (Wijnholds 2003)—with the United States using about $20 billion from its Treasury's Exchange Stabilization Fund (ESF) for a bilateral loan.

The crisis, however, had serious social costs, with the population suffering a considerable deterioration in the standard of living as real wages plummeted. The economic cost can be measured by the sharp fall in output in 1995, the large increase in external debt from US$75 billion in 1993 to US$100 billion in 1995, and the large cost of restructuring the banking sector, estimated at close to 20 percent of GDP. Bailing out weak banks and the concomitant increase in domestic debt were necessary to avoid a systemic crisis of the financial sector.

During the repeated financial shocks to emerging markets starting with the Asian crisis of 1997, followed by the Russian crisis of 1998, the Brazilian crisis of early 1999, and the Argentine default of December 2002, Mexico was the least affected country in Latin America. This was, to a large extent, due to the reform package adopted in the wake of the 1994 crisis, and to the government's efforts to avoid contagion as the various crises hit (Blejer and del Castillo 2001). It was also due to Mexico's proximity and increased integration with the United States through the North American Free Trade Agreement (NAFTA).[6]

Thus, since its independence Mexico has been able to secure foreign financing due to its rich resources, its proximity to the United States, and optimism about the country's economic prospects, with creditors often misjudging its ability to pay, most notably by overestimating its capacity for future export earnings.

Debt No Longer a Forefront Concern

A decade after the 1994 crisis, and amid financial crises in other countries in the region, the debt issue is no longer a pressing problem for Mexican policymakers, the IMF, or international investors. This is reflected in a lack of interest in the issue by local and international journalists. Many argue that foreign debt ratios in relation to GDP are well below the level of the 1994–1995 crisis. Furthermore, the slowdown in 2001, after vigorous growth in 2000, took place in a context of financial and price stability, or, as the minister of Finance has pointed out, "as part of the business cycle, rather than a crisis situation" (Gil Díaz 2002).

By being one of only two Latin American countries blessed with investment grade by all rating agencies since February 2002,[7] in 2003 Mexico has had access to credit at less than 200 basis points (or 2 percent) over U.S. Treasury Bills. The upgrade to investment grade has permitted Mexico's inclusion in the key U.S. fixed-income benchmark (the Lehman Aggregate) and has allowed the country to broaden its investors' base to include high-grade institutional investors, such as mutual and pension funds, which can only buy investment grade instruments.

After limited financial intermediation following the banking crisis in 1995, commercial bank credit to the private sector expanded in 2002–2003. At the same time, with inflation at about 4 percent, the lowest level in thirty-four years, and with short-term interest rates (28-day Cetes) bottoming out in June 2003 at less than 5 percent (and fluctuating around 6 percent in 2004), Mexico has managed to develop a market for domestic debt as an alternative source of financing for the public sector. The development of a yield curve for public sector bonds as maturities increased created a benchmark for private sector debt placements. Thus, the domestic capital market has become a competitive financing alternative for private sector companies as well, which were previously financing themselves through foreign borrowing or through suppliers' credits, given the paucity of bank lending.

Another factor explaining market confidence in Mexico is the Bank of Mexico's large international reserves amounting to close to US$60 billion at the end of 2003, covering almost 150 percent of estimated short-term external debt by residual maturity.

Withering Foreign Debt

At the end of 2003, the stock of public sector foreign debt (excluding debt relating to off-budget transactions) stood at slightly below US$80 billion, representing 13 percent of Mexico's GDP. The stock of foreign debt has been falling. While in the five years following the 1982 crisis it amounted to almost 50 percent of GDP on average, in the comparable period following 1994 it fell to 23 percent. During the 2000–2003 period it fell to a low 13 percent of GDP, thus greatly diminishing the exchange rate risk.

For the last few years the government has focused on extending the maturity of its foreign debt by issuing long-term Global Bonds, including a thirty-year bond and a Global Floating Rate Bond (at Libor plus 70 basis points) in 2003. This has facilitated the construction of a United Mexican States (UMS) yield curve of different maturities in the dollar capital markets. In 2003, two other noteworthy developments with respect to foreign debt included, first, the inclusion of collective action clauses (CACs) providing for "majority enforcement and majority restructuring provisions" to facilitate debt restructuring in the unlikely event of debt difficulties, and second, the cancellation of Brady Bonds by issuing new bonds at better terms in the international capital markets. In addition to recovering its collateral, this operation represented an estimated savings of US$1.2 billion.

These developments attest to Mexico's good debt management and are a reflection of investors' confidence in the country's sound economic policies. The average maturity of the federal government external debt, representing about three-fourths of public sector debt, increased to 10.3 years in 2003 (compared to 9 years in 2000).

Vigorous Domestic Debt

On the domestic front the main objectives were to increase the average maturity of the public debt, to reduce the vulnerability of public finance to interest- and exchange-rate shocks, and to promote the development of domestic financial markets. Under a budgetary policy of zero net foreign indebtedness, issuing domestic debt has not only been a way to finance the budget deficit, but also a means to effectively channel the large resources of institutional investors, particularly pension funds, into the domestic capital market.

To achieve this, the government has continued to extend the yield curve by issuing longer-term fixed-rate bonds of 20-year maturity in pesos, in addition to the 3- , 5- , 7- , and 10-year bonds issued since 2000. Practically all net domestic borrowing took place through issuance of long-term fixed-rate domestic currency denominated development bonds (Bonos de Desarrollo). As a result, the proportion of fixed-rate bonds increased to 33 percent of the total stock (from 26 percent in 2002).

Domestic debt (excluding debt related to off-budget transactions), which averaged 15.5 percent in 1989–1994, returned to that level in 2001–2003, after having fallen to 10.4 percent in the in-between period. By 2003, domestic debt represented 16.5 percent of GDP, about twice the level in 1996. Increases in domestic debt in 2003 financed the public sector deficit, replaced external debt, and financed the Program for Voluntary Separation through which the government reduced its public service by close to 50,000 positions. In 2004, the government plans to accelerate the swap of domestic debt for foreign debt to reduce the vulnerability of public finances to changes in the international capital markets and exchange-rate fluctuations.

By end of 2003 the average maturity of debt issued in the domestic market had increased to 908 days, from 539 days at the end of 2000. By April 2004, the average maturity had increased by 60 additional days. At the same time, the proportion of long-term fixed-rate debt (Bonos de Desarrollo) grew to about 31 percent (from 0 percent in 2000).

Has the Debt Problem Really Withered Away?

Looking at the traditional definition of public sector debt (which, as we said, excludes debt relating to off-budget transactions), many analysts have concluded that Mexico's debt problems are over (e.g., Blásquez and Santiso 2004). Under this restrictive definition, Mexico's debt stock (external and domestic) was just below 30 percent of GDP at

Figure 11.1   **Traditional Public Sector Debt, 1982–2003** (in percent of GDP)

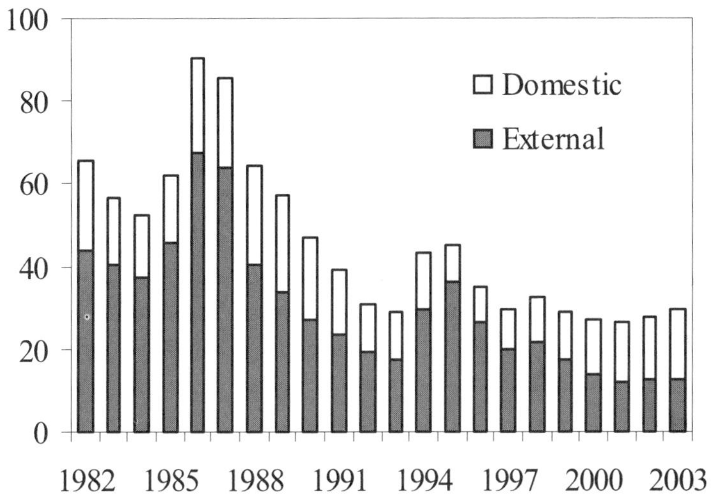

Sources: Secretariat of Finance and Public Credit and our own estimates.

the end of 2003. Although this level is significantly lower than the 45 percent of GDP on average during the 1994–1995 crisis, and even lower than the one during the 1982–1983 crisis (over 60 percent of GDP), the ratio has been growing since 2000 when it bottomed at 26.5 percent of GDP. Furthermore, at 30 percent of GDP in 2003, public sector domestic debt was at a similar level as in 1993 (see Figure 11.1).

Two points arise from this analysis. First, is this definition of debt adequate for cross-country comparisons? Second, does this level of debt really reflect the actual and contingent liabilities of the public sector? The traditional (restricted) definition does not satisfy either of these two criteria. For that reason, the IMF and some of the ratings agencies have focused on a broader definition that takes into consideration off-budget transactions. Recognizing this—and in an important effort to improve the transparency of the fiscal accounts—the authorities started to report the PSBR in 2001, the critical ratio for analysis of the fiscal stance of the consolidated public sector (including off-budget transactions). In January 2002 the government started to report the public sector net debt data incorporating these off-budget transactions (net of public sector assets).

A More Comprehensive Debt Concept

While with the restricted traditional definition, total public sector debt fell from 43 percent of GDP on average in the 1994–1995 period to 27 percent in 2002–2003; if we include off-budget transactions, the "augmented public sector debt" averaged 48 percent of GDP in 2002–2003 (see Figure 11.2).

Figure 11.2   **Public Sector Debt, 1982–2003** (in percent of GDP)

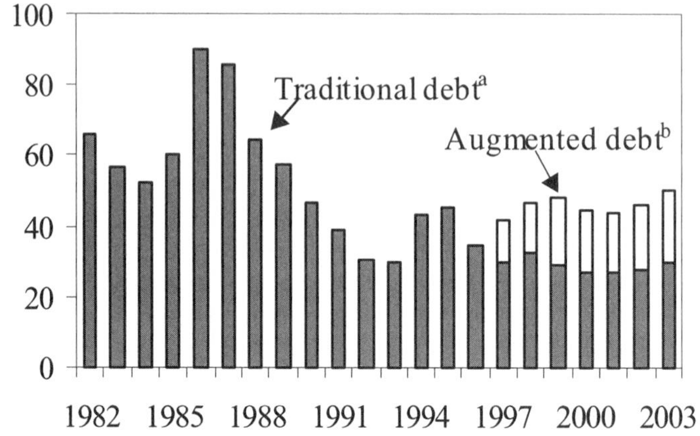

Sources: Secretariat of Finance and Public Credit and our own estimates.
[a]Excludes off-budget transactions.
[b]Includes off-budget transactions.

By the end of 2003, the augmented public sector debt stock, incorporating off-budget transactions relating to the banking bailout program (FOBAPROA/IPAB),[8] rescue of toll roads (FARAC), and investments in the energy sector (PIDIREGAS), which are explained below, amounted to over 50 percent of GDP, a significant increase from 46.2 percent in 2002. Even this ratio is an underestimate since off-budget transactions are reported (and hence included) on a net rather than gross basis.[9]

On the positive side, although the debt level in 2001–2003 remained unchanged from that of the previous three years, the composition improved: the share of investment through PIDIREGAS has practically doubled since 2000 to 5.1 percent of GDP in 2003, while that of IPAB and debtor support programs has remained unchanged. This indicates that the share of finance costs associated with banking restructuring is slowly falling.

Since most PIDIREGAS debt is external, public sector external debt (including off-budget transactions) reached 18 percent of GDP in 2003. This ratio is about the same as that reported in 1993 (see Figure 11.3). Including off-budget transactions, domestic debt increased to 32 percent of GDP in 2003. Increases in domestic and external debt together have added 6 percentage points of GDP to public sector debt since 2000 (see Figure 11.4, see page 186).

In the aftermath of the 1994 crisis, several factors led to off-budget transactions. First, the government undertook a comprehensive program to minimize banking sector problems and maintain credibility with depositors.[10] Although the government does not guarantee IPAB's debt, IPAB (Spanish acronym for the Insti-

Figure 11.3 **Public Sector External Debt, 1982–2003** (in percent of GDP)

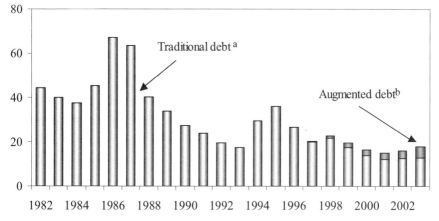

Sources: Secretariat of Finance and Public Credit and Table 11.2.
[a]Excludes off-budget transactions.
[b]Includes off-budget transactions.

tute for the Protection of Bank Savings, "Instituto de Protección al Ahorro Bancario") fulfills a public policy role as the deposit insurance institution for distressed financial institutions, and the government has the legal obligation to ensure that IPAB meets its liabilities. This is the reason why it should be considered a contingent liability of the government. As we mentioned earlier, the cost of the banks and depositors rescue operation added about 20 percent of GDP to the stock of Mexican domestic debt. These liabilities today are still estimated at about 12 percent of GDP. The rescue of the toll roads and other programs add close to 4 percent of GDP to public sector domestic debt.

Second, at a time when access to international capital markets was severely curtailed, the country was obliged to comply with fiscal targets imposed by the IMF, and as opening up the energy sector to private ownership was restricted by the Constitution, the Mexican authorities decided to finance part of its large infrastructure needs off-budget. To do so, Mexico embarked on the ingenious financing scheme known as PIDIREGAS (Spanish acronym for Energy Projects with a Deferred Fiscal Impact, "Proyectos de Impacto Diferido en el Registro del Gasto"). It allowed the government to defer the fiscal impact of the investment by attracting private long-term financing into strategic and highly profitable projects in the energy sector, where requirements were large.

There are two types of PIDIREGAS. Only the first one, known as a Direct Investment Project (DIP), affects the stock of public sector debt. DIP is a project built and financed by the private sector for the construction of energy infrastructure (electricity and oil). Upon completion, ownership of the project is transferred

Figure 11. 4   **Augmented Public Sector Debt, 1997–2003** (in percent of GDP)

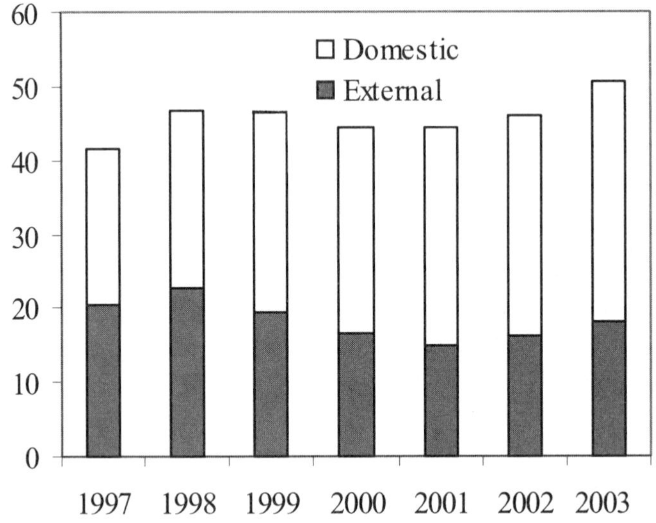

Sources: Secretariat of Finance and Public Credit and our own estimates.

to the government in exchange for payment ("turnkey operation"). Payment is either done in full (rarely) or, more generally, a stream of payments takes place over a number of years. The government includes the obligations for the first two years in its public sector debt accounts and assumes that the rest will be self-financed through the projects' own revenue. There are explicit clauses in these contracts requiring that, under special circumstances, the government buys out the operation. Because of this, the obligations beyond the first two years are included as contingent liabilities of the government.

Remaining Vulnerabilities

Mexico's remaining vulnerabilities relate mainly to its low growth, fiscal weaknesses, increasing debt levels, lagging structural reform, and loss of competitiveness. The political transition initiated by the Zedillo government, the macroeconomic framework established following the 1994 crisis, and the leadership role that Mexico is playing among emerging markets in financial matters have not led to sustained growth, nor to a systematic improvement in social conditions. Mexico grew at only 0.7 percent annually on average in 2001–2003, compared to 5.1 percent during the three previous years, and 3.5 percent during the full Zedillo administration (1994–2000) (despite a close to 7 percent fall in 1995). Income per capita fell in 2001–2003. Although GDP grew by close to 4 percent in 2004, the IMF (2004) projects lower medium-term growth.

Efforts at fiscal consolidation to bring the PSBR down have not largely succeeded. On the one hand, despite fiscal discipline, the traditional budget (excluding nonrecurrent revenue) was hardly reduced in the 2001–2003 period, averaging 0.8 percent of GDP (as compared to 1.0 percent in the previous three years). On the other hand, off-budget expenditure related to PIDIREGAS increased. Thus, at 3.5 percent of GDP, the PSBR has been practically unchanged during this period. Despite the reactivation of growth in 2004, the PSBR was still over 3 percent of GDP, a level comparable to that of 2000.

To make matters worse, fiscal flexibility is low. At about 11 percent of GDP, the tax burden remains low, even by regional standards. More worrisome, after having peaked at 36 percent of total revenue in 2000, oil still accounts for about one-third of them, practically unchanged from 1998–2000. This is despite major efforts at improving tax and customs collection, which paid off with an 11 percent increase in value added tax (VAT) collection in 2003.

Had the government succeeded in its reform proposals of end-2001 and end-2003 to eliminate most of the exemptions and zero rates in the VAT, and to set a uniform VAT rate for all goods and services, the tax system would have been more efficient, the increase in revenue would have been more sustainable, oil dependency would have decreased, and long-term solvency would have been assured.[10] Fiscal reform packages approved by Congress, however, have fallen short of what the government proposed and what the country needs.

For Mexico to grow in a sustained and vigorous way,[12] capacity in the energy sector needs to increase in line with growing demand. Unless tax revenue is increased significantly, reforms to open up the sector to private sector participation are needed. At the present time, public investment is clearly insufficient to cover the human and physical infrastructure needs. In fact, public investment fell from 2.8 percent of GDP in 1998–2000 to 2.4 percent in 2001–2003, a very low level indeed.

Other structural reforms to move toward a fully funded public sector pension system,[13] expand flexibility in the labor market, make the judiciary more efficient and improve governance are also important to attract foreign direct investment, reverse the fall in investment in relation to GDP from its peak in 1997,[14] and create high-quality employment to improve social conditions. The Fox administration's inability to pass tax and structural reform through Congress has contributed to the country's loss in competitiveness, has inhibited the consolidation of public sector finances and continues to be a downward risk going forward.[15]

Vulnerabilities also remain with regard to both public sector external and domestic debt. The zero net foreign indebtedness budgetary policy has served the country well and has reduced foreign exchange risk. However, we have seen that the stock of foreign debt has continued to grow, due to the depreciation of the currency, off-budget operations, and slow growth. This ratio is about the same as that prevailing in 1993. Domestic debt has tripled since 1993. Despite the maturity extension, about 20 percent of the domestic debt remains short-term

(Cetes of less than one year) and an additional 35 percent (Bondes) bear interest rates linked to short-term Cetes rates. Furthermore, 8 percent of this debt is issued at rates of interest linked to the inflation rate, so that they bear a fixed real rate of interest (Udibonos).

Debt Benchmarks

Including private sector external debt amounting to 10 percent of GDP, the total external debt ratio reached 28 percent of GDP in 2003. As Reinhart, Rogoff, and Savastano (2003) have pointed out, countries with a high debt intolerance caused by repeated episodes of high indebtedness, default, and instability have a low safety threshold for external debt, perhaps as low as 15–20 percent of GDP. Mexico's debt tolerance has probably increased from the low levels reported for 1970–2000 due to major financial reform in the last few years and growing integration with the United States. Nevertheless, debt intolerance is a legacy of the Mexican past and should not be totally ignored. Thus, we should not underestimate vulnerabilities relating to foreign debt in Mexico.

Public sector debt (including all external and domestic off-budget transactions) has surpassed the 50 percent level, a level that has been associated with debt problems in other countries, most recently in Uruguay.[16] Based on casual observations of sovereign debt defaults in emerging markets over the last thirty years, the IMF (2003) found that while the level of public debt at the time of the default has varied substantially, in many cases it has been quite low. In 55 percent of the defaults recorded, public debt the year before was below 60 percent of GDP—the benchmark established for European Union members in the Maastricht Treaty—and in 35 percent of the cases the default actually occurred at a debt ratio of less than 40 percent of GDP. In fact, they found that the median public debt-to-GDP ratio in the year before a default was about 50 percent of GDP.

The authorities posit that the public sector debt in Mexico is significantly lower than that of other OECD members, but the comparison may not be valid. Although Mexico's prudent macroeconomic policies, good debt management, much-improved financial system, and close integration with the United States have lowered the perception of risk,[17] other factors make the comparison difficult. OECD countries have lower sovereign risk, less volatility in spreads and interest rates, and are less prone to the regional and other economic and political shocks that Mexico is subjected to from time to time. Furthermore, the share of external debt in total public sector debt in Mexico, at 36 percent, remains well above the 25 percent average level of OECD countries (IMF 2003). In order for Mexico to compare itself with other OECD countries, fiscal flexibility should increase by making fiscal revenue higher and less volatile, interest cost as a share of public sector revenue should continue to fall,[18] and the share of domestic debt at short maturities and variable interest rates should drop significantly.

Concluding Remarks

Growth prospects are critical to any analysis of debt sustainability and debt vulnerability. Mexico's inability to find a path of sustainable growth is particularly troublesome amid increasing public sector debt levels, its lack of fiscal flexibility, its low savings from the oil bonanza, strong pressures to increase spending in human and physical infrastructure, and the nation's lagging reform agenda. Average growth of 2 percent in the Fox administration and prospects of 3 percent growth in coming years are still insufficient to make a difference.

There should be no room for complacency in dealing with Mexico's fiscal and debt matters. This is particularly true since Mexico's benign international environment of high oil prices and low interest rates may not last forever. Furthermore, external and political shocks cannot be ruled out, and political noise, as elections get closer in 2006, makes adoption of necessary reforms unlikely. To improve the fiscal stance and ensure debt sustainability, to make the country more competitive internationally and enhance growth prospects, and to increase human development and the living conditions of the population at large, certain fiscal and structural reforms are imperative. Congress should ignore these issues only at its own risk.

Notes

I am grateful to Reyna Gutiérrez, director of Debt Statistics at the Ministry of Finance and Public Credit of Mexico for historical data and for her valuable assistance in understanding Mexican debt methodology. I am also grateful to Javier Murcio and Onno Wijnholds for comments and suggestions. Errors, however, remain my own.

1. While the PSBR in 2000 was 3.3 percent of GDP (see Table 11.1), the IMF (2004) estimates a PSBR of 3.1 percent in 2004.

2. Reinhart, Rogoff, and Savastano (2003) note that during the 1824–2000 period, the debts of Mexico were either in default or undergoing restructuring for almost half the time, while those of Venezuela and Colombia were in default almost 40 percent of the time, and those of Brazil and Argentina almost a quarter of the time.

3. As 1999 Nobel laureate Robert A. Mundell predicted in his fall 1976 courses at Columbia University, monetary and exchange rate instability followed and foreign debt accumulated rapidly.

4. On August 6, a two-tier foreign-exchange system was set up and one week later, dollar-denominated deposits in the Mexican banking system were made payable in pesos only. On August 20, the secretary of Finance, Jesús Silva-Herzog, requested a three-month moratorium on principal payments, as well as the formation of an "advisory group" of creditors to negotiate the restructuring of the foreign public sector debt. On September 1, private banks were nationalized and foreign exchange controls were imposed. The administration of Miguel de La Madrid, which assumed power on December 1, adopted a drastic stabilization program to bring the public sector imbalance to 8.5 percent of GDP in 1983, from 18 percent the year before (Zedillo 1986).

5. For a detailed analysis of policy inconsistencies that led to the 1994 crisis, see Blejer and del Castillo (1998).

6. Gil Díaz (2003) showed how Mexico's economic cycle has increasingly followed

Table 11.1

Mexico: Selected Economic and Financial Indicators, 1997–2003

	1997	1998	1999	2000	2001	2002	2003
Income and prices (as indicated)							
GDP (billions of Mexican pesos)	3,538.3	4,197.2	5,017.9	5,799.0	6,000.6	6,569.6	6,918.6
GDP (billions of US$)	437.7	425.5	527.4	605.8	656.4	637.1	613.5
GDP per capita (US$)	4,395	4,787	5,398	6,212	6,403	6,673	6,190
Real GDP (percent change)	6.7	5.0	3.6	6.6	−0.2	0.9	1.5
Investment/GDP	25.2	23.5	23.8	23.8	20.9	20.3	21.5
Savings/GDP	23.4	20.0	21.1	20.8	18.0	18.1	20.1
Population (in millions)	94.3	95.8	97.3	98.7	100.3	101.9	103.5
Open unemployment rate percent (end period)	2.8	2.6	2.0	1.9	2.5	2.8	3.5
Consumer prices (percent change)	15.7	18.6	12.3	9.0	4.4	5.7	4.0
Price of oil (US$/bbl)	16.5	10.2	15.7	24.8	18.6	21.5	24.7
Exchange rate (end of period)	8.1	9.9	9.5	9.6	9.1	10.3	11.3
Exchange rate (average)	8.0	9.0	9.7	9.5	9.4	9.7	10.8
External indicators (as percent of GDP)							
External current account balance	−1.8	−3.5	−2.7	−3.0	−2.9	−2.2	−1.4
Net international reserves (billions of US$)	28.0	30.1	30.7	33.6	40.9	48.0	57.4
Merchandise trade balance	0.6	−7.9	−5.6	−8.0	−10.0	−7.9	−5.6
Exports	16.9	17.6	16.3	17.3	15.4	15.9	17.3
Petroleum and derivatives	2.6	1.7	1.9	2.7	1.9	2.3	3.0
Manufacturing (including net proceeds from maquila)	13.4	14.9	13.6	13.8	12.8	13.0	13.4
Imports	−16.8	−19.5	−17.4	−18.6	−16.9	−17.2	−18.2
Current account receipts (CAR)a	18.0	18.3	20.7	25.0	24.4	24.6	26.4
Foreign direct investment (billions of US$)	12.8	12.3	13.2	16.4	26.6	14.4	10.7
Gross financing needs (billions of US$)b	73.8	62.2	56.8	62.3	72.7	72.3	63.9
Gross international reserves (billions of US$)	28.9	31.9	31.8	31.7	35.6	44.8	50.7
Money, credit, and equity (apc or as indicated)							
Broad money (M4a)	28.3	25.1	19.6	12.9	16.0	10.5	12.8

Treasury bill rate (28–day Cetes)	21.9	26.9	24.1	17.0	12.9	8.2	6.8
Real interest rate	6.3	7.7	12.3	8.6	8.5	2.6	2.2
EMBI spread (basis points)	402.0	741.0	363.0	392.0	308.0	331.0	199.0
Stock prices (Dec 02 = 100)	118.9	73.5	138.3	106.7	128.0	108.7	144.0
Fiscal indicators (as percent of GDP)							
Traditional (budget) public sector balance (inc. NRR)[c]	-0.7	-1.1	-1.1	-1.1	-0.7	-1.2	-0.5
Primary balance	3.3	1.5	2.6	2.6	2.6	1.8	2.3
Interest	4.0	2.6	3.3	3.5	3.1	2.7	2.8
Public sector investment	3.0	3.1	2.6	2.6	2.4	2.4	2.3
Nonrecurrent revenue (NRR)	1.0	0.4	0.4	0.4	0.7	0.7	0.6
Public sector balance (exc. NRR)	-1.7	-1.5	-1.5	-1.5	-1.4	-1.9	-1.1
PSBR or augmented public sector balance (exc. NRR)[d]	-6.6	-6.4	-6.3	-3.7	-3.8	-3.4	-3.6
Fiscal indicators (as percent of noted denominator)							
Public sector interest payments/revenue	17.8	14.2	17.2	16.9	15.7	12.9	11.9
Central government interest payments/revenue	20.0	15.5	18.9	18.1	16.0	15.4	14.1
Central government tax/revenue	9.5	9.6	10.4	10.0	10.9	11.1	11.1
Public sector oil revenue/GDP	8.1	6.0	6.2	7.4	6.8	6.2	8.3
Public sector oil revenue/revenue	36.4	32.3	32.5	36.0	34.1	29.6	35.9

Sources: Secretariat of Finance and Public Credit (SHCP); National Institute of Statistics and Geography (INEGI); Bank of Mexico; IMF; and our own estimates.

a Includes earnings of foreign exchange from exports of goods and services and transfers (remittances). Maquila exports are included on a net basis.

b Defined as the sum of the current account deficit, debt amortization (including ST debt), and gross reserve accumulation.

c Includes the Federal Government and entities under direct budgetary control (PEDBC). The latter includes PEMEX, CFE (Comisión Federal de Electricidad), LFC (Luz y Fuerza del Centro), Roads and Bridges, National Lottery, IMSS (Instituto Mexicano del Seguro Social) and ISSSTE. Nonrecurrent revenue such as privatization proceeds are included as revenue.

d Includes the traditional budget, entities under indirect budgetary control (PEIBC), and off-budget transactions. It also includes privatization and other nonrecurrent revenue as financing rather than revenue.

Table 11.2

Mexico: Public Sector Indicators, 1997–2003 (as a percent of nominal GDP)

	1997	1998	1999	2000	2001	2002	2003
Excluding off-budget transactions							
Public sector debt[a]	29.6	32.5	29.2	27.1	26.6	27.9	29.4
By type of debt:							
External[b]	20.2	21.7	17.5	14.0	12.2	12.4	12.9
Domestic[c]	9.4	10.8	11.7	13.2	14.4	15.5	16.5
By maturity:							
Long-term	85.9	84.3	87.5	85.6	84.9	84.0	86.9
Short-term	14.1	15.7	12.5	14.4	15.1	16.0	13.1
By debtor:							
Non-financial public sector	23.1	25.8	23.8	22.8	22.9	24.2	28.1
Federal government	18.9	21.3	20.0	19.2	19.4	20.6	24.2
Public entities	2.5	2.7	2.2	2.1	1.8	1.8	2.0
Local government	1.6	1.7	1.6	1.5	1.7	1.7	1.9
Financial public-sector (development banks)	6.5	6.6	5.4	4.3	3.7	3.7	1.4
Federal government assets	2.5	3.2	2.7	2.5	1.8	1.8	1.5
External	2.1	2.4	1.7	1.3	0.6	0.5	0.3
Domestic	0.4	0.8	1.0	1.2	1.2	1.3	1.2
Net public sector debt[d]	27.1	29.2	26.5	24.6	24.8	26.2	27.9
External	18.1	19.3	15.8	12.6	11.7	11.9	12.6
Internal	9.0	9.9	10.6	12.0	13.2	14.2	15.3
Including off-budget transactions							
Augmented net public sector debt[e]	37.2	41.2	42.8	40.1	40.3	41.7	45.4
Budgetary sector and development banks[f]	25.2	26.8	23.7	22.8	22.6	23.4	24.4
IPAB[g]	8.1	9.6	13.2	11.2	11.6	10.8	11.4

Debtor support programs[h]	0.8	0.8	1.0	1.0	1.0	0.8	0.5
PIDIREGAS[i]	5.1	3.7	2.6	2.6	2.1	1.1	0.3
Funds and trusts[j]	3.7	3.0	2.5	2.5	2.8	2.9	3.1
Public sector assets	3.1	2.8	2.4	2.8	3.9	3.9	2.7
Federal government	1.5	1.8	1.8	2.5	2.7	3.2	2.5
Development banks[k]	1.6	1.0	0.6	0.3	1.2	0.7	0.2
Augmented public sector debt[l]	50.5	46.2	44.3	44.4	48.3	46.9	41.6
External debt	18.0	16.1	14.8	16.6	19.6	22.8	20.5
Domestic debt	32.4	30.1	29.5	27.9	28.7	24.1	21.1
Debt service							
External debt service (as percent of GDP)	5.0	4.1	5.4	5.7	5.5	7.0	9.1
External debt service (as percent of CAR)	39.3	33.1	44.9	44.1	36.9	37.8	50.6
Internal debt service (as percent of GDP)	14.1	15.3	17.3	14.1	13.2	10.8	8.1
Total debt service (as percent of GDP)	19.0	19.2	22.8	19.8	18.8	17.2	17.0
Total interest payments (as percent of GDP)	2.7	2.8	3.4	3.8	3.6	2.9	3.7
Total interest payments (as percent of public sector revenue)	25.7	25.3	27.5	29.7	24.5	16.7	17.7
External interest payments (as percent of CAR)	8.9	8.4	9.5	10.4	8.8	8.1	8.3
Memorandum items:							
Net augmented public sector debt[m]	47.3	43.5	41.9	41.6	44.4	42.9	38.9
Off-budget transactions (net)[n]	21.0	18.3	17.7	17.3	19.1	14.4	12.0
Effective interest rate on external debt (percent)	6.4	6.4	7.6	8.1	6.7	6.5	7.2
Gross official reserves in percent of short-term debt[o]	214.9	158.0	135.1	133.5	165.7	146.8	158.7

Sources: Secretariat of Finance and Public Credit; National Institute of Statistics and Geography; Bank of Mexico; IMF; and our own estimates.

aTraditional (gross) definition (including federal government, entities under direct budgetary control (PEDBC) including PEMEX and CFE, and development banks adjusted to include local government debt.

bIncludes the debt of the federal government, PEDBC (including other public sector which is negligible) and debt of the development banks (Nafin, Bancomext, Banobras and Banrural).

(continued)

Table 11.2 (continued)

[c]Includes debt of the federal government and the local government (states and municipalities) and is denominated in pesos.

[d]Net of federal government assets.

[e]SHCP augmented definition of net debt. Excludes local governments. Includes off-budget transactions on a net basis.

[f]This differs from the definition in a for two reasons: first, the coverage is broader (includes both external and domestic debt of the federal government, entities and development banks but the difference is very small. Second, it is a net value, and in additional to the federal assets, the assets of the entitites and development banks are taken into account to calculate the net value.

[g]IPAB is the Mexican equivalent of the U.S. FDIC.

[h]Debtor support programs refer to payment discounts, restructured debt in UDIs and fixed real rates offered to debtors. They are administered by IPAB but with federal government resources.

[i]PIDIREGAS includes the Master Trust and direct projects relating to Pemex and CFE.

[j]Includes FARAC (toll road rescue), Fovi, Fira, Fonatur, and funds.

[k]Calculated as the difference between a and f, assuming domestic debt of PEDBC and other public sector is negligible.

[l]This measure of gross public sector debt is still an underestimate since it includes off-budget transactions on a net basis only (since the SHCP reports it this way). Including IPAB on a gross value would add 0.5 percent of GDP to total public sector debt in 2003.

[m]Assets of the federal government and development banks are used in this calculation.

[n]Off-budget transactions include IPAB, PIDIREGAS, debtor support programs and funds and trusts operations on a net basis.

[o]In percent of short-term debt by residual maturity (excluding pre-payment of public sector debt). Historical data include all prepayments (IMF data).

that of the United States and Canada. While the correlation between the industrial cycles in Mexico and the United States was only 0.50 in 1994, this correlation had increased to 0.99 in 2001–2002.

7. Moody's was the first to upgrade Mexico to Baa3 (March 2001) and it upgraded it to Baa2 in early 2003. S&P was last.

8. The government acted mostly through FOBAPROA, a trust managed by the central bank. In May 1999, IPAB was created to replace FOBAPROA. In July 2004, banks and the government agreed on the exchange of FOBAPROA debt for new bonds, ending a long period of uncertainty for the financial system (see IMF 2004).

9. These ratios also include debt of local governments, which is not included in the SHCP net public sector debt data.

10. In fact, there was not a single bank run during this crisis. The strategy to avoid losses by depositors included debtor-support programs for the restructuring of credits, a dollar liquidity facility aimed at banks with relatively high levels of external liabilities, a temporary capitalization program to compensate for the loss of capital due to the increase in nonperforming loans, and other more permanent capitalization schemes (Ortiz 2002).

11. As the Chilean experience indicates, unifying VAT rates could have resulted in a large increase in revenue, while fiscal equity could have improved by compensating the most vulnerable through well-targeted assistance programs. The Chilean government has managed to bring people out of poverty more rapidly than any other country in the region with a single-rate VAT with no exemptions.

12. The Bank of Mexico has repeatedly mentioned the need for reform if the economy is to grow fast and in a sustained way.

13. This is another source of contingent liabilities that, because of the difficulty in estimating, is not normally included in the PSBR.

14. Investment fell to slightly less than 21 percent of GDP in 2001–2003, 1 percent of GDP lower than in the three years following the 1994 crisis (1995–1997), and 3 percent lower than in the following period (1998–2000). Investment grew, however, in 2004 but it was still significantly lower than at the peak in 1997.

15. Part of the problem may have been the inability of the government to build support for the reforms. Another important part, however, is that, as congressmen cannot be reelected since it is prohibited in the Constitution, they are not accountable for another term and have no real incentive to adopt reforms that might have a political cost in the short run. This is likely to change since there seems to be support for a constitutional amendment allowing for reelection, which requires two-thirds of the votes in Congress.

16. Uruguay's public sector debt to GDP in 2001 was slightly over 50 percent of GDP and the PSBR was close to 4 percent of GDP. Uruguay was kept at investment grade by the three major ratings agencies until February 2002, four months before the peak of the banking crisis, ignoring contagion factors from Argentina and Brazil, the lack of fiscal flexibility, and the inability of the government to adopt structural reforms that could have made the country less vulnerable to external shocks (del Castillo 2004).

17. Bond index spreads fluctuated between 175 and 205 basis points in 2004.

18. Public sector interest as a proportion of revenue fell to 13.5 percent in 2001–2003, as compared to 16.1 percent in the previous three years.

References

Bank of Mexico. Available at www.banxico.org.mx.
Blázquez, Jorge, and Javier Santiso. 2004. "Mexico: Is It an Ex-Emerging Market?" *Journal of Latin American Studies,* no. 36.

Blejer, Mario I., and Graciana del Castillo. 1998. "Déjà Vu All Over Again: The Mexican Crisis and the Stabilization of Uruguay in the 1970s." *World Development* 26, no. 3.
———. 2001. "Contagion: From Higher Risk to Risk Aversion and the Danger of Protectionism." In *The Political Economy of the East Asian Crisis and its Aftermath,* ed. Francisco Rivera-Batiz and Arvid J. Lukauskas. Boston: Edward Elgar.
Dawson, F.G. 1990. *The First Latin American Debt Crisis.* New Haven, CT: Yale University Press.
del Castillo, Graciana. 2004. "Assessing Sovereign Risk." In *Covering Globalization: A Reporter's Handbook,* ed. Anya Schiffrin and Amer Bisat. New York: Columbia University Press.
Gil Díaz, Francisco. 2002. "The Mexican Economy: Recent Developments and Future Challenges." Presentation made by the Minister of Finance to investors on Wall Street.
———. 2003. "Creating a Favorable Investment Climate: Mexico's Experience." Presentation made by the Minister of Finance at the Inter-American Development Bank, December.
INEGI. Instituto Nacional de Estadística, Geografía e Informática. Available at www.inegi.gob.mx/inegi/default.asp.
International Monetary Fund (IMF). 2004, *Staff Report for the 2004 Article IV Consultation,*Washington, DC, September. Available at www.imf.org/external/pubs/ft/scr/2004/cr04419.pdf.
———. 2003. *World Economic Outlook,* Chapter 3: "Public Debt in Emerging Markets: Is It Too High?" Washington, DC, September.
Mexico, Secretaría de Hacienda y Crédito Público (SHCP). 2003. "Informe sobre la situación económica, las finanzas públicas y la deuda pública." México. Available at www.shcp.gob.mxleofp/index.htm.
Ortiz, Guillermo. 2002. "Recent Emerging Market Crises—What Have We Learned?" Per Jacobsson Lecture, July 8, Basle, Switzerland.
Reinhart, Carmen, K.S. Rogoff, and M.A. Savastano. 2003. "Debt Intolerance." *Brookings Papers on Economic Activity,* no. 1. Also published as NBER Working Paper, No. 9908. Cambridge, MA: NBER.
Standard & Poor's. 2003. "Instituto Para la Protección al Ahorro Bancario" (December 12).
Wijnholds, J. Onno de Beaufort. 2003. "Five Financial Crises: Lessons for Prevention and Resolution." In *Ontwikkeling En Overheid* (Development and the Public Sector), ed. A.P. Ros and H.R.J. Vollebergh, pp. 5–17. The Hague: Sdu Publishers.
Zedillo, Ernesto. 1986. "Mexico's Recent Balance-of-Payments Experience and Prospects for Growth." *World Development* 14, no. 8 (August).

12

JORDY MICHELI THIRIÓN AND RUBÉN OLIVER ESPINOZA

Changing Patterns in Mexican Science and Technology Policy (1990–2003)

Still Far From Economic Development

Should a developing nation have a science and technology policy? And what should it be? As recently as twenty years ago, influential Mexican policymakers observed that there should be a division and specialization of labor in scientific activities, with rich countries investing in expensive basic research and developing nations investing in technologies that adapted basic research to their individual conditions. At the same time, there was limited support for science policy. In 1990, only 44 percent of Mexicans thought that scientific advances would help mankind; 50 percent thought so in 2000.

Micheli and Oliver write that the structural reforms in Mexico incrementally transformed science and technology policy as part of the general liberalization and structural reforms in the country's economy, linking it to research and development efforts that were expected to make the nation more competitive. During this period, Mexico adopted the recommendations of the Organization for Economic Cooperation and Development (OECD) for defining and measuring the national science and technology effort, creating a new science and technology (S&T) policy planning the supply of research, development, and innovation according to the needs for research and development (R&D) and innovation in the economy and society, designing new mechanisms to channel the results of these efforts to those who needed them, and for reorganizing the National Council of Science and Technology.

These efforts were made despite the economic crisis of 1994–1995 and the recession in 2001. Public expenditure for science and technology grew more than twice as rapidly as gross domestic product (GDP) growth, increasing from 0.28 percent of GDP in 1990 to 0.41 percent in 2000. By the year 2004 science and technology policy was supported by a new law designed to eliminate uncertainty about the continuation of S&T policy. The law declares that S&T is a state policy, meaning that it is mandatory. S&T policy now is conceived of as a system of science and technology made of stable agents with well-defined and monitored relationships.

Recent attempts to improve linkages between the public and private sectors in regard to S&T policy have had varied results. At the National Autonomous University of Mexico (UNAM), the change in outlook that arose from the linkages between the university and the private sector changed the structure of decision making and scope of employment at the university. These changes were resisted, and in 2000, the emphasis on linkages with the private sector was abandoned: groups of scientists had criticized the policy of linkages on the grounds that UNAM was becoming privatized. Instead, the university implemented a new policy that was dominated by these scientists: more resources for existing scientists and for the formation of human resources.

The continuing transformation of the Instituto Mexicano del Petróleo (IMP) into a "learning community" at the service of the oil industry, provides an opposite example of strategy about both institutional development and linkages with the private sector. In 2000 the IMP was recognized as a public research center and at the same time it adopted the civil service career employment system, which ensures long-term employment. In 2001, the IMP's functions were modified to permit them to grant M.A. and Ph.D. degrees in several fields. It also was allowed to market its goods and services and form strategic alliances with both profit and nonprofit entities.

These efforts are gradually having a positive effect. Although from 1990 to 2000, patenting requests made by Mexicans dropped by an annual average of 3.9 percent and patenting requests by foreigners grew 15.9 percent, scientific production (number of journal articles) grew by an average of 12 percent, accompanied by a 2.9 percent increase of the scientific work force. Micheli and Oliver believe that it is urgent to take a new step in S&T policy, employing fine-tuning approaches and strategies, and especially embracing the idea that innovation occurs in the firm—not in public R&D laboratories—and that therefore, the principal agent of a public policy technology is the enterprise, as is commonly accepted in the OECD countries.

The government of Vicente Fox has promoted a new science and technology policy (S&TP) that proposes an innovative institutional framework for that activity and consolidates some basic trends of a gradual change that took place during the nineties. This chapter provides a general and brief description of the main changes that characterize the new policy, and the most significant processes that preceded it.

From the early 1990s to 2003, under the presidencies of Carlos Salinas de Gortari, Ernesto Zedillo, and Vicente Fox, Mexico incrementally transformed science and technology policy as part of the general liberalization and structural reforms in the country's economy. Mexico needed these reforms because its semi-industrialized economy had been rapidly exposed to globalization (Alzati 1992; Micheli 1993). The nation had to become more efficient in order to compete in both domestic and international markets. It therefore modified its science and technology policy to link it to R&D efforts that were expected to make the nation more competitive. These efforts were made despite the economic crisis of 1994–1995 and the recession in 2000 (see Figure 12.1).

Figure 12.1 **Mexico S&T Public Expenditure in the Context of Macroeconomic Growth, 1991–2003** (billion pesos, year 2000 prices; annual rate of growth in percent)

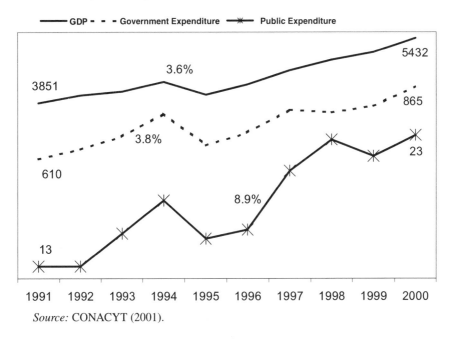

Source: CONACYT (2001).

During the nineties the public expenditure for activities defined as science and technology increased: its 8.9 percent annual growth between 1990 and 2000 exceeded that of gross domestic product growth (3.5 percent) and that of the total government expenditure itself (3.8 percent). By the year 2004, science and technology policy was seen as a public policy that was stronger than it had been in the past both because of this growth and because of the fact that it is supported by a new law (2002) that defines the functioning and responsibilities of the several S&T interconnected actors under a "system criterion." Otherwise, the law itself declares the policy in S&T as a state policy, meaning that it is mandatory.

The expected result is the elimination of uncertainty about the continuation of government attention to S&TP, which now is conceived of not as something amorphous and haphazard but as a system of science and technology made of stable agents with well-defined and monitored relationships. This is just a step toward promoting a national commitment to innovation, a concept that public authorities in the economic field have not yet embraced. As a result, it is often difficult for them to incorporate the mainstream thinking regarding science, that technological change and the world's economic sustained development are processes increasingly determined by innovative efforts (Edquist 2002).

The Transition of Science and Technology Policy:
Concepts and Budget

The efforts to transform Mexican S&TP started in the beginning of the 1990s (Micheli 1996) during the change in Mexico's political and economic orientation and structure. The import substitution model of development and of the Keynesian state was abandoned and replaced by a new discourse supporting the new policy of S&T mainly because of the overwhelming need to relate this policy to the current views of Mexico's needs. The swift incorporation of Mexico to the North American Free Trade Agreement (NAFTA) and the OECD highlighted the existence of enormous gaps between the technological-scientific effort and performance of Mexico and the other countries. This led to Mexico's adoption of new approaches and practices for the evaluation and management of science and technology. For example, the government implemented the OECD's "Frascati Manual," which contains the concepts and methodology for defining and measuring the national science and technology effort. This brought the first reorganization of S&T policy that was undertaken in the 1990–1994 National Program of Science and Technology pressuring public scientific and R&D institutions to establish links with enterprises and with the private sector in general.

In 1994, the OECD surveyed the scientific and technological system in Mexico. The two main recommendations were in the fields of the policy and the institutional structure. The first recommendation was to create a new S&T policy planning the supply of research according to the needs for R&D and innovation in the economy and society, and to design new mechanisms to channel the results of these efforts to those who needed them. The second recommendation was to reorganize the National Council of Science and Technology (Consejo Nacional de Ciencia y Tecnología–CONACYT) in order to cut the inefficiencies in his operation, and at the same time to place it at a superior and autonomous level in the government hierarchy.

These recommendations were not fully accomplished, but the authorities began to implement them. The OECD's *Survey on Mexico* for the year 2000 emphasized Mexico's low level in R&D and innovation mechanisms in comparison to other OECD nations. The survey underscored the weak participation of the business sector in R&D, and the low level of cooperation between this sector and universities and specialized centers. It concluded that an absence of human and financial resources as well as structural distortions hampered Mexico's transition to a knowledge-based economy.

The evaluating activity of the OECD encouraged the study of tendencies of the innovation systems and the policies applied to science and technology of other nations. A new generation of Mexican scholars added to the model of science that states that technology follows from science in a linear way. The new model is based on the idea that R&D and innovation in general are complex processes embedded in national institutional frameworks (Cimoli 2000).

Figure 12.2 **Human Resources and Scientific Production, 1990–2000**

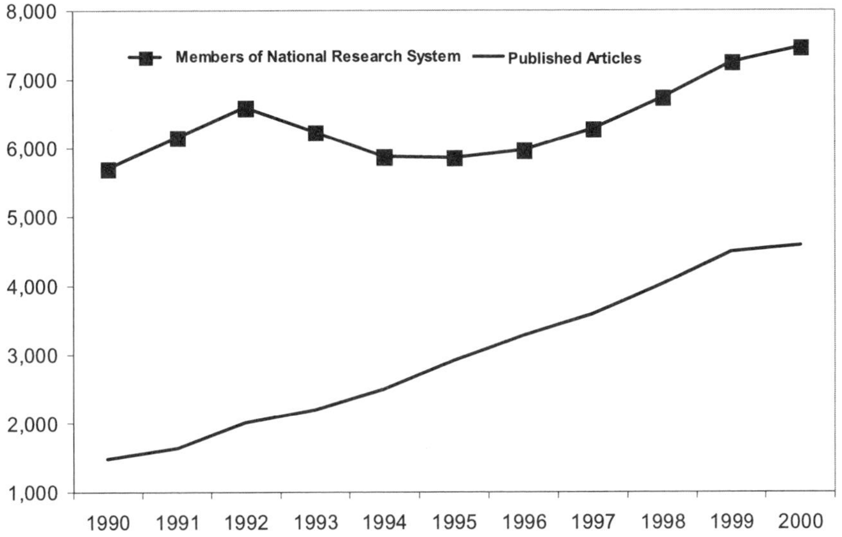

Source: CONACYT (2000).

The importance of S&T to many aspects of Mexican life is incorporated in the evolution of the budgetary structure of R&D during the 1990s. The federal expense on science and technology (FES&T) is the sum of the National Council of Science and Technology's budget and other particular budgets from the several government ministries that assign resources to science and technology, such as Energy, Health, and Agriculture. The FES&T represented on average 2.33 percent of the total public expense from 1990 to 2000, and 0.37 percent with respect to the national economy (GDP), growing from 1.74 percent of the total expense by the public sector and 0.28 percent of GDP in 1990 to 2.68 percent and 0.41 percent, respectively, in 2000. This sudden growth during the 1990s became a stable pattern from 2000 to 2003, that is, in President Fox's administration. Table 12.1 shows the panorama from 1990 to 2003 and illustrates both periods already mentioned (i.e., growth and stability).

In the same manner, the federal expense on science and technology breaks down into three major components: (1) 58 percent of the total went to experimental R&D, defined as creative and systematic labor oriented to knowledge increase in order to employ it in the search for new solutions to national problems; (2) 21.5 percent went to scientific and technological services, defined as the set of activities related to experimental R&D that contributes to generation, diffusion, and application of science and technology; for instance, services provided by museums, zoos, botanical gardens, among others; topographic, geological and hydrological research; oil and mineral resources discovery, and so

Table 12.1

S&T Federal Expenditure, 1990–2003

	1990	1995	1996	1997	1998	1999	2000	2001	2002	2003[a]
As percent of public sectors expenditures	0.28	0.35	0.35	0.42	0.46	0.41	0.42	0.41	0.41	0.42
GDP	1.74	2.23	2.19	2.53	2.96	2.64	2.68	2.56	2.42	2.53

Source: Mexico, Presidencia de la República (2003).
[a]Estimated.

on; and (3) 20.5 percent were the expenses on scientific and technological education, defined as the activities of technical education provided after junior high school and as far as college and graduate school and the systematic production of engineers and scientific human resources. Now, consider that R&D is the largest component of federal expense on S&T, but at the same time it had the slowest speed of growth during the 1990s. This is an important fact because this particular budgetary effort is more clearly conceived of as expenses oriented to innovation as a systematic process.

There was an important change in the pattern followed by the final destination expenditures on R&D because of the decrease of importance of the educational sector (53 percent to 27 percent in the period 1993–1999). Thus, R&D resources were reorganized: government research centers obtained the largest share of funds (35 percent to 45 percent), and to a lesser degree, the productive sector obtained them (11 percent to 28 percent).

Institutional Reengineering: The "National System of S&T"

During the next decade, the new authorities directing CONACYT generated institutional changes following the idea of a "national system of science and technology." They would seem to recognize, at least implicitly, that increasing the budgetary effort was not enough. It was also necessary to define the proper conditions for the budget to achieve the desired result by taking account not only of funds, but also of those who would use them: scientific organizations, professional associations, and regions gathered under a "system" criterion.

During the beginning of the present administration, the S&T institutional framework was reengineered, starting with promulgation of a new Science and Technology Law in 2002 that defined an array of actors and the rules for monitoring their effort and performance. This was accompanied by the creation of an independent budgetary "drawer" in 2003, which clusters the specific science and technology public resources. The total S&T budget in 2003 was 22,308.4 million pesos (about 2.03 billion dollars). S&T expenditures are distributed among several agencies. The structure of the S&T budget is 38.8 percent from CONACYT and 28.3 percent from the Ministry of Public Education. The residual 32.9 percent is shared among others ministries, mainly Energy, Agriculture, Health, Environment, and Economy (*Poder Ejecutivo Federal 2002*).

From the point of view of public administration capability, this opens a new epoch for CONACYT, creating the proper management and monitoring mechanisms that enable it to carry out its new role in the S&T system as defined by the law. The new Science and Technology Law is a branch of the Third Constitutional Article, which declares that science and technology, including public education, should be obligatory, supported and promoted by the state. The first articles establish the general purposes. The main goal is to create a framework for regulation, especially for channeling the financial resources to science and technology that is embedded in a structure or "national system of science and technology," as the law itself defines it. The science and technology policy should have several "strategic" goals: first, to enhance the S&T capabilities in order to solve "fundamental national problems"; second, to connect S&T activity to production; third, to develop strategic areas of knowledge; fourth, to decentralize S&T activity; fifth, to make S&T a part of the "society's general culture"; and, finally, to promote processes that enable the rational use of federal government resources. In sum, the new policy should follow objectives within education, culture, economy, federalism, and budgetary rationality.

According to these goals, the law defines a national system of science and technology based on government policy that takes account of the Special Program on Science and Technology, which is the particular strategy for the period ending in 2006. There are three main goals: to have a state policy, to increase the technological and scientific capacity of Mexico, and to increase innovation by firms and, consequently, their ability to compete. The special program is based on the regional programs from the federal states, the organizations, and specific actors that manage economic resources, the institutional actors that perform the research, and the set of norms that regulate the relationship among all these elements of the system.

The S&T law also creates a General Council of Scientific Research and Technological Development, Consejo General de Investigación Científica y Desarrollo Tecnologico, headed by the president of Mexico, nine ministers, and CONACYT's director. This General Council is in charge of the definition of state policy. The law defines the set of instances that permit the institutionalization of the tasks of the several actors that make decisions about scientific and technological research in Mexico. These include organizations and bodies that comprise the traditional "scientific community," the state governments, and the organizations located in an official record as apt to receive the public budget that CONACYT administers (see Box 12.1).

Illustrating the Transition in Two Representative Institutions

Establishing relations with the private sector has been a complex process for the diverse representative institutions that comprise the science and technology system. The most important transformation has been the shift in concept from emphasizing the supply of existing services by research centers to responding to client firms' requests for the development and execution of projects in which the clients define the economic value of the knowledge created by the research centers. This shift has broadened the range of services that can be offered, ranging from the provision of tests, measurements, and small innovations to assistance in disputes over ownership of innovations.

Simultaneously, during the 1990s, the discussion about how to create better links with the private sector encountered responses that indicated ignorance and mutual distrust between the universities, the science and technology system, and

Box 12.1

S&T Institutional Reengineering: Instruments and Actors

Institutional Body	Purpose	Actors
National Council for Scientific Research and Technological Development	To define the scientific and technology state policy	The republic president, nine ministries, the director of CONACYT, the president of the scientific and technological consulting forum plus four *ad honorem* members
Scientific and Technological Consulting Forum	Autonomous and permanent consulting body for the executive power and the CONACYT	The traditional institutional actors defined generally as the "scientific community"
Groups and Research Centers National Net	To actualize, at a micro level, efforts and actors of the scientific and technological policy	Groups and research centers voluntarily integrated to the net
Science and Technology National Conference	To coordinate CONACYT and the states governments	States governments
Scientific and Technological Institutions and Enterprises National Registration	CONACYT is responsible for the construction of a statistical apparatus about S&T activities	Any actor (center, enterprise, group, etc.) that wants to receive funds must be registered previously
Committee to Define the Application of the Firms Technological Development Fiscal Stimulus	To provide the rules for the application of a 30 percent stimulus in the general tax on revenues, for enterprises that have expenses on R&D	An intergovernmental committee, with CONACYT, economy, financing, and education ministries

the private sector. In this context, it generally has been large firms that have been able to establish better relations, because they have used a strategy of relying on the installed capacities of the universities to provided innovations that are marginal for the firms.

The common denominator in all of these situations has been the difficulty of maintaining both the increasing stimuli that are meant to be guaranteed by the public sector and are used to reward scientific production, and the business practices of negotiation, which yield uncertain results, used by the private sector.

At the National Autonomous University of Mexico (UNAM, Universidad

Nacional Autónoma de México), which is without doubt the most influential public university in the Mexican educational and political system, Casas and De Gortari (1997) found that the change in outlook that arose from the linkages between the university and the private sector gave rise to changes in the scope of the organization of academic employment, in traditional structures of university decision making, and in the employment of its economic resources. One of the most significant changes is the process of decentralization in which each dependency of the university defines its own means and programs and links with the private sector as a function of the traditional networks between researchers and external clients. Nonetheless, UNAM's actions "do not delineate [a] coordinated policy of linkages with the private sector" (p. 226).

As part of UNAM's attempt to adapt to the new context of science and technology policy, the university in 1997 created a structure designed to improve the relationship with the private sector. This group was headed by experts in developing these linkages, and the effort took place under the leadership of the rector, Francisco Barnés de Castro, with the aim of increasing the multiple capacities of the university's several academic departments and research institutes. However, in 1997 the new rector, Juan Ramón de la Fuente, had a different priority, which was the reestablishment of a climate of tranquility that had been broken by political conflicts within the university. Thus, in 2000, the emphasis on linkages with the private sector was abandoned amid criticism by groups of scientists that UNAM was becoming privatized. Instead, the university implemented a new policy that was dominated by these scientists: more resources for existing scientists and for the formation of human resources.

A contrasting example is the continuing organizational transformation of the Instituto Mexicano del Petróleo (IMP). The IMP was created in 1965 as a public decentralized organization with the objective of carrying out research and development of technology, providing technical services, training, and dissemination of its knowledge. During most if its existence, the IMP has functioned under the stewardship of PEMEX (Mexican national oil company); its operations were determined by PEMEX's needs, and IMP's business activities were subordinated to PEMEX's decisions. The initial vision of making IMP an organization that promoted technological development for PEMEX was limited because priority was given to providing technical services, and because for PEMEX, the need for new products and technologies has not been a priority item.

At the beginning of the 1990s, IMP was polarized between both pure research and research that was not related to the need for innovation. The IMP generated 546 patents between 1970 and 2000, however this activity was not reflected in a stream of innovations that flowed to the market and provided commercial options for the IMP.

The challenge was, then, to reconstitute the IMP as a profitable organization in regard to knowledge, research and development, services, and marketing of its services and patents. The IMP carried out an organizational transformation, defining itself as a "learning community" at the service of the oil industry, with the objective of "transforming knowledge into innovations for industry." (IMP 2002) In 2000 the IMP was recognized as a public research center according to the Law on Science and Technology, and at the same time it adopted the civil service career employment system that ensured long-term employment and, added to the awards and prizes of the scientific career system, provided a stimulus to employees to utilize all of their capacities within the IMP. In 2001, the IMP's functions were modified to permit the training of specialists in science, and chemical and petrochemical engineering, granting them M.A. and Ph.D. degrees. It also was allowed to market its goods and services and form strategic alliances with both profit and nonprofit entities.

It adopted "knowledge management" techniques, promoted a redefinition of its job categories in function of the competencies that they required, and formed flexible work groups that were oriented toward obtaining economic profits by "providing value added to its clients." The IMP's organizational program was punningly called ACEITE (oil, in Spanish), the acronym for Administración del Conocimiento e Inteligencia Tecnológica. It defined its catalogue of products, focusing on core competencies, and achieved International Standard Organization certifications of quality for its internal management processes. It encouraged the increase in the capabilities of both new and existing personnel, who numbered 5,400 people. Those with postgraduate degrees grew from 289 in 1997 to 762 in 2002. It established diverse strategic alliances with Battelle (1998), GX Technology (2001), and the Instituto Francés del Petróleo (2002). In 2002, the IMP billed $230 million dollars. However, the largest part of its business is still the sale of diverse technical services to PEMEX; exploration and production and the IMP's research and development potential are not manifested in an ability to competitively provide innovations. The transactions between the powerful PEMEX and the IMP are not likely to be arms' length transactions, and the transformation of the IMP into a commercially viable enterprise has yet to be demonstrated.

The cases of both UNAM and IMP illustrate the great difficulties encountered by Mexican public organizations when they attempt to adapt themselves to the new conditions imposed by the economy and by those that the new science and technology policy tried to incorporate during the 1990s and the first years of the twenty-first century.

Conclusion: The Challenge Remains the Same

Mexican S&T policy has been reengineered and transformed to the extent of being a mandatory public policy as defined by the Constitution. This represents a crucial point for the incremental innovations that this policy has performed since the early 1990s.

However, we have remarked that the amounts of funding destined for the activities of science and technology have grown in comparison to the economy as a whole. The underlying motivation for this institutional reengineering is to generate a series of rules of interaction among the several agents of science and technology in Mexico, looking for a quality criterion in the public S&T budget. The two main goals of the S&T budget are the production of high-standard knowledge and technological goods, and the upgrading of human capital for scientific and technological activities. It is interesting to compare that aspiration with some basic trends: first, according to the main purposes of the federal expenditure on S&T, from 1990 to 2000, the financing for the general advancement of science has remained basically as the largest designation, with about 50 percent of the budget; second, the production and conservation of energy has increased from 20 to 28 percent; and, third, industrial development grew from 5.5 percent to 10 percent of the S&T budget. In the same period, patenting requests made by Mexicans dropped by an annual average of 3.9 percent, while the patenting requests by foreigners grew 15.9 percent. Scientific production (number of journal articles) grew by an average of 12 percent, accompanied by a 2.9 percent increase of the scientific work force.

In the early 1990s, fresh ideas arrived for S&T policy: the market forces would transform the productive sector into a more competitive one, and the S&T sector should follow this process by transforming and creating the opportunities that enterprises could catch for business. However, time has passed and the apparatus for creating knowledge and transforming it into innovation is still far from the innovation activity as an economic force.

Mexican S&T policy is made and administered by the General Council of Scientific Research and Technological Development, described above. Nonetheless, although this authority maintains the general purpose of the S&TP, it does not recognize the tendencies and opportunities that could be present in specific sectors, building dynamic advantages with the support of S&T. In that sense, it is a policy far from the trajectories seen in the other OECD countries, which are carrying out high investment rates in S&T, but close to this economic effort, developing an analytical approach to defining strategic sectors or goals, strongly supporting small and medium enterprises, and upgrading financing mechanisms and in particular the aim of obtaining the commercial results of the innovative activities of the OECD (2002).

The outlook for Mexican science and technology policy is profoundly marked by the confused political panorama that began during the Fox presidency. In 2004, the PAN parliamentary group prepared an initiative for a new law devoted to promoting innovation and technological development. This is interesting because it suggests a novel preoccupation to the extent that it conceives a technology and innovation policy exclusively directed at firms. Its objectives are to promote and generate a significant increase in private investment in research and development, to create and impel the regional development of firms linked to scientific and basic technology, and to increase the national capacity to innovate. The proposed legislation focuses on the creation of a national public-private fund that generates several strategies to support firms' research and development activities. This initiative was suggested by a small group of entrepreneurs interested in the pickup of high-technology industry in the northern zone of Baja California (the cities of Tijuana, Ensenada, and Mexicali). This group was headed by technicians and politicians affiliated with PAN, who previously promoted the Prosoft Program (Programa Nacional de Software), managed by the Secretaría de Economía. Its goal is the substantial elevation of Mexico's ability to produce software.[1]

Public intervention in science and technology is increasingly characterized by political rivalries in Mexico. One can consider this as a manifestation of a new democratic spirit, but the risk is that those rivalries take the place of evaluation and strategic vision in guiding decisions, or lack thereof, as the last four years of experience have shown.

The challenge is still here: should S&T policy benefit from the new conditions and be an active agent in the forthcoming economic and social restructuring the country needs? Poverty, education, governance, energy, information, and the environment are the critical issues for the evolution of Mexico in the twenty-first century. As a state policy, future S&T public efforts have the opportunity to abandon the timid adherence to government budget limitations and to become a driving force for the needed transformation by a political and visionary leadership founded on knowledge and strategic thinking. Lamentably, in the past decade it is hard to find arguments to substantially neglect the validity of what was written in Micheli's 1996 article (p. 181): "There was a prevailing lack of scrutiny with regard to the policies needed in order to create national ability in technological innovation."

It becomes urgent to take a new step in S&TP, employing fine-tuning approaches and strategies, especially embracing the idea that innovation occurs in the firm—not in public R&D laboratories—and, therefore, the principal agent of a technology-oriented public policy is the enterprise, as is commonly accepted in other OECD countries.

Note

1. The PAN initiative regarding the proposed law collides with other political parties in the Chamber of Deputies; PRD, for example, considers this proposal as another step toward the privatization of science and technology, and therefore threatening UNAM's modus operandi (the PRD representatives in the Congress Commission of Education and Science and Technology are UNAM professors and their union leaders). In contrast, PRD prefers to provide aid to the production of science, under the assumption that this would strengthen Mexican technological development, and it believes that firms would obtain greater benefits from the creation of special subsidies for technological innovation without undertaking substantial revision of existing laws.

References

Alzati, Fausto. 1992. "Una política científica y tecnológica para la modernización." *Tecnoindustria.* México: CONACYT (November–December).
Casas, Rosalía, and Rebeca de Gortari. 1997. "La vinculación en la UNAM, hacia una nueva cultura académica basada en la empresarialidad." In *Gobierno, academia y empresas en México. Hacia una nueva configuración de relaciones,* ed. Rosalía Casas and Matilde Luna. México: Plaza y Valdés Editores.

Cimoli, Mario. 2000. *Developing Innovation Systems. Mexico in a Global Context.* London and New York: Continuum.

CONACYT (Consejo Nacional de Ciencia y Tecnología). 2000. *Informe general de actividades científicas y tecnológicas.* México: CONACYT.

———. 2001. *Indicadores de actividades científicas y tecnológicas.* México: CONACYT.

———. 2003. *Programa de trabajo institucional* México: CONACYT.

Edquist, Charles. 2002. "Innovation Policy in the System of Innovation Approach: Some Basic Principles." In *Knowledge Complexity and Innovation Systems,* ed. M.M. Fischer and J. Frölich. New York: Springer-Verlag. México: IMP.

IMP (Instituto Mexicano del Petróleo). 2002. *Principales líneas estratégicas* (documento). México: IMP.

Mexico, Presidencia de la República. 2003. *Anexo del Tercer Informe de Gobierno.*

Micheli, Jordy, ed. 1993. *Tecnología y modernización económica.* México: UAM Xochimilco, CONACYT.

———. 1996. "Technology Policy for a Weak Market." in *Changing Structure of Mexico,* ed. Laura Randall. Armonk, NY: M.E. Sharpe.

OECD (Organization for Economic Cooperation and Development). 2002. *Science, Technology and Industry Outlook.* OECD Publishing.

Poder Ejecutivo Federal. 2002. "Decreto de Presupuesto de egalsos de la Federación, 2003." *Diario oficial de la federación.* México, December 31.

III

Changes in Sectors

13

Antonio Yúnez-Naude and
Fernando Barceinas Paredes

The Reshaping of
Agricultural Policy in Mexico

Inefficient agriculture is a hallmark of poor nations. A major process in developing a nation is not necessarily reducing the share of agriculture in gross domestic product, but increasing the efficiency of agriculture without causing massive and abrupt increases in unemployment.

The Mexican government addressed the concern for efficiency in 1992 by making it possible to sell ejido *lands, which could not be sold between 1917 and 1992. It also facilitated trade, most notably by entering the NAFTA agreement in 1994. And it adopted some policies to provide a multiyear safety net for producers of basic grains and oilseeds in 1991 and in 1994. It also increasingly initiated programs to increase the capabilities and well-being of persons in the rural sector.*

The government has long viewed small properties, whether privately owned or owned as ejidos, as inefficient. The reasons for low yields, however, are in part the conditions faced by small producers and go beyond the inability to use their property as collateral, as was the case of ejido producers before the 1992 agrarian reform. Consequently, only 5 percent of ejidos were sold under the agrarian reform by 2001 because a large share of ejido land has low productive value except for nonagricultural uses. Change in land ownership did not provide a major explanation for structural change in agriculture from 1994 to 2002.

Yúnez-Naude and Barceinas state that in terms of the composition of crops, yields, imports, and prices faced by farmers, the rural-agricultural economy of Mexico was not structurally transformed by agrarian reform and the implementation of NAFTA. Instead, they state that the agricultural sector experienced year-to-year changes in production, trade, yields, and prices since the 1980s.

Agricultural employment fell from 26 million in 1980 to 22.6 million in 1990 to 15.8 million in 2000. The Fox government in 2002 promised, as had many earlier governments, to provide a level playing field for agriculture by giving Mexican farmers increased access to credit; subsidizing energy costs, which were higher than those in the United States and Canada, and creating a framework to face unfair competition from dumped imports.

Yúnez-Naude and Barceinas state that there is not yet a clear agreement between the political forces in Mexico about whether agricultural development can be achieved by agricultural policies alone, or whether broader development policies are needed to achieve economic and political goals in rural Mexico.

During the last two decades, Mexico has witnessed radical changes in public policies toward agriculture and the rural economies. We propose that rural-agricultural economy of Mexico was not structurally transformed by these reforms and the implementation of NAFTA (North American Free Trade Agreement); instead, this sector experienced year-to-year cumulative changes since the 1980s (the exception being the effects on agricultural exports and rural out-migrations caused mainly by the macroeconomic crisis of 1995–1996).

This chapter focuses on the crop component of Mexican agriculture. It is divided into three parts. In part one, below, we summarize major reforms and present the basic characteristics of Mexico's crop production. In part two we review the evolution of the agricultural and rural economies, confront these trends with the expected effects of liberalization policies, and propose answers to unpredicted trends.[1] We conclude the chapter by discussing the current situation of agricultural and rural policy reforms.

The Structure of Mexico's Rural Economy and Major Reforms

The Mexican agricultural sector has both entrepreneurial farmers and peasant or family producers. The latter are rural households making joint production and consumption decisions for staples; agriculture is just part of their income-earning activities. In general, peasant producers have limited land, do not have access to irrigation or to formal credit, and—due to poor communications and transport limitations—face high transaction costs in some markets. In contrast, entrepreneurial or commercial farmers operate in a context that enables them to make decisions in the same way as farmers in the developed world: their production is specialized, produced for a profit and for the market in a context of no or low transaction costs. Their stronger position in the Mexican economy and society makes it more likely that they will be able to influence the formation and obtain the benefit of government policies.

The heterogeneity of rural production in Mexico is reflected in the data of the 1990 Agricultural Census (no agricultural census was done in 2000): 59 percent of the 3.45 million of farmers producing crops had less than 5 hectares of land and 42.3 percent had limited property rights (they are *ejidatarios* and *comuneros,* the beneficiaries of land redistribution of the Mexican Revolution of last century); 48.5 percent of the 3.8 million agricultural units produce foodstuffs for their own consumption. The dual character of the agriculture of Mexico can also be approximated using data on yields, distinguishing production under irrigation from production under rain-fed conditions and taking into account that the former is a commercial activity whereas rain-fed lands are basically peasant lands (Table 13.1). For example, the yield of corn—the basic staple for human consumption in Mexico—under irrigation was 2.7 times higher with respect to yields on rain-fed lands during the first years of the 1990s and the difference rose to 3.2 times during NAFTA. (In the next section we discuss the evolution of national crop supply.)

Major Reforms

In order to modernize agriculture by transforming or eliminating inefficient producers unable to face competition in international markets, the Salinas government created new institutions and programs, privatized and eliminated state enterprises related to agriculture, and signed the 1994 North American Free Trade Agreement (NAFTA) with Canada and the United States (Table 13.2). Many of these initiatives were expected to reduce rural poverty and help farmers adjust to the new, less regulated and more open market structure. Critics of the government policy opposed its probable destruction of jobs and of rural traditions (Randall 1996).

The Ejidal Reform

The most widely known reform is the modification of property rights in 1991 by the reform of the *ejido* system of landholding under which land was distributed to peasants from the 1930s until the 1980s. Up to 1991, farms in Mexico were either privately owned or had limited property rights. The latter farms, known as ejidos, were created as a result of land redistribution following the Mexican Revolution of 1910. An ejido is formed by several small landholdings, each of which is assigned to a member of the ejido, although some of the ejidos also have common lands. Most of the members of the ejido are small farmers, and a high proportion of the ejidos' lands in Mexico are rain fed and dedicated to staple production. Prior to the ejidal reform, the ejidatarios were not allowed by law to sell or lease their lands, nor even to hire workers, although they did so.

The ejidal reform began to be implemented in 1992. It meant amendments to Article 27 of the Constitution of Mexico, and the main changes are the following:

- An end to the government's constitutional obligation to distribute land to the landless.
- An end of expropriation of private lands.
- Land rights disputes among ejidatarios or between ejidatarios and private landholders will be settled by decentralized, autonomous agrarian tribunals and not by the Ministry of Agrarian Reform.

Table 13.1

Mexico: Evolution and Structure of Crop Production, 1983–2003[a]

Product	Period	Production (thousand of metric tons)			Cultivated area (thousand of hectares)			Yields (tons/cultivated hectares)		
		Total	Irrigated	Rainfed	Total	Irrigated	Rainfed	Total	Irrigated	Rainfed
Crops for the domestic market										
Corn	1983–90	12,472	2,932	9,540	8,076	994	7,082	1.54	2.95	1.35
	1991–94	16,885	6,488	10,397	8,294	1,553	6,741	2.04	4.18	1.54
	1995–96	18,189	5,997	12,192	8,859	1,343	7,516	2.05	4.46	1.62
	1997–00	17,844	5,957	11,886	8,649	1,175	7,474	2.06	5.07	1.59
	2001–03	19,846	6,661	13,055	8,285	1,121	7,213	2.40	5.94	1.81
Other[b]	1983–90	13,574	8,835	4,739	5,985	2,113	3,872	2.27	4.18	1.22
	1991–94	11,889	7,578	4,311	5,128	1,737	3,391	2.32	4.36	1.27
	1995–96	12,987	7,263	5,724	5,666	1,454	4,212	2.29	4.99	1.36
	1997–00	14,528	8,225	6,303	5,841	1,425	4,416	2.49	5.77	1.43
	2001–03	15,628	8,139	6,958	5,507	1,332	4,203	2.84	6.11	1.66
Vegetables[c]										
Tomatoes	1983–90	1,759			76			23.06		
	1991–94	1,584			80			19.73		
	1995–96	1,942			74			26.18		
	1997–00	1,940			72			26.97		
	2001–03	1,964			69			28.64		
Other	1983–90	1,202			85			14.09		
	1991–94	1,480			100			14.78		
	1995–96	1,486			93			15.98		
	1997–00	2,111			121			17.39		
	2001–03	2,321			122			19.07		

Fruits[d]

Traditional									
1983–90	1,458	1,235	223	145	117	29	10.04	10.58	7.83
1991–94	1,525	1,305	220	135	105	29	11.33	12.40	7.49
1995–96	1,525	1,341	184	116	95	22	13.12	14.18	8.49
1997–00	2,010	1,795	215	120	99	21	16.77	18.17	10.18
2001–03	1,662	1,664	250	105	89	21	17.45	18.68	12.14
Tropical									
1983–90	2,241	976	1,265	236	107	129	9.50	9.12	9.82
1991–94	2,454	1,115	1,340	267	118	149	9.20	9.48	8.97
1995–96	2,722	1,251	1,472	279	123	156	9.75	10.14	9.45
1997–00	2,847	1,318	1,528	284	127	157	10.02	10.35	9.75
2001–03	1,400	763	926	204	75	70	6.87	10.20	13.18
Citrus									
1983–90	2,776	941	1,835	292	106	186	9.50	8.85	9.87
1991–94	3,512	1,219	2,293	371	134	237	9.48	9.10	9.69
1995–96	4,357	1,856	2,501	406	154	252	10.74	12.04	9.94
1997–00	3,919	1,966	1,954	365	159	206	10.75	12.36	9.50
2001–03	3,329	1,857	2,055	397	145	203	8.38	12.84	10.11

Sources: Mexico, Ministry of Agriculture (n.d.) Databases (SAGARPA-SIACON) and "Anuario estadístico de la producción agrícola 1999–2002."

[a] The data for irrigated and rain-fed lands are for the period of 2001–2002.

[b] barley, beans, sorghum, soybeans and wheat.

[c] More than 90 percent of production is under irrigation (89 percent for tomatoes). Total includes: asparagus, broccoli, carrots, cauliflower, cucumbers, garlic and onions. Peppers are not included because of reclasifications during the period that do not allow comparisons.

[d] Traditional: grapes, melons, strawberries and watermelons; Tropical: guavas, mangos, and papayas (includes avocados); Citrus: lemons and oranges.

Table 13.2

Policy Reforms and New Institutions for Agriculture and the Rural Economy of Mexico, 1985–2003

Policy	Description	Years
Mexico joins GATT	By 1990–91, most licenses to import agricultural products were abolished. In 1991–94 most agricultural commodities were subject to tariffs fluctuating between 0 and 20 percent	1986–94
Institutional reforms and the government's new role	Privatization of state companies: seed and production of fertilizer, grain storage and marketing of coffee, sugar and tobacco ASERCA (1991) was created to give marketing support and services to producers	From 1988–99
Reform of the Agrarian Law	Land redistribution ends Recognizes the individual rights of each ejido	1992
North American Free Trade Agreement (NAFTA), two separate agricultural agreements: Mexico-Canada and Mexico-United States	Defines which are the obligatory conditions for market access and for export subsidies Each country has the right to choose its own internal subsidies, phytosanitary measures, rules of origin and regulations for packing and tagging products. Consistency with the World Trade Organization and with the Uruguay Round Import and export licenses are abolished and substituted by tarification In January 2008 all tariffs will be eliminated by NAFTA members	1994
PROCAMPO (Program of Direct Support for the Countryside), part of ASERCA	Direct payments to the producers of basic crops that compensate producers for the loss of input subsidies, price supports and import protection Grants annual direct payments per hectare to those producers who continue to produce, based on historical acreage for nine crops	Winter 1993–94

Elimination of producer price supports, abolition of CONASUPO	In 1991 guaranteed prices for wheat, sorghum, soy beans, rice, barley, safflower, sesame seed and sunflower were eliminated, and in 1999 support prices for beans and corn producers were abolished	1991–99
Creation of the Ministry for Social Development	PROGRESA: monetary transfers to poor rural female household heads for nutrition, school and health services (from 2001 the program is extended and called OPORTUNIDADES)	1991
Alliance for the Countryside (Alianza para el Campo)	A set of programs designed to support farmers with productive potential in an open economy	1995
	Federalized. Each state is responsible for the application of Alliance's programs Farmers in the programs have to contribute to its financing	
Agri-food Armour	To protect Mexican farmers from impacts of U.S. Farm Bill of 2002	2002
Privatization of rural credit	Reduction of official credit and credit subsidies. Creation of Financiera Rural and abolishion of BANRURAL	1991–2003
National Accord for the Countryside	An agreement between the Fox Administration and farmer and peasant organizations to define policies for rural development	2003

- Ejidatarios can obtain individual certificates of title to their land parcels if the ejido has agreed to participate in the PROCEDE (Program for the Certification of Ejido Land Rights and the Titling of Urban House Plots). Once certified, ejidatarios have the right to legally sell, rent, sharecrop, or mortgage their land as collateral for loans.
- Ejidatarios will no longer be required to work their ejido parcels personally, whatever they decide to do with them; they can enter into joint ventures with investors (individuals and/or private companies), or they can form associations among themselves to increase the size of the productive unit and maximize economies of scale.
- The government will continue to enforce legal limits on maximum property size to prevent excessive concentration of privatized ejido land.
- Opening of the ejido sector to foreign direct investment, and elimination of the prohibition against formation of production associations between foreign private investors and ejidatarios (Randall 1996; and Saldívar in press).

The amendment of Article 27 of the Mexican Constitution seeks to give security to those who own land, to enhance well-defined property rights for this asset and, along with the latter, to develop the land market. One expected consequence of the ejidal reform is to drastically reduce the number of small farmers engaged in agricultural production (Cornelius and Myhre 1998).

The new legal framework has been implemented by the creation of the Agrarian Attorney General and by PROCEDE. PROCEDE has been implemented since 1992 to measure, map, and issue certificates of use for ejido land. PROCEDE is intended to confirm ejidatarios' patrimonial holdings and to make it easier for them to enter into joint ventures, borrow money, and carry out other legal transactions. The Salinas administration maintained that PROCEDE would conclude its work in a couple of years. By 2002, 76 percent of ejidal lands had been certified, and the process of certification is still under way after more than ten years of the ejidal reform because in order to assess ownership rights, PROCEDE has to confirm the boundaries of ejidos and of individual parcels, resolve internal disputes, and distribute titles. This has given new life to disputes about boundaries, the rightful ownership of land that has been illegally used for loan collateral (Saldívar in press), the inheritance rights of non-ejidatario women or children, and conflicts with absentee ejidatarios.

Once a person's land is certificated, it can be transferred to someone else within the family or within the ejido through a sale. Then the certificate can be converted to a private property title by requesting that the entire ejido assemble and vote for majority approval. If permission is granted and a title issued, the proprietor of the land has a "complete right" to the land (*derecho pleno*) and can then sell it to anyone as private property and it would pass outside the ejido (Saldívar in press). As of 2002, only 3.86 percent of the ejidal lands had derecho pleno (Secretaría de la Reforma Agraria 2003), but leasing out of ejidal lands has increased since the reform. According to the 1997 National Ejido survey, from 1994 to 1997 there was a 19 percent increase in rental transactions by ejidatarios. By 1999, 51.4 percent of rural territory was still under ejido regime and just 5 percent of ejidatarios had sold their land (Appendini 2001).

Jones and Ward (1998) argue that changes in ownership patterns have been much more modest than the expected impacts of ejidal reform not only because of the slow pace of land titling, but also because except in urban and suburban ejidos, where the land is coveted by private real estate developers, and in profitable irrigated land, ejido land has low productive value: fewer people than anticipated wish to purchase it.

Abolition of Producer Price Supports and the Creation of
New Institutions and Programs

One major player in government intervention in agriculture was the National Company of Popular Subsistences (CONASUPO—Compañía Nacioncal de Subsistencias Populares). Since its creation in the mid-1960s, CONASUPO was fundamental in Mexican agricultural policies, shaping food production, storage, consumption, and rural incomes. Before the reforms, the company's programs involved eleven agricultural field crops (termed basic crops): barley, beans, copra, corn, cotton, rice, sesame, sorghum, soybeans, sunflower, and wheat. By supporting prices for the producers of these crops, by processing, storing, and distributing these crops, and by regulating their trade through direct imports, CONASUPO exerted control over an important component of Mexico's food chain.

President Miguel de la Madrid (1982–1988) began the elimination of CONASUPO and by 1995–1996, most CONASUPO subsidiaries and financial activities were dismantled, privatized, or transferred to farmers; by 1999, the liquidation of CONASUPO was practically complete (Yúnez-Naude 2003).

In 1991, an agricultural marketing agency, Support Services for Agricultural Marketing (ASERCA, Apoyos y Servicios a la Comercialización Agropecuaria), was created, independent of CONASUPO but part of the Agricultural Ministry (SAGARPA—acronym for the Mexican Secretariat of Agriculture, Livestock, Rural Development, Fisheries and Food Products). ASERCA was a key element in the process of eliminating CONASUPO interventions in the markets for the eleven crops that were under the company's control. The functions of ASERCA have been directed toward marketing supports for grain and oilseeds for designated regions, assistance in negotiating contracts between producers and purchasers, stimulation of contracts to cover the risk of price changes, provision of information about markets, and promotion of exports. ASERCA does not buy or store agricultural commodities, as CONASUPO did. ASERCA is also in charge of a program of direct income transfers to farmers and called PROCAMPO (Program for Direct Support to the Countryside, or Programa de Apoyos Directos al Campo) (SAGARPA 2000).

In practice, ASERCA gives marketing supports to commercial producers of basic crops in surplus regions. This is the case of the northern Mexico surplus-producing states, which in 2002 received 89 percent of the marketing assistance budget. Producers of corn in the state of Sinaloa, sorghum in the state of Tamaulipas, and wheat in the state of Sonora have received especially large shares of these funds (see de Ita 2003 for the case of corn in Sinaloa). Until the spring–summer season of 2000 the government and commercial producers from surplus regions negotiated a certain price. Then, in a public bid, interested buyers asked for a subsidy in order to commit themselves to buying a certain amount of the crop in question at the negotiated price. Hence, marketing supports of ASERCA are not decoupled from production and they could have helped to maintain or even promote the commercial production of these crops, notwithstanding competition from the United States allowed by NAFTA.

A major reform in Mexican state intervention in staple production was implemented parallel to the creation of ASERCA. It consisted of the elimination of guaranteed prices that CONASUPO had traditionally awarded to the producers of basic crops, so that from 1991 to 1999, price interventions by CONASUPO were limited to beans and corn, and in 2001 subsidies for tortillas were eliminated.

Some months before NAFTA was signed, the income support program for all farmers producing basic crops (PROCAMPO) was implemented. The program is decoupled from production since the transfer is based on cultivated area with basic crops and its amount is independent of yields (in pesos of 2003 and using a conversion of 10 pesos per U.S. dollar (USD), the transfers have been around 100 USD per hectare). PROCAMPO is planned to last until 2008 when full liberalization under NAFTA will be reached, and its main objective is to facilitate producers' transition from price supports for basic crops to a food economy open to foreign competition. Each year payments are made to around 3 million producers who work approximately 14 million hectares of land (Knuston and Ochoa 2003).

In addition to ASERCA and PROCAMPO, the Zedillo administration created Alliance for the Countryside (Alianza para el Campo) in 1995. Alliance's main objective is to increase agricultural productivity and to capitalize farmers and to encourage sanitary projects to integrate farmers into commercial food production. A major purpose of Alliance is to enhance farming efficiency and to promote substitution of fruits and vegetables for basic crops in cases in which farmers have a potential comparative advantage in producing such crops in the context of an open economy. Alliance has a decentralized character, with state-level control of its programs and contributions to the funding by participating farmers.

Trends in Rural Credit

Rural credit is another subject of policy reforms. The Salinas administration decided to sharply reduce official credit subsidization, with the expectation that private credit institutions would fill the credit requirements of Mexican farmers.

Notwithstanding this, the two main official rural credit institutions—BANRURAL (Rural Bank) and FIRA (Fideicomiso Relacionado con la Agricultura)—were not abolished, and in 2003 the Fox administration replaced BANRURAL with Financiera Rural (Rural Financing, a government bank) in an effort to increase rural credit and to avoid the persistent high rates of default of credits granted by BANRURAL, whose assets/liabilities were taken over by Financiera Rural.

Credit subsidies and official credit coverage for working capital given to farmers by public financial institutions for rural development declined sharply during the nineties. In the 1980s and before the deepening of the reforms, the government granted credit subsidies to farmers and provided 55 percent of total credit given to the agricultural sector. Since 1990, government credit has been sharply reduced, and private credit increased to more than 73 percent of the total during the 1990s (Yúnez-Naude and Barceinas 2002). In addition, the proportion of agricultural credit in total credit granted in Mexico has been declining—from 5.9 percent in 1994 to 2.8 percent in 2002 (Puyana and Romero 2004)—and rural banking in Mexico is imperfect and segmented; the limited supply trends indicate that the banking crisis of 1994–1995 was a major factor impeding the increase of private credit to agriculture that was expected to accompany the economic and ejidal reforms.

PROCAMPO and Alliance for the Countryside supports of commercial farmers were used as substitutes for credit, and credit restrictions may have limited the option that liberalization provided to farmers to change their production to competitive crops under the reforms and NAFTA. Both domestic investment in agriculture and U.S. investment in Mexico's field crops remained low (Bolding, Calderon, and Handy 1999; Casco and Rosensweig 2000).

Agricultural Trade Liberalization

The first step the Mexican government took toward trade liberalization was to join the General Agreement on Tariffs and Trade, or GATT, in 1986: by 1990–1991, most licenses to import agricultural products were abolished, and in 1991–1994 most agricultural commodities were under a tariff regime. NAFTA began implementation in January 1994. For the agricultural sector, two separate agreements were negotiated: one between Mexico and Canada, and the other between Mexico and the United States of America.

Under NAFTA, trade in some agricultural commodities was liberalized in January 1994; others—considered as sensitive by the signing governments— were subject to a process of year-to-year liberalization, so that full free trade was reached in January 2003 for barley and will be attained in January 2008 for beans, corn, and powdered milk. Mexico imposed tariff rate quotas for the imports of barley, dry edible beans, corn, and powdered milk, whereas the United States included seasonal tariffs as well as tariff rate quotas for several fresh vegetables and fruits imported from Mexico. Beginning in 1995, quota levels grew and above-quota tariffs were reduced until they reached free trade in January

2003 for barley and will reach it for the other commodities in January 2008 (Yúnez-Naude and Barceinas 2002).

NAFTA does not imply specific commitments with regard to domestic marketing support reductions or export subsidies; it includes dispute settlement mechanisms in its Chapters 19 and 20 that establish binational panels to review anti-dumping and countervailing (AD/CVD) actions between two countries when requested by an involved party. The role of these binational panels is limited to determining whether a country appropriately follows its own national AD/CVD laws in making a particular determination. National AD/CVD laws of the United States were not changed, and Mexico adapted these laws to be in accordance with its trade liberalization policies. Although national AD/CVD laws cannot be questioned by the review panels, the process provides an alternative to having national courts handle appeals of AD/CVD decisions. This provides the possibility of greater impartiality of the review (Leycegi and Ruiz Cornejo 2002; Perry et al. 2003).

Social Programs That Affect the Rural Poor

Parallel to the process of economic liberalization of the rural economy, specific policies to aid the rural poor were created. The first one was the National Solidarity Program (Programa de Solidaridad Nacional, PRONASOL), founded in 1988, followed by the creation of the Ministry for Social Development (SEDESOL) in early 1990s. The Salinas government decentralized the administration of these policies during 1992 to 1994, and President Ernesto Zedillo initiated a major change in the social development programs in 1997 with the creation of PROGRESA (Program for [rural] Education, Health, and Nutrition).

PROGRESA's objective was to contribute to human capital formation, focusing on the poorest rural families, by providing transfers in money and in kind to poor rural female household heads if they sent their children to school, took care of their nutrition, and brought them to health centers on a regular basis.

In the National Program for Social Development (2001–2006), the administration of President Vicente Fox adopted the concept of human development from United Nations Development Program (PNUD) and calls its social strategy CONTIGO. CONTIGO puts together governmental efforts aimed at enhancing human development: promoting the capacities of the people (education, health, and nutrition); generating income opportunities (infrastructure, credit, and employment); helping to form assets (housing, savings and property titles); and social protection (insurance, social security, and attention to collective risks). CONTIGO extends the objectives of the previous administrations by expanding the activities of PROGRESA (now called OPORTUNIDADES) to the urban sector (UN Program for Development 2003). (See chapter 29 in this book.)

The economic crisis of 1995–1996 worsened the condition of Mexico's poor. By 2002, however, they had regained the conditions of 1992. Rural poverty has generally been worse than urban poverty. This can be seen by using SEDESOL's three poverty lines: a "food-based" poverty line (income required to acquire enough food to cover nutritional needs); a "capabilities" poverty line, which also includes the income required to acquire basic education, health, housing, dress, footwear, and transportation; and an "assets-based" poverty line, which also includes other needs. Table 13.3 shows that in 1992 almost 30 percent of rural households were under food-based poverty (35.6 percent of individuals); if we add poverty in capabilities the incidence rises to 35 percent of households (42 percent of individuals); and if we include poverty in assets the percentage increases to 57 percent (65 percent). Rural poverty increased in 1994 and even more in 1996 (for example, taking the three poverty lines together, in 1994, 64 percent of rural households were poor; in 1996, 73 percent). Rural (and urban) poverty began to decrease in 1998, and in 2002 rural poverty was at the levels of 1992.

Evolution of the Rural Sector: 1980–2002/3

The basic economic reasoning behind the expected effects of liberalization policies is that they affect costs, prices, and profits, leading to changes in resource allocation of the country in question and therefore to structural transformation in trade and national supply. The trade liberalization in North America was expected to lead to a decrease in the prices of goods that Mexico imported at the same time that the Mexican government removed its price supports of crops, forcing Mexican producers of products that could be imported to compete with farmers in Canada and the United States. Greater competition will increase productivity and/or reduce Mexico's supply of these crops and its farmers would tend to replace their production of goods that can be imported with those that can be exported, causing an increase in the supply of the latter.

The above implies that NAFTA and internal policy reforms were expected to provoke considerable growth in agricultural trade in North America (for the Mexican case, this would be especially so with the United States). It was also predicted that employment created by increasing the production of goods that could be exported would be insufficient to absorb the displaced workers from the farms that produced goods that could be imported, leading to a rise in rural out-migration. For example, Mexico's former undersecretary of Agriculture, Luis Tellez, predicted that about one-half of the Mexican rural population—around 16 million people—will be forced to move "within a decade or two" (*New York Times,* November 27, 1991). These projections assumed macroeconomic stability, a condition that the Mexican economy did not have from the end of 1994 to 1996 (Audley et al. 2003).

According to predictions, the prices of Mexican crops that are bought in international trade in constant 1994 pesos have followed U.S. prices and have diminished (Table 13.4). However, we found no structural change in this relationship during the reforms and NAFTA. Our findings also indicate that convergence be-

Table 13.3

Mexico: Poor Households and Individuals Under Poverty, 1992–2002 (in percent)

	1992			1994			1996		
	Urban	Rural	National	Urban	Rural	National	Urban	Rural	National
Households									
Food based poverty	10.2	29.5	17.4	7.2	30.0	16.1	20.1	43.3	28.8
Poverty in capabilities[a]	14.0	34.8	21.8	12.8	38.1	22.7	27.7	51.3	36.5
Poverty in assets[b]	36.5	56.7	44.1	35.6	64.2	46.8	53.2	73.4	60.8
Individuals									
Food based poverty	13.5	35.6	22.5	9.7	36.8	21.1	26.5	52.4	37.1
Poverty in capabilities	18.4	41.8	28.0	17.1	46.2	29.4	35.0	60.2	45.3
Poverty in assets	44.0	65.0	52.6	43.6	72.0	55.6	61.9	80.8	69.6

	1998			2000			2002		
	Urban	Rural	National	Urban	Rural	National	Urban	Rural	National
Households									
Food based poverty	16.4	43.8	26.8	9.8	34.1	18.6	8.5	28.5	15.8
Poverty in capabilities[a]	22.8	49.3	32.9	16.2	41.4	25.3	12.2	36.5	21.1
Poverty in assets[b]	47.7	68.6	55.6	37.4	60.7	45.9	35.4	59.4	44.1
Individuals									
Food based poverty	21.3	52.1	33.9	12.6	42.4	24.2	11.4	34.8	20.3
Poverty in capabilities	29.0	57.6	40.7	20.2	50.0	31.9	16.0	43.8	26.5
Poverty in assets	55.8	74.9	63.9	43.8	69.3	53.7	42.0	67.5	51.7

Source: SEDESOL Web site: www.sedesol.gob.mx.

aIncludes food-based poverty.

bIncludes poverty in capabilities and food-based poverty.

Table 13.4

Mexico: Evolution of Producer Prices of Major Basic Crops, 1980–2001[a]
(1994 pesos)

Year	Barley (grain)	Corn	Sorghum (grain)	Soybeans	Wheat	Palay rice
1980	946	1,257	1,122	1,926	914	1,472
1981	1,080	1,343	992	2,112	928	1,227
1982	963	1,189	890	1,883	847	1,196
1983	1,047	1,140	1,087	1,998	856	1,339
1984	1,138	1,245	1,710	2,155	931	1,379
1985	1,130	1,229	1,006	2,012	869	1,371
1986	1,254	1,171	760	2,094	750	1,279
1987	1,024	1,341	768	2,638	710	1,330
1988	858	943	746	2,049	783	1,002
1989	935	986	714	2,023	819	1,057
1990	935	1,014	783	1,357	844	908
1991	860	959	833	1,719	795	828
1992	816	894	1,038	1,200	722	666
1993	746	821	866	1,064	658	582
1994	679	656	1,205	857	611	688
1995	743	809	661	1,092	669	790
1996	783	791	881	1,172	978	891
1997	630	619	554	1,018	597	693
1998	569	570	739	901	541	647
1999	487	492	766	833	463	600
2000	458	468	644	557	454	453
2001	473	440	1,006	536	357	430

Source: Mexico, Ministry of Agriculture (n.d.).
[a]Deflated by the National Consumer Price Index or INPC.

tween Mexican and U.S. prices of these crops was present before and during NAFTA. However, the adjustment of these two sets of prices takes a long time (at least twenty months), and furthermore, the periods of convergence have not decreased during NAFTA (see Yúnez-Naude and Barceinas 2004).

As expected, the volume of production of major exported vegetables and fruits has grown continuously since the early nineties (see Table 13.1). This is explained by an increase of both total area planted and yields for each of the major exported crops.

What is striking is that, in contrast with the predictions, national production of the most imported and important basic crops grown in Mexico (barley, beans, corn, sorghum, soybeans, and wheat) also increased throughout the deepening of internal reforms and NAFTA during the 1990s and the first years of the twenty-first century. This is explained by a continued increase in yields obtained in the production of these crops. For example, during the period of 2001–2003 the production of the six basic crops under consideration was 36 percent higher than in

1983–1990, yields increased 21 percent, and the cultivated area remained practically the same. Yields on irrigated land were greater than those obtained on rain-fed lands, and this difference has deepened since the second half of the 1990s: in 1983–1990 and 1991–1994 average metric tons per hectare of the studied six basic crops under irrigation were 2.9 higher than yields obtained under rain-fed conditions, and the relation increased to more than 3.4 times since 1997.

The supply from irrigated lands increased sharply during 1991–1994 with respect to the previous eight-year period (19.5 percent), but it remained around 14 million metric tons from 1995 to 2003. Parallel to this, cultivated area decreased by more than 20 percent, meaning that yields increased for crops produced under irrigation. Production under rain-fed conditions had a different trend, since it has grown during the whole period under study: average production of crops during 2001–2003 was 40 percent higher than in 1983–1990 as a result of both an increase in planted area and in yields. Another difference is that whereas production and cultivated area under irrigation declined during the macroeconomic crisis of 1995–1996 with respect to the previous four-year period (–5.7 percent and –15 percent respectively), supply and cultivated area in rain-fed lands increased during the same period (21.8 percent and 15.7 percent). These contrasts suggest a different reaction of farmers producing basic crops, depending on the access they have to water (a question that is discussed subsequently, with special reference to corn).

Corn has remained the major crop produced in Mexico: during 1983–1990 it accounted for almost 48 percent of total supply of the six major basic crops and 57 percent of the area cultivated with these crops. After a sharp rise of corn supply and cultivated area under irrigated lands during 1991–1994 (121 percent and 56 percent with respect to 1983–1990), production and cultivated area under irrigation have remained practically the same since 1995–1996 and up to 2001–2002. As for rain-fed corn, cultivated area during the period of reforms and NAFTA has remained similar with respect to 1983–1990, whereas production grew during the macroeconomic crisis of the mid-1990s and during 2001–2003 (one purpose of the next section is to propose hypotheses pertaining to these unpredicted trends).

Similar trends are observed when considering separately each of the six basic crops, although soybean production suffered from a disease in 1995. Barley production grew, especially under rain-fed conditions, but wheat production, which is usually produced under irrigation, fell (Yúnez-Naude and Barceinas 2002.)

Cultivated Area and Yields

Based on the fact that agricultural production is the result of cultivated area and yields, we applied an econometric test (a Chow test) to study empirically whether or not structural change in these two latter variables and for major exported and imported crops took place beginning with NAFTA implementation. The period covered is from 1980 to 2002. Our results show that of the eight major exported vegetables, only tomatoes and broccoli experienced structural change in cultivated area: tomatoes showed a statistically significant decrease in production, whereas broccoli had a significant rise in output and in yields. For the case of fruits we could only apply the test to melons and watermelons. Both underwent a positive structural change in yields, but not in planted area.

The only basic crop that experienced a structural change in cultivated area was sorghum produced in rain-fed lands. The total cultivated area planted with this grain (i.e., when irrigated sorghum is included) increased significantly. Barley produced under irrigation is the only basic crop whose yields increased significantly, in contrast to the significant fall in yields for soybeans.

The above econometric evidence does not contradict previous observations on tendencies in the production of major exported and imported crops. Furthermore, they suggest that, overall, no structural change has been present in the field crop subsector of Mexico after more than ten years of reforms and NAFTA.

In addition to the above trends, labor productivity in crop production—measured by value added divided by employment—has increased continuously from late 1980s to 2001. Agricultural real wages have experienced a different evolution: they decreased from 1980 to 1997 (especially during the macroeconomic crisis of 1995–1996) and had a slight increase from 1997 to 2001 (Puyana and Romero 2004).

Agricultural Trade

The participation of trade in the agricultural supply of Mexico has increased considerably: from an average of 19.7 percent during 1991–1994, to around 35 percent from 1997 to 2002 (this share jumped to almost 40 percent during the macroeconomic crisis of 1995–1996). Agricultural trade between Mexico and the United States has also increased beginning with NAFTA, especially since 1997. During this period the value of imports at constant U.S. dollars has grown faster than that of exports, and the agricultural trade deficit of Mexico with the United States has increased (Yúnez-Naude and Barceinas 2002).

As expected, the volume of Mexican exports of major fresh vegetables and fruits has grown considerably during NAFTA; for vegetables by 80 percent during NAFTA with respect to 1991–1993 and by 90 percent for fruits. The volume of imports of the six major basic crops has grown even faster than Mexican exports of fruits and vegetables: it doubled from 1994 to 2001 with respect to 1991–1993 (Table 13.5).

Taken together, the volume of imports of barley, beans, corn, sorghum, soybeans, and wheat accounted for 27.5 percent of Mexico's production during 1983–1990, for 29.8 percent in the following four-year period, for 34.7 percent during 1995–1996, and for almost 50 percent from 1997 to 2003 (since Mexican exports of these crops is almost nil, the figures approximate to Mexico's consumption of these crops).

Increasing food imports were expected to happen with internal liberalization and NAFTA, but they are currently the basis of concerns about food self-sufficiency in Mexico. Of particular interest is the case of corn because of the controversy

Table 13.5

Mexico: Evolution of Trade of Major Exported and Imported Crops, 1983–2001
(thousands of metric tons)

Period	Exports		Imports		
	Vegetables[a]	Fruits[b]	Basic crops[c]	Corn	Total
1983–1990	931	382	3,998	3,160	7,157
1991–1993	1,020	545	7,050	979	8,029
1994–2001	1,835	1,036	10,962	5,223	16,185

Source: United Nations Food and Agriculture Organizatiion (FAO) Web site.
[a]Asparagus, cauliflower, carrots, cucumbers, eggplants, garlic, onions, peppers, tomatoes, and spinach.
[b]Avocados, cantaloupe, citrus (limes, lemons, and oranges), mangoes and guavas, papayas, pineapples, strawberries, and watermelons.
[c]Barley, beans, sorghum, soybeans, and wheat.

about whether or not yellow corn imports from the United States—mainly for processing—compete with Mexican production of white corn—mainly for the Mexican population's diet (see Puyana and Romero 2004; Zahniser and Coyle 2004). The Mexican government has not charged the agreed tariff under NAFTA when corn imports from the United States exceeded the established quota. If the official position is valid, imported yellow corn at low prices has not posed competition to Mexican farmers of the basic crop. Furthermore, since yellow corn is used for animal feed, cheap imports of the grain could benefit the livestock sector of Mexico and reduce meat imports. Moreover, as income grows, demand for meat increases. The Mexican government could argue that cheap corn imports under NAFTA promote food self-sufficiency in Mexico. The problem lies in the fact that corn is still the basic food for millions of poor Mexicans and an important segment of its production is by small farmers. The issue is further complicated by the following two facts: corn production and consumption are part of the culture of Mexico, and corn imports could pose a threat to the prevailing biodiversity of the crop in Mexico (Dyer and Yúnez-Naude 2003).

As expected, Mexico's agricultural trade has increased during NAFTA. However, this trend could have been present before NAFTA. So we conducted an econometric study to test whether NAFTA has caused structural change in the agricultural trade of Mexico. Contrary to what has been commonly argued, our results show that neither total agricultural imports nor imports of corn, sorghum, oilseeds, and wheat have experienced structural change in their trade from 1980 to 2002. The result is particularly striking for corn, because no tariffs were charged on over-quota imports of the grain (see Puyana and Romero 2004).

In contrast to imports, and, as predicted, total exports and exports of major vegetables and fruits experienced structural change. Notwithstanding this, the dates of this type of change (November or December 1994, and June 1995) make us suspect that this could have been due more to the sharp devaluation the peso suffered during the mid-1990s than to NAFTA.

Rural Employment and Out-Migration

Employment in the agricultural sector of Mexico decreased by approximately 2 percent during 1993–2002 with respect to 1984–1993 (Audley et al. 2003). Although this was in accordance with expectations, the question is where these displaced workers found alternative jobs.

Preliminary results of a household survey in towns and villages with 500 to 2,500 people all over Mexico show that rural out-migration (both within Mexico and to the United States) increased significantly during the 1990s compared to the previous decade, especially following the peso devaluation. This increase also may reflect several other factors, including the reform of the ejido system of property rights (see http://precesam.colmex.mx and Taylor and Dyer 2003).

Most rural migrants to the rest of Mexico go to cities, so that increasing numbers of people born in rural Mexico are working in nonagricultural activities. We can add to this the argument of Polack (Audley et al. 2003) that the insufficient growth in manufacturing employment during the nineties, and its inability to absorb these rural migrants, means that they work in urban informal services, and those with friends and relatives in the United States decide to migrate north (Randall 1962; Taylor and Yúnez-Naude 1999; Taylor, Yúnez-Naude, and Hampton 1999).

The Political Economy of Agricultural Reforms

The agricultural reforms in Mexico and their effects after two decades of implementation, have led to increased research and a more sophisticated understanding of agricultural processes (Aceves Dávila 2000, 2003; García 2001; Rosenzweig 2003; Robinson et al. 1991; and Schwentesius et al. 2003). For example, corn production and cultivated area on "traditional" rain-fed lands has grown since 1995–1996 with respect to the previous ten years, but in contrast to irrigated corn, yields have remained practically the same (Table 13.1). Although de Janvry, Fafchamps, and Sadoulet argued in 1991 that peasant production is not directly affected by price changes, in 2003 Dyer and Taylor argued that the sales of corn by government rural stores to local households at low prices affected peasants producing this crop for the market, forcing them to reduce production and provoking drops in local land and labor prices. Lower land rental rates allowed subsistence farmers to lease commercial farmers' land to produce corn for their families' consumption.

The response of some of the traditional farmers to the agricultural and political conditions of the 1990s included the Zapatista uprising as well as the use of pressure groups to change government policy. For example, in late 2002 and early 2003 farmer, peasant, and worker organizations pressed for increasing supports to the rural sector, the revising of some of the liberalization policies, including the corn component of NAFTA, and the end of imports of genetically altered corn.

The political unrest led to policy changes in 2002, first in the Blindaje Agropecuarío "Agro-food Armour" (AFA), and later in the "National Accord for the Countryside" (Acuerdo Nacional para el Campo), signed in April 2003 by the government and by farmer's and peasants' organizations (Dyer and Dyer 2003).

The AFA was designed to place Mexican agriculture on the same basis as U.S. agriculture, mirroring the U.S. Farm Security and Rural Investment Act (FSRIA) of 2002. The AFA is intended to provide a multiyear income safety net for the producers of basic grain and oilseeds and to subsidize energy so as to equalize the costs of electricity and diesel paid by Mexican farmers with the costs paid by their Canadian and U.S. counterparts. The AFA also meant changes in Mexican Trade Law to create an effective framework to face unfair competition from dumped imports (see Knuston and Ochoa 2003; Hobbs 2003). The government also promised to provide Mexican farmers with increased access to credit at lower interest rates.

Ten ministries participate in the federal budget for rural development, the most important ones being the Ministry of Agriculture or SAGARPA (which in 2003 received 35 percent of the budget), the Ministry of Education (15 percent), the Ministry for Social Development or SEDESOL (12 percent), the Ministry of Ecology (8 percent), and the Ministry of Health (7 percent). In addition, state and county (municipal) governments receive federal finance for rural development (11 percent of the budget for 2003). In 2003, most of SAGARPA's budget went to ASERCA (46 percent) and to crops (18 percent), livestock (6 percent), and fisheries (5 percent), and practically all of SEDESOL's budget related to rural development is used for poverty alleviation (53 percent) and for its rural welfare programs (42 percent) (Grupo Consultor de Mercados Agrícolas, 2004).

This could ease the conditions in the countryside. Although there has not been structural change in agriculture, the changes in rural Mexico during the last decade have been painful. There is not yet a clear agreement between the political forces in Mexico about whether agricultural development can be achieved only through agricultural policies, or whether broader development policies are needed to achieve economic and political goals in rural Mexico.

Notes

This chapter contains results from research conducted with the financial support from Mexico's National Council of Science and Technology (CONACYT), the Ford and Hewlett Foundations, and UC MEXUS. We thank Gabriela Soto and Ana Pulido for their support.

1. We include in the chapter a review of the changes on agricultural employment, credit, and poverty, as well as of land property rights. However, we do not study empirically whether these trends reflect structural change because of unavailability of data (for similar reasons, we have not studied the sugar and livestock subsectors).

References

Aceves Dávila R. 2000. "El campo que nos tienen prometido . . . Notas para una nueva agenda para la organización económica del medio rural." *Manuscript for Internal Discussion* (November). Ministry of Agriculture.

————. 2003. "Tres años de gobierno de Vicente Fox: Una evaluación de las políticas públicas y el Acuerdo Nacional para el Campo." Paper presented at the seminar, "Los Primeros Tres Años del Gobierno de Vicente Fox: Una Evaluación." Mexico City: El Colegio de Mexico and Konrad Adenauer Foundation, December.

Appendini, Kirsten. 2001. "The Challenges of Rural Mexico in an Open Economy." In *Mexico's Politics and Society in Transition,* ed. J.S. Tulchin and Andrew Selee. Boulder, CO: Lynne Rienner.

Audley, J., D. Papademetriou, S. Polasky, and S. Vaughan. 2003. *La promesa y la realidad del TLCAN: Lecciones de México para el Hemisferio.* Washington, DC: Carniege Endowment for International Peace.

Bank of Mexico. n.d. *Indice nacional de precios al consumidor* (INCP). Available at www.bancodemexico.gob.mx.

Bolding C., J. Calderon, and C. Handy. 1999. "U.S. Invests in Mexico's Processed Food Industry." *Food Review* 22, no. 2 (May–August).

Casco, A., and A. Rosensweig. 2000. *La política sectorial agropecuaria en México: Balance de una decada.* Mexico City: Instituto Interamericano de Cooperación para la Agricultura (IICA).

Cornelius, Wayne. A., and David Myhre. 1998. *The Trasformation of Rural Mexico. Reforming the Ejido Sector.* La Jolla: University of California, San Diego. Center for U.S.-Mexico Relations.

Dyer, G., and D. Dyer. 2003. "Policy, Politics and Projections in Mexican Agriculture." Comment presented at the Ninth Policy Disputes Information Consortium Workshop, Montreal, April.

Dyer, G., and J.E. Taylor. 2003. "Rethinking the Supply Response to Market Reforms in Agriculture: Household Heterogeneity in Village General Equilibrium Analysis from Mexico." Working Paper, Department of Agricultural and Resource Economics, University of California–Davis.

Dyer, G., and A. Yúnez-Naude. 2003. "El TLCAN y la conservación de la diversidad del maíz en Mexico." North American Commission for Environmental Coorperation. Available at www.cec.org/symposium, March.

García Salazar, J.A. 2001. "Efecto de PROCAMPO sobre la producción y saldo de comercio exterior de maíz," *Agrociencia* 35, no. 6.

Grupo Consultor de Mercados Agrícolas. 2004. "Productividad y competitividad del sector granos en México." Paper presented at the workshop "Diálogo para el Desarrollo Rural." World Bank, Morelos, Mexico, May 17–18.

Hobbs, J.E. 2003. "Traceability and Country of Origin Labeling." Paper presented at the Ninth Policy Disputes Information Consortium Workshop, Montreal, April.

de Ita, A. 2003. "Los impactos socioeconómicos y ambientales de la liberación comercial de los granos básicos en el contexto del TLCAN: El caso de Sinaloa." Paper presented at the Second North American Symposium on Assessing the Environmental Effects of Trade, Mexico City, March 25–26.

de Janvry, A., M. Fafchamps, and E. Sadoulet. 1991. "Peasant Household Behavior with Missing Markets: Some Paradoxes Explained." *Economic Journal,* 101.

Jones, Gareth A., and Peter M. Ward. 1998. "Deregulating the ejido: The Impact on Urban Development in Mexico." In *The Transformation of Rural Mexico: Reforming the Ejido Sector.* La Jolla: Center for U.S.-Mexican Studies, University of California, San Diego.

Knuston, R., and R. Ochoa. 2003. "Convergence, Harmonization and Compatibility Under NAFTA: A 2003 Status Report." Paper presented at the Ninth Policy Disputes Information Consortium Workshop, Montreal, April.

Leycegi, B., and M. Ruiz Cornejo. 2002. "Treading Remedies to Remedy Trade." Paper presented at the Eight Agricultural and Food Policy Information workshop, "Keeping the Borders Open." Puerto Vallarta, unpublished revised version.

Mexico, Ministry of Agriculture. n.d. Databases (SAGARPA-SIACON) available at www.siea.sagarpa.gob.mx//sistemas/siacon/SIACON.html.

Mexico, Ministries of Economy and Agriculture. 2002. *Acciones de política agropecuaria y comercial para enfrentar los efectos de la Ley Agrícola 2002 de EE.UU. y la apertura comercial en el TLCAN en productos sensibles.* (Agro-food Armour [AFA]). Mimeo.

Perry, G., D. Lederman, L. Serven, and W. Maloney. 2003. "Lessons from NAFTA for Latin America and the Caribbean." Available at http://lnweb18.worldbank.org/external/lac/lac.nsf/. Chapter 3.

PRECESAM (Program for the Study of Economic Change and Sustainability in Mexican Agriculture) http://precesam.colmex.mx.

Puyana, A., and J. Romero. 2004. "Evaluación integral de los impactos e instrumentación del capítulo agropecuario del TLCAN. Antecedentes y desempeño del sector agropecuario a partir del TLCAN." *Preliminary Report,* February.

Randall, Laura. 1962. "Labour Migration and Mexican Economic Development." *Social and Economic Studies* 11, no. 1 (March).

———, ed. 1996. *Reforming Mexico's Agrarian Reform.* Armonk, NY: M.E. Sharpe.

Robinson, S., M.E. Burfisher, R. Hinojosa-Ojeda, and K.E. Thierfelder. 1991. "Agricultural Policies and Migration in a U.S.–Mexico Free Trade Area: A Computable General Equilibrium Analysis." *Working Paper No. 617.* Berkeley: University of California–Berkeley, Department of Agricultural and Resource Economics. December.

Rosenzweig, A. 2003. "Changes in Mexican Agricultural Policies: 2001–2003." Paper presented at the Ninth Policy Disputes Information Consortium Workshop. Montreal, April.

SAGARPA. n.d. Available at www.sagarpa.gob.

———. Databases available at www.siea.sagarpa.gob.mx//sistemas/siacon/SIACON.html.

———. 2000. www.attrition.org/mirror/attrition/2000/06/05/www.intoaserca.gob.mx/aserca.htm.

Saldívar Tanaka, L. In press. "A reforma agrária Mexicana: Do ejido à privatização." In *Ofensiva e resistência na America Latina, África e Ásia,* ed. Dias Martins. Brazil: Boitempo.

Schwentesius, R., M.A. Gómez Cruz, J.L. Calva Tellez, and L. Hernández Navarro, comp. 2003. *¿El campo no aguanta más?* Mexico City: Universidad Autonoma de Chapingo.

Secretaría de la Reforma Agraria. 2003. *Colección de cuadernillos de informacion agraria básica.* Mexico.

Taylor, J.E., and G. Dyer. 2003. "NAFTA, Trade and Migration." Unpublished paper prepared for the Migration Policy Institute Project, The Carnegie Endowment for International Peace, NAFTA@10, July.

Taylor, J.E., and A. Yúnez-Naude. 1999. *Education, Migration and Productivity: An Analytic Approach and Evidence for Rural Mexico.* Development Center Studies. Paris: OECD.

Taylor, J.E., A. Yúnez-Naude, and Steve Hampton. 1999. "Agricultural Policy Reforms and Village Economies: A Computable General Equilibrium Analysis from Mexico." *Journal of Policy Modeling* 21, no. 4.

United Nations Food and Agricultural Organization, FAO and SAGARPA. 2000. *Evaluacion de la Alianza Para el Campo: Informe Global.* Available at www.rlc.fao.org/prior/desrural/document/alianza.htm.

United Nations Program for Development (PNUD). 2003. *Informe sobre el desarrollo humano. Mexico 2002.* Mexico: Mundi Prensa.

Yúnez-Naude, A. 2003. "The Dismantling of CONASUPO, a Mexican State Trader in Agriculture." *World Economy* 26, no. 1.

Yúnez-Naude, A., and F. Barceinas Paredes. 2002. "Lessons from NAFTA: The Case of Mexico's Agricultural Sector," *Report to the World Bank.* Available at http://wbln0018.worldbank.org/lac/lacinfoclient.nsf/1daa4610322912388525683 1005ce0eb/2e11a4d12a57e2ee85256c4d006d9b66/$FILE/Yunez%20Text%20Final.pdf

———. 2004. "Agricultural Trade and NAFTA: the Case of Mexico." In *The First Decade of NAFTA: The Future of Free Trade in North America,* ed. Kevin Kennedy. Lansing, MI: Transnational Publishers.

Zahniser, S., and W. Coyle. 2004. "U.S.–Mexico Corn Trade During the NAFTA Era: New Twists to an Old Story." Available at www.ers.usda.gov. May.

14

JUAN QUINTANILLA MARTÍNEZ AND
MARIANO BAUER E.

Mexican Oil, Gas, Electricity Generation, and Energy Consumption

The nationalization of the Mexican oil industry, and later the electric power indus-try, made these industries symbols of national identity. The importance of these industries therefore was seen as greater than their impact on output, employment, government income, or the foreign debt. Policy decisions for these industries none-theless depended on technical as well as political factors. Bauer and Quintanilla describe the administrative and productive structure of the energy sector, and pro-vide a detailed analysis of the factors that constrain its development.

The Mexican oil company, PEMEX, in 2002 provided 38 percent of govern-ment fiscal revenues and 9 percent of total exports that mainly were sent to the United States. Mexico sent heavy crude oil to a PEMEX-Shell jointly owned refinery in Texas, where it was transformed into gasoline and returned to Mexico, providing almost 20 percent of Mexico's gasoline. It is anticipated that Mexico's modernization of its energy sector and reduction of imports of oil and gas prod-ucts will require investment of an estimated $168'000 million* ($168 billion) from 2002 to 2011.

Although Mexico has sufficient proved reserves of oil and gas for the next few years, their adequate development is not likely under present circumstances. Thus, new arrangements for foreign investment have been made and new ones are being developed. Additional ways of making investment in the oil, gas, and electric power industries attractive may require changes in government ownership and control of the energy sector.

---

*As the word "billion" has a different meaning in countries other than the United States, we prefer to write x'xxx million as this would be understood equally by readers every-where. To avoid the confusion between the decimal point used in the United States and the decimal comma used in Europe, the comma is replaced by the apostrophe.

Policy, Economics, and Geology

Until now, the constitutionally based state monopolies of the Mexican Oil Company (PEMEX—Petróleos Mexicanos), the Federal Commission of Electricity (CFE—Comisión Nacional de Seguridad Nuclear y Salvaguardas), and the Light and Power of the Center (LFC—Luz y Fuerza del Centro), have dominated the energy sector. Although these public companies have generally developed oil, oil products, natural gas, and electricity infrastructure sufficient for Mexico's needs, it is undeniable that lately they have begun to fall short, mainly due to insufficient investments by previous administrations. Also, it is undeniable that the energy sector must be expanded and modernized in order to meet the demand that is expected in the near future.

Mexican oil, gas, and electricity have a role in the nation's history that goes beyond their economic, technical, and geologic components. Beyond the constitutional mandate, they are often identified as key elements of the nation's sovereignty and, indeed, of its national identity. Consequently, reforms of the legal framework, such as those that allowed independent power producers and deregulated the transmission and distribution of natural gas (Quintanilla 1996), are subject to discussion and objections that transcend economic and technical parameters, as well as to getting clouded by party politics. This is currently the case of the multiple services contracts that PEMEX is offering to develop nonassociated gas fields, and of the reforms to the power sector proposed by the present administration to Congress.

In this chapter, we describe the Mexican energy system, projected future energy demand, and institutional (legal) changes to increase investment, and give an update on the changing legal framework together with some conclusions.

The Mexican Energy System

Figure 14.1 shows the structure of control and administration of the Mexican energy system. It is headed by the Energy Secretariat (SENER—Secretaría de Energía), which is in charge of the country's energy planning. Under it there are the Energy Regulatory Commission (CRE—Comisión Reguladora de Energia) in charge of the regulatory matters in the areas of natural gas, electricity, and liquefied petroleum gas (LPG); the National Nuclear Safety Commission (CNSNS—Comisión Nacional de Seguridad Nuclear y Salvaguardas), in charge of the control of nuclear materials and their applications; and the National Commission for Energy Savings (CONAE— Comisión Nacional para el Ahorro de Energía), in charge of energy efficiency standards, promotion of nonconventional energies and energy-saving actions in industry, and other-end use sectors, as well as three national research institutes: the Mexican Petroleum Institute (IMP—Instituto Mexicano del Petróleo) in the areas of oil and gas, the Electrical Research Institute (IIE—Instituto de Investigaciones Eléctricas) in the area of electricity and renewable energies,

Figure 14.1   **Structure of the Mexican Energy Sector**

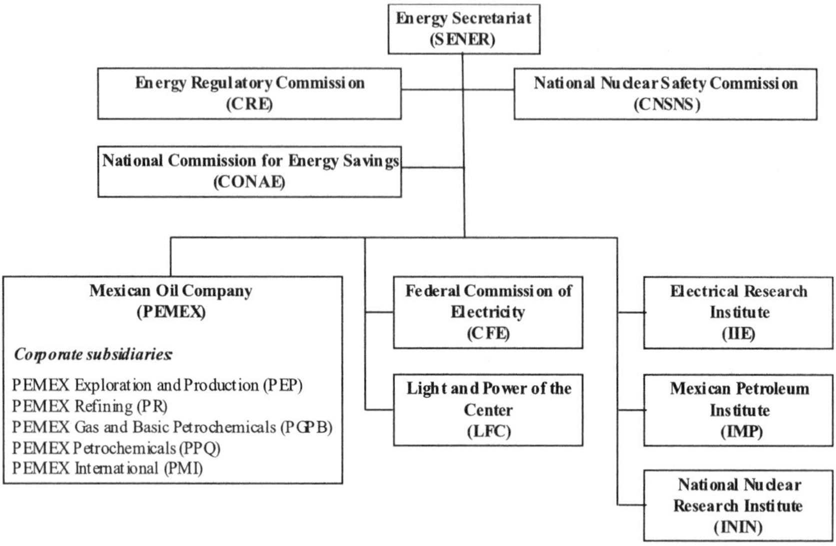

Energy Secretariat
(SENER)

Energy Regulatory Commission
(CRE)

National Nuclear Safety Commission
(CNSNS)

National Commission for Energy Savings
(CONAE)

Mexican Oil Company
(PEMEX)

Corporate subsidiaries
PEMEX Exploration and Production (PEP)
PEMEX Refining (PR)
PEMEX Gas and Basic Petrochemicals (PGPB)
PEMEX Petrochemicals (PPQ)
PEMEX International (PMI)

Federal Commission of Electricity
(CFE)

Light and Power of the Center
(LFC)

Electrical Research Institute
(IIE)

Mexican Petroleum Institute
(IMP)

National Nuclear Research Institute
(ININ)

and the National Nuclear Research Institute (ININ—Instituto Nacional de Investigaciones Nucleares) in the nuclear area and its applications.

Additionally, three state-owned companies are under the control and coordination of the Energy Secretariat: PEMEX, in charge of the exploration, production, transformation, distribution, and commercialization of oil and oil products as well as the production and first-hand sales of natural gas; and CFE and LFC, in charge of the generation, transmission, distribution, and marketing of electricity in the country. PEMEX is a holding company. Its subsidiaries and their activities are: PEMEX Exploration and Production (PEP—PEMEX Exploración y Producción) explores and develops the oil and natural gas reserves of Mexico; PEMEX Refining (PR—PEMEX Refinación) transforms crude oil into a variety of oil products; PEMEX Gas and Basic Petrochemicals (PGPB—PEMEX Gas y Petroquímica Básica) processes, transports, distributes, and commercializes natural gas and natural gas liquids, LPG, and some basic petrochemical raw materials; PEMEX Petrochemicals (PPQ—PEMEX Petroquímica) produces a variety of petrochemical raw materials; and PEMEX International (PMI—PEMEX Internacional) provides commercial services for international trade to the four PEMEX subsidiaries.

The Energy Sector in the Economy

In 2002 PEMEX provided about 38 percent of government fiscal revenues, 1.2 percent of the GDP, and employed 141,628 people. Its contribution to the trade balance is shown in Table 14.1. Crude oil and oil products represented 9 percent

Table 14.1

Net Trade Balance, 2001–2003 (million US$)

	2001	2002	2003
Total exports	158,443	160,763	165,355
From maquiladoras	76,881	78,098	77,745
From the rest of the activities	81,562	82,665	87,610
Oil and oil products exports	12,799	14,476	18,634
Crude oil	11,591	13,109	16,812
Oil products and petrochemicals	1,208	1,367	1,822
Nonoil and oil products exports	145,644	146,287	146,722
Farming and livestock	3,903	3,866	4,795
Extractives	388	389	517
Manufacturing	141,353	142,031	141,409
From maquiladoras	76,881	78,098	77,745
From the rest of the activities	64,472	63,933	63,664
Total imports	168,396	168,679	170,958
From maquiladoras	57,599	59,296	59,058
From the rest of the activities	110,798	109,383	111,901
Consumption goods	19,752	21,178	21,509
Intermediate use goods	126,149	126,508	129,212
From maquiladoras	57,599	59,296	59,058
From the rest of the activities	68,550	67,212	70,154
Capital goods	22,496	20,992	20,237
Net trade balance	−9,954	−7,916	−5,603
From maquiladoras	19,282	18,802	18,688
From the rest of the activities	−29,236	−26,718	−24,291
Without oil exports	−22,752	−22,392	−24,237
Tourism income	8,401	8,858	9,457
Tourism net balance	2,699	2,798	3,204
Transfers from temporary workers	8,895	9,814	13,266

Sources: INEGI (n.d.); Mexico, Presidencia de la República (2003); and Banco de Mexico (n.d.)

(8.15 percent crude oil and 0.85 percent oil products) of total exports. Nonoil exports were 2.4 percent farming and livestock, 0.24 percent extractive activities, and 88.36 percent manufacturing. The manufacturing contribution is divided into maquiladora (in bond) exports (48.58 percent) and the rest of the activities (39.78 percent). Total imports exceed total exports with a very important portion of intermediate-use goods and smaller imports of consumption and capital goods. Clearly, the net trade balance is negative, being positive for the maquiladora sector but negative for the rest. In the case of petrochemicals the balance (including PPQ) was negative by an amount of US$4'800 million, originated by an apparent consumption of 23.8 million tons and a domestic production of 16.2 million tons. Petrochemical exports accounted for US$2'300 million with a PEMEX participa-

Figure 14.2   **Hydrocarbon Reserves and Reserves-to-Production Ratio, 1938–2002**

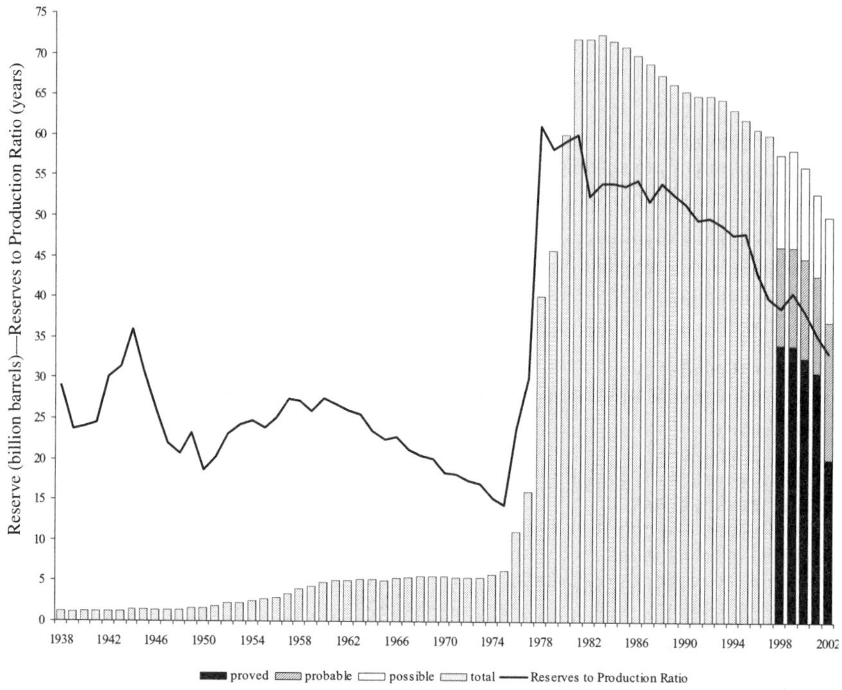

proved ▬▬ probable ▨▨ possible ▢▢ total ▢▢ —— Reserves to Production Ratio

Source: PEMEX (various years).

tion of US$112.9 million while imports accounted for US$7'100 million with a PEMEX participation of US$45.9 million.

In 2002 the power sector, CFE, and LFC, provided 1.15 percent of the country's GDP, employed 86,050 persons, and contributed a marginal amount, in energy terms, to the trade balance.

Oil and Gas Reserves and Production

Mexico's total hydrocarbon reserves reached a peak of 72.5 billion barrels of crude oil equivalent (see Figure 14.2) in 1984. At the beginning of 1986, total hydrocarbon reserves began to decrease as a result of the rate of extraction and the lower level of new discoveries, revisions, additions, and developments.

Any discussion of hydrocarbon reserves should be based on a precise knowledge of remaining reserves. This knowledge may vary in depth. Indeed, the question regarding the extent of the total hydrocarbon reserves in Mexico has led to an unprecedented detailed study on the subject. For one, since 1995 PEP intensified efforts to broaden its knowledge of the main reserves in the country through the use of sophisticated numerical models and the acquisition of new seismic and petrophysical information. The economic objective of these specialized technical activities is to maximize the value of reservoirs throughout their productive lifetime. Additionally, other circumstances also converged in this effort. First, two international technical associations, the Society of Petroleum Engineers (SPE) and the World Petroleum Congress (WPC), integrated a joint workgroup in 1994 to set forth reserve definitions and criteria and guidelines to estimate such reserves. Second, in 1995, PEP decided to standardize the criteria for the estimation of Mexico's reserves using the best practices accepted by the petroleum industry.

The three aforementioned circumstances resulted in new estimates, obtained from 1996 to 1999, which were based on the approved definitions and guidelines of SPE and WPC and those of the American Association of Petroleum Geologists. In an effort of transparency, PEP audited the new estimates through well-known specialized firms such as Netherland, Sewell and Associates, Inc. (NSAI) and the firm DeGolyer and MacNaughton. The participation of the second consultant was with the purpose of utilizing the services of the firm that twenty-five years earlier, in 1978, conducted the first external evaluation of the reserves in the Paleocanal de Chicontepec, located between the states of Puebla and Veracruz within PEMEX's North region.

According to this change of methodology, Figure 14.2 shows, for the years 1998 to 2002, the total hydrocarbon reserves of Mexico disaggregated into proved, probable, and possible, according to the SPE and WPC requirements. Regarding the reserves for 2002, the lower value of these reserves results from the application of not only the already mentioned SPE and WPC requirements, but also of the criteria of the Securities and Exchange Commission (SEC).[1] As a consequence, the 8'925.2 million barrels of oil equivalent (Mboe) of the Chicontepec area classified as proven at the beginning of 2002 had to be reclassified as probable (5'392.1 Mboe) and possible (3'534.1 Mboe) reserves at the beginning of 2003. Nevertheless, reserves classification is a dynamic subject. For example, in the next three years, due to the perforation of the already authorized development wells, a portion of the current probable and possible reserves at Chicontepec will be reclassified as proven, as has been the case in other oil and gas areas.

As of January 1, 2003, Mexico's total hydrocarbon reserves amounted to 50'032.2 Mboe, classified as follows: 20'077.3 Mboe are proved reserves, 16'965.0 Mboe are probable, and 12'990.0 Mboe are possible. By type of hydrocarbon, the composition of this reserve is 72.5 percent crude oil, 18.8 percent dry gas, 6.9 percent plant liquids, and 1.8 percent condensates. These reserves are located in four regions—two onshore and two at sea. Total crude oil reserves consist of 53 percent heavy crude (less than 27 API degree[2]), 38 percent light crude oil (between 27 and 38 API degree), and 9 percent extra light crude (over 38 API degree). In the case of the natural gas, 79 percent of the total reserves of gas are associated gas and 21 percent nonassociated gas.

The reserves-to-production ratio[3] is shown as a continuous line in Figure 14.2.

Remaining reserves at the beginning of 2003 compared to the 2002 production, yields a reserves-to-production ratio of 33 years for the total hydrocarbon reserves, 25 years for the added proven and probable reserves, and only 13 years for the proven reserves. If this analysis is carried out for the nonassociated gas, it results in 18 years for the total reserve, 11 years for the proven plus probable reserve, and 8 years for the proven reserve alone. If a similar analysis is carried out for the light and lighter crude oil, excluding Chicontepec's reserves, the reserves-to-production ratios are 23, 19, and 14 years, respectively. Despite the fact that these figures assume constant rates of production, which is not the case due to the fact that oil fields decrease their production over time, the results show the importance of the current policy for exploration and development of new fields of nonassociated gas and light oil.

In 2002, the total production of crude oil was 3.177 million barrels per day (Mbd); in 2003 it increased by 6.08 percent to 3.37 Mbd, which represents a historical maximum. A large portion of the total gas production is associated gas; however, the associated gas contribution has been declining since 1998 when its contribution reached its highest value. On the other hand, nonassociated gas is present in some actives[4] of the South and North regions and its contribution has been increasing as a result of the developments in the Burgos active. As a result of the reduction of flared gas, the index of gas use was 94.0 percent in 2002 against the 92.3 percent for the year 2001. It is expected to reach an index of gas use of 98 percent by 2006.

The existing infrastructure in PR, the refining subsidiary, consists of 6 refineries, 77 sales centers, 5'564 gas stations, 5'266 km of crude oil pipelines, and 8'944 km of derived products pipelines. PGPB, the gas-processing subsidiary, operates 19 sweetening and 14 cryogenic plants, integrated in 9 gas processing centers, all of them located on the coast of the Gulf of Mexico. PPQ, the petrochemical subsidiary, operates 43 plants in 8 petrochemical complexes. In 2002 the production was 5.89 Mt and the internal sales 2.2 Mt.

Power Capacity and Generation

The National Electric System consists of nine areas, seven of them interconnected (93.9 percent of the total capacity) and two isolated (the Baja California peninsula). The isolated areas remain as independent systems due to technical and economical reasons that do not justify their interconnection. However, the Baja California System is interconnected to the electrical grid of the occidental region of the United States.

Mexico's total power capacity in 2002 was 41'184.3 MW,[5] including 3'495 MW from independent power producers (IPP). Hydroelectric power accounted for 23.35 percent of the total capacity, thermal for 76.65 percent, and wind for 0.01 percent. Of the total thermal capacity, 64.97 percent is based on hydrocarbons, 6.31 percent on coal, 3.31 percent on nuclear, and 2.05 percent on geothermal.

Thermal capacity is strongly based on steam plants burning mainly fuel oil. However, since 1997, as a result of the energy policy and of environmental considerations, some of these plants, especially those located near urban areas (such as the Metropolitan Areas of Mexico City, of Guadalajara City in the state of Jalisco, and of Monterrey City in the state of Nuevo León) and other "critical areas," have been converted to burn natural gas instead of fuel oil.

Another consequence is that the power capacity expansion in the last six years has used the combined cycle[6] natural gas–fired technology, except for some small increase in turbo gas and internal combustion capacity and some specific hydro projects. The IPPs have developed their contribution to the National Electric System's existing power capacity on the basis of combined cycle natural gas–fired technologies.

The existing dual power capacity, plants that burn fuel oil and/or coal, in 2001 began a conversion program from fuel oil to imported coal as a consequence of the energy and environmental policies. Geothermal capacity shows a small increase, 100 MW with respect to the capacity in 1999. Nuclear shows an increase of 50 MW with respect to the 1998 capacity, mainly due to some improvement along the generation steps in Laguna Verde nuclear power plant. Wind current operation capacity is 2.2 MW.

At the end of August 2002, private producer's capacity in operation was 8'327 MW. According to the information provided by the Energy Regulatory Commission (CRE), up to August 2002, there were 251 entitled permits, all of them entitled to private producers, representing a total of 19,703 MW, with a structure of: independent producers (8'759 MW), cogeneration (2'096 MW), self-supply (5'925 MW), importing (153 MW), exportation (2'171 MW), and others (599 MW). The structure by type of technology is dominated by combined cycle. Steam turbines, gas turbines, fluidized bed, hydraulic turbines, internal combustion, and wind are the technologies included in the permits to the private producers.

In 2002, as in the past, the gross generation was dominated by fossil fuels; they represent 80.1 percent while nuclear 4.85 percent, hydraulic 12.37 percent, geothermal 2.68 percent, and wind a very small amount. The National Electric System gross generation was 201.06 TWh, including 22.55 TWh from the IPPs. After own uses, imports, exports, and transmission and distribution losses the net electrical energy delivered to end use was 160.2 TWh.

The Energy Balance

For an average over selected years during the period of 1988 to 2002, fossil fuels represented 86.67 percent of the domestic production plus imports plus inventory changes (see Table 14.2); hydrocarbons accounted for 84.83 percent and coal for 1.84 percent. Other primary sources were: hydraulic 2.94 percent, biomass 3.58 percent, geothermal 0.62 percent, uranium 0.70 percent, and wind with a marginal contribution.

Table 14.2

Energy Production, Supply, and Consumption, 1988–2002

	1988		1990		1995		2000		2002	
	PJ[a]	%	PJ	%	PJ	%	PJ	%	PJ	%
Domestic production	7,929	97.7	8,072	97.3	8,156	95.0	9,619	91.2	9,625	93.0
Hydrocarbons	7,205	88.7	7,278	87.7	7,216	84.0	8,557	81.1	8,639	83.5
Coal	130	1.6	142	1.7	173	2.0	227	2.1	220	2.1
Hydraulic	225	2.8	252	3	284	3.3	342	3.2	259	2.5
Biomass	318	3.9	313	3.8	331	3.9	342	3.2	344	3.3
Geothermal	50	0.6	55	0.7	58	0.7	61	0.6	56	0.5
Nuclear			31	0.4	93	1.1	90	0.9	107	1.0
Wind										
Imports	180	2.2	247	3.0	377	4.4	893	8.5	900	8.7
Inventory changes	10	0.1	–21	–0.3	54	0.6	38	0.4	–176	–1.7
Exports	–3,166	–39	–3,002	–36.2	–3,012	–35.1	–3,858	–36.6	–3,884	–37.5
Others (spills, flaring, etc.)	–54	–0.7	–134	–1.6	–88	–1	–189	–1.8	–112	–1.1
Maquila and net exchange							–61	–0.6	–76	–0.7
Total internal supply	4,899		5,161		5,487		6,442		6,276	
End use	PJ	%	PJ	%	PJ	%	PJ	%	PJ	%

Transformation	1,608	32.8	1,626	31.5	1,647	30	2,359	36.6	2,226	35.5
Oil sector	818	16.7	725	14	577	10.5	896	13.9	780	12.4
Power sector	800	16.3	896	17.4	1,057	19.3	1,431	22.2	1,436	22.9
Coke sector	−10	−0.2	5	0.1	14	0.3	33	0.5	10	0.2
End use sectors	3,291	67.2	3,535	68.5	3,840	70	4,083	63.4	4,051	64.5
Industrial	1,464	29.9	1,466	28.4	1,531	27.9	1,518	23.6	1,460	23.3
Transport	1,072	21.9	1,275	24.7	1,399	25.5	1,614	25.1	1,634	26
Residential, commercial, and public	652	13.3	701	13.6	816	14.9	836	13	850	13.5
Agricultural	103	2.1	93	1.8	94	1.7	116	1.8	106	1.7

Source: Mexico, SENER (various years).

[a]Petajoule (PJ) is approximately equal to 1.676×10^5 barrels of oil equivalent (boe).

On the other hand, also on the average and after exports of crude oil, oil deriva-tives, natural gas, coal, and electricity, the structure of the internal energy supply was 87.45 percent fossil fuels and 12.58 percent nonfossil fuels. The supply distri-bution of the different fuels is: oil (52.43 percent), natural gas (26.24 percent), and coal (3.5 percent). Other primary sources are: biomass (5.73 percent)—sugar cane bagasse (1.5 percent) and fuel wood (4.23 percent), geothermal (1 percent), hy-draulic (4.72 percent), uranium (1.13 percent), and a very small contribution from wind. Noncommercial fuel wood still plays a significant role. It is the sole source of energy for many small rural communities and, on the negative side, contributes to the country's deforestation problem.

The generation of electricity accounts for 22.9 percent of the country's total energy consumption. Fossil fuels (coal, fuel oil, diesel, and natural gas) account for the 79.07 percent of the total consumption in the sector, nuclear 5.3 percent, hydraulic 12.84 percent, geothermal 2.79 percent, and wind with a very small amount (less than 1 percent).

Table 14.2 shows that in 2002 the country's total energy consumption was 6'276 PJ, of which the power sector consumed 2'018.2 PJ, producing 734.1 of electricity (a gross power generation of 201.6 TWh). For the same year, the structure of the fossil fuels mix was dominated by fuel oil (39.02 percent) followed by natural gas (26.21 percent), coal (13.09 percent), and diesel (0.75 percent). Therefore, the Mexican power system relies strongly on fossil fuels and, as a consequence, be-comes an important contributor to the country's greenhouse gas emissions.

In 2002, internal energy consumption (Table 14.2) showed that the energy sec-tor itself—the oil and gas sector (PEMEX), the power sector (CFE) and (LFC), and the coal processing sector—accounted for 35.46 percent, leaving 64.54 per-cent for end use. Of the latter, transport took 26.04 percent; industry took 23.26 percent; the residential, commercial, and public sector took 13.54 percent; and, finally, agriculture took 1.7 percent. Industry's energy consumption includes feed-stocks (i.e., nonenergy uses), which in 2002 represented 15.2 percent of the total consumption of the industrial sector. The transport sector has been the most im-portant sector from the energy consumption point of view, followed by the indus-trial sector, the power sector, the oil sector, and the residential, commercial, and public sector. This trend will continue in the foreseeable feature.

Internal Energy Demand

Mexico's internal energy demand, supplied mostly from domestic resources, is predominantly and increasingly dependent on oil products and natural gas. (See Figure 14.3, where internal energy supply is shown as a continuous line along the right-hand axis; exports are shown as negative along the left-hand axis). In 2002, Mexico supplied 100 percent of its crude oil apparent consumption, 86.3 percent of natural gas, 85.2 percent of refined products, and 68.1 percent of total petrochemicals.

Figure 14.3 **Domestic Production, Imports, and Exports by Energy Source, 1998–2002**

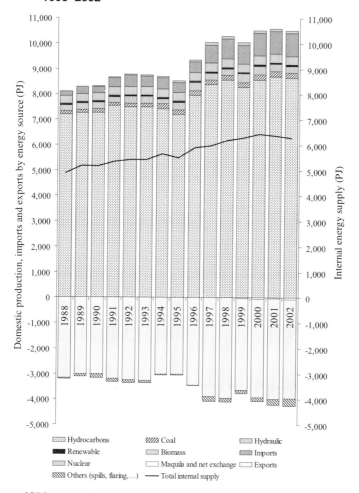

Source: JQM, prepared on the basis of *National Energy Balances,* Mexico, SENER, (various years).

Exports

Mexico is an important crude oil exporter. Since 1975 the country has been self-sufficient in the supply of crude oil. In 2002, the amount of crude oil exported was 1.66 Mbd, 2.7 percent lower than in 2001 (82.3 percent of heavy crude, 14.8 percent lighter, and 2.9 percent light) as a result of the measures adopted to reduce the global supply and stabilize the international oil market. Crude oil exports (3'562 PJ) represent over 50 percent of total production and are directed to over twenty countries.

From 1988 to 2002 the United States has been the main client for Mexican oil, followed by Spain, Japan, and the San José Agreement nations. Under this agreement, Mexico and Venezuela each guarantee to supply up to 80'000 barrels of crude oil per day to seventeen Latin American countries (Argentina, Barbados, Bolivia, Colombia, Costa Rica, Ecuador, El Salvador, Grenada, Guatemala, Haiti, Honduras, Jamaica, Nicaragua, Panama, Peru, Dominican Republic, and Uruguay) included in the agreement. Also, in 2002, exports of oil products (313 PJ) account for 155'900 barrels per day and marginal amounts, 10 PJ in total, of natural gas, nonenergy products, and electricity.

Imports

Mexico is becoming increasingly dependent on outside sources for the satisfaction of its energy needs for oil products, LPG and natural gas, petrochemicals, as well as some other nonenergy products such as asphalts and lubricants. However, gasoline imports have decreased lately due to the increase of domestic production following the reconfiguration of refineries (to produce more gasoline and jet fuel and less fuel oil and heavy distillates) and the larger contribution from the "maquila (in-bond) mechanism." This mechanism consists of sending mostly heavy crude oil (130'000 barrels per day in 2002) to the PEMEX and Shell jointly owned Deer Park refinery in Texas, and returning oil products (mainly, gasoline and diesel). In 2002, the maquila mechanism contributed 19.2 percent and 3.6 percent of the total supply of gasoline and diesel, respectively.

On the other hand, natural gas imports have increased at the expense of fuel oil, and it is expected that they will grow rapidly as a consequence of the investment limitations for extraction and processing, the expected demand from the power and industrial sectors, the current energy policy, and the environmental considerations, as mentioned in the section on power capacity and generation.

Imports of total petrochemical products have been growing in the past few years, reaching 10.3 million tons in 2002, despite Mexico's production capacity of 33.8 million tons, of which only 48 percent was used. On the one hand, the production of basic petrochemicals by PPQ declined over the last eleven years as a result of the lack of investment after the federal government announced its intention of selling this subsidiary, or at least of turning it into a joint venture with private investors. Both proposals were blocked by Congress. There was also a lower supply of raw materials such as natural gas and ethane, as well as a lower demand for some of its products, and a temporary suspension of operations of some plants due to the lack of maintenance. On the other hand, there was a steady increase of imports of the specialized products that the private secondary petrochemical industry did not produce due to the shortage of basic feedstocks or the lack of investments.

Net Trade Balance

The Mexican total trade balance in hydrocarbons is positive; however the net imports of oil products, LPG, and natural gas has increased. It will continue to be positive depending on several factors, such as the amount of crude oil production and exports; oil products and natural gas exported and/or imported; their international price; the existing oil and gas reserves as well as the incorporation of additional ones; the oil and gas processing, transportation, and distribution capacities, and the internal demand for oil products and natural gas, among others. Additionally, other considerations apply, such as development and availability of the required technology for extraction and processing of crude oil and gas; or to the trade-off between producing refined hydrocarbon products that have a high added value versus producing crude oil and natural gas for export, with the inherent vulnerability to international prices.

Projected Future Energy Demand

Government energy policy reflects projections about the nation's economic needs, the assessment of geological petroleum and gas reserves, and the availability of investment, technology, and manpower. It also includes concerns about the economic and social development of oil- and energy-producing regions, as well as environmental impacts. For example, PEMEX devotes significant resources not only to develop cleaner fuels, but also to water preservation and road development for the benefit of rural communities, and to the preservation of ecological reserves, among other actions. As an example, in 1999 it donated US$550'000 to sustain the action plan of the biosphere reserve Pántanos de Centla in the state of Tabasco, US$150'000 to Campeche's environmental protection plan, which includes the preservation of the marine turtle, and US$75'000 to the city of Coatzacoalcos to complete its potable and waste water plants, to the benefit of 30'000 people (Gómez Ávila et al. 2001), among other things. In 2002, donations amounted to US$30 million, in addition to US$60 million invested in the social development of the areas next to Pemex's installations (PEMEX 2003).

Assessment of projections of future energy demand is difficult because of their great sensitivity to assumptions about the economy's demand for oil and gas, refined products, and electricity, and to assumptions about the domestic energy resources. Indeed, assumptions about supply depend, in turn, on the technical definitions of proven and economically viable reserves, that is, those reserves where there is a high probability that oil may be profitably produced with existing technology at probable prices.

Very recent analyses (Quintanilla et al. 2003a, 2003b, 2003c, 2003d; Bauer, Mar, and Elizalde 2003; Bauer et al. 2003; Elizalde and Bauer 2003; Mexico, SENER 2002a, 2002b, 2002c, 2002d) show that the energy dependency will grow in the medium term and might even cancel the positive balance for the country in the long term if proper and on-time actions are not taken. These studies cover the areas of crude oil, natural gas, liquefied petroleum gas, oil products, the power sector, and the entire Mexican energy system (domestic production, imports, exports transformation, transportation, distribution, and end use). They reflect the official energy policy, that is, the replacement of fuel oil by natural gas in the power and industrial sectors, the introduction of natural gas in the residential sector and to some extent in the transport sector, and the reconfiguration of refineries.

Comparative Assessment of Energy Options and Strategies Until 2025

A study by Quintanilla and others (2003a) comprises a reference scenario and three alternative scenarios. Under the reference case or Unlimited Natural Gas Supply Scenario (see Table 14.3), the crude oil market share decreases from 68.2 percent in 1999 to 62.7 percent in 2025 as a consequence of the nonassociated gas growth share to 11.9 percent in 2025 from 4.5 percent in 1999; associated gas decreases from 13.9 percent in 1999 to 12.8 percent in 2025, as shown in Table 14.3. The highest growth rate for market share is that of nonassociated gas (5.2 percent), followed by coal (3.7 percent), crude oil (1.0 percent), geothermal (0.8 percent), and sugar cane (0.2 percent). The first unit of the Laguna Verde nuclear power plant is scheduled to close in 2025 (unless its operation is extended, as is currently occurring for many nuclear plants in other countries).

Oil production in 1999 amounted to 2.91 Mbd and it is projected that in 2025 it will be 3.8 Mbd (see Table 14.4)—a growth rate of 1 percent. The assumptions under which this oil production is projected were: (1) country's total refining capacity is set to 1.6 Mbd and no capacity additions along the entire projection period; (2) the driving oil product is gasoline; (3) maquila mechanism capacity is set to the maximum capacity of the current agreements; (4) excess demand of gasoline, after domestic refining and maquilas' contribution, are satisfied through imports; and (5) oil exports will increase at a decreasing growth rate, in 6.94 percent from 1999 to 2000 up to 0.55 percent from 2024 to 2025.

The gasoline and diesel imports have become an essential component of supply for the domestic market, a fact that forces the refining industry to become strong in order to face the challenges of a dynamic internal market in a modern and flexible form. In 1999, after self-consumption the gasoline yield of the National Refining System (NRS) was 25.34 percent. The existing refining capacity (1.54 Mbd of atmospheric distillation) was not enough to provide the required gasoline production from the country's refineries. By year 2007, Mexico's refineries are expected to have an additional capacity over 160'000 barrels per day from Minatitlán and Salina Cruz refineries and a gasoline yield of 32.8 percent. Mexico's total refining capacity will be 1.7 Mbd. Under these conditions there will be a deficit of refining capacity of 27'000 barrels per day in regard to satisfying the internal demand for gasoline. This deficit could be covered by a reduction in the gasoline exports; however such action will impact the estimate of the aggregated value of oil. After 2008, also to satisfy the internal demand for gasoline and with a gasoline yield of 39 percent, the total refining capacity will have to increase to the following total

Table 14.3

Projection of the Total Primary Energy Supply, 1999–2025 (reference case)

	1999 PJ	2000 PJ	2005 PJ	2010 PJ	2015 PJ	2020 PJ	2025 PJ
Crude oil	6,352	6,567	7,610	7,796	7,958	8,103	8,232
Associated gas (includes flaring)	1,295	1,338	1,551	1,513	1,622	1,651	1,678
Nonassociated gas	422	446	874	1,391	1,364	1,478	1,568
Condensates	125	125	125	125	125	125	125
Coal	273	298	367	442	515	599	705
Sugar cane bagasse	92	91	91	93	94	96	98
Firewood	252	252	252	252	252	252	252
Nuclear	108	108	108	108	108	108	54
Hydro	336	342	314	346	346	346	346
Geothermal	58	67	75	75	72	72	72
Wind	n.s.	1	1	1	1	1	1
Solar	n.s.	n.s.	n.s.	n.s.	n.s.	n.s.	n.s.
Total	9,312	9,635	11,366	12,140	12,457	12,829	13,130

Source: Quintanilla et al. (2003a).
n.s. = nonsignificant.

Table 14.4

Crude Oil and Natural Gas Primary Energy Supply, 2005–2025 (reference case)

	2005	2010	2015	2020	2025
Crude oil (Mbd)	3.49	3.58	3.65	3.72	3.78
Condensates (mbd)	92.87	92.87	92.87	92.87	92.87
Associated gas (includes flaring; Mcfd)	3,710.39	3,618.82	3,880.50	3,950.79	4,013.82
Nonassociated gas (Mcfd)	2,580.45	4,107.45	4,028.85	4,363.49	4,629.27
Natural gas imports (Mcdf)	1,570.68	1,770.74	3,405.07	5,160.02	7,673.92

Source: Quintanilla et al. (2003a).

Table 14.5

Natural Gas Demand Projection Scenarios, 2005–2025

	2005 Mcfd	2010 Mcfd	2015 Mcfd	2020 Mcfd	2025 Mcfd
Low demand	7,015	9,624	—	—	—
Domestic supply	6,001	7,749	—	—	—
Imports	1,014	1,875	—	—	—
High demand	7,285	10,542	—	—	—
Domestic supply	6,268	8,657	—	—	—
Imports	1,017	1,885	—	—	—
Unlimited	7,862	9,497	11,314	13,474	16,317
Domestic supply	6,291	7,726	7,909	8,314	8,643
Imports	1,571	1,771	3,405	5,160	7,674
Limited	7,862	9,497	10,859	11,884	13,725
Domestic supply	6,291	7,726	7,909	8,314	8,643
Imports	1,571	1,771	2,950	3,570	5,082
Nuclear	7,830	9,496	11,125	13,280	16,127
Domestic supply	6,291	7,726	7,909	8,314	8,643
Imports	1,539	1,770	3,215	4,966	7,483
Renewable	7,856	9,437	11,155	13,161	15,808
Domestic supply	6,291	7,709	7,909	8,314	8,643
Imports	1,565	1,729	3,245	4,847	7,165

Sources: SENER (2002a); and Quintanilla et al. (2003a).
Notes:
Low Demand: Base minimum equilibrium scenario (see SENER 2002a).
High Demand: High accelerated natural gas production scenario (see SENER 2002a).
Unlimited: Reference case or unlimited natural gas supply (see Quintanilla et al. 2003a).
Limited: Limited natural gas supply starting 2010 (see Quintanilla et al. 2003a).
Nuclear: Nuclear scenario (see Quintanilla et al. 2003a).
Renewable: Renewables scenario (see Quintanilla et al. 2003a).

capacities: 1.9 Mbd for 2008; 2.5 Mbd for 2015; 3.2 Mbd for 2020; and 4.1 Mbd for 2025. According to the current PEMEX plans, by 2012 there is expected to be a new refinery with a capacity of 150'000 barrels per day. Therefore, the needed accumulated increase of the refining capacity will be 2.4 Mbd by 2025 with respect to the expected refining capacity in 2007 (1.7 Mbd). The elimination of the expected gasoline exports will have the effect of lowering the required refining capacity, by 2025, to 2.1 Mbd.

Table 14.5 shows the most recent natural gas demand projection scenarios. The scenarios' low demand and high demand are reported in SENER (2002a) and cover the horizon from 2002 to 2011. The scenarios presented for unlimited natural gas, limited natural gas, nuclear, and renewable energy cover the horizon from 1999 to 2025 (Quintanilla et al. 2003a). The growth trend of natural gas demand is similar for all scenarios. The difference between the SENER (2002a) and the Quintanilla et al. (2003a) scenarios for the first years is the result of a difference in the power sector expansion capacity, the technical parameters for the expansion candidates, and the retirement schedules for the existing plants.

The projections by Quintanilla et al. (2003a) of natural gas production were developed under the following assumptions: (1) total capacity of gas plants is fixed and equal to 5.1 Bcfd; (2) total capacity of fractionating plants is also fixed and equal to 554 Mcfd, (3) natural gas exports are marginal with a decreasing pattern; and (4) there are no capacity additions for gas and fractionating plants along the entire projection period. Additionally, the ratio of crude oil to associated gas is kept constant and equal to the average value of the last few years.

The effects of the Quintanilla et al. (2003a) alternative scenarios on natural gas demand are shown in Table 14.5. The results for the period 1999–2011 are the same as in the unlimited natural gas scenario; however for the period 2012–2025 there are several effects on the natural gas projections coming from the alternative scenarios.

Total economic system cost[7] and incremental cost (see Table 14.6) for the reference case and alternative scenarios are at present value with a discount rate of 10 percent. A screening curve analysis with four power expansion candidates (gas turbine, combined cycle, nuclear, and dual coal-fired with flue gas desulphurator [FGD]) in the power sector was carried out under the assumptions of 8, 10, and 12 percent discount rates.

For a discount rate of 10 percent, the nuclear option is always the most expensive, followed by the dual coal-fired unit with FGD. For capacity factors lower than 20 percent, gas turbine units are the most attractive ones. For capacity factors greater than 20 percent, combined cycle units are the most attractive and the other alternatives are not attractive at any capacity factor.

For a discount rate of 8 percent and at very high capacity factors, dual plants are more attractive than gas turbines. The most economical pair of candidates is gas turbines for low-capacity factors (peak loads) and combined cycle units for high-capacity factors (base loads). Finally, for a 12 percent discount rate the results are, in essence, the same as for the reference case with small differences in the initial and final value of each candidate.

In the limited natural gas scenario, the power sector expansion changes to a maximum of 3 combined cycle units each year and introducing between 4 and 6 coal-fired units each year for a total 17.7 GW. The cumulative capacity of combined cycle units is 44.8 GW as compared to 62.2 GW in the unlimited natural gas scenario. The gas limitation on the generation by fuel type becomes effective in 2009. The share of natural gas generation reaches 56 percent as compared to 82 percent in the reference case. This will have the effect of reducing the pressure for the development of the needed infrastructure for natural gas production, process-

Table 14.6

Total Economic System Cost and Emissions Reductions

Scenario	Total economic system cost NPV billion US$	Incremental cost NPV billion US$	Total CO_2 reductions million ton	CO_2 cost-effectiveness US$/ton CO_2
Reference case— Unlimited natural gas	708.45			
Limited natural gas supply	710.71	2.26	−314.47	
Nuclear	708.69	0.24	48.11	4.98
Renewables	708.87	0.42	82.18	5.06

Source: Quintanilla et al. (2003a).
Notes: See note 7 for an explanation of the term total economic system cost. Since we are talking about carbon dioxide emissions reduction with respect to the reference case, a minus sign indicates an emissions increment of the corresponding alternative scenario with respect to the reference case.
NPV = Net Present Value.

ing, transportation, and distribution; however it will transfer part of this pressure to the development of the corresponding infrastructure for imported coal reception, transportation, and distribution. The total economic system cost (see Table 14.6), also at present value and at a 10 percent discount rate, is higher than in the reference case by US$2.26 billion. The shift away from natural gas to imported coal comes at an environmental cost. Compared to the reference case, power sector carbon dioxide (CO_2) emissions are forecast to reach about 238.7 Mt by 2025, which is about 45.85 Mt or 23.6 percent higher than the reference scenario.

In the case of the nuclear scenario, nuclear power also replaces base-load[8] gas-fired generation and leads to lower natural gas imports and lower emissions. When the nuclear unit does come on line (2012), it is base-loaded into the system and generates a constant level of 34 PJ of electricity per year. The system-level analysis shows that nuclear replaces effectively base-load gas combined-cycle capacity and between 33–37 PJ of gas-fired generation. This represents a reduction in the imports of natural gas, 189.6 Mcfd, and an additional consumption of uranium of 31.3 tons per year. Total economic system cost (see Table 14.6), also at present value and at a 10 percent discount rate, is higher than under the reference scenario with an incremental cost of US$239.67 million. CO_2 emissions reductions vary between 3.6 and 4.0 Mt per year. Total cumulative emissions reductions are 48.11 Mt of CO_2. The cost-effectiveness[9] of nuclear technology as a greenhouse gas mitigation technology is therefore US$4.98/ton CO_2.

The renewable-energy scenario includes wind and solar photovoltaic (PV) energy. The role of solar PV will be very limited. By 2025, solar will generate only about 1.2 PJ of electricity, equivalent to 195 MW of installed PV capacity. Wind is forecast to penetrate the market relatively rapidly, approximately 4.9 percent of total generation, that is, 78.3 PJ by 2025. At the assumed average capacity factor of 26.2 percent, about 9'500 MW of wind capacity will be needed to generate this power. Wind replaces marginal gas-fired generation by up to 93.3 PJ (2025), that is, about 19 percent more than wind electricity and a reduction of imported gas. The reduction grows as wind generation increases and reaches approximately 180 PJ by 2025, equivalent to a reduction in the natural gas imports of 509 Mcfd with respect to the reference scenario. The total economic system cost (Table 14.6), also at present value and at a 10 percent discount rate, is higher than under the reference scenario with an incremental cost of US$415.65 million. The accelerated penetration of renewable power generation results in CO_2 emissions that are up 10 million tons per year (2025) below the reference case levels. The total cumulative emissions reductions in the period from 2005 to 2025 are equal to 82.18 million tons. The cost-effectiveness of solar and wind as a greenhouse gas mitigation technology is therefore US$5.06/ton CO_2.

Technical-Economical Analysis of the Environmental Impact and Corresponding Sustainability Indicators of the Use of Natural Gas in Mexico

Mexican natural gas policy has been the subject of two studies at the Mexican Petroleum Institute. The first study (Bauer et al. 2003) compares the natural gas policy scenario (SENER) with a "business as usual" one (BAU), in which the same energy demand is satisfied throughout with a fuel mix corresponding to the one existing in 2002. The main results are:

- *Oil products.* There exists a mismatch between the natural gas policy and the development plans of the oil sector. The increases in production and processing capacities as planned lead in the SENER scenario to the need to import in 2010 up to 1.85 Bcfd of natural gas, even if the production of associated and nonassociated gas reaches 8.98 Bcfd, as PEMEX projects. On the other hand, in the BAU scenario, there would be a capacity to export up to 2.04 Bcfd with the same production, although imports of fuel oil would reach 599'000 bd (barrels per day). Gasoline demand as high as 1.32 Mbd could ensue by 2010 if the annual average GDP growth rate reaches 3.7 percent, versus a production capacity of only 660'000 bd (Bauer, Mar, and Elizalde 2003).
- *Costs.* The difference in costs between the SENER and BAU scenarios is extremely sensitive to the price of natural gas. In the SENER case, the lower cost of basing the expansion of the power sector on natural gas combined cycle plants can be upset quickly by an increase from 3 to 5 dollars per MBtu. The same occurs for the import–export balance of natural gas and oil products, which can easily reach a deficit of over 5 billion dollars for a NG price of 6 dollars per MBtu.

The second study (Elizalde and Bauer 2003) extends to 2025 the SENER natural gas scenario (SENER 2002a), and compares it to two alternative ones: a coal scenario in which the expansion of the power sector from 2010 on allows a diversification based on coal and dual power plants; and a "nuclear and hydro" scenario where the diversification relies on nuclear, hydro, and geothermal plants. The natural gas balance yields an import to demand ratio in 2025, of 53, 42, and 50 percent for the SENER, coal, and "nuclear and hydro" scenarios, respectively, unless the necessary investments in exploration and production are made to tap the extensive resources foreseen.

Institutional (Legal) Changes to Increase Investment

Considerable investment is necessary for Mexico to change from being a net importer of natural gas, oil products, and petrochemicals to a significant exporter. Moreover, reliance on natural gas imports might expose Mexico to price volatility similar to that which has been observed in the United States recently (Greenspan 2003) or risk disruptions in its gas markets.

According to energy sector estimates, the expansion and modernization of the energy sector for the period 2002–2011 will require investments of US$ 168'200 million. PEMEX will require US$107'500 million and the power sector US$61'700 million (see Table 14.7). In the last five years, an important amount has gone to exploration and development in order to increase proven oil and gas reserves and production; the remainder has gone to the reconfiguration of refineries and to natural gas processing and distribution. In the case of natural gas, PEMEX set up a Strategic Gas Program (US$12'000 million) with the purpose of increasing production capacity by 800 Mcfd by 2003 and by 3.5 Bcfd by 2008.

Credit is the main financial source of PEMEX, because the major part of its expansion of capacity is carried out by the use of resources of third parties. These include PIDIREGAS type projects (Long-Term Productive Infrastructure Projects with Deferred Impact on the Budget—Proyectos de Impacto Diferido en el Registro del Gasto); credits from banks, contractors and suppliers; and funds from the emissions of bonds. The PIDIREGAS[10] projects create payment liabilities for the government that must be included in the federal budget each year and are, therefore, accounted for as public debt.

Recently, to develop the nonassociated natural gas potential of the Burgos Basin, which would reduce the dependency on natural gas imports, PEP created the mechanism called Multiple Services Contracts (MSCs). Their objective is to group in a single contract with one company or consortium—national, foreign, or mixed—all exploration, development, and production services in an assigned block, instead of contracting them separately with the resulting effect of a costly and inefficient follow-up, analysis, and evaluation of the contracted services. To respect the explicit prohibition of risk-sharing contracts, the hydrocarbons produced within a work area shall be the exclusive property of PEP, the contractor shall own

Table 14.7

Energy Sector's Investment Requirements, 2002–2011

	Billion US$	Observations
Total energy sector	168.2	
Oil sector total	107.5	
PEMEX Exploration and Production	85.8	Emphasis on exploration to increase proven reserves and production of light crude oil and non-associated natural gas. Exploration and producíion of nonassociated natural gas is financed, mainly, through the mechanism called Multiple Services Contracts (MSC).
PEMEX Refining	16.2	Emphasis on supply and fuels quality as well as maintenance of the refineries and equipment. Part of the required investment will be financed through budget allocations and the rest through the PIDIREGAS scheme.
PEMEX Gas and Basic Petrochemicals	4.5	Emphasis on natural gas strategic and integral projects as well as PIDIREGAS amortization.
PEMEX Petrochemicals	1	Investments programmed for the next 3 years.
Power sector total	60.7	
Generation	22.8	
Financed Public Works	12.2	These investment projects will be representations of the direct investment projects option of the PIDIREGAS scheme commented on in the text.
Independent Power Producers	10.4	These investment projects are representations the conditional investment projects option of the PIDIREGAS scheme undertaken by CFE and pays for the power it receives via budget allocation as discussed in the text.
Public Sector Investment (budget)	0.2	
Transmission	14.9	
Financed Public Works	6.8	Same observations as in the case of Generation Financed Public Works.
Public Sector Investment (budget)	8.2	
Distribution	13.2	
Financed Public Works	2.8	Same observations as in the case of Generation Financed Public Works.
Public Sector Investment (budget)	10.3	
Maintenance	8.3	
Other investments	1.5	

Sources: PEMEX (2002); México, SENER (2002d).

neither the production nor the reserves within the work block, and the contractor shall receive in cash the compensation for the gas produced and for financial interests as set in the contract. The MSCs are classified as PIDIREGAS projects oriented to the development of the nonassociated natural gas potential.

In the case of the power sector, despite the 1992 amendments by the Congress to the Public Electricity Service Ruling Act, the sector's monopolistic conditions and the restrictions of the current legal framework have made private investment in self-supply, cogeneration, and small production unattractive. As a result of the lack of a market in which generators may sell their surplus energy in a competitive manner, projects are only cost-effective when capacity is allocated for self-supply.

Private financing for new generation capacity has been obtained through independent power producers (IPPs) that bid for long-term power purchase agreements. Under this type of contract, the CFE bears the investment risks because producers receive compensation for capacity throughout the contract term (twenty-five years), even when power plants are not used. In addition, if electricity is produced at a lower cost due to technological developments within five or ten years, CFE has to continue paying the price agreed to in the long-term power purchase agreement.

Finally, because the total natural gas production, including the projected increase in associated gas, may not be sufficient to supply the expected demand, CFE has contracted the construction of a gasification plant in Altamira, on the shore of the Gulf of Mexico, to import liquified natural gas (LNG) for an amount of 450 Mcfd, mainly to assure the supply to the new IPPs in the area. This increase is needed to respond to the deregulation issued in 1995 that limited PEMEX to production and first-hand sales and opened the transport and distribution of natural gas to private participation (Quintanilla and Bauer 1996).

The Changing Legal Framework: An Update

Policy and decision makers have attempted to increase foreign investment through changes in the legislation that governs the energy sector. Consequently, structural changes have been taking place in Mexico's gas and power sectors since 1992, the most important one being the opening to independent power producers (Quintanilla and Bauer 1996). Since then, the Energy Regulatory Commission has issued the following regulatory instruments for the natural gas industry:

1. Provisions for the participation of PEMEX and individual parties in natural gas regulated activities: the participation in transportation, storage, and distribution is subject to a permit regime.
2. Price and rate determination directive for natural gas regulated activities: among which first-hand sales are subject to a price cap methodology and determined with reference to international markets and consideration of gas transportation costs in Mexico.

3. Accounting directive for natural gas regulated activities: establishes the general accounting principles for permit holders and includes an account catalog that must be used, in accordance with generally accepted accounting principles in Mexico. This directive is intended to standardize the information that PEMEX and permit holders submit to the Energy Regulatory Commission, in order to facilitate its regulation and comparison.

4. Geographic zone directive for natural gas: establishes the general procedure used by the Energy Regulatory Commission to determine geographic zones for natural gas distribution purposes. Geographic zones are established considering a number of economic, technical and urban planning factors in order to ensure the development of profitable and efficient distribution systems, according to national and regional development programs.

5. Natural gas first-hand sales directive: specifies the criteria and procedures that must be followed by PEMEX and its subsidiaries for natural gas first-hand sales. The general terms and conditions for first-hand sales are governed by the following principles: (a) transparency and balance in the contractual relation between PEMEX and natural gas buyers; (b) monitoring that PEMEX does not impose unilateral or discriminatory conditions; and (c) establishment of reciprocal conditions between PEMEX and natural gas buyers.

6. Official Mexican Standards (Normas Oficiales Mexicanas, NOM): between 1998 and 2002, the Energy Regulatory Commission issued eleven NOMs related to natural gas and to develop the specifications that inspection units, testing or calibrating laboratories, and certifying organizations should use to determine the degree of compliance with the official standards.

The continuation of the current restrictions (fiscal and operational among others) imposed by the federal government on PEMEX will curtail its possibilities of growing and participating in a competitive way as a world-class company. From 1998 onward, due to the high transfers from PEMEX to the government's fiscal income, PEMEX has reported losses after taxes and dues. In the long term this can reduce the access of PEMEX to international financial markets and as a result make it more expensive to finance its growth.

Therefore, proposals to change the structure in which PEMEX operates have been suggested. These include the modification of the legal and control frameworks under which PEMEX operates, administrates, and finances its activities by (1) a change in the fiscal regime of PEMEX; (2) greater management autonomy; and (3) the definition of new mechanisms of association with third parties—national and foreign—for the development of projects along the whole productive chains. So far, Congress has not agreed on any such measure. At present, the only concession granted to PEMEX for the 2004 fiscal year (January–December), is to keep for development 40 percent of any revenue arising from export prices above US$20 per barrel.

Conclusion

According to conservative estimates, the expansion and modernization of the energy sector would require investments of US$168'200 million from 2002 to 2011 in order to reach economic growth goals. The state cannot continue financing the energy sector's investment requirements on its own, due to either macroeconomic or income distribution issues. The limitations imposed on state-owned companies and the effects of these limitations on the competitiveness of the domestic industrial sector are becoming increasingly evident. An example is the increased dependence on imports to supply the petrochemical sector, public and private, while on the public side PEMEX both has been prevented from divesting its petrochemical branch and has been restricted for several years in its investments because funds needed for this purpose are diverted to finance other government activities. This contrasts with the development of other countries' energy sectors, where competition has been encouraged by allowing private investment in activities previously reserved for the state.

If private participation increases reliability, efficiency, and competitiveness in the energy sector, then it seems crucial for the state to provide adequate conditions for the private sector to participate in the development of the required energy infrastructure over the next years and to guarantee that benefits are passed on to the population. In order to accomplish this, the state's regulatory role must be strengthened through clear and predictable rules, as well as solid, transparent, and reliable institutions. To allow public and private companies to compete on equal footing, the following actions must be undertaken to this effect: (1) redefine the areas reserved exclusively to the state and focus public companies' effort on those areas, (2) open new areas to private investment and focus the public sector's efforts on priority areas, and (3) separate vertically and horizontally state-owned companies and transform them into various public institutions and companies with an authentic business sense, and (4) introduce effective competition conditions.

Exposing the Mexican oil sector to a complete and immediate open market could be disastrous because in the short term it could lose part of its protected market for oil products that provides a major part of its revenues (over 64 percent in 2002), and in the long term it therefore would not be able to share in the expected expansion for the lack of investment. It is necessary and indispensable to strengthen it as a first step and afterward to decide on further steps. Foreign oil companies would like to have full access to the upstream areas of the industry and be contractually bound in production-sharing agreements (upstream refers to the early stages in the operations of a business or industry, as exploration and production in the oil business). Also, they would like to be allowed direct entry into the Mexican market for petroleum products and to open gas stations with supply from their own refineries. Therefore, if Mexico considers such initiatives and decides to make changes in its legal framework, it is important to ask many questions, such as: Will the concessionaires be obligated to sell their products to PEMEX? Could they sell them directly to the market? Could they be allowed to export them? Would they have to use PEMEX facilities for transportation and distribution or they would have to build their own systems?

The more sensitive area of proposed electric power sector reform lies in the changes to the Constitution. Subjects of intense debate are concepts such as sovereignty, strategic areas, whether the state should have a monopoly over all aspects of the electric power industry—as originally understood under its constitutional obligation to provide this "public service"—and if so, the question is of how this monopoly should be exercised. Or, if a monopoly is not the preferred form of ownership and control, how the electric sector should be regulated beyond the exclusions to the concept of public service, which opened the sector to IPPs and self-supply in 1993 but kept a hold on distribution and marketing (Quintanilla and Bauer 1996).

If the final decision is to open the electricity sector to private investment in generation, distribution, and marketing, equal conditions must be guaranteed to public and private companies. The private sector will not risk investment if it must confront monopolistic structures or regulations that may eventually regulate them out of existence. As a consequence, it will become of central importance to transform CFE and LFC and create new state-owned companies, with a clear business sense, that may compete among themselves as well as with private companies.

Notes

This chapter is based on a longer work that is available on request from Juan Quintanilla (juaquin@servidor.unam.mx) or Mariano Bauer (mbauer@fisica.unam.mx.).

1. The SEC's criteria, in the case of clastic (sedimentary) reservoirs and in the absence of pressure proofs showing the continuity of the hydrocarbon column, recognizes as proven area only the immediate area adjacent to the productive zone. Therefore, the SEC guidelines do not recognize as necessary and sufficient elements the integration of seismic and well information to the geological-petrophysical models as a demonstration of the continuity of the reservoirs. On the other hand, they manifest that the pressure measurements are indispensable elements to classify a reserve as proven as well as the clear desire to produce such a reserve in a reasonable time span. The application of this definition to reservoirs deposited in clastic sedimentary environments, conducts to classify as proved the immediate vicinity of the productive area.

2. Conventional crude oil flows naturally or can be pumped without being heated or diluted. Crude oil commonly is classified as light, medium, or heavy, referring to its gravity as measured on the American Petroleum Institute (API) Scale. The API gravity is measured in degrees and is calculated using the formula $(141.5/sp) - 131.5 = $ API Gravity, where sp is the specific gravity. The higher the API gravity, the lighter the compound. Light crudes generally exceed 38 degrees API and heavy crudes are commonly labeled as all crudes with an API gravity of 22 degrees or below. Intermediate crudes fall in the range of 22 degrees to 38 degrees API gravity.

3. The reserves-to-production ratio is commonly used in the oil industry; the meaning of this term is the ratio of the remaining total reserves at the beginning of a given year to the total oil production during the previous year.

4. An active, from the administrative point of view, is a subdivision of each region. Presently, there are seventeen actives: three in the northeastern marine region, three in the southwestern marine region, seven in the onshore southern region, and four in the onshore northern region.

5. According to the listing of units of measure, MW is a million watts (W). A watt is a

unit of power with dimensions of energy divided by time. In electrical terms, 1 watt is the power delivered to a resistor by an electric current of 1 ampere when the resulting voltage drop is 1 volt. This is the reason that in electrical applications energy is often measured in kilowatt-hours (kWh) or similar units. To give an idea of this amount of energy from everyday experience, 1 kWh represents the energy delivered by ten 100-W light bulbs left on for only one hour.

6. The combined-cycle power plants are integrated by two types of generating units: gas turbine (Bryton cycle) and steam. At the end of the thermal cycle of the gas turbine unit, the waste gases have an important amount of thermal energy that can be recuperated in a heat recovery unit and used to increase the water temperature and take it to the steam phase (Rankine cycle); this steam is used to generate electricity. Due to the combination of these two thermodynamic cycles, they receive the name of combined cycle.

7. We use the term *total economic system cost* for the following reason. Since we try to model consumer behavior in response to prices, we model full consumer prices. Taxes and subsidies are a big component of consumer prices, which really are transfer payments from one sector to another. So when we do an economic analysis we need to exclude transfer payments. This is why we call it total economic system cost.

8. Base load means the constant or permanent load on a power supply.

9. A cost-effective project or technology is one that optimizes economic efficiency and minimizes the associated greenhouse gas emissions.

10. The economic crisis of December 1994 caused a drastic reduction in public revenues and budget allocation, as well as highly limited access to international financing markets. Under these economic circumstances, the PIDIREGAS program was initiated with the purpose of attracting private sector capital and long-term financing to develop strategic and highly profitable projects and a more flexible governmental budgetary instrument to carry out strategic projects. The central concept was to prevent strategic projects from being subject to budgetary cuts or delays due to economic volatility impacting Mexico's public finances. The PIDIREGAS scheme results in multiyear project approval capability. Legal amendments were made in December 1995 that allowed the creation of the PIDIREGAS program. Prior to implementation of PIDIREGAS, Mexico's state-owned energy entities developed and financed new construction projects via public funding or direct bilateral/multilateral funding sources. Therefore, project development was dependent on annual budget allocations. The requirements of a project to qualify for PIDIREGAS consideration are: (1) be strategic for the nation; (2) generate significant cash flows (these have to be more than sufficient to cover future financing costs); and (3) have the ability to secure long-term financing. PIDIREGAS are not necessarily limited to energy-related infrastructure projects, but to date they have been exclusively used for such projects. They must comply with all the laws and provisions that govern and/or impact PIDIREGAS projects and the project approval process. PIDIREGAS modalities in use are: (1) direct investment projects (projects that are built and financed during the construction period by the private sector; upon completion, ownership is transferred to the public sector entity in exchange for full payment or a stream of payments); and (2) conditional investment projects (projects that are built, financed, owned, and operated by the private sector; under these projects, the public sector entity is contractually bound to purchase the goods or services produced by the private sector entity over a specified number of years; an example of these are the long-term power purchase agreements between the CFE and the IPPs). More details on PIDIREGAS can be found in IPD (2002).

Acronyms and Abbreviations

AAPG   American Association of Petroleum Geologists
CFE   Federal Electricity Commission (Comisión Federal de Electricidad)

CNSNS   National Nuclear Safety Commission (Comisión Nacional de Seguridad Nuclear y Salvaguardas)
CONAE   National Commission for Energy Savings (Comisión Nacional para el Ahorro de Energía)
CRE   Energy Regulatory Commission (Comisión Reguladora de Energia)
GDP   gross domestic product
GHG   greenhouse gas
IAEA   International Atomic Energy Agency
IIE   Electrical Research Institute (Instituto de Investigaciones Eléctricas)
IMP   Mexican Petroleum Institute (Instituto Mexicano del Petróleo)
ININ   National Nuclear Research Institute (Instituto Nacional de Investigaciones Nucleares)
IPP   independent power producer
LFC   Light and Power of the Center (Luz y Fuerza del Centro)
LPG   liquefied petroleum gas
LNG   liquefied natural gas
NRS   National Refining System (Sistema Nacional de Refinación)
PEMEX   Mexican Oil Company (Petróleos Mexicanos)
PEP   PEMEX Exploration and Production (PEMEX Exploración y Producción)
PGPB   PEMEX Gas and Basic Petrochemicals (PEMEX Gas y Petroquímica Básica)
PMI   PEMEX International (PEMEX Internacional)
PPQ   PEMEX Petrochemicals (PEMEX Petroquímica)
PR   PEMEX Refining (PEMEX Refinación)
SEC   Securities and Exchange Commission
SENER   Energy Secretariat (Secretaría de Energía)
SPE   Society of Petroleum Engineers
WPC   World Petroleum Congresses

Units of Measure

m   thousand (10 to the 3rd power)
M   million (10 to the 6th power)
T   tera (trillion, 10 to the 12th power)
P   peta (quadrillion, 10 to the 15th power)
boe   barrel of oil equivalent
mboe   thousand barrels of oil equivalent
Mboe   million barrels of oil equivalent
Btu   British thermal unit
Mbtu   million British thermal unit
d   day
yr   year
bd   barrels per day
Mbd   million barrels per day
cf   cubic feet
cfd   cubic feet per day
Mcfd   million cubic feet per day
Bcfd   billion cubic feet per day
t   ton

Mt	million ton
W	watt
MW	million watt
GW	gigawatt
Wh	watt-hour
MWh	million watt-hour
GWh	gigawatt-hour
TWh	trillion watt-hour
J	Joule
PJ	Petajoule

Conversion Factors

1 boe = 5,201 cubic feet of natural gas
1 year = 365 days
1 PJ = 167.6 mboe

References

Banco de Mexico. n.d. Available at www.banxico.org.mx.

Bauer, M., E. Mar, and A. Elizalde. 2003. "Transport and Energy Demand in Mexico: The Personal Income Shock," *Energy Policy* 31. no. 14.

Bauer, M., E. Melgar, R. Villaseñor, M. Magdaleno, A. Elizalde, E. Mar, E. Ceballos, G. Yánez, S. Martínez, L. Tavera, V. Mora, M.E. Ruiz, G. González, J.L. López, C. Gallardo, G. Bravo, J. Gazca, A. Melgarejo, and M.E. Palmerín. 2003. "Technical-Economical Analysis of the Environmental Impact and Corresponding Sustainability Indicators of the Use of Natural Gas in Mexico." *Proceedings of the 22nd World Gas Conference Tokyo 2003.* International Gas Union.

Elizalde, A., and M. Bauer. 2003. "Natural Gas Demand in Mexico's Electric Generation Sector: Restructuring of the Power Industry and Forecasts to 2025." *Proceedings of the 22nd World Gas Conference Tokyo 2003.* International Gas Union.

Gómez Ávila., S., N. Rodríguez M., F. Guzmán, and M. Bauer. 2001. "Petróleos Mexicanos: A National Oil Company Committed to Improve Its Environmental Performance," *World Energy: The Ethical Dimension,* ed. World Energy Council. London.

Greenspan, Alan. 2003. "Natural Gas Supply and Demand Issues, Testimony of Chairman Alan Greenspan Before the Committee on Energy and Commerce." U.S. House of Representatives, Washington, DC, June 10.

INEGI. n.d. Available at www.inegi.gob.mx.

International Project Development Latin America, Inc. (IPD). 2002. "PIDIREGAS: Viability or Crisis, International Project Development Latin America, Inc." Tercer Seminario Anual de Energía y Derecho, organized by Instituto Tecnológico Autónomo de México and Academia Mexicana de Derecho Energético, Mexico, October.

Mexico, Presidencia de la República. 2003. *Tercer Informe de Gobierno.*

———. Secretaría de Energia (SENER). Various years. *Balance nacional de energía.*

———. 2002a. *Prospectiva del mercado de gas natural 2002–2011.* México: SENER.

———. 2002b. *Prospectiva de petrolíferos 2002–2011.* México: SENER.

———. 2002c. *Prospectiva de gas licuado de petróleo 2002–2011.* México: SENER.

———. 2002d. *Prospectiva del sector eléctrico 2002–2011.* México: SENER.

PEMEX. 2002. *Memoria de Labores.* PEMEX, México, March.

———. 2003. *SEGURIDAD, SALUD Y MEDIO AMBIENTE—Informe Annual 2002.*

————. Various years. *Statistical Yearbook.* PEMEX, México.

Quintanilla, Juan. 1996. "Mexican Oil and Energy." In *Changing Structure of Mexico,* ed. Laura Randall. Armonk, NY: M.E. Sharpe.

Quintanilla, Juan, V. Aguilar, J. Fernández, E. Ibars, H. Cadena, I. Jiménez, G. Serrato, R. Ortega, C. Martín del Campo, L. Conde, E. Mar, and A. Rodríguez. 2003a. *Comparative Assessment of Energy Options and Strategies Until 2025.* México: Secretaría de Energía. (To be published by the International Atomic Energy Agency [IAEA], Vienna, Austria.)

Quintanilla, Juan, V. Aguilar, J. Fernández, E. Ibars, H. Cadena, I. Jiménez, R. Ortega, C. Martín del Campo, and A. Rodríguez. 2003b. "Comparative Assessment of Energy Sources for Electricity Supply Until 2025." México: Secretaría de Energía. (To be published by the International Atomic Energy Agency [IAEA], Vienna, Austria.)

Quintanilla, Juan, G. Conzelmann, V. Aguilar, J. Fernández, G. Serrato, R. Ortega, C. Martín del Campo, L. Conde, and E. Mar. 2003c. "Mexico's Long-Term Energy Outlook—Results of a Detailed Energy Supply and Demand Simulation." Paper presented at 23rd International Association for Energy Economics (IAEE) North American Conference, Mexico, October 21.

Quintanilla, Juan, G. Conzelmann, V. Aguilar, J. Fernández, E. Ibars, H. Cadena, and I. Jiménez. 2003d. "Powering Mexico's Future—An In-Depth Look at Long-Term Electricity Market Developments." Paper presented at 23rd International Association for Energy Economics (IAEE) North American Conference, Mexico, October 21.

15

Oscar F. Contreras

Industrial Development and Technology Policy

The Case of the Maquiladoras

The ability of the Mexican government to form and implement industrial policy is strongly influenced by the huge flow of funds, goods, and services between Mexico and the United States. Oscar Contreras analyzes how Mexico used firms called maquiladoras to promote its economic development.

Goods produced by maquiladoras have U.S. tariff benefits when they are exported to the United States. At first, promoting exports produced by maquiladoras was successfully used to promote employment in the northern border area of Mexico.

In time, Mexico created other export promotion programs and expanded the areas in which maquiladoras could be established. The broadening and deepening of the maquiladoras and of export promotion contributed to the establishment of the North American Free Trade Agreement (NAFTA)—a move that increased the growth of many maquiladoras but was not a panacea for Mexican economic development.

Mexican exports face competition from other nations that have lower labor costs than Mexico at the same time that their technology is similar to Mexico's. This leads Dr. Contreras to suggest that in order to be productive and competitive, Mexico must specialize in high value-added and knowledge-intensive industries. He argues that Mexico needs policies to encourage Mexican suppliers to provide inputs to Mexican export industries. Maquiladoras have begun to use more Mexican management, and process and product engineering, although few research and development activities have transferred to Mexico. Dr. Contreras concludes that the market by itself cannot provide the knowledge and services needed for economic development that could be provided by industrial, scientific, technological, and educational policy.

The maquiladora export industry in the North region of Mexico generated a substantial part of Mexican industrial growth during the last twenty-five years.[1]

Maquiladoras are firms that import raw materials, components, and machinery without paying duties, in order to process or assemble them in Mexico and then reexport them, principally to the United States.

The maquiladora program originally was part of the Mexican government's temporary strategy to reduce unemployment in the border zone with the United States. The emphasis on employment dominated Mexican maquiladora policy from 1965 to 1988. After this year, other objectives were added, among them that of incorporating Mexican firms as suppliers of inputs to maquiladoras.

The employment objectives were achieved. Maquiladora policy, however, could not substantially increase Mexican capacity to supply the inputs it needed from Mexico itself, since it favored imports from other nations for processessing and export. For foreign enterprises that established maquila operations in Mexico, this scheme was very advantageous because it allowed them to dramatically reduce their labor costs in comparison to what they would have paid in the United States if they had not moved to Mexico.

After some years these enterprises acquired enormous importance for the Mexican economy. And although at the beginning their activities were largely labor intensive with only a low technological content, many plants that are operating today have up-to-date technologies, with a modern organization and well-trained labor force that includes several tens of thousands of technicians and engineers. Despite this, one of the persisting problems is the maquiladora's low capacity to generate productive links to local firms.

In 2001, an economic recession began in Mexico that largely was the result of the economic recession in the United States. Toward the third quarter of 2002, employment in maquila firms had fallen by 22 percent and the number of maquiladora plants by 20 percent, but conforming to the U.S. economy, the sector began to show signs of improvement as employment began to increase. In mid-2004, maquiladoras showed a total of 2,800 plants and 1,130,000 jobs.

However, there are indications that the decrease that began in 2001 is not only a business cycle problem, since Mexico has confronted strong competition from China, Central America, and the Caribbean. Many analysts indicate that the industrialization strategy based on maquiladoras is worn out, at least in the sense of a competitive industrial model based on labor costs. Apparently, the only option is the shift to a more advanced scheme based on specialization in more knowledge-intensive and high value-added industries.

How Many Maquiladoras Are There, Where Are They, and What Do They Do?

The Mexican government has developed several programs to promote exports. The maquiladora program is the most important. Another program is the Program of Temporary Imports for Exportation (PITEX), established on May 3, 1990. The signing of NAFTA followed in January 1994. During the 1990s, the PITEX program was increasingly important, above all for export firms that were not located in border regions, but even so the maquiladora program continued to be the source of 60 percent of Mexican exports carried out under this type of promotion of exports programs. Table 15.1 only includes firms officially registered as maquiladoras. There were eight times as many firms in 2000 as in 1975, and eighteen times as many workers.

Growth was greatest during the 1985–2000 period, which not only had the greatest increase in output and employment, but also was a period in which the original concept of "maquiladora industry" was substantially transformed, as much in productive processes as in industrial organization and legal definition. At the end of 2000, there were more than 3,700 firms, employing more than 1.3 million workers. During these years, the maquiladoras became the main source of creation of industrial jobs, and the second most important source of foreign exchange, representing half of Mexican exports and 40 percent of manufacturing employment.

This growth was especially important because it occurred during a period of stagnation of manufacturing employment in Mexico. In 1985–2000, employment in maquiladoras grew at an annual rate of 13 percent, while the increase in the rest of the manufacturing sector was less than 1 percent per year. In 1985, the total value of Mexican exports was a little more than 27 billion dollars, of which 19 percent came from maquiladoras. Fifteen years later, in 2000, the total value of exports was six times that amount, and maquiladoras represented 48 percent of the country's exports.

The maquila activities that grew most rapidly were the manufacture of auto parts and apparel, although the electronic industry had the major share of firms and employees. During the 1985–2000 period, employment in manufacture of auto parts grew at an annual rate greater than 20 percent, while apparel increased 14 percent and electronics 10 percent annually.

With regard to the regional distribution of maquiladoras, despite the increasing tendency to establish plants in the interior of Mexico, today 77 percent of firms and 83 percent of employment are located in the six U.S. border states.

Despite almost uninterrupted growth since their beginning, maquiladoras began to decline rapidly at the end of 2000, spreading alarm among businessmen and politicians in Mexico. However, the decline stopped in 2003 and the activity of the maquiladoras substantially recovered in 2004.

In October 2000 employment reached its highest level with 1,338,970 employees. But from November 2000 to December 2001, more than 250,000 jobs were lost (INEGI 2004). By mid-2002, employment in maquiladoras had fallen 20 percent from the October 2000 peak and production by 30 percent. The electronics sector was the most impacted, especially in the border region (U.S. GAO 2003). Nonetheless, when the U.S. economy began to recover, this negative tendency partially stopped, and by mid-2004, there were 2,800 firms and 1,130,000 employees.

Table 15.1

Regional Economic Performance in the NAFTA Era (selected variables)

Variable	Year/period	Major regions*						
		Northern Border	Central–North	Central–West	Central	Southeast	South	Nation
GDP share	1980	19.1	4.6	13.8	39.3	11.8	11.4	—
	1993	21.4	5	15.3	37.8	9.6	10.9	—
	1998	22.9	4.8	15.5	36.6	9.4	10.8	—
	2001	23.4	4.7	15.5	36.6	9.2	10.7	—
Real GDP avg. annual growth	1993–2001	4.28	2.33	3.34	2.79	2.5	2.82	3.15
FDI share**		25.3	0.9	5.5	65.6	1	1.6	—
FDI (bn. dls.)	1994–2001	25.49	0.86	5.56	66.01	1.05	1.63	100.6
Maquiladora plants share	1993	87.4	2.8[a]	1.9[b]	1.2[d]	1.2[f]	0	—
	1998	79.3	4	6.8[c]	2.4[e]	2.2[f]	2.29[g]	—
	2003	78.6	2.6	8.1[c]	2.2[e]	3.1[f]	2.89[g]	—
Maquiladora plants (average annual growth)	1990–1994	4.31	0.7	2.39	13.62	20.96	—	5.33
	1994–2003	2.87	4.08	25.4	8.98	15.7	—	4.03
	1994–2000	7.46	14.78	41.55	18.54	28.75	—	9.54
	2000–2003	–6.30	–17.31	–6.91	–10.14	–10.42	–9.89	–7.0
Exports share***	1996	45	1.6	5.2	41.1	2	5.1	—
	1998	50	1.8	5.5	34.4	1.5	6.7	—
	2002	42.3	1.2	7.1	41.7	1.3	6.4	—
	1996–2002	46.3	1.4	5.9	38.3	1.5	6.6	—

Exports average annual growth	1996–1999	5.73	0.02	3.54	−4.28	−12.69	19.73	2.09
	1996–2002	−0.79	−4.89	6.01	0.93	−5.52	4.92	0.15
Exports (U.S.$ billions)	1996–2002	289.8	8.84	36.88	239.47	9.14	41.26	625.39

Source: Based on information from INEGI, Bancomext y Secretaría de Economía.

* Definition of regions: Northern Border (Baja California, Sonora, Chihuahua, Coahuila, Nuevo León, and Tamaulipas); Central-North (Sinaloa, Durango, Baja California Sur, and Zacatecas; Central-West (Jalisco, Colima, Aguascalientes, Nayarit, Guanajuato, Querétaro, and San Luis Potosí); Central (D.F., México, Hidalgo, Morelos and Tlaxcala); Southeast (Veracruz, Tabasco, Quintana Roo and Campeche); South (Chiapas, Oaxaca, Guerrero, Michoacán, and Puebla).

** Includes new investment and importation of fixed assets by the maquiladoras. In the registration of FDI by states, investments are assigned to the state where the headquarters of the firms is located, which in some cases does not coincide with the state where the investment actually takes place.

*** Includes only exports for which a place (state) of origin has been identified. That portion on average amounts to 70 percent of total exports during the period. The database is produced by Bancomext.

[a]Baja California Sur and Durango; [b]Jalisco; [c]Jalisco, Guanajuato, and Aguascalientes; [d]Mexico State; [e]Mexico State and Federal District; [f]Yucatán; [g]Puebla.

Maquiladoras as a Strategic Element of Mexican Industrial Policy (1989–2001)

The maquiladora industry began in 1965 as a combination of two government instruments: the U.S. tariff provisions 806.30 and 807.00 (later replaced as HTS 9802 in 1989), and the Border Industrialization Program in Mexico (Programa de Industrialización Fronteriza). This scheme was very attractive for U.S. firms because it allowed them to maintain their competitiveness in the world market by operating with substantially lower costs when they moved part of their productive process to Mexico. This segmentation of the production process was possible thanks to advances in communications and transport, which made it possible to maintain efficient coordination and strict supervision of geographically diverse productive processes.

For Mexico, the main objective was to attract foreign firms along the northern border to create employment for workers forced to return to Mexico at the end of the Bracero Program in the United States. The Mexican government confronted an emergency situation by creating a "policy of exception" with temporary coverage of delimited regions. It was claimed that in the medium term, the assembly plants would create productive links and promote Mexican industrialization using local inputs; the regional delimitation of the program responded exclusively to the conditions of the north border, since in the rest of Mexico industrial policy continued to be centered on protection of Mexican industry by means of fiscal and tariff instruments.

In spite of the government's intention of promoting links to other Mexican firms, no instrument was designed to achieve this goal. The focus of government policy was limited to combating unemployment and generating foreign exchange. Using this point of view, government created regulations of maquiladora activities during the initial phase: in 1966, the government established the rules that allowed the temporary importation of machinery and inputs in the border area;[2] in 1971, a new rule authorized the establishment of firms in regions outside of the border and the creation of firms with 100 percent foreign capital,[3] and in 1977 it defined coordination mechanisms for the compliance with the rules applicable to this type of firm.

During the initial period, legal changes were defining the administrative norms and operating mechanisms of the maquila regime, but always with the view of maquiladoras as transitory industries in a "situation of exception."

The first important change occured in 1983, when a new decree established that maquiladoras were Mexican mercantile societies; from then on, official documents considered them as a factor of industrial development and not only as assembly enclaves for creating employment. This point of view was reinforced in a 1989 decree, when maquiladoras came to be considered as instruments for transfer of technology and promoters of industrial competitiveness (CEPAL 1996).

In 1994, the previous decree of 1989 was modified to adjust it to the provisions of NAFTA, and in 1996, it was again modified, this time to stimulate the development of Mexican firms that supply inputs of services, parts, and raw materials. In 2001, Provision 303 of NAFTA took effect, which gave rise to a series of adjustments that will be discussed below.

All of these legal changes were related to structural changes in the maquiladoras, and to their increasing importance for the Mexican economy. This model, designed as an emergency measure, was being transformed both in its rules and in their application, until it became the basis for industrial development in the northern region of Mexico and for the most dynamic industrial exports of the nation.

Technology and Industrial Learning

The typical image of maquiladoras during the 1970s and first years of the 1980s is that of simple assembly plants, in which unskilled manual labor, a low level of technology, and low salaries predominated.

However, beginning in the 1980s, many of the new plants (above all in the electronics and auto parts industries) introduced production technologies based on microelectronics, robots, and information technologies. Some plants began to use automatic insertion machines, computerized quality control equipment, programmable systems for moving materials, and "pick-and-place" robots. This type of technology began to be used when it was an exception in a context characterized by a broad predominance of manual labor. However, in the electronics and auto parts industries the utilization of flexible technologies and automation spread rapidly (Wilson 1992; Carrillo and Hualde 1998; Lara 1998; Contreras 2000).

A recent investigation reported that in 2002, 56 percent of electronics and auto part firms utilized the best technology available in the world market, 40 percent had a high grade of automation, and 68 percent of these firms were using sophisticated software for enterprise resource planning (Carrillo 2004). The same study mentioned that these enterprises, on average, had 24 programmable machines and 5 robots per plant, and identified a total of 72 research and development centers in Mexico. (For a discussion of Mexico's policy of linking research and development to the needs of firms, see Chapter 12 in this volume).

The utilization of advanced technologies produced a change in the composition of the labor force, requiring a larger number of skilled workers, technicians, and engineers. In 1980, technicians made up 9 percent of the maquiladoras' workforce; in mid-2004 this had reached 12.5 percent. But in some activities and regions, the employment of technicians is higher, as in the case of electronics maquiladoras, 14 percent of whose workers were technicians. As far as regions go, the share of technicians in the labor force of maquiladoras in Guadalajara reached 20 percent in 2004, Mexicali, 17 percent, and Ciudad Juárez 15 percent. Similarly, the constant expansion of industry required the recruitment of a large number of directors and administrators. According to one study, in the cities of Tijuana and Ciudad Juárez alone, 500 new management positions were created each year during the nineties, and 7 of 10 of these positions were filled by Mexican engineers and administrators (Contreras 2000).

This industrial trajectory gave rise to an intense learning process that became a regional comparative advantage (Ohno and Okamoto 1994). Industrial learning had two principal sources: the technical and professional training of the employees, based on the school system and the firms' training programs, and, the shared experience of these employees within the firms and in local society, which is sometimes described as "social capital" (Contreras and Kenney 2002).

Even though many transnationals in sectors such as electronics and auto parts preferred to centralize decision making and research-and-development activities in their own countries, beginning in the 1990s not only U.S. firms but also those transnationals from other nations began to decentralize some of these activities. The main reasons were the search for strategic advantages, such as the availability of human capital (for example, the cost of engineers and managers), the increase of sales in local markets, and the fulfillment of commercial and legal requirements (Eden and Monteils 2002). In the case of maquila operations in Mexico, the decentralization of research and development is incipient, but the transfer of process and product engineering is very advanced (Alonso, Carrillo, and Contreras 2002), as is the transfer of the main managerial functions (Contreras and Kenney 2002).

The Impact of NAFTA

During the first years of NAFTA (1994–2000) maquiladoras grew rapidly. In the first six years of the agreement, employment grew 110 percent, while in the six previous years growth had been 78 percent (Sargent and Matthews 2003). However, as Gruben (2001) has shown, this growth cannot be directly attributed to NAFTA (see Chapters 5, 6, and 8 in this volume).

It is possible to establish an alternate explanation of maquiladora development: NAFTA gave rise to converging processes that favored this growth. On the one hand, the rules for regional content that penalized the use of inputs from nations outside the three NAFTA countries provided an incentive for the manufacture of parts and components in Mexico. Together with the rules of origin, the agreement, by eliminating barriers to trade and investment, favored strategies of organization of production that involved the geographic space of NAFTA as an integrated economic region. These strategies are evident above all in the automotive and electronics industries, but they also occurred in other industries, such as computer equipment and clothing manufacture. The transnational firms rationalized their regional or world production, placing a greater emphasis on aspects such as the quality of the labor force and organizational innovations (Eden and Monteils 2002).

The new rules for investment and trade, as well as the new business climate generated by NAFTA, above all in the period of economic growth in the United States, were the factors which, taken together, unchained an unprecedented growth of maquiladoras. This included the installation of several hundred Japanese,

Korean, and other Asiatic supply firms that were established in Mexico to supply the assembly plants and comply with the new regional content rules. Sargent and Matthews (2003) mentioned three specific aspects of the regulatory structure of maquiladoras that were directly affected by NAFTA: (a) beginning in 2001, the maquiladoras could sell 100 percent of their output in Mexico; (b) the rules of origin established percentages of required regional content to qualify as duty-free products in the United States, even though in some cases the inputs from other regions could be considered as "regional" if they were processed in Mexico; and (c) from 1994 to 2000 it was possible to legally avoid the payment of Mexican taxes, but in 2001 Article 303 took effect. It prohibited the duty-free importation of inputs that were not produced in the NAFTA nations.

The entering into effect of Article 303 gave rise to one of the most conflictive episodes related to NAFTA. In an attempt to maintain the competitiveness of maquiladoras and other export firms, the Mexican government developed various Sectorial Programs (PROSEC) that established low taxes (between 0 and 5 percent) for some inputs. However, the information about the rules of operation of these programs was very incomplete, and many firms could not be declared eligible for them. This added another factor of uncertainty to an atmosphere that already was characterized by confusion and pessimism owing to the U.S. recession and the growing competition from China.

Prospects

The decline of maquiladoras in 2001 unleashed an intense debate in Mexico about the future of this model of industrialization on the grounds that it appeared to be highly vulnerable to fluctuations in the international environment. The decline is attributable to diverse factors: the cyclical behavior of the U.S. economy; the growing competition from China, Central America, and the Caribbean; the strengthening of the peso, which eroded maquiladoras' competitiveness; and the constant changes in fiscal policy, which created a climate of uncertainty for investors.

According to the U.S. General Accounting Office, by 2002 Mexico had lost market share in 47 of 152 categories of U.S. imports, while China gained market share in 35 of these 47 categories, including toys, furniture, electrodomestic equipment, certain kinds of television and video equipment, clothing, and textiles (U.S. GAO 2003).

In addition, the incorporation of China into the World Trade Organization significantly reduced tariffs on imports of Chinese goods to the United States. As a result, many Japanese and Korean maquiladoras revised their strategies: instead of producing electronic components in Asia, assembling them in Mexico, and selling the final product in the United States, some firms were already moving production and assembly to Asia to supply the U.S. market from this location (Sargent and Matthews 2003).

Although on a smaller scale, something similar occurred with regard to competition from Central American and Caribbean countries. Beginning in 2000, the treatment authorized by the United States for the Caribbean Basin Initiative (CBI) eroded Mexico's ability to compete in the U.S. market for clothing, especially because these nations had labor costs much lower than those of Mexico (U.S. GAO 2003).

In contrast to the assembly of components or the manufacture of clothing, there is a large range of products that it is more difficult to move to China or Central America. Whether because of the coordination that must be located close to the market for just-in-time production (as is the case in the auto parts industry) or because of transport costs (as in the case of television sets larger than 27 inches), Mexico continued to have competitive advantages directly linked to its geographic location.

However, it began to be evident that the nation's development could not be sustained only by the maquiladoras. After almost forty years of the maquiladora program, the average of Mexican inputs excluding labor is less than 5 percent, which reflects the absence of an industrial policy capable of promoting endogenous development by means of this strategy. Moreover, recent studies report clear tendencies that the eruption of China into the world market is severely affecting countries and regions that specialize in labor-intensive manufactures exports (Blázquez, Rodríguez, and Santiso 2004; Dussel 2004).

As has been mentioned, in some products and regions, industrial upgrading and learning processes are developing in Mexico as a result of the transfer of engineering, management, and other key functions to Mexican firms. But this system of complementarities that broaden local capabilities has not been generalizad. The trajectory of some regions, such as Tijuana and Ciudad Juárez, in some specific products constitutes a clear example of the potential for local development of world-class capacities for manufacturing, but also shows the limits of an industrialization model that is incapable of generating local linkages.

In the past, the "Asian Tigers" developed their local industries making use of the presence of maquiladora firms. In the 2000s, some emerging economies such as India and Ireland are successfully developing world-class information technology industries. As these and other experiences of advanced local development in the context of a world market have shown, the market by itself is not a substitute for industrial policy, nor of scientific, technological, and educational policy.

Notes

The author thanks the Center for U.S.-Mexican Studies of the University of California, San Diego, for research support.

1. The North region includes the six states on the northern border of Mexico. See the Tamayo-Flores definition in Table 1.2.

2. The zones in which it was permitted to establish maquiladora plants included that so-called Free Zone, which included the peninsula of Baja California and part of the state of Sonora, as well as the "border strip," a strip of territory 20 kilometers from the border.

3. Before, only 49 percent could be owned by foreigners.

References

Alonso, Jorge, Jorge Carrillo, and Oscar Contreras. 2002. "Aprendizaje tecnológico en las maquiladoras del norte de México." *Frontera Norte* 14, no. 27 (January–June).

Blázquez-Lidoy, Jorge, Javier Rodríguez, and Javier Santiso. 2004. "Angel or Devil? Chinese Trade Impact on Latin American Emerging Markets." Paper presented at Columbia University, Institute of Latin American Studies and the Weatherhead East Asian Institute, October 6.

Carrillo, Jorge. 2004. *Principales estadísticas de la industria maquiladora. Encuesta sobre aprendizaje tecnológico y escalamiento industrial.* Tijuana: El Colegio de la Frontera Norte.

Carrillo, Jorge, and Alfredo Hualde. 1998. "Third Generation Maquiladora? The Delphi–General Motors Case." *Journal of Borderland Studies* 13, no. 1 (Spring).

CEPAL (Comisión Económica para América Latina). 1996. *México: La industria maquiladora.* Santiago de Chile: Colección Estudios e Informes de la CEPAL.

Contreras, Oscar. 2000. *Empresas globales, actores locales: Producción flexible y aprendizaje industrial en las maquiladoras.* México: El Colegio de México.

Contreras, Oscar, and Martin Kenney. 2002. "Global Industries and Local Agents: Becoming a World Class Manager in the Mexico-USA Border Region." In *Communities Across Borders*, ed. Paul Kennedy and Victor Roudometof. London and New York: Routledge.

Dussel, Enrique. 2004. *Los efectos económicos de China para México y Centroamérica.*

Eden, Lorraine, and Antonie Monteils. 2002. "Regional Integration: NAFTA and the Reconfiguration of North American Industry." In *Regions, Globalization and the Knowledge-Based Economy*, ed. Paul Kennedy and Victor Roudometof. Oxford: Oxford University Press.

Gruben, William. 2001. "Was NAFTA Behind Mexico's High Maquiladora Growth? *Economic and Financial Review* (Third Quarter). Available at www.dallasfed.org/research/efr.

INEGI (Instituto Nacional de Geografía, Estadística e Informátioca). 2004. Available at http://dgcnesyp.inegi.gob.mx/bdine/bancos.htm. Consulted September19.

Lara Rivero, Arturo. 1998. *Aprendizaje tecnológico y mercado de trabajo en las maquiladoras japonesas.* México: Miguel Ángel Porrúa–UAM Xochimilco.

Ohno, Koichi and Yumiko Okamoto. 1994. *Regional Integration and Foreign Direct Investment: Implications for Developing Countries.* Tokyo: Institute of Developing Economies.

Sargent, John, and Linda Matthews. 2003. "Boom and Bust: Is It the End of Mexico's Maquiladoras?" *Business Horizons* (March–April).

U.S. GAO. 2003. *Mexico's Maquiladora Decline Affects U.S.–México Border Communities and Trade; Recovery Depends in Part on Mexico's Actions.* Washington, DC: U.S. General Accounting Office.

Wilson, Patricia. 1992. *Exports and Local Development: Mexico's New Maquiladoras.* Austin: University of Texas Press.

16

FERNANDO REIMERS

Principally Women

Gender in the Politics of Mexican Education

Increasing efficiency of education is a major goal in Mexico, as in much of Latin America. Education provides much of the human and social capital needed for effective participation in society and at work. Fernando Reimers argues that serious improvements in the quality of education must focus on questions of purpose as well as of efficiency in the delivery of education. Too often the concern with efficiency overrides fundamental questions about the purposes of schools. Often policy reforms to address efficiency make unwarranted assumptions about contextual conditions that can turn the intended purposes of those policies on their heads; for instance, the current popularity of policies to expand the decision making authority of principals assumes that they have incentives and are capable of improving instruction in schools. Reimers shows how in Mexico there are serious problems that undermine the effectiveness of school principals: part of the explanation for the lack of efficiency in education lies with social attitudes that favor men and make it difficult for women to advance in their professions. This in turn creates deep problems for the purpose of teaching students an egalitarian and tolerant set of values, essential to effective citizenship in a democratic society. In this chapter Reimers demonstrates how to productively combine a focus on the purposes of schools with a focus on the efficiency of education delivery.

Women principals run schools whose students achieve at higher levels and have more effective and inclusive organizational cultures yet women are less likely to be promoted to the principalship than men. At the root of this situation are patriarchal and corrupt politics that undermine the foundations of the Mexican public education system and limit the opportunities for professional advancement for women. The National Teachers' Union (SNTE) long supported the dominant government party (PRI). Together with educational administrators, it controls appointments and other conditions of employment.

A top official in the Ministry of Education in the Fox (PAN) administration recently reported that "The union is a business for selling jobs. The inherited jobs open the possibility that those who get them are not good teachers." Moreover, to become a principal, a teacher must help the union. The demands of union leadership, with work in evenings and on weekends, are hard to meet given other social expectations of women in Mexico. One interviewee reported, "We all know what goes on for women in the cantinas and with the sindicato and how some union leaders expect sexual favors from women in order to help them advance in their careers."

In Mexico, as in other countries in Latin America, most principals of elementary schools are men despite the fact that schools run by men are less effective than those run by women. For example, women principals run schools whose students achieve at higher levels and that have more effective and inclusive organizational cultures. Moreover, most elementary school teachers are women, and female teachers have higher levels of professional preparations and teach students who achieve at higher levels. At the root of this paradox—that those who are better at running schools are less likely to be promoted to manage them—are patriarchal and corrupt politics that undermine the foundations of the Mexican public education system. This paradox is problematic for several reasons. On the surface, because it leads to inefficiency. More importantly, this paradox is problematic because it shapes a powerful moral lesson for all students, boys and girls: that merit and ability in the quest for social and professional advancement are secondary to the ascribed characteristics of individuals and to the unfair and misguided traditional values of patriarchy. In Mexico, as in other places in Latin America, politics plays an important role in the appointment of candidates to the positions of teacher and principal. As a result, the odds of appointment and promotion depend on a number of characteristics other than the demonstrated competency to teach. Because of this, it is not uncommon that teachers are often required to spend time away from teaching as a way to pay dues to their political patrons. This chapter examines empirical evidence on the different likelihoods that men and women teachers have of being promoted to principal of an elementary public school in Mexico. It examines how schools managed by men and women differ, and discusses whether those differences relate to the processes that regulate the promotion of teachers to principals, to the experiences and competencies of teachers, or to the incentives attracting teachers to the profession.

Almost a century ago, John Dewey explained that how we teach is what we teach (Dewey 1916). The organization of schools provides powerful models to students about how individuals associate to accomplish tasks, about the roles different people play, and about how difference is valued, or not, as a resource to support collective action. As argued in the classic study of educational change by Seymour Sarason, the relationships among professionals in the school, between them and the students, and among all of them and the society outside the school define school culture (Sarason 1971). That principals play a role in shaping school culture is obvious; less obvious is the specific form this role takes in different contexts. A recent study of the role of principals in Paraguay highlights the fact that research on the principalship in developing countries is extremely scarce (Borden 2002). Research in the United States and other early industrialized nations, in contrast, consistently points to school instructional leadership as one of the sources of school effectiveness (Blasé and Blasé 1999). Many of the approaches of school reform developed over the last decade in the United States, consequently, point to inducing changes in leadership, to redistributing leadership, and to developing new collaborative relationships and dialogue that reshape shared meaning and expectations among school professionals—in effect, to changing the culture of schools (Levin 1998).

There are several related sets of reasons to look carefully at social interactions, leadership, and shared meanings in the school. One reason to look at school culture and social relations is that it is in this social context that teachers carry their work. As teachers talk to colleagues, principals, and parents, these conversations hold the potential to affect how they conceptualize their work (Lawrence-Lightfoot 2003). This is the reason that contemporary ways of thinking about how to support the professional development of teachers emphasize these conversations as central to empowering teachers to teach for understanding. "Teachers learn by doing, reading, and reflecting (just as students do); by collaborating with other teachers; by looking closely at students and their work; and by sharing what they see." (Darling-Hammond and McLaughlin 1995, 598). At a practical level, one reason to study the role of principals in Mexico is that strategies for school improvement increasingly depend on decentralizing decision-making authority to the school under the assumption that this will most directly support initiatives that will lead to enhanced opportunities for student learning. The popular strategy to decentralize decision making to principals assumes that principals are competent and that they have incentives to attend to the learning opportunities for the students in the schools they manage. If there is a weak alignment between their selection and future professional prospects and the learning opportunities of their students, as suggested in this chapter, this challenges the essential premise that schools will improve if principals' decision-making authority is enhanced. This strategy is consistent with views of educational improvement that suggest that education is a very complex and poorly understood business and that as a result it makes sense to move away from input-based policies to policies that focus on incentives to improve outcomes and that delegate the task of improvement to local actors such as principals (Hanushek 1995). On the surface, this shift in policy approach is predicated on the assumption that principals and teachers have the capability to improve instruction, something that assumes that the incentives to hire them are in line with securing those capabilities.

Another reason to look at the gendered social interactions in schools is that students learn from them. The conversations in the classroom between teachers and students are only a small part of the context that enables students to develop personal knowledge and meaning. Students learn about gender relations by observing how other students treat each other, how teachers and school staff treat them and their peers inside and outside the classroom, and how their parents are treated by teachers and school administrators. The playground, the school entrance, the hallways, the cafeteria, and the school lavatories are, because of the social interactions that take place in them, learning environments that matter to students. The nature of these interactions provides not just powerful lessons to students, but a context that influences how what happens inside the classroom is constructed by students. When schools offer students a strong sense of community, students are more engaged with school work and are more likely to act ethically and responsibly and to develop appropriate social and emotional competencies (Schaps, Battistich, and Solomon 1997; Solomon et al. 2000.) A number of current comprehensive reform strategies in the United States have a strong component of community building. James Comer's School Development Program, Henry Levin's Accelerated Schools Program, and Eunice Shriver's Community of Caring Program are examples.

A third reason to look at social interactions in schools, particularly at how teachers and principals relate to parents and community members, is that students' lives outside school influence how they engage with school work. Building bridges of trust and communication between the worlds of home and school can support the academic engagement of students (Henderson and Mapp 2002).

A fourth, perhaps more compelling reason to look at these social interactions and shared meanings, and this encompasses some of those mentioned earlier, is that they define what the school is about. Thomas Sergiovanni has explained that in order to support deep change in the operational core of schools, it is more effective to think of them as communities than what is most common, which is to see them as bureaucracies or markets (Sergiovanni 1994, 1998). It is in this view of schools as communities committed to the good of all students that Anthony Bryk, Valeria Lee, and Peter Holland find the explanation for the greater effectiveness of Catholic schools with low-income students in the United States (Bryk, Lee, and Holland 1993). As explained by Stromquist, examining gender relations is central to understand whether the institutions of education contribute to democratic citizenship (Stromquist 1996, 407). This is particularly important in Mexico as there is evidence that teachers in Mexico do not take the development of gender equity as an important objective of schools. In a random survey of elementary school teachers conducted in 2002 only half of them mentioned that one of their objectives was to promote gender equity in their schools (Fundación en Este Pais 2004).

The culture of Mexican schools provides students with powerful moral lessons on what is important, the role of agency, and the value of difference or the sense of justice in the purposes of schools. The massive expansion of schooling that took place in Mexico during the twentieth century was predicated in part as an instrument to explicitly shape new social relationships among different social groups in communities. The state-sponsored National Teachers' Union (Sindicato Nacional de Trabajadores de la Educación, SNTE) actively enlisted teachers to work toward national integration, the economic transformation of rural communities and the consolidation of a national and centralized political system (Arnaut 1998, 208). Particularly in rural communities teachers were, especially between the 1920s and 1940s, commonly expected to play the roles of community leaders and agents of change. A study of rural teachers after 1921 describes their work as follows: "Of course teachers had to teach reading, writing and basic numeracy to their pupils, segregating boys from girls, with occasional references to the history of Mexico. But their task went beyond that. The most important task was to reinforce the social organization of the town and motivate people to collaborate in tasks of collective interest, such as opening a post office, building roads, increasing productivity in farming and crafts, and influencing family relationships to make them more pleasant" (Bonfil 1997, 237; my translation).

This historical reference is important because it suggests that the teaching profession was constructed as having a significant political role. Political groups and interests were thus invested in shaping the selection and advancement of teachers because they were expected to play an important political role. The gendered nature of political relationships—the differences of how men and women were groomed for political leadership—thus also played a role in the gendered nature of the education profession. In this way, public schools were set to reproduce gender relations in a patriarchal society.

The persistence of patriarchal norms in Mexican politics is illustrated by the media responses to a meeting of women political leaders that took place on October 6, 2003. "Among the participants there were former governors, ex-leaders of political parties, deputies, senators, feminists, writers, representatives of social organizations, and even the First Lady, constituting what was called the Grupo Plural. The next day the media announced the meeting with an avalanche of sexist comments questioning the participants' intentions, and accusing them of hiding the 'real' purpose of their meeting. Most of the articles, editorials, TV and radio news that covered the event ridiculed, mocked, and disqualified these twenty-one women, and, in a sense, all women interested in politics and political power . . . The Grupo Plural was accused of being a 'Club de Lulu' (the Little Lulu's Club, referring to an only-women club), and hiding political intentions of some of its members . . . the meeting was called El Aquelarre ('witches' sabbath')" (Cardenas 2004, 4–5). Attitudes toward gender equity appear to be more conservative in Mexico than in most other Latin American countries. A gender equality scale based on the World Values Survey places Mexico below Colombia, Argentina, Peru, the Dominican Republic, Venezuela, Chile, and Uruguay; only El Salvador and Brazil have lower scores on this scale representing values in favor of gender equality (Inglehart and Norris 2003).

Because schools were to serve patriarchal politics, men were more likely to be promoted for political leadership. Male teachers were thus more likely to be favored by the political groups who expected those promoted in this way to serve their political purposes. The disproportionate advancement of men in the education profession, particularly to the positions of principals and supervisors, created educational environments that were obviously unfair and inefficient, both in terms of their educational purposes, and arguably also in terms of their political and larger social purposes. This process placed men in positions of authority over women teachers, many of whom would be more qualified and competent than their male supervisors.

Engendering Leadership in Schools

Thirty-seven percent of Mexican principals are women,[1] much lower than the percentage of sixth-grade teachers (43 percent) and significantly lower than the total percent of female teachers (63 percent). Furthermore, and paradoxically, the percentage of female principals is lower among those appointed more recently: among those principals with more than 20 years of experience 43 percent are women, whereas among those with 11–20 years of experience and those with less than 10 years of experience, 22 percent are women. Among teachers who teach only one grade (86 percent of the total), the percentage of female teachers diminishes consistently as the grade increases, from 74 percent in the first grade to 54 percent in the sixth grade. The disproportion of female teachers in several grades is inequitable for various reasons. Teaching in lower grades is more demanding and has lower prestige than teaching in higher grades. Classes in lower grades typically have more students than those in higher grades. It is in the earliest grades that the problems of inadequate development of pre-literacy skills, inadequate readiness, and deficient pedagogies translate into high rates of student failure. As children are retained in a grade, the age heterogeneity of the class increases; this further increases the complexity of teaching at those levels. Teachers teaching in higher grades enjoy not only the benefits of working with the students who have "survived" until the highest ends of the system—and the consequent satisfaction derived from working with students who are academically more successful—but, because they have smaller classes, they also have more time for other activities, including participating in professional development courses and cultivating the support of union leaders, all of which eventually translate into greater support for being promoted as principals.

This gendered division of school work models gendered roles to students, who see that the chances that a teacher will become principal are almost three times greater for males than for females. These differences send powerful signals about the role of merit and ability in qualifying people for leadership positions, particularly as proportionately more female teachers are qualified to teach than their male counterparts (98 percent versus 96 percent), and as female teachers have higher education levels and more teaching experience. Among teachers, those with only a high school degree or less are 7 percent men versus 3 percent women. By contrast, 60 percent of the female teachers have a degree from a normal teacher training school, compared to 52 percent of the men. A normal teacher education degree is a professional degree, for primary school teachers it represents 4 years of education. Until 1984, students in normal schools had completed 9 years of basic instruction; after 1984 the requirements were increased to 12 years of basic instruction prior to being admitted in normal schools. On average, female teachers have 17 years of experience, whereas male teachers have 15. The lower probability that women will become principals is significant not just relative to the higher qualifications of female teachers in Mexico, but also relative to other countries in Latin America, where the percentage of women teachers who are appointed principals is higher. Furthermore, while in most countries in Latin America the percentage of female principals increases among the younger cohorts, this is not the case in Mexico. The percentage of principals who are women in Mexico is 57 percent among those older than 61 years, 52 percent for those ages 51 to 60, 36 percent for those ages 41 to 50, and 47 percent for those between 31 and 40. In Brazil it increases from 38 percent among those older than 61 to 51 percent among those between 31 and 40.[2] It appears that the processes that explain the under-representation of advancement of women from teaching positions to the positions of principals in Mexico are resilient and have not improved over time.

Two processes influence the more limited representation of women among principals in Mexico: first, the processes resulting in lower proportion of female teachers in Mexico than in other countries in Latin America, and second, the processes resulting in the lower odds in Mexico of women teachers being promoted to principal. The ratio of the percentage of female teachers to the percentage of female principals in Mexico, an index of proportionality in the gender composition of both roles, is one of the lowest among all countries in Latin America (see Table 16.1), particularly in public schools and significantly more unequal in rural areas.

In urban schools in the capital in Argentina, for example, 97 percent of the third- and fourth-grade teachers are women, and 93 percent of the principals are women, thus the percentage of female teachers relative to the percentage of female principals is 95 percent (an index of 100 percent would indicate perfect equality in proportionality in women's representation among principals relative to their representation among teachers). In the capital of Mexico, in contrast, the percentage of female teachers is 71 percent, that of female principals 40 percent, for an index of inequality of representation of 57 percent. It is surprising that there are such gender inequalities in the opportunities women have to teach and to run schools in Mexico since women are more likely to choose the teaching profession as a vocation than men. Whereas 81 percent of the women teachers polled say they chose to teach because they felt a vocation to do so, only 62 percent of the men polled give this reason to choose the profession. In contrast, 24 percent of the men say they chose teaching because they needed a job, while only 11 percent of the women give this reason. Among the men, 8 percent say teaching was the only professional option in their community, while only 3 percent of the women say they chose teaching because it was the only option.

Among principals, the same pattern of differences between men and women in the motivations to choose the teaching profession is observed: 81 percent of the

Table 16.1

Percentage of Teachers and Principals Who Are Female and Ratio of Percentage of Female Teachers to Percentage of Female Principals in Several Latin American Countries (third and fourth grade, 1998)

Country	Mega-Public	Mega-Private	Urban-Public	Urban-Private	Rural
Teachers					
Argentina	97	89	95	92	96
Bolivia	78	59	74	87	5
Brazil	100	100	100	98	100
Chile	84	79	88	75	81
Colombia	91	89	77	88	66
Cuba	94	na	94	na	9
Honduras	100	100	92	100	69
Mexico	71	97	72	75	57
Paraguay	na	na	95	93	96
Peru	73	88	71	56	57
Dom. Rep.	85	88	74	87	65
Venezuela	91	100	92	89	81
Principals					
Argentina	93	71	96	78	88
Bolivia	75	42	79	51	0
Brazil	91	56	93	83	99
Chile	5	61	4	3	43
Colombia	75	5	48	46	64
Cuba	75	na	79	Na	68
Honduras	31	83	61	100	62
Mexico	4	71	41	81	35
Paraguay	na	na	87	89	69
Peru	35	56	33	68	23
Dom. Rep.	48	6	44	100	41
Venezuela	62	42	69	72	56
Ratio of percentage of female principals to percentage of female teachers					
Argentina	95	8	101	85	92
Bolivia	96	72	107	58	0
Brazil	91	56	93	85	99
Chile	6	77	45	39	53
Colombia	82	57	62	52	97
Cuba	81	na	84	na	76
Honduras	31	83	66	100	9
Mexico	57	74	57	109	61
Paraguay	na	na	92	96	72
Peru	48	64	47	122	4
Dom. Rep.	57	69	59	115	63
Venezuela	69	42	75	81	69

Source: Author's calculations using database of UNESCO (1998).
Note: The category mega refers to cities with more than 1 million people. Urban refers to cities with less than one 1 million people.

women principals say they chose teaching because they felt a vocation, compared to 63 percent of the men; 12 percent of the women did so because they needed a job, compared to 23 percent of the men; and 4 percent say they did because it was the only option in their community, compared to 8 percent of the men.

Why would the union-dominated boards that select teacher candidates favor men who choose teaching out of economic necessity or because there are no other options in their communities, over women who are attracted to the profession of teaching? The gender dynamics in the politics of the union are a largely unexplored topic worthy of examination. In a presentation I made to a hundred leaders of the national teacher union (Sindicato Nacional de Trabajadores de la Educacion SNTE) in June of 2002, the most senior members of the leadership, I remarked on the fact that less than 10 percent of them were women. In a follow-up discussion over dinner with the most influential of those leaders, including one woman in a group of twelve, I brought up the question.

The woman in the group explained that the demands of union leadership, with work on evenings and weekends, are hard to meet given other social expectations of women in Mexico. Only to underscore the complex nature of the social processes that construct gender bias, however, the president of the union is a woman. In May of 2004 I asked the Secretary of Education of a northern state in Mexico (paradoxically a woman) why there were not more women in her position, and shared with her some of the findings I report in this chapter. She explained, "It's very simple. In order to advance professionally in education, and to be promoted, everyone needs the support of the *sindicato*. A lot of the business of the *sindicato* is done in the cantinas on Friday nights and weekends. It is not easy for women to do this work and fulfill their other obligations to their families. In the environment of the cantinas there are very few women teachers and because of this they are often treated and expected to behave in ways that are not compatible with the honorability of a woman in Mexico. So this makes it very discouraging for women to seek leadership in the union. It's very difficult to talk about these things in Mexico even though we all know what goes on for women in the cantinas and with the *sindicato* and how some union leaders expect sexual favors from women in order to help them advance in their careers."

Why is the teachers' union so important to the professional opportunities of women, and of men, in Mexico? The Mexican teachers' union, the SNTE, is controlled primarily by groups within the party that ruled Mexico during seven decades, the Partido Revolucionario Institucional (PRI). Teacher selection and assignment to schools in Mexico are done by joint committees of the SNTE and the educational administrators in each state. Because the SNTE also influences appointments of educational administrators, they have an important role in selecting and assigning new teachers.

While there is no systematic research on this topic, common lore among educators in Mexico is that initial assignments are typically to the most marginalized rural areas and that as teachers gain experience they can request to be transferred to schools that are located in urban centers until they "crown" (*coronar* is the expression used by teachers in Mexico, literally to crown) their service in the center of the capital of the state. It takes approximately twelve years for a teacher to end up in an urban school from the initial appointment to a rural school, but the actual velocity of this shift varies across teachers for reasons that are not transparent to those outside the inner workings of these committees. However, many teachers who graduate from the more prestigious normal schools do not begin their careers in rural areas. The teachers' union plays a decisive role in processing and authorizing these requests for transfer. There is very limited research on how patrimonial politics and union politics influence teacher supply and retention in Mexico, but some of the extant research suggests that the union has often pursued its own corporate and political objectives and advanced the political interests of the Mexican government at the expense of the professional interests of teachers (Arnaut 1996).

The Mexican Teachers' Union, the single organization that has represented teachers since the mid-1940s, plays a very large role in hiring, retaining, and promoting teachers. This is achieved through large union representation in the positions of school principals and supervisors, and in the system of teacher selection and transfers and promotions, which shape the careers of teachers (Arnaut 1998, 207); the "*comisiones mixtas,*" is where union representatives and administrators decide on teacher appointments and transfers. "Most teachers believe that, after completing their education in the normal school, their basic source of professional development is their daily work. But their daily work is related to the Union. There is no teacher that does not have an intense and frequent relationship with the affairs of the Union. And it could not be otherwise for the relationship with the Union influences their income and their being able to stay in the profession, their job, their working conditions, expectations for promotion, benefits payment of their salary and even processing of their ability to retire with benefits." (Arnaut 1998, 209–210; my translation).

From an educational standpoint, the lower likelihood of women to be promoted to principals is problematic not only because this reduces the exposure of girls and boys at an early age to women in higher-status professional roles, but also because students in schools headed by female principals have higher academic scores, more of them obtain good scores on curriculum-based tests, and they are less likely to repeat grades than students in schools headed by male principals. Female principals are also more likely to live in the community in which the school is located (51 percent versus 44 percent). Female teachers have higher expectations for the educational attainment of students than male teachers—29 percent of them expect students to reach high school or college, compared to 18 percent of male teachers. In schools with higher concentrations of low income students, female principals are slightly more likely to hold more positive views of students' dedication to school work; 34 percent of them find students motivated, compared to 28 percent of their male counterparts. There are no differences in what male and female principals say they do, as characterized by the percentage of them that talk with teachers about instruction or other matters or who visit classrooms. Nor are there gender differences in terms of how principals perceive relations between teachers and principals.

The processes that explain the limited participation of women in teaching and particularly in managing schools are probably multifaceted. They may include social expectations and customs of a patriarchal society. They may also reflect the large role of the male-dominated teachers' union in shaping teacher appointments and the expectations that teachers should be involved in union partisan activities, which often take place on evenings and weekends. If combining the expectations of holding a teaching job with the traditional social expectations placed on women in patriarchal societies is challenging, the additional expectations of evening and weekend duty in union politicking place demands that are extremely difficult to meet. This is not to suggest that the men who combine their teaching and union duties do a poor job, just that they can more easily perform these two sets of obligations because patriarchy places different burdens on them as far as how the material demands of attending to the needs of a family and keeping up a household are distributed. Supportive of the hypothesis that the union plays a role in the opportunities of women to be principals is the striking contrast in the percentage of female principals in public schools and private schools, where the union plays no role. Whereas in urban public schools 44 percent of the principals are women, in private schools almost twice as many (79 percent) are women. In rural areas and indigenous schools, where even more traditional values characterize local leadership, the percentage of women is even lower—33 percent in rural schools and 19 percent in indigenous schools.

The blatant inequalities in the opportunities for women to be teachers and principals in Mexico are problematic not merely because they challenge the basic sense of fairness of a modern democratic society, and the basic human rights of women, but especially because there is evidence that female principals run their schools more effectively than their male counterparts. There are, for example, differences in how safe teachers perceive a school to be depending on whether the principal is a man or a woman. When the principal is a woman, male teachers are as likely to find the school safe for staff and for students as are female teachers. However, when the principal is a man, female teachers are less likely to say that the school is a safe place for staff and students (80 percent) than when the principal is a woman (87 percent). These differences hold for each of the different kinds of schools in Mexico (public, rural, and indigenous). There are no differences in the percentage of female or male principals who find their school a safe place for staff and students.

It is hard to determine whether these opinions are held because unsafe schools are less attractive to female candidates for the position of principal, or because female candidates lead schools in ways that are conducive to safer environments, or because the same influences that lead supervisors and appointment boards to disproportionately advantage men in their opportunities for promotion to principal exert other corruptive influences in the schools in ways that jeopardize the sense of community and safety in the school for teachers and students. What is entirely clear is that children and teachers in schools run by men are more likely to perceive the school as unsafe. We cannot discount the possibility that a factor that contributes to making schools unsafe is the fact that they are run by men, particularly given that it is female students and teachers who are most likely to find those schools unsafe.

One of the ways in which schools run by men appear to limit gender equity is that there are fewer women in those schools teaching in the higher grades. Perhaps there are school cultures that are less likely to block the opportunities for women's career advancement. It is possible that female principals open opportunities for other women to teach in higher grades, which in turn consolidates a culture of greater parity. In schools where the principal is a woman, it is more likely that women will teach in the highest grades; this is the case in the school in every kind of school. In urban public schools, for example, 65 percent of the sixth-grade teachers are women where principals are women, compared to 53 percent where principals are men. The gap is 83 percent versus 65 percent in private schools, 62 percent versus 25 percent in rural schools, and 44 percent versus 12 percent in indigenous schools. Given the point made earlier about the advantages associated with teaching in the higher grades, the greater parity in opportunities for teachers to teach in all grades where principals are women increases women's opportunities to be promoted to the position of principal more so than do the conditions existing in schools where principals are men.

Not only is female leadership associated with a safer sense of community in the school, there are also better relations with the community outside the school where women are principals. Participation of parents and students is more likely when the principal is a woman, in all kinds of schools. The percentage of schools with a student association in urban public schools is 43 percent when the principal is a woman, compared to 38 percent when it is man. In private schools the respective figures are 55 percent versus 52 percent, in rural schools 44 percent versus 41 percent, and in indigenous schools 57 percent versus 49 percent.

Similarly, female principals are more likely than male principals to report that the parent association functions appropriately in the school. In urban public schools the figures are 83 percent versus 79 percent; in urban private schools the gap is smaller, 94 percent versus 93 percent; in rural schools 82 percent versus 77 percent; and in indigenous schools 73 percent versus 70 percent.

Participation in general, of students and parents, is also more likely when the principal is a woman than when it is a man. In addition, the quality of participation may be higher with female principals as suggested by the fact that the gap in student scores in a curriculum test is greater between schools where parents participate and those where they do not in schools where the principal is a woman than in schools where the principal is a man.

Engendering Teaching

Since principals are promoted from the ranks of teachers, the different chances of men and women to be principals can originate in the transition from teacher to principal (in the decision of who should be promoted), in the experiences and opportunities that teachers face before being appointed principals, or in the selection into the teaching profession. The previous sections in this chapter have suggested that norms governing the transition from teaching to becoming a principal play an important role. Are there additional differences associated with the gender of teachers that exist before this transition?

In a society such as Mexico, where men and women have different social and economic opportunities, it is reasonable to examine whether teacher gender influences who joins the profession. Presumably, where the occupational options for women are fewer than for men, one could expect the general quality of female teachers to be higher than that of men because women of higher levels of general ability would choose education whereas men of higher ability would have other professional options available to them. Indicative of social customs that constrain women's work, the proportion of women who work for pay in Mexico is half that of men (42 percent versus 82 percent) (ECLAC 2003, 174). This gap remains even within groups with similar levels of schooling. For instance, among those with some college education, 83 percent of the men work, compared to 55 percent of the women. Among those who work, on average women earn significantly less than men, even when they have comparable levels of education. In urban areas, for example, college-educated women who earn wages earn 60 percent of the earnings of their male counterparts (ECLAC 2003, 193).

Relative to this highly inequitable context in the work opportunities facing men and women in Mexico, teaching offers women more equal opportunities. Forty-three percent of the sixth-grade teachers in Mexico are women (63 percent of all the teachers are women, with the proportion of women teaching declining at higher grades). Consistent with the hypothesis that the teaching field attracts women of greater general ability than their male counterparts, students of female teachers have higher levels of literacy on the curriculum-based tests than students of male teachers. Students also rank the effectiveness of their female teachers higher (see Table 16.2).

The gap between students of male and female teachers is greater for students with two literate parents than for students who have only one or no literate parent. Students with two literate parents score a full point more on a curriculum based language test administered to students in the sixth grade, on average, when they have a female teacher. This gap is a half a point for students with only one literate parent and a third of a point for students with two illiterate parents. The advantage of having female teachers is about twice as large for girls as it is for boys, in each of the categories of parental literacy. When examined separately by type of school, this gap in student achievement by teacher gender holds in urban schools, but not

Table 16.2

Mean Differences in Student Reading Literacy[a] and in How Students Rank Teacher Efficacy by Gender of the Teacher (percent)

Gender of teacher		Average Spanish	>11	Understands teacher	Teacher answers	Understands norms	Teacher helps	Learns much	Teacher expectations
Female	Mean	12.00	52.08	56.25	66.01	49.57	67.61	68.32	87.57
n = 1,063	Std. Deviation	2.91	28.47	19.27	20.36	20.02	19.38	17.59	14.66
Male	Mean	10.56	37.49	51.25	64.73	45.43	60.69	64.72	82.97
n = 1,398	Std. Deviation	2.74	28.73	22.44	23.77	23.44	23.39	22.88	19.97
Total	Mean	11.18	43.77	53.41	65.32	47.31	63.69	66.28	84.97
n = 2,467	Std. Deviation	2.90	29.54	21.30	22.37	22.18	22.06	20.87	18.02

Source: Author's calculations using database of EVEP, Mexico, Secretaría de Educación Pública (2000).
[a]Class average and percentage who attain more than 11 points on an exam with scores ranging from 0 to 25.

in rural or indigenous schools. This suggests that, in contexts where teachers are highly educated and where schools are adequately endowed with instructional resources, students, and particularly girls, benefit more from having female teachers. In schools where teachers have lower levels of education, and where minimal instructional conditions are sorely deficient, the characteristics associated with teacher gender cannot compensate for those deficits.

Conclusion

Even though there are more female than male teachers in Mexico, and females have higher levels of education and more experience, they are less likely to be promoted to position of principal. This, in itself, sends a powerful message about the role of merit and ability in career advancement to all students, and about the gendered division of work in schools. Students in schools headed by female principals have higher levels of reading literacy and are less likely to experience academic failure. Female principals are more likely to live in the community where the school is located and hold higher expectations for the educational attainment of their students. Male and female teachers find schools safer for themselves and for students when the principal is a woman. In schools headed by female principals, women are more likely to teach in the upper grades of elementary schools. The superior results of students in schools with female principals, and the better climate as reported by professional staff in these schools, could be the results of two different processes. One possibility is that because women in Mexico have more limited opportunities to work, those attracted to teaching and to being a principal are more competent than their male counterparts, who have more options. An alternative is that there are indeed gendered differences in the leadership styles of women and men that make female principals more effective. While the evidence examined does not allow for a definitive answer to this question, the low percentage of female principals suggests that there is potentially much room for improvement in school management that would increase the opportunities for women to be promoted to the positions of principal until the "reserve" of highly talented female principals is exhausted, should the first process suggested be the main cause for the differences. The real question that needs urgent attention is, "Why aren't more women being appointed as principals in Mexico?" This will be a difficult question to answer and to act upon because it challenges the cultural and political norms and traditions that govern how public resources in education are used and, more basically, the very different social opportunities that men and women face in Mexico.

Notes

1. The figures provided in this chapter that refer only to Mexico reflect the author's analysis of data collected by the Dirección General de Evaluación of the Secretaría de Educación Pública, through nationally representative surveys of schools in which students were tested and principals and teachers were interviewed. Unless otherwise noted, the data

reported here correspond to the administration of these surveys in the year 2000. Comparative data for Mexico and other Latin American countries reflect the author's analysis of data collected by the United Nations Educational, Scientific, and Cultural Organization's (UNESCO) Office for Latin America and the Caribbean in a survey of primary schools in the region administered in 1998.

2. These figures are the author's calculations of data in UNESCO's 1998 survey of primary schools.

References

Arnaut, A. 1996. *Historia de una profesión. Los maestros de educación primaria en México 1887–1994.* México: Centro de Investigación y Docencia Económica.
———. 1998. "Los maestros de educación primaria en el siglo XX." In *Un siglo de educación en México,* ed. P. Latapi, vol. 2. México. Fondo de Cultura Económica.
Blasé, J., and J. Blasé. 1999. "Principals' Instructional Leadership and Teacher Development: Teachers' Perspectives." *Education Administration Quarterly* 35, no. 3.
Bonfil, R. 1997. "Ser maestro en el siglo XXI." Ponencia presented a en el V Seminano de Política Educativa, Fundación SNTE.
Borden, A. 2002. "Primary School Principals in Paraguay: Looking Through the Window or Walking Through the Door?" Unpublished Ph.D. dissertation, Harvard Graduate School of Education.
Bryk, A., V. Lee, and P. Holland. 1993. *Catholic Schools and the Common Good.* Cambridge, MA: Harvard University Press.
Cárdenas, L. 2004. "Women and Political Power in Mexico." Unpublished Master's thesis dissertation, New School University, New York.
Darling-Hammond, L., and M. McLaughlin. 1995. "Policies That Support Professional Development in an Era of Reform," *Phi Delta Kappan* 76, no. 8.
Dewey, J. 1916. *Democracy and Education.* New York: The Free Press (first edition 1916).
ECLAC (Economic Commission for Latin America and the Caribbean). 2003. *Social Panorama of Latin America 2001–2002.* Santiago de Chile: Economic Commission for Latin America.
Fundación Este Pais. 2004. *Encuesta Nacional sobre Conocencias, Actitudes y Valores de Maestros y Padres de Familia de la Educación Básica en México.*
Hanushek, E. 1995. "Interpreting Recent Research on Schooling in Developing Countries." *The World Bank Research Observer* 10, no. 2 (August).
Henderson, A., and K. Mapp. 2002. *A New Wave of Evidence: The Impact of School, Family, and Community Connections on Student Achievement.* Austin, TX: National Center for Family and Community Connections with Schools. Southwest Educational Development Laboratory.
Inglehart, R., and P. Norris. 2003. *Rising Tide: Gender Equality and Cultural Change.* Cambridge: Cambridge University Press.
Levin, H. 1998. "Accelerated Schools: A Decade of Evolution." In *International Handbook of Educational Change,* ed. A. Hargreaves, A. Lieberman, M. Fullan, and D. Hopkins. Dordrecht, Boston, London: Kluwer Academic Publishers.
Lawrence-Lightfoot, S. 2003. *The Essential Conversation: What Parents and Teachers Can Learn from Each Other.* New York: Random House.
México, Secretaría de Educación Pública. Dirección General de Evaluación. 2000. Database EVEP.
Sarason, S. 1971. *The Culture of the School and the Problem of Change.* Boston: Allyn and Bacon.
Schaps, E., V. Battistich, and D. Solomon. 1997. "School as a Caring Community: A Key to

Character Education." In *The Construction of Children's Character, Part II: 96th Yearbook of the National Society for the Study of Education,* ed. A. Molnar. Chicago: University of Chicago Press.

Sergiovanni, T. 1994. *Building Community in Schools.* San Francisco, CA: Jossey-Bass.

———. 1998. "Organization, Market and Community as Strategies for Change: What Works Best for Deep Changes in Schools." In *International Handbook of Educational Change,* ed. A. Hargreaves. Dordrecht, Boston, London: Kluwer Academic Press.

Solomon, D., Victor Battistich, M. Watson, E. Schaps, and C. Lewis. 2000. "A Six-District Study of Educational Change: Direct and Mediated Effects of the Child Development Project." *Social Psychology of Education* 4.

Stromquist, N. 1996. "Gender Delusions and Exclusions in the Democatization of Schooling in Latin America." *Comparative Education Review* 40, no. 4.

UNESCO–Laboratorio Latinoamericano de la Calidad de la Educación. 1998. Database Santiago.

IV

Resources and the Environment

17

JAVIER DELGADO, ARON JAZCILEVICH,
SILKE CRAM, CHRISTINA SIEBE, NAXHELLI RUIZ,
GABRIELA ANGELES-SERRANO, AND MARCOS HERNÁNDEZ

The Environment

Or How Social Issues Affect the Commitment of Environmental Tasks

The Mexican government is increasingly aware of environmental issues, perhaps reflecting the inclusion of the environment in international trade treaties and the recent signing of international environmental accords. Government spending on protecting the environment has risen, and was 0.6 percent of gross domestic product in 1999–2002. After allowing for the cost of exhaustion of resources and degradation of the environment, gross domestic ecological product was 90 percent of gross domestic product in 2002.

Mexican citizens' attitudes toward the environment are complex. Five percent belong to an environmental group; 3 percent do unpaid work for it. Support for the environmental movement comes from those who are young, well educated, and have high incomes. Although a majority of Mexicans would contribute to organizations or pay increased taxes if they were sure that the funds would in fact be used for the environment, from 1990 to 2000 they were decreasingly willing to do so. Almost three-quarters of Mexicans, especially those who were older, less educated, and poor, thought that "the government should reduce environmental pollution, but it should not cost me any money."

More than half of Mexicans support the environmental movement and, perhaps because of the impact of air pollution on health, 55 percent think that protecting the environment is more important than economic growth or creating jobs. These opinions are consistent with the increasing number of environmental groups and the creation of the "green ecologist" political party (PVEM, Partido Verde Ecologista de Mexico). Delgado, Jazcilevich, Cram, Siebe, Ruiz, Ángeles, and Hernández provide basic information on the location and extent of soil and air pollution, and the impact of government administration on pollution and on groundwater extraction and the use of urban land. They argue that the analysis of environmental problems is inappropriate because it focuses on "cities as points" rather than the broader "cities as areas" that form part of broad regional corridors impacted by the same problems.

The authors that state the "appropriate task" for the government in regard to pollution problems is not well defined. Even if it were, the regulation of urban growth and of ecological requirements was divided into two laws that delegated the responsibilities and functions to different government organizations, without providing for much coordination between them.

Only one-third of Mexico's cities have prepared the required urban development and ecologic regulation plans. The authors conclude that "each of the 'task networks' for water, soil, and air is subordinated to political pressures that prevent it from carrying out its task. Mexico's environmental problems cannot be resolved until the nation creates organizations capable of carrying out their 'appropriate tasks.'"

Institutional Capacity

Economic growth often brings with it deterioration in the environment, damaging a nation's ability to maintain growth, protect the environment, and carry out "sustainable development." Attempts to limit the damaging concomitants of growth depend on the institutional capacity of the state. In this chapter we first present a summary description of contamination in Mexico, and then analyze Mexico's institution-building capacity and its impact on (1) urban expansion, (2) underground water extraction, (3) soil contamination, and (4) air pollution.

During the 1980s, as in almost all of Latin America, Mexico underwent a profound economic crisis—the lost decade—and the breakdown of the welfare state. Together, these events changed the rules of the game between the state and civil society as well as within the state itself (Stiglitz 1998). In this context, the state's ability to manage public affairs became highly fragile. The functions of government were decentralized—with very little participation of nongovernmental organizations—which made it difficult to establish politicians' responsibility for their own actions and the consequences of their decisions, summarized in the broad concept of "accountability."

The new complexities of government make it difficult to carry out sustainable development, which assumes an overall vision of development that may be difficult to carry out because of insufficient coordination of efforts among those involved—the "task network"—in their implementation. The idea of sustainable development was popularized in 1987 by the Bruntland Commission report "Our Common Future" and was reaffirmed in 1992 by the United Nations Declaration on Environment and Development. The sustainable development paradigm assumes the adoption of development strategies at municipal, regional, and worldwide levels that establish the long-term self-sustaining ability to fulfill economic and social needs.

A self-sustaining development model is advocated as a means of avoiding the negative impacts of economic growth on the environment. Damage to the environment in the countryside includes deforestation, erosion of agricultural soil, an in-

Table 17.1

Physical Balance of Natural Resources, 1997–2002

	Resource	Measurements units	1997	2002	Annual rate
	Forest[a]	Billions of m³ of timber	2.38	2.28	–0.87
	Oil (total reserves)[a]	Billions of barrels	56.51	50.03	–2.40
Exhaustion	Water availability[a,b]	Billions of m³	–5.95	–6.64	–2.23
	Air Contamination by primary emissions[c]	Millions of tons	40.16	53.92	6.07
	Soil contamination by municipal garbage[c]	Millions of tons	31.51	35.82	2.60
	Water contamination by uncontrolled sewerage discharge[c]	Billions of m³	19.22	21.61	2.37
Degradation	Soil erosion[d]	Millions of tons	637.1	768.73	3.83

Source: INEGI (2002).
[a]Opening balance + or – change equals closing balance.
[b]"Water availability" is the water that can be used for human purposes without affecting the level of groundwater. For instance, suppose that it rains 100 litres in a year. 20 litres are evaporated and 20 are taken by the vegetation. That means that 60 remaining litres should go to the aquifer.If we extract 10 litres of underground water for human activity that means that we have a "water availability" of 50 litres. But If we extract 70 litres, the level of groundwater will have been reduced by 10. In both 1977 and 2002, the level of groundwater fell.
[c]Flow of contaminating emissions.
[d]Loss of nutrients.

discriminate use of fertilizers and insecticides, intensive extraction of groundwater, and contamination of the main hydrological basins. Damage to the environment in the cities includes air pollution as well as pollution generated by the irresponsible management of toxic and dangerous wastes, and above all, by a severe institutional distortion that makes it difficult to incorporate public goods and interests when regulating urban expansion.

Although there is no precise methodology to collect and systematize environmental data in a national scope, a government assessment states that the stock of natural resources such as wood and crude oil fell at an annual rate of 0.87 percent and 2.40 percent, respectively, from 1997 to 2002. In the same period, overexploitation of groundwater grew at an annual rate of 2.23 percent. The annual rate of increase of contamination was 6.07 percent for contaminants to the air, 2.60 percent for contaminates thrown on the soil, 2.3 percent for water contamination, and 3.83 percent for soil erosion (see Table 17.1.) (INEGI 2002).

Considered as a whole, the cost of environmental impacts on air, soil, and water reached 10.3 percent of the gross domestic product (GDP) in 1996 and diminished to ten percent in 2002. Most of this cost must be charged to the degradation processes, which was 9.4 percent, and fell to 9.1 percent in 2002. The cost of exhaustion was 0.9 percent of GDP in both years (INEGI 2002).

We analyze environmental problems by focusing on the institutional capacity of the government agencies responsible for urban environment policies. This allows us to evaluate the results of programs and policy proposals and to question the effectiveness of organizations and of their leadership (Hildebrand and Grindle 1994). The concept of institutional capacity building leans on the identification of the public agency that is responsible for carrying out appropriate tasks in a context of actors and influences at various levels. The fulfillment of those tasks depends on the interdependence of agencies, bureaus, support organizations, and other groups involved in a "task network."

According to Hildebrand and Grindle (1994), the first level of analysis within organizations is human resources, followed by the organization itself, responsible for carrying out its appropriate task within the group of organizations with which the primary organization must have relationships in order to achieve an efficient functioning of the task network. The second level of influence is the institutional context of the public sector, and the third level, the general economic, political, and social environment that imposes exogenous restrictions on a public organization and affects the carrying out of its tasks.

Urban or Ecological Policy? The Ultimate Dilemma of Mexico's Urbanization

Mexico's recent urbanization is characterized by an unprecedented geographic distribution of its rural and urban populations. The earlier stage of urban concentration followed the center–periphery pattern based on four large cities—Mexico, Guadalajara, Monterrey, and Puebla—and an extensive rural area. This pattern was gradually abandoned during the 1970s and by the middle of the 1980s the largest cities' population growth diminished, while the small and medium cities' population growth surged unexpectedly (Graizbord 1984).

Explanations of this "clean break" with the past can be summarized in two positions: for those who understand *urban systems as points,* changes are explained as a result of different phases of evolution of central places—urbanization, suburbanization, disurbanization (Geyer and Kontuly, 1993; Garza 2000); for those who consider the whole territorial extension and not only the points, *cities as areas* explains these evolutionary changes (Tuirán 2000; Sobrino 2003; Delgado 2003).

This is important because diffuse urbanization brought with it the administrative fragmentation of suburban and exurban[1] space in spite of the fact that those new spaces constituted a diffuse regional corridor. As we will show in this chapter, these diffuse corridors formed the basis of extensive agglomerations, defined ex-ante within an area of 50 kilometers around official metropolitan zones[2] and within 25 kilometers in the case of cities of more than 50,000 people whose urban area included only one city. These "cities as area" results are completely different when seen from the "cities as points" approach.

State of Urban Sprawl

The Center and North regions have a similar number of urban areas (43 and 44), but the population of the Center is double that of the North. That means that, at the national level, only the center presents a higher number of people and number of suburbs and exurbs in its territory. The Central region has half of its rural population within its suburban and exurban area (see Table 17.2). This appears to prove that the settlements—urban, rural or mixed[3]—are agglomerating around the principal cities, whether or not they are "metropolitan." Eight of these agglomerations have outstanding influence on the surrounding areas: four in the Greater Central region (Mexico City, Bajío, West, and Pacific) two in the South region (Gulf and Poza Rica), and two more in the North region (Zacatecana and Regia), as shown in Map 17.1. In the Central region, suburban and exurban areas are almost continuous from the Gulf to the Pacific cluster. They form the most extensive and dense wide agglomeration of the country and include 11 metropolitan zones and 18 cities larger than 50,000 inhabitants. This does not mean that there is a conurbation (continuity) along the agglomeration; instead, it means that "the city" has exploded into a wide exurban territory as predicted by Gottman in 1961. This amazing scope of Mexican urbanization has cradled the best known cities from the pre-Hispanic era to the present. However, it has not been considered by current urban policies: they are still attached to the "cities as points" paradigm.

Existing Land Regulation Laws for Urban and Exurban Space

Faced with this increasingly complex territorial organization, the regulation of urban expansion was hindered by the separation between the regulation of urban growth and that of ecological requirements in the two laws that delegated the responsibilities and functions to different government organizations, without providing for much coordination between them. These laws are the *Ley General de Asentamientos Humanos* (LGAH) for the urban field and the *Ley General del Equilibrio Ecológico y Protección al Ambiente* (LGEEPA) for the environmental field. (The third law [*Ley de Planeación*] is a general law that includes other fields [economy, social, political] that are not analyzed here.)

Supervision of urban areas is provided by the General Law of Human Settlements (LGAH, Ley General de Asentamientos Humanos), approved in 1976 and reformulated in 1993. The primary organization is the Department of Social Development (SEDESOL, Secretaría de Desarrollo Social). It is charged with proposing the urban development policy that every state government should consider in issuing its own State Urban Development Program. Finally, the municipalities must encourage and verify the control of urban sprawl at the local level. No agency exists to sanction the infringement of urban control policies (see Figure 17.1). The LGAH contains rules governing federal, state, and municipal government; requires

Table 17.2

Suburban and Exurban Spaces by Region, 2000 (thousands of inhabitants)

		North		Center		South		Subtotal	
		Localities	Population	Localities	Population	Localities	Population	Localities	Population
Urban spaces	Metropolitan zones	10	9,212.0	13	29,119.9	8	3,572.6	31	41,904.6
	More than 100,000	19	6,378.8	8	2,031.7	11	2,851.3	38	11,261.8
	50,000–100,000	15	1,095.6	22	1,570.7	11	715.1	48	3,381.4
	Subtotal	44	16,686.4	43	32,722.3	30	7,139.0	117	56,547.8
Suburban and exurban spaces	30,000–50,000	4	105.1	7	260.8	5	189.8	16	555.7
	15,000–30,000	13	262.4	57	1,162.0	23	474.4	93	1,898.8
	Mixed	117	601.6	599	3,040.8	345	1,768.9	1,061	5,411.4
	Rural	15.108	1,140.2	20677	4,123.7	16,388	3,183.9	52,173	8,447.9
	Subtotal	15,242	2,109.3	21,340	8,587.3	16.761	5,617.2	53,343	16,313.8
Beyond exurban spaces	Urban	37	1,091.5	55	2,070.1	51	1,223.7	143	4,385.3
	Mixed	272	1,516.3	403	2,132.8	393	1,968.1	1,068	5,617.2
	Rural	55,679	3,301.5	35,317	4,801.6	53,724	6,515.9	144720	14,619.1
	Subtotal	55,988	5,909.3	35,775	9,004.5	54,168	9,707.7	145,931	24,621.6
National	Urban[a]	98	18,145.5	162	36,215.2	109	9,026.9	369	63,387.7
	Mixed[b]	389	2,118.0	1,002	5,173.6	738	3,737.1	2,129	11,028.7
	Rural[c]	70,787	4,441.7	55,994	8,925.4	70,112	9,699.9	196,893	23,067.0
	National	71,274	24,705.2	57,158	50,314.2	70,959	22,463.9	199,391	97,483.4

Source: Based on INEGI (2000).

Notes: Metropolitan zones: clusters of municipalities with a continuous urban area over two or more municipalities. They often are greater than 50,000 people.

Mixed: localities in which population is between 2,500 and 15,000 inhabitants.

Rural: localities with less than 2,500 inhabitants.

[a] Includes rural and mixed localities included within metropolitan municipalities.

[b] Does not include mixed localities included within metropolitan zones.

[c] Does not include rural localities included within metropolitan zones.

Map 17.1   **Suburban and Exurban Spaces in Mexico, 2000**

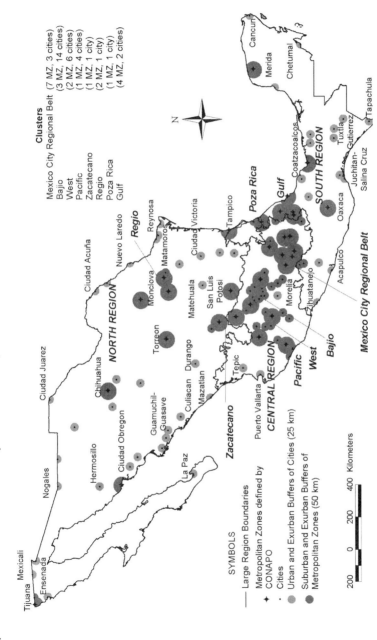

Source: The authors based on INEGI (2000).

the individual state to create territorial reserves needed to prevent urban expansion, and transfers the regulation of urban areas to the municipal governments. The lack of clarity of this law as regards proposed financial instruments and regulatory proposals is frequently criticized (Ramírez 1989). In effect, the difficulty in regulating urban growth is determining who should pay for "common lands" and how payments are to be made, and how to enforce the requirement that real estate be used according to the provisions of these laws.

In addition, at the beginning of the 1980s, the Planning Law (Ley de Planeación) was promulgated and the National System of Democratic Planning was created to decentralize geographic planning and management, giving these functions to municipal governments. The amendment of Article 115 of the Constitution allowed the formulation of the first National Urban Development Plan, which required the elaboration of regional, municipal and local plans. Almost two decades later, only twenty-eight cities larger than 50,000 people (of a total of 117 cities) in the national urban system had a plan of urban development, whether or not they followed it, and these plans had little relation to the ecological organization of suburban and exurban space, which was governed by a different law and a different bureaucracy.

In effect, the General Law of Ecological Equilibrium and Environmental Protection (LGEEPA), which regulates the environment and not only pollution of the environment, was passed in 1988 and revised in 1996. The Department of the Environment and Natural Resources (SEMARNAT, Secretaría de Medio Ambiente y Recursos Naturales) is responsible for administering it. This law provides a standard that is imposed on other sectoral legislation with environmental aspects (Quintana 2000), and thus may be contradictory to the Planning Law, because it does not specify those interactions.

In effect, there is no complementarity between urban and environmental legislation, because the key concepts in these laws differ, despite the fact that they refer to the same topic and the same territory. "Urban" refers to the regulation of "population centers" defined according to the "urbanized area" ("cities as points") that could include "territorial reserves" and eventually nearby "conservation areas." In contrast, ecological regulations are applied only *outside* of urban centers" ("cities as area") in a territory that is defined according to its natural resources and that prevails over any social factor associated with it. Suburban and exurban space refer to territory that overlaps in both laws, which gives rise to the difficulty in regulating the use of this land. Diffuse urbanization has erased the demarcation between both areas, since it raises the questions, Who applies the rules in diffuse suburban and exurban areas? Or even better, Who is responsible for organizing these areas?

The law foresees that the local (municipal) authorities are responsible for attaining this compatibility, yet these authorities are the weakest link in the chain—the least technically and politically capable of confronting the challenge of the most extensive urbanization known until now. Unlike what happens with the "urban situation," in this case there is an agency that applies sanctions to the invaders, the Attorney's Office for Environment and Land Management (PAOT, Procuraduría

Figure 17.1   **Capacity Building for Managing Environmental Regulations of Urban and Exurban Lands**

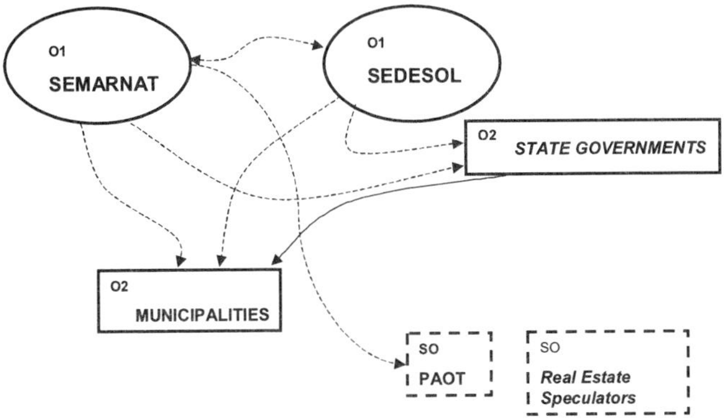

O1	Primary organizations	(Other organizations and agents that
O2	Secondary organizations	influence the appropiate task fulfillment)
SO	Support organizations	

SEMARNAT   Department of the Environment and Natural Resources
SEDESOL   Department of Social Development
PAOT   Attorney's Office for Environmental and Land Management, Federal District

Ambiental y de Ordenamiento Territorial del Distrito Federal), but only for the Federal District (see Figure 17.1).

This pressure is accentuated regarding the definition of city borders. It has always been difficult to be technically precise in defining the "city limits," but it is also clear that the control of the periphery's expansion is made even more difficult by the discretionary powers of the authorities and their corruption of those who promote unregulated urbanization. It is very common to find massive and irregular operations incorporating rural land into urban areas, which gives enormous profits to its promoters and giant problems to local authorities who successfully "control" expansion.

The different conceptualizations of the two laws appear to respond more to the requirements of the process of decentralizing regulatory and executive functions, shifting them to states and municipalities, but this exercise fragments the main task: controlling urban expansion in suburban and exurban spaces.

The insufficiency of current regulation is confirmed by observing that only 18 of the 31 metropolitan zones and only 37 of the 85 cities with more than 50,000 inhabitants have an Urban Development Plan. Control over urbanization in suburban and exurban spaces is also insufficient because only 6 entities have decreed an Ecologic Regulation Plan—another 3 are technically terminated, and 5 are being created—and the remaining 19 states have no ecological regulation. In the North region, two states that contain transnational corridors—including the free trade highway—have no ecological regulation.[4] In the South region, the major biodiversity reserve, no state has a plan, while the Center region has 5 decreed, one terminated, and another is being prepared (see Table 17.3). This lack of ecological planning highlights the

Table 17.3

Presence of Urban Development Plans and Ecological Regulation Plans in Mexico

	Presence of urban development plans (UDP)				Presence of ecological regulation plans (ERP)			
	Yes		In preparation	No	Decreed	Technically completed	In preparation	Without ERP
Region	Before 1996	1996–2003						
North								
Metropolitan zones	3	3	0	4	Baja California[b]	Coahuila Sinaloa	Zacatecas[a] San Luis Potosí[a]	Baja California Sur, Sonora, Chihuahua, Nuevo León, Tamaulipas, Durango
Cities	13	7	1	13				
Central								
Metropolitan zones	3	3	1	6	Tlaxcala, Colima,[b] State of México, Michoacán,[b] Hidalgo	Jalisco	Aguascalientes[a]	Querétaro, Puebla, Guanajuato, Morelos, Distrito Federal, Nayarit
Cities	2	7	1	20				

South						
Metropolitan zones	1	5	1	1	Yucatán	Guerrero, Oaxaca, Chiapas, Quintana Roo, Campeche, Tabasco
Cities	5	3	1	12	Veracruz	

Sources: Based on information supplied by Department of the Environment and Natural Resources (SEMARNAT) and Department of Social Development (SEDESOL), Mexico.

[a]Includes urban development subjects.

[b]Does not include urban development subjects.

fact that although it is often stated that water is necessary for almost all human activities, in fact we do not know much about how to conserve it.

On How an Already Obsolete Paradigm Could Complicate Compliance With a Necessary Public Policy: The Case of Water

Mexico is undergoing increasing and increasingly diffuse urbanization. Although it requires sufficient water to maintain this pattern of urbanization, the extraction of water resources has been carried out with a policy that has not succeeded in controlling the negative effects on the environment.

According to the official point of view, which we do not share, one of the most important problems of groundwater use is water scarcity, which is frequently referred to as "overexploitation of groundwater"; the other problem is its contamination (CNA 2004). We believe, however, that the problems associated with the use of groundwater exist both when groundwater is overexploited and when it is not overexploited.

The Situation of Groundwater in Mexico

In order to plan and manage surface and groundwater resources, the National Water Commission (CNA) regroups the 314 river basins of the country into 37 hydrological regions placed under 13 administrative regions. In the case of groundwater, 653 aquifers were defined (CNA 2004). Since planning regions correspond to political districts and aquifers are geo-forms, the delimitations hardly coincide. Additionally, because of the number and differences between actors involved in each region, this fragmentation has made it difficult to diagnose, manage, and make decisions about water.

As Table 17.4 shows, Administrative Hydrological Regions (RHA, Regiones Hidrologicas Administrativas) do not coincide with the state lines (see Table 17.4), where Roman numerals identify each different RHA and its proportion included by region. For example: RHA I, II VI, and VII are totally (100 percent) included in the North region, but only 22 percent of RHA VIII is included there, while the rest (78 percent) belongs to the Center region. The most fragmented RHA is IX, which is divided into the North region (75 percent), Center (19 percent), and South (6 percent). Reading the table by rows, different states may be affected by different impacts. For example, in the North region, the state of Coahuila is affected by "Springs, lakes, and river base flow decrease" and by deterioration of habitat, but it is not affected by the other four impacts, while none of the states in the North region are affected by land subsidence.

Some 76 percent of Mexico's surface water is principally used in agriculture, while 70 percent of groundwater resources and water stored in damns are destined mainly for urban and public consumption or energy generation for a total annual consumption of 75 km^3 (CNA 2004). This owes more to Mexican geography than

Table 17.4

Environmental Impacts Related to Groundwater Extraction by Region and Administrative Hydrological Region

Regions and Administrative Hydrological Regions (RHA)	Land subsidence	Springs, lakes and river base flow decrease	Deterioration of habitat (wetlands, riparian zones, special vegetation, etc.)	Change in the quality and temperature of the water	Soil salinization	Intrusion of seawater
North I, II, VI and VII (100%) III (94%), IX (75%) VIII (22%)	BC Norte	Coahuila	BC Sur, BC Norte, Coahuila, Sonora	BC Sur SLP Sonora	Sonora	BC Norte, BC Sur Sonora
Center XIII (100%) VIII (78%), IV (75%) IX (19%), X (14%) III (6%)	México, DF, Querétaro Jalisco	México, DF, Puebla, Jalisco Michoacán Aguascalientes	México, DF, Jalisco Michoacán Aguascalientes Michoacán	Guanajuato Aguascalientes México, DF, SLP	México, DF Guanajuato Querétaro, SLP Aguascalientes	
South V, XI, XII (100%) X (86%), IV (25%) IX (6%)	Chiapas	Oaxaca Guerrero Yucatán	Oaxaca, Campeche Yucatan Quintana Roo	Yucatán Guerrero Quintana Roo	Veracruz Yucatán	Yucatán Oaxaca

Sources: Based on internal dossiers of CNA SEMARNAT/CNA (1996, 1999, 2001, 2004); INEGI (2002), and expert judgment. We thank Dr. Joel Carrillo Rivera. Map Digitalization Tonatiuh Suárez.

Note: Roman numerals identify the different RHA and its proportion included by region. The proportion that every RHA have in each State is different and some have not been included here. RHA I, II, VI, and VII are totally included in the North region, while the most fragmented RHA is number IX, divided into the North region, Center and South. SLP = San Luis Potosí; BC = Baja California; DF = Federal District.

to a public policy decision: a large part of the nation—principally in the North—is arid (31 percent) and semi-arid (33 percent), so that pumping water is the only possible way of supplying it. Where water is more abundant, surface water extraction has been abandoned due to the great contamination of streams and rivers or geographical peculiarities caused by a lack of surface water resources.

Many of the hydrological regions are found in arid and semi-arid zones: 14 regions (43 percent of the total consumption) have less rainfall than 500 mm annually and 8 of them (8 percent) have less than 250 mm (CNA 2004). In contrast, the temperate and tropical regions (South, Southeast, and Coastal regions), where the per capita volume of water is adequate and even excessive (with rainfall greater than 1,000 mm yearly), suffer floods, mudflows, and contamination of rivers and other bodies of water.

In Mexico overexploitation is related to a continuous groundwater level drawdown that may cause one or more of these effects: (1) drying out of springs, lakes, and rivers; (2) disappearance/damage of groundwater-dependent habitats; (3) water quality deterioration and temperature increases; (4) soil salinization; (5) seawater intrusion; and (6) undesirable effects on land such as subsidence, collapses, and soil cracking. In the institutional realm, for the purpose of evaluating the effects of groundwater extraction, it is overexploited if it exceeds by more than 10 percent its natural capacity of renewal in the long run (CNA 2004).

Groundwater is highly overexploited, particularly in those aquifers that provide more than half of the water consumed in Mexico (see Map 17.2). Historically, the intensive use of groundwater began in 1940, during the most favorable period of the use of the earlier economic development model. Barely eleven years later, the first overexploited aquifers were already reported (Escolero 1993), with 30 reported in 1975, and 102 in 2003. Since this tendency is intensifying and continuing, the control of extraction to avoid or mitigate overexploitation and its related effects seems to be the appropriate task of water management institutions. This task is carried out through a market-related approach in order to encourage efficient usage and sustainable rates of extraction, although there are no appropriate water balances and ecological studies (OECD 2003).

Nevertheless, due to the diversity of problems and factors involved in the "overexploitation situation," it may not be enough to try to solve those problems under the "safe-yield" extraction approach (Chávez-Guillén 1992). In effect, as some scholars have demonstrated, most problems associated with overexploitation may be present even if less than 10 percent of the aquifer water that has been replenished has been used (Sophocleous 1997; Custodio 2000; Kendy 2003). That has led experts to the conclusion of the obsolescence of the prevalent paradigm.

For example, environmental problems linked to overexploitation are located in the North—with less availability of water resources—but they are also to be found in the South, where more water is available (see Map 17.2). According to CNA, natural availability reaches 1,897 m^3 per capita per year in the North, Northeast, and Central regions, and some 13,566 m^3 per capita per year in the Southeast.

Map 17.2   Environmental Problems Related to Groundwater Extraction

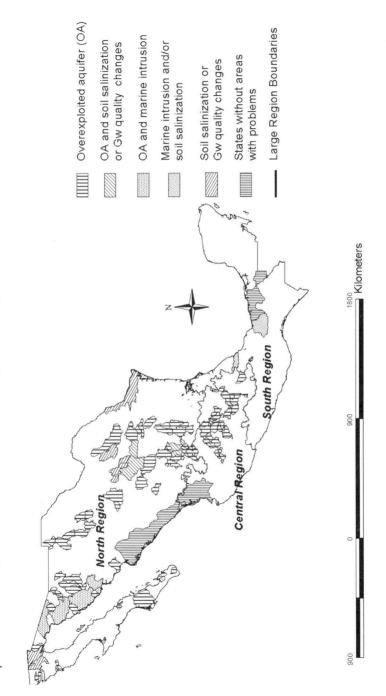

Overexploited aquifer (OA)

OA and soil salinization
or Gw quality changes

OA and marine intrusion

Marine intrusion and/or
soil salinization

Soil salinization or
Gw quality changes

States without areas
with problems

Large Region Boundaries

North Region

Central Region

South Region

N

900   0   900   1800
Kilometers

Source: Based on CNA (2004).

It is true that those effects frequently emerge under a continuous extraction situation. But due to variable geographic conditions, each effect is manifested in a particular way. For example, in Chiapas or Yucatán groundwater extraction causes subsidence or ecosystem damage, but it hardly can be related to groundwater depletion since these states are in a region that has abundant groundwater. Besides, *land* subsidence problems are also present in regions with less water, such as Querétaro and Mexico City (see Table 17.4).

In addition, overexploitation is also related to the high costs of extraction, social conflicts produced by the competition for the use of water resources—especially in neighboring states or municipalities—health problems, and ecological deterioration. Given the variety of negative effects associated with overexploitation, it is necessary to question its relevance as an indicator of the condition of groundwater as has been done in other countries (Custodio 2000).

In spite of the efforts realized, there is marginal success in remedying associated ecological impacts even in those regions with a fine availability of water. It is probably true that an inappropriate institutional capacity that includes the lack of trained personnel of appropriate equipment, the existence of general laws that do not have corresponding programs or other instruments required to manage them, or an inappropriate approach to the management of the resource may be the cause of this failure (Tortajada 2001; OECD 2003).

Many Organizations, Few Results

According to the National Water Law, the federal government is responsible for regulating the extraction and use of national waters. In order to "prevent or remedy the overexploitation of aquifers," zones have been established where further extraction is limited or prohibited, or the zone declared as a "water reserve" (*Ley de Aguas* 1994). To carry out this objective, various secondary tasks have been elaborated: (1) establishing a record of users of water (REPDA, or Water Rights Public Register); (2) transferring the cost of extraction and disposition of waste to users of water in order to generate financial resources, on the basis of market-based rates (tariffs); (3) prohibiting or limiting extraction of water in overexploited aquifers or river basins in order to decrease pumping rates; (4) persuading those involved in inefficient water usage activities of the benefits of shifting to other more profitable activities with a more efficient use of water; and (5) implanting technical and administrative methods to relieve overexploitation, such as the simultaneous use of surface and groundwater, artificial recharge (groundwater replenishment), reuse of wastewater, inter-basin transferences of water, etc.

Since 1995 the Department of the Environment and Natural Resources has been the primary organization charged with carrying out the appropriate tasks of managing water resources and controlling those associated negative ecological impacts. However, this role has now been assigned to the National Institute of Ecology (INE, Instituto Nacional de Ecología), and—at the same time—to the National

Figure 17.2 **Capacity Building for Groundwater Extraction Management**

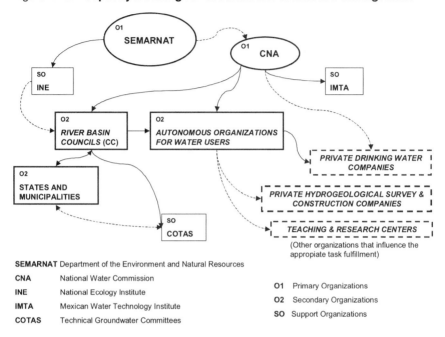

SEMARNAT Department of the Environment and Natural Resources
CNA National Water Commission
INE National Ecology Institute
IMTA Mexican Water Technology Institute
COTAS Technical Groundwater Committees

O1 Primary Organizations
O2 Secondary Organizations
SO Support Organizations

Water Commission (CNA, Comisión Nacional del Agua), both of which are under SEMARNAT'S jurisdiction (see Figure 17.2).

SEMARNAT was created in 1989 and charged not only with the control of water extraction but also with the administration of biodiversity and of the "natural capital" associated with preventing or mitigating the negative impact on ecosystems that resulted from the diminution of the water supply. On the other hand, the INE and another agency, the Mexican Institute of Water Technology (IMTA, Instituto Mexicano de Tecnología del Agua) (Molina and Molina 2002), were created as "support organizations" that share the same objective in terms of developing and transferring technology and methodology to achieve a management of resources that would conserve them or mitigate or reverse a situation in which they were exhausted.

However, there are no clear rules for coordination of these three dependencies nor are there precise instruments to carry out the assigned task in an articulated form between them; a high proportion of their budgets is wasted in the quantification of "water scarcity" through "safe yield balances."

Some of the CNA's goals overlap with those of various secondary and support organizations. For example, the Autonomous Organizations for Water Usage (OOA, Organismos Operadores Autónomos) was created to deal with the public supply of water, treatment of wastewater, and collection of payment for these services. OOA members are technically and financially able to make their own assessments on controlling the extraction of water, within the limits imposed by the CNA. They must also promote the participation of diverse private companies—private drinking water and consulting—as well as obtain additional resources. Consequently they use the market outlook of businessmen. However, they have no responsibilities for the local impact produced by their extraction activities; this responsibility is still assigned to the regional dependencies of CNA.

Other agencies such as the River Basin Councils (CC, Consejos de Cuencas) were conceived of as a link between the CNA, the dependencies of federal, state, or municipal entities, and the representatives of water users from the various hydrological basins. The twenty-six River Basin Councils include those using the river basin water and the corresponding federal, state, and local organizations.

The River Basin Councils make use of the Technical Groundwater Committees (COTAS, Consejos Técnicos de Agua Subterránea) as assisting organizations for the management of hydraulic resources that come from aquifers (CNA 2004). The COTAS include all those involved in making decisions about a specified management policy or action. This is an attempt to construct "social capital," a decision-making ability that is capable of achieving a consensus about a given management strategy, considering local conditions (Kemper 1998). Active participation by these actors is closely linked to a perception of scarcity; for this reason, the connotation of "overexploited aquifer" could explain the success of the management measures that they propose.

Finally, it must be said that no multidisciplinary studies are encouraged; further, very little attention is paid to studying and preventing ecological damage due to water extraction. Despite this, there have been many attempts to increase the participation of research and educational centers that still play a marginal role in making water policy (Arreguín 1998).

In synthesis, the diversity of problems and interrelations associated with the extraction of groundwater cannot be objectively evaluated in terms of the paradigm of "safe yield" and the prevention of overexploitation. Instead, it is necessary to focus on how questions relating to water are being managed. The constant change of organization strategies and creation of new agencies—typical of policy in Mexico—could be the reason for the inefficiency in the carrying out of these tasks. Some scholars believe that the current administrative attitudes regarding water management in Mexico respond more to the political commitments acquired at the Earth Summit than to a decision to resolve problems (Tortajada 2001).

Other Undesirable Impacts of Development: Soil Pollution

Various human activities contaminate the soil. Agriculture and cattle raising, industry and mining are outstanding examples, as are activities related to urban life—transport and the disposal of solid and liquid wastes. Agriculture pollutes the soil through the application of pesticides, manures and fertilizers, while irrigation with wastewater introduces diverse contaminants into the soil, such as organic compounds, heavy metals, salts, and pathogens. Manufacturing industry also emits organic compounds, such as PCBs (polychlorinated biphenyls), heavy metals, acid deposition and radioactive wastes. The gaseous emissions from urban transport lead to acid rain and introduce heavy metals and organic compounds into the soil. Cities dispose of their solid wastes, which have organic compounds, heavy metals, parasites, and salts. Oil extraction produces accidental spills of crude oil and brines, and mining produces tailings and slag and atmospheric pollution from smelting operations.

In combination, these substances could contaminate agricultural cultivation and thus food. They also could provoke direct and indirect toxic effects in soil-based organisms and in natural vegetation. Consequently, the productive capacity of the soil could be reduced, the aquifers could be contaminated by the percolation of pollutants, and bodies of surface water could be affected by erosion of contaminated soil. Some wastes also could provoke the emission of greenhouse gases with a "global warming effect," as well as other numerous adverse effects on human health, especially for children who eat contaminated soil.

Soil contamination usually occurs in specific small areas, only agriculture and long-distance atmospheric transport spread contaminants over a broader area. Identifying the location of soil-polluted areas requires very detailed cartography. In Mexico there have been studies of specific cases using various methodologies in some local areas, but the results of these studies cannot readily be extrapolated to the rest of the nation. In our essay, we present our own estimates of the current state of regional and national soil contamination, using specific indicators of human activities that are related to it. The data used are those published by the government.

The oil industry is the most important part of extractive industries; 97 percent of oil extraction takes place in Tabasco and Campeche in the South region (see Table 17.5). Oil exploration and extraction and its transport to refineries, as well as inadequate management of oil wells, often leads to accidental spills. The contaminants that they add to the soil are hydrocarbons; heavy metal components of crude oil, such as vanadium and nickel; and other metals contained together with high concentrations of soluble salts in the brine (Cram et al. 2004; Zavala et al. 1996).

The extraction of heavy and precious metals has been an important economic activity in Mexico for centuries. Tailings have thus been piled up around the mines. Some of them are currently eroding and contaminating the surrounding areas with heavy metals. Mining is principally located in the North region, followed by the Central region. In the South it is restricted to Guerrero and Oaxaca. Examples of heavy metal contamination have been documented for some mining districts such as Molango (Cram et al. 2003), Zimapán (Méndez and Armienta 2003), Guanajuato (Ramos et al. 2004; Armienta et al. 2003), Baja California (Carrillo and Drever 2000) and Zacatecas (Fernández 2003; Sommer et al. 2000).

Contaminants of the atmosphere such as sulphur dioxide and nitrous oxides

Table17.5

Potential Contamination of the Soil Due to Mining and Oil Extraction

Human activity	Unit	Great region			Nationwide
		Central	North	South	
Crude oil extraction	Thousand barrels per day	0	23	700	723
Natural gas production	Thousand cubic feet per day	0	554	2,291	2,845
Mining:					
Gold	Tons per year	4.6	19.4	1.9	25.9
Silver	Tons per year	427	1,029	1,151	2,607
Lead	Tons per year	14,829	91,007	64,863	170,699
Copper	Tons per year	2,841	361,195	23,589	387,625
Zinc	Tons per year	51,937	212,407	112,053	376,397
Iron	Thousand tons per year	3,929	2,245	0	6,174

Sources: Based on data from INEGI (1999) and PEMEX (2003).

emitted from diverse industrial activities affect surrounding soils in the form of acid deposition. The bitter gas–processing centers and fuel oil and coal-burning thermoelectric plants emit important precursors of acid deposition.[5] In Mexico, 81 percent of natural gas extraction and 99 percent of its processing are carried out in the South region (see Table 17.5), especially in the states of Veracruz, Chiapas, and Tabasco. Specific studies in the Northern Zone of Chiapas (Siebe and Cram 1999; Siebe, Ainsworth, and Cram 2001) and in the state of Guerrero (Siebe, Ainsworth, and Cram 2001; Siebe and Fernández 2003) document the multiple effects of soil contamination produced by a gas-processing center and by a thermoelectric center, respectively.

Automotive transport vehicles also emit precursors of acid rain into the atmosphere. In earlier years, leaded gasoline added this element to land bordering roads. Tires add heavy metals such as cadmium and zinc to asphalt, and some additives to tires contain molybdenum; the burning of diesel and gasoline adds nickel and polycyclic aromatic hydrocarbons to the soil as a result of their emission into the atmosphere. The required installation of catalyzers in automotive vehicles in the past decade has reduced the emission of gaseous pollutants into the atmosphere, but instead platinum is now introduced into the environment, because catalyzers contain platinum. We chose the number of gasoline stations in each state as an indicator of transport activity. The Center region has the largest number of stations, followed by the North, while the South has the least (see Table 17.6).

In regard to the contamination produced by agriculture (see Table 17.7) the Central region sells the largest quantity of solid or liquid insecticides, principally in the Federal District and Puebla. This area produces 45 percent of pigs and 65 percent of birds, whether they are raised for eggs or for their flesh. Almost all of the excrement produced by aviculture and part of that from pigs is reused in the production of concentrated cattle feed. However, an important part of the excrement produced in pig and dairy farms needs to be disposed of. Some of it is used as soil amendment, but a general practice in Mexico is also to discharge it without treatment into superficial water bodies, where it causes severe pollution. Excessive application of animal manure to agricultural land brings with it the formation of nitrates that percolate to the aquifers and also can form gases such as ammonia and nitrous oxides that are sources of contamination of the atmosphere. In the dairy regions of La Laguna (Durango), Tizayuca (Mexico State), and in several municipalities of Jalisco, Michoacán, and Yucatán that have a high density of pig farms, diagnostic studies of contamination should be carried out. Excrement of pigs and poultry, in particular, could also contain important concentrations of hormones and antibiotics that should be tested to estimate the quantity of these concentrations. There are not yet studies of this topic in Mexico.

The Central region also has the largest share of land irrigated with wastewater (see Table 17.7), especially in Hidalgo. It is estimated that only 7 percent of domestic sewage and 8 percent of industrial sewage is processed in water treatment plants (Jiménez 2001). In Mexico, 26 percent of wastewater is reused in agricul-

Table 17.6

Indicators of Soil Contamination From Industrial, Urban, and Transport Activities

Human activity	Unit	Great region			Nationwide
		Central	North	South	
Petrochemical plants	Number of products	750	610	10,153	11,513
Oil refineries	Thousand barrels per day	472	314	457	1,243
Gas processing plants	Thousand barrels per day	0	4.4	382	386.4
Thermoelectric plants	Megawatts	6,445	11,075	7,106	24,626
Gas station	Number of stations	2,396	2,175	993	5,564
Solid waste generation:					
Municipal waste	Thousand tons per year	18,915	8,557	3,040	30,512
	Tons per inhabitant	0.38	0.37	0.13	0.31
Hazardous waste	Thousand tons per year	2,738	556	413	3,707
	Number of waste generating companies	15,614	8,657	3,009	27,280
Illegal and abandoned waste disposal sites	Number of sites	42	85	39	166

Sources: Based on data from thermoelectric plants that use fossil fuel (coal or oil), INEGI (1999); PEMEX (2003); and GTZ/COMIA (2003).
Note: This data represents total production. Since there is no information for Mexico as a whole about degree or extension of soil contamination, we use some specific indicators for urban, agriculture and industrial activities to represent the potential soil contamination in Mexico.

Table 17.7

Indicators of Soil Contamination From Agricultural and Farming Activities

Human activity	Unit	Central	North	South	Nationwide
			Great region		
Use of solid pesticides	Tons per year	17,502	3,406	58	20,966
Use of liquid pesticides	Thousand liters per year	5,806	3,615	298	9,719
Pesticides/cultivated land:					
Autumn-winter cycle	Kilograms per hectare	12.50	1.21	0.02	3.20
	Liters per hectare	4.15	1.29	0.13	1.48
Spring-summer cycle	Kilograms per hectare	3.02	0.93	0.01	1.36
	Liters per hectare	1.00	0.98	0.05	0.63
Use of wastewater for irrigation:					
Annual volume	Millions cubic meters	1,168	434	15	1,618
Irrigated surface	Hectares	117,361	37,453	1,386	156,200
Manure generation:					
Pigs	Million tons per year	5,548	3,076	3,856	12,480
Birds (eggs and flesh)	Million tons per year	2,505	762	603	3,870
Bovine cattle	Million tons per year	80,197	97,178	113,038	290,413

Sources: Based on data from a survey in agrochemical stores provided by SEMARNAT (Department of the Environmental and Natural Resources) (2000); SIAP (n.d.); Arango (1990).

Note: Calculated through the number of cattle heads (INEGI 1999) multiplied by 10 (bovine), 0.8 (pigs) and 0.018 tons of manure generated per animal per year (HydroAgriDuelmen 1993).

ture without previous treatment. In other words, sewage is treated by land treatment to a great degree, since the municipalities have no other means of water treatment. The generation of sewage sludge in Mexico is therefore low. Wastewater that is not used for irrigation is discharged directly into surface water. The reuse of wastewater in agricultural land over a long period of time promotes the accumulation of heavy metals in the arable layer of soil (Siebe 1994). It also introduces excessive quantities of nutriments, salts, and detergents. This has been documented for Irrigation District 03 in the state of Hidalgo (Siebe and Cifuentes 1995).

Existing Rules to Protect the Soil

Mexico has official rules that regulate the disposition of wastes that indirectly protect the soil. They have been established from 1994 onward and include the management of urban, industrial, and mining wastes, as well as the discharge of wastewater and emissions into the atmosphere. However, the maximum load of soil amendments such as manure and agro-industrial wastes is not specified. Only the rules governing sewage sludge specify loads and maximum permissible concentrations of several pollutants, and these were approved in 2002. Today, in mid-2004, there is only a projected rule governing the direct protection of the soil that would establish maximum allowable limits of contaminants and would include methods of cleanup and restoration of sites affected by them. In this next section we analyze the case of the control of contamination of soils by hydrocarbons.

The Contamination by Hydrocarbons and a Delayed "Mexican Standard"

The scientific estimate impact of oil spills on the environment and of the areas affected by them has been evident since the beginning of the 1990s; from that time, some actions to mitigate the damage were undertaken without knowledge of their effectiveness with any scientific certainty. Mexico today has neither cleanup standards nor regulations that are needed to limit the impact of oil spills or to restore the soil that they contaminate. As a result, there are intolerable concentrations of pollutants that need to be remedied. The Mexican Official Standards (NOM, Normas Oficiales Mexicanas) should establish the maximum level of contamination that is permitted, using the definitions elaborated by the National Committees of Standards (CNN, Comités Nacionales de Normalización). Because there is no specific standard for hydrocarbons, the determination of whether or not a soil was contaminated was first guided by using a 1993 generic rule that established "the limits which make a waste dangerous" and that could be used to decide whether the soil should be restored or used for a purpose other than the one that contaminated it. The use of such a general rule covering wastes rather than one covering the soil hampered efficient control of the environment.

The government body responsible for enforcing the prevention and control of soil contamination in 1998 therefore formed an interinstitutional and multidisciplinary working group to fill in the gaps in existing legislation. Its main objective was to establish criteria for the restoration of contaminated soils, apply sanctions to those who contaminated the soil, and require them to restore it (SEMARNAP/PROFEPA 2000). This work was completed in 2000. It is a document with no legal effect, but it served in 2002 as the basis of a temporary measure "that established the maximum permissible limits of contamination of lands affected by hydrocarbons, the characterization of the site and procedures for its restoration." This document guided the preparation of a NOM that was expected to become law in mid-2004, but has not yet been approved.

SEMARNAT is responsible for setting the rules of environmental protection, but these responsibilities are actually carried out by a broad and complicated network of organizations (see Figure 17.3) in procedures that take a long time to implement and are subject to pressures from many interested parties. The factors that limit the carrying out of the network of tasks include the fact that there is little transparency in the process of adopting a NOM. Moreover, it takes a long time to issue a NOM and establish oversight to see if it is in fact obeyed. Applying sanctions where appropriate is not easy. There is little continuity of personnel and consequently of operating rules, and in general, the administrative weaknesses noted above for protection of the environment are also present with regard to pollution resulting from hydrocarbons. This is consistent with Mexico's lack of an adequate environmental strategy. Civil society does not participate sufficiently in protecting the environment. Studies and action at the national level are needed to bring the diverse groups responsible for contamination together and make them comply with environmental rules.

Urban Expansion, Transportation, and Air Pollution

We now turn to the impact of urban expansion and transportation on contamination of the atmosphere. Topography, local climate, demographic growth, industrialization, and socioeconomic development all pollute the air of large cities, such as Mexico City. The principal source of emission of the precursors of ozone—the atmospheric contaminant that most often exceeds the prescribed limits in Mexico City—is public and private transport, which contributes 40 percent of the atmosphere's *volatile organic compounds* (VOCs) and 80 percent of its *nitrogenous oxides* (NOx's). According to official sources, the total number of vehicles in the metropolitan area is about 3 million. We will separately review the characteristics of public and private transport to focus precisely on the multiple social and political dimensions of the problem (Molina and Molina 2002).

Mexico City's mass transport system has decayed since the 1980s. This has led to the displacement of the subway as the principal means of transport and its replacement by collective automotive vehicles known as *combis* and *microbuses,* which has resulted in more emission of contaminants. In 1983 the subway trans-

Figure 17.3 **Capacity Building for Soil Hydrocarbon Pollution Control**

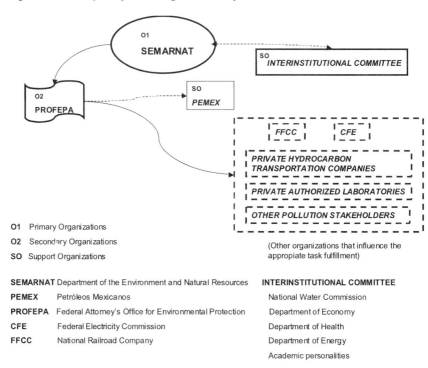

O1 Primary Organizations

O2 Secondary Organizations

SO Support Organizations

(Other organizations that influence the appropiate task fulfillment)

SEMARNAT Department of the Environment and Natural Resources	**INTERINSTITUTIONAL COMMITTEE**
PEMEX Petróleos Mexicanos	National Water Commission
PROFEPA Federal Attorney's Office for Environmental Protection	Department of Economy
CFE Federal Electricity Commission	Department of Health
FFCC National Railroad Company	Department of Energy
	Academic personalities

ported 25 percent of all passengers; by 1999 it carried barely 15 percent. The subway's share of the number of trip segments fell from 70 percent in the 1980s, but this share now is transported by combis and microbuses. In 1986, buses transported an average of 5.6 million people daily, but in 2000 this was only 413,000 in the metropolitan area. Emission control of combis and microbuses is scarce, their maintenance low, and their wear and tear high. Currently the majority use gasoline, but some have been converted to natural gas to reduce emissions and others have been converted to liquefied petroleum (LP). The LP conversions have been counterproductive because of faulty installations that produce emissions because of gas leakage. Thus, in 2002 the total emissions of combis and microbuses contributed 6 percent of NOx's and 10 percent of VOCs, although they represent 1.6 percent of the total of vehicles (CAM 1996). Also, because there is no established system of bus stops, it is difficult to quantify these vehicles' influence on the deterioration of the average speed of vehicles in the city, and since no in-depth study to determine emissions of public transport has been carried out, the real volume of emissions for which these vehicles are responsible could be significantly larger than current estimates.

The case of taxis is very similar, given that they circulate freely, looking for passengers, instead of staying in specified sites and moving only when they are asked to provide service. Taxis emit 5.4 percent of NOx's and 8 percent of VOCs, although they represent 3.4 percent of the total of vehicles. It should be noted that there are more than 25,000 unregistered taxis, so taxis' emissions are underestimated too.

The diverse and inadequate characteristics of Mexico City's road network also impact the emission of contaminants into the atmosphere. There is no differentiation between regional and metropolitan roads (around 30 percent of traffic is through-traffic that does not have a destination in the city); the access roads to the "Periférico" and other primary streets in the city are incomplete; there is an insufficient number of primary roads that cross the city; and roads connecting the city with suburban areas in the state of Mexico are not integrated into the city's road system, provoking enormous congestion at the borders between the two. Contamination would be much less if the city road network were well constructed and public transport more efficient.

The political power of those who benefit from the current system is very great. Nonetheless, current plans are that in 2004 special bus lanes (Metro-Bus) will be first constructed on Insurgentes Avenue within the Federal District, a main north–south thoroughfare about 40 km long that continues inside the state of Mexico. (The bus lanes will continue into the state of Mexico, but under current plans, the metro bus will not.)

Depending on the results other similar lanes could be constructed. This would be the first effort to rationalize and improve the efficiency of high-capacity public transport in the city since the construction of the subway in 1969 and its expansion during the 1980s. However, it does not seem that the operation of the Metro-Bus will be coordinated between the Federal District and state of Mexico. Traditionally, transport and urban agencies in the two localities make their own plans with little coordination between them. As a result, buses, taxis, and metro do not continue service through the administrative limits and do not follow any coordinated plan.

Another predictable problem, given the lack of compliance with the law by owners of combis and micros, is that they will probably operate routes adjacent to the Metro-Bus lane with no planned stops, competing unfairly and decreasing the efficiency of the Metro-Bus system.

Private cars, which account for 72 percent of a total of 3 million vehicles, contributed in 1988 with 23 percent of NOx's and 17.2 percent of VOC emissions. Starting with the use of three-way catalytic converters in 1993 thanks to the introduction of gasoline with no lead content by the Mexican Oil Company (PEMEX, Petróleos Mexicanos), the emission of VOCs and NOx's was reduced. Right now an estimated 50 percent of the automotive fleet has three-way catalytic converters and this is considered to be the main reason for the decrease in the maximum of the ozone concentrations by about 30 percent from 1991 to 2004. However, the number of new vehicles continues to increase at an average rate of 4 percent and their average speed is decreasing, due to congestion, increasing commuting time and placing the engines of the vehicles at their least efficient operating point. Average speed in the city in 2003 was around 22 km per hour. It is believed that in ten to fifteen more years the relative advances achieved until now in VOC and NOx emissions reductions will be lost (Jazcilevich et al. 2003).

A Complex Appropriate Task Network to Control Air Emissions

We now review the construction of institutional capacity and its impact on the environment. In 1993 the standard for the maximum of ozone in the air was set at 0.11 parts per million (ppm) during one hour per year. Ozone is a secondary contaminant formed from reactions of VOCs and NOx's in the presence of sunlight. It is an oxidant that affects the respiratory system and damages lung tissue. Among the impacts of ozone on health are loss of lung capacity, asthma attacks, coughs, irritation of the eyes, and headaches. Chronic exposure to ozone affects the immune system and provokes premature aging of the lungs and respiratory tract. Even though the level of concentration of ozone and its precursors has been reduced in the last ten years in Mexico City, it violates the norm on more than 80 percent of the days each year (INE 2000; Boletín RED-SIMAT 2003).

Institutional Capacity

Although the appropriate task network to control ozone levels in the air is well defined, except for the case of water, success in the control of air pollution has been modest because the functioning of the organizations that are supposed to limit it has been obstructed by political motives. SEMARNAT was created to take charge at the national level of environmental problems (see Figure 17.4).

SEMARNAT issues the regulations governing pollutants emitted by automotive vehicles, but verification of compliance with the regulations is left to the governments of the Federal District and state of Mexico, which verify compliance every six months. Since the inspection stations in the Federal District are in better condition than those in the state of Mexico, car owners prefer to have their vehicles tested in the state of Mexico, and the share of inspections carried out in the Federal District has fallen. In response, the Federal District government required vehicles registered in Mexico City to be tested at Mexico City inspection stations. An audit of the inspections program indicated that in some inspection centers the failure rate is much lower than others (6 percent versus 22 percent) indicating a severe problem in the current inspection program (Klausmeier and Pierce 2000).

An institution created for the task of dealing with the air pollution problem in the metropolitan area is the Metropolitan Environment Commission (CAM, Comisión Ambiental Metropolitana). Its purpose "is to coordinate and follow up policies, programs, projects and actions to preserve and restore the environment" (Molina and Molina 2002). Notwithstanding the magnitude of this task, the CAM does not have a specific budget or a defined operative organizational structure: every two years, the responsibility of presiding over the CAM shifts between the governments of the Federal District and the state of Mexico.

Figure 17.4   **Capacity Building for Air Pollution Control in Mexico City**

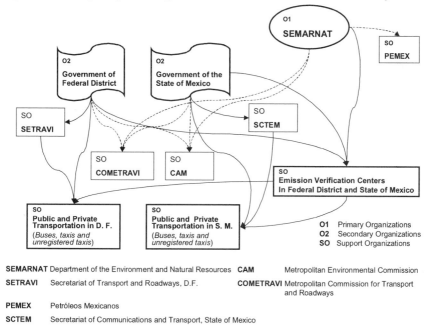

SEMARNAT	Department of the Environment and Natural Resources
SETRAVI	Secretariat of Transport and Roadways, D.F.
PEMEX	Petróleos Mexicanos
SCTEM	Secretariat of Communications and Transport, State of Mexico
CAM	Metropolitan Environmental Commission
COMETRAVI	Metropolitan Commission for Transport and Roadways

Another organization important for air pollution control is the Metropolitan Commission for Transport and Roadways (COMETRAVI, Comisión Metropolitana de Transporte y Vialidad) (Molina and Molina 2002), responsible for coordinating transport issues between the state of Mexico and the Federal District. It has not been successful mainly because of the great disparity of services between the two entities. As an example, the subway (metro) serves the Federal District area but not the state of Mexico, except for the suburban trains (Lines A and B), which offer a limited service. For more information about CAM and COMETRAVI, see Molina and Molina 2002.

It should be noted that neither COMETRAVI nor CAM has any enforcement capability; enforcement is left to the governments of Federal District and state of Mexico. Figure 17.4 shows the interrelationships between the different government and the other organizations described above. Note that COMETRAVI and CAM depend on the state of Mexico and Federal District, but no organization falls under their jurisdiction.

We believe that government institutions with key tasks such as coordinating air pollution and transport policies in metropolitan Mexico, such as CAM and COMETRAVI, lack the organization and power necessary to accomplish their task. The state of Mexico and the Federal District have shown that they are not capable of coordinating air pollution control and transport policies, and have wasted precious money and human resources. If it were not for the introduction of cars with catalytic converters, the situation would be much worse. Unfortunately, as the car population grows and the car inspection programs degrade, the air pollution problem might worsen with time.

Conclusion

In spite of the absence of adequate information, our chapter suggests that the "appropriate task" regarding water and urban development is unclear; that the organization that should control land use for urban development is not well defined; and that each of the "task networks" for water, soil and air is subordinated to political pressures that prevent it from carrying out its task.[6] Mexico's environmental problems cannot be resolved until the nation creates organizations capable of carrying out their appropriate tasks.

Notes

1. Most European authors refer to this area as *periurban;* in this chapter we use *exurban* and *suburban,* terms that may be more common in North America.
2. A metropolitan zone is formed by a central city and its suburban areas characterized by some continuity of the urban landscape. It encompasses the whole municipality limits, including unbuilt areas. Most metropolitan zones are formed by two or more municipalities. There were thirty-one metropolitan areas defined in Mexico by the National Population Council (CONAPO) in the 1995 census, *La distribución territorial en México,* available at www.conapo.gob.mx.
3. Mixed are localities of between 2,500 and 15,000 inhabitants.
4. In effect, the state of Nuevo León, which the NAFTA corridor passes through, does not yet have an ecological plan.
5. *Acid rain* is a most common term, but it only refers to wet deposition. Since dry deposition also occurs, it is better to say acid deposition than acid rain.
6. *Land use* refers to urban sprawl, although we use *soil* when it refers to the pollution of a specific place.

References

Arango, J.M. 1990. *Panorama general sobre la reutilización del agua en el riego agrícola en México. Taller Internacional Reuso del Agua en la Agricultura. Experiencia México-Israel.* Los Berros Estado de México: CNA/IMTA.
Armienta, M., O. Talavera, O. Morton, and M. Barrera. 2003. "Geochemistry of Metals from Mine Tailings in Taxco, Mexico." *Bulletin of Environmental Contamination and Toxicology* vol. 71, no. 2.
Arreguín, J. 1998. *Aportes a la historia de la geohidrología en México, 1890–1995.* México: CIESAS; Asociación Geohidrológica Mexicana.
Boletín RED-SIMAT (Sistema de Monitoreo Atmosférico de la Ciudad de México). 2003. Resumen Estadístico del 1er Semestre de 2003." *Boletín de la Red de Desarrollo e Investigación sobre Calidad del Aire en Grandes Ciudades* 3, no. 4 (January–July).
CAM (Comisión Ambiental Metropolitana). 1996. *Inventario de emisiones de la Zona Metropolitana del Valle de México.*
Carrillo, A., and I. Drever. 2000. "Arsenic Content and Groundwater Geochemistry of the

San Antonio–El Triunfo, Carrizal and Los Planes Aquifers in Southernmost Baja California, Mexico," *Environmental Geology* 39, no. 11.

CNA. 2004. *Estadísticas del Agua en México.* 2d ed. México: Comisión Nacional del Agua.

Cortinas de Nava, C. 2003. "Los contaminantes orgánicos persistentes." México: Cámara de Diputados del Congreso de la Unión.

Cram, S., L. Olvera, J. Ramírez, A. Herre, Y. Ramos, and C. Siebe. 2003. *Mangantransport in der Landschaft in Abhängigkeit von der Bodennutzung im Bergbaubezirk Molango, Mexiko.* Deutsche Bodenkundliche Gescellschaft (DBG)-Mitteilungen (ISSN–0343–1071) 102, 2. Oldenburg, Germany.

Cram, S., C. Siebe, R. Ortíz, and A. Herre. 2004. "Mobility and Persistence of Petroleum Hydrocarbons in Tropical Peat Soils in Southeastern Mexico." *Soil and Sediment Contamination* 13, no. 5.

"Cuesta degradación ambiental 623 mil 75 milliones: INEGI." 2004. *La Jornada,* June 5, 24.

Custodio, E. 2000. "The Complex Concept of Overexploited Aquifers," *Uso intensivo de las aguas subterráneas: Aspectos ecológicos, tecnológicos y éticos.* Papers of the Groundwater Project. 2d ed., series A. Spain: Fundación Marcelino Botín.

Delgado, J. 2003. "La urbanización difusa, arquetipo territorial de la ciudad-región." *Sociológica* 18, no. 51 (January–April).

Escolero, O. 1993. "Panorámica del agua subterránea en México." In *El agua: Recurso vital,* ed. UTM. Oaxaca: México: Universidad Tecnológica Mixteca.

Fernández, L. 2002. "Especiación de arsénico y su relación con la actividad enzimática en los suelos de las inmediaciones de una presa de jales en el estado de Zacatecas." Unpublished master's thesis, Facultad de Ciencias, UNAM, México.

Garza, G. 2000. "Ámbitos de expansión territorial." In *La ciudad de México en el fin del segundo milenio.* México: El Colegio de México.

Geyer, H., and Th. Kontuly. 1993. "A Theoretical Foundation for the Concept of Differential Urbanisation." *International Regional Science Review* 15, no. 2.

González-Morán, T., R. Rodríguez, S.A. Cortés. 1999. "The Basin of Mexico and Its Metropolitan Area: Water Abstraction and Related Environmental Problems." *Journal of South American Earth Sciences* 12.

Gottman, J. 1961. *The Urbanized Northeastern Seabord of the United States.* New York: Twentieth Century Fund.

Graizbord, B. 1984. "Perspectivas de una descentralización del crecimiento urbano en el sistema de ciudades de México." *Revista Interamericana de Planificación* (SIAP), 18, no. 71 (Guatemala).

GTZ/COMIA (Deutsche gesell schaft fur Technische Zusammenarbeit/Comisión Méxicana de Infraestructura Ambiental). 2003. "La basura en el limbo: Desempeño de gobiernos locales y participación privada en el manejo de residuos urbanos." Deutsche gesell schaft fur Technische Zusammenarbeit (GTZ)—Comisión Méxicana de Infraestructura Ambiental (COMIA) *GTZ—Proyecto de apoyo a la gestión de residuos sólidos en el estado de México.* México.

Hildebrand, M., and M.S. Grindle. 1994. "Building Sustainable Capacity: Challenges for the Public Sector." *Pilot Study of Capacity Building (INT/92/676).* Cambridge, MA: Harvard Institute for International Development, United Nations Development Program.

INE. 2000. *Almanaque de datos y tendencias de la calidad del aire en ciudades mexicanas.* México: Instituto Nacional de Ecología, JICA (Japan Internacional Cooperation Agency), INE and CENICA (Centro Nacional de Investigación Ambiental).

INEGI. 1999. *Estadísticas del medio ambiente.* Vol. 1. México: Instituto Nacional de Estadística, Geografía e Informática.

———. 2000. *Resultados Definitives.* XII Censo depoblación y vivienda. Instituto Nacional de Geografía e Informática, México (CD). Available at www.INEGI.gob.mx.

———. 2002. Sistema de cuentas económicas y ecológicas de México, 1997–2002. Available at www.inegi.gob.mx/prod_serv/contenidos/espanol/bvinegi/productos/derivada/ economicas/medio%20ambiente/2002/sceem_2002.pdf.

INE/SEMARNAT. (1997). *Estadísticas e indicadores de inversión sobre residuos sólidos municipales en los principales centros urbanos.* México: Instituto Nacional de Ecología/ Sec. del Medio Ambiente y Recursos Naturales.

Jazcilevich, A., A. García, L.G. Ruiz, X. Cruz, J. Delgado, C. Téllez, L. Chias. 2003. "An Air Quality Modeling Study Comparing Two Possible Sites for the New International Airport for Mexico City." *Journal of the Air and Waste Management Association* 53.

Jiménez, B. 2001. *La contaminación ambiental en México: Causas, efectos y tecnología apropiada.* México: Editorial Noriega-Limusa.

Kemper, K. 1998. "Water as an Economic Resource–Institutional Aspects of Water Resources Management." *Memoria del Simposio Internacional de Agua Subterránea,* ed. J. Castellanos, J. Carrillo, and C. Hernández. Sociedad Mexicana de la Ciencia del Suelo, León, México.

Kendy, E., 2003. "The False Promise of Sustainable Pumping Rates (Technical Commentary)." *Groundwater* 41, no. 1.

Klausmeier, R., and D. Pierce. 2000. "Audit of Vehicle Emission Control Programs." *Report to Comisión Ambiental Metropolitana, México.* De la Torre Klausmeier Consulting Inc. and ICF Consulting.

Ley de Aguas Nacionales y su reglamento. 1994. Comisión Nacional del Agua (CNA). México, Distrito Federal.

Méndez, M., and M. Armienta. 2003. "Arsenic Phase Distribution in Zimapán Mine Tailings, Mexico." *Geofísica Internacional* 42, no. 1.

Molina, L., and M. Molina, eds. 2002. *Air Quality in the Mexico Megacity. An Integrated Assessment.* Cambridge, MA: Kluwer Academic Publishers.

OECD. 2003. "Economic surveys, Mexico." *Country Reviews,* November. Organization for Economic Cooperation and Development.

PEMEX. 2003. *Petróleos Mexicanos. Anuario estadístico.* Available at www.pemex.com.

Quintana, J. 2000. *Derecho ambiental mexicano. Lineamientos generales.* México: Editorial Porrúa.

Ramírez, J.M. 1989. "Los objetivos de la Ley General de Asentamientos Humanos." In *Una década de planeación urbano-regional en México 1978–1988,* ed. G. Garza. Centro de Estudios Demográficos y de Desarrollo Urbano, El Colegio de México.

Rodríguez, K. 2001. "El marco jurídico urbano en México. Un recuento de sus complejidades y algunas propuestas de reforma." Unpublished master's thesis in urban studies. Centro de Estudios Demográficos y de Desarrollo Urbano, El Colegio de México.

Ramos Arroyo, Y.R. (2004), Caracterización geoquímica de depósitos de jales del distrito de Guanajuato, Tesis de doctorado, UNAM, México.

SEMARNAT (Secretaría del Medio Ambiente, Recursos Naturales y Pesca—Procuraduría Federal de Protección al Ambiente) /PROFEPA. 2000. "Disposiciones y procedimientos para la caracterización y restauración de suelos contaminados." México: Procuraduría Federal de Protección al Ambiente.

SIAP. n.d. Servicio de Información y Estadística Agroalimentaria y Pesquera.

Siebe, C. 1994. "Acumulación y disponibilidad de metales pesados en suelos regados con aguas residuales en el Distrito de Riego 03, Tula, Hidalgo." *Revista Internacional de Contaminación Ambiental* 10.

Siebe, C., and E. Cifuentes. 1995. "Environmental Impact of Wastewater Irrigation in Central Mexico. An Overview." *International Journal of Environmental Health Research* 5, no. 2.

Siebe, C., and S. Cram. 1999. "Monitoreo edafoecológico de las actividades de PEMEX en el estado de Tabasco. Proyecto Ambiental de la región Sur (PARS), Informe final." Instituto Mexicano del Petróleo, Universidad Nacional Autónoma de México y Battelle.

Siebe, C., C. Ainsworth, and S. Cram. 2001. "Impact of Emissions from a Gas Processing Facility on Soils in Mexico." 4th International Conference on Environmental Chemistry and Geochemistry in the Tropics, Townswille, Australia, May 7–11.

Siebe, C. and N. Fernández. 2003. *Umweltwirkung von Schwefel und Schwermetalle-missionen eines Thermokraftwerks: eine Fallstudie aus México.* Deutche Gesellschaft fur Technische Zusammenarbeit. DBG-Mitteilungen, Oldenburg, Germany, 102, 2.

Sobrino, J. 2003. "Rurbanización y localización de actividades económicas en la Región Centro del país, 1980–1988." *Sociológica* 18, no. 51 (January–April).

Sommer, I., H. Fernández, H. Rivas, and M. Gutiérrez. 2000. "La geoestadística como una herramienta en estudios de contaminación de suelos. Estudio de caso: Afectación de suelos por As, Cd y Pb contenidos en jales mineros." *Revista Internacional de Contaminación Ambiental* 16, no. 4. Mexico.

Sophocleous, M.A. 1997. "Managing Water Resources Systems: Why Safe Yield is Not Sustainable." *Groundwater* 35, no. 4.

Stiglitz , J.E. 1998. "More Instruments and Broader Goals: Moving Toward the Post-Washington Consensus." The 1998 WIDER (World Institute for Development Economics Research) Annual Lecture, Helsinky. January. Available at http://wwwz.gsb.columbia.edu/faculty/jstiglitz/papers.cfm.

Tortajada, C. 2001. "Capacity Building for the Water Sector in México: An Analysis of Recent Efforts." *Water International* 26, no. 4: 490–98.

Tuirán, R. 2000. "Tendencias recientes de la movilidad territorial en algunas zonas metropolitanas de México. *El mercado de valores, perspectiva del sistema urbano mexicano* I, vol. 55, no. 3 Año LX (March).

Zavala, C., S. Ortiz, O. Trejo, and V. Botello 1996. "Contaminación del suelo por hidrocarburos en el campo petrolero Samaria, Tabasco." In *Golfo de México: Contaminación e impacto ambiental,* ed. V. Botello, G. Rojas, J. Benítez, and L. Zárate. Universidad Autónoma de Campeche, EPOMEX (Programa de Ecología, pesquerías y oceanografia del golfo de México) Sene Cientifica 5, Campeche, México.

Web sites:

Servicio de Información y Estadística Agroalimentaria y Pesquera (SIAP), www.siap.sagarupa.gob.mx.

PEMEX, *Annuario estadístico 2003*, www.pemex.com.

18

DAVID BARTON BRAY, SKYA ROSE MURPHY, AND
MELISSA CORNEJO

Beyond Islands?

Sustainable Rural Development in Mexico

Most Mexicans would like to protect the environment. The most environmentally friendly way of doing so is by using sustainable development methods of production.

David Bray, Skya Murphy, and Melissa Cornejo state that development, sustainable or otherwise, is sorely lacking in rural Mexico. In 2002, agriculture provided 3.6 percent of gross domestic product and accounted for 4.5 percent of environmental damage: 2.4 percent from a decrease in timber-yielding assets, 1.7 percent from soil erosion, and 0.7 percent from over-extraction of groundwater. A strong case can therefore be made for using sustainable development techniques that maintain or enhance the natural resource base.

Production responds to profits; one way of obtaining them is by producing in environmentally friendly ways that allow producers to sell in niche markets that pay premiums for "organic, fair trade, and sustainable" production. These premiums are available for production for the market, but not for subsistence. Consequently, as much as 10 percent of national coffee production is organic, while it has been difficult to introduce sustainable practices to subsistence agriculture and corn production. When some corn farmers introduced sustainable techniques, yields grew from 800–1,000 kilograms per hectare in the mid-seventies to up to 6,000 kilograms per hectare in 2003, turning corn into a cash crop and creating biologically diverse farms.

Some communities of ejido farmers have organized themselves into forestry enterprises and others have joined with private partners and public agencies to promote ecotourism. Success has depended on natural, human and social capital, and on strong institutions. Bray, Murphy, and Cornejo believe it is possible that among small farmers only those who have found new markets for environmentally based production will survive in the medium term.

The purpose of development is to alleviate poverty and promote economic growth that contributes to increasing levels of social and economic welfare at the family level. The purpose of sustainable development is to do this while maintaining or enhancing the natural resource base on which production depends. By these standards, development, sustainable or otherwise, is severely lagging in rural Mexico. Poverty in Mexico continues to be disproportionately rural: over half of Mexico's rural population lives in extreme poverty, and nearly 90 percent lives below the moderate poverty line (Cervigni 2001). Natural resources are also increasingly degraded, with an estimated 85 percent of total land area affected by erosion in 1993. By 1999, some 60 percent of national territory had been severely affected by desertification (Gilbreath 2003). The most recent authoritative study of deforestation found that the rate of forest loss in the 1976–2000 period has been 0.25 percent for forests and 0.76 percent for tropical forests, implying an average annual loss of 865,211 acres including both types of forest (Velázquez et al. 2002).

Rural Mexico had traditionally received relatively high levels of government support, but over twenty years of policies of trade liberalization and reduction in government support for agriculture and rural development have taken their toll. Small farmer reliance on the government for an array of supports in marketing, fertilizers, price, and credits made it extremely vulnerable to the 85 percent reduction in state investment in the agricultural sector, in real terms, between 1980 and 1989 (Kelly 2001). Since the signing of the North American Free Trade Agreement (NAFTA) in 1992, corn prices were cut in half, while at the same time the income support mechanism known as PROCAMPO lost half of its value in real terms (Nadal 2000). The price of coffee, the most important cash crop in the poorest southern states, fell 58 percent since 1994. In the face of these income declines, producer organizations are seeking ways to diversify production into niche markets. More environmentally friendly alternatives are a way to tap into the price premiums available through organic, fair trade, and sustainable production.

These efforts include certified organic agriculture, community forest management for timber and nontimber products, and ecotourism, among other initiatives. Nongovernmental organizations (NGOs), international assistance, and Mexican government programs such as the Fondo Nacional para Empresas Sociales (FONAES 2003) have all promoted these alternatives. Some organic fruit and vegetable producers, organic coffee producers, community forest enterprises, and community-based ecotourism operations have survived the shocks of liberalization and have become higher-quality and more efficient producers who have found niche markets. But do these efforts really amount to much in the face of the overwhelming macroeconomic and globalizing forces at work in the Mexican countryside? Are they really economically and ecologically viable models, or are they just artificial "islands of sustainability" (Bebbington 1997) propped up by NGOs, international foreign assistance, and government subsidies? In this chapter we will explore the current status of these initiatives and assess whether sustainable rural development is a realizable goal or just a phrase to beguile NGOs and academics, while the subjects of their attention "vote with their feet," fleeing rural poverty to urban Mexico and the United States.

Development of any kind requires the creation and mobilization of capital in its various forms (Bell and Morse 2000). To frame our discussion on sustainable rural development, we will employ the concepts of natural, social, and human capital. We focus on natural, social, and human capital because financial and physical capital have been much more difficult to obtain for the rural poor than natural, social, and human capital. These three kinds of capital are defined as follows:

1. *Natural capital: Land, ecosystem services, and amenities such as recreation, biological diversity, and natural resources.* Rural communities do not rely on activities that require expensive inputs, but instead live from direct exploitation of their physical environment, where natural capital provides crops, food, energy, construction materials, and a safety net through marketing of nontimber forest products (NTFPs) (Toledo 2003). Conservation and development efforts frequently focus on rebuilding degraded natural capital through soil and forest enrichment projects of various kinds.

2. *Human capital: Health, education, traditional knowledge, technical expertise and know-how.* Human capital in the form of training is frequently a focus of NGO, government, and international aid programs. In this vein, Southgate (1998, 140) has argued that "No cause of poor economic performance in Latin America . . . is more important than inadequate human capital formation. . . . Environmentally sound production of agricultural commodities and timber . . . often requires the sophisticated understanding and management of biological processes. Obviously, adoption of improved systems is discouraged if knowledge is lacking."

3. *Social capital: The networks, relationships, cultural norms, and organizations that enable collective action.* In southern Mexico in particular, indigenous traditions of democratic governance of *ejidos* and *comunidades,* which are the two main forms of rural land tenure in Mexico, combined with the contemporary ejido derived from Mexico's agrarian reform process, form the basis for "pro-poor" social capital (Fox 1996). The impact of social capital on local organizations is suggested in the Chinanteco region of Oaxaca, where 472 public works were constructed exclusively by local communities using locally generated funds from 1992 to 1997, compared to only 100 government-funded public works built during the same period (Beltrán 2003).

Sustainable Agriculture

Sustainable agriculture projects can be divided into those that focus on subsistence and those that focus on market production. For many years, most of the focus of Mexican NGOs in agriculture was on how to increase or restore food self-sufficiency through the documentation and analysis of traditional agricultural techniques (Toledo et al. 1991; Leff and Carabias 1993). More recently, there has been a greater focus on using both traditional means and introduced technological packages to achieve soil enrichment using techniques such as green manures, composting, minimal use or elimination of agrochemicals, and containment of erosion with filtration ditches (Gliessman 2002; Toledo 2003). However, many NGO efforts at promoting sustainable subsistence agriculture have great difficulty showing significant results (Robles Guadarrama and Almeida Monterde 1998).

However, some subsistence-oriented projects have achieved at least localized success in convincing some farmers to adopt more sustainable practices. Perhaps one of the most noteworthy successful cases is the ejido Vicente Guerrero in Tlaxcala (Ramos-Sánchez 1998; Bray 2000). Vicente Guerrero (VG) is a small ejido in Tlaxcala with 108 ejidatarios on only 200 hectares of land. Reportedly all 108 of the VG ejidatarios now have varying degrees of soil conservation and other sustainable practices on their plots. This may make VG the only ejido in Mexico that has entirely transformed its agriculture to more sustainable practices. In the 1970s, VG had the reputation of being one of the poorest ejidos in Tlaxcala when an NGO leader named Rogelio Cova began promoting deep tilling methods in horticulture. In 1978, four farmers from VG went to Guatemala for training in sustainable agriculture by the U.S.-based NGO World Neighbors. When war engulfed Guatemala in the mid-1980s, two of the Guatemalan farmer-trainers came to live in VG for seven years. The combination of the training and the arrival of the Guatemalans launched a transformation of the ejido. Focusing on terracing, integral pest management, improved pasture grass, nitrogen-fixing trees and crops, gardens, and management of backyard livestock, VG slowly became a model of sustainable agriculture ejido (Ramos-Sánchez 1998).

All of this has had a dramatic impact on corn yields. When they started in the mid-1970s, corn yields were in the 800–1,000 kilograms/hectare range, while today they get up to 6,000 kilograms/hectare, turning corn into an important cash crop. Further, VG representatives speak passionately about the defense of small-scale farmer seed sources and note that "Biodiversity in the farm plots is what allows us to control the pests and build soil fertility" (Bray 2000). The result of over twenty years of training is, among other things, a much more variegated landscape, with windbreaks, greater numbers of trees, small nature reserves, and more abundant wildlife. But VG is very much the exception rather than the rule in rural Mexico. These NGO-driven experiences seldom seem to easily or spontaneously spread beyond the farmers who have received the intensive training and other support, a point to which we shall return at the end of this chapter.

An example of a situation where the introduction of more sustainable practices in subsistence agriculture appears to have been successful in the short term without market production is the case of the Association of Organic Producers of the Perlas

River and Blue Mountains in a remote area of Chiapas. Here, almost all 260 members of the organization have adopted green manures and other soil conservation practices under a program supported first by Conservation International and later by the U.S. Fish and Wildlife Service over a several-year period. This represents an unusually rapid adoption of the new technology, and there may be sound economic reasons why this has occurred. In terms of opportunity costs, Rio Perlas may be at an opposite extreme from the situation in Tlaxcala. Opportunity costs for investments in sustainable subsistence agriculture in Tlaxcala are apparently quite high, while they are quite low in Rio Perlas. In 2000, rural wages in Rio Perlas were only 25 pesos a day, compared to 100 pesos in Tlaxcala, meaning that labor investments in sustainable agriculture had lower opportunity costs in Rio Perlas (Bray 2000).

The experience of VG shows that sustainable practices can have an impact on corn productivity, but examples such as VG and Rio Perlas are rare and localized. A specialized activity that is needed for the future sustainability of corn production is the protection of the biodiversity of corn, which contains adaptations to the great variety of growing conditions found in Mexico. Although the number of varieties planted has dwindled, Mexico continues to be a huge *in situ* conservation center of corn diversity (Eilitta et al. 2003). In the case of many communities, "up to eight varieties of corn are used in a reduced surface" (Nadal 2000). At the same time, this genetic resource is threatened by the introduction of genetically modified corn into rural Mexico, although this assertion has also been the source of considerable contention (Chapela 2001; Quist and Chapela 2001).

But unlike the difficult struggle to establish more sustainable practices in subsistence crops, it is in the presence of the price stimulus in high-value niche markets that we find the clearest and most encouraging evidence of transitions to more sustainable production patterns. The most easily tracked manifestation of sustainable agriculture is certified organic production (Torres-Torres and Delfín 1997). The growing international markets for certified socially and ecologically sustainable food is providing new markets for some Mexican rural communities ("The State of Sustainable Coffee" 2003). Organic agriculture climbed dramatically from 25,000 hectares in 1996 to 115,000 hectares in 2003 (Secretaría de Agricultura, Ganadería, Desarrollo Rural, Pesca y Alimentación 2002), although it remains a tiny percentage of the total. It is reported that there are some 35,000 organic growers in at least ten states and government support of organic agriculture is increasing.

There have been few studies of organic production and export of fruits and vegetables. However, available figures suggest an average 20 percent annual growth in the market for 1990–1996 from a very small base (Marsh and Runsten 2000). Income from organic was recently estimated at about 140 million dollars per year (Secretaría de Agricultura, Ganadería, Desarrollo Rural, Pesca y Alimentación 2002). Marsh and Runsten (2000) provide one of the few case studies of export organic horticulture, a successful partnership between an ejido cooperative in Baja California Sur and Californian organic farmers, where both benefit from higher incomes. The main explanations for the success of the venture are the provision of high-quality technical and financial support from U.S. partners, their explicitly social mission, and the existence of a niche market for organic tomatoes and basil in the winter.

However, it is the export of organic (and now "shade" coffee) that is the largest and best-documented case of sustainable agriculture in Mexico (Bray, Plaza-Sanchez, and Murphy 2002). Mexico is the leading world producer and exporter of organic coffee ("The State of Sustainable Coffee" 2003) and organic coffee reached 10 percent of Mexican coffee production in 2000, increasing family incomes by 25 percent (Fleischer 2002), despite the fact that certification can be a difficult concept to implement at the community level (Mutersbaugh 2002).

Social and human capital have been extremely important in establishing the organic coffee sector in rural Mexico. Almost all of the organic coffee production is from organized small farmers, not from individual large farms, and the training delivered by these small farmer organizations has been crucial in raising the quality of the production and processing. The organic coffee transition in Mexico has also been a transition to higher quality (Bray, Plaza-Sanchez, and Murphy 2002). In the conclusion of this chapter we will examine the implications of the apparent variations in success of the subsistence and market-oriented strategies in the promotion of agricultural alternatives.

Community Forest Management

It has been estimated that as much as 80 percent of Mexico's forests are in the hands of ejidos and agrarian communities: Mexico has over 2,000 communities with legal logging permits, as of 2002 (Juan Manuel Torres-Rojo, personal communication). Until the 1970s, Mexican forest communities had little control of their forests, since the government continued giving logging concessions to private companies and state-owned enterprises. In the mid-1970s, however, government reformers, community protests, and student activists combined to push a pro-community forestry agenda forward (Wexler and Bray 1996) and with the passing of the 1986 forest law, logging concessions were eliminated entirely. In most less-developed countries, community forest management refers to firewood production or nontimber forest products (NTFPs); Mexico appears to be unique in the degree of community participation in management of lands over which they have clear title and which are dedicated to the production of timber, an industrial process that is usually considered to be beyond the capacity of local communities (Bray 2003). The implications and characteristics of community forest management for timber are covered in Bray et al. (2003) and in Bray, Merino-Pérez, and Barry (forthcoming) and will not be further discussed here. Nonetheless, it is a clear example of how natural, social, and human capital, combined with Mexico's agrarian revolution during the twentieth century, create a sector that is making important strides towards socially equitable and ecologically sustainable rural production.

Nontimber Forest Products (NTFPs) and Bioprospecting

An NTFP is any forest product that is not timber and is used for subsistence or commerce (Neumann and Hirsch 2001). There are around 1,300 nontimber forest products that are used by indigenous communities in Mexico (Toledo 2003). The largest group of NTFPs are used primarily for subsistence purposes and have very small, irregular markets. Only twelve of the total number are regulated for commercial extraction by the Mexican environmental agency, Secretaría de Medio Ambiente y Recursos Naturales (SEMARNAT) (Torres-Rojo 2000).

An example of one of the few NTFPs with established commercial markets is *pita* (*Aechmea magdalenae*), a fiber from the leaf of a bromeliad native to lowland tropical forest traditionally used for ropes and bags (Ticktin 2000). In the south, organizations originally formed to market coffee are making use of their social and human capital to produce pita, whose domestic market has exploded with a fashion trend inspired by a popular Mexican music group, La Onda Grupera, that incorporates belts, hats, and boots embroidered with the fiber (Methodus 2003). In 2003, NGOs and community-based organizations from Veracruz, Oaxaca, and Chiapas formed an organization to expand markets for pita by creating new products and investigating its biology, distribution, and fiber yield (Methodus 2003). Its success lies in its high market value, contributing 13 percent of the income of producers in the Chinantla region of Oaxaca with only about one-half hectare in production, equal to the income generated from two hectares of coffee (Edouard 2003). The majority of NTFPs do not share pita's commercial success, but do continue to supply subsistence needs to the poor who depend on forests.

Transportation difficulties, low product price, lack of financial instruments, and difficulty accessing markets, as well as lack of community organization, are cited as the most common constraints limiting the successful commercialization of NTFPs in Mexico. The lack of clarity in forest policy governing NTFPs and lack of institutional support at the government level, as well as the extensive process required to legally extract and sell wild species in Mexico, are also obstacles for many communities seeking to profit from the conservation of their forests.

Bioprospecting was once thought to be another important avenue for increasing the value of standing forests by finding chemical compounds in plants and microbes that could be used to develop pharmaceuticals, but this has proved to be problematic. A high-profile effort funded by the U.S. National Institutes of Health in Chiapas collapsed because of opposition by public opinion and local communities and questions over intellectual property rights (Nigh 2002; Barreda 2003).

Ecotourism

According to the Secretaría de Turismo, tourism is currently the third largest source of foreign currency receipts in Mexico, providing over 8 billion dollars of income in 2000, equal to 8.9 percent of Mexico's gross domestic product (Secretaría de

Turismo n.d.). For most of the last thirty years tourism policy was focused on the promotion of large "megaprojects" such as Cancún and Cabo San Lucas (Healy 1997). However, by the 1990s, the limitations of the mass beach tourism model were beginning to be felt. All of the large beach resorts reported polluted waters and urban congestion (Clancy 2001). It also became clear that little tourism money filtered out into rural areas. However, consumer interest in travel categories such as adventure, nature, and ecotourism began to increase. The Secretaría de Turismo (SECTUR) (Clancy 2001) reports that foreign tourists spent 51.2 million dollars on ecotourism activities, which included adventure tourism and nature tourism, during 2000. However, this represents only 0.62 percent of the 8.2 billion dollars spent by foreign tourists in traditional tourism that same year (O'Boyle 2003).

According to SECTUR, there are seven states in which ecotourism activities are most prominent; it also reports 442 private ecotourism and adventure tourism operators throughout Mexico. However, there are only fifteen registered community ecotourism enterprises (www.sectur.gob.mx), suggesting that not many of these ecotourism operators are taking people to communities that are organized with their own enterprises to receive them, but anecdotal information suggests the number of communities that are trying to develop ecotourism initiatives is much higher.

Although ejido communities have built upon social capital and some have much experience in organizing themselves into forestry enterprises, it is challenging for ejidos to meet the expectations in a service industry like tourism. However, there are emerging positive experiences of communities partnering with private enterprise and public agencies, as well as establishing more autonomous community-based ecotourism enterprises, that suggests that this relatively low impact industry will offer another employment option for some communities.

Conclusion

Some sectors of sustainable agriculture are clearly moving beyond isolated examples of success. As noted, organic coffee is thought to now compose as much as 10 percent of the national production, and there is anecdotal evidence that in the current ongoing crisis of low prices, organic farmers are surviving while conventional coffee farmers are abandoning production. It was noted that progress in introducing sustainable practices in subsistence agriculture and corn production is far more difficult and time consuming. It may take several years of persistent effort before there are visible results on more than a tiny scale. Why are these practices so slow? If it can have such positive impacts over the long run, why is there not a clearer demonstration effect? Part of the answer can be found in contrasting these efforts with the relatively rapid spread of organic coffee production, driven by important price differentials between organic and regular coffee in particular periods, demonstrating *market-driven* adoption.

By contrast, the market by definition does not offer any premium for the products of subsistence agriculture. Efforts to introduce sustainable practices in corn face an uphill battle because economic payoffs are probably a minimum of three to five years in the future, with probable higher labor costs in the interim. Thus, efforts to promote more sustainable practices in subsistence agriculture are necessarily *value-driven,* that is, driven by a desire to preserve traditional values and reintroduce traditional practices in agriculture in the early years. Representatives of VG in interviews frequently recurred to statements about how they were trying to preserve traditions and a way of life, speaking passionately about peasant values. A sustained application of this approach eventually has payoffs in the marketplace, as witnessed by the seven-ton corn yields in VG. But there were apparently few economic incentives in the first years to drive such a transition. Thus, one can deduce that the opportunity costs of investing in improving subsistence agriculture are high. This highlights the fact that it takes real and continuing subsidies to achieve these kinds of transformations in subsistence agriculture. If these investments are not made, and even in contexts where the opportunity costs are lower, such as Chiapas, advances in sustainable subsistence agriculture are likely to remain only islands (Bray 2000).

Community forest management for timber has also clearly had important success in Mexico in communities where the timber resource is substantial for historic reasons, with NTFPs having a far spottier record. Ecotourism is an emerging opportunity with some signs of success, although it is still too early to judge how widespread it will become as an option. This review also affirms the importance of natural, social, and human capital in sustainable natural resource management. In addition to the comments about social capital above, Southgate (1998) has correctly observed that "strong institutions make sustainable resource management possible." In the case of the small farmer organizations developing more sustainable alternatives in Mexico, human capital formation supports social capital formation.

In this chapter we have attempted to answer Bebbington's (1997) question about whether rural sustainable development efforts can be anything more than islands of sustainability in a sea of degradation. The answer for Mexico appears to be that sustainable rural development is moving beyond being mere islands to become a significant new alternative for important numbers of farmers, but only under certain conditions. The withdrawal of state subsidies has put most Mexican agriculture in an increasingly precarious position, and among small farmers it may be only those who have found new markets for environmentally based production will survive in the medium term.

References

Barreda, A. 2003. "Biopiracy, Bioprospecting, and Resistance: Four Cases in Mexico." In *Confronting Globalization: Economic Integration and Popular Response in Mexico,* ed. T.A. Wise, H. Salazar, and L. Carlsen. Bloomfield, CT: Kumarian Press.
Bebbington, A. 1997. "Social Capital and Rural Intensification: Local Organizations and Islands of Sustainability in the Rural Andes." *Geographic Journal* 163.

Bell, S., and S. Morse. 2000. *Sustainability Indicators: Measuring the Immeasurable.* London: Earthscan.

Beltrán, E. 2003. *Indigenous Monographs: The Chinantecs.* Mexico City: Instituto Nacional Indigenista (INI).

Bray, D.B. 2000. "An Evaluation of Five Sustainable Development/Wildlife Management Training Projects with Three Different Small Farmer Organizations in Mexico: A Report to the U.S. Fish and Wildlife Service, Office of International Affairs, 1997–2000." Unpublished report.

Bray, D.B., L. Merino-Pérez, and D. Barry, eds. Forthcoming. *The Community Forests of Mexico.* Austin: University of Texas Press.

Bray, D.B., J.L. Plaza-Sánchez, and E.C. Murphy. 2002. "Social Dimensions of Organic Coffee Production in Mexico: Lessons for Eco-Labeling Initiatives." *Society and Natural Resources* 15.

Bray, D.B., L. Merino-Pérez, P. Negreros-Castillo, G. Segura-Warnholz, J.M. Torres-Rojo, and H.F.M. Vester. 2003. "Mexico's Community-Managed Forests as a Global Model for Sustainable Landscapes." *Conservation Biology* 17, no. 3.

Cervigni, R. 2001. "Biodiversity." In *Mexico: A Comprehensive Development Agenda for the New Era,* ed. M.M. Giugale, O. Lafourcade, and V.H. Nguyen. World Bank: Washington, DC.

Chapela, I. 2001. "Transgenic Corn Found Growing in Mexico." *Nature 413.*

Clancy, M. 2001. *Exporting Paradise: Tourism and Development in Mexico.* New York: Pergamon Press.

Edouard, F. 2003. "Apropriación de sistemas agroforestales y gestión del territorio en la región de la Chinantla." Methodus Consultora, Oaxaca.

Eilitta, M., L.E. Sollenberger, R.C. Littell, and L.W. Harrington. 2003. "On-Farm Experiments with Maize-Macuna Systems in the Los Tuxtlas Region of Veracruz, Mexico. I. Macuna Biomass and Maize Grain Yield." *Experimental Agriculture* 39.

Fleischer, G. 2002. "Toward More Sustainable Coffee: Consumers Fuel Demand for More Sustainable Agriculture." *Rural Development Department Agriculture and Technology Notes* 30 World Bank.

FONAES. 2003. "Proyectos de Ecoturismo." Available at www.fonaes.gob.mx.

Fox, J. 1996. "How Does Civil Society Thicken? The Political Construction of Social Capital in Rural Mexico." *World Development* 24.

Gliessman, Stephen R. 2002. *Agroecología: Procesos Ecológicos en Agricultura Sostenible.* Turrialba, Costa Rica: CATIE.

Gilbreath, J. 2003. *Environment and Development in Mexico: Recommendations for Reconciliation.* Washington, DC: CSIS Press, Center for Strategic Studies.

Healy, R.G. 1997. "Ecotourism in Mexico: National and Regional Policy Contexts." Paper prepared for the annual meeting of the Latin American Studies Association, Guadalajara, Mexico.

Kelly, T.J. 2001. "Neoliberal Reforms and Rural Poverty." *Latin American Perspectives* 28.

Leff, E., and J. Carabias, eds. 1993. *Cultura y manejo sustentable de recursos naturales.* Mexico City: Centro de Investigaciones Interdisciplinarias en Humanidades, Universidad Nacional Autónoma de México.

Marsh, R., and D. Runsten. 2000. "The Organic Produce Niche Market: Can Mexican Smallholders Be Stakeholders?" In *Resource Management, Production and Marketing in Rural Mexico,* ed. G.R. Gómez and R. Snyder. University of California, San Diego. La Jolla, CA: Center for U.S.-Mexican Studies, University of California.

Methodus. 2003. *Memoria: Asamblea constitutiva del Consejo de Organizaciones de Pita de la Selva el Sexto Encuentro.* Methodus Consultora, COPPITA, and CONABIO RBC, Oaxaca City, Mexico.

Mutersbaugh, T. 2002. "The Number Is the Beast: A Political Economy of Organic-Coffee Certification and Producer Unionism." *Environment and Planning* 34.

Nadal, A. 2000. *Mexican Corn: Genetic Variability and Trade Liberalization.* Mexico City: PROCIENTEC/Colegio de Mexico.

Neumann, R.P., and E. Hirsch. 2001. *Commercialisation of Non-Timber Forest Products: Review and Analysis of Research.* Bogor, Indonesia: Center for International Forestry Research.

Nigh, R. 2002. "Maya Medicine in the Biological Gaze: Bioprospecting Research as Herbal Fetishism." *Current Anthropology* 43, no. 3.

O'Boyle, M. 2003. "Talking About a Revolution." *Business Mexico* 13, no. 3.

Quist, D., and I. Chapela. 2001. "Transgenic DNA Introgressed into Traditional Maize Landraces in Oaxaca, Mexico." *Nature* 414.

Ramos-Sánchez, F.J. 1998. *Grupo Vicente Guerrero de Españita, Tlaxcala.* Mexico City: Red de Gestión de Recursos Naturales and the Rockefeller Foundation.

Robles Guadarrama, C.A., and E. Almeida Monterde. 1998. *Experimentación campesina y tecnología sustentable en Los Tuxtlas.* Mexico City: Red de Gestión de Recursos Naturales and the Rockefeller Foundation.

Secretaría de Agricultura, Ganadería, Desarrollo Rural, Pesca y Alimentación. 2002. *La agricultura orgánica en México.* Mexico City: Subsecretaría de Desarrollo Rural, Dirección General de Servicios Profesionales.

Secretaría de Turismo. Available at www.sectur.gob.mx/wb2/sectur/wb2/sectur/sect 9190ecoturismoenmexico. Accessed March 28, 2005.

Southgate, D. 1998. *Tropical Forest Conservation: An Economic Assessment of the Alternatives in Latin America.* New York: Oxford University Press.

"The State of Sustainable Coffee." 2003. DevNews Media Center. World Bank.

Ticktin, T. 2000. "Ethnoecology of *Achmea magdalenae (Bromeliacaceae):* A Participatory Investigation into the Sustainable Harvest and Conservation of a Non-Timber Rainforest Product." Unpublished Ph.D dissertation in plant science. McGill University, Montreal.

Toledo, V.M. 2003. "The Multiple Use of Tropical Forests by Indigenous Peoples in Mexico: A Case of Adaptive Management." *Conservation Ecology* 7.

Toledo, V.M., J. Carabias, C. Mapes, and C. Toledo. 1991. *Ecología y autosuficencia alimentaria.* Mexico City: Siglo Veintiuno Editores.

Torres-Rojo, J.M. 2000. *Diagnóstico de los recursos forestales no maderables en Oaxaca, Durango, Michoacán, Jalisco y Guerrero.* Mexico City: Centro de Investigación y Docencia Económicas (CIDE).

Torres-Torres, F., and Y.T. Delfín, eds. 1997. *La agricultura orgánica: Una alternativa para la economía campesina de la globalización.* Mexico City: Plaza y Valdés Editores.

Velázquez, A., J.F. Mas, J.R. Díaz, R. Mayorga, G.C. Alcántara, R. Castro, T. Fernández, and J.L. Palacio. 2002. "Patrones de cambio de uso del suelo y tasas de deforestación en México." *Gaceta Ecológica del Instituto Nacional de Ecología* 62.

Wexler, M.B., and D.B. Bray. 1996. "Reforming Forests: From Community Forests to Corporate Forestry in Mexico." In *Reforming Mexico's Agrarian Reform,* ed. L. Randall. Armonk, NY, London: M.E. Sharpe.

19

MARGARET WILDER AND SCOTT WHITEFORD

Flowing Uphill Toward Money

Groundwater Management and Ejidal Producers in Mexico's Free Trade Environment

The opening of the Mexican economy involves not only efficient production, but also changes in the environment that occur as the crops produced change in response to free trade agreements. Wilder and Whiteford examine the impact of free trade on groundwater irrigation districts in northern Mexico. In particular, they consider two trade agreements in different contexts, the North American Free Trade Agreement (NAFTA)(in Baja California and Sonora) and Mexico's free trade agreement with Chile (in Sonora). These case studies are important because agriculture uses approximately 80 percent of Mexico's water, and groundwater districts are threatened by water shortages from natural and human causes. The free trade agreements have had an uneven impact throughout Mexico, especially in major irrigation districts where producers have disproportionately benefited from production of more water-intensive crops, and binational concerns about water supply and quality are increasingly critical. The demands for water conservation and less intensive agriculture are directly in conflict with the demands of the market, which call for water-scarce arid regions such as those in northern Mexico to produce water-consumptive export crops, such as asparagus, which are benefited by free trade agreements, and profits have fallen under competition from the Chilean free trade agreement with Mexico. Asparagus uses as much water as grapes; its production is helping to deplete the valley of Caborca's groundwater aquifer at a very fast rate. Asparagus has therefore become a conflictive crop within the region because of the presence of transnational companies and other "outsiders" in the asparagus sector and the impunity of asparagus producers in observing required water restrictions. In addition to a prolonged drought, the Caborca aquifer has become severely overdrafted due in large part to state policies that supported and promoted cultivation of more water-consumptive crops. Moreover, grape produc-

ers have complied with water-use restrictions more than have asparagus produc-ers, and grape production has more local economic impact than asparagus pro-duction. Wheat producers in Mexicali and Sonora have suffered from increased wheat imports from the United States under NAFTA, and binational water quality and supply issues threaten the source of high-quality irrigation water in Mexicali. Wilder and Whiteford call for greater engagement between Mexico and the United States to find sustainable solutions to binational groundwater issues, to increase control of pumping groundwater and inclusion of water management issues in new trade treaties.

Free trade and liberalization strategies have ushered in a new era of significant challenges for Mexico's ejidal producers.[1] Even in northern irrigation districts with a relative wealth of advantages, including a location close to Mexico's major trade partner, the United States, use of advanced technological packages, and especially access to irrigation water, ejidal farmers face nearly insurmountable obstacles to remaining on their land as active producers. Water management in the ejido sector has been dramatically transformed not only by explicit revisions to federal water legislation (first adopted in 1992, the same year as the ejido reforms), but also by the Article 27 ejido reforms that allowed ejidatarios legally to rent or sell their property, and by a host of free trade accords into which Mexico has eagerly en-tered over the last decade.[2]

Although NAFTA is the best known of these initiatives, other free trade accords have been as important or even more so within specific local regions and particular crop sectors in shaping changes in resource use and economic and social relations. The relationship between free trade and groundwater use and management has, to date, received insufficient attention. In the contemporary moment, Mexico is ex-periencing challenges to the future environmental sustainability of its productive and urban sectors, and, to risk an understatement, water is a significant component of the environmental landscape. In this chapter, we examine the impacts of free trade agreements on groundwater use and management by ejidal producers within Mexican irrigation districts. We argue, first, that the role played by water in the transformation of agriculture is integral to understanding major shifts in Mexico's political-economic landscape, and second, that Mexico's hearty embrace of free trade has intersected with other components of its liberalization strategy to create an economic straitjacket for ejidal producers. As Mexico enters into more free trade agreements with countries that enjoy comparative advantages in distinct ar-eas, ejidal producers are exposed in increasingly complex ways to volatile interna-tional market prices and rules. Moreover, the imperatives of free trade that lead to the intensification of groundwater use and movement into more highly water-consumptive crops are on a collision course with the contravening demands of more sustainable use of water resources.

The first section of this chapter provides an outline of Mexican liberalization strategies, including the sweeping water reforms and adoption of multiple free trade agreements. The second section analyzes the current water situation in Mexico. In the third section, we focus on case studies of ejidal groundwater use and management in northern irrigation districts in the states of Sonora and Baja California, which are among the largest irrigators in Mexico. In the fourth and final section of the chapter, we assess the implications of our findings for the sustained economic viability of ejidal producers.

Free Trade and Water Reforms

In recent years, Mexico has vigorously pursued a free trade agenda, entering into a total of twelve free trade agreements in the eleven-year period of 1994 to 2005 (Mexico, Secretaría de la Economía 2005).[3] Beginning with its 1986 entry into the General Agreement on Tariffs and Trade (now the World Trade Organization, WTO), Mexico began an economic opening that was crowned by its entry into NAFTA with Canada and the United States on January 1, 1994. As important as NAFTA assuredly is, it is not the only significant free trade accord, and in particular regional contexts, other free trade accords can be distinctly more influential, as we will see in our case studies. The economic liberalization strategy encompassed a broad range of measures beyond free trade, including changes in fiscal policy, privatization of state-owned industries, elimination of many subsidies, reduction in state-provided rural credit, the disappearance of guaranteed crop prices, and a reduced role for the state. After seventy-one years of control by the Party of the Institutionalized Revolution (PRI), economic liberalization was accompanied by political opening during this period, culminating in the July 2000 election of President Vicente Fox of the opposition National Action Party (PAN). Liberalization was also applied to the environmental sphere, as major land and water reforms were introduced to legislation governing water rights, water management, and ejido land tenure. It is within the scope of other chapters in this volume to address the implications of the ejido reforms per se; however, we will provide a brief overview of the water reforms to set the context for understanding their impact within the ejido sector.

The National Water Law of 1992

A new National Water Law (Ley de Aguas Nacionales) was published in the *Diario Oficial* (Mexico's Congressional Record) on December 1, 1992, and became effective the following day.[4] The new law profoundly altered Mexico's prevailing water policy through its emphasis on greatly increased water user participation in managing the resource; its vision of a retrenched role for the federal government in managing water and an enhanced role for state and local governments; its emphasis on private investment in waterworks infrastructure and private sector management of urban water systems; its establishment of formal water rights markets; and its focus on recuperation of full costs of systems management and operation from water users. Within the urban sphere, the law called for decentralization of water services to the municipal or state (from the federal) level, and allowed for privatization of urban water services.[5] Within the rural sphere, the law established a "transference" program to transfer management authority from the federal government to water users in irrigation districts, and implemented full cost recovery policies. The law established formal water markets and allowed for private sector participation in irrigation works construction, operation, and maintenance.

In order to design and implement the new water program, a redesigned federal water management agency, the National Water Commission (or Comisión Nacional del Agua, CNA) was created in 1989 and in 1995 merged as part of the Secretariat of the Environment and Natural Resources (Secretaría de Medio Ambiente y Recursos Naturales, SEMARNAT). Several other major organizations constitute the state framework for water management: the River Basin Councils (Consejos de Cuenca), the Mexican Institute of Water Technology (IMTA), the Technical Committees of Underground Water (COTAS), and the Autonomous Users' Organizations. (An excellent discussion of how these organizations ideally interface is presented in Chapter 17 of this volume.)

The free market orientation of Mexico's water reform should be understood in the context of a global water reform prescription being written by the World Bank and other international financial institutions for developing countries around the world. For example, a 1998 World Bank study of bank-financed water user management programs, such as the transference program in Mexico, involved projects in twenty countries, including Mexico, Chile, Peru, and Colombia in Latin America, as well as Egypt, Tunisia, Albania, Armenia, China, the Phillipines, Nepal, Turkey, Mali, Niger, and Senegal (Easter 1998). The World Bank provided Mexico with US $350 million as a loan, supplemented by another US$200 million from the Inter-American Development Bank to finance the water reform program, representing close to 50 percent of total projected costs (Pineda Blancarte 2000, 67).[6] Given the global reach of World Bank influence in shaping water reform programs, Mexico's experience may be illuminative for other regions experimenting with dramatic market-oriented reforms in water management and policy.

Apart from financial pressure applied by the World Bank, Mexico had its own reasons for choosing to institute dramatic changes in water management and policy. By the early 1980s, Mexico's irrigation infrastructure was in a state of serious deterioration. Although irrigation had been the largest single item in agricultural budgets over the previous six decades, most of the money had been channeled into extension of irrigation, rather than maintenance of the existing infrastructure. It was estimated that half the irrigation supply never reached the intended cultivated lands (Cummings et al. 1989; Buras 1996). Distribution canals were silting up in areas affected by erosion; salinization was a growing problem, especially in coastal areas; and there was a perennial insufficiency of water supply, exacerbating rural–urban conflicts (Buras 1996; Yates 1981). A World Resources Institute study called the rehabilitation required by the failing infrastructure a "staggering" problem, estimated to cost 302 billion pesos (Cummings et al. 1989). Maintenance of the systems was often neglected by the users, who had the responsibility for upkeep, and this led to expensive water loss. The distribution of water was conducted within particular social contexts, underscoring the fact that irrigation communities are complex social systems. For example, in Mexico, district committees in charge of distributing water were often highly political. Although in some cases water was distributed equitably, in others it was allocated according to acreage sown, or directly to local bosses and their friends (Yates 1981; Whiteford and Enge 1989). Mexico's irrigation system required an overhaul that the federal government was financially unable to address, setting the stage for a new approach to water management that involved transferring the huge budgetary outlays associated with modernization to entities other than the federal government.

The Water Situation in Mexico

Mexico's uneven distribution of water supply and demand represents a final element critical to understanding the drive toward modernization of irrigation systems. Mexico's water resources are distributed very unequally among its geographic regions, and water is available almost in inverse proportion to where it is needed to serve the population. Mexico has a population of 97.3 million (INEGI 2000), of whom 75 percent live in urban areas and 25 percent live in rural areas (CNA 2001). The Southeast of Mexico, which occupies 20 percent of the land surface and contributes about 10 percent of gross domestic product (GDP), receives more than half the rainfall, while the North, with 30 percent of the surface and nearly 30 percent of GDP, receives only 4 percent of the country's annual rainfall. The Central Region with 11 percent of the surface, contributes nearly 55 percent of GDP (Romero Lankao 2001). This pattern of mismatch between supply and demand results in "a profound division between a 'south' rich in water and a 'north' subject to chronic scarcity" (Búrquez and Martínez 2000). Climatic conditions such as highly variable precipitation due to periodic and prolonged droughts and extreme hydrologic phenomena such as hurricanes and floods affect much of Mexico. Adequately meeting water needs is difficult under these natural supply conditions, especially in periods of drought (CNA 2001). In 2000, twelve Mexican states were declared federal emergencies due to the prolonged drought (Becerril, Muñoz, and Camacho 1999).

The quality of both surface and groundwater is a growing issue in Mexico. With over 70 percent of residential wastewater and 85 percent of industrial wastewater not treated, natural water systems have become increasingly contaminated. In agriculture, the use of black waters, high levels of pesticides, and fertilizers, in particular nitrogen, in irrigated regions combined with natural salinity in soils has contributed to water quality problems. The contaminated water is both a public health problem and a threat to many agricultural regions.

Overall, water usage in Mexico is highly inefficient, with as much as 40 percent of total water supply unaccounted for and not recovered through revenues (Wilder 2002). Approximately 38 percent of water is lost through system inefficiencies, and water revenue recovery is low. Agriculture consumes far more of Mexico's water than any other sector, approximately 80 percent of the total, followed distantly by urban/public use at 12 percent and industrial use at 8 percent (CNA 2001). Agriculture generates a disproportionately small share of national GDP, at just 4 percent, yet it is a significant employer at about 21 percent of the economically active population (CNA 2001). Although agriculture's contribution to national GDP is modest, irrigated agriculture is responsible for 50 percent of the value of total national production; it represents 70 percent of Mexico's agricultural exports and 80 percent of employment within the rural sector (Contijoch 1999). With 6.3 million hectares (ha) under production, Mexico is the seventh-largest irrigator in the world in terms of area irrigated (CNA 2001).

The groundwater situation is especially imperiled. Nationally, natural groundwater recharge is estimated to be 75 km^3/year with use estimated at 28 km^3. As a national average, the extraction rate is equivalent to only 37 percent of the natural recharge (renewable volume of water through rainfall and absorption runoff). However, the CNA cautions that this global figure does not reveal the "critical situation that exists in arid regions," where the balance between extraction and recharge is negative (i.e., more groundwater is extracted than is naturally recharged) and the groundwater aquifers are being mined to serve growing urban and agricultural needs. Groundwater resources are important for both urban and agricultural uses. Seventy percent of the water delivered to cities is from groundwater sources, serving approximately 75 million people. Fully 66 percent of the groundwater extracted is destined to irrigate one-third of the total irrigated surface of the country (CNA 2001). Aquifer overdrafting has steadily worsened over the last twenty-five years, tripling from 32 aquifers in states of overdraft in 1975 to 96 in 2000 (CNA 2001). Overdrafting of aquifers has resulted in severe ecological damage, including the exhaustion of natural springs, the disappearance of lakes, the reduction in underground rivers, and the elimination of native vegetation and loss of ecosystems (CNA 2001).

Aquifer water quality has declined due to saline intrusion and industrial and agricultural contamination. For example, aquifer water in some parts of the Mexicali Valley contains levels of pesticides that pose serious health problems for residents who consume the water for drinking (Whiteford and Cortez forthcoming). In other regions of Mexico, the water has become too saline to use directly on the fields for irrigation.

Many irrigated zones have seen abatement of groundwater levels of dozens of meters, increasing the cost of extraction (due to the need to use higher-powered and higher-energy-consuming pumps), thereby making traditionally grown crops much more expensive to cultivate. Urban population growth contributes to aquifer overdrafting as well.

Regional Groundwater Situation

Within the CNA's northwest region (containing all of Sonora and seven munici-palities in the border state of Chihuahua), 88 percent of the water extracted from surface and groundwater sources is for irrigated agriculture. One-third of the ground-water aquifers within the northwest region are overdrafted, the most severely be-ing those of Caborca, Guaymas, Costa de Hermosillo, and Sahuaral. In the arid Sonoran desert, average annual rainfall is only 476 mm, falling even lower in the northern half of the state around Caborca and along the western coast of Sonora. Similarly, the Mexicali aquifer is one of six severely overdrafted aquifers in Baja California and 85 percent of water supply is used for agriculture. Average annual rainfall in Baja California, at only 196 mm, is even lower than the Sonoran aver-age, and only about one-quarter of Mexico's national average (CNA 2001).

Ejidal Producers, Water Management, and Free Trade:
Cases From Northern Irrigation Districts

The fundamental assumption that underlay Mexico's water reforms, ejidal reforms, and free trade agenda was that entrepreneurial producers could take advantage of the market opportunities opening to them—the country's most efficient producers would advance and progress under the modernization strategy. Producers in north-ern irrigation districts like Mexicali and Altar-Pitiquito-Caborca (hereafter Caborca) are among the nation's most advantaged, given their proximity to U.S. markets, access to irrigation, sophisticated technological package and training, and experi-ence with commercial production.[7] In short, these producers ought to be among the strongest and most competitive. We argue, however, that the liberalization strat-egies have not benefited producers and have particularly disadvantaged the ejidal sector of farmers. Caborca is located in the northwest coastal region of Sonora, with groundwater irrigation from a total of 831 wells. The irrigation district in-cludes a total of about 3,800 producers, with approximately two-thirds *ejidatarios* and one-third private farmers (IMTA 1990). Half of the ejidatarios have very small landholdings averaging 3.03 ha, and only 2 percent of ejidatarios have holdings greater than 20 ha. Among private farmers, 24 percent have average parcels of about 89 ha, and 21 percent have very small holdings averaging 3.3 ha (IMTA 1990). The actual amount of land in private control is much larger than these offi-cial figures indicate due to renting of ejidal land and the common use of *prestanombres*—a practice whereby persons allow private producers to use their names as landholders—to avoid parcel size limitations imposed by agrarian law. In Caborca, 60,000 ha are open to cultivation, but only about half are currently under cultivation due to water restrictions. Caborca producers are organized into two water modules, operated by an Association of Water Users. Caborca's crop production is quite diverse, with asparagus, raisins, fresh grapes, industrial grapes, olives, and wheat as the district's principal crops. About one-third of Caborca's cultivable area (12,500 ha) is in pressurized irrigation systems—such as drip (*goteo*) and sprinkler (*aspersión* and *micro-aspersión*) systems—which allow a high degree of crop diversification due to the ability to control more precisely water and fertilizer applications.

Production costs vary widely among different crops produced in Caborca, and thus production is highly stratified among different kinds of producers and land tenure groups. Asparagus, by far the most lucrative crop grown in Caborca, is dominated by large private producers who sell on a contract basis to transnational companies (such as Dole Foods and Lee Brands). Fresh grapes are grown by private and ejidal producers, as well as *colonos* (colonists) who, as smallholders with clear title to their land parcels, share characteristics with both private and ejidal farmers. Wheat production is similarly the province mostly of private farmers. Relatively lower production costs induce ejidatarios and colonos to produce mainly industrial grapes (for sale to brandy producers like Domecq), raisins, and olives. Ejidatarios and colonos in Caborca dominate Mexico's raisin market, producing fully 95 percent of all raisins consumed in Mexico (Wilder 2002). The land tenure structure of production is critical to understanding the complex nexus of relations between distinct free trade agreements and producer groups in Mexico.

The Mexicali Valley is located in the northwestern states of Baja California and Sonora, bordering the U.S. states of California and Arizona. The rich alluvial soils of the Colorado River delta and water from the Colorado River, supplemented by pumped groundwater, support the region's vast agricultural activity. It is one of the major wheat-producing areas in Mexico, but growers in the Mexicali Valley also cultivate cotton, vegetables, and alfalfa and sorghum for cattle feed. The city of Mexicali, one of the fastest growing urban centers in Mexico and a major maquiladora (assembly plant) location, dominates the area. The valley has over 200,000 ha. of irrigated land, with 13,349 ejidatarios and smallholders in over 200 communities scattered throughout the region. Ejido lands represent about 61 percent of this total, with ejido holdings averaging 15.25 ha., compared with 12.69 ha. for smallholders (Whiteford et al. 1998).

While the Colorado River provides 85 percent of the water for agriculture, groundwater is of particular importance because of its high quality. The Mexicali–Mesa de Andrade aquifer that provides water for Mexicali Valley also passes under the Imperial Valley on the U.S. side of the border. Ten to 12 percent of the recharge of the aquifer comes from water that seeps from the irrigation canals and ditches in the Imperial Valley. The Metropolitan Water District, which includes much of Los Angeles and San Diego, has purchased 106,000 acre-feet of water annually from the Imperial Irrigation District, which would capture water by the use of water conservation methods, especially the paving of the All American Canal and other major canals. In the first years of the agreement a maximum of 200,000 acre feet will be transferred from the Imperial Valley to major urban centers for domestic use. Because conservation methods have been adopted on the U.S. side of the border, the water table in the Mexicali Valley is not being recharged at the same rate and it is dropping rapidly, threatening production of ejidatarios growing water-intensive vegetables for the U.S. markets. Nevertheless, there are no international agreements to govern the management and regulate the use of binational groundwater. Some have called the competitive pumping of binational groundwater the beginning of border water wars. For ejidatarios whose livelihood depends on the groundwater, the binational resource management collaboration has been called into question.

One of the consequences of the modifications of the Mexican Water Law in 1992 is that ejidatarios and small private producers (*pequeños proprietarios*) are organized into water modules for water management (Whiteford and Bernal 1996). Despite initial opposition in some regions, the modules have, in some regions, evolved into potentially significant political units capable of pressuring and influencing the CNA, municipal governments, River Basin Councils (Consejos de Cuenca), and even international negotiations. The pumping of groundwater and the transfer of water in the Imperial Irrigation District has sparked political mobilization of impacted modules.

Because Mexicali is located next to the United States, NAFTA has the potential to influence water use in a second significant way. Once water becomes a good in commerce, which can happen in a number of ways, it has the potential to reduce the control of the federal government and local organizations of access to and allocation of water. Given the scarcity of water in the region and discussions in California about water markets and privatization of water rights, it is very possible that farmers in Mexicali or the Imperial Valley could sell water to their counterparts on the other side of the international border. Of equal concern are the rights of foreign companies to pollute water resources in Mexico if antipollution regulations are put in place after the signing of NAFTA.

The North American Free Trade Agreement

The North American Free Trade Agreement is, of course, the 800-pound gorilla in any discussion of free trade and water management in Mexico. However, we argue that as significant as NAFTA is, Mexico's other major forays into free trade agreements with major competitors has exposed producers to a more complex array of challenges that particularly affect ejidatarios.

NAFTA and other trade agreements, as we mentioned earlier, have created the potential for the Mexican government and local water user associations to lose control of water management. According to the text of NAFTA, "unless water, in any form, has entered into commerce and become a good or product, it is not covered by the provisions of any trade agreement including NAFTA. And nothing in the NAFTA agreement would obligate any NAFTA Party to either exploit its water for commercial use, or begin exporting water in any form" (Joint Statement of NAFTA Countries, December 1993, quoted in Gleick et al. 2002, 18) Yet when water is packaged and sold—in plastic bottles, tanks, or for agriculture—it is immediately covered by the NAFTA rules. It is possible that a single license or permit to export water could open up water to be sold as a commodity.

Ongoing trade and investment regulations have the potential to "place restrictions on the ability of governments to manage water resources and services" (Mann 2003, 4). The potential implications of these agreements for sovereign management of Mexican water, and even for local and watershed management of water resources, are significant and must be addressed.

The impact of NAFTA on Mexican agriculture has been uneven, with specific regions and producers of specific commodities absorbing the negative impacts while others prosper. For example, when faced by highly subsidized rice production in the United States, more than 30,000 rice producers in Mexico had to abandon rice cultivation and almost half of the rice processing mills closed. Since NAFTA was enacted, corn exports by U.S. farmers to Mexico have grown by over 240 percent. On the other hand, vegetable production for the U.S. market has expanded by 80 percent and fresh fruit production by 90 percent. Both fresh and frozen vegetables are grown predominately by large producers, while corn and to a lesser degree rice producers are ejidatarios and small landholders.

Wheat is a principal battleground in the NAFTA wars, and farmers in Sonora and Baja California, the two major wheat growing states in Mexico, are in the advance guard, trying to shore up defenses against their well-subsidized U.S. and Canadian competitors. Due to the significance of wheat for a powerful set of Mexican farmers and to the need to protect a critical grain producing sector, the government has ironically—in this era of free trade and elimination of subsidies —been forced to continue offering a supported price for wheat that is considerably higher than international market prices, which fail to cover wheat growers' costs. For example, in 2000, although the international price for wheat was US$96/ ton, the Mexican government was forced to pay about US$133/ton to stave off social unrest among wheat farmers, who were closing highways in protest over the untenable low prices (Wilder 2002). While contending with low international wheat prices, wheat growers must deal at the same time with rising water and agricultural input costs.

Wheat exports to Mexico from the United States have expanded rapidly during the NAFTA era, by 182 percent. Equally significant is the shift from the export of wheat for bread to durum wheat, which is used for pastas. Within Mexico too, there has been a significant shift to durum wheat for the production of pasta, much of which is exported to the United States: "Since enactment of NAFTA, pasta processing has been among the largest recipients of foreign direct investment (FDI) inflows in Mexico, aside from the manufacturing and service sector. Mexico's exports of all pasta types to the United States have increased by approximately 50 percent since NAFTA took effect" (Vaughan 2003, 62). Wheat production in Caborca and Mexicali is based on irrigation, with much of the water coming from groundwater from rapidly lowering aquifers. Of course, the same could be said for the United States, where major wheat production is dependent on the Ogallala Aquifer, a huge aquifer threatened by nonsustainable use.

In Caborca, the cost of producing a hectare of wheat increased by 134 percent from 1994 to 2004, and water costs increased by 89 percent over the same period. In 2000–2001, the Fox administration eliminated the subsidy for wheat transport, amounting to a reduction of almost 10 percent of the national wheat price per ton (Wilder 2002). Due to Caborca's severe water restrictions, which were implemented after the 1994 transference of the irrigation district to water users, most ejidatarios in Caborca have fallowed their wheat fields in favor of continuing their more lucrative grape production. Thus, the private sector dominates the remaining wheat production in the region now. Mexican wheat growers are losing domestic market share to their international competitors, who sell at lower prices than the government-supported price industries must pay to buy Mexican wheat, resulting in increased wheat imports into Mexico.

Grapes and Asparagus

The tale of grapes and asparagus in the Caborca region is an intertwined and convoluted one involving both groundwater use and free trade. In August 1999, five years after NAFTA adoption, Mexico signed a free trade agreement (FTA) with Chile. Like the wheat growers, grape producers are concerned about free trade and the loss of government protections, but in their case it is the Chilean FTA that is problematic. With the stringent grape quality standards imposed by U.S. buyers, Mexican producers were already wary of the barriers to exporting their fresh grapes. Local officials voiced concern that Mexican grapes were experiencing a suspiciously high rejection rate at the border, based not upon quality problems but "lack of a perfect shape" or similarly insignificant reasons, leading officials to believe that U.S. inspectors were looking for ways to stem grape imports (Wilder 2002). Prior to the free trade accord with Chile, grape buyers were standing on Caborca curbsides ready to buy grapes at good prices as soon as they were harvested. Since the entry of Chilean raisins into the Mexican market, the price of raisins has dropped and Chile has made inroads on Mexico's market share. As 95 percent of Mexico's raisins come from Caborca alone, the "globalized" issue of raisin trade has a very specific regional impact. Even more, the effects of increased free trade with Chile has affected one particular kind of producer, the ejidatario and colono who are heavily invested in raisin production since raisins cost less to produce than fresh grapes. The global linkage with Chile translates into a very specific local impact not only on a particular *region* of Mexican production but on a very particular *group* of ejidatario producers (Wilder 2002). Fresh grape growers have also expressed their grave concern about the entry of Chilean grapes into the Mexican market, and are urging the federal government to pursue allegations of dumping against Chilean growers. A morning in November 2001 found Caborca's grape producers awaiting a first-ever visit by the secretary of agriculture to the region, during which Secretary Javier Usabiaga Arroyo was to be presented with a report voicing concerns over Mexico's free trade policies, beginning with the statement that "The initiation of these treaties has provoked, since the year 2000, the most severe crisis that regional agriculture has ever suffered from," and arguing that "the treaties with Chile and the European Union need to be reviewed to find some way of establishing safeguards that protect our activity" (ASUDIR 2001). On the other hand, fresh grape growers benefited from NAFTA court protection in June of 2000 when they were cleared of any wrongdoing after Coachella County growers in California accused their Mexican counterparts of dumping grapes on the U.S. market.[8] If they had been found guilty of dumping, access to U.S. grape markets might have been closed to Mexican producers for a period of three years. The failed U.S.–Mexico dumping allegation, the allegations by Mexico that Chile is dumping grapes and raisins on its domestic market, and the anecdotes about informal reasons for the U.S. rejecting of grape imports from Mexico all underscore the uneasiness of producers on both sides of the border about agricultural protection. This points to agricultural protection as a two-edged sword that cuts both ways, depending upon one's geo-economic positioning. Thus, we see Caborca farmers campaigning for new protections for their crops with the Mexican government, while in the same breath calling for protections against Chilean produce (Wilder 2002).

Asparagus and fresh grape growers have benefited from the removal of import duties under NAFTA. Duties placed on the importation of asparagus into the United States that had been set at 25 percent in 1993 were completely phased out during the 1990s, creating a boon for Caborca producers. The region has about 5,700 ha. in asparagus, representing 41 percent of the surface in asparagus nationally (ASUDIR 2000). Mexicali is also a major source of asparagus for the export market, with the number of hectares of asparagus under cultivation rising rapidly since the signing of NAFTA. Caborca fills a critical gap in the world asparagus market as it is able to supply asparagus during the January through March period when neither the other Mexican regions nor California can do so. Asparagus production is concentrated virtually entirely within the private producer sector, including a large amount of activity from transnational companies; only one ejido is involved in asparagus production. Asparagus costs 2.5 times as much to produce as fresh grapes, and 5 times as much as industrial grapes and raisins. The cost of producing one hectare of asparagus rose 130 percent from 1996 to 2002, and the cost of irrigation for asparagus rose by 186 percent over the same period (Wilder 2002).

Asparagus is helping to deplete the valley of Caborca groundwater aquifer at a very fast rate. It has therefore become a conflictive crop within the region. Two other factors help fuel the conflict that has developed between grape and asparagus producers: the presence of transnational companies and other "outsiders" in the asparagus sector, and the impunity of asparagus producers when it comes to observing required water restrictions. In 1994, after the irrigation district was transferred from the federal government to the Irrigation District Water Users' Association (Asociación de Usuarios del Distrito de Riego, ASUDIR), the association promptly implemented a strict water reduction plan due to the falling water table and severely overdrafted state of the aquifer. In addition to a prolonged drought, the Caborca aquifer has become severely overdrafted due in large part to state policies that supported and promoted cultivation of more water-consumptive crops.

State-sponsored grape production in the region began in the 1960s, even while it was recognized since the mid-1950s that the aquifer was in danger. In the 1980s, new arrivals from the Mexicali Valley—"outsiders"—came into the region and began cultivation of asparagus, a much more water-consumptive crop than grapes. Asparagus water demands affected water levels and supply throughout the region, not just those of asparagus producers themselves. Although asparagus and grape production were well under way when the free trade accords of the 1990s were signed, NAFTA made attractive the option of expanding production with the elimination of U.S. import tariffs. By 1995, under the water reduction program, each water rights holder was required to reduce consumption every year, meaning in practice that cultivated area had to be reduced as well. Although the area in grapes declined slowly but steadily from 1995 on through 2000, the area in asparagus continued to climb throughout the same period. Clearly asparagus producers were expanding production and using more water (by renting ejidal or other well rights) commensurate with the expansion, a fact that angered grape producers in the region. As one prominent private grape producer stated,

> Asparagus has become a very conflictive crop for this region. The American [e.g., Dole Foods] and Japanese [e.g., Lee Brands] transnational companies are involved in asparagus production, and they manage things differently. They use tons of water and buy up water rights. . . . If it goes well with grape farmers, we feel it in the community. People buy a new car or open a little business. But with the asparagus business, we don't feel anything. Thousands of workers come in from other parts of Mexico and the buses come and drop them off with their checks at the door of the bank or the changing house, and they cash their checks, get back on the bus, and leave town. Something like four-fifths of the area in asparagus is owned by foreign companies. (personal interview, private producer/ community leader, June 20, 2001)

A local ejidal producer said: "The worst thing is that the American companies are buying up ejidal lands. They've got too many wells. They take away our water and they're going to leave us without any water. But everything they're doing is legal" (personal interview, ejidatario, June 26, 2001).[9] An official with the ejidatario producers' union noted pointedly: "The problem of the region is asparagus." (Wilder, personal interview, ejidal producers' union official, June 20, 2001). Despite lax enforcement in earlier years, there was some evidence in 2001 that local irrigation district officials had stepped up enforcement on the asparagus producers to bring them in line with the water reduction plan requirements.

The current water situation for Caborca ejidatarios is bleak, based upon a number of considerations. Water supply is dominated by private producers who own

86 percent of the 831 wells in the irrigation district. On average, there is only one well to support every twenty-seven ejidatarios, where there are 1.29 wells for every private producer. Moreover, 85 percent of the largest, most powerful wells (of 8 to 12 inches in diameter) are owned by private producers. Added to this picture of private sector control of irrigation water supply is the existence of numerous long-term (typically ten-year) well rentals by ejidos seeking money to pay off accumulated debt. According to a senior irrigation district official, "one hundred percent" of those who rent wells are private producers. Many ejidatarios have had their electricity (for pumping water up from irrigation wells) cut off due to inability to pay, a situation worsened by the phased elimination of electrical subsidies, which means that electrical costs actually increase each month, even for the same amount of water pumped. According to a local official with the federal electricity commission, about half of the community had its electricity cut off at some point during the year 2001 (Wilder 2002). The ejidatario sector was responsible for three-fourths of the 450 million pesos in accumulated overdue debt in Caborca in 2001. Many ejidatarios have therefore abandoned production, unable to keep the pumps turned on and needing to make payments on their debt, and have turned to working in the asparagus fields for the private producers. One woman ejidataria stated that debt is the reason her ejido has rented out its well: "Just one well is rented. . . . The contract is with a private asparagus producer." She stated that the well is commonly owned by twenty-one families in two groups (societies of productive responsibility). The group receives 80,000 pesos (about US$8,000) annual rent, divided among the twenty-one families, meaning that each family earns only about US$381 each year from the well rental. Many of the families stated they use the income earned from the well to pay off some of their debt; thus, although the income does ease their financial burden, the well rental does not translate into disposable income that helps ejido families advance (Wilder, personal interview, June 21, 2001).

Implications and Conclusion

The Mexican water legislation passed to help Mexican agriculturalists be more efficient has changed the organization of large irrigation districts. In concert with the host of other liberalization strategies the government has pursued throughout the last ten years (including entry into numerous free trade agreements and the ejido reforms), this has created a raft of challenges for ejidatario producers. Although groundwater is a rapidly declining resource in some of the most productive agricultural regions of the country, its management and mismanagement has not received sufficient attention from Mexican authorities. The increased population pressure in large cities in central and northern Mexico translates into rising water demand and greater rural–urban conflict over scarce water resources. In Mexico, cities have priority rights to water over agriculturalists, which intensify the pressure on groundwater resources. Mexico's wholehearted embrace of free trade has benefited some producers and regions while creating new obstacles for many others, particularly ejidatarios who frequently are concentrated in lower-value crop production due to lack of resources and limited access to credit.

NAFTA and other FTAs have had an uneven impact throughout Mexico, even in major irrigation districts where producers have shifted production to more water-intensive crops that require a greater investment of capital, including funds needed to pay for pumping groundwater. Subsidies paid to farmers in the United States have created an uneven field of competition for grains. Apart from NAFTA, other trade agreements, such as Mexico's FTA with Chile, can have specific sectoral impacts on particular crop sectors and producer groups, even while others in the same local region are benefiting from other free trade agreements. The demands of nature, which call for water conservation and less intensive agriculture, seem to be directly in conflict with the demands of the market, which call for water-scarce arid regions such as those in northern Mexico to produce water-consumptive export crops.

The benefits and losses associated with free trade will become increasingly complex as producers are exposed to competition from more markets with the entry into additional free trade agreements. There is a need for greater government control over the pumping of groundwater and, in the border region, creative engagement with the United States to manage groundwater in a sustainable, transparent, and equitable fashion. This is especially important as pressures on groundwater sources grow with increased agricultural trade and urban demands for water.

Finally, Mexico has to engage with the water management issues inherent in the NAFTA agreement itself. New agreements are now being drafted, providing an opportunity for Mexico to build on what it has learned about the trade and investment agreements. Governments' sovereign rights and those of local water management organizations must be protected in a fashion not presently in use. In the process, greater transparency and accountability need to be built into the system. Given the critical importance of water in Mexico, these changes should be a priority.

Notes

1. An ejido is a communal landholding organization that normally has at least twenty members. Ejidos were created in the decades following the Mexican Revolution (1910–1920) to redistribute productive land to landless peasants. The massive land redistribution and creation of the ejido system is a major legacy of the revolution.

2. The terms "ejido reform(s)" or "Article 27 reform(s)" are generic expressions that refer to three separate legal reforms that took place in 1992 and 1993 (Jones 1996, 189). The principal change was the reform of Article 27 of the Constitution, adopted January 6, 1992. The second was the new Agrarian Law (Ley Agraria) of February 26, 1992. Finally, new Agrarian Law regulations (*reglamentos*) were adopted January 6, 1993.

3. Mexico has the following active free trade agreements: NAFTA (with the United States and Canada), January 1, 1994; G-3 (with Colombia and Venezuela), January 1, 1995;

Bolivia and Costa Rica, both on January 1, 1995; Nicaragua, July 1, 1998; Chile, August 1, 1999; European Union and Israel, both on July 1, 2000; Northern triangle (with El Salvador, Guatemala, and Honduras), on March 15, 2001, and June 1, 2001; Northern European nations, July 1, 2001; Uruguay July 15, 2004; and Japan, on April 1, 2005 (Mexico, Secretaría de la Economía 2004).

4. The law was the regulatory structure (*reglamentaria*) that had been established in paragraphs 5 and 6 of Article 27 of the Mexican Constitution (Tellez 1993, 104). It replaced the former Federal Law of Waters (Ley Federal de Aguas) that had been in effect since 1972, with several modifications in 1986 (Vargas and Sanchez 1994, 9), which in its turn had supplanted the earlier water legislation titled the Law of National Property Waters (Ley de Aguas de Propiedad Nacional) dating to 1936 (Vargas and Sanchez 1994, 9).

5. See Pineda 1999 for an excellent discussion of the limitations of municipalization and privatization in a multiple-city study.

6. The transference program was carried out in Mexico by the National Water Commission (CNA) under the auspices of the World Bank's Program for Investment in Irrigation and Drainage, and had a total budget of US$1.195 billion. The World Bank provided 29 percent (US$350 million) as a loan to Mexico (World Bank Loan 3419 ME) and the Inter-American Development Bank lent another 17 percent (US$200 million) (Pineda Blancarte 2000, 67). The original loan was for the period 1991–1994, and was subsequently extended through June of 2000 (Pineda Blancarte 2000, 67). The World Bank loan was directed toward three areas: (1) development and technology transfer; (2) capacity-building; and (3) communication and user participation. The loan funded Mexico's Institute of Water Technology (IMTA) to carry out the ambitious program (Pineda Blancarte 2000, 66–72).

7. The Caborca case study is based primarily upon a dissertation study focusing on the impacts of national water reforms on local producers, primarily ejidatarios, completed in two irrigation districts in Sonora, Mexico, the Rio Yaqui Irrigation District (041) and Altar-Pitiquito-Caborca Irrigation district (037) (see Wilder 2002). The Mexicali case study is based upon a decade of work looking at the impacts of water and agricultural reforms on ejidatario producers in the Mexicali Valley (Baja California and Sonora) (see Whiteford and Bernal 1996; Whiteford et al. 1998).

8. "Dumping" is defined as selling a product in a country's national market at prices lower than those at which the same product is sold internationally, or selling a lower-quality product. For example, Mexican grape producers complained that Chileans were dumping their raisin backlog—*rezago*—at cheap prices on the Mexican market.

9. Both this comment and the prior one reflect a local belief that foreign companies own land and operate within Caborca. In a strictly legal sense, however, this may not always be the case. For example, a Dole Foods official I met with stated that they own no land in Caborca and do not even officially have an asparagus operation in Mexico, nor do they actually buy the asparagus until it crosses the U.S. border. The role of the Dole Foods official and his tiny staff was strictly to ensure quality control so that the asparagus harvest would be sure to meet Dole's quality standards. Similarly, a group of Mexican entrepreneurs (originally from Mexicali) also has a major asparagus operation and although it sells to Lee Brands, it is not strictly speaking controlled by Lee Brands. Nevertheless, despite these strict legal distinctions, there clearly is a strong sense within the larger community that these two transnational companies are actively benefiting from local production based on water from the shared groundwater aquifer. For a more in-depth discussion, see Wilder (2002).

References

ASUDIR. 2000. *Plan emergente, Distrito de Riego Caborca (037)*. Caborca, Sonora. Asociación de Usuarios de Riego.

————. 2001. *Programa Integral Para la Rehabilitación y Modernización de la Región Agricola de Caborca, Sonora.* Caborca: Asociación de Usuarios de Riego (ASUDIR).
Baker, Randolph, Christopher A. Scott, Charlotte de Fraiture, and Upali Amarasinghe. 2000. "Global Water Shortages and the Challenge Facing Mexico." *Water Resources Development* 16, no. 4.
Becerril, Andrea Alma, E. Muñoz, and Carlos Camacho. 1999. "Declaran a Aguascalientes calientes zona de desastre debido a la 'sequía.'" 1999. *La Jornada*, June 13. Mexico, D.F.
Buras, Nathan. 1996. "The Water Resources of Mexico: Their Utilization and Management." In *The Changing Structure of Mexico*, ed. L. Randall. Armonk, NY: M.E. Sharpe.
Búrquez, Alberto, and Angelina Y. Martínez. 2000. "El desarrollo económico y la conservación de los recursos naturales," In *Sonora 2000 al debate: Problemas y soluciones, riesgos y oportunidades*, ed. I. Almada Bay. Hermosillo: El Colegio de Sonora.
CNA (Comisión Nacional de Agua). 2001. *Programa Nacional Hidráulico, 2001–2006.* Mexico, D.F.: Comisión Nacional de Agua.
Contijoch Escontria, Manuel. 1999. *El programa de ferti-irrigación de la Alianza para el Campo.* Primer Foro Internacional Sobre el Finciamiento de la Modernización de las Areas de Riego. Hermosillo, Sonora, October.
Cummings, Ronald G. 1989. *Waterworks: Improving Irrigation Management in Mexican Agriculture.* Washington, DC: World Resources Institute.
DeJanvry, Alain, Gustavo Gordillo, Elisabeth Sadoulet, et al. 1997. *Mexico's Second Agrarian Reform: Household and Community Response, 1990–1994.* San Diego: Center for U.S.–Mexico Studies, University of California Press.
Easter, William. 1998. *Irrigation Improvement Strategy Review: A Review of Bankwide Experience Based on Selected "New Style" Projects.* Washington, DC: World Bank.
Gleick, P., and G. Wolff. 2002. *The New Economy of Water: The Risks and Benefits of Globalization and Privatization of Fresh Water.* Oakland, CA: Pacific Institute.
IMTA. 1990. *Características de los distritos de riego, 1990.* México, D.F.: Instituto Mexicano de la Tecnología del Agua.
INEGI. 2000. *General Census of Population and Housing, Preliminary Results.* México D.F.: Instituto Nacional de Estadística e Informática.
Jones, Gareth. 1996. "Dismantling the Ejido: A Lesson in Controlled Pluralism." In *Dismantling the Mexican State?*, ed. Rob Aitkin, Nikki Craske, Gareth A. Jones, and David E. Stansfield. New York: St. Martin's Press.
Mann, Howard. 2003. "Who Owns 'Your Water'? Reclaiming Water as a Public Good Under International Trade and Investment Law." International Institute for Sustainable Development, August.
Mexico. Secretaría de la Economía. 2004. www.economia-snci.gob.mx/sphp_pages/faci_negocios/ficha_publica_tlcs.htm, viewed on April 1, 2005.
Pineda Blancarte, Victor Manuel. 2000. "Credito externo en apoyo a la transferencia de los distritos de riego en México." In *Memorias: Congreso Internacional de Transferencia de Sistemas de Riego, Mazatlan, Sinaloa, Mexico. April 2–9, 2000*, ed. E. Palacios Velez. México, D.F.: Comisión Nacional de Agua.
Pineda, Nicolas. 1999. "Urban Water Policy in Mexico: Municipalization and Privatization of Water Services." Unpublished Ph.D. dissertation, University of Texas at Austin.
Romero Lankao, Patricia. 2001. "Mexico: Water for the 21st Century, Main Tendencies and Challenges." Paper presented at the 62nd National Conference of the American Society for Public Administration.
Scott, Christopher A., and Tushaar Shah. 2004 "Groundwater Overdraft Reduction Through Agricultural Energy Policy: Insights from India and Mexico." *Water Resources Development* 20, no. 2.
Tellez, Luís, ed. 1993. *Nueva Legislación de Tierras, Bosques y agues.* México, D.F.: Fondo de Cultura Económica.

358 RESOURCES AND THE ENVIRONMENT

Vargas, Sergio, and Marco Antonio Sanchez. 1994. *La Nueva Política Hidroagrícola.* Mexico, D.F.: Instituto Mexicano de la Tecnología del Agua (IMTA).

Vaughan, Scott. 2003 "The Greenest Trade Agreement Ever? Measuring the Environmental Impacts of Agricultural Liberalization." *NAFTA's Promise and Reality: Lessons from Mexico for the Hemisphere.* New York: Carnegie Endowment for International Peace.

Whiteford, Scott, and Alfonso Cortez. 2005. "Good to the Last Drop: The Political Ecology of Water and Health on the Border." In *Globalization, Water and Health: Resource Management in Times of Scarcity,* ed. L. Whiteford and S. Whiteford. Santa Fe, NM: School of American Research.

Whiteford, Scott, and Francisco Bernal. 1996. "Campesinos, Water and the State: Different Views of La Transferencia." In *Reforming Mexico's Agrarian Reform,* ed. L. Randall. Armonk, NY: M.E. Sharpe.

Whiteford, Scott, and Kjell Enge. 1989. *The Keepers of Water and Earth: Mexican Rural Social Organization and Irrigation.* Austin: University of Texas Press.

Whiteford, Scott, Heliodoro Díaz Cisneros, Francisco Bernal, and Esteban Valtierra. 1998. "The Struggle for Land and Water: Arid Land Ejidos Bound by the Past, Marginalized by the Future." In *The Transformation of Rural Mexico: Reforming the Ejido Sector,* ed. David Myhre and Wayne Cornelius. La Jolla: University of California, San Diego, Center for U.S.-Mexican Studies.

Wilder, Margaret. 2002. "In Name Only: Water Policy, the State and Ejidatario Producers in Northern Mexico." Unpublished Ph.D. dissertation, University of Arizona.

Yates, Paul Lamartine. 1981. *Mexico's Agricultural Dilemma.* Tucson: University of Arizona Press.

V
Legal, Political, and Social Change

20

HUGO ALEJANDRO CONCHA CANTÚ

The Justice System

Judiciary, Military, and Human Rights

In 1990, only 53 percent of Mexicans had quite a lot of confidence in the Justice System. There are thirty-three Mexican judiciaries: one federal, one from the Federal District, and thirty-one from the Mexican states. There also have been many other "ancillary" institutions, such as the police corps, prosecutors, penitentiaries, human rights commissions, and even executive offices that have "administrative courts," controlled by the president. These courts have been in charge of labor, agrarian, administrative, and electoral conflicts against the state within a trial, sued for the lack of provision of the services it is supposed to deliver. Federal justice could and still can review and alter any type of legal construct with regard to local elections made by the local legislature and interpreted by local judiciaries.

Judicial institutions had limited jurisdiction and excluded political questions: the existence of political rights became uncertain when there were no means for protecting them. Moreover, the president appointed the justices of the Supreme Court. Judicial reform came about in part because independent judiciaries were seen as essential to achieve economic competitiveness. Thus, on December 6, 1994, President Ernesto Zedillo sent Congress a constitutional amendment that reduced the Supreme Court of Justice from twenty-six to eleven seats and selected its members by the Senate choosing each justice from three names that the president presented for its consideration. Each justice would have a single term of office of fifteen years. The reform also created a Judiciary Council that absorbed all the administrative tasks the Court used to handle.

In 1996, the Electoral Court, previously part of the executive branch, became part of the federal judiciary and procedural means were created to demand the protection of federal courts against the violation of political rights. As a result, since the mid-nineties the country started having a federal judiciary with an acceptable degree of independence that fulfilled its duties on time, although difficulties remain because judiciaries lack information and statistical systems, performance indicators, and sustained efforts for training and professional edu-

cation. A shortage of funds led to the selection of reform goals linked to those aspects related to economic interests or to their funding feasibility. Hugo Concha states that efficiency was improved, but sometimes fast proceedings produce erratic resolutions. A new factor in the continuing judicial reforms is the role of international agencies and organizations: for the first time, judiciaries are able to obtain money from donations or international loans. It should be noted that military courts have a separate justice system that remains as the only exception from regular jurisdiction of civil justice.

Human rights in Mexico consist of both traditional civil liberties and of social rights that particularly protect workers and peasants. Nonetheless, there was a formal recognition by the government that there were more rights than those established in its Constitution. These rights derived from multiple international agreements signed by Mexico, but these new rights mainly were ignored. Finally, in the nineties, President Carlos Salinas de Gortari created an organization based on the Swedish "ombudsman" to denounce authorities that were committing abuses. Although in practice it is polemical, the mere fact of knowing about such abuses is a clear sign of improvement.

The Mexican Justice System and Its Difficult Transformation

One decisive element in any major political and economic transformation is the justice system. This refers to the set of state institutions in charge of securing the actual existence and enforcement of citizens' rights and their protection against possible violations by establishing legal remedies and penalties.

The importance of this element in a process of structural change is diverse and difficult to systematize for analysis. Each case would inevitably present its own logic and characteristics. It is important, however, to present some of the most significant expressions of the complicated relationship between structural adjustments and a justice system. The most obvious case is the one in which the institutions comprising the justice system are included in the process of reform or change. In recent decades, most Latin American countries have undergone major processes of change involving their courts, their police corps, their prosecutor offices, and many other instances related to the protection of human rights. Extreme living conditions, marginalization, poverty, and increased crime rates have demanded urgent attention from governments. As can be seen, the relationship between these conditions and the justice system is direct and positive.

Another common scenario is the one in which the justice system is not part of the process of change, but is affected directly by the process. In such a situation, a major transformation of the political and economic structure would impact the rights of people, sometimes widening or improving their scope and in other cases, limiting it. In this case, the failure or success of the overall process is indirectly linked to the justice system. Some examples can be found in Latin America during the multiple economic adjustments that were made in the 1980s and 1990s (privatizations, reductions of the state subsidiary components), without considering aspects related to insecurity or to the widening of political participation. In these cases, the changes were highly unpopular and led to social problems. Also, the process of democratization in some countries has been hindered by its lack of direct impact on the rights and living conditions of the people. Thus, the situation of the set of institutions devoted to the protection of human rights is a major theme for the success of political and economic adjustments. The most striking lesson is that these institutions need to be considered (their structure and functions) along with the effects and impact of the changes being made in other dimensions.

Mexico presents an interesting and, simultaneously, complex case for the study of these institutions. In some moments, judicial institutions have been pivotal in the process of change, and at some other moments, these institutions have been left out, producing such negative effects that they now constitute one of the most important concerns in the process of economic and democratic consolidation. This chapter attempts to reveal both trends in which the justice institutions have been crucial for the process of change, and other instances in which their exclusion has produced negative consequences.

It is important to mention that despite its possible variation in each country's configuration, the judicial branch is at the core of any justice system; its long-established institutions are designed to solve social conflicts of every type and to determine the interpretation of "justice" each time they do so, by applying the law. At their side, but never replacing their role as the true administrators of justice, there are many other "ancillary" institutions, such as the police corps, prosecutors, penitentiaries, human rights commissions, and even direct executive offices such as labor or interior departments. The military is also an important institution, not only because but also because it has, as will be addressed, a special jurisdiction of its own.

This chapter directs its attention, primarily, to judicial institutions in Mexico (formally and functionally), as the main components of the justice system, but also will address some aspects of the other institutions in the system as well. Specifically, it refers to the military, not because the army has played a particular political role in Mexican contemporary history, but mainly because of a dual motive: first, the armed forces affect the administration of justice by being a key component of public security and social stability, and second, because the military is the only institution that maintains an isolated subsystem of justice that cannot be reached by ordinary courts.

The Mexican case, despite its particularities, presents an interesting example that differs from the more frequent occurrence in Latin American history of the military as the opposite face of legality and respect for societal rights. With the exception of Mexico, authoritarianism in the region has always been embodied by the armed forces. Some reflections are necessary in this regard in order to understand the particular situation of Mexico.

Finally, as it is impossible to analyze every institution integrating the Mexican justice sector in this work, this chapter will present some brief considerations about the protection of human rights in general, combining the institutional analysis of the judiciary and the military with a general view of the object being protected.

The Mexican Judiciaries

After its inception as an independent nation, Mexico adopted, in 1824, the form of a constitutional state, where the exercise of political power followed the design of the U.S. Constitution, creating the three classical branches of power—legislative, executive, and judicial—within a federal pattern. However, this political structure had its own peculiar elements as the result of the combination of the new republican institutions just created and the legal and cultural legacy of the Spanish colonial rule, as happened with most Latin American countries. Therefore, Mexico was founded bringing together innovation and continuity, that is, creating modern political institutions without a complete rupture with its past according to its legal, hierarchical, and patrimonialistic culture.

Institutions such as popular sovereignty and separation of power were established without putting aside the civil law tradition.[1] This meant that Mexico gave the highest importance to its legislative branch as the body composed of the true representatives of the people, and to its main product, the written statute or code, in the Rousseauian tradition of understanding legislation as the "expression of the popular will." This form of positioning one branch of government above the others, which had the unavoidable duty of obeying the law (legislation), hindered the possibility of controlling the legislative body and providing an equilibrium among the three powers, which is a key element for the functioning of a system based on checks and balances. The law, then, was identified with legislation, and the judiciary was its servant.[2]

This peculiar design endured, throughout the different constitutions that were put into place during the nineteenth century (characterized by struggles between conservatives, supporters of a centralized state, and liberals, in favor of a federal system) and up to the creation of the present Constitution, in 1917. As a result of continuous political struggles, control and domination became the first and foremost requirement of any group that came into power. Late nineteenth- as well as most of twentieth-century Mexican history is an account of political centralization and relentless control, putting aside every aspiration for pluralism or liberty that could become as challenge to the established government. From 1833 to 2000, Mexico was ruled in an authoritarian fashion.[3] Even now, after a true democratic transition (2000), President Fox, coming from a traditional opposition party, has been hesitant to abandon the use of authoritarian methods of governance. Despite the fact that one of the main rallying cries of his campaign was the need for comprehensive political and constitutional change, his administration has not drafted such an initiative.

Within this context of legislative superiority and political subordination of the judiciary to the executive branch, the thirty-three Mexican judiciaries (one federal, one from the Federal District, and thirty-one from the Mexican states) have been institutions that have struggled to survive, but their functioning throughout Mexican history has been unique and distant from the traditional models of judicial analysis.

Power and Control

The analysis of Mexican judiciaries can be divided in two main periods of its contemporary history (postrevolutionary, from 1920 on). The first period is characterized by the existence of an authoritarian and corporatist state, controlled by one party, with the president of the country as its undisputed leader. During this period, 1920–1994, judiciaries worked as part of the political machinery, fulfilling particular objectives related to stability and control.

The second period, 1995–2004, as described in the next section of this chapter, is the one in which the country's severe and centralized form of government started to erode by a steady process of economic and political liberalization, pushed by multiple internal and external demands. In this phase, judiciaries were part of the overall transformation, giving birth to a new type of institution characterized by its commitment to independence and efficiency, coming closer to the ideal type of a liberal institution, but still missing some components needed to become a democratic institution.

On the political side, the system was based on the merging of the government (federal and local) and the hegemonic party. Any presidential system is based on the leadership of the executive power,[4] but the Mexican design overstressed this leadership, turning this branch of government into a very powerful political figure. The president not only possessed the formal powers and roles that the Constitution bestowed on him as head of the federal executive branch—such as commander-in-chief of the army, supreme chief of the federal bureaucracy (with the capacity to appoint and fire every member of the cabinet and highest federal officials), and the representative of the country internally as well as in the international arena—but he also was, informally, the supreme leader of the party. He controlled the party by selecting all the political candidates for the elected positions, from municipal officials to local and federal representatives, senators, governors, and principally his own successor (this practice became commonly known as the *dedazo,* indicating the physical act of pointing to the presidential heir). In sum, there was no important political decision in which the Mexican president did not participate, directly or indirectly.[5] Mexico thus developed an institutional machinery that to a certain degree achieved the impossible: a "constitutional" and at the same time authoritarian government.[6]

Mexican judiciaries were, in a certain way, victims of the design. According to modern constitutional theory, adopted formally by the Mexican state, the judiciary has the mission of solving social disputes according to the law, and also of controlling the government when its acts (including legislation) violate individual rights. For this reason, independence from any possible interference, public or private, is a necessary condition for what can be called liberal judicial functioning. Although it is difficult to assert that Mexican judiciaries fulfilled the liberal aspiration of becoming true guardians of human rights, it would be wrong to assert that they were useless or utterly dysfunctional. Mexican judicial institutions had, in the constitutional and legislative texts, all the powers that judiciaries need to work, but their function was limited in different ways. Nonetheless, they were key institutions for the functioning of the peculiar political system.

The Mexican Federal System

The idea of a balanced political system based on the notion of shared checks and balances was de facto inexistent in Mexico, but this situation did not affect social perceptions and the ordinary use of courts. Even though the hegemonic role of the president was present within the judicial structure and operation, both federally and locally, the Mexican federal judiciary was always seen as a key reference for evaluating the performance of the president in turn.

The federal judiciary and especially its highest body, the Supreme Court of Justice, enjoyed a reputation if not of true independence, at least of a certain distance from political decisions. Besides, the idea that legal decisions are not political has been enforced by the excessive formality existent in a civil law country. Lawyers and, especially, high-ranking judges, could argue that they were outside the political arena. Again, what was visible in the law, at first sight, was distorted by other subtle means: at the end, the law was subordinated to political decisions.

The first and most important limitation to federal justice was its jurisdiction—in other words, the definition of the area in which federal courts could intervene. Following the French model, Mexico established "administrative courts." These institutions function as courts, but belong to the executive apparatus, which means that the designation of their judges and the allocation of their budget were a responsibility of the president. The conundrum was very convenient for political purposes, because these courts were in charge of different and crucial areas of justice such as labor, agrarian, administrative (conflicts against the state within a trial, sued for the lack of provision the services it is supposed to deliver), and electoral. Political power appropriated these areas of justice, leaving the judicial branch seriously handicapped.

A second element also limited the jurisdiction of federal courts by excluding political questions. In Mexico as in the United States, legal conflicts that deal with political themes are known as political questions, mainly legal conflicts about political (electoral) rights. Originated as a consequence of a period of excessive political activism, this barrier was a major burden for political participation. The existence of political rights became uncertain when there were no means for protecting them.

The third venue where the exaggerated power of the president affected the federal judiciary was the designation of the highest-ranking judges, the justices of the Supreme Court. This situation not only affected the independence per se of the justices, who had a moral debt to the person that appointed them, but it created an unstable atmosphere. The president was directly responsible for every sort of political career in the country, so it was natural for justices to have expectations about their political future. Many justices ended up as senators or as governors from their state of origin. In the end, the Supreme Court of Justice was, in many ways, one more political space subordinated to the presidential will. Still, there are many registered cases of Court decisions against the executive power, though to fully understand this apparent inconsistency, it is important to mention the next set of controls of a procedural nature.

According to the Constitution, the Supreme Court was charged with interpreting the Constitution each time a case was solved, but this important function was, and still is, severely restricted. Although every federal and local judge was supposedly entitled to interpret the Constitution, this is understood as having the obligation of obeying the Constitution as well as the legislation derived from it. Only the Supreme Court could really create, ultimately, constitutional interpretations. Any other court resolution, federal, administrative, or local, could be revised by the Court, which had the sole capacity to create mandatory precedents.[7]

In Mexico, parties, lawyers, and judges cannot use judicial precedents except for certain resolutions of the Supreme Court. When courts resolve a legal conflict, they are obliged to provide a reason for their view of the facts and justify the way in which the law (legislation) should be applied. Judges cannot cite, as legal sources for this type of justification, other peer or judicial resolutions. In other words, the doctrine of *stare decisis* (the principle stating that precedent decisions are to be followed by the courts) does not exist in Mexico. This is a way of restricting the scope of judicial resolutions, thus weakening courts' positions and linking their performance to the written law (legislation). Clearly, this situation constrains the notion of judicial "law creation" and in contrast underlines the idea of judicial mechanization.

Only the Supreme Court of Justice is allowed to establish certain kinds of legal precedents known as *jurisprudence* (which has nothing to do with the common meaning of jurisprudence, and means constitutional doctrine done by the Court). A "jurisprudential thesis" is formed when a specific topic is solved by the unanimous vote of the Court members, and in five consecutive occasions without interruption. Although these special precedents are formally mandatory for every inferior court, lawyers and judges frequently ignore their existence and do not use them. Also, frequent changes of the members of the Court and changes of the justices' opinions have created a universe of ambivalent and contradictory precedents.

The Court's power to modify social life is further limited by Mexican legislation that added one more fundamental restriction: a specific judicial resolution cannot be applied to anyone except the parties involved in each particular case.[8] Even a Supreme Court resolution involving constitutional interpretation, when *jurisprudencia* is created, could not be applied to similar cases. If a particular individual believed her case was similar to one already solved by the Court, she would have to litigate to obtain a particular resolution.[9]

The final relevant procedural obstacle was the most evident one: excessive procedural formalism. Many cases brought to federal judiciaries were simply rejected or discarded[10] for procedural reasons (Fix Fierro 1994). Excessive requirements made practically any case liable to be excluded from legal treatment, or made proceedings slow and difficult to follow, creating uncertainty and increasing their costs.

Finally, the budget had a very important place among controls over the judiciary. Budgetary allocation was in the hands of the president and, formally, in those of the representatives he has appointed. From salaries to material resources, the institution and its members were constrained in every possible way.

A Look at the States

The situation of local judiciaries was worse than that of the federal institution. They not only suffered the direct will of the president and his particular caprices, but they also had to confront the local version of the system in which they were seen as institutions dependent on the governor of each state. If the large set of controls was effective at the federal level, locally the subordination had no limits in all the country, despite regional cultural differences.

Direct political controls were clear obstacles for judicial independence. In Mexico the distinction between a "Supreme Court" (Suprema Corte) and a "Superior Tribunal" (Tribunal Superior de Justicia) entails diverse institutions. Precisely, according to the explanation that will follow regarding the *amparo directo,* the Mexican federal design did not contemplate local supreme courts, having jurisdiction over certain issues without any superior review, and in their place superior tribunals were established, whose resolutions were subject to review by federal courts. The idea of supreme courts, with supreme local interpretative powers was rejected, and governors decided, without any type of intermediary, on the appointment, resignation, and retirement of local judges, from municipal to the members of the local Superior Tribunal. Also, the institution had to maintain a continuous servile attitude in its desperate request to obtain sufficient financial resources, which was in the hands of the governor.

Procedural obstacles for local judiciaries were very similar, and also had a very important federal component. Not only was there the same hierarchical structure established within these local institutions, but a federal hierarchical mechanism was also established in order to balance the possible excesses committed by the governor and the goals decided by federal authorities. Moreover, judiciaries were not only seen as a target themselves for federal intervention, but also as the ideal means by which federal authorities could intervene in a variety of local activities and interactions, and as a subtle way for sending messages with specific meanings to local authorities. As can be seen, local judiciaries were used and manipulated by different political actors who impeded them from functioning as they were supposed to do, according to the federal and local constitutions. Again, a sophisticated legal device achieved this complicated goal of providing and delimiting rights, the judicial *amparo* or *amparo directo*.

The amparo lawsuit in Mexico is a very interesting proceeding that originally adapted the habeas corpus from the common-law system as a judicial procedure in civil law countries to protect fundamental rights. At present, however, there are two types of amparo. The amparo indirecto is the basic means used to demand immediate protection by federal courts (district judges, dispersed throughout all the territory) when a constitutional right has been violated by an authority. The amparo directo is the proceeding by which administrative (labor, agrarian, or administrative) or local resolutions can be reexamined by federal courts (circuit courts, located in certain cities throughout the country).[11] This type of trial is known as *cassation* and is considered a major element of the constitutional right to due process. This means that a superior court (federal circuit courts) can be asked to review any local resolution, even the ones coming already from the highest local appeals court, the Superior Tribunal. Despite the fact that the underlying rationale for this procedure was the protection of the constitutional order from ample local political discretion, it is true that a major impediment was established to providing a healthy federalism. States were excluded from the possibility of constructing their own interior legal orders because, ultimately, federal justice could review and alter any type of legal construct made by the local legislature and interpreted by local judiciaries.

Consequently, until the mid-nineties, Mexican judiciaries have been working as efficient institutions at the service of a corporatist and authoritarian state using both substantial and procedural methods of control. Yet the idea that judiciaries were useless institutions, or that they did not operate as liberal institutions, is quite inexact. They were very useful institutions for state purposes and logic, and they formally kept working as any liberal judiciary, according to and strictly following legal prescriptions. It was the excessive regulation and formalism that finally distorted the overall work of Mexico's courts, transforming them into institutions of social control.

The Logic of Change: New Institutions for New Demands

As has been widely analyzed in this book, different groups forced the liberalization of the country, first in its economic dimension (1982–1994)[12] and, following that, in its political dimension (1994–2000).[13] In 2000, as it has been discussed in other chapters of this book, the country finally achieved a formal transition to democracy with the presidential victory of Fox, a candidate from a different political party (PAN) than the one that had been in power since the end of the revolutionary war (PRI). From 2000 the country has been debating how to consolidate this important transformation beyond a mere change of actors.

The justice system and, specially, its judiciaries, was an important component of the reform efforts that followed the liberalization processes. By 2004, although judicial institutions had changed in some important aspects, they remained untouched in others due to the specific interests and goals that the promoting groups were trying to protect and meet, which has led to further calls for integral judicial reform.

Economic liberalization was the result of the weakness of the postrevolutionary model. Domestic and international demands for competitiveness and growth could not be met by the state in 1982, which succumbed to a financial crisis that combined with a depressed economy. The lack of financial resources made it impossible for the Mexican state to continue funding an enormous welfare apparatus for both individuals and industries, the latter being part of the import substitution model that subsidized inefficient industries by means of elevated tariffs and import restrictions.

In the new scenario, economic policy was adapted to the requirements of a competitive international economy. Among the many changes implemented, there was consensus about the relevance of a general transformation of the institutions that could guarantee economic transactions and investments. Judiciaries were major elements of this reform because they were directly responsible for the protection of private economic transactions and contracts, as well as for the guarantee for copyrights. To achieve these goals, judicial institutions needed adjustments regarding their efficiency and their independence. Efficiency was a key goal because it was clear that Mexican judiciaries needed to achieve more and better results in opportune periods of time (Fix Fierro 1998). On the other hand, independent judiciaries were seen as essential because economic competitiveness required a liberal model where conflicts were resolved with neutrality, without interference of the government or other interested parties (Russell and O'Brien 2002).

Among the transformations that afterward became part of political liberalization, there was the need for a judiciary that could be trusted to solve electoral conflicts, protect political rights, and provide a place in which political differences could be resolved with the acceptance of the different political forces. Independent judiciaries throughout the country become symbolic of the protection of the new democratic recognition of plurality and differences.

*The Federal Reform of 1994–1995 and the Electoral
Court Reform of 1996*

On December 6 of 1994, only five days after being sworn in as the eighteenth president of Mexico,[14] Ernesto Zedillo sent Congress the initiative for a constitutional amendment that would substantially reform the judicial branch of government in its structure and functions. In May 1995, the same legislature received and passed two secondary regulatory statutes regarding the federal judiciary,

Figure 20.1   **The Judicial Reform of 1994**

Judicial Reform 1994–1995

     I.   Federal judicial branch restructuring.
    II. Extension of constitutional control mechanisms.
   III. Separation of administrative tasks in a different organ.
   IV. Establishment of a professional judical career.

Amparo	**Constitutional Controversies** and **Unconstitutional Actions**
Amparo Directo: Review of jurisdictional resolutions. *Amparo Indirecto*: Protection of individual and social rights.	

consolidating the legislative modifications known as the "Judicial Reform of 1994–1995."[15]

Although the content of this reform is technically vast and complex, it is important to list its most important aspects (see Figure 20.1). First, the reform altered the structure of the federal judiciary, particularly the Supreme Court of Justice. The number was severely reduced from twenty-six to eleven, by the forceful retirement of most of its former members. The members of the new Court were selected by a new method, according to the reform. Now, the appointment was made by the Senate, which chose each justice from three names that the president presented for its consideration. Each justice would have a single term of office of fifteen years, as part of a system of gradual renovation that sought to end the use of the Court as a political platform (Fix Zamudio 1995).

Second, the nature of the Supreme Court and, consequently, the functioning of the entire federal system of justice, was also altered. The reform provided two new mechanisms to guarantee the protection of constitutional provisions, supplementing the traditional judicial review or amparo lawsuit. These new constitutional tools are called "constitutional controversies" and "unconstitutional actions," mechanisms that extend legal protection against a concentrated use of power. In both cases, the Court became the ultimate referee in conflicts that involve different political actors.

"Constitutional controversies" addresses conflicts between different actors in the constitutional system (federal branches of government, states, or municipal governments). Any branch of government, at the federal or local level, can demand that the Supreme Court of Justice rule on the constitutionality of actions taken by another branch of government if these actions are seen to invade the

Figure 20.2 **Constitutional Controversies**

Constitutional Controversies (*Controversias Constitucionales*)
Article 105, 1.

Object: To protect the faculties given to each level of government in the Constitution.

Possible Plaintiff:	Possible Defendant:
Federal branch of government	Federal branch of government
Local branch of government	Local branch of government
Municipal branch of government	Municipal branch of government

plaintiff's area of jurisdiction or impose an unfair obligation on the plaintiff. The idea established in the Constitution is that any political organ from any level of government can ask the Court to intervene and guarantee the constitutional separation of powers of the federal system (see Figure 20.2). An interesting procedural feature within this constitutional control is that only when the conflict arose between the federal branches of government, between different states, or in matters regarding municipal governments being contested by a state or by the federal government could the eventual resolution by the Court have general effects, and only if this passed by 8 of the 11 possible votes of the Supreme Court justices. In every other possible combination of controversies, the Court resolution would only be obligatory to the parties involved.

"Unconstitutional actions" enables numerous political agents to ask the Court to invalidate a specific statute even before its concrete individualization through a particular case (as happens with judicial review). In contrast to constitutional controversies, unconstitutional actions are procedural mechanisms that can be used by one-third (33 percent) of any legislative body, that is the Senate, the Federal Congress, or any state legislature, as well as the Attorney General of the Nation, or any registered political party, demanding that the Supreme Court of Justice rule about the contradiction between a law and the Constitution (see Figure 20.3). The Supreme Court resolution in this type of case would necessarily have general effects, in as much the contested law would be declared utterly invalid.

In any case, the introduction of these new constitutional controls pointed out an effective widening of the Supreme Court role as a constitutional guarantee through political controls (controversies and actions). Before these new mechanisms were included, the only control was the amparo lawsuit, a different type of mechanism because this has been in the hands of the society at large and not in the hands of specific political actors. The amparo lawsuit proceeds basically against any act of government that violated a fundamental right.

Third, as a way of strengthening the new Court and making it more efficient and independent, the reform created a new organ, the Judiciary Council (Consejo

Figure 20.3 **Unconstitutional Actions**

Unconstitutional Actions (Acciones de Inconstitucionalidad)
Article 105, 2.

Possible Plaintiff	Object of Complaint
33% of Congress 33% of any local legislature (including the Federal District legislature) The Attorney General Any registered political party	Any legislation or legislative project that is in contradiction with the Constitution

de la Judicatura), which absorbed all the administrative tasks the Court used to handle, such as budgetary allocation, appointment of judges and creation of new judicial organs, disciplinary matters, and the judicial career. Among all these new powers, the one to establish and manage a professional judicial career is fundamental as a means to fortify its independent nature, avoiding any appointment from outside the judiciary. It is important to mention that in order to achieve this objective, a huge bureaucratic structure was created (Melgar 1996).

These changes were a conscious, coherent attempt by the executive to transform the judicial branch into an effective, stronger, and independent actor. Independence could only be attained by establishing a distinctive operational logic, professional guarantees for the members of this branch through a set of new rules and procedures, as well as new instruments for the new political composition of the country brought about by the process of liberalization. By doing this, the state would not only expand the number of players within the political system, but would create a separation between the political sphere and the legal sphere.

In 1996, another important reform underscored aspects that had been excluded in the improvement of the electoral system and, thus, the establishment of formal democracy in the country. The first of the new modifications was the inclusion of the Electoral Court, previously part of the executive branch, in the federal judiciary. Along with this incorporation there was the creation of procedural means to demand the protection of federal courts against the violation of political rights, putting an end to a long vacuum.

As a result, since the mid-nineties the country has had a federal judiciary with an acceptable degree of independence from exterior influences that fulfills its duties on time. These important achievements do not mean that it has become fully professional, doctrinally consistent, transparent, accountable and open to other views, and, above all, accessible to most citizens. The relative progress made by the first reforms simply created a dynamic in which new multiple challenges became evident and new problems emerged.

A Look at the States

The Federal Reform of 1995 triggered multiple processes of local reform all around the country. In many cases these were the outcome of the same type of pressures to transform the judiciaries into more efficient and independent institutions, and in some other cases the impulse came from specific political pressures or simply as a response to what was going on in the rest of the country. With the existing differences in design and roles, the federal model of reform could not be repeated, but the conditions that pushed for the reform were present in the all the different local contexts. Nevertheless, the relevance of local reform movements is critical to the justice system. In spite of the multiple limitations upon local jurisdiction, commercial law is the major area of local jurisdiction in terms of the number of trials, followed by civil, family, and criminal affairs. Most of the conflicts related to contract defaults, breaches of obligation, or bank and financial actions are taken to commercial or civil jurisdiction. The outcome was thirty-two distinct reform processes taking place in the country that were trying to underline the efficiency of the institutions and, to a minor degree, their independence.[16]

The results of all these processes of reform are better mechanisms for systematic performance, for better allocation of the scarce financial resources, and for disciplinary sanctions. Structure and equipment are constant objectives for improvement, as well as work conditions. Among the major setbacks for efficiency, judiciaries face a lack of information and statistical systems, performance indicators, and sustained efforts toward training and professional education.

A major problem that has come to light in these processes is that of finances. Notwithstanding that every judicial branch in the country improved its budget and found new financial sources, such as direct federal government allocation, as well as capital investments, the long marginalization of the institution from active service to the population still could not be remedied with existing material resources. This presented a fundamental dilemma for the state, which needed to modernize its institutions in order to become reliable and attractive to further investment and capital flows, but lacked the resources for this objective. This element has constituted a factual barrier to almost every state effort to persist in seeking changes without caring for the degree of importance of each particular change. This means that the selection of reform goals, in this first period, was linked to those aspects related to economic interests (related with efficiency, mainly) or to their funding feasibility, restricting other types of urgent needs.

Judicial independence has improved less than efficiency. The judicial reforms made many fragmented improvements in appointment procedures, individual work guarantees and conditions for stability, proper retirement conditions, and internal nonintrusive atmospheres (referring to interference by lawyers or superior judges through informal channels), but did not create integral models that combine all of the above. Reform processes may also underscore the subordinated position of the judiciary if the reform process is too limited in its scope, because after a reform is enacted, it is difficult to bring it back for a new discussion.

Judicial Reform

The reform processes initiated in the mid-nineties produced relevant improvements that can be empirically presented, but still have been insufficient to the needs, demands, and expectations of the vast majority of the population. Many of the specific results of such movements had drawbacks: Efficiency was improved at the cost of quality. Independence from external private or political actors has increased, but this has also exposed the lack of capacity for sound and systematic work, leaving instead weak, inconsistent, and defective judicial resolutions that do not provide better justice, qualitatively speaking. The untouched internal authoritarian structure has not been helpful in creating more responsible and autonomous judges. The law is supposed to provide legal security, but some of the improvements are now creating a new type of uncertainty coming from fast proceedings that produce erratic resolutions.

True, it is now very difficult to imagine the situation of Mexico without a strong and active Supreme Court intervening in all sorts of political conflicts through its new set of constitutional powers, or the social costs if Mexico had not modernized many of its court offices and processes in order to deal with the higher number of conflicts. But it is also true that the rule of law is still an ideal far from reality for the majority of the population.

Many of the problems untouched by the initial reform processes are now being emphasized by continuous demands for an institution that is physically accessible and also legally available and easy to use. In this particular area, judiciaries in Mexico need to continue their transformation in order to protect individual and social rights.

For these reasons, it is possible to continue talking about judicial reform in Mexico, but as a process that is promoted by new actors and with new objectives. A new factor in the continuing judicial reform is the role of international agencies and organizations, which has no precedents in the area of judicial modernization. For the first time ever, judiciaries are able to obtain money not only from their traditional sources (budget, direct federal government allocation, as well as their own capital investments),[17] but also from donations or international loans from the American government through U.S. AID and its multiple projects, the World Bank and its project on local justice modernization, the Bank of Inter-American Development, the European Union, the Spanish government through the projects of its National Judiciary Council, and the Konrad Adenauer Foundation, to cite the most important ones.

The next stage of the reform process would need to transit from the new design and procedural innovations to easier, more understandable rules and accessible institutions. This is true for the justice system as a whole, which includes administrative courts, prosecutor and police institutions, jails, juvenile detention centers, and human rights commissions. The success of this ample reform would be conditioned upon the incorporation of all the actors.

In a newly designed judiciary, stronger local courts would be needed in order to reinforce the overall system, providing different ways of guarding constitutional provisions beyond the mere intervention of the federal courts. The enormous administrative judicial apparatus would eventually need to become part of the judicial branch. Prosecutor's offices and police corps would need to become more professionalized and better acquainted with modern systems of criminal justice.[18] Public security would necessarily become one of the new priorities in the reform agenda, which would emphasize the transformation of the criminal system as a way to recovering confidence and social peace.

In procedural matters, a main concern is the need to update and simplify the amparo procedure,[19] both in its dimension of constitutional protection of human rights, and in its dimension as a federal review over local jurisdiction. For this purpose, comparative experiences might prove useful in order to provide better models of coordination where the stability of states as well as constitutional guarantees for citizens are preserved. Locally, many states have complicated agendas for their own legislative review and update.

One of the most important challenges to be addressed is the need to work with judges' attitudes and willingness to be part of a changed institution. Resistance to change normally arises from fear, ignorance, and insecurity. This is a phenomenon widely present in Mexican judiciaries that is becoming the principal obstacle to further transformation. If judiciaries are going to play a significant role in a new democratic context, their members, on all levels, need to believe in their role. They need to realize that the institution has changed and will continue to change from an essentially authoritarian body to one of service and reliability.

The Mexican Military

The military has played an important role of deference and safeguarding in the country's transformation. This role has been discreet and respectful of civil authorities and their decisions without any attempt to become involved as a political actor. Even in the cases of direct military involvement, this has been an explicit act of others, undertaken to bring the military into the political arena, rather than an act of the military's will.[20] In sum, the Mexican armed forces have remained silent and loyal actors in turbulent times of transformation, despite the fact that some changes have altered their own stability.

Very little is known about the Mexican military in general. Its traditional closeness and aversion to publicity has impeded the realization of systematic research on something more than formal, public information, with the clear exception of sociologist Roderick Ai Camp's work (*Generals in the Palacio: The Military in Modern Mexico,* 1992), several historical accounts, and some technical descriptions of the laws and rules that organize the military.[21] In general, with very few exceptions, this secrecy has been accepted both by members of the military and by the society at large (see the following section).

Until 1946, the presidency of the country was in the hands of the military. At the same time, the military was one of the four sectors (together with the workers, the peasants, and the social sector) that originally constituted the PRM (Partido de la Revolución Mexicana), the official political party that in 1946 became the PRI (Partido de la Revolución Institucionalizada). It was in that same restructuring of 1946 that the military also abandoned its formal place in the party's internal composition.

The military then ceased playing a formal role in the political process, doing so as part of a silent agreement based on a trade-off between loyalty on the part of the military and multiple concessions from the state. In that sense, the retreat of the military from political life was formal and apparent. The military has received all sorts of privileges such as installations, facilities, equipment, a reasonable budget, and even political positions in the Congress and Senate. For many years it was not unusual for some governors to belong to the army. Nevertheless, these positions were never openly bestowed because of people's military status, but on a supposed individual basis, simply to candidates elected by the official party. This silent agreement was very comfortable for the military and for its political counterpart. The military remained loyal to the system and at the same time they could avoid the burden of an institutional political presence. On the contrary, it has been quite common to hear the pledges to loyalty and institutional life by high-ranking military officials every time they have an opportunity to make public declarations in civic ceremonies, as a way of maintaining their tacit pact.

However, the comfortable positioning of the military has also carried some costs. By remaining in a silent and apparently marginal position, the military changed its member composition. Middle- and upper-class youth stopped viewing the military as a reasonable option for their development, while it became attractive to lower-middle-class and poor sectors of the population. This changed social composition affected any real possibility of the army's regaining its position as a decisive political actor.

It is almost inevitable to compare the Mexican army's role with that of other Latin American armed forces. While most Latin American countries have active armed forces that have been directly responsible for democratic breakdowns and multiple human rights abuses, in Mexico the military never took such actions. The silent agreement, as well as the favorable economic and social conditions that Mexico enjoyed for many years, brought relative peace and stability. It is illustrative that the Mexican army never grew to disproportional size, as happened with most of its Latin American counterparts. With the exception of fighting illegal drugs and the response to student unrest in 1968 (see next section), the Mexican army has enjoyed a good reputation in the society, especially after its role in disaster situations, such as the 1985 earthquake, as indicated in opinion surveys.[22]

Because of its particular nature as the state's armed extension and its mission to maintain order and peace, the military became central in the country's long fight against drug trafficking. Unfortunately, the results have not been positive. Despite the enormous amounts of money and forces directed to this effort, the uncommon and disproportionate war between a clandestine and invincible enemy supported by international networks and funds, and a traditional and limited army, has frequently dragged many of its members into corruption and treachery. Every year it is known that several army officials and soldiers have accepted bribes from drug gangs.[23] The challenge is probably impossible to win as long as the international drug market persists with the same intensity.

Military Justice and Human Rights

As happens with many other countries, the Mexican army enjoys a privileged position not only de facto but also in the constitutional order. As part of what is supposed to be needed for disciplinary matters and independence from political affairs, the military has the only special jurisdiction that the Constitution allows to exist,[24] hence the existence of military justice. According to the Constitution this type of jurisdiction exists only for the military and for disciplinary reasons, and cannot, under any circumstances (except for the emergency situations described by the Constitution itself in Article 29), be extended to ordinary citizens. Any crime or misdemeanor committed by military members is subject to be treated by military courts and not by ordinary courts. Criminal cases in which the military participated can only be seen by this type of jurisdiction, and sanctions are determined only for military members. In cases where one party belongs to the military but the other is an ordinary citizen, the case shall be analyzed by an ordinary criminal court.

Regarding their position in the justice system, accusations of human rights abuses by the military are frequent, but most of these accusations have lacked empirical support. On the other hand, accusations against the military for abuses upon members of civil society are uncommon. With clear and very controversial exceptions, the Mexican military has remained excluded from this type of event. One major exception is the military involvement in the student massacre that took place in Mexico City in 1968 and that has been subject to investigation by a special prosecutor appointed in 2001 (by the new government), involving not only high-ranking military officials but even the secretaries of Defense and Interior, and the former president Luis Echeverría as the military commander-in-chief at the time. But, in general, very little is known about the functioning of military justice in specific cases.[25]

Mexico's Human Rights: Justice's Never-Ending Story

All the institutions comprising the Justice system in Mexico theoretically are linked to protecting the existence and implementation of the set of rights considered as basic for the life and normal development of any human being. Again, however, the Mexican institutional configuration did not correspond to this ideal model of human rights for two reasons. The first one was the specific and restrictive definition of human rights that the Constitution and its interpreters adopted, and the second was the controlling effect that the authoritarian system had over the institutions in charge of protecting these rights.

The constitutional text of 1917 practically adopted the Bill of Rights that existed in the previous Constitution (1857) and added social rights. The rights contained in the first section of the Constitution were a list of the traditional civil liberties. These liberties constitute rights that citizens need in order to interact with their peers (expressing beliefs, associating, moving from one place to another, interacting in every type of activity, etc.) and to participate in the formation of the national will (voting, expressing beliefs, associating, being voted for, etc.). In sum, these were individual rights necessary to create a modern state based on the existence of a market economy and democratic rule.

The social rights included in the postrevolutionary Constitution were a direct result of political compromises between the victorious groups. These were rights protecting the most vulnerable groups existing in the country, whose previous lack of legal protection led them to participate in the civil confrontation.[26] At the time, these were the rights envisaged for the working class, and they encompassed both individual rights for workers and collective rights for unions in Article 123, sections A and B, respectively. In addition, a special communal form of property and land-use rights for peasants was established through the creation of the *ejido* by Article 27. The rationale of these rights was to alter the liberal notion of individual rights, which created distortions and extreme inequality between the middle classes and those groups that could not enjoy their liberties due to their extremely poor living conditions. With these social rights, these groups could demand an active participation of the state in order to ameliorate the disastrous social effects of the market economy created by the liberal economic model.

At first, the inclusion of social rights in the Constitution was seen as an innovation toward the creation of a welfare state. But political realities gave way to other effects. First, individual rights were not accompanied by the necessary means of protection. The amparo lawsuit existed, but with many limitations and the exclusion of political rights. And second, while direct subjects interested in the protection of a specific liberty claimed the protection of individual rights, it was difficult to protect social rights because of the problem of diffused title-holders. This means that besides, their use by workers, unions, cooperatives, or peasant communities (ejidos), social rights also became the domain of authorities acting as the state's representatives for such rights. For instance, every time a radical measure was taken, like land confiscation, social rights were used as justification. Social rights became a political instrument to legitimate an array of state actions. Even their use by workers or peasants could be manipulated and politicized if it was convenient, due to the fact that this type of case was processed in labor and agrarian courts, both of which are part of the administrative apparatus (see the earlier section, "The Mexican Federal System").

By 1990, human rights in Mexico were neither recognized in all their scope nor truly protected by Mexico's ineffective, government-controlled, and, many times, corrupt authorities. While these dramatic conditions survived for many years, there was a formal recognition by the government that there were more rights than those established in the constitutional text. These rights derived from multiple international agreements and conventions that Mexico had signed and ratified. But these new rights were by and large ignored by most actors and judges.

Finally, in the 1990s, in an attempt to gain legitimacy and support for an ambitious project of economic reform, President Carlos Salinas de Gortari decided to do something regarding human rights. Immediately after becoming president, he created the National Commission of Human Rights, an institution that had been promoted for years by academic experts, based on the Swedish "ombudsman." The new institution was designed as an autonomous constitutional organ to avoid any government interference. Though limited in its enforcement powers, it was designed as a moral actor to denounce authorities that were committing abuses. From its creation to the present, the commission has fulfilled a decisive role, although it has not escaped controversy. In the end, the nature of this institution is polemical.

Despite many areas in which human rights violations are still registered, the mere fact of exposing them is a clear sign of improvement. Multiple domestic and international organizations work with authorities in cooperative efforts, or simply denouncing their faults. Every year there is the potential for several different reports on human rights coming from distinct sources such as Mexican authorities, international actors like the United Nations (through special envoys), and independent organizations such as Amnesty International.

So far, institutional responses have been insufficient as far as protecting human rights in Mexico and regardless of the comparative progress made in recent years. The country still registers critical numbers in marginal poverty and in discrimination against indigenous populations and women (for example, the unexplainable and unacceptable murders that have been committed in Ciudad Juárez), just to mention some of the most obvious. For years to come, justice and human rights will undoubtedly constitute the most important challenge for the country. In order to meet this challenge, a major institutional work will be needed involving a major constitutional reform, but also, beyond the law, every social actor will need to realize that without improvements in this area, democracy will remain one more concept without social meaning.

Notes

1. For a clear and succinct explanation of the legal civil law tradition and its components, see Merryman (1969). For a comparative study between legal traditions, see the classic study of René (1978).

2. Despite the fact that the Mexican judiciary seems to have been designed in the same manner as the American model, the final product was far from the Madisonian conception of an institution that checked the majoritarian excesses (*The Federalist papers,* no. 78).

3. The years refer to the following periods, broadly speaking: Antonio López de Santa Anna (ruler from 1833 to 1855 with several interruptions), to Benito Juárez (president from 1858 to 1872), to Porfirio Díaz (president of the country from 1876 to 1911), and the post-revolutionary rule of the PRI (Partido de la Revolución Institucionalizada, generally speaking, from 1920 to 2000).

4. That is the main reason why, for pedagogical purposes, presidential systems are always contrasted with parliamentary systems, in which the president and (or) the prime minister share many of these attributes with other actors, and the system is more controlled by different means.

5. For a complete analysis of this type of presidential system, known as presidentialism, see Carpizo (1978), and Marván (1997). The former makes the distinction between the formal, constitutional powers and those informal powers, referred to as "meta-constitutional."

6. The real mystery of the system came from the contrast between Mexico and most other Latin American countries in the twentieth century, where the rule of law was replaced by clear-cut military dictatorships. The odd Mexican political phenomenon drew, throughout the years, the attention of social scientists and intellectuals. Writer Octavio Paz called it "the philanthropic ogre," and Mario Vargas Llosa the "perfect dictatorship."

7. However, it is important to mention that Mexican constitutional doctrine, as the one created by the Court, has been weak, fragmented, inconclusive, and contradictory for many reasons, some of them related to the explanation stated in this work. For a major analysis of this topic, see the work of the current justice José Ramón Cossío Díaz (2002).

8. This requirement, known as the "Otero formula," developed in the nineteenth century as a check to the Court's excessive political intervention (during what is known as the Iglesias period, 1872–1877).

9. This element presents a plausible thesis for several cases in Mexican judicial history in which the Court "confronted" an act or a piece of legislation coming directly or indirectly from the executive office. Explained either as surprising "relative" judicial independence (González Casanova 1979; Fix Fierro 1994), or as the acts of suicidal or heroic justices, these cases benefited the system and its institutions. In such cases, both the executive and the judiciary could proclaim their adherence to their legal obligations in a fully legal and democratic context. The cases lost by the executive meant little, quantitatively, in the universe of presidential orders and decisions, but carried much weight, qualitatively in terms of prestige and legitimacy.

10. It is important to underline that these two concepts are different in procedural terms. Rejected cases are normally those that do not pass a first formal review of their requirements according to the law. Discarded cases are those that a judge after accepting its entrance into a legal process, decides to dispose of, when they present a problem for continuing a procedural stage, for instance the nonfulfillment of precise terms or acts to be done.

11. Judicial review in this sense is a totally different concept from the one developed by the American doctrine. While the latter refers specifically to the power of the Supreme Court to review the Constitution, in Mexico judicial review simply means the power of federal courts to review other courts' resolutions, or judiciaries reviewing judicial acts.

12. This is in very general terms, considering 1982 as the year when a major economic breakdown occurred, ending with Mexico's entrance to the GATT (General Agreement on Tariffs and Trade), and 1994, the year when NAFTA (the North American Free Trade Agreement) came into force.

13. Although these dates can be subject to debate because there is a long story of gradual opening of the system to the participation of opposition parties (principally since 1977), I

am considering them because 1994 is the year in which the electoral authority (IFE, Instituto Federal Electoral) became independent from government control, and 2000 the year when a candidate from an opposition party won the presidential race.

14. Considering the contemporary political period initiated since the establishment of the current Constitution in 1917.

15. The first one is the regulatory statute of constitutional Article 105, sections I and II (Ley Reglamentaria de las Fracciones I y II del Artículo 105 de la Constitución Política de los Estados Unidos Mexicanos), regarding the new judicial mechanisms known as "constitutional controversies" and "unconstitutional actions," which are explained further on. The second one was the Organic Statute of the Federal Judiciary (Ley Orgánica del Poder Judicial de la Federación), which defines the general structure of the judicial branch.

16. A complete description of the elements of each of these reform processes as well as certain indicators of their evaluation cannot be made in this chapter for space reasons, but are discussed in detail in Concha Cantú and Caballero Juárez (2001).

17. Since the mid-nineties most states in Mexico started to pass new laws that allow judiciaries to retain the interests derived from fees, parole, bail, deposits, tuitions, and so forth, and use them as their own resources. At the same time, it is important to mention that judiciaries own diverse properties that are used and produce rents and interests.

18. A contemporary trend in Latin America has promoted, in the last ten years, the transformation of criminal justice systems from inquisitorial institutions into accusatorial ones, based on oral and concentrated trials. In the former "inquisitorial" model (still existing in Mexico), prosecutors have all the power in the investigation of a crime and the initial presentation of the file to the judge, thus influencing the latter's actions and opinions in a decisive way. In the "accusatorial" model, like the American system, no person can be convicted until his or her culpability is demonstrated before a judge, making the judge the only guardian of rights. Since April 2004, the Mexican Federal Executive presented Congress with an extensive initiative to reform the Constitution and a legislation package directed at transforming the basis of criminal justice, especially in the area of criminal prosecution and police.

19. It is important to mention that there is wide consensus about this particular need. For instance, in 2000 former chief justice Genaro David Góngora Pimentel invited a group of specialists to formulate the draft of a new amparo law, which in the end was not accepted by Congress.

20. The Fox administration chose this type of route, appointing a general to the post of attorney general of the nation, as a way of showing that this government was really serious in its commitment to fight organized crime. Unfortunately, this purpose has not been accompanied by evident results.

21. Historical works related specially to the revolutionary period are full of descriptions and analysis of the military (e.g., Katz 1998), but again there are no works of this nature related to contemporary military history. Regarding descriptions of military legislation, see the work of López Saucedo (2002).

22. The confidence levels gained by the military are evident in different contemporary surveys, such as the *Encuesta Nacional sobre Cultura Política y Prácticas Ciudadanas 2003*, elaborated by Secretaría de Gobernación (www.segob.gob.mx/), the *Encuesta Nacional Ciudadanos y Cultura de la Democracia. Reglas, Instituciones y Valores de la Democracia,* conducted by the Instituto Federal Electoral, 2000, or the one conducted by Hugo Concha, Héctor Fix Fierro, and Diego Valadés, *Cultura de la Constitución en México. Una Encuesta Nacional de Actitudes, Percepciones y Valores* (Instituto de Investigaciones Jurídicas, Comisión Federal de Mejora Regulatoria y Tribunal Electoral del Poder Judicial de la Federación, 2004).

23. A major scandal became widely known when the General José de Jesús Gutiérrez Rebollo, in charge of drug fighting as the general director of the Instituto Nacional de

Combate a las Drogas, was prosecuted for his involvement with drug lords' operations in February 2000.

24. The connotation of "special" refers not to a special type of conflicts, but to the situation in which these conflicts are not solved by ordinary courts but by military courts. According to Article 13 of the Mexican Constitution, "No person shall be judged by special legislation or special courts. No person or corporation can have a special jurisdiction, or enjoy compensation that differs from those established by the law. Military jurisdiction shall exist for those crimes and misdemeanors against military discipline, but military courts shall never and for no reason, extend their jurisdiction over people who do not belong to the military. When a person is involved in a military crime or misdemeanor, the case shall be reviewed by civil authorities."

25. This secrecy was brought to light recently by a scandal involving General José Francisco Gallardo Rodríguez, who was sentenced to prison time by a military court for supposed crimes against the army in 1993. He was liberated only after his case was admitted for review by the Inter-American Commission of Human Rights in 2002. After his liberation, however, the issue remained silent and distant from public opinion.

26. This is true at least in what is considered to be the second stage of the Mexican Revolution, known as the social revolution (1914–1918), in which the fight spread to every region and every group, demanding a new type of social and political configuration than the one existing during the dictatorship. The first stage was the political revolution (1911–1914), led by Francisco Madero against the dictatorship of Porfirio Díaz.

References

Carpizo, Jorge. 1978. *El sistema presidencial mexicano.* México: Siglo XXI.

Concha Cantú, Hugo Alejandro, and José Antonio Caballero Juárez. 2001. *Diagnóstico sobre la administración de justicia en las entidades federativas: Un estudio institucional sobre la justicia local en México.* México: Instituto de Investigaciones Jurídicas.

Cossío Díaz, José Ramón. 2002. *La teoría constitucional en México.* México: Fontamara.

David, René. 1978. *Major Legal Systems of the World Today.* New York: The Free Press.

Fix Fierro, Héctor, ed. 1994. *A la puerta de la ley. El estado de derecho en México.* México: Cal y Arena–CIDAC.

———. 1998. "Courts and Efficiency: A General Investigation with Evidence from Three Continents." Unpublished doctoral dissertation, law department, Bremen University.

———. 2004. *Courts, Justice and Efficiency: A Socio-Legal Study of Economic Rationality in Adjudication.* London: Hart.

Fix Zamudio, Héctor, and J.R. Cossío Díaz. 1995. *El poder judicial en el ordenamiento mexicano.* México: Fondo de Cultura Económica.

González Casanova, Pablo. 1979. *La democracia en México.* México: Era.

Katz, Friederick. 1998. *The Life and Times of Pancho Villa.* Stanford, CA: Stanford University Press.

López Saucedo, Antonio. 2002. *Teoría jurídica del ejército y sus lineamientos constitucionales.* México: Instituto de Investigaciones Jurídicas.

Madison, James, and Alexander Hamilton. 1961. *The Federalist Papers* [editor's note: based on McLean edition of 1788]. New York: New American Library.

Marván Laborde, Ignacio. 1997. *¿Y después del presidencialismo? Reflexiones para la formación de un nuevo regimen.* México: Océano.

Melgar Adalid, Mario. 1996. *El consejo de la Judicatura Federal.* México: Porrúa.

Merryman, John. 1969. *The Civil Law Tradition. An Introduction to the Legal Systems of Western Europe and Latin America.* Stanford, CA: Stanford University Press.

Russell, Peter H., and David O'Brien. 2002. *Judicial Independence in the Age of Democracy.* Charlottesville: University Press of Virginia.

21

JOSEPH L. KLESNER

Institutionalizing Mexico's
New Democracy

*The presidential victory of Vicente Fox in 2000 ended one-party domination of the
Mexican presidency. Joseph L. Klesner writes that political reforms made possible the
establishment of new political parties and allowed the electoral victory of parties other
than the long-dominant Institutional Revolutionary Party (Partido Revolucionario
Institucional, PRI) by removing the PRI from control of the authorities that supervised
elections during the 1990s. The Federal Electoral Institute has increased the transparency of elections by involving ordinary citizens in running the polling stations and by
installing advanced information systems for rapid disclosure of the election results.*

*Mexican political reform facilitated the establishment of new parties by providing
generous funding. The resulting multiparty system, however, leads to difficulties in passing legislation. The political reform did not change the requirement of "no reelection" of
government officials, so that great power remains in the hands of the presidency because
each elected or appointed official must look for a new position in three or six years.*

*This concentration of power also results in part from changes in the number of
legislators and in the way in which they are selected. The Chamber of Deputies initially
had 300 members in single-member district seats. By 1986, 200 members were added
in proportional representation seats. The Senate includes two senators from the party
that won the election, one from the party that came in second, and thirty-two additional senators nationally elected by proportional representation from party lists. No
single party controls Congress; moreover, power has shifted to municipalities with
results that vary from greater control by local bosses to increasing control by citizens
who demand to know where their increased taxes and fees are being spent.*

*The fragmentation and stalemate of the government led to a strong decline
from 1990 to 2000 in confidence in Congress, the civil service, and political parties, accompanied by increased general confidence in government and in experts
making decisions. This suggests that there is increasing public concern for efficient decision making that could lead to the elimination of the "no reelection"
clause and to the reconsideration of how elections are financed and the criteria
for national recognition of political parties.*

Vicente Fox's unexpected victory in the July 2000 presidential election brought to culmination Mexico's protracted transition from one-party authoritarian rule to democracy. The nation's prolonged, at times glacial movement toward democracy involved the emergence and growth of a civil society committed to citizen involvement in shaping Mexico's future; a gradual liberalization of the public sphere, particularly in the realms of freedom of speech and of the press; and the slow growth of opposition political parties. However, despite progress in the late 1980s and 1990s by the Mexican citizenry in developing new channels of political participation and in liberalizing the political regime, most critics of the long-ruling PRI argued that Mexico could not be considered a democracy until there had been alternation of parties in the control of the powerful presidency. If President Fox accomplishes nothing else in his political career, he will be remembered and honored by millions of Mexicans as the man who ousted the PRI from Los Pinos, Mexico's White House, and thereby brought democracy to his people.

Although alternation in the presidency may be a sign of a transition to democracy, the consolidation of that democracy requires more than alternation in the party controlling the presidency. Indeed, an overly powerful presidency has characterized the seventy-one years of PRI rule, and democratization of Mexico's regime will necessarily include downgrading the role of the presidency. Despite physical features and a demeanor that suggest he can be a strong leader, Fox has not been an overly powerful president, in part because he has lacked the support of the traditional wing of his political party, the National Action Party (Partido Acción Nacional, PAN). If anything, the alignment of political forces in Mexico today suggests that the days of all-powerful presidents —limited-term dictators, in the words of Frank Brandenburg (1964, 161ff.)— are past, at least for the near future.

To replace an all-powerful presidency, Mexicans must build new institutions of democracy. In the past decade, political elites and activists have strived to create (or recreate) the institutions, both formal and informal, of democratic governance. In this chapter I will address institutional change, focusing on the political reforms that made presidential alternation a possibility, on developments within the major political parties that will make them more effective instruments of democratic representation, and on the divided government that has accompanied the reemergence of a Congress with real legislative powers. In addition, I will explore the geographical dispersion of power in Mexico, examining the forces that have begun to replace its overly centralized regime with the federalism that the nation has long incorporated in its Constitution, considering both the creeping federalism that has come with the growth of opposition party strength in states and localities, and the formal deconcentration of central power that is known as the new federalism. First, though, before turning to the significant changes that have come to the Mexican political regime in the past decade, I will explain the structural bases of Mexican authoritarianism so that the changes associated with Mexico's democratization can be better set in their context.

Table 21.1

Changing Characteristics of the Mexican Political Regime

Mexican authoritarianism	Emerging democracy
One-party dominance (1929–1994)	Three-party system (1995 to present)
Presidentialism (1934–1997)	Divided government (1997 to present)
Excessive centralism (until 1990s)	New federalism (1984 to present): Greater financial autonomy of *municipios* Increasing opposition control of state and municipal governments (1989 to present)
Corporatism (1936–1990s)	Declining importance of major interest associations of labor and peasantry (1980s to present) Greater independent influence of business (1988 to present)
Clientelism (until 1994)	Emergence of popular organizations (1985 to present) Erosion of sources of patronage (1980s to present)
Corruption (continuing)	Repeated pledges to eliminate corruption
Electoral fraud (until 1994)	Independent electoral authorities and clean elections (1994 to present)
Weak judiciary subordinate to executive(continuing)	Efforts to strengthen judiciary (1995 to present)

Note: See text for definitions of terms. Dates may overlap because reforms have been introduced before old regime characteristics change definitively.

The Bases of Mexican Authoritarianism

Mexican authoritarianism rested on one-party domination of the political system. (Table 21.1 summarizes the features of Mexican authoritarianism, not all of which I can discuss in this short chapter.) From the time of President Lázaro Cárdenas (1934–1940), the former ruling party was organized into three sectors, one for peasants, another for the workers, and a third for state bureaucrats. This organizational structure made the PRI a corporatist institution. By incorporating these organizations of peasants, workers, and bureaucrats into the PRI, Cárdenas gave them privileged access to decision makers. At the same time, however, the incorporation of these groups within the party, especially of their leaders within the PRI hierarchy, made them vulnerable to co-optation and control. In particular, labor and peasant leaders were co-opted by the PRI national leadership—offered personal political opportunities in return for exercising restraint in their demands on behalf of their constituents.

The PRI's corporatist organization also had the advantage of providing to the party unparalleled capacity to turn out voters on election day. Local representatives of the peasant confederation served as political bosses in their villages and state capitals, providing the party with unusual support in getting rural voters to the polls and ensuring that they voted for the ruling party. Labor union leaders were similarly able to convince their membership to vote for the PRI.

Under Cárdenas, the powerful position of the presidency within the political regime became cemented too. The Mexican presidency held a formidable set of powers. The president's formal Constitutional powers are not more extensive than those held by most presidents in other Latin American political systems (Mainwaring and Shugart 1997), but Mexican presidents enjoyed "metaconstitutional powers," a "series of prerogatives [that] corresponds to the 'unwritten' norms of the Mexican system. They allow the president to centralize his power progressively through a distortion of constitutional mechanism" (Garrido 1989, 422). Such powers set up a characteristic of Mexican politics that scholars have labeled "presidentialism," which is defined by Roderic Ai Camp (1999, 11) as "the concept that most political power lies in the hands of the president and all that is good or bad in government policy stems personally from the president."

The Mexican Congress is charged with the responsibilities of auditing the public accounts of the previous year, approving the budget of the coming fiscal year, and voting on all bills introduced to it by the president or by members of the Chamber of Deputies or the Senate, the two houses of the bicameral legislature. In the formal rules about making laws established in the Mexican Constitution, a bill becomes a law there in ways similar to the United States: bills must pass both houses of Congress; they can be approved or vetoed by the president; and if they are vetoed, the veto can be overridden by a two-thirds vote of both houses. However, until very recently, studying the way a bill becomes a law in Mexico did not require the same attention to executive–legislative relationships that we have given it in the United States. Before the 1990s, the Mexican Congress had not rejected a bill introduced by the president since the 1930s.

How can we explain presidentialism, this seemly unprecedented domination of the legislature and other national institutions by the president with his metaconstitutional powers? When we take into account the incredible advantages accruing to the PRI of having been the incumbent party since 1929 (it took credit for all of the benefits of economic development that had come to Mexico) and its capacity to mobilize voters because of its corporatist incorporation of peasants, workers, and urban popular groups, we should not be surprised that a PRI nomination was equivalent to an appointment to that "elected" position—for federal congressional candidates or for those running on the PRI ticket for governor, state assembly member, mayor, or membership on the municipal council. If we then remember that post-revolutionary Mexico has forbidden reelection to the many positions just mentioned, it becomes easier for us to understand why the president was so powerful (Cosío Villegas 1978). Politicians cannot develop support bases in constituencies that will return them to office in the way that U.S. politicians can.

Each "elected" PRI politician thus had to be looking for a new position, either elected or appointed, within three (for municipal offices, state assembly members, or federal deputies who serve in the equivalent of the U.S. House of Representatives) or six years (for governors or federal senators). Likewise, because each new president brought a new administration with him, those appointed to political positions in the bureaucracy knew that they must plan to be appointed to some new position—probably in another area of the bureaucracy—or be nominated for an elected post within six years. Who controlled these appointments and nominations? Ultimately, the president. However, for younger politicians to gain presidential approval, bosses in their *camarillas,* or political groups, could provide essential support to indicate that an aspiring politician was worthy of appointment to a lesser elected or appointed position. Candidates for political jobs therefore were "clients" of bosses, and, ultimately, of the president. Hence, clientelism became an essential means of ascent in a system in which political recruitment was dominated from the top by the president.

In this situation, the reasons for Congressional subordination to the president become clear. Even though the PRI typically had ample majorities in the Congress, which PRI deputy or senator wanted to demonstrate opposition to a presidentially initiated bill? What would a vote against a bill proposed by the president accomplish? Since a member of Congress could not be reelected, why would he or she care about constituents' reactions to a bill that might not be favorable to their district? But, since his or her career required getting another position within three or six years, why would he or she risk antagonizing the president by voting against a presidential initiative?

This logic produced an impressive record of legislative accomplishment for Mexican presidents. As mentioned above, between the 1930s and the late 1990s, no bill initiated by the president was turned down by the Mexican Congress. Opposition members of Congress usually spoke against bills emanating from the presidency, but to little practical effect, especially if the national media paid little attention to their speeches, which was generally true before the 1970s.

Mexico's 1917 Constitution also enshrined the concept of the "free municipality," local government that has autonomy in making local laws and policies, but *municipios* (equivalent to U.S. counties, the lowest level of government in Mexico, whose size varies tremendously, from municipios in Oaxaca with fewer than 1,000 residents to Guadalajara's nearly 2 million) were subordinate to the federal government in the same way that the Congress was dominated by the president. This local political subordination to the center developed despite the strong regionalism that has characterized Mexico.

The long record of central government domination of the states can be attributed to three factors. First, the federal government raises by far the greatest proportion of tax revenues, which it then "shares" with states and localities. Indeed, after 1947, the federal government came to control practically all sources of government revenue (Courchene, Díaz-Cayeros, and Webb 2000). However, federal revenue sharing need not be proportional to the amount of taxes that a state or locality contributes to the federal budget. Thus, state and local governments had to be careful about their relationship with the federal government, especially with the all-powerful executive, for fear of being allocated relatively small shares of federal revenues (Rodríguez 1997). Second, once the PRI was formed and came to control political recruitment throughout the nation, further political advances for state governors and other aspiring politicians in a state then depended on staying in the good political graces of the president. While there were still regional strongmen in the 1930s and 1940s, fewer and fewer of these regional power brokers could withstand presidential wishes as the PRI-dominated political system developed through the 1950s and 1960s. Third, like other elected officials in Mexico, governors cannot be reelected and thus they have been constrained in the degree to which they have been able to build local political machines that would be support bases for resisting central government demands. In effect, because most or all state governors have had further political ambitions (if not for themselves, then at least for their closest followers, often their own children) that they would pursue through the PRI, the president had the de facto power to appoint and to remove governors. Thus, the power of the Mexican presidency extended beyond the federal government to the states and the municipalities.

These features of Mexican authoritarianism came under assault during the nation's protracted transition to more democratic rule. Because of space limitations I cannot address all features of the political regime and their change over the past two decades—for example, I will not discuss the growing role of women in politics (see Chapter 22 in this book) or the part that nongovernmental organizations and social movements have played in the transition to democracy. Instead, I will focus on political reforms and challenges by the political opposition that have fundamentally altered electoral politics and the means of representation that electoral politics permit, especially in the political parties; the changing balance of power between the president and Congress; and the emergence of a more real federalism in Mexico.

The Record of Political Reform

Mexico's protracted transition to democracy has had a "two steps forward, one step back" character. While oppositionists often hoped to make sudden advances —as in 1988, when Cuauhtémoc Cárdenas (son of Lázaro Cárdenas, and a maverick who left the PRI in 1987 and established the Party of the Democratic Revolution —PRD, or Partido de la Revolución Democrática—in 1989) seemed poised to defeat the PRI's presidential candidate, Carlos Salinas de Gortari—those efforts never quite succeeded in producing the ouster of the PRI until July 2000. The PRI held onto power in no small part because it controlled the institutions that oversaw the legal process by which individual politicians succeeded each other in power. Mexico has used elections to produce citizen consent for transitions of power at the federal, state, and local levels since the 1910 revolution. Because those elections were supervised by federal and state electoral agencies controlled by the PRI until 1996, opposition parties and candidates often charged they had been cheated out of legitimate victories and thus long felt that the electoral playing field was tilted against them.

Beginning in 1977 (when newly elected president José López Portillo had the somewhat embarrassing triumph that came with winning his 1976 election uncontested) but accelerating in the 1990s, a process of political reform-making gradually removed the PRI from control of the authorities that oversaw elections. Electoral reforms addressed two main features of the electoral regime. First, the federal electoral authority—for decades known as the Federal Electoral Commission, which became the Federal Electoral Institute (IFE) in 1990—had been headed by the secretary of the Interior (Gobernación) since 1946 and always included a majority of members in one way or another linked to the PRI. The Federal Electoral Commission approved parties' petitions for registration and oversaw the voting on election day, recording (or not) procedural irregularities and certifying the election results. To the extent that the PRI won office by electoral fraud, its control of the electoral authority permitted those victories.

In the 1990s, the opposition pushed hard to reduce the extent of PRI control of the IFE, first succeeding in removing the president's power to appoint the membership of the IFE's executive committee in 1994, and then entirely removing the secretary of the Interior from the management of the IFE in 1996. These gains by the opposition were achieved because President Salinas de Gortari (1988–1994) needed to reach political accommodations with the PAN, the largest opposition party, in order to pass the more fundamental elements of his neoliberal economic reforms in the Congress, and because of President Ernesto Zedillo's (1994–2000) commitment to democratize a country whose presidency he controlled only after a series of truly unexpected events, including the assassination the PRI's first 1994 presidential candidate, Luis Donaldo Colosio. From 1996 forward, a professionalized IFE led by citizen councilors approved by all major political parties has run Mexico's electoral processes. The IFE has promoted the transparency of the electoral process by involving ordinary citizens in running the polling stations on election day and by installing advanced information systems for the rapid and broad dissemination of election results.

Second, as the ruling party for seven decades, the PRI enjoyed many perquisites of incumbency, including often-inappropriate access to state coffers to fund party functions, including campaign financing. Although earlier electoral reforms had made more public monies available to opposition parties for campaign efforts, new reforms adopted in 1996 made a qualitative difference in the character of opposition campaigns. By the 1996 electoral law, private sources of campaign finance are supposed to be limited to 10 percent of total campaign spending. The remainder of campaign funds come from the government, distributed by the IFE to parties according to a formula based in part on past election performance; the large sums allocated to federal campaign financing reflect the Zedillo administration's efforts to drive private financing out of Mexican electoral politics (Preston and Dillon 2004, 277–78). Although the PRI remained favored by this public campaign-financing scheme, its advantages over the other parties were greatly reduced. Similarly, the parties gained greater access to free time on television and radio, again according to a formula based on past performance. With these new sources of campaign finance, the PRD produced a much-improved campaign to elect Cuauhtémoc Cárdenas as Mexico City mayor in 1997 and Vicente Fox won the presidency behind a lavishly financed campaign, funded partly by the federal contributions mentioned above and partly by his political action committee, Mexico's first of the genre, called Amigos de Fox.

These reforms have changed Mexico's electoral system from one of the most suspect in the world to a system that the parties and the citizenry can trust to mount a fair electoral contest, in which the votes cast by Mexican citizens will be faithfully and rapidly reported. While finding exactly comparable survey evidence is difficult, in 1988 nearly six in ten Mexicans expected that widespread fraud would take place in that year's election, while prior to the 2000 election two-thirds expected the process would be clean and fewer than 17 percent reported that they thought there had been fraud after the elections had taken place (Domínguez and McCann 1996, 157; Mexico 2000 Panel Study). Yet making Mexico's elections both clean and fair has been an expensive process. For example, the IFE oversaw the distribution of some US$306 million in public funds to the parties in the year 2000 alone, including sums of over US$5 million to several small parties whose genuine electoral support base is miniscule (Crespo 2000). Both political analysts and the public at large have begun to view these expenditures as too high for a developing country like Mexico.

Future electoral reforms will likely address the scale and formula for public funding of parties and the electoral process. In particular, many analysts and major party leaders have grown concerned that establishing new political parties has become a business for opportunistic political operators. Lavish federal financing of parties that meet minimal conditional registration requirements—an organization petitioning to become a party has to show that it has at least 3,000 members in each of 10 of the 32 states, or at least 300 in each of 100 of the 300 federal electoral districts—has led to a proliferation of small parties without clear ideological or programmatic positions. A good example of the political opportunism rampant among small parties in Mexico that such critics seek to curb is the Green Ecological Party of Mexico (PVEM, Partido Verde Ecologista de México), Fox's coalition partner in 2000, which defected shortly thereafter and ran as a coalition partner of the PRI in 2003. Critics point out that the PVEM's leader, Jorge González Torres, and his family have been the main beneficiaries of the party's appropriation of the green label for a party that is largely pro-business. Other examples abound of political operatives seeking to establish parties in order to feed from the public trough.

Developments in the Political Parties

For seventy-one years the PRI was the party in power. During that time its leaders and activists developed the view that the PRI was the governing party and that its role in Mexican society was to recruit and develop future Mexican leaders. Indeed, one view of the PRI was that it was the electoral organ of the ruling elite, designed principally to produce electoral legitimacy for the continued rule of a small but somewhat open group of civilian politicians—not a real political party at all. The idea that the PRI might lose an election did not begin to take hold within the party until well into the 1990s.

On the other side of the electoral picture stood opposition parties that seldom won significant elected positions. As time passed, those parties—although they held distinct ideological positions and policy preferences—came to see themselves and to be seen by voters as primarily anti-regime parties, or pro-democracy parties (Molinar Horcasitas 1991). A distinct division of the party system into pro-regime and anti-regime camps emerged by the 1990s, deepened by the electoral conflict of 1988. The PAN and the PRD came to be seen as offering two different versions of an anti-regime message—a moderate but pro-democracy, pro-business stance by PAN, and a more intransigent, anti-PRI, pro-economic nationalism on the part of PRD.

The anti-regime message drew a wide range of Mexicans who became floating opposition voters, choosing the party for which they voted based upon which seemed most efficacious to them in a particular election. Table 21.2 shows some dimensions of this floating opposition vote as well as the relative steadfastness of PRI partisans. The table divides those who voted in the 2000 presidential race into three groups: those who remained loyal to the party for which they voted in the 1997 mid-term Congressional elections; those who defected from their 1997 party choice to vote for Fox; and those who did not vote in 1997 but cast a ballot for Fox in 2000. The greater loyalty of those who call themselves PRI partisans is notable, as is the extent to which PRI voters come from the category of those who always cast their vote for the same party. In contrast, the defectors tend to come from the ranks of the politically nonaligned—independents—and tend to report that they switch their votes from party to party. In the pivotal 2000 election, Fox gained many votes from new voters or from those who had not gone to the polls in 1997, as the last column of Table 21.2 indicates.

Table 21.2 thus suggests that Fox owed his victory to voters who did not have a history of party loyalty. There were and are many loyal partisans in Mexico; slightly over half of voters can be relied upon to cast their ballots for the same party in two consecutive elections. However, in a three-party system with significant numbers of unattached voters and former opposition voters who do not have the same degree of commitment to the parties for which they have voted as do PRI partisans, electoral success can depend much on the ability of the parties to run successful campaigns. In 2000, Fox and the PAN ran a brilliant campaign. In 2003 they did

Table 21.2

Political Characteristics of Loyalists and Defectors, 1997–2000 (percent)

	Loyalists			Defectors		Non-
Partisanship in 2000	PAN/ Fox	PRI/ Labastida	PRD/ Cárdenas	PRI to Fox	PRD to Fox	voter to Fox
PAN	76.0	2.7	0.7	26.5	43.0	54.9
PRI	1.1	86.5	0.8	27.7	2.8	5.0
PRD	0.3	0.4	75.8	1.1	14.0	1.8
None/other/do not know	22.6	10.4	22.7	44.7	40.2	38.3
Total	100.00	100.00	100.00	100.00	100.00	100.00
Self-reported party loyalty:						
Always vote for the same party	65.9	89.1	65.6	29.3	17.3	36.2
Sometimes vote for one party, some- times another	29.5	9.8	28.2	63.9	76.2	46.7
Neither/do not know/no answer	4.6	1.1	6.2	6.8	6.5	17.1
Total	100.00	100.00	100.00	100.00	100.00	100.00
Percent of total sample*	15.5	20.0	5.9	4.5	2.9	14.8

Note: *Table excludes voters for smaller parties (3.0% of the total sample); 1997 PAN voters (2.3%) and 1997 non-voters (16.8%) who voted for any other party in 2000; and those who could not remember or would not report their 1997 vote (13.7%). To ascertain partisanship, the Mitofsky/Consulta exit poll asked, "Normally, do you consider yourself *panista, priísta,* or *perredista?*" (Normalmente usted se considera panista, priísta or perredista?).

not, with the result that fewer than six in ten Fox voters chose PAN Congressional candidates in the most recent mid-term elections and the PRI took the largest share of the votes cast by new voters ("Impera disinterís en abstencionistas," 2003).

Since the early 1990s, then, a three-party system has gradually emerged to re-place one-party dominance. Since 2000, we can hardly use the term "opposition" in this new three-party system, for none of the three parties is truly an opposition party—each holds key elected executive positions at various levels of government and all share power in the federal Congress. With the end of the regime–opposition distinction, however, come significant challenges to each party in terms of identity and strategy.

PRI

Consolidating democracy in Mexico must involve making the PRI into a true po-litical party that can offer the electorate a distinct vision of Mexico, not just an

Table 21. 3

Distribution of State and Local Elected Positions as of 2004

Party	Percent of state legislators	Number of governors	Percent of population under party governors	Percent of population under party municipal governments
PRI (Institutional Revolutionary Party)	45.6	17	57.4	40.1
PAN (National Action Party)	26.1	9	22.8	32.3
PRD (Democratic Revolutionary Party)	18.7	5*	15.7	18.0
Other	9.6	1**	4.0	9.5

Sources: Partido Acción Nacional, *Presencia de Gobierno* (Mexico City, April 2004); Consulta Mitofsky, *Los congresos estatales* (Mexico City, May 2004).

*The PRD's total includes the position of head of the Federal District government, equivalent to a governorship.

**The governor of Chiapas was supported by a coalition of the PAN, the PRD, and several smaller parties.

organization beholden to presidential will. The values of Mexican voters are complex and differ according to their characteristics (see Chapter 2 in this book), a point that was not well understood by the PRI of old that largely saw itself *as Mexico*—it was the party of the majority, and its ideological position was frequently little more than that. Perhaps as a result, until mid-2004, the time of this writing, the former opposition parties have made more progress in learning the ways of governing than the PRI has in learning to be a party of opposition. Both the PAN and the PRD governed at the state and local level in the 1990s, experiences that have produced party leaders with a record in government, most notably President Fox himself, the former governor of Guanajuato. Table 21.3 provides information about the portions of Mexico governed by each political party as of April 2004.

The PRI faces the test of turning its 2000 defeat into the motivation to rebuild as a genuine political party that seeks votes by appealing to those who cast them with policy prescriptions, rather than just the clientelist favors it so often dispensed in the past but which are now in rather shorter supply with the PRI's diminished access to government coffers. There are two major challenges before the PRI, both having important consequences for the Mexican party system and Mexican democracy. First, in the absence of a president from the PRI to serve as de facto party leader, can the party resolve party leadership struggles without falling apart? Thus far the evidence suggests that it can, but major tensions exist between PRI leaders who identify with current party president Roberto Madrazo (who seeks to make the PRI into a social democratic party, but whose democratic credentials are very suspect given his violations of campaign financing restrictions when he ran for governor of Tabasco in 1997), and Madrazo's rivals, some of whom are still identified with former presidents Salinas and Zedillo and failed PRI presidential candidate Francisco Labastida.

Prior to the 2000 presidential election, party leaders pushed forward a new party rule that PRI presidential candidates had to have held electoral office before becoming the PRI's nominee—none had done so since the time of Luis Echeverría (1970–1976), including Salinas and Zedillo. In addition, the PRI introduced a national party primary to select its presidential nominee, with the encouragement of then-president Zedillo. These reforms mean the party is no longer the instrument of the president—but of course, the PRI no longer holds the presidency. Internal party struggles are now much more in the open than ever before; the extent to which they are resolved according to clearly defined norms of democratic contestation remains suspect.

Related to problems about party leadership is the challenge of defining the PRI's policy platform and ideological orientation now that it is no longer simply the "party of the majority." Under Salinas and Zedillo, the PRI put through Mexico's neoliberal economic program, turning its back on a long history of populism. Many supporters of the neoliberal restructuring continue in the party. While some populists left the PRI with Cárdenas in 1988, many still remain in the party, and other newer leaders—such as Madrazo—see promise in a strategy of recreating the PRI as a social democratic party. The PRI can probably also be something of a catchall party—indeed, when in power it played this role in terms of recruitment and efforts to appeal broadly to the whole electorate. The question is in which the PRI will situate itself in a party system where the PAN will sit to the right of center and the PRD to the left—is there room in the middle?

PAN

The PAN has a long history of disagreement between those party leaders who feel committed to maintaining the PAN's ideological purity as a party in the mainstream of Catholic social teaching with a commitment to democracy—effectively, a Christian Democratic position—and those who have urged the party to strive for electoral victory and government power even if it means broadening the party's social and ideological bases and making compromises with former enemies. Many of the former group of PAN leaders are sons and daughters or grandsons and granddaughters of PAN leaders of the 1950s and 1960s; they regard the latter group as "barbarians of the north," since many relatively newer PAN members come from northern states and from the business community and are regarded as impolitic—

more interested in simply getting things done or "throwing the bastards [PRI] out" than in doing so with grace.

Fox is a quintessential barbarian. His ascension to the presidency has not come without serious tensions with more socially conservative and traditional PAN leaders. To ensure that he would win the PAN's presidential nomination in 2000, Fox created the first Mexican political action committee, Amigos de Fox, which so intimidated his rivals for being the party's standard bearer that no one else ended up contesting the nomination. Within the party, the PAN operates according to well-defined democratic procedures, but it is important to note that those rules pertain to party members only. The PAN has the smallest membership base of the three main parties, reflecting stringent rules designed to keep out of the PAN those regarded as not sufficiently serious about the responsibilities of party membership and those regarded as not sufficiently prepared ideologically. Fox, for instance, was formally selected as PAN presidential nominee by a party primary in which only party members participated; had there been a rival, Fox could have lost even though he was clearly very popular with the general electorate. Many newer PAN members believe the party must embrace as much of Mexico as possible in order to continue to win important electoral posts, and they favor easing the barriers to party membership, essentially making the PAN a catch-all party, even if one situated on the center-right of the ideological spectrum. More traditional party members fear that allowing too many new members into the PAN will blur its focus. Fox's victory has meant that the barbarian wing of the party is on the rise, but it does not mean that PAN has fully committed to being one of two or three catch-all parties in the Mexican party system.

PRD

The PRD's origin as the organizational manifestation of the (Cuauhtémoc) Cárdenas movement—initially involving secession of a portion of the PRI's left wing—has created a different set of challenges for the major party of Mexico's often fractious left. To a large extent, supporting the PRD has been synonymous with supporting Cárdenas in his challenge to the PRI. However, Cárdenas never defeated PRI candidates in his three tries for the presidency (or was denied a fairly won victory in 1988 and defeated in his two subsequent races) and he is aging. Fierce struggles have taken place within the PRD for leadership after Cárdenas. At the same time, Cárdenas has resisted suggestions that he step back from another presidential candidacy. Moreover, the PRI no longer controls the presidency, so the PRD (like the PAN) must put forward a platform containing issues other than ousting the PRI.

The PRD's control of the Mexico City government means that it and its popular mayor, Andrés Manuel López Obrador, can reward supporters and lure potential voters with public spending projects. But whether spending in the capital can effectively convince voters the length and breadth of Mexico that the PRD is a credible alternative to either the PAN or the PRI remains to be seen. The PRD, too, is tending in the direction of a catch-all party, in this case for the left, but in catching many former PRI activists as well as people from many other progressive currents, it has built into its organization much of the fractiousness that has historically characterized the Mexican left.

As a self-consciously democratic party, the PRD has sought to establish clear formal rules that guide the party's internal life, in contrast to the murkiness of procedures and the imposition of candidates from above in the PRI that caused so many current PRD members to flee the PRI. Unfortunately, the PRD's fractiousness has led to intense rivalries that have sometimes promoted violations of the party's democratic procedures; elections for party president in 1999 had to be nullified because of fraud, for example. Also threatening to the health of the party has been the role of Cuauhtémoc Cárdenas, whom everyone recognizes for leading the struggle against PRI hegemony to found an independent party of the left, but who has played something of a caudillo role within the PRD, insisting on running for president again in 2000 after two defeats and refusing to rule out a fourth candidacy in 2006.

Divided Government

As I described above, the keys to presidential dominance during the PRI's heyday were the PRI's complete control of the Congress combined with the principle of no reelection. Prior to 1977, almost all Congressional seats (both Chamber of Deputies and Senate) were chosen by a single-member-district winner-take-all system like that used in the United States. As the dominant party, the PRI won all or nearly all such seats. Nomination by the PRI for a Congressional seat became tantamount to election, but no member of Congress could serve more than one term consecutively. As the effective leader of his party, the president could exercise enormous power over members of Congress who relied upon him for their next nomination to elected office or appointment in his administration. Consequently, the Congress never rejected presidential initiatives and rarely modified them in significant ways.

In the long process of political reform that began in the mid-1970s, Mexico's legislative bodies were made more representative of the political forces in the nation by the creation of new legislative seats in the Chamber of Deputies originally reserved for minority parties (i.e., those other than the PRI initially; after a 1986 reform, the PRI too had access to the *plurinominal* seats, as they came to be called). This "mixed member proportional" system was first used in West Germany and has been introduced recently in Japan and Russia. In Mexico, 100 such seats in the Chamber of Deputies (the lower house of the federal Congress) were introduced in 1977, and another 100 were added in 1986, on top of the 300 single-member district seats that were usually nearly all won by the PRI. Thus are now 500 deputy seats, each elected every three years: 300 from single-member districts, 200 from lists in proportional representation races.[1] The Senate, whose members are elected every six years at the same time as the president, also has been made more representative. Each state now has three senators, two elected from the party that finishes first in the Senate race in that state and one from the party that finishes second. These 96 senators are joined by 32 more who are elected nationally by proportional representation from party lists. The party lists for both senators and deputies are drawn up by the national party leadership; not surprisingly, the highest positions on the lists are usually occupied by party leaders themselves so that they can be assured election to the upcoming Congress.

In the political reforms of the 1990s, the opposition parties pushed the Salinas and Zedillo governments to change the proportional representation formula so that the overrepresentation of the PRI was diminished. In 1996, the Zedillo government acquiesced to a formula by which a party had to win at least 42 percent of the popular vote in order to take the majority of the Chamber of Deputies; the 42 percent figure was arrived at after intense negotiation between electoral experts in the Zedillo administration and the political parties.

In 1997, its first election under this new "governance" formula, the PRI failed to win 42 percent, with the result that a coalition of opposition parties could deny the president and the PRI passage of laws. Since 1997, Mexico has had divided government: Fox may have won 44 percent of the popular vote in 2000, but his Alliance for Change coalition (his PAN and the PVEM) failed to win 42 percent of the Congressional vote, receiving 38.3 percent of the deputy vote and 222 seats between them, well short of the 251 needed to form a majority. In 2003, the PAN suffered an electoral setback and is thus even further from being able to support President Fox's initiatives than during the first half of his term. Furthermore, the PRI has a stronger position in the Senate than in the Chamber of Deputies. Table 21.4 illustrates PRI dominance of the Chamber before 1997 and divided government since then.

During the seven decades of PRI hegemony and dominance of the presidency, the formal powers of the Congress atrophied. Its investigative powers were rarely invoked, committee debate of bills was often pro forma, and submission of significant bills by the Congress was uncommon. Since 1997 the Mexican Congress has been rebuilding its capacities as a legislative body—for example, by holding oversight hearings on a variety of executive and former ruling party misdeeds—but the Congress remains stymied by the principle of no re-election. For example, the heads of major committees in the legislature are first-term members of Congress, or have not been members of that house of Congress in a decade.

Experts on the Mexican Congress differ in their evaluations of its accomplishments since 1997. They write that although the Mexican Congress has taken on a considerably larger volume of business than was the case before 1997, in particular legislation concerning dual nationality, health care, and pension reforms (Weldon 2004), it has not passed several significant reform measures that Mexico should address in its transition away from PRI rule, such as further

Table 21.4

Distribution of Seats in the Chamber of Deputies, 1991–2003

Party	1991	1994	1997	2000	2003
PRI (Institutional Revolutionary Party)	320	300	239	208	224
PAN (National Action Party)	89	119	121	205	151
PRD (Democratic Revolutionary Party)	41	71	125	54	97
PVEM (Mexican Green Ecological Party)	—	0	8	17	17
PT (Workers Party)	—	10	7	8	6
Others	50	0	0	8	5
Total	500	500	500	500	500

Sources: Grayson (2003, 4–5); Weldon (2004, 13).

electoral reforms (elimination of the no re-election clause, among others) and fiscal reform (Dresser 2003; Lawson 2004; see also Chapter 9 in this book). When the Fox government sought to pass a set of laws to address the complaints of indigenous peoples, as most prominently expressed by the Zapatista National Liberation Army (EZLN) in Chiapas, the administration found its bill eviscerated by PAN legislative leaders, who were upset by not having been consulted by the president on the legislation, as well as by congressmen from other political parties.

Mexico is saddled with a constitutional structure in which a presidential system coexists with a Congress in which no party holds a majority. It suffers from the further challenge that past presidents enjoyed large majorities in that Congress. Thus, a pattern of policymaking in which presidents can dictate to Congress has become the norm by which current presidential performance is measured. Not pushing through major policy initiatives may look like presidential failure when it is little more than a reflection of current political constraints. At the same time, President Fox has made errors in his handling of both his own party and the PRI. PAN and PRI legislators and their leaders have some incentive to pursue effective public policies because they can then go to the electorate with evidence of their parties' accomplishments in meeting Mexico's urgent challenges. Fox, however, has not effectively courted either rivals within his own party or in the former ruling party, with the consequence that major policy and political reform initiatives remain to be introduced in Congress or have been held up there.

Facing the check of no majority in the Congress, President Fox has chosen to appeal to the people to try to put pressure on the Congress to pass his legislative agenda. His presidency has been marked by frequent trips outside the capital to trumpet the administration's policy agenda (Dresser 2003). The Congress, especially because it does not face re-election pressures, lacks incentive to listen to a citizenry that Fox has riled up, if indeed he has convinced average Mexicans of the merits of his legislative initiatives. However, members of Congress have reason to listen to their party leaders, for those individuals will make decisions about their future nominations for elective office or for administrative appointments when and where their parties hold power. And those party leaders have little incentive to cooperate with the president, whose failure can open opportunities for their own success as candidates for office in the next presidential election.

Speculation about the inability of President Fox to improve relations with Congress reflects the fact that some felt that the president has chosen to assist the presidential aspirations of his wife, Marta Sahagún, at the expense of forming good working relationships with congressional leaders in the PAN and the PRI—although in July 2004 both the president and Mrs. Fox have declared that she has no intention of seeking Mexico's presidency. Poor relations also are tied to Fox's contentious relationship with the PRD's possible candidate for the presidency in the 2006 elections, Mexico City mayor Andrés Manuel López Obrador. Still others claim that the poor relations stem from President Fox's severe back pain, which may impair his political abilities. Yet others note that neither Fox nor his predecessor, Zedillo, had much political (as opposed to administrative) experience prior to assuming the presidency, and hence have had difficulty in the intensely political negotiations that go on as legislative bargains are hammered out. Regardless of the reasons for Fox's difficulties with Congress, most observers regard the current situation as a standoff in which major areas of public policy are not being addressed. The Congress seems to be checking the president more than facilitating the passage of major pieces of legislation. Even if the Congress were not checking President Fox's efforts for partisan political gain, though, other patterns of decision making that have evolved in Mexican society, such as the pact making that Soledad Loaeza discusses in Chapter 3 of this book, threaten to undermine any president's ability to choose a specific policy, advocate its passage as a Congressional act, and implement it. Most parties affected by a policy now know how to organize to protest decisions that adversely affect them, and if the administration does not effectively negotiate with affected parties beforehand, they can and will use direct political action and the media in an attempt to block implementation of policies with which they disagree.

Creeping Federalism

The extreme centralism of PRI rule during the 1940s through the 1970s has succumbed to two parallel processes—the first, a devolution of power from above that I will describe in the next section, and the second, a series of challenges to the former ruling party emanating from opposition victories at the local and state levels in the 1980s and 1990s. Given the PRI's advantages in national politics during its prime, we should perhaps not be surprised that the opposition parties put considerable effort into contesting PRI rule at more local levels of government where smaller campaign funds could be effective and less formidable organizational challenges could be overcome. The PAN, in particular, followed a strategy of "creeping federalism" in its growth during the 1980s and 1990s. During the later 1990s, the PRD, too, began to win local and state office more frequently, in part by winning over the political organizations of failed contenders for the PRI's nomination to state and local office.

Mexico has over 2,400 municipios, the lowest level of government in the nation, equivalent in many ways to the U.S. county. The PRI remains in power in the vast majority of the smaller municipios. Although the PAN won a few important town halls in 1982–1983, in the aftermath of Mexico's economic collapse of that period, the PAN made its major gains after 1988 and especially after the economic crisis of 1994–1995. By 1998, the PAN governed over 300 municipios. More important, though, the PAN governed most of the largest cities in Mexico. By 1999, the PAN had governed in 25 of the 30 largest municipios outside of Mexico City (Lujambio 2000). Moreover, before the 2000 elections, it had won the governorships of several important states: Baja California, Guanajuato, Chihuahua, Jalisco, Nuevo León, Querétaro, and Aguascalientes, and it added Morelos and Yucatán to its list in 2000 and 2001. From these mayoral and gubernatorial positions, PAN leaders were able to develop their skills as political executives and the party was able to build its organizational base to challenge the PRI nationally. This was, effectively, its strategy of "creeping federalism"—coming to power nationally by gradually winning over Mexicans in localities, states, and regions. As part of this strategy, the PAN successfully negotiated increased federal revenue sharing with municipios as part of its legislative approach during the last three years of the Zedillo administration, gaining more money for local governments in exchange for support on a controversial bank bailout bill.

The PRD found early electoral popularity in central and southern Mexico, winning several town halls in the state of Michoacán in 1989 and the early 1990s as well as in Oaxaca, Chiapas, and Veracruz (Rodríguez 1997). Political conflict and violence characterized the PRI–PRD relationship during the Salinas administration, and the federal government clearly treated the PAN more favorably than the PRD as each challenged the PRI in local and regional settings. The Salinas government also clearly used funds from its National Solidarity Program (PRONASOL), ostensibly designed to encourage local initiative in projects to improve the lives of the poor, in an attempt to win voters back from the PRD in the southern states. (For an evaluation of PRONASOL, see Chapter 29 in this volume). The electoral victory of the PRD's Cárdenas in the election for Mexico City mayor in 1997 caused a series of disappointed contenders for the PRI's gubernatorial nominations to bolt from the PRI to the PRD in 1998 and 1999, in part reflecting the long-term frustration with the PRI's national leadership for imposing candidates on states and localities. These prominent local PRI leaders brought their supporters and local organizations to the PRD, which led to PRD victories (often at the head of alliances of various opposition parties of both national and state-level orientation) in Zacatecas, Baja California Sur, and Tlaxcala, all outside of the party's earlier electoral bases in the south and the capital city area. The PRD also won Michoacán in 2001 behind the candidacy of a second Lázaro Cárdenas, son of Cuauhtémoc and grandson of the famous president, his namesake, both of whom had earlier governed that state.

With their victories in local and state elections (see Table 21.3), the PAN and the PRD have sought to provide good government of a kind that had lapsed in many settings under the PRI. In doing so, local PAN and PRD governments have sometimes been stymied by hostile PRI governors who have withheld revenues they were supposed to share with localities. In addition, providing good government may in many cases mean needing to gather more revenue in order to be able to offer the services required in Mexico's burgeoning cities, which is difficult because the federal government has controlled income and value-added taxes and sought to use those revenues for its own purposes. Opposition governments in the early 1990s were generally successful in improving the provision of services, however, with the consequence that in many cases those governments remained in the hands of the PAN or the PRD (Rodríguez and Ward 1995). Yet, as the stories of continuing drug trafficking in various Mexican states and the murders of over two hundred young women in Ciudad Juárez indicate, bringing parties other than the PRI to power in states and localities does not immediately bring an end to Mexico's endemic problems in the areas of preventing and punishing crime or with other inadequately provided public services.

The New Federalism

Not all of the movement away from centralism comes from opposition challenges to the former ruling party, however. The federal government itself has sought to decentralize the regime since at least a 1984 municipal reform law promoted by the Miguel de la Madrid (1982–1988) administration. In this reform initiative, de la Madrid and his government followed a time-honored PRI approach of preemptive reform—creating reforms to deflect criticism from the PRI-led federal government that, as most observers could easily argue, had become too centralized by the late 1970s. Local governments had gained most of their income from federal revenue sharing, reaching a point in 1983 where 64 percent of local government revenues came from that source (Rodríguez 1997). The 1984 reform gave greater financial autonomy to municipios, which obtained exclusive control of revenues from property taxes and any fees they might charge for public services (water and sewage rates, garbage collection fees, and so forth).

As I mentioned above, there are limits to the income that can be generated from property taxes and fees imposed on already poor people. Consequently, the state and local share of total government revenue raised remains quite low— on the order of 5 percent. States are especially squeezed in the federal fiscal equation, for they cannot effectively raise revenue from the sources reserved to local governments nor from the major federal tax sources—the income and value-added taxes (Ward and Rodríguez 1999). So they too rely on federal revenue sharing.

This decentralization brought with it improvement in public administration by reducing clientelist practices and by introducing modern management practices. Also, local government has become more transparent, especially regarding fiscal accounts, as citizens demand to know where their increased taxes and fees are going (Rodríguez 1997).

The movement for decentralization discussed above, in combination with the general democratization explored in this chapter, has had some negative consequences for Mexico. As Wayne Cornelius and his collaborators have argued (Cornelius, Eisenstadt, and Hindley 1999), the unraveling of centralized authoritarianism in Mexico has meant that the central government's control of law and order at the regional, state, and local levels has weakened. In some cases this means the injustices associated with PRI domination of state or local affairs have ceased, or at least been replaced with more benign rule by the PAN, the PRD, or some coalition of local political forces. In other cases it means that new strongmen have emerged, able to resist the federal authorities and inclined in some instances to align themselves with drug traffickers and other criminal elements. In other words, the loosening of central power has not in all cases led to greater democracy and to more just law and order at the local level; in some cases, quite the opposite has resulted.

Conclusion

During the 1990s and at the beginning of the new century, significant institutional change has come to Mexican politics. One-party domination has given way to three- (and more) party competition. Divided government has replaced presidential supremacy. A highly centralized political regime has been followed by renewed emphasis on federalism. In most ways, Mexico can be said to have democratized in the years since the controversial election of 1988.

Democracy does not always mean easier policymaking; indeed, it usually means that more actors have an opportunity to attempt to veto policy initiatives. Democracy does not always mean better public policies either, although democracies are usually more responsive to citizen demands than nondemocracies. Democracy does mean, however, that more Mexicans have an opportunity to compete for public office and to participate effectively in the choice of national and local officials.

Note

1. To select the 200 proportional representation seats (called *plurinominal* in Mexico), the country is divided into five multimember districts (or "circumscriptions") of forty seats each. Each party poses a list of forty candidates. The seats then are elected by proportional representation within the region—if in region 1 the PAN wins 25 percent of the votes, it receives ten seats—and the top ten candidates on its list go to the Chamber of Deputies.

References

Brandenburg, Frank. 1964. *The Making of Modern Mexico.* Englewood Cliffs, NJ: Prentice Hall.

Camp, Roderic Ai. 1999. *Politics in Mexico.* 3d ed. New York: Oxford University Press.

Consulta Mitofsky. 2004. *Los congresos estatales.* Mexico City. May.

Cornelius, Wayne A., T. Eisenstadt, and J. Hindley, eds. 1999. *Subnational Politics and Democratization in Mexico.* La Jolla: Center for U.S.-Mexican Studies, University of California–San Diego.

Cosío Villegas, Daniel. 1978. *El sistema político mexicano.* Mexico City: Joaquín Mortiz.

Courchene, Thomas, Alberto Díaz-Cayeros, and Steven B. Webb. 2000. "Historical Forces: Geographical and Political." In *Achievements and Challenges of Fiscal Decentralization: Lessons from Mexico,* ed. Marcelo Giugale and Steven B. Webb. Washington, DC: World Bank.

Crespo, José Antonio. 2000. "Raising the Bar: The Next Generation of Electoral Reforms in Mexico." In *Policy Papers on the Americas,* vol. 9, no. 1. Washington, DC: Center for Strategic and International Studies.

Domínguez, Jorge I., and James A. McCann. 1996. *Democratizing Mexico: Public Opinion and Electoral Choices.* Baltimore, MD: Johns Hopkins University Press.

Dresser, Denise. 2003. "Mexico: From PRI Dominance to Divided Democracy." In *Constructing Democratic Governance in Latin America,* 2d ed., ed. Jorge I. Domínguez and Michael Shifter. Baltimore, MD: Johns Hopkins University Press.

Garrido, Luis Javier. 1989. "The Crisis of *Presidencialismo.*" In *Mexico's Alternative Political Futures,* ed. Wayne A. Cornelius, Judith Gentleman, and Peter H. Smith. La Jolla: Center for U.S.-Mexican Studies, University of California at San Diego.

Grayson, George. 2003. "Distribution of Seats in the Chamber of Deputies."

"Impera desinterés en abstencionistas." 2003. *Reforma,* July 7.

Lawson, Chappell. 2004. "Fox's Mexico at Midterm." *Journal of Democracy* 15, no. 1.

Lujambio, Alonso. 2000. *El poder compartido.* Mexico City: Océano.

Mainwaring, Scott, and Matthew Soberg Shugart, eds. 1997. *Presidentialism and Democracy in Latin America.* New York: Cambridge University Press.

Mexico 2000 Panel Study. Directed by Miguel Basáñez, Roderic Camp, Wayne Cornelius, Jorge Domínguez, Federico Estévez, Joseph Klesner, Chappell Lawson (Principal Investigator), Beatriz Magaloni, James McCann, Alejandro Moreno, Pablo Parás, and Alejandro Poiré. Support for the Mexico 2000 Panel Study was provided by the National Science Foundation (SES-9905703) and *Reforma* newspaper.

Molinar Horcasitas, Juan. 1991. *El tiempo de la legitimidad: Elecciones, autoritarismo y democracia en México.* Mexico City: Cal y Arena.

Partido Acción Nacional. 2004. *Presencia de gobierno.* Mexico City, April.

Preston, Julia, and Samuel Dillon. 2004. *Opening Mexico: The Making of a Democracy.* New York: Farrar, Straus and Giroux.

Rodríguez, Victoria E. 1997. *Decentralization in Mexico: From Reforma Municipal to Solidaridad to Nuevo Federalismo.* Boulder, CO: Westview.

Rodríguez, Victoria E., and Peter M. Ward, eds. 1995. *Opposition Government in Mexico.* Albuquerque: University of New Mexico Press.

Ward, Peter M., and Victoria E. Rodríguez. 1999. *New Federalism and State Government in Mexico.* U.S.-Mexican Policy Report No. 9. Austin: LBJ School of Public Affairs, University of Texas.

Weldon, Jeffrey A. 2004. "Changing Patterns of Executive–Legislative Relations in Mexico." In *Dilemmas of Change in Mexican Politics,* ed. Kevin Middlebrook. La Jolla, CA: Center for U.S.-Mexican Studies, University of California–San Diego.

22

María Luisa Tarrés

The Political Participation of Women in Contemporary Mexico, 1980–2000

The increasing participation of women in politics reflects a movement away from traditional values. Only 42 percent of Mexicans believe that men are better political leaders than women. This view is most often held by older, less educated, and low-income men. Five percent of Mexican women belong to women's groups, compared to 2 percent who belong to political parties, while 5 percent belong to local community action groups and 7 percent to groups concerned with health. This trend reflects a remaining resistance to women in political parties, inadequate attention to health at the national level, and the increasing importance of nongovernmental organizations in a government that increasingly looks outside of the legislature to resolve issues.

Increasing the representativeness, and therefore legitimacy, of government requires greater incorporation of women in political parties and greater responsiveness to their demands. Nonetheless, this takes place sporadically, in different locations, in a society marked by conflicting values about women. Eighty-nine percent of Mexicans believe that both a husband and a wife should contribute to household income, while 34 percent say that when jobs are scarce, men should have more right to a job than women, a view that is held most often by older, poorer, less educated men—and is probably held by those who kill women maquiladora workers in northern Mexico.

María Luisa Tarrés writes that the number of children born to an average Mexican woman by the end of her reproductive life fell from 6.8 in 1970 to 3.8 in 1970 to 2.4 in 2000, reducing the time women spent in child care from 23 years in 1970 to 10 years in 2000, and freeing women to have more education, employment, and participation in group activities.

A major development beginning in the 1980s was the formation of national alliances of women's groups. The preparation for the Beijing Conference on Women in 1995 facilitated meetings between feminist and nonfeminist women who represented many different groups. They urged that their demands be included in the agenda of the presidential candidates for the 2000 elections. The integration of women into political processes has often occurred in new groups, such as the Zapatistas, who included "The Revolutionary Law of Women" in their program; the organizations formed for aid after the 1985 earthquake in Mexico City; and the Partido de la Revolución Democrática (PRD), formed in 1989. The PRD established and sometimes observed quotas of 30 percent of the candidacies, which later encouraged other political parties to do the same. Nonetheless, few women have important positions within the political system.

Tarrés concludes that "the elites who govern the political system have not adequately integrated women and other sectors into the political process; this failure casts doubt on the political system's capacity of representation."

The Condition of Mexican Women and Their Political Participation

Mexican women participate in the society in which they live, but their participation in politics nonetheless differs from that of men. Although increasing numbers of Mexicans have been integrated into the nation's development and modernization, during the last twenty years the nation's structural inequality has increased and has not favored women; they constitute 60 percent of the poor, but are scarcely present in political policymaking institutions, a field that historically is reserved for men.

The small representation of women in politics is explained both by a culture that subordinates them because they are women and by a system in which a small elite—the "revolutionary family"—monopolized power and the enjoyment of its benefits from the time of the revolution (1910–1917) until the year 2000, thanks to a system of exchanging favors that allowed a controlled circulation of government offices among its members. Women were only included in this system of controlling political participation when there were men who helped them and when they were capable of fulfilling their functions within political groups that discriminated against them because of their gender (Martínez Fernández 2001). The political elite was efficient in reproducing itself for seventy years, controlling the government, achieving stability and developing the nation, but it did not succeed in representing the diversity of political orientations, gender, class, and ethnic groups that characterize Mexican society.

In this context, the participation of women in formal mechanisms of the political system was cyclical and limited until the crisis of that system became acute in 1988 and moved toward a democratic regime in which women and other excluded groups, such as indigenous peoples, hoped to exercise their rights and be represented. Political representation, however, is won, not granted. For this reason, it is necessary to consider a series of factors that came into play during this period enabling women as a group to enter the public arena and then be recognized as subjects of government policy.

The condition of women changed between 1980 and 2000 because society modernized. Although inequality has been a structural factor for centuries, economic growth and social policies produced significant improvements in the standard of living. The unequal distribution of the benefits of development became more acute from the 1980s until 2000, when 10 percent of population had 38.7 percent of the nation's wealth, while 60 percent only had 25.13 percent. Poverty was characterized by work carried out in the informal sector, without social security, labor rights, or union organization, and by the early incorporation of children into the labor force.

Notwithstanding the fact that the general law of population (Ley General de Población) was promulgated in 1974 and that, as a result, the National Council of Population was created to promote birth control, it was only in the 1980s that, in spite of the fact that poverty was feminized, modernization benefited women because of their increasing access to education, paid employment and family planning.

Education

Increasing enrollment in basic education has greatly reduced illiteracy in Mexico during the last three decades. In 1970, 28 percent of men and 35 percent of women over age fifteen were illiterate. In 1990, the percentages fell to 11.7 percent for men and 15.6 percent for women, and in 2000, the illiteracy rate fell to 8.7 percent for men and 11.6 percent for women (INEGI 2002b). Despite this improvement, the difference in favor of men persists not only in the illiteracy rates, but also in the formal school system: women abandon both primary and secondary school at higher rates than men. Women's access to higher education is a recent development in cities, mainly among middle-class women whose earlier destiny was motherhood and marriage. Today, women's enrollment in higher education, which grew at an annual rate of 6.6 percent between 1990 and 2000, is equal to 48.7 percent of university students. Although this rate is close to that of men, profound differences are evident when enrollment is analyzed according to profession: women predominate in education and the humanities, social science, and health, while men for the most part are enrolled in engineering, sciences, and so forth (INEGI 2002b).

The improvement in women's education has not transformed the sociocultural processes that reproduce gender inequality, an inequality that is strongest in regions that are rural, poor, or have a high concentration of indigenous groups, where women are undervalued and less is spent on their education.

Participation in the Labor Force

Households headed by men fell from 83 percent in 1970 to 64 percent in 2000, at the same time that urbanization and financial needs led to the increasing participation of women in the officially recognized paid labor force. This has increased from 17 percent of women in 1970 to 31.5 percent in 1980, reaching 36 percent in 2000 when 47 percent of the women of working age were housewives, and the rest were in school (INEGI 2002b).

Family Planning

Family planning is the only public policy directed specifically at women since 1974; it probably is the factor that has offered the greatest opportunity for the autonomy of women, because it contributed to the reduction of very high rates of fertility. It is worth recording that in 1970 a Mexican woman at the end of her reproductive life on average had 6.8 children, a number that fell to 3.8 children in 1980, to 3.2 in 1990, and to 2.4 in the year 2000. This signifies an enormous gain of autonomy in a woman's life when it is noted that in 1970 with 6.8 children a mother invested at least twenty-three years in their care, without the possibility of doing anything else, while today ten years are spent (Tarrés 1997).

The Background of Increased Women's Participation in Politics

The increased participation of women in political activity was both one of the causes and, later, a result of the loss of power by the old political elite. This process was highlighted by the student movement in 1968, a movement that was principally composed of middle-class participants who questioned authoritarianism and infiltrated political institutions. The movement, which culminated in the assassination of and repression of hundreds of demonstrators in Tlatelolco, led to openings or limited modifications of the political system, as did each of the later crises. The government of President Luis Echeverría (PRI, 1970–1976) incorporated the former leaders of the student movement in its administration.

President José López Portillo (PRI, 1976–1982), who won the presidency in uncontested elections, began political reform in 1977. The government continued to control elections, but at the same time opened political and legal channels to the participation of the opposition, especially that of the left, and broadened civil liberties and freedom of the press. The opening of political processes allowed new opposition parties to register, such as the Partido Revolucionario de los Trabajadores (PRT), which nominated Rosario Ibarra de Piedra, a woman activist for human rights, as candidate for president in 1982.

The implicit principle of this reform, however, was simple: the opposition had the right to participate in the legislature but could not govern or be a majority since that was supposed to put the nation's stability at risk. During the government of Miguel de la Madrid (PRI, 1982–1988) the nation lived through a broad crisis that was met by economic adjustment measures and limits on public spending that made it impossible to redistribute resources and led to constant demonstrations and undermined the government's legitimacy. There was also pressure to modify electoral laws that prevented the opposition from winning. This gave rise to conflicts in the north of Mexico, where PAN had its roots, and also in Oaxaca, where the left controlled some towns, such as Juchitán.

Despite the limited increase in democracy, in 1988 President Carlos Salinas de Gortari (PRI, 1988–1994) won the election from Cuauhtémoc Cárdenas by fraud, and President Ernesto Zedillo (PRI, 1994–2000) recognized that his competition for the presidency was inequitable because of the enormous amount of resources that he had compared to the other candidates.

In 1996, President Zedillo carried out the "definitive reform," which was formalized in the Federal Code of Electoral Institutions and Procedures and Other Electoral Rules (Código Federal de Instituciones y Procedimientos Electorales y Otros Ordenamientos Electorales). This generated confidence that electoral rules would be followed. In 1997, the Federal Electoral Institute (Instituto Federal Electoral, IFE) recommended that political parties nominate women to 30 percent of candidacies, which had been initiated by following the PRD's establishment of this quota for both internal party positions and candidacies.

This year (1997) saw the first election carried out under nationwide rules, completing a process begun twenty years earlier. For the first time in Mexico's history, elections for deputies were competitive, and political parties of various leanings had equal conditions of participation in the elections. Moreover, the votes were counted.

Beginning in the 1980s, women's groups that previously had not been linked created national alliances that included groups of urban settlements, feminists, intellectuals, indigenous peoples, workers, and peasants in a new movement that differed from earlier ones because it was multiclass and multi-ethnic in a country marked by inequality and discrimination. The mobilization of women permitted the creation of a public identity that broke with the existing stereotypes about a woman's role as a mother, wife, and housewife by showing women's capacity for political mobilization, generating leaders and managers, and placing their demands related to gender into public debate. For example, during the mobilization process between the 1980s and 2000, women activists and social leaders joined political parties and founded public institutions created to benefit women. Some leaders created feminist associations, such as the Diversa Agrupación Política Feminista, Mujeres en Lucha por la Democracia, and Mujeres y Punto. This type of organization allowed the creation of electoral alliances with traditional political parties and the integration in their agendas of women's interests. Finally, women members of social movements were legislators or candidates for political office. The great majority of these representatives came from the educated middle classes, leaving most women without representation.

Later, these facts would become part of the debate about the democratization of society and the political system in Mexico's civil society in which feminism and issues relating to women had been cast as a divisive element.

The preparation for the Beijing Conference on Women in 1995 facilitated the encounter between feminist and nonfeminist women who served as officials, politicians, and representatives of nongovernmental organizations. These women urged that their concerns be included in the agenda of the presidential candidates for the 2000 elections. With the establishment of a multiparty political system and with a competitive electoral democracy starting with the election of President Vicente

Fox (PAN 2000–), a slow and difficult transition was begun toward the constitution of a democratic regimen that would integrate the demands of women that challenged traditional values. This transition was slow and difficult, because President Fox was the candidate of a political alliance created around the conservative and Catholic Partido Acción Nacional (PAN), and the Catholic hierarchy influenced the members of the government and of the governing party. Moreover, a majority of Mexicans consider issues related to gender to be "women's things."

The Development of the Women's Movement

After Mexican women obtained the right to vote in 1953, the Mexican feminist movement declined until the 1970s, in part because of the integration of the women in the development process, but above all because of the nature of the institutional political system that excluded and repressed those who were not integrated into the ranks of the official party. This exclusion broke the solidarity and influence of the networks and organizations that had given women access to the formal political system (Tarrés 2004). These reappeared in public life thanks to the feminist movement that developed during the student movement of 1968 and that became increasingly important between the 1980s and the end of the 1990s, when national feminist demands and proposals were understood by the rest of society. In this way, from the 1980s onward, feminists were able to establish links with women's movements in low-income urban neighborhoods, and with peasants and Indians, workers and unionists, who demanded better living conditions or fought against their exclusion from power. It is thus possible to delineate three periods that highlight women's concerns and the presence of a permanent women's movement in Mexico: (1) the 1982 financial crisis and the 1985 earthquake in Mexico City; (2) the movement for democracy focused on the 1988 elections; and (3) the greater opening of the Mexican economy and the Zapatista rebellion of the 1990s.

The Crises of the 1980s

The 1982 financial crisis and its consequences, the reduction of the social budget, and the 1985 earthquake in Mexico City stimulated the development of the women's movement because the feminists formed aid groups that included the condition of women in the discussion of how to overcome them. The groups that were formed were nongovernmental organizations that worked with the Movimiento Urbano Popular (MUP) in Mexico City and with other groups in the rest of the nation on health, education, and other social issues. The organizations whose work was most outstanding during this period are Acción Popular de Integración Social (APIS), Grupo de Educación Popular con Mujeres (GEM), Mujeres para el Diálogo, Colectivo Revolucionario Integral, NOSOTRAS, Madres Libertarias, Colectivo de Lucha Contra la Violencia Hacia las Mujeres (COVAC), and Cuarto Creciente A.C. (Sánchez Olvera 2002, 133–141).

The entry of feminist activists, who came from groups, movements, and left-wing parties to the lower-income neighborhoods and to the countryside, allowed new relations with the women of the ecclesiastical base communities (CEBs) that acted at the local level. The contact of these CEB women with feminists produced a silent revolution: in a very short time, they began to incorporate feminist notions in Catholic liberation theology (Tárres 2004). The repercussions were enormous: during these years there were about 10,000 base communities functioning throughout the nation (Muro González 1994) and the majority of their members were women.

Perhaps the case that best exemplifies the linkage of feminists with the base communities is that of Chiapas, where the Zapatistas incorporated socioeconomic, ethnic, and gender issues into their demands. The Revolutionary Law of Women was integrated into the Zapatista program. It proclaims women's right to equality with men in education, work, and political participation, and emphasizes women's right to make their own childbearing decisions, to choose their spouses, not to be forced to marry according to custom, and not be beaten and violated by family members or strangers ("Chiapas" 1994, 14–15). From 1985 onward there was an increase of ten feminist organizations per year in all states[1] and a great number in Mexico City, not counting the hundreds of women's organizations in the nation that were not focused on gender issues.

The activity of women also was expressed in the opening of courses and research and teaching programs in universities and centers of higher education. Women were increasingly present in radio, television, and printed media. They created journals and other publications with national or state circulation. At the end of the 1980s, the "practical networks of the movement" (Red Nacional de Mujeres, Red en Contra de la Violencia de las Mujeres, Red Feminista Campesina, Red de Educadoras Populares, etc.), created an awareness of national linkages among women's groups and reinforced women's autonomy in public life. Thus, the networks allowed the establishment of relations with academic and professional institutions, officials in the public administrations, legislators, and other persons aware of the demands of the women's movement.

The opening of new relations between middle-class feminists and organizations of the progressive Catholic Church, left-wing groups, and workers led to great activism. In this period there were ten national and sectoral conventions of peasant women and women from low-income neighborhoods with an average attendance of 500 women at each one, and at least fifty local or regional meetings of popular feminist groups. In these meetings, discussions were held about the nature of classes and gender in feminists' demands and the "Popular Feminism" movement was established. The movement united feminist discourse with popular demands. The link between middle-class women and low-income sectors for the first time produced a transclass movement in Mexican society—a highly stratified society with many cultural and racist prejudices. Formation of this linkage was made difficult by a lack of confidence and by frequent conflicts, but wishes for alliances centered on the common experience of being a woman predominated.

After the 1985 earthquakes in Mexico City, women from low-income sectors and feminists worked together to consolidate their public presence. Two new women's contingents appeared: women from low-income neighborhoods from the center of the city initially formed the Coordinadora Unica de Damnificados (CUD) and later formed diverse neighborhood associations; and women from the seamstresses' union joined forces when confronted the loss of their jobs after various workshops were buried in the debris. The Movimiento Urbano Popular (MUP) is another organization whose participation was important in forming the Regional de Mujeres del Valle de México in 1984, giving rise to a series of activities centered on the analysis of the subordination of women in the family and on forging tools to enter government and other organizations. The MUP's success in making the role of women visible today seems obvious and shows that the links of its members with the feminists broadened their scope of action and their discourse so that, from this moment on, these would not be limited to basic needs. Several of MUP's members later had important positions in their organizations, in offices representing people in legislative spaces, and in the administration of the city (Espinosa 1986; Sánchez Olvera 2002).

The constant presence of women's groups on various fronts made their efficiency in the solution of problems of citizenship clear, and legitimized these women since their members were recognized as interlocutors for the state and for other social and political movements.

From this time on, the mutual influence of the diverse sectors (popular, worker, feminist) became clear and it was possible to begin to talk about the public presence of the women's movement. In 1986, the manifestation of the International Day of the Woman for the first time was not convoked by feminists, but by women from low-income neighborhoods, and brought together the largest number of participants ever seen at this event—50,000 women. From then on, the traditional marches of feminists (for choice about childbearing, abortion, and against violence) would be coordinated by women from the urban movement and by workers in various unions. From this date, two tendencies were outlined in the national feminist movement that would be expressed with clarity in the Fourth Encuentro Feminista Latinoamericano y del Caribe, which took place in 1987 in Taxco with more than 2,500 participants. This meeting facilitated the movement of feminists toward the definition of joint interests related to political and social citizenship of women.

The constant mobilization of women in the decade of the 1980s generated a unifying experience. In the urban organizations, women demanded to be recognized as leaders, and upon not being listened to by men, they created "women's management," leaving these organizations without women members until they provided for their inclusion in managerial positions.

The intense popular mobilization was accompanied by a process of political maturation that not only allowed the integration of the women's question in the discourse about class but also allowed the redefining of the role of the state by left-wing feminists who shifted their attitude from conceiving the state as an adversary to a willingness to negotiate with the state. Their experiences with women from low-income sectors smoothed the way to understanding that this relation was necessary if one claimed to work with sectors whose basic needs were involved. Further, the political opening that characterized these years offered women leaders and directors opportunities of participation in politics or in government administration without fear of repression.

The Movements for Democracy Before and After the 1988 Election

Electoral fraud was denounced throughout Mexico in the 1988 presidential election, when the votes for Cuauhtémoc Cárdenas were not acknowledged even as society was demanding democracy. Moral indignation permeated national discussion and generated enormous disquiet among women about participating in politics. In this period, two organizations reacted against official authoritarianism: one, with the clear intention of mobilizing women from the viewpoint of gender, was the Coordinadora Benita Galena, which grouped together thirty-three women's, urban, union, NGO, and political party organizations; and the other was the Asociación Civil Mujeres en Lucha por la Democracia, which for several years brought together independent women at the margin of the parties. Later, both would remain linked to the PRD, which inherited the PRI's left-wing defectors. This is relevant because since its creation in 1989, the PRD established principles, programs, and statutes in which it promised equality of rights, the liberation of women, and the denunciation of discrimination by sex, age, and ethnic group.

The entry of members of the MUP and of organizations created to combat the 1985 electoral fraud facilitated the democratization of the PRD since women in these groups aided some leaders who, like Amalia García or Rosario Robles, did not have sufficient power to establish the gender perspective in their organization. This not only benefited the militants of PRD in later elections, but also influenced the other parties to establish minimum quotas for the equal access of women to representative positions in internal party leaderships. (Stevenson 1999).

The 1988 presidential elections coincided with the legislative elections, and there were increases in the percentages of women elected to Congress. The proportion of women deputies elected was 12.2 percent, a figure slightly higher than that of 1985; this increased to 17 percent in 1997. Women senators constituted 12.5 percent in 1985 and three years later rose to 15.6 percent. Although some parties approved mechanisms to assure that 30 percent of their candidates were women, between 1997 and 2000 women obtained a smaller percentage because the majority of women candidates were registered either as alternates or in electoral zones where the party had little or no presence. Thus, although 87 women deputies had been in the prior legislature, the number fell to 80 in 1997–2000.

In the 2003 elections, the Federal Elections Institute supervised the quotas, so that women gained 22 percent of the positions and did not reach the desired 30 percent. PAN and PRD respected the rules, and their women candidates obtained 29 percent and 28 percent of the positions, respectively. PRI had the largest number of representatives, and only 15 percent of its women candidates were elected (Gómez Tagle 2003).

The Greater Opening of the Mexican Economy and the Zapatista Rebellion of the 1990s

The 1990s had a special significance for the women's movement because its demands were institutionalized thanks to the legitimacy granted by the Action Program approved in Beijing in 1995. The demands regarding gender were spread and began to be implanted and administered by groups that the women's movement had not believed would endorse them. This situation, however, presented new challenges to the women's movement because it did not control the orientation of policies that were later developed and it was necessary to create new strategies to enable the women's movement to impact decisions. In addition, the condition of Mexican women had changed.

The governments of Presidents Carlos Salinas de Gortari (1988–1994) and Ernesto Zedillo (1994–2000), changed the Constitution. The privatization of government firms, the changes in Article 27 that modified ejidal rights by permitting the legal sale of ejidal land,[2] the renewal of relations with the Catholic Church and the Vatican, and general deregulation are decisions that the government took in the name of modernization and of the integration of the nation into the global economy. The popular discontent with this situation erupted in 1994 on the 1st of January with the appearance of the Zapatista Liberation Army (EZLN, Ejército Zapatista de Liberación Nacional).

The experience of the Zapatista movement was a very important example for the women's movement and for feminism in general. Indigenous women, despite their poverty and subordination to men, created a document that contained concrete proposals oriented toward questioning their traditions with respect to gender and subordination of women to older men. The Zapatista Revolutionary Law Regarding Women (Ley Revolucionaria de mujeres) was integrated into the Zapatista Project. It demanded that women, notwithstanding their race, creed, color, or political affiliation, had the right to participate in the revolutionary battle. Moreover, it stated their right to education, work, and political participation within and outside of the community, but above all it called for the recognition of their personal autonomy, thus emphasizing their right to decide the number of children that they wanted to have, to choose their spouse, to not be forced to enter into matrimony according to custom, and to not be beaten or raped by family members or strangers. By demanding the right to choose whom to marry, the women in the Zapatista movement weakened the traditional authority of their fathers, who by custom decided whom their children should marry.

Even though this movement emerged as a result of many factors, it is clear that the claims of indigenous women expressed the relationship that they had developed with the left and with the CEBs starting in the 1980s. Thus, during the 1990s, women's issues were defined and incorporated into national policies. This was not accidental. Through persistent mobilization, feminists and other women were able to legitimate their demands thanks to (1) alliances with social and political actors who fought for democratization of the political regime, (2) the presence of political parties that began to compete for votes and needed to include women in their programs in order to obtain their support, and (3) an international environment that legitimated women as political subjects who had rights.

The mobilization of the Zapatistas was also a response to Article 27, which ended agrarian reform and severely restricted women's access to land and credit, for which they had fought since 1971, when women obtained juridical equality with respect to granting of lands that was extended to their access to credit in 1979 (Arizpe and Botey 1986). The legal change harmed them more than it did men when one considers that it is men who owned the land and could profit from selling it.

The deregulation and opening of the economy led to the establishment of hundreds of maquiladora firms in the north of Mexico. Their employees were predominantly very young women who came from the countryside to urban areas, and, for the first time, encountered the possibility of enjoying a certain amount of independence by working for pay. However, beginning in 1993 in Chihuahua, some of these workers were "disappeared" and/or raped and/or murdered. Mothers and family members of these women organized, and little by little organizations of women in Chihuahua and in all of Mexico were mobilized to demand justice. Between 1993 and 1998 there were 56 murders, and from 1998 to 2000 there were 370 murders; 400 women are still listed as missing. The demand for justice in local, state, and national institutions has not been met, so that for several years aid from international sources has been sought. The impossibility of resolving these murders shows the limitations of a social movement in an institutional context that is dominated by a culture of discrimination.

After women from several sectors of Mexican society participated in the Beijing meeting in 1995, they pressed the government to implement the accords that they had signed. Thus, public policies began to be generated that were oriented to gender equality. There was an important group of women's and feminist organizations that redefined their position toward the state and decided to maintain an equilibrium between what was "politically correct and what was possible," which signified taking advantage of state resources to strengthen their organizations. This contributed to the institutionalization of the demands for gender equality, and to the professionalization of leaders, with the result that the leaders of the social movement tended to be replaced by women experts, legislators, and government officials. This implied that the original creators of the project were not in charge of its implementation.

The last years of the 1990s were times of increasing public dialogue about gender and of the establishment of alliances between women with different party memberships and policy positions. The first experience of this type was the reform of the law on sexual crimes; afterward, it became a model of political action favoring women's interests that went beyond partisan concerns. From there, agreements between women's groups were reached on various themes related to gender: a campaign of affirmative action called "gaining spaces" was begun whose principal objective was the establishment of quotas in political jobs; agreements were established to create a policy of recognition and respect for diversity, in which gender did not imply inequality of opportunities. Other examples of joint actions and agreements are indicated in Table 22.1.

These agreements impacted legislative proposals that covered items such as violence against women, sexual and reproductive rights, and sustainable development, as well as proposals for earmarked budgets for improving income, health, education, the law of quotas for political positions, and aid to indigenous and rural women.

Is Mobilization to Obtain Representation in Formal Politics Enough?

Despite the success of the women's movement in spreading its discourse and demands in the public sphere, and women's important presence in the process of transition to democracy, Mexican women have not obtained equitable representation in politics (see Table 22.2). The reproduction of structures that discriminate against women is entrenched in political parties, although women's participation at the local level tends to be equal to or greater than that of men. In the PRD, 33.3 percent of the positions in the National Executive Committee are occupied by women; in the PRI, 21.9 percent, and in PAN, 20 percent. The participation of women in public administration has increased, but has not been translated into effective access to managerial positions. Although 53 percent of women officials are heads of a department, only 3 percent of them have positions in higher-level jobs and only two of the cabinet posts such as the minister of the environment and minister of tourism were headed by women. In the judiciary of the 8,895 registered jobs in the year 2000, only 37.5 percent were held by women and only one of the eleven members of the Supreme Court of Justice is a woman. The representation of women in politically elected positions is and has been relatively low, despite advances in legislation (see Table 22.3).

Immediately after women gained the right to vote, in the legislative period from 1955 to 1958, the proportion of women deputies was 2.5 percent. In 1970–1973, the percentage rose to 7.3. In the three last legislatures there was a small increase: in 1994 women were 14.1 percent of the total; in 1997, 17.4 percent, which fell to 16 percent in the year 2000 (INEGI 2002b, 367–368). The 1997–2000 legislature has shown the greatest growth in the representation of women in the three major political parties in the Chamber of Deputies and the Senate. In 2001 and 2003, the number of women deputies fell, but the number of women

Table 22.1

Agreements Among Women's Groups and Developments Aiding Women, 1993–2000

Year	Name of agreement	Purpose	Groups involved
1991	National Convention of Women for Democracy	To promote the nomination of women as political party candidates. 39 candidates were nominated; none won	Nongovernmental organization and political parties of the left: PRT, PT, and PRD
1992	Gaining Spaces	First attempt to obtain a percentage of women within the decision making organs of political parties and in the list of candidates for election	Women from nongovernmental organizations and political parties
1993	From A to Z	"Women walk a ways together before our policy differences separate us"	The group consisted of independent feminist and feminists who belong to a political party (from the PRI and from the PRD).
1996	National Program of Women: Alliance for Equality	Government organization to formulate programs and policies to improve the condition of women in regard to health, education, povery, violence, participation, and rights	National Population Council (CONAPO) incorporated diverse social organizations that worked with, by and for women
1997	"We advance a step"	Agreement of political parties to promote and legislate reforms to benefit women	DIVERSA Feminist Political Organization, a legislator and a candidate for deputy from political parties
1997	Commission on Gender Equality	To include consideration of gender in national laws, policies and programs. To develop a new political culture on the basis of women's rights	Deputies from various political parties, whose origin is PRI: 15, PAN 7, PRD 6, PT 1, PVM 1. In the commission, there were only 4 men, all from PAN
1998	Mexican Women's Parliament	To promote new laws benefiting women; to oversee and evaluate the implementation of public policies concerning gender	Deputies and Senators, feminists, and women from civil society
2000	Pact between women: Towards a Legislative Agenda.....For Gender Equality	Strengthening women's viewpoints in the legislature, regarding labor, reproductive health, sustainable development, combatting violence based on gender and helping Indian women within the governance of the government (e.g., not including religious matters)	Representatives of political parties, feminist and women's organizations

Table 22.2

Women's Representation in the Mexican Legislature, 1976–2003

Presidential period	Legislature	Chamber of Deputies					Senate				
		Men	As a % of total	Women	As a % of total	Total	Men	As a % of total	Women	As a % of total	Total
1976–1982 José López Portillo	L (1976–1979)	215	91.1	21	8.9	236	59	92.2	5	7.8	64
	LI (1979–1982)	368	92	32	8	400					
1982–1988 Miguel de la Madrid Hurtado	LII (1982–1985)	358	89.5	42	10.5	400	58	90.6	6	9.4	64
	LIII (1985–1988)	358	89.5	42	10.5	400					
1988–1994 Carlos Salinas de Gortari	LIV (1988–1991)	441	88.2	59	11.8	500	54	84.4	10	15.6	64
	LV (1991–1994)	455	91.2	44	8.8	499	60	93.7	4	6.3	64
1994–2000 Ernesto Zedillo Ponce de León	LVI (1994–1997)	426	85.9	70	14.1	496	112	87.5	16	12.5	128
	LVII (1997–2000)	413	82.6	87	17.4	500	109	85.2	19	14.8	128
2000–2006 Vicente Fox Quesada	LVIII (2000–2003)	420	84	80	16	500	106	82.8	22	17.2	128
Total		4,892		566		5,448	786		86		872

Sources: Based on data from PRONAM (1997); PROEQUIDAD (2002); INEGI (2002).

Table 22.3

Mexican Women Legislators, by Party Affiliation, Legislative Chamber, and Session, 1988–2003

Presidential period	Legislative session	Legislative chamber	PRI	PAN	PRD	PVEM	Independents and other	Total
1988–1994 Carlos Salinas de Gortari	LIV 1988–1991	Chamber of Deputies	37	11	0	0	11	59
		Senate	9	0	1	0	0	10
		Total LIV	46	11	1	0	11	69
	LV 1991–1994	Chamber of Deputies	27	7	5	0	5	44
		Senate	4	0	0	0	0	4
		Total LV	31	7	5	0	5	48
1994–2000 Ernesto Zedillo Ponce de León	LVI 1994–1997	Chamber of Deputies	42	12	16	0	0	70
		Senate	14	1	1	0	0	16
		Total LVI	56	13	17	0	0	86
	LVII 1997–2000	Chamber of Deputies	38	15	29	3	2	87
		Senate	13	3	3	0	0	19
		Total LVII	51	18	32	3	2	106
2002–2006 Vicente Fox Quesada	LVIII 2000–2003	Chamber of Deputies	33	25	13	8	5	84
		Senate	10	6	2	4	0	22
		Total LVIII	43	31	15	12	5	106
1988–2003		Grand Total	227	80	70	15	23	415

Sources: Based on data from PRONAM (1997); PROEQUIDAD (2002); INEGI (2002a).

senators increased (see Table 22.3). It is not surprising that the PRI had the largest number, because it is the dominant party. What is surprising is the growth in the number of women in the PRD, which increased from 5 deputies and no senators in 1991 to 29 deputies and 3 senators in 1997 as a result of its internal quotas, which were respected at that time. The representation of women in PAN slowly grew from 1994 to 1997, reaching 25 deputies and 6 senators in 2000. The number of women senators was the same in 2000 as a result of the temporary alliance of PAN and PVEM, when PVEM elected 5 women deputies. Although advances occurred in the legislature between 1994 and 2000, it must be pointed out that the majority of women legislators were relegated to secondary positions in the working commissions of the legislature (Rodríguez 2003). Even though quotas nominally established a 30 percent minimum for either gender, the percentages of the last years still showed limited participation of women because though the political parties accepted the quotas, they named a large number of women to jobs as alternate candidates so that they were not elected in the same proportion as men.

Mexico is a federal nation, and in 2004 there was not a single woman governor until the PRD candidate Amalia García was elected governor of Zacatecas on July 4, 2004, to take office on September 12 of that year. She is the first militant left-wing feminist to be elected governor in free elections.[3] There have only been four women governors in the history of the nation and one woman mayor of the Federal District. Two were elected, and two were interim governors. The elected governors were Griselda Álvarez, governor of Colima (1979–1985), and Beatriz Paredes, governor of Tlaxcala (1987–1992). The interim governors were Dulce María Sauri in Yucután (1991–1994) and Rosario Robles, who replaced Cuauhtémoc Cárdenas as regent of Mexico City (1999–2000). All four are feminists.

The discrimination is enormous on the municipal scene, since women have never been more than 5 percent of the mayors, which is paradoxical, because Mexican women act at local levels. Women comprise 14.5 percent of the members of state congresses. (INEGI 2000). In the labor unions there is a profound disequilibrium in powerful positions and there are strong barriers to women's access to management positions and to having their needs and claims considered in the unions' agenda. This includes the unions of the maquiladoras, where women are the largest share of union members, but their representation in union elected office is very low.

We have shown that women participate massively in neighborhood associations, but as in other cases do not easily reach management positions. Neither the increase of women in paid jobs nor the increase in their education nor their access to birth control nor their increasing autonomy have been sufficient to break their subordinate status in formal politics.

The political class has not accepted their demands and rights to equitable representation as something natural. Twenty years after the electoral reform began, clean elections and political alternation in government are assured, so that an alternative to government by the PRI is possible. Yet the political elites still are not creating institutions, mechanisms, and values that would assure the equitable participation of women. The political class that has embraced political party pluralism and clean elections does not differ from the previous one in favoring its own members and discourses over outsiders, and is reluctant to change its personnel, diversify its agenda, and integrate in an egalitarian manner those who are different, such as women. The inertia of the national political system teaches the elite merely to react to crises; this failure to integrate women and other sectors into the political process casts doubt on the political system's capacity of representation.

Notes

1. Mexico is a federal republic that has thirty-two states and a Federal District, where the City of Mexico and the federal government are located. The ten feminist organizations per year were created in the thirty-two states.
2. For the historical details of women's limited access to *ejido* land and management, see Stephen (1996).
3. Amalia García was one of the founders of the Unified Socialist Party of Mexico (PSUM, Partido Socialista Unificado de México) in 1982. She was an early member of the PRD in 1989, and became its president in 1998. She participated from an early age in the feminist movement, aiding its proposals in the PRD as a deputy and as a senator. She is part of the political elite: her father was the PRI governor of Zacatecas and later represented Mexico as its ambassador in several nations.

References

Arizpe, Lourdes, and Carlota Botey. 1986. "Las políticas de desarrollo agrario y su impacto sobre la mujer campesina en México." In *La mujer y la política agraria en América Latina*, ed. M. León and C.D. Deere. Bogotá: Siglo Veintiuno, Editores ACEP.
"Chiapas: El alzamiento de las mujeres indígenas." 1994. *Debate Feminista* 9 (March).
Espinosa, Gisela. 1986. "La organización de mujeres del Movimiento Urbano Popular 1983–1985." México: Ponencia.
Gómez Tagle, Silvia. 2003. "La discriminación de la mujer." *La Jornada* 21 (August).
INEGI, Instituto Nacional de las Mujeres. 2000. *El enfoque de género en la producción de estadísticas sobre participación política y toma de decisiones*. México: INMUJERES.
———. 2002a. *Memoria de los foros de consulta PROEQUIDAD*. México: INMUJERES.
———. 2002b. *Mujeres y hombres*. México: INEGI.
———. 2002c. *Primer informe de labores 2000–2001*. México: INMUJERES.
Martínez Fernández, Alicia Inés. 2001. "De invitadas a protagonistas: La integración de las mujeres a la política en el México moderno." Unpublished Ph.D. dissertation, centro de estudios sociologicos. México: El Colegio.
Muro González, Víctor Gabriel. 1994. *Iglesia y movimientos sociales en México, 1972–1987. Los casos de Ciudad Juárez y el Istmo de Tehuantepec*. México: El Colegio de Michoacán.
PROEQUIDAD. 2002. *Memoria de los foros de consulta*. México: Programa nacional para la igualdad de oportunidades y no discriminación contra las mujeres (2000–2006).
PRONAM. 1997. *Más mujeres en el Congreso*. México: Programa Nacional de la Mujer (1995–2000).
Randall, Laura. 1999. *Reformando la reforma agraria mexicana*. México: El Atajo; UAM–Xochimilco.

Rodríguez, Victoria E. 2003. *Women in Contemporary Mexican Politics*. Austin: University of Texas Press.

Sánchez Olvera, Alma Rosa. 2002. *El feminismo mexicano ante el Movimiento Urbano Popular: dos expresiones de lucha de género (1970–1985)*. México: UNAM, Plaza y Valdez.

Stephen, Lynn. 1996. "Too Little, Too Late? The Impact of Article 27 on Women in Oaxaca." In *Reforming Mexico's Agrarian Reform*, ed. Laura Randall. Armonk, NY: M.E. Sharpe.

Stevenson, Linda. 1999. "La política de género en el proceso de democratización en México: Eligiendo mujeres y legislando delitos sexuales y acciones afirmativas, 1988–1999." *Estudios Sociológicos. CES-El Colegio de México*, vol. XVII, no. 50 (Mayo-Agosto).

Tarrés, María Luisa.1997. *La voluntad de ser: Mujeres en los noventa*. México: PIEM–El Colegio de México.

———. 2001. "Las organizaciones del movimiento de mujeres en la reforma política." *La sociedad civil: De la teoría a la realidad*, ed. Alberto Olvera. México: El Colegio de México.

———. 2005. "Discurso feminista y movimiento de mujeres en México (1970–2000)." In *Miradas Feministas a las mexicanas del siglo XX*, comp. Marta Lamas. Colección Biblioteca Mexicana, FCE, CONACULTA.

23

ROBERTO BLANCARTE

Religion, Church, and State in Contemporary Mexico

An examination of survey data for several years leads some observers to believe that the election of Vicente Fox in 2000 changed the way in which religious belief and behavior is presented in Mexico, increasing people's willingness to admit that they believed in God. This would have taken place despite the historical contention for power between church and state that marked most of Iberian and Ibero-American history. In fact, we are observing a long liberal tradition that emphasizes distinction between private and public spheres, religion and politics and as a consequence church and state affairs. In Mexico, "revolution" and "religion" represented frequently conflicting symbols and structures. The 1917 Constitution that had denied the legal personality of the Church was amended in 1992 to recognize it, recovering at the same time the liberal tradition. This took place at the same time that other religions gained adherents, and could be viewed as a step taken to prove that Mexico demonstrated its attachment to the basic values shared by all OECD members: an open market economy, democratic pluralism and respect for human rights. Mexico was admitted to the OECD in 1994.

In 2000, 90 percent of Mexicans included in the World Value Survey said religion was very important in their lives; although there was some variation during the period, in 1980–2000 three-quarters of Mexicans said that they are a religious person and about 55 percent said that they attended religious services once a week, with church attendance having little influence on the belief in God.

The important shift is the increase in values associated with being Protestant or not having a religious belief. Basañez and Moreno report that this group of Mexicans tend to be more trustful and autonomous than Catholics, who are less trustful and are more dependent. This shift away from Catholic beliefs is consistent with a 32 percent increase in confidence in government and a 14 percent increase in confidence in churches from 1990 to 2000. Yet these figures understate the place and the role of religion in Mexico that must be understood in the context of the historical importance of the lay or secular state.

Roberto Blancarte emphasizes other aspects of religious individuals' and orga-

nizations' behavior. He notes that two-thirds of non-governmental organizations in Mexico have a religious origin or influence. However, only 54 percent of Mexicans believe that churches give adequate answers to social problems, reflecting the fact that a good deal of Mexican behavior differs from that recommended by the Catholic Church: 53 percent of rural women use contraceptives; 20 percent have had an abortion. The Fox administration's attempts to use administrative means to give the Catholic bishops a privileged role in the definition of public policies—as of mid 2004—have failed.

Roberto Blancarte distinguishes between religious individuals and the Catholic Church. Individuals have contributed to democratizing society and expanding human rights. The Catholic Church has defended the conscience when it is attacked by the state; the state has defended free conscience by ensuring civil and religious liberties. The acknowledged role of religion in social issues as well as individual behavior has increased, while the direct role of the Catholic Church, now in competition with other religions, has decreased.

Religion in Mexico is at once everywhere and nowhere. Although the religiosity of Mexicans is unquestionable, the place of religion is (curiously or paradoxically) unclear. We cannot state that the individual's conscience is the only place where religion thrives. In Mexico, religion counts in different ways. Religion is a social issue with an impact on the collective life of individuals: for instance, at the national level, two-thirds of the nongovernmental organizations in Mexico have a religious origin or some kind of religious influence. The role of these organizations has been and will continue to be crucial to defining how religion counts, in both the democratic life of the country and areas of social life that are particularly sensitive, such as the defense of human rights.

Recognizing that religion is a social phenomenon does not mean that the public policies of a country should respond to the specific doctrines of the main national denominations or to those pertaining to the majority church. That would certainly seem obvious given the increasing religious plurality of the country. Protestants, for example, have historically demanded guarantees of respect for religious plurality and fair juridical treatment, and until recently, they did not intend to influence the sociopolitical arena. The Jewish community has demanded freedom to develop its own culture, a way of life whose adhesion to national values can go unquestioned. It is also important to note the increase of other religious minorities and their growing importance, particularly on the northern and southern borders of the country.

The Catholic Church for its part has oscillated between establishing a privileged relationship with the government—in an attempt to shape the public policies of the state—and advocating a defense of the poor and of human rights. At the same time, paradoxically, the conditions that allow religion to play a role in Mexico have derived so far from the existence of a secular state, which has guaranteed religious freedom and fair treatment to its citizens.

The victory of the National Action Party (PAN) in 2000 led to the formation of a government heavily influenced by conservative Catholic thought. This has led to confrontations concerning social policy, especially key themes such as reproductive health, sexual rights, and education, and to the redefinition of the role of religion in Mexico (Blancarte 2004).

Historical Background

Legal Structure

During the last five centuries, religion in Mexico has thrived under an apparent and contradictory monopoly of the goods of salvation at the institutional level, and a profound diversity of religious manifestations that coexist, intertwine, and feed on that monopoly. The key to understanding the weak institutional control of the Catholic Church in Mexico and the rest of Latin America is the endemic scarcity of priests, a fact that also accounts for the strength of popular religions and the shapes religiosity adopts in the region.

During the colonial period, the church presence was concentrated in the center and west of Mexico. This generated scarce pastoral care and a Catholicism characterized by ritualism rather than doctrine, by the subsequent development of a popular Catholicism with a marked autonomous and at times anti-clerical trend, and by the control and management of religion by the state.

In the mid-nineteenth century, the liberal political parties associated the rejection of any form of agreement with the church with religious freedom. Freedom of religion in most Latin American countries was not the result of increased social tolerance, but of political circumstances that led to identifying such freedom with the separation of the Catholic Church and the state.

In Mexico, the 1857 Constitution and the Laws of Reform of 1859–1861 establish the separation of church and the state. In the twentieth century, the 1917 Constitution imposed by the revolutionaries stated that churches did not exist from a juridical standpoint, and that religion could be practiced only at temples or in homes, never in the streets. Religion was not legally a public or a social matter. Religious ministers were subject to political restrictions, and political parties could not have any religious or denominational references. An individual's religion became a form of belief linked solely to spiritual matters, which eliminated the social character of religious expressions. The conflict that these provisions generated manifested itself in the form of solid opposition by the church to the revolutionary regime, which peaked with the Cristero revolt (1926–1929).

In 1938, during the Lázaro Cárdenas administration (1934–1940), the Mexican Catholic hierarchy supported the government's expropriation of oil. This led to a new stage called *modus vivendi* in which the church accepted the state monopoly in social matters, in exchange for governmental tolerance of church educational activities (Blancarte 1992).

The 1992 constitutional reforms and the July Law on Religious Associations and Public Worship eliminated the most anti-clerical provisions, although it maintained the laicism of the Mexican state. In September of the same year, President Carlos Salinas de Gortari established diplomatic relations between Mexico and the Holy See.

In general, the objective of the 1992 amendments to the Constitution of 1917 was to eliminate the anti-clerical character of the 1917 Constitution, particularly concerning the juridical recognition of churches and religious associations. The main reforms consisted in eliminating from Article 3 the prohibition against private schools imparting religious instruction, as well as that against religious congregations or ministers of religion opening or running primary schools, and eliminating from Article 5 the prohibition against establishing monastic orders.

The new Article 24 eliminated the requirement that believers must attend religious ceremonies, devotions, or acts only at temples or at home. Article 27 had prohibited churches regardless of denomination, to purchase, possess, or administrate real estate or capital. The 1992 reform modified that article and now establishes that religious associations "will have the capacity to purchase, possess, or administrate exclusively the assets that are essential to accomplish their purposes, in accordance with the requirements and limitations set forth by regulatory law."

Article 130 recognized as legal entities churches and religious groupings, and eliminated the prohibition on ministers of religion criticizing government authorities or fundamental laws of the country during a public "or a private meeting." The reformed version of the article merely states that "Ministers of religion will not oppose the laws of the country or its institutions during public meetings, religious ceremonies or through religious propaganda and publications," and grants ministers the right to be elected, but still prohibits political parties from having religious affiliations.

Finally, concerning freedom of speech, before 1992 church periodicals could not comment on national political affairs or inform about acts performed by government officials or individuals directly associated with the operations of public institutions (Blancarte 1993, 2002). This prohibition, and that against foreigners becoming ministers of any religion, disappeared after the reform. Ministers continue to be prohibited from conducting proselytizing activities in favor of or against a political candidate, party, or association, or from opposing the laws of the country or its institutions, during public meetings, religious acts, or acts of religious propaganda. Moreover, Article 268 of the Federal Electoral Code also states that the Federal Electoral Institute will inform the Department of the Interior about instances in which ministers "try to persuade the electorate to vote in favor of or against any political candidate or party, or to abstain from voting, inside places of public worship or at any other venue." (Mexico, Instituto Federal Electoral 1987).

In sum, Mexico in 2004 is a country with a deeply religious population; it is mostly Catholic and particularly devoted to the Virgin of Guadalupe, but with a strong Evangelical presence and a growing religious plurality. Mexico also has deeply rooted laicism and an increasingly secularized society; its inhabitants emphasize more and more the importance of the separation of church and state, of the public and the private, Mexico is a country where freedom of conscience is painfully but persistently making headway (see Chapter 2 in this volume on the relation of religion to values that favor modernization).

The Evangelical presence is indicated by the fact that twelve years after the 1992 reform, there are roughly six thousand juridically recognized "religious associations" (religious associations achieved legal status in 1992), more than half of which (about 52 percent) are Protestant or Evangelical, whereas a little more than 47 percent belong to the Roman Catholic Church. Various other religious associations, ranging from the Church of Jesus Christ of the Latter-Day Saints (Mormons) to associations of Jews, Muslims, Hindus, Jehovah's Witnesses, Orthodox, Buddhists, and others, constitute the remaining 1 percent of associations. This panorama has contributed to enhancing the public presence and social activity of the various religious denominations, particularly minority cults.

In 2004, the topics of religion and of the relationship between state, churches, and religious associations are no longer taboo. The same holds true for politicians' religious ascription, which has produced widespread confusion in establishing the difference between the public and the private, the legal and the illegal, between what is socially accepted and what is politically condemned. In any case, the fact is that nowadays only a few are surprised or scandalized to hear that the president professes Catholicism, which does not mean that the people approve of attempts to mold public policies according to personal beliefs. In like manner, the fact that some governors or government officials (such as Pablo Salazar Mendiguchía, governor of Chiapas) are Protestant or Evangelical is no longer regarded with fear or concern. Furthermore, the coalition of the PAN (the right-wing, political party with Catholic affinity) with other opposition parties, including the left, led to the election of the governor of Chiapas in 2000. The fact that the PAN was backing a Protestant was proof of an increasingly secularized political environment.

Religion, Authoritarianism, and Democracy

Throughout the second half of the twentieth century, the Catholic bishops tried to contribute to the creation of a civic culture by fighting against abstaining from voting and by promoting responsible voting. Many bishops assumed (and continue to do so) that the secularization of the state was the result of the lack of participation of Catholics as such in the political life of the country. Both then and now, they attributed to that lack of participation the fact that a liberal, anti-clerical elite ruled the country, supposedly contradicting the wishes of the Catholic majority.

Throughout the slow democratization process of the country, symbolically triggered by the student revolt of 1968, the participation of lay Christians has been remarkable, as has been the case in most Latin American countries. In fact, these developments would push many lay Catholics to get involved in base communities, liberation theology movements, or even armed groups. For their part, clearly alluding to the repeated cases of electoral fraud committed by the then ruling party, the Mexican Episcopate, in its May 1968 Pastoral Letter on the "development and integration of the country" (Conferencia del Episcopado Mexicano 1968), maintained that "systems to discourage the free exercise of citizen life" abounded. The impact of this letter was so immediate that only a few months later, a congress that encompassed the main lay Catholic organizations of the country also called for creating "authentic, free, and operating unions" and declared that Catholics were entitled to participate actively in politics, "as Mexicans and as Christians" (Blancarte 1995a).

This democratizing drive would also affect the church itself because in the late sixties some of its members began to question its hierarchized ecclesiastical structures, the traditional Catholic social doctrine, and what some thought to be the Episcopate's lack of social commitment. The church was demanding, on the one hand, more freedom and democracy for the Mexican society. On the other hand, according to the Second Vatican Council teachings, the church was facing the demands of many of its members, priests and laymen alike, that urged it to "create free opinion forums," as well as to "democratize" or eliminate some ecclesiastical structures that were too rigid or authoritarian according to the Vatican II teachings (Vatican Council 2d 1962–1965). Progressive sectors of the church tried to organize themselves in associations such as Christians for Socialism (Christians por el socialismo) and Priests for the People (sacerdotes para el Pueblo), creating a more independent social movement inspired by the Gospel but not under ecclesiastical control. On the other hand, Catholic Action (Acción Católica), traditionally submissive to the hierarchy, continued to operate under "disciplined participation in the hierarchical apostolate," and the Episcopate kept on insisting on the need for revitalizing the civic spirit of Catholics in order to accomplish constitutional reforms in matters of ecclesiastical affairs, while seeking to restore discipline and impose their hierarchical authority.

By the mid-1980s, the Episcopate as a whole, encouraged by Pope John Paul II and his visit to Mexico in 1979, began to insist not only on the responsible exercise of the right to vote, but also on defending the vote cast. In other words, instead of just overseeing the elections, the Episcopate started evaluating their validity. In the early 1990s, more than half of the nongovernmental organizations involved in electoral transparency and vigilance activities belonged or were in some way related to Christian groups.[1] During this decade leading to the downfall of the Institutional Revolutionary Party (PRI) regime, some bishops promoted "democracy workshops" in order to expand civic and democratic culture among the faithful, and fought the state's authoritarianism. The workshops consisted in most cases of practical teachings to avoid electoral fraud. Through nongovernmental and extra-ecclesiastical organizations, lay Catholics—rather than the bishops—adopted political positions that promoted political change based on general Christian concepts.

Nevertheless, the role of the Christian message displays its complexity in other issues, where the Catholic hierarchy has been more reluctant to grant freedoms. Positions on women's rights are often taken as the most important current indicator of church attitudes toward modernization. At any rate, in Mexico, the Catholic Church's permanent opposition to women's rights has influenced the debate on sexual and reproductive rights. In the 1970s, some of these rights were recognized, but only because they were linked to governmental plans targeting a reduction of the birthrate and to family planning campaigns. The General Law on Population, published in January 1974, and the creation of the National Population Council, generated distrust among the bishops, who criticized the planned-parenthood program because according to them it was at risk of "becoming a pro-contraception campaign." They accused the government of going along with what world powers dictated and with multinationals that manufactured contraceptives. The Episcopate went so far as to declare that demographic policies, contraceptive campaigns, and sterilization and abortion campaigns were all part of a "smoke screen that hides the maneuvers of dominant countries whose political and economic interests are unmasked in times of crisis" (Conferencia del Episcopado Mexicano 1975). It also opposed sexual education in the schools, which was being disseminated through new textbooks (Blancarte 1992). The Mexican Episcopate's opposition to sex education and reproductive rights became their leitmotif in the following decades, as the Vatican became increasingly conservative on these issues.

An example of the complex relationship between religion, freedoms, and rights is the case of the Chiapas. In the early 1990s, its governor attempted to modify the State Penal Code to include abortion as a legal family planning method. The immediate reaction of Samuel Ruiz, bishop of San Cristóbal de las Casas, was to argue that this initiative—if passed—would go against the rights of indigenous women, who would be forced by the government to interrupt their pregnancies in an attempt to achieve more stringent population control within indigenous communities. This created a conflict that led the Catholic Church to distance itself from the civil government and to limit its informal role in curbing the growing social agitation in indigenous communities. The result, in small part attributed to this process, was the indigenous uprising that broke out in Chiapas on January 1, 1994.

The Religious Panorama in the Year 2000

Numbers

In 1950, 98 percent of the Mexican population was Catholic. In the last three decades of the twentieth century, particularly between 1990 and 2000, the trend toward religious plurality increased. Although the number of Catholics has significantly increased, in relative terms such growth is smaller than that of other religions. The number of Mexican Catholics increased from 70 to 85 million (approximately 20 percent), whereas the number of Evangelicals or Protestants and members of the nonevangelical biblical churches (which include Mormons, Adventists, and Jehovah's Witnesses) increased from 3.5 to more than 6 million (roughly 70 percent) (INEGI 2000).

In Mexico, the current religious plurality includes more than just Catholics, Protestants, or Evangelicals. According to the 2000 census, 87.99 percent of Mexico's almost 100 million people profess Catholicism, whereas the remaining 12 percent profess another religion or none at all. The Protestant and Evangelical churches that represent 5.2 percent of the population constitute the most important group. The vast number of Evangelical churches includes a highly varied mosaic of denominations; on the other hand, that churches (somewhat arbitrarily) classified as Pentecostal or Neopentecostal[2] have become stronger, whereas the historical churches (Methodist, Baptist, Presbyterian, etc.) occupy a solid but smaller niche in the ambit of Protestantism. Agnostics and atheists constitute 3.52 percent of the people.

Three churches classified as nonevangelical biblical churches encompass 2.13 percent of individuals aged five and older; 58.85 percent of these are Jehovah's Witnesses. An additional 600,000 are Seventh-Day Adventists and 220,000 are Mormons. The Jewish community in Mexico includes 60,000 individuals, placing it among the largest Jewish communities in the Americas, just behind those in the United States and Argentina. Finally, the census also showed that around 300,000 individuals belong to other religions (Islam, Hare Krishna, Buddhism, Shintoism, New Age, etc.). By 2005, according to the Undersecretary of Population, Migration, and Religious Affairs, there were more than 6,200 religious associations registered in the Department of Interior (Secretaría de Gobernación) (Uttutra 2005).

In regard to geographical data, central Mexico had the highest number of Catholics in the country, continuing the tradition begun in the colonial period; the two most Catholic states are Guanajuato and Aguascalientes, followed by Jalisco, Querétaro, and Zacatecas, as well as Michoacán, where approximately 95 percent of the population is Catholic. In contrast, the states with the largest Protestant presence are those in the south-southeast, headed by Chiapas (with less than 64 percent of Catholics), Tabasco, and Campeche (both with almost 14 percent of Protestants), closely followed by Quintana Roo, Tamaulipas, Yucatán, Baja California, Oaxaca, Morelos, and Chihuahua (INEGI 2000).

Although Catholicism has survived the attacks of other religions relatively well, the others are gaining adherents in a consistent fashion. This may help to explain the efforts by the Catholic Church to canonize the Indian Juan Diego, who reportedly became the instrument of the miracle of the Virgin of Guadalupe; these efforts particularly targeted the indigenous groups and communities of the country. Juan Diego officially became a saint in July 2002 (*Milenio Diario* 2002).

Beliefs

According to recent surveys, roughly two-thirds of the population believes that the church has considerable or too much power; however, they trust more in the church than in other social or political institutions—the object of their trust being the institution, not the priests (Blancarte in press). Additionally, in Guadalajara, in the state of Jalisco, regarded as the center of Mexican Catholicism, two-thirds of the population believes that the family is the ideal institution to transmit values that are deemed fundamental in their children's upbringing, whereas only 7.2 percent regard the church as the prime source of education on values (de la Torre Castellanos 1999).

Some studies are beginning to shed light in matters of ascription and with regard to religious beliefs and their influence on the behavior of Mexicans. In a recent study, Gabriela Rodríguez (2002) states that the selective appropriation of urban symbols and lifestyles, of foreign and domestic cultural offers has led peasants to reflect upon religious regulations, while clinging to the need for the saints' indulgence and to magical-religious beliefs. In addition, Rodríguez writes that more than 53 percent of rural women use contraceptive methods, and 1 in 5 women have received an abortion. Young people said they trust more in physicians and teachers than in priests.

Furthermore, most Mexicans, Catholics and non-Catholics, believe that public management should be clearly separated from personal convictions. A recent survey indicates that 79 percent of Mexicans believe that abortion should be legal under any or certain circumstances, whereas only 21 percent of the interviewees consider that abortion should be illegal under any circumstance.

As to what group should be most heard by legislators when creating abortion-related laws, 48 percent of the interviewees answered that women should be the most heard; 29 percent, "the society"; 14 percent, the physicians; and only 7 percent, the church. Eighty percent of the informants said it was wrong that legislators passed laws according to their religious beliefs. Mexicans did not declare that they were against legislators professing the belief of their choosing, but stated that they should restrict their preferences to the ambit of their conscience, separate from their decisions, when designing a policy in public health. They stated that legislators should regard abortion as a public health issue, not a moral one.

Consequently, in twenty-first-century Mexico, the separation between the political and the religious spheres, and the distinction between public management and personal belief, are essential principles of social life. From this perspective, political institutions must guarantee freedom of conscience, a primordial element of religious freedom that has emerged as a fundamental value. This framework also helps to explain the increase in strength of the secular Mexican state, which has taken place in spite of government changes and the aggressive attacks of the religious sectarian right wing.

The Churches and the Secular State in the Current Political Transition

Vicente Fox's electoral victory on July 2, 2000, and his subsequent ascent to the presidency on December 1 of the same year, created expectations of change among some groups and fear among others with regard to religion because, for the first time in many decades, Mexico would have an avowedly Catholic president. The erroneous notion that President Fox wanted, and was able, to change the state–church relations was the basis of these expectations of change and fears about the new government's conservative inclinations. As time would later prove, nothing guaranteed the feasibility of that change, even if there had been a specific program to achieve it. For example, there was strong opposition to eliminating rape as a condition for abortion in Guanajuato when Vicente Fox was president-elect of Mexico which showed the limits of his mandate to change church–state relations.

On March 25, 2000, in the midst of the presidential campaign and the Catholic Church's Jubilee, the Mexican Episcopate published a pastoral letter entitled "From the encounter with Jesus Christ to solidarity with all" (Conferencia del Episcopado 2000). At this time, the public opinion interpreted this pastoral letter as an open endorsement of PAN presidential candidate Fox by most of the Episcopate, and as a sign of an implicit alliance between Fox and the Catholic hierarchy.

Candidate Vicente Fox contributed to this perception by sending a letter in May 2000 to religious authorities of various churches in which he presented a list of ten promises ranging from defending the right to life from the moment of conception until natural death (which meant a condemnation of abortion and euthanasia), to granting religious associations access to communication media ("Ofrece Fox a la Iglesia apertura apoyo total," 2000). Many of those promises were hard to keep because no political party had an absolute majority in the Congress elected on July 6, 2000. Nonetheless, Fox's "ten promises" were regarded by many as proof of the alliance between religious conservatism and followers of the PAN or (at least) between the Catholic Church and candidate Fox.

President Fox's appointment on December 2000 of Javier Moctezuma Barragán, who was a member of the PRI, to head the Sub-Secretariat of Religious Affairs (Sub-Secretaría de Asuntos Religiosos) helped to appease those who regarded the arrival of Fox as a threat to the secular state and the separation of state and church. Nevertheless, as time went by, some troubling signs would show that the government's impotence to change laws in matters of religion would translate into multiple endeavors to transform surreptitiously and through merely administrative means the policy on issues pertaining to the state–church separation. Examples of this abound: namely, the attempt to restitute nationalized property (the former Palace of Archbishopric) to the church; efforts to impose the Catholic Church's doctrinal vision on public policies; campaigns allegedly endorsed by the daughter of the president promoting sexual abstinence instead of sexual education; and the disruption of constitutional order by allowing major public servants to attend religious ceremonies in their official capacity.

The most evident example of this surreptitious strategy to alter Mexican state policy on religion was the attempt in 2003 to publish the regulations of the Law on Religious Associations and Public Worship, announced by the Sub-Secretaría de Asuntos Religiosos. The Fox administration, in view of the fact that it had not been able to change the aforementioned law, formulated another set of administrative regulations against the spirit in which the law was created, especially in matters regarding separation of political spheres and religion.

The law on Religious Associations and Public Worship declares, "Federal, state, and municipal authorities . . . will not attend in their official capacity any public religious act or activity." This law, which reflects a tradition that is almost a century and a half old, seeks to avoid confusing roles and to distinguish clearly between religious positions and beliefs held by officials, and their performance as public servants. This is what most Mexicans wish for and have voiced many times. Therefore, within the national context, this precept becomes critical to distinguish also between religious and political spheres, between state and churches. The Fox government tried to introduce the following text in the regulation: "An authority will attend in their official capacity any public religious act or activity when during the conduction of the said act or activity the authority performs any kind of juridical act, exercising to that end their legal attributions or faculties" (Secretaría de Gobernación 2003). In short, the inclusion of this paragraph would allow President Fox and his officials to attend religious ceremonies legally. This article evidently would have violated the spirit of the law, because it was seeking to eliminate the separation of official capacity and private acts. In the end, heavy criticism by civil society and political parties forced the vice-minister for Religious Affairs to endorse a regulation according to the law and the Constitution, respecting the separation of spheres. Thus, President Fox cannot go to mass in his capacity as president (for example, no mass to celebrate the beginning of his mandate), but can attend religious services as any other citizen.

The "New Relation": What Is Desirable and What Is Feasible

As president of Mexico, Vicente Fox had to distinguish between what he had wanted to do and what he could actually achieve. Yet, although in legal terms the results have so far been nil, the symbolic change, or the introduction of a conservative perspective into public administration, is not negligible. In addition to the impossibility of changing the juridical framework of the reforms established in 1992, and President Fox's ability to make only minor administrative changes that undoubtedly account for the nonexistence of a new relationship between churches and the current administration, other (perhaps weightier) causes were more important, namely:

1. *An incompatibility of the neoliberal economic model with the Catholic social doctrine.* The present federal government is ultimately a mix—possible but incompatible in the long term—of the neoliberal social scheme and the Christian social doctrine. Neither the Catholic Church nor any other religious association will endorse an economic model that broadens the gap between the rich and the poor and leads to social injustice. They will not support political measures that, solely based on economic gain, may well cause deeper social distress, including

unemployment, corruption, and violence. Therefore, in spite of the evident close-ness between the Catholic Episcopate and Vicente Fox, and the fondness many religious leaders have for this president, the churches have distanced themselves from the announced economic program.

2. *The secular nature of the state.* "Laicity," or the lay state, can be defined as *a social regime of coexistence whose political institutions are mainly legitimized by popular sovereignty and not [anymore] by religious elements* (Blancarte 2000). The Mexican lay or secular state has remained a central element of public life because it constitutes a tool the people seized to ensure respect for freedom of conscience, expression, belief, and worship. In that regard, the building of the lay or secular state is linked to the defense of civil liberties and rights inherent to religious freedom.

The most conservative groups have attacked the secular state by comparing it to an entity that promotes anti-religious or areligious ideologies. These attacks show little understanding not only of the raison d'être and function of the secular state in a democratic society, but also of its trajectory in the specific case of Mexico. The "new relation" between the Fox administration and the churches, delimited by the historical, legal, and social framework established by the 1857 and 1917 Constitu-tions, cannot ignore the secularity of the Mexican state.

3. *The secularization of society.* Secularization of modern societies can be mea-sured in several ways, one of which being the distance between the moral policies established by ecclesiastical institutions and the quotidian behavior of the faithful. The role of individual conscience has become larger; this allows differentiating between religious doctrine and individual behavior, regardless of church affilia-tion. Consequently, believers frequently oppose the opinions of their own reli-gious leaders. Many indicators point to the noticeable process of secularization of the Mexican society.

Religion and the Secular State in Twenty-first–Century Mexico

The great tragedy of the relationship between the Mexican state and the Catholic Church, which has had repercussions for all the churches and religions in the country, lies in the appalling lack of understanding of the role of the state's laicism. The inability of the Mexican Catholic Episcopate to understand the modern world trans-lates into a distorted conception of the secular world and the lay state. Evidently, perceiving the state as anti-religious (or rather, anti-clerical) is the result of nine-teenth-century struggles that imbued the state with anti-religious and anti-clerical tinges in Latin American countries, much to the Catholic Church's chagrin. Defin-ing laicist education as a "secular religion" that is also "imposed and intolerant" is the clearest evidence of episcopal intransigence, of how the prelates have not been able to accept the wishes of the Catholic majority. Under these circumstances, the likelihood of improving the Catholic Church–state relations, particularly in Mexi-can society, seems quite remote.

Religions are, in that regard, much more than institutional expressions of the churches. In Mexico, religion plays a central role in the lives of the people. Nonetheless, we cannot infer from this centrality that there is a connection between religious beliefs and sociopolitical behavior.

Furthermore, many Mexicans—parishioners and members of lay groups of different churches, often supported by the churches themselves—have contributed to democratizing the country and to expanding human rights. However, religious leaders and hierarchies have rarely endorsed these efforts. Nevertheless, the intrinsic internal plurality in the churches has always allowed the social commitment inspired by religious faith to express and strengthen itself. Hence, free conscience is acquiring a growing importance as a means to face any form of civil or ecclesiastical power, or their collusion to the detriment of freedoms in the country.

Based on the above, both civil and religious liberties in Mexico exist within the framework of triangular relations between the state, the churches, and the conscience of the people. On occasion, the churches have defended the conscience when attacked by the state. Nonetheless, in Mexico, it has been the secular state, painfully constructed throughout the course of many decades, that has defended free conscience by creating ample spaces for civil and religious liberties, hence its paradoxical centrality and importance as guarantor in the search for expanding rights and the multiple expressions of civic-religious liberties.

Notes

1. That was the case with the large conglomerate of organizations that formed Alianza Cívica in order to watch over the 1994 elections. Personal interviews were carried out during the 1994 electoral process by the author.

2. Pentecostal churches are those that seek the manifestation of the Holy Spirit for the renewal of the individual. The Holy Spirit manifests itself through ordinary (music, teachings) or extraordinary charismas (speaking in tongues, healing, or prophesy). These churches have deeply transformed Protestantism in Mexico and the world through a type of religiosity that places more emphasis on the emotional, thus establishing direct contact with various forms of popular religiosity.

References

Banamex. Forthcoming. *El factor religioso. Tercera encuesta nacional de valores.* México: Banamex.

Blancarte, Roberto. 1992. *Historia de la iglesia católica en México.* Fondo de Cultura Económica.

———. 1993. "Religion and Constitutional Change in Mexico, 1988–1992," *Social Compass, International Review of Sociology of Religion,* 40, no. 4. Sage Publications.

———. 1995a. *Religión, iglesias y democracia.* México: La Jornada Ediciones-Centro de Investigaciones Interdisciplinarias en Humanidades de la UNAM.

———. 1995b. "The 1992 Reforms of Mexican Law on Religion: Prospects of Changing State-Church Relations," Riordan Roett, ed., *The Challenge of Institutional Reform in Mexico.* Boulder London: Lynne Rienner.

———. 2000. *Laicidad y valores en un Estado democrático.* (Compiler) El Colegio de México-Secretaría de Gobernación.
———. 2002. "The politics of regulating religion in Mexico: The 1992 constitutional reforms in historical context," Derek H. Davis, ed., *Church-state relations and religious liberty in Mexico: Historical and contemporary perspectives.* Dawson Institute of Church-State Studies.
———. 2004. "Vicente Fox y el Estado Laico: El zorro en el gallinero." Samuel Schmidt (coord.), *Fox a mitad del camino.* Aguilar-Nuevo Siglo.
Conferencia del Episcopado Mexicano. 1968. "Carta pastoral del Episcopado Mexicano sobre el desarrollo e integración del país," *Christus* 33, no. 390.
———. 1975. "Declaración del Episcopado Mexicano sobre el respeto a la vida humana." *Documentación e Información Católica* 3, no. 38.
———. 2000. "Carta Pastoral. Del encuentro con Jesucristo a la solidaridad con todos; El encuentro con Jesucristo, camino de conversión, comunión, solidaridad y misión en México en el umbral del tercer milenio." CEM.
de la Torre Castellanos, Rene. 1999. "El catolicismo: ¿un templo en el que habitan muchos dioses?" In *Creyentes y creencias en Guadalajara,* comp. Patricia Fortuny Loret de Mola. México: CONACULTA, CIESAS, INAH.
INEGI (Instituto Nacional de Estadística Geografía e Informática). 2000. *Estados Unidos Mexicanos: XII censo general de población y vivienda 2000.* México: INEGI.
México, Instituto Federal Electoral. 1987. "Código federal de instituciones y procedimentos Electorales." Diario oficial de la Federación, 12 de Febrero.
Milenio Diario. 2002. "Juan Diego ya es santo" July 31.
"Ofrece Fox a la Iglesia apertura apoyo total," *Reforma,* May 7, 2000.
Rodríguez, Gabriela. 2002. "Jóvenes, cristianismo y cultura laica." Ponencia presentada en el seminario internacional los retos de la laicidad y la secularización en el mundo contemporáneo (Paper presented at the International Seminar on the Challenges of Laicism and Secularization in the Contemporary World). El Colegio de México, February 26–27, 2002.
Secretaría de Gobernación. 1992. Ley de asociaciones Religiosas y Culto Público. *Diario Oficial de la Federación, Órgano del Gobierno Constitucional de los Estados Unidos Mexicanos.*
———. 1997. Constitución Política de los Estados Unidos Mexicanos. México.
———. 2003. Proyecto de Reglamento de la Ley de Asociaciones Religiosas y Culto Público. México.
Urrutia, Alonso. 2005. "No se retiró el registro a la iglesia de la Santa Muerte por presiones." *La Jornada,* May 3. Available at www.jornada.unam.mx/imprimir.php?fecha+ 20050503&nota+045n3soc.php.
Vatican Council II. 1962. *Documentos Conciliaires, 1962–1965.*

24

FRANCISCO ZAPATA

Mexican Labor in a Context of Political, Social, and Economic Change, 1982–2002

From 1990 to 2000, Mexican confidence in labor unions decreased, but union membership—sometimes in "sweetheart" unions in which labor leaders and businessmen increase their benefits at the expense of workers—increased. Mexicans increasingly said that hard work, thrift, and competition were very important. They were dissatisfied with their household finances. The share of the population in the labor market increased from 25 percent in the 1960s to about 56 percent in 2003. Both a weak economy and the importance of fringe benefits and government social spending increasingly led Mexicans to value having and keeping a job more than its characteristics, ranging from good pay to good hours and personal development. Fewer Mexicans believed that it was fair to pay a more efficient worker more, and more Mexicans believed that workers should follow a superior's instructions only if they are right. There was much less support for political actions involving lawful demonstrations, unofficial strikes, and occupations of buildings and factories, which is important because labor has traditionally used political means to achieve its objectives.

These seemingly conflicting views reflect different tendencies in government policies impacting labor. Francisco Zapata writes that labor, business, and the state have interacted efficiently to control inflation, limit salary increases, and suppress strike activity, bypassing the legislature; therefore, political parties do not play the significant role they play in other national contexts on matters related to labor questions. The negotiations to join the North American Free Trade Agreement (NAFTA) decreased union control of hiring and work conditions, and payment systems were adjusted to reflect changes in productivity by replacing hourly wages by piece-rate systems in order to offer the best chance to companies in their struggle to be competitive in the international market.

During the Fox government, tenured employment, labor control of hiring and firing decisions, and the forty-eight hour workweek, among others, were modified and supplemented by direct assistance to the poor and jobless. Thus, in spite of change at the top, the corporatist structure was maintained. The labor leadership increasingly was identified with the official neoliberal policy and with the managers of the companies. This did not lead to a general discontent among rank-and-file workers at the shop-floor level, but reflected itself in their electoral behavior. In fact, the leadership of the Mexican Labor Confederation lost positions in its representation in the Chamber of Deputies in congressional elections in 1988 and thereafter. This decreased their leverage within the Institutional Revolutionary Party (PRI) and the government. However, there have not been any initiatives to establish collective bargaining between business and labor without state intervention.

Francisco Zapata summarizes the situation in early 2004, writing that protests take place almost on a daily basis in Mexico City and in other cities of the country, making manifest the fact that the social situation is not improving. In addition, if access to the decision-making process in regard to questions of labor is denied to labor organizations, and especially if the labor leadership continues to lose its central importance as a political mechanism in generating consensus among workers, as it has in the last few years, then expectations for a stable labor climate cannot be optimistic.

In the twenty years from 1982 to 2002, Mexico experienced frequent turbulence and underwent profound transformations in the political, social, and economic spheres. Defeat of the Partido Revolucionario Institucional (PRI, Institutional Revolutionary Party) in the 2000 presidential election; devaluations in 1982, 1987, and 1994; stock exchange debacles in 1987 and 1995; triple-digit inflation; adjustment policies; eruption of the Zapatista movement in Chiapas on January 1, 1994; political assassinations in 1994; trade liberalization from 1986 to 1993 (when NAFTA was signed); guerilla movements; privatization of state enterprises in the steel, telecommunications, and banking sectors; and changes in foreign investment regulations, to mention only a few factors, had strong impacts upon trade union action, collective bargaining negotiating capacity, and especially on the historic link between the labor movement and the political system. They were the result of economic factors, of the changing ideology and role of the state, and of the transformation of the political attitudes of Mexican citizens.

The Macroeconomic Scenario: 1982–2002

Economically speaking, the Mexican gross domestic product (GDP) experienced negative growth rates in 1982, 1983, 1986, 1995, and 2001, and very low positive rates in the other years (see Table 24.1). Inflation levels reached their peak in 1987. They tended to decrease after the signing of the Pacto de Solidaridad Económica on December 15, 1987, a pact committing business, labor, and the state to price and wage controls and other economic matters (exchange rate, reduction of subsidies, etc.) (Zapata 1999). Since 1996, inflation has decreased to single-digit levels, reaching a minimum of 3.8 percent in 2003. Open unemploy-

Table 24.1

Mexico: Annual Variations in Economic Indicators, 1980–2002 (in percent)

		GDP-	OUE							UCLF (1980
Year	GDP	PC	Men	Women	Total	I	MS	MES	PRO	= 100)
1980	8.3	4.9	3.8	5.9	4.7	29.8	−14.5	—	—	—
1981	7.9	5.5	3.5	5.6	4.2	28.7	− 6.3	—	—	—
1982	−0.6	−3.0	3.9	4.9	4.2	98.8	− 9.0	0.9	—	—
1983	−4.2	−6.5	5.3	7.6	6.1	101.6	−17.4	−21.0	—	—
1984	3.6	1.2	4.9	7.0	5.6	65.5	− 5.6	− 7.3	—	—
1985	2.6	0.2	3.6	5.8	4.4	57.7	− 1.7	1.5	106.7	68.3
1986	−3.8	−5.9	3.7	5.3	4.3	86.2	− 8.7	− 5.8	104.3	66.1
1987	1.8	−0.5	3.4	4.8	3.9	131.8	− 5.2	− 0.3	107.1	64.7
1988	1.3	−0.7	3.0	4.5	3.5	114.2	−11.9	0.6	110.9	60.3
1989	3.3	1.4	2.6	3.6	2.9	20.0	− 6.3	9.1	118.7	61.1
1990	4.5	2.5	2.6	3.0	2.7	26.7	−10.4	2.1	126.2	59.2
1991	3.6	1.7	2.5	2.9	2.7	22.7	− 4.6	6.7	133.4	59.1
1992	2.8	0.9	2.7	3.0	2.8	15.5	−10.2	9.7	141.3	60.3
1993	0.6	−1.2	3.2	3.7	3.4	9.8	− 6.4	7.9	134.1	58.2
1994	3.0	1.3	3.6	4.0	3.7	−11.0	−0.8	3.4	—	—
1995	−7.0	−8.6	6.1	6.5	6.2	52.6	−21.1	−12.3	—	—
1996	5.4	3.7	5.3	5.9	5.5	27.7	− 8.0	− 6.9	—	—
1997	6.8	5.1	3.5	4.2	3.7	15.7	− 1.3	0.0	—	—
1998	5.0	3.3	3.0	3.7	3.2	18.6	0.0	3.3	—	—
1999	3.7	2.1	2.4	2.6	2.5	12.3	− 0.3	1.4	—	—
2000	6.8	5.2	2.1	2.4	2.2	9.0	4.7	5.5	—	—
2001	−0.4	−1.9	2.4	2.5	2.4	4.4	0.0	4.1	—	—
2002	1.2	−0.3	2.7	2.8	2.8	5.4	0.8	2.7	—	—

Sources: Gross domestic product (GDP) and GDP per capita: Oficina Internacional del Trabajo (1994–2002); open unemployment (men, women and total): INEGI (1985–2002); minimum salaries and median salaries: Comisión Económica para América Latina, (all years since 1980). Productivity in manufacturing and unitary cost of labor force: INEGI (1994).

Note: Gross domestic product (GDP); gross domestic product per capita (GDP-PC); open unemployment by sex (OUE); inflation (I); minimum salaries (MS); median salaries, 1980–2002 (MES); productivity in manufacturing (PRO); unitary costs of labor force (UCLF).

ment fluctuated from a minimum of 2.5 percent to a maximum of 6.1 percent of the population aged twelve years and, on average, has remained around 3 percent all through this twenty-year period.

Minimum real salaries[1] decreased during the entire period; median real salaries decreased relatively less, but their level in 2002 was about less than half of what it had been twelve years before; contractual real salaries tended to follow the same pattern of median salaries. Data presented in Table 24.2 show that minimum sala-

Table 24.2

Minimum Day and Hourly Salaries in Mexican Pesos and U.S. Dollars, 1990–2002

Year	A Nominal minimum salary (pesos per day)	B Exchange rate minimum (monthly average closing) (Mexican pesos per dollar)	C Salary per day in U.S.$ B/A	D Minimum salary per hour in U.S.$ C/B
1990	9,138.89	2,948.20	3.099	0.3874
	(1–1/15–11)	(Nov. 1990)		
	10,786.58	2,959.40		0.4556
	(16–11/31–12)	(Dec. 1990)	3.644	
1991	10.786,58	3,073.10		0.4387
	(1–1/10–11)	(Nov. 1991)	3.509	
	12,084.02	3,071.00		0.4918
	(11–11/31–12)	(Dec. 1991)	3.934	0.4848
1992	12,084.02	3,115.40 (Dec)	3.878	0.5256
1993*	13.06*	3.1059 (Dec)	4.204	0.3279
1994	13.97	5.3250 (Dec)	2.623	
1995	14.95	6,8175		0.2741
	(1–1/31–3)	(March 1995)	2.192	
	16.74	7.6425		0.2737
	(1–4/3–12)	(Dec. 1995)	2.190	
	18.43	7.6425		0.3014
	(4–12/31–12)	(Dec. 1995)	2.411	
1996	18.43	7.9172		0.2909
	(1–1/31–12)	(Dec. 1995)	2.327	
	20.66			0.3286
	(1–4/2–12)	7.8509	2.628	
	24.30			0.3864
	(3–12/31–12)	7.8509	3.091	
1997	24.30	8.0681	3.011	0.3764
1998	27.99			
	(1–1/2–12)	9.9404	2.815	0.3519
	31.91			
	(3–12/31–12)	9.8650	3.234	0.4043
1999	31.91	9.5143	3.353	0.4192
2000	35.12	9.6098	3.654	0.4192
2001	37.57	9.0710	4.141	0.5177
2002	42.50	9.5000	4.470	0.5599
Averages			2.775	0.3909

Sources: (A) Comisión Nacional de los Salarios Mínimos (2001); México, 2001 and (B) Banco Nacional de México (2001). Exchange rate (monthly average closing: U.S.$1= $ Mexican pesos).

*As of January 1993, 1,000 Mexican pesos became one Mexican peso.

ries, which were equal to 52 cents an hour (in dollar terms) in 1993 decreased to 27 cents an hour at the end of 1995. Between 1996 and 2002, hourly minimum salaries increased from 30 cents an hour to 51 cents, a significant increase, which reflected the appreciation of the Mexican peso in relation to the U.S. dollar and a very modest increase in real pesos. It is important to mention that minimum salaries play a role with respect to median and contractual salary levels by fixing a floor in terms of which the others are negotiated.

Labor Market Dynamics

In the year 2000, the Mexican economically active population (EAP) (equal to the population between twelve and sixty-five years of age) reached 34 million people (from a total population of approximately 97 million people), of which 15.8 percent worked in the primary sector (agriculture and mining), 27.8 percent in the secondary sector (manufacturing, construction, electricity and water services), and 53.4 percent in the tertiary sector (communications, trade, personal services, and bureaucracy). This process of massive incorporation into the labor market was a function of survival strategies of families who needed to get more of their members into remunerated occupations to ensure a livelihood. This also meant that many people had to search for jobs, thus forgoing educational opportunities or retirement possibilities. This process resulted in a highly intensive use of manpower as reflected in an increase in the rate of participation[2] in the labor market, from around 25 percent in the 1960s to about 56 percent today, something that occurred all through the 1990s, in other Latin American countries for the same reasons. In some countries, such as Colombia, Panamá, Uruguay, and Venezuela, the rate is even higher, around 63 percent.

These data can be placed in the context of a drawn-out process of structural change that has been taking place in Mexico in the last decades. The evolution of the sectoral distribution of the employed population shows that, in addition to an increase in the rate of participation, changes occurred in the structure of nonagricultural employment where the growth of informal labor has to be underlined (see Table 24.3). Also, the proportion of self-employed people remained around 38–39 percent while people employed in the formal sector remained at 60 percent of total nonagricultural employment (see Table 24.4).

Therefore, short-, medium-, and long-term changes are to be considered if one is to understand that not all the labor impacts we will analyze here are related to the 1982 economic crisis. Events of the period 1982–2002 are also to be understood within a general process of social, economic, and political change where, obviously, one cannot dismiss what happened within the period but neither can one forget the framework in which it was happening (Centro de Estudios Sociológicos 1990).

**Impacts of Economic and Labor Market Changes
on the Labor Relations System**

Economic and labor market changes had an impact on the labor relations system. Important clauses from collective contracts that favored union control of work

Table 24.3

Mexico: Sectoral Distribution of the Economically Active Population, 1895–2000 (in percentages and percent decade variation)

Year	Agriculture	% Var.	Industry	% Var.	Services	% Var.	Total
1895	62.50	—	14.55	—	23.0	—	4,761,914
1900	61.93	–0.1	15.66	7.6	22.4	– 2.6	5,131,051
1910	67.15	8.4	15.05	–3.8	17.8	–20.5	5,337,889
1921	71.43	6.4	11.49	–23.7	17.0	– 4.5	4,883,561
1930	70.20	–1.8	14.39	25.2	15.4	– 9.4	5,165,803
1940	65.39	–7.0	12.73	–11.5	21.9	42.2	5,858,116
1950	58.32	–10.8	15.95	25.3	26.0	18.7	8,272,093
1960	54.21	–7.0	18.95	18.8	27.2	4.6	11,332,016
1970	39.39	–27.3	22.95	21.1	37.7	38.6	12,955,057
1980	25.98	–34.0	20.35	–11.3	53.7	42.4	21,941,693
1990	22.6	–13.0	27.9	37.1	46.1	–14.2	23,403,413
2000	15.8	–30.0	27.8	0.0	53.4	15.8	33,730,210

Sources: INEGI (1985, vol 1, 251); and INEGI (2000).

Table 24.4

Mexico: Structure of Nonagricultural Employment, 1990, 1995, 2000 (percent)

Sector	1990	1995	2000
Informal sector			
Self-employed	19.0	20.9	18.3
Domestic employment	4.6	5.3	3.7
Small companies	14.8	17.0	17.2
Total	38.4	43.2	39.2
Formal sector			
Public sector	19.4	16.1	14.5
Large private companies	42.3	40.7	46.4
Total	61.6	56.8	60.8

Source: Oficina Internacional del Trabajo (OIT) (2002).

processes and the operation of internal labor markets (in particular, in relation to hiring and layoff procedures) were deleted and clauses related to the flexibilization of labor conditions (Zapata 1998) were added with the purpose of adapting labor to the new economic conditions. These policies were applied together with an intensified anti-union offensive that was facilitated by the weakening of the bargaining position of unions, largely a result of the changes in the structure of the

EAP and of the weakening of corporatist arrangements, as we will see later on. In particular, when the NAFTA negotiations were under way (1991–1993), these pressures were exerted on both labor and business so that government officials in charge would have a consensus on which to rely.

This has put into question the historic trade-off that resulted from the political structure consolidated during the Lázaro Cárdenas presidency (1934–1940), where corporatist arrangements established a system of reciprocal advantages for the state and organized labor, trading political support and employment opportunities, free access to education and health facilities for unionized workers and peasants, and other benefits (Middlebrook 1995).

Starting in the 1940s and still operational today, these arrangements included, among other benefits, the creation of a national social security system (1940) that provided both free health and retirement benefits for salaried workers through institutions such as the Instituto Mexicano del Seguro Social (IMSS, Mexican Institute for Social Security) and the Instituto de Servicios y Seguridad Social de los Trabajadores al Servicio del Estado (ISSSTE, Social Security Institute for Workers at the Service of the State), created in 1960.

The corporatist arrangement also included political aspects that are fundamental to understanding the way in which the PRI ruled Mexico from 1920 to 2000. The PRI structure includes (to the present) three "sectors": the labor (*obrero*), peasant (*campesino*) and popular (*popular*) organizations, under an umbrella which, until the 2000 presidential elections, was very much managed by the president of the republic, who had the decisive voice in naming the party president and a direct influence on nominations for political positions at all levels of the public bureaucracy (federal, state, and sometimes even at the local, municipal level). This arrangement also implied privileges for the labor leadership, which obtained positions in the PRI congressional representation as members of the "labor sector." The same occurred for the leaders of the peasant organizations and for the middle class (or "popular sector") leaders of labor, peasants, and popular sector who enjoyed these privileges.

In the 1980s and 1990s, these arrangements also reinforced the policies of the Ministry of Labor that tended to impose salaries systematically below increases in the cost of living and repressed strikes. The ministry also instructed the Juntas Federales y Locales de Conciliación y Arbitraje (JFLCA, Federal and Local Conciliation Boards) to block union pressures in contract negotiations for salary increases above the limits fixed by the Secretaría de Hacienda y Crédito Público (SHCP, Ministry of the Treasury). At the same time, there were changes in the institutional framework, where the role of institutions such as the Comisión Nacional de Salarios Mínimos (CNSM, National Commission for Minimum Salaries) became associated with rubber-stamp measures rather than with their traditional function as places of bargaining the terms of the commitment of social and political actors to the corporatist arrangement (Murillo 2001).

Thus, to the present, labor, business, and the state have interacted efficiently to control inflation, limit salary increases, and suppress strike activity. The corporatist arrangement, defined in terms of state control over labor, peasant, and business interests, continues to bypass the legislature, and therefore political parties do not play the significant role they play in other national contexts on matters related to labor. Thus, in the Mexican political system, corporatist and representative democracy institutions have coexisted for long decades and, in large measure, continue to do so until the present.

In general terms, these arrangements were and are operational because the central actors of the corporatist system (state, labor, peasants, and business) have interacted with one another on the basis of a nonideologically motivated consensus. This consensus resulted from the existence of a very long history in which these actors performed other "plays" in other "circumstances," more functional than contemporary ones, and were able to confront the new challenges with these shared perspectives. The existence of this method of structuring political support provided support for the implementation of the economic strategy followed in the last twenty years, which, seen retrospectively, was quite effective.

Finally, in spite of the reduction in social expenses forced by the overall decrease in public spending, and in spite of the fact that this reduction has affected the operation of health services, education and scientific research, social security, and other institutions that chose survival strategies limiting their capacity to face the demands of a growing population (+3.3 percent increase of urban population between 1981 and 1987), the arrangement has continued to operate, even with a non-PRI president.

In the labor relations field, the transformation of labor markets, both external and internal, modified the way in which matters such as horizontal and vertical mobility, layoffs, subcontracting, and payment systems were managed. In all these matters, the common denominator was associated with higher degrees of control by the firm over decision making at the shop-floor level, geared toward achieving higher levels of flexibility to respond to changes in markets both national and international. For example, payment systems were adjusted to reflect changes in productivity. Hourly wages were discarded in favor of piece-rate systems.

All of the above considerations and facts are indicators both of persistence and changes within the institutional system of labor relations and of its interrelations with the political system. A series of processes, combined and linked to one another, developed in parallel: on the one hand, the reduction of public spending and of social expenses questioned the capacity of the state to continue to play its role in the political alliance with the labor movement, the peasantry, and the middle classes. It became harder to find the financial resources with which to face the increasing demands of those social groups in terms of subsidies for food consumption, public transportation, education, health, and, in more general terms, to facilitate social mobility. Indeed, one can argue that this package of nonmonetary benefits contributed to satisfy the needs of approximately half of the economically active population—that belonging to the so-called "formal sector" of the labor market. This explains why wages, in spite of continuing to decrease in real terms, were not the central preoccupation of Mexican workers, who preferred to focus their demands on the conservation of these nonmonetary benefits rather than on monetary matters. It also can contribute to explaining why Mexico has had difficulties in deregulating the social net at the same pace that other countries, such as Chile, did in the last two decades.

On the other hand, tensions at the level of the corporatist structure, within the political leadership, also resulted in divisions in the so-called "revolutionary family" between the renovators or modernizers and the traditional, patrimonialist leadership. It is within this context that one can analyze the role of unions in the present phase of the implementation of the modernizing strategy (from the year 2000 onward), which we will undertake now.

Corporatism in the Late 1990s: Continuity or Breakup?

To evaluate the present status of the relation between the modernizing project and trade union action, one can start with the hypothesis that unions, employers, and the state continue to interact within the corporatist structure that was established in the thirties, during the Cárdenas presidency (1934–1940), as we stated before. We will argue that recent political events, such as the success of Vicente Fox in winning the Mexican presidency in the year 2000, defeating the PRI candidate, did not substantially change the relations among these actors and with the state. Trade unions and business chambers continued to recognize their subordination to the state, now controlled by Fox and the PAN (Partido Acción Nacional, National Action Party), and at the same time contributed to the implementation of its objectives.

From this point of view, neither the profound economic crisis of 1994–1995 nor Fox's success modified the structures of interaction among these actors, especially because, in the latter case, it was not accompanied by a PAN majority in the Chamber of Deputies. Those institutions where these players interact face to face, such as the CNSM, the IMSS, or the ISSSTE, as well as those organizations that represent labor and business, reveal the static nature of those relations and the rhetorical character of much of what is said and done.

A good example of this situation has been the debate concerning reform of the Ley Federal del Trabajo (LFT, Federal Labor Law) (Loyzaga 2002),[3] where, in spite of the fact that many good intentions of reform were expressed so as to make it compatible with the new economic model, nothing substantial has happened given the political costs that those reforms would imply for any Mexican president. Since 2000, then, labor reform continues to be stalemated in spite of the efforts by the Ministry of Labor to move it forward.

In the Fox government, this can be explained by the commitments that the new administration established with the corporatist labor leadership shortly before Fox was inaugurated on December 1, 2000. These commitments closed the door on the implementation of the principal elements of labor reform, such as (a) flexibilization of labor contracts (establishing short-term work contracts and part-time jobs),

(b) establishing of unilateral decision-making procedures by managers on hiring and firing decisions, (c) decreeing secret balloting for union executive committees, and last but not least, (d) maintaining the privileges of the Ministry of Labor to deny or grant legal registration to unions.

Thus, the new president confirmed his commitment to the institutions that administer corporatism, in spite of the economic restrictions to spending that derived from the 2001–2003 recession. Through this strategy, which implied maintaining spending levels for education, health, and other social priorities, some of the negative impacts of the adjustment and restructuring processes were corrected and became instrumental for labor peace and for the relative economic stability of Mexico. This response was similar to the strategy adopted in 1994 and 1995, when the corporatist institutions were able to cope with the intense turbulence that occurred in the country. Also, in spite of Fox's success, this did not mean that the PRI vote in municipal, state, and federal elections left the party without support.

On the contrary, notwithstanding political turbulence in 1994[4] and 2000, and the recent economic recession, the propensity of Mexican citizens to vote for the PRI in the legislative elections of 1994, 1997, 2000, and 2003 remained stable. Indeed, in the July 2003 legislative elections, the PRI increased its congressional representation in the Chamber of Deputies, both in absolute and relative terms, in relation to the 2000 election.

These measures point toward the existence of a consensus where the historic trade-off of the period 1940–1982 was reformulated in a way that some of the benefits that were dysfunctional to the new economic model—such as tenured employment, labor control of hiring and firing decisions, the forty-eight-hour workweek, among others—were modified while new ones, more associated with direct assistance to the poor and jobless, were included in the package to ensure cogency to the political alliance. This shows that the intervention of the Mexican state is being partially modified to be compatible with trade liberalization, privatization of state-owned companies and deregulation of labor relations. Thus, labor, business, and the state did not fundamentally change their traditional forms of interaction; this did not mean, however, that they refrained from making adjustments at the margin. Thus, in spite of change at the top, these actors were able to maintain the corporatist structure in operation.

All this means that the corporatist arrangement continues to play a fundamental role in the maintenance of the core elements of the political structure, while modifying its forms of operation in light of the change in the political adscription of the new leaders. Thus, the defeat of the PRI at the presidential level did not imply a defeat of the PRI as a political organization.

Challenges to the Labor Movement on the Shop Floor

In addition to the rearticulation of the historic link between the Mexican labor movement and the state, framed within the corporatist alliance, the labor movement had to face challenges on the shop floor that need to be addressed. Indeed, technological modernization, massive layoffs, and revision of collective contracts in sectors such as steel, telecommunications, and automobile production implied strong internal adjustments and flexibilization of labor procedures both between and within companies. In these sectors, the labor leadership was willing to accept drastic modifications to collective contracts, aligning itself more and more with the official neoliberal policy and with the managers of companies.

Surprisingly, this did not result in generalized discontent among rank-and-file workers at the shop-floor level, but it did reflect itself in their electoral behavior. In fact, the leadership of the Confederación de Trabajadores de México (CTM, Mexican Labor Confederation) lost positions in its representation in the Chamber of Deputies, especially at the national level, in the 1988, 1991, 1994, 1997, and 2000 congressional elections. This involved a decrease in the CTM's leverage within the PRI and the government.

Thus, the present status of the labor leadership is very ambiguous: while it is losing its capacity to deliver the working-class vote to the PRI, it nevertheless maintains access to the political system and has a privileged position with respect to the president of the republic, who continues to be the central element in the corporatist structure, at least in relation to the labor movement.

However, this does not mean that other political parties such as the Partido de la Revolución Democrática (PRD, Party of the Democratic Revolution) or the PAN succeeded in co-opting the labor leadership or in obtaining electoral support from the working classes: surprisingly, neither of these parties has a significant and stable labor following. Electoral results do not show a specific appeal of candidates from these political parties to the working classes.

The loss of political power on the part of unions was particularly clear in the case of strikes. Between 1982 and 2002 many strikes took place where the margin of maneuver that the labor movement enjoyed up to that moment was seriously undercut. Perhaps the workers that were affected first by the co-optation of labor leaders by the PRI and PAN were on the one hand, those at Fundidora de Hierro y Acero de Monterrey (Correa Villanueva 1986), where, in 1986, the government decided to declare the company bankrupt and thereby close it. On the other hand, a similar strategy was applied to restructure the national airline, AeroMéxico (Vasquez 1992), also in 1986, but here, instead of the company being closed, workers were rehired after the collective contract had been purged of clauses that worked against its competitiveness. Until 1987, these two cases were illustrative of the way in which the government used strikes to radically modify labor relations in both companies. Given the dramatic economic situation that the country was experiencing at that moment, workers could not face the radical "flexibilization of labor relations"[5] that the government implemented and that was associated with various mechanisms, located both inside and outside the factory.

After President Salinas took office on December 1, 1988, this strategy was applied to other companies such as the Cananea copper mine, the steel companies that were going to be privatized such as Siderúrglca Lázaro Cádenas-Lastruchas S.A. (SICARTSA) and Altos Hornos de México (AHMSA), and especially Teléfonos de México (TELMEX), the telecommunications monopoly. In different ways, the renegotiation of the terms of collective contracts was preceded or was followed by long strikes or conflicts that had to face either state or federal officials who intervened in the internal life of the respective unions by modifying union statutes, demoting uncooperative leaders, and repressing public meetings. The relatively high level of conflict derived from the profound changes that were being introduced into collective contracts. These changes included changes in clauses that had to do with the labor process, with internal labor markets, hours of work, overtime, and subsidies that companies gave to unions. SICARTSA and AHMSA plants, located in the states of Michoacán and Coahuila respectively, pointed toward the tensions that arose when the government searched for the restructuring of prevailing labor conditions without negotiation with the respective union locals (Davillé 1990; Martínez Aparicio 1992). Later, in 1990, beer-producing workers at the Cervecería Modelo plant in the Federal District struck as a consequence of violations to the collective contract, and in 1992, autoworkers at Ford Motor Company and Volkswagen also struck as a consequence of the establishment of unilateral flexibilization by corporations. One general characteristic of these strikes was that they started as a result of contract revisions that were judged to be detrimental to workers and union leaders, or because workers questioned the authority of their leaders to negotiate better salaries and conditions of work.

As has been shown by many analysts, the objective pursued by the government through the policies of the Ministry of Labor was to eliminate contractual clauses that maintained high levels of rigidity in the operation of factories, or to make strikes very costly by systematically refusing to discuss demands that were not compatible with macroeconomic policy. Clauses such as union control of hiring (closed shop) and immunity for labor leadership during the terms in office were deleted from contracts. At the same time, the ministry opted for a discretionary application of the Federal Labor Law in matters such as layoffs, which became easier to implement through the use of arbitrary indemnifications that were not calculated according to years of service as the law provides (instead, workers were given lump sums of indemnification), or by the repression of strikes, where both the local and federal conciliation boards tended to favor business over union interests.

For example, in the automobile sector (Montiel 2000; Von Bülow 1998), modifications took place in the amount and rhythm of work, in the horizontal and vertical mobility of workers, in the degree of unilateral intervention by managers in the supervision of work, and in several other aspects that regulate work at the shop-floor level. It is to be noted that in this process of flexibilization no new clauses related to the regulation of technological change were introduced, something that reveals that the type of flexibilization going on in Mexico was not related to policies that searched for productivity increases or the involvement of workers in the organization and production processes, as some governmental rhetoric suggested.

Also to be noted is that most changes had to do with the control of workers within the firm—especially with the terms of hiring temporary personnel, promotion procedures, and horizontal mobility—and involved decisions about the proportion of union and nonunion personnel within total employment. In most cases it was possible to see an increase of managerial rights in the factory. This went together with increases in supervisory personnel (nonunion) and changes in the statute concerning each type of personnel.

Also, in Petróleos Mexicanos (PEMEX), the state oil company: while in the seventies a significant portion of the technical personnel of the company was unionized, at the end of the eighties they were de-unionized and returned to the status of *personal de confianza* (managerial personnel). This change implied that PEMEX had recovered its authority over this critical mass of workers who, during the time they were a part of the national union, had been very militant in the defense of their demands (Novelo 1991; Loyola and Martínez 1994).

In the case of SICARTSA, privatized in 1991, the negotiation of the 1989 collective contract culminated in the strike mentioned above (August–September 1989), which was not successful in blocking changes in ten clauses referring to types of work, payment of salaries, work on holidays and compulsory rest, vacant jobs, voluntary retirement, and the administration of the resources of the company. In all these themes, the common denominator was the search for greater unilateral decision-making capability of management and the objective of making SICARTSA attractive for investors. In addition, the new contract stipulated the absolute freedom of the company to manage resources and install new equipment while it compelled the union to provide the workers that the company required. Last but not least, the failure of the strike was clear when the union was forced to accept the dismissal of 1,775 workers as well as the suppression of the same number of jobs in the company. Thus restructured, SICARTSA had no difficulty in finding bidders when it was put up for sale at the end of 1990.

Other cases of restructuring point to other changes that resulted from the flexibilization of collective contracts in relation to very concrete aspects of factory life. Some of these changes were the introduction of flexible hours of work, the decrease in the number of days of vacation, the flexibilization of shift work, the number of rest periods during working hours, the elimination of payments that the company made to social security organs on behalf of workers, and the elimination of clauses that had to do with preferential or voluntary retirement.

Finally, many privileges that had been enjoyed by unions and their leaders, such as donations (automobiles for example) or long-term absences from work for the members of executive committees, were restricted. The same thing happened to members of health and hygiene committees and with the money that usually was allotted to athletic activities.

This process reflects the deep modifications that were introduced in collective contracts to make working conditions less rigid so as to offer the best chance to companies in their struggle to be competitive in the international market.

Conclusion

On the basis of what has been said here, one can observe a continuing decrease of the historic leverage that the Mexican labor movement had within the political system and a deterioration of the power of local unions, where rank-and-file workers lost the influence they could command on shop-floor workers. These processes resulted in an increase of labor militancy at the Volkswagen-Puebla factory in July–August 1992, at the Ford-Cuautitlán and Ford Hermosillo plants in 1993–1994, as well as in other industrial plants.

Given the stagnation of the Mexican economy in the 1995–2002 period, this scenario has tended to spread. All sorts of protests take place on almost a daily basis in Mexico City and in other cities of the country, and all coincide in making manifest that the social situation is not improving. In addition, if access to the decision-making process is denied to labor organizations, and especially if the labor leadership continues to lose its central importance as a political mechanism in generating consensus among workers, as it has in the last few years, then expectations for a stable labor climate cannot be optimistic.

Also, if layoffs increase, if subcontracting becomes a general practice, if flexibilization of conditions of employment continues to be implemented, if salary levels are not linked to productivity, and if the trend of labor authorities to intervene in favor of business continues, then it is possible that the patience that both unions and workers have shown until now will diminish.

This situation is exacerbated because there have been no initiatives directed toward collective bargaining where business and labor interact without the intervention of the state and within the enterprise. On the contrary, the distance has tended to increase as the example of the maquiladora industry in the western northern border indicates: indeed, especially in those facilities located in cities such as Tijuana and Ciudad Juárez, workers do not even know there is a union that represents them. Still worse, workers do not know that there is a collective contract because unions are artificially created by spurious confederations and contracts are written by personnel managers in collusion with those labor leaders (Quintero 1992, 1998). The total absence of workers from union life and the union practices mentioned leads to an unprecedented situation: a labor movement without workers, something that seems to be the project of some managers and union leaders in the western northern border of Mexico. We should qualify this statement by saying that this is not the case in maquiladoras located in the eastern northern border cities such as Matamoros, where a more legitimate labor leadership exists. There, collective contracts reflect worker demands, and labor leaders such as Agapito González lead unions that practice very different strategies from the ones implemented in the western part of the border region.

At the end of this brief reflection, we can state that profound changes are taking place in the historic relationship between labor and the Mexican state. Both as a result of the internationalization of the national productive and financial apparatus and of tensions within the political alliance that succeeded in representing diverse social interests in the country, one can see a tough period ahead where neither the new economic model nor the modifications to the corporatist arrangement have a guaranteed future.

Notes

1. *Minimum salaries* are fixed every December by the Comisión Nacional de Salarios Mínimos (National Commission of Minimum Salaries), a tripartite institution composed of labor, business and state representatives. In Table 24.2, we show their nominal amount from 1990 to 2001, including increases that correspond to periods when inflation got out of hand and minimum salaries had to be readjusted several times within a single year. To show their dollar equivalent we calculated their amount through the use of the exchange rate for each value of the minimum salary. *Median salary* corresponds to the salary level obtained by more than 50 percent of the economically active population. *Contractual salaries* derive from collective bargaining agreements, gathered by the Mexican Association of Industrial Relations Executives, which indicates that workers subject to collective contracts have the highest levels of income in the country.

2. The *rate of participation* is equal to the ratio of the economically active population to the population aged twelve years and older: in 2002, it fluctuated around 56 percent.

3. The Ley Federal del Trabajo (Federal Labor Law) was passed in 1931 and regulates Article 123 of the 1917 Mexican Constitution. It was revised in 1970, but it did not experience fundamental modifications with respect to labor union rights such as organization, strikes, minimum salaries, and so forth.

4. One has to underline that the indigenous revolt in Chiapas of January 1994; the assassination of Luis Donaldo Colosio, PRI presidential candidate in March 1994; and the assassination of José Francisco Ruiz Massieu, secretary general of the PRI in September 1994, among other events, all contributed to the destabilization of the political system. In spite of it all, Ernesto Zedillo, the substitute candidate for Colosio, won the presidential elections in July 1994.

5. "Flexibilization of labor relations" is an umbrella expression that can be associated with decisions on hiring practices, payments systems, unilateral decision making by managers irrespective of union prerogatives, capacity to respond to changes in the market, and so on. All of its connotations point toward the objective of making the enterprise capable of confronting change in an efficient way.

References

Banco Nacional de México. 2001. *Exchange rate (monthly average closing: US$ 1= $ Mexican pesos)*. Available at www.banamex.com.mx. July.

Centro de Estudios Sociológicos. 1990. *México en el umbral del milenio*. México: El Colegio de México.

Comisión Económica para América Latina. 1980–2003. *Balance de la economía latinoamericana*. Santiago: CEPAL. Annual publications.

Comisión Nacional de los Salarios Mínimos. 2001. *Salarios mínimos 2001*. México.

Correa Villanueva, José Luis. 1986. "La liquidación de Fundidora Monterrey y la reconversión industrial," *Cuadernos Políticos* 47 (July–September).

Davillé, Selva. 1990. "Historia de la sección 271." In *Negociación y conflicto laboral en México*, ed. G. Bensusán and Samuel León. México: Fundación Friedrich Ebert y FLACSO-sede.

INEGI. 1985. *Estadísticas históricas de México.* Vol. I. México: Instituto Nacional de Estadística, Geografía e Informática.

————. 1985–2002. *Cuadernos de información oportuna.* Mexico: INEGI.

————. 1990. *XI Censo General de Población y Vivienda.* México: INEGI.

————. 1994. *Indicadores de la competitividad de la economía mexicana,* no. 5. México: INEGI.

————. 2000. *Perfil Socio-Demográfico, XII Censo General de Población y Vivienda, 2000.*

Loyola, Rafael, and Liliana Martínez. 1994. "Petróleos Mexicanos: La búsqueda de un nuevo modelo empresarial." *Estudios Sociológicos* 12, 35 (May–August).

Loyzaga, Octavio. 2002. *Neo-liberalismo y flexibilización de los derechos laborales.* México: Universidad Autónoma Metropolitana–Miguel Angel Porrúa Editores.

Martínez Aparicio, Jorge. 1992. "SICARTSA: De la reconversión a la modernización, 1986–1990." *El Cotidiano,* no. 45 (January–February) 1992.

Middlebrook, Kevin. 1995. *The Paradox of Revolution, Labor, the State and Authoritarianism in Mexico.* Baltimore, MD: Johns Hopkins University Press.

Montiel, Yolanda. 2000. *Un mundo de coches: Nuevas formas de organización del trabajo. Estudios de caso.* México: Centro de Investigaciones Superiores en Antropología Social (CIESAS).

Murillo, Victoria. 2001. *Labor Unions, Coalitions and Market Reforms in Latin America.* Cambridge: Cambridge University Press.

Novelo, Victoria. 1991. *La difícil democracia de los petroleros: Historia de un proyecto sindical.* México: Centro de Investigaciones Superiores en Antropología Social (CIESAS), Ediciones El Caballito.

Oficina Internacional del Trabajo (OIT). 1994–2002. *Panorama Laboral,* nos. 1–8. Lima, Peru.

Quintero, Cirila. 1992. *El sindicalismo en las maquiladoras tijuanenses.* México: Consejo para la Cultura y las Artes.

————. 1998. "Sindicalismo en las maquiladoras fronterizas. Balance y perspectivas." *Estudios Sociológicos* 16, no. 46 (January–April).

Vásquez, César. 1992. "La aviación: Una reconversión en los aires." *El Cotidiano,* no. 46 (March–April).

Von Bülow, Marisa. 1998. "Reestructuración productiva y estrategias sindicales. El caso de Ford-Cuautitlán (1987–1994)." In ¿*Flexibles y productivos? Estudios sobre flexibilidad laboral en México,* ed. Francisco Zapata. México: El Colegio de México.

Zapata, Francisco, ed. 1998. ¿*Flexibles y productivos? Estudios sobre flexibilidad laboral en México.* México: El Colegio de México.

————. 1999. "Trade Unions and the Corporatist System in Mexico." In *What Kind of Democracy? What Kind of Market? Latin America in the Age of Neoliberalism,* ed. Philip Oxhorn and Graciela Ducatenzeiler. University Park: Pennsylvania State University Press.

25

PIA M. ORRENIUS

Mexico-U.S. Migration

Economic Effects and Policy Impact

International migration is a continuing theme in Mexican history. In the early 1960s, a Mexican author predicted that in the future, blonds from the United States would cross the Rio Grande river to work in Mexico. His prediction was partly accurate: some gray haired Americans retire to Mexico, while large numbers of working-age Mexicans migrate to the United States as the two nations move from a free trade agreement for goods and services toward a common market with free movement of capital and labor. A de facto common market largely exists, mainly legally for the exchange of goods, services, and capital, but often illegally for the movement of labor.

Pia Orrenius writes that in 2003, there may have been 10 million Mexican-born residents in the United States. When they arrived, they typically had limited education and poor English skills, and clustered in low-wage jobs; they had at most a small adverse impact on U.S. wages. With assimilation, their skills and wages improved.

Mexico has lost more than 10 percent of its prime working-age labor force in the last few decades. It has benefited to the extent that emigrants help the families and communities that they leave behind, but it has been damaged to the extent that some communities die out when they lose their working-age population. In 2003, $13.3 billion was transferred by migrants in the United States to Mexico; 48 percent went to rural areas. These money transfers are the country's second source of income after oil exports.

U.S. attitudes toward immigration vary. State and local governments say that they lack funds to adequately provide health and education for (sometimes illegal) immigrants. There is fear of a dilution of U.S. culture, as well as a desire to reduce the use of illegal identification cards and of underground economic activity. The 1996 Immigrant Responsibility Act added Border Patrol agents, allowed the removal of illegal immigrants without a hearing or judicial review, and greatly expanded the definition of deportable crimes. Stricter border en-

forcement has contributed to a record number of migrant deaths along the U.S.– Mexico border.

Despite the controversy over illegal immigration, many U.S. employers want to hire Mexican workers. Consequently, a legalization program is being proposed as part of a new immigration policy. President Vicente Fox supports a guest worker arrangement—a temporary visa program whereby Mexican workers will be matched to U.S. jobs for a limited amount of time. Devoting funds to workplace enforcement and creating a way for employers to legally meet their need for low-skill workers are more viable long-term solutions than are current policies. Meanwhile, extending legal status to currently undocumented workers is the only practical solution to a complicated problem where alternative solutions such as mass deportations or pursuing the status quo do not really benefit anyone—immigrants or natives.

The U.S.–Mexico border is one of the few in the world where a highly industrialized nation directly borders a developing country. As a result, labor and capital markets in both countries have become increasingly interdependent, and no more so than in the last thirty years. The rise of Mexico–U.S. migration, the establishment of the maquiladora industry, and Mexico's entry into the World Trade Organization (WTO, formerly General Agreement on Tariffs and Trade or GATT) and NAFTA (North American Free Trade Agreement) have forged permanent economic links between the two countries.

It is interesting that, while the media often focus on problems in the binational relationship, trends in recent years have served the two economies and their citizens well. Mexico, home to a labor surplus and capital shortage relative to the United States, has seen an exodus of workers and an inflow of capital. The mid-1990s ushered in the first extended period of macroeconomic stability since the 1960s, with low levels of inflation, stable debt, and a strong peso. The electoral process saw its first party change in seventy years with the election of Vicente Fox in 2000.

The United States, meanwhile, has filled millions of primarily low-skilled jobs with immigrant workers from Mexico. The immigrant influx has revitalized inner cities and contributed to a boom in residential housing markets and the service industry. As a result of immigrant labor, U.S. natives have enjoyed lower prices on everything from food and child care to hotel rooms and new homes. During the 1990s boom, regions with a slow-growing native labor force, such as states in the western Midwest, New England, and mid and south Atlantic regions, depended on immigrant workers for sustained economic growth. Meanwhile, U.S. manufacturers and investors continue to benefit from locating production plants in low-cost Mexico.

While the flow of capital between the United States and Mexico is sizable and interesting in and of itself, it does not have nearly the economic, social, and political implications of the massive migration flows the two countries have experienced in the last two decades. The rest of this chapter will give a brief overview and recent history of Mexico–U.S. migration and U.S. policy responses; it will then discuss the economic effects on both home and host country. In concluding, policy alternatives such as an amnesty or guest worker program are assessed.

Overview of Mexico–U.S. Migration

In 2003, the total number of Mexican-born residents of the United States, including illegal immigrants, was between 10 and 11 million. Mexicans make up about 30 percent of all immigrants and 3.5 percent of the U.S. population as a whole. The large presence of Mexican immigrants in the U.S. population is impressive, but the rate of increase in that population is even more significant. In 1980, the Mexican foreign-born numbered only 2.2 million. The annual average net inflow of illegal immigrants from Mexico rose from about 200,000 in the 1980s to over 400,000 in the 1990s. Legal immigration from Mexico has also reached record levels. Between 1990 and 1999, 2.8 million green cards went to Mexicans who immigrated or adjusted their status; this compares to 1 million during the 1980s. Between 2000 and 2002, an additional 600,000 Mexicans have received legal permanent residency. Of course, since many Mexican immigrants arrive as undocumented immigrants and then legalize; adding illegal and legal immigration across time is often double counting.

Illegal immigration from Mexico is a fairly recent phenomenon. Up until the mid-1960s, with the exception of the Great Depression years, there were few restrictions on Mexico–U.S. migration. The nature of northward migration changed with the end of a binational guest worker program, the Bracero Program, in 1964, and the adoption of a family-based immigration policy in 1965. Once the Bracero Program was terminated, the legal avenue by which hundreds of thousands of Mexicans came to work temporarily in the United States was gone. It was replaced with an immigration policy not based on the U.S. economy's needs, but on the principle of family reunification for U.S. citizens and prior immigrants. The result was a rise in Mexican undocumented immigration. Between 1965 and 1980, the undocumented immigrant population rose from a few hundred thousand agricultural laborers to between 1 and 2 million largely urban workers. The problem worsened after 1977, when country-specific quotas limiting the number of legal immigrants into the United States were extended to the Western hemisphere, including Mexico.

Since then, the majority of Mexico–U.S. migration has been undocumented or "illegal." In a 2003 report, the U.S. Immigration and Naturalization Service (INS) estimated that 69 percent of illegal immigrants in the United States are from Mexico (INS 2003). This implies a 2003 population of Mexican undocumented immigrants of around 5.5 million. Other estimates range as high as 7 or 8 million.

The characteristics of this large population lie at the root of the controversy that surrounds Mexican immigration. Mexican immigrants tend to be near the bottom of the U.S. skill distribution and are disproportionately employed in low-wage jobs in the agriculture, construction, and service industries. Low levels of education and poor English skills are among the reasons why Mexican immigrants, at least initially, are clustered in low-wage jobs. However, research has also shown that the wages of immigrants grow faster than those of natives, so their situation improves considerably with time in the United States (Borjas 1994; Duleep and Regets 1997). Legal status and U.S. citizenship among immigrants are also linked to higher educational outcomes, incomes, and rates of home ownership.

The U.S. Policy Response to Rising Illegal Immigration from Mexico

The rise in immigration from Mexico came about despite the implementation of several U.S. policies to curb it. The first of these was a 1986 law intended to put an end to illegal immigration. The Immigration Reform and Control Act (IRCA) legalized over 2 million undocumented immigrants from Mexico through an amnesty program, instituted employer sanctions for businesses that hired undocumented workers, and increased funding for the Border Patrol. The law stipulated that employers verify a worker's ability to legally work in the United States upon hiring him or her, but instead of curbing the demand for undocumented workers, the law caused a booming market for fake documents such as fraudulent green cards and social security numbers. The fake documents allowed employers to comply with the law by "verifying the applicant could legally work," while ensuring continued job opportunities for undocumented immigrants.

The second policy response came in the early 1990s. While the legalization of millions of undocumented immigrants in 1987–1988 initially seemed to slow illegal immigration, migrant apprehensions along the U.S.–Mexico border began to rise steadily again after 1990. The amnesty program had removed legalized migrants from the typical inflows of illegal immigrants, making border apprehensions look low and IRCA appear successful in curbing illegal immigration. Ultimately though, the failure of IRCA to deter undocumented immigration led to a Border Patrol offensive consisting of a massive crackdown implemented in border cities and aimed at diverting migrants out of cities where they could hide, into the wilderness where they could be easily spotted and detained. To this end, the Border Patrol launched a series of offensives, starting with Operation Hold-the-Line in El Paso in 1993 and Gatekeeper in San Diego in 1994.

Current policies, while they have not notably slowed the pace of illegal immigration, have had many adverse effects. Stricter border enforcement has contributed to record number of migrant deaths along the U.S.–Mexico border (Cornelius 2001). Many of these deaths are due to exposure to extreme temperatures as migrants take circuitous routes through dangerous deserts and over mountains in order to get into the United States. A rising number of deaths are also due to abuse and carelessness at the hands of human smugglers who transport migrants in sealed rail cars and trucks or abandon them in the wild. Smuggling has flourished as the Border Patrol has increased both the personnel and the technology it uses to enforce the border.

A third policy response to increasing immigration—legal and otherwise—from Mexico and other countries, was a set of 1996 laws that included the Illegal Immigration Reform and Immigrant Responsibility Act (IIRIRA) and the Welfare Reform Act. IIRIRA was instrumental in the continued crackdown on illegal immigration. The law added Border Patrol agents, allowed the removal of certain illegal immigrants without a hearing or judicial review, and greatly expanded the definition of deportable crimes.

The passage of IIRIRA reflects the U.S. move toward limiting the rights of noncitizens. The Welfare Reform Act, also passed in 1996, similarly reflects this trend. This law made most legal immigrants ineligible for federal public assistance programs such as food stamps and Supplemental Security Income (illegal immigrants have always been ineligible for most government transfer programs although they have access to emergency medical services and public schools). These laws contributed to a sudden surge in the number of eligible immigrants applying for citizenship in the mid to late 1990s, reversing a long trend of declining citizenship rates among legal immigrants. More recently, legislation passed in the wake of the 9/11 terrorist attacks follows the trend toward restricting the rights of noncitizens. As these changes are implemented and divulged, the incentives among legal permanent residents to naturalize should only continue to grow stronger.

What Drives Mexico–U.S. Migration

Policy responses to date have not been successful in curbing illegal immigration from Mexico because deep-rooted economic and social factors drive this migration. Average wages in Mexico are about one-ninth of those in the United States. This sizable wage gap, combined with proximity to the United States and readily available jobs, has led many Mexicans to choose to migrate for work in the United States. Moreover, the turbulent pre-1996 Mexican economy periodically led to surges in out-migration as crisis years were characterized by devastating devaluations and high unemployment.

One debate that has been put to rest regarding Mexican immigrants is whether they immigrate in order to receive welfare benefits. The fact that Mexican immigrants have high labor force participation rates—significantly higher than comparable U.S. natives—and are typically ineligible for public assistance programs, reinforces the fact that the majority migrate to work. In fact, research using Mexican household survey data indicates that the expected value of U.S. welfare and medical services does not help explain immigration from Mexico (Massey and Espinosa 1997).

Family reunification also drives a substantial fraction of Mexican immigration as immigrants come to the United States to live with relatives. Surveys indicate that women and children have comprised an increasing proportion of the Mexican immigrant inflow in recent years. Many of these family members are migrating to join a head of household who migrated earlier for economic reasons.

Economic Effects of Migration on Mexico and the United States

While discussion typically focuses on immigration's economic impact on the United States, the impact of the out-migration of millions of Mexican workers and their families is felt in both home and host country. Mexico has lost over 10 percent of its prime working-age population to the U.S. labor market in just a few decades. Despite the fact that Mexican immigrants typically fall into the low end of the U.S. skill distribution, they are closer to the middle of the Mexican income distribution, meaning their absence translates into a loss of both human and physical capital. Nevertheless, the economic consequences of emigration at the source are positive in many cases, particularly when out-migration does not become too pervasive and migrants keep ties to their home communities. At very high rates of out-migration, communities lose their economic base along with their working-age populations, and can begin to decline or die out.

More often than not, migrants keep ties to their origins, and Mexican communities have prospered with U.S. migration. Money earned in the United States allows migrants to support families back home, to cushion income shocks, and to save and invest. Many migrants remit a substantial fraction of their wages, allowing for both a higher and more stable standard of living among relatives remaining in the home country. Remittances to Mexico surpassed $13 billion in 2003, with about 18 percent of all Mexican adults receiving funds remitted from the United States (Suro 2003). A portion of remittances are also used for investment purposes. Savings from a job abroad can be used to buy a house or start a business, helping immigrants and their families to overcome the incomplete capital markets that prevail in Mexico. One study estimates that while only about 6.5 percent of migrant remittances and savings go directly to productive ends, the indirect effect of remittances on investment in the local production of goods and services is much larger (Massey and Parrado 1994).

Extensive emigration has also had price and distribution effects. As workers leave, the supply of labor shifts inward, pushing Mexican wages up. This wage effect is what drives neoclassical economic models to predict that wages in different regions should equalize, after adjusting for amenities and cost-of-living differences, when labor is perfectly mobile. Although data suggest Mexican real wages are barely higher than they were in 1980, they are still higher than they would have been had there been no emigration. Also, since migrants are not randomly selected from the population but are self-selected, out-migration has distributional effects. Since the high and low ends of the income distribution do not typically migrate, the low end due to budget constraints and the high end because skill transferability is limited between the two countries, the Mexican income distribution has probably widened slightly as a result of mass out-migration (Chiquiar and Hanson 2003).

It is important to note that the economic effects of Mexico–U.S. migration depend critically on not only how many people migrate, but also on how long they stay abroad. Early Mexico–U.S. migration was characterized by its circularity and temporary nature, while present-day out-migration is of longer duration and often permanent. Return migration has declined as year-round employment has become more common, farm work less prevalent, border crossings more difficult, and spouses and children have joined the migration stream. As a result, migrants return less frequently than in the past.

Large-scale Mexico–U.S. migration has also had significant impact on the U.S. economy, particularly in the gateway states such as California, Texas, and Illinois, where Mexican immigrants have tended to settle. Economic theory dictates that, under standard assumptions, immigration results in lower wages for comparable native-born workers and prior immigrants. The magnitude of the decline in wages depends on the degree of substitution between immigrants and other workers. Because most Mexican immigrants are relatively unskilled, they are most substitutable for other low-skilled workers and hence have the largest impact on low-skilled natives and prior immigrants.

Despite theoretical predictions, however, researchers have found at most a small adverse effect of immigration on wages. There are several reasons why downward pressure on wages might be small. First of all, existing workers may respond to immigrant inflows by moving out of gateway labor markets, changing jobs, or going back to school to learn new skills. Second, producers respond to inflows of immigrant labor and lower wages by increasing production of goods that utilize that type of labor. This shifts out the demand for labor and pushes wages partly back up. Third, if immigrants and natives produce different goods, there should not be much of an adverse wage effect. This occurs if immigrants are complements to natives in production, instead of substitutes. Since many Mexican immigrants have not completed the equivalent of high school, do not speak English fluently, and are not legal residents, they are not substitutes for most American workers. Of course, over time, immigrants learn the language, obtain more skills, and acquire legal residency. Clearly, as immigrants assimilate, they become more substitutable for natives (Orrenius and Zavodny 2003).

The undocumented nature of much of Mexico–U.S. migration can have some additional labor market effects, although to date these appear to have been limited. First, unauthorized workers can be exploited by their employers, who may pay them at rates below the minimum wage, not pay them for overtime hours, or not pay them at all. This type of abuse has been limited in the United States for two important reasons: one, in order to encourage reporting of worksite abuses, authorities have not typically inquired about the immigration status of complainants; and two, job opportunities are typically plentiful so unhappy workers seldom last long in jobs where they are treated unfairly. Strong immigrant networks, by providing information and support to family members and friends, also help in situations like this.

Because there has been so much low-skilled immigration, there is concern that Mexican immigration is causing U.S. income inequality to rise. "Between-group" inequality, or differences in average earnings between age, experience, or education groups (such as between high school graduates and college graduates), began increasing in 1979 before leveling off during the mid-1990s. Immigration has likely contributed to this increase by lowering the wages of less-educated workers, but again, the effect appears to be small. The consensus among economists is that immigration accounts for about 10 percent of the increase in U.S. earnings inequality (Council of Economic Advisers 1997).

Concern about the fiscal impact of Mexican immigration is more warranted since low-skilled immigration imposes fiscal burdens on state and local governments, although less so at the federal level. For example, a major study sponsored by the National Research Council on the impacts of immigration concluded that the net fiscal impact of immigrants in California in 1994–1995 was about $1,178 per native-born household (Smith and Edmonston 1997). This was largely due to an increase in public education costs (mainly resulting from children born to immigrants) and because immigrants are more likely to be poorer than native-born households and therefore pay less in taxes while (legal) immigrants receive more in transfer payments, such as welfare. Immigrants also tend to use publicly provided health care since few low-paying jobs provide employer-paid benefits such as health insurance. In addition, the study concluded that immigrants from Latin America pose a larger fiscal burden than other groups, in part because of higher fertility rates.

Implications for Immigration Policy

The fact that undocumented immigration from Mexico has been growing for such a long period of time—over thirty years—suggests that policymakers have found it more costly to implement effective policy changes than to allow the status quo to continue. While there has been a relatively small negative impact on native workers, employers and immigrants and consumers have all largely benefited from Mexican immigration.

There are three main concerns, however, that suggest policy changes may be necessary. First, the fiscal burden of immigration has been increasing at a time when state and local governments are struggling to adequately finance public schools and health care providers. Second, there is increasing worry regarding the economic assimilation of large numbers of immigrants, particularly Hispanics who tend to have lower education levels than other color and ethnic groups. Third, the terrorist acts of 9/11 have prioritized national security. While Mexican immigrants are not typically seen as a threat to security, there is a clear need to control the borders, minimize the underground economy and limit the use of false identification cards. The Real ID Act, passed in early 2005, addresses some of these concerns by stipulating that states have to ensure an individual is legally present in the country before issuing any form of state identification, including a driver's license.

As a result of economic, fiscal, and national security concerns, a consensus is building that the United States needs to overhaul its immigration policies. Many U.S. lawmakers, including President George W. Bush, are calling for some form of legalization program as part of the new policy. Legalization would speed up assimilation and increase national security, although it would not do much to alleviate the fiscal burden some immigrants impose. Mexico is also pressing for policy changes in the United States. Early on, President Vicente Fox supported a guest worker arrangement—a temporary visa program in which Mexican workers would be matched to U.S. jobs for a limited amount of time. A temporary worker program is also central to President Bush's January 2004 proposal, although it would not be limited to Mexico. Bush suggests that where employers demonstrate they are unable to hire a U.S. worker, they should be able to hire a willing foreign worker.

Existing illegal immigrants would be eligible for the temporary worker program. These guest workers would have to work and return home again and, while they could apply for green cards in a normal way, the program would not provide the path to permanent residency. In contrast, another immigration proposal introduced in May 2005 by Senators McCain and Kennedy, would make guest workers —including formerly illegal immigrants—eligible for green cards.

Skeptics of immigration reform point out that, in 1986, IRCA was composed of both an amnesty and a small agricultural guest worker program—the H2A visa program. Despite these provisions, it is clear that IRCA failed in its primary goal to stop undocumented immigration. In 2003, there were at least 9 million undocumented immigrants present in the United States, most of them working. The key point, however, is that IRCA failed not because it implemented an amnesty and a guest worker program, but because it did not enforce another of its provisions, namely, employer sanctions.

Any credible reform has to rely on increased interior enforcement of immigration laws where employers have to verify an applicant's legal status before hiring the worker. This could be done by simply requiring that the worker's Social Security number be checked on a central government-run database. The government, in turn, would have to follow up by actually enforcing this law and punishing noncompliance.

Under a policy where work-based visas are provided and there is employment verification and worksite enforcement, the demand for illegal immigrant workers would be sharply reduced; there would be fewer illegal immigrants and more border enforcement could be devoted to terrorism and drug smuggling rather than illegal immigration. Emphasis on border enforcement has done little to reduce illegal crossings but has cost millions of dollars and hundreds of lives. Devoting funds to workplace enforcement and creating a way for employers to legally meet their need for low-skill workers are more viable long-term solutions than current policies. Meanwhile, extending legal status to currently undocumented workers is the only practical solution to a complicated problem in which alternative solutions such as mass deportations or pursuing the status quo do not really benefit anyone—immigrants or natives.

References

The views expressed in this chapter do not necessarily reflect those of the Federal Reserve Bank of Dallas or the Federal Reserve System.

Borjas, George J. 1994. "The Economics of Immigration." *Journal of Economic Literature* 32, no. 4 (December).

Chiquiar, Daniel, and Gordon Hanson. 2003. "International Migration, Self-Selection, and the Distribution of Wages: Evidence from Mexico and the United States." Mimeo.

Cornelius, Wayne A. 2001. "Death at the Border: Efficacy and Unintended Consequences of U.S. Immigration Control Policy." *Population and Development Review* 27, no. 4 (December).

Council of Economic Advisers. 1997. *Economic Report of the President.* Washington, DC: Government Printing Office.

Duleep, Harriet Orcutt and Mark C. Regets 1997. "Immigrant Entry Earnings and Human Capital Growth: Evidence from the 1960–1980 Censuses." *Research in Labor Economics* 16.

Immigration and Naturalization Service (INS). 2003. *Estimates of the Unauthorized Immigrant Population Residing in the United States: 1990 to 2000.* Washington, DC: Immigration and Naturalization Service.

Massey, Douglas S., and Kristin E. Espinosa. 1997. "What's Driving Mexico–U.S. Migration: A Theoretical, Empirical and Policy Analysis." *American Journal of Sociology* 102, 4 (January).

Massey, Douglas S., and Emilio Parrado. 1994. "Migradollars: The Remittances and Savings of Mexican Migrants to the U.S." *Population Research and Policy Review* 13, no. 1 (March).

Orrenius, Pia M., and Madeline Zavodny. 2003. "Does Immigration Affect Wages? A Look at Occupation-Level Evidence." Federal Reserve Bank of Dallas Working Paper 03–02.

Smith, James P., and Barry Edmonston. 1997. *The New Americans: Economic, Demographic, and Fiscal Effects of Immigration.* Washington, DC: National Academy Press.

Suro, Robert. 2003. *Remittance Senders and Receivers: Tracking the Transnational Channels.* Washington, DC: Pew Hispanic Center.

26

CONSUELO CASTRO

Understanding Mexican Philanthropy

Individual Mexicans increasingly participate in nongovernmental organizations that represent their interests in improving social conditions. In a nation where 7.1 percent of gross domestic product was spent on public order and security, Mexican businesses have sought to ameliorate these conditions and also to improve their image by including social awareness in their governance, marketing, and advertising. The media have held telethons to benefit the disabled, prizes were given for individual and corporate philanthropic activities, and networks of philanthropic groups were established.

A remarkable and imitated development was the suggestion in 1990 by businessmen in Chihuahua that the state government levy a tax on payrolls to create a social Trust Fund. This was done in 1994, and since 1996 more than $25 million has been given for projects in Chihuahuan communities. In 1994, a tax treaty with the United States allowed U.S. individuals and corporations to deduct their donations to Mexican tax-exempt organizations from the income that they earned in Mexico.

Corporate foundations sponsor education, research in science and technology, culture, and community development. The government encourages the creation and growth of philanthropy by provisions in the income tax law that authorize organizations to receive tax-deductible donations when they are dedicated to aiding the poor, the disabled, children, elderly, formal education, fine arts, environmental activities, and, starting in 2006, human rights. The organizations are required to supervise the use of funds. In some cases, state and federal governments provide economic resources, so that both direct spending and "tax expenditures"—in the sense of forgone tax receipts, which came to .0259 percent of gross domestic product (GDP) in 2002—are devoted to philanthropic causes.

These social causes are recognized as being in the public interest, with the consequence that the government would be required to develop them by authorizing incentives and inviting the nonprofit organizations to participate in public policies. Some wish the nonprofit sector to have a greater role in decision making, on the grounds that they have more contact with community and knowledge of its needs and problems.

The nonprofit sector in Mexico is increasing steadily. Nonprofit organizations not only increase in number but contribute to the construction of a solidly based society by promoting new forms of collaboration between the government and corporate sectors in order to search for solutions to the social problems that confront them.

The principal objective of this chapter is to summarize these advances and indicate some special features. We will discuss topics such as business initiatives, the creation of community foundations, the participation of the media, and the framework in which philanthropy develops in Mexico.

Today, nonprofit organizations are unquestionably important for the social development of Mexico. Despite the complexity of this topic, we will provide an overview that allows the reader to have a general idea of the development of Mexican philanthropy in recent years.

Size of the Nonprofit Sector

In this new century, the tendency toward an increasing number of nonprofit organizations incontrovertibly continues to increase. Proof of this is that, in 1996, only 2,364 organizations were registered in the Directory of Philanthropic Institutions of the Mexican Center of Philanthropy (CEMEFI) in all of Mexico, and in 2005, this directory had information about more than 9,500 organizations. It is interesting to point out that among these, 703 appeared under the category "Foundations." However, it must be explained that this title neither means that they have an endowment of their own to carry out their work, nor that they provide funds.

On the other hand, the Tax Administration Service (SAT) of the Finance Ministry publishes the list of organizations and trusts that have been authorized to receive tax-deductible donations that are indicated in the *Diario Oficial de la Federación*.[1] In 1995 this list included information about approximately 1,500 organizations; this quadrupled in number in 2002 to almost 6,000. Within this group, 67 percent (at least 4,000) organizations provided assistance. Organizations that provided economic resources to other organizations, according to the SAT, increased to 257, and those that aided public works increased to 103 organizations. Among those organizations that give grants, the recently created business and community foundations are outstanding.

Business Foundations

Business foundations have increased in Mexico as a result of a greater awareness of the social responsibility of business as part of their growth and permanence in the market.[2] In Mexico, businesses have contributed to philanthropy for many years, principally by providing financial resources to organizations. Recently, to make these actions more consistent, business foundations have been created.

Today, it is possible to observe how businesses in diverse branches of industry and commerce create foundations: in the construction industry, Fundación Apasco;

in telecommunications, Fundación Telmex; in the financial area there are foundations with a long history such as Fundación Bancomer and Fomento Cultural Banamex. Some multinational firms have replicated the plans and practices of their behavior in their country of origin: for example, Fundación Coca Cola created in 1997; Fundación Ronald McDonald, A.C. created in 2001, and Fundación Wal-Mart, created in 2003, among others.

Equally important, the media have created their own foundations, as is the case of the large television enterprises in Mexico: Fundación Televisa and Fundación TV Azteca use the facilities of their respective enterprises to make a broad sector of the Mexican population aware and directly involved in charitable works. These foundations organize media fundraising campaigns for different causes such as drug abuse, conservation of endangered species, and disabled persons.

Some of these business initiatives are undertaken jointly. For example, since 1966 Ford of Mexico together with its Distributors' Association created a nonprofit organization, Ford Civic Affairs Committee and Ford Mexican Distributors Association (Comité de Asuntos Cívicos de Ford y de la Asociación Mexicana de Distribuidores Ford, A.C.), mainly to help education. One of their accomplishments is that 198 schools were built and are maintained up to today. Another example is the Foundation of the Confederation of the Chambers of Industry (CONCAMIN, Fundación Concamin, A.C.), which acts for the businesses its organization represents in philanthropic actions.

An action without any precedent, not only in Mexico but also in many other nations, is the outstanding work of all of the industries in the state of Chihuahua. After a flood in Chihuahua (the capital city of the state of Chihuahua) that severely affected the region in 1990, business leaders made a proposal to the local government to levy state taxes on payrolls and create a Social Trust Fund of the Chihuahua Business Community. This initiative was approved by the Chihuahua State Congress in 1994 (Act 266/94 XI P.O.) and since then, a share of the payroll tax of nearly 29,000 corporations is oriented toward social objectives through the foundation of Chihuahuan Entrepreneurs (Fundación del Empresariado Chihuahuense, A.C), which is a vehicle of the trust fund. Since 1996, the foundation has granted more than 25 million dollars to projects in the Chihuahuan communities.[3]

Corporate foundations in Mexico originate in a wide variety of types of organizations; their philanthropic works also are diverse: education, research in science and technology, culture, and community development. It is hoped that that the trend of creating community business foundations will continue to increase.

Community Foundations

In order to avoid the dispersion of efforts, in Mexico, as in other nations, attempts are made to increase the impact of philanthropic activities by concentrating them in a defined geographic area. This gave rise to the process of the "community foundations" that have recently been created in Baja California Norte, Chihuahua,

Coahuila, Guanajuato, Morelos, Oaxaca, Puebla, Querétaro, Quintana Roo, Sonora, and Sinaloa. CEMEFI has aided both these and the business foundations since their creation, by means of diverse mechanisms. Community and business foundations are especially important because they are relatively new models of directing important financial resources to the community. All of these initiatives take place within a fiscal regime explained in the next section.

Regulation and Philanthropy

The fiscal regime governing "civil society" organizations is of great importance for their functioning and development, as fiscal regulation is a means of the government either stimulating or inhibiting an activity.[4]

One of the most important fiscal incentives for nonprofit organizations is the authorization to receive tax-deductible donations according to the Mexican Income Tax Law. Authorization is granted by the Taxation Administration Service of the Finance Ministry (SAT). Organizations dedicated to the following activities may obtain this authorization:[5]

- charitable activities such as attention to the poor, particularly the disabled, children, and the elderly;
- formal education recognized by the Ministry of Education;
- scientific and technological research registered at the National Council on Science and Technology (CONACYT);
- promotion of fine arts;
- environmental activities; and
- promotion of human rights (starting 2006).

The recently enacted Federal Law on Promotion of Activities of Civil Organizations has helped to promote changes such as the inclusion in the fiscal legislation of tax incentives to organizations such as these dedicated to human rights in order that they may be authorized to receive tax-deductible receipts in the near future, when it is hoped that the tax law itself will be changed. Until that time, human rights organizations still did not have tax incentives. Thus, there are some important activities that have been left off of this list of federal tax exemptions. One issue that deserves our special attention was the lack of incentives for organizations that promote "human rights." According to the Human Rights National Commission (CNDH) Directory, there are about 800 organizations identified under this category. No wonder that these organizations had a short existence, or that there are signs that their professionalization process was incipient to the point that some have not yet been legally incorporated.

Therefore, it was a challenge to persuade fiscal authorities of the benefits of giving incentives to these organizations; it was also important for the federal government to establish a fiscal regime that is consistent with its national and international stance of support of human rights.

Returning to tax-exempt organizations: they are required to include in their bylaws clauses stipulating that their objectives are social in nature, not geared to profit; that they do not distribute profits among their associate members; and that in case of dissolution, the organization's entire endowment will be transferred to other organizations with the same status or to governmental entities. It is also stipulated that charitable organizations may not intervene in election campaigns or be involved in propaganda activities or those aimed at influencing legislation, in accordance with Article 97 of the Income Tax Law. However, the publication of an analysis or research that is not designed to win adherents or technical assistance for a government agency that requests it is not considered to be influencing legislation.[6] There are three categories of organizations authorized to receive tax-deductible donations based on the Income Tax Law:

- Entities such as foundations, boards of trustees, and trusts that economically support other tax exempt organizations.[7]
- Entities that directly operate their own programs.[8]
- Entities that grant scholarships for studies in institutions that are officially recognized or validated by the Public Education Ministry, or if the studies take place abroad, are recognized by the National Council on Science and Technology (Consjo Nacional de Ciencia y Techología, CONACYT). The scholarships should be awarded through a competitive process open to the public in general.[9]

As mentioned in previous lines, the list of organizations that are newly authorized as tax exempt, as well as organizations whose tax-exempt status has been renewed, is published periodically in the *Diario Oficial de la Federación,* the official government gazette, and remains in effect for a year.

Organizations that are authorized to receive donations are subject to special tax requirements, the objective of which is that the organizations provide effective supervision of the use of funds. This is a device for accountability that is important not only for the government but also for society as a whole.

It is also important to mention that with the Income Tax Treaty entered into between Mexico and the United States in 1994, it is possible for U.S. citizens and corporations resident in the United States to deduct their donations to Mexican organizations with exempt status if they have income from Mexico. The treaty also facilitates the grant-making process for foundations to Mexican organizations according to the Internal Revenue Service procedures for American international grants.

Law of Promotion for Nonprofit Organizations

In order to officially consolidate the will of the state to support the nonprofit sector according to its present situation and needs, a bill called "Law of Promotion for

Nonprofit Organizations' Social Activities" has been promoted at the federal as well as state level during the past ten years by a group of civil society organizations.[10]

After having gone through the one-decade process of promoting the bill, at the federal level, the Congress finally approved the Law of Development of Activities of Civil Organizations. This law was enacted and published in the official journal on February 9, 2004.[11] According to the law, the social causes taken care of by civil society organizations, including human rights, community development, and civic education, among others, are to be recognized as being in the public interest and therefore with rights and obligations, and consequently the authorities would be required to develop them by means of authorizing incentives and establishing mechanisms for their participation in public policies.

This law establishes a federal registry for nonprofit organizations and an information system listing not only the nonprofit organizations' data but also with information on programs, subsidies, and all kind of incentives given by the governmental entities. The registry is expected to facilitate the Finance Ministry's actual requirements for certifying nonprofit organizations' activities in order to qualify for tax-exempt status.

The law also created an Inter-Ministry Commission with the purpose of coordinating, designing, and following up on the promotional actions of the federal government. It is composed by the Ministry of Social Development, the Ministry of Finance and Public Credit and the Ministry of Foreign Affairs. This commission was formally installed by a decree published in the *Diario Oficial de la Federación* on May 14, 2004.

On the other hand, in December 2004, a Consultative Council was also created in which nine nonprofit organizations, four academic, scientific, and cultural representatives and two members of the House of Representatives participate. This board is able to make suggestions to the Inter-Ministry Commission on issues regarding the registry and the promotion activities. We are confident that the new law will facilitate, in the near future, the implementation of new forms of collaboration between the government and the nonprofit sector. The access to mechanisms making the incentives and subsidies to nonprofit organizations public at the federal level certainly assures transparency and therefore strengthens civil society organizations.

The Media and Philanthropy

The media are important for their contributions to charitable causes, the use of their facilities through telethons and news campaigns to raise funds for charitable activities, and as a source of information about charitable activities by many organizations.

In recent years, the topic of philanthropy has come to occupy a greater space on radio, television, and in the press. Perhaps one of the most impressive examples of the relevance of the media's assistance to a social cause is the financial campaign carried out by the Teletón organization in its mission of aiding handicapped persons.[12] More than 428 media organizations joined in publicizing this campaign, which raised US$18,585,001 (equal to 207,408,620 pesos) in 2001, US$19,522,977 (217,876,247 pesos) in 2002, US$22,200,658 (247,759,351 pesos) in 2003, and US$33,256,235 (349,190,470 pesos) in 2005.[12] The amount raised was announced to the public daily by the media. This was useful not only as an indication of the economic importance of the sector, but also enhanced the accountability of these resources: during the campaign, results showing the number of people assisted at the rehabilitation centers as well as its costs were announced.

In 2002, CEMEFI identified at least 2,000 news items related to nonprofit organizations in general and to their activities, and in April 2003 alone reported having recorded US$5,428,172 (equal to 60,578,402 pesos) from different sources that appeared in the media.

This provided the novel result that the public was openly informed of these amounts. It should be mentioned that in this sense, corporations have actively incorporated social responsibility as part of their governance, marketing, and advertising, promoting the awareness of sponsored causes and frequently disclosing donations. Practices such as advertising that a percentage of the total price paid by the costumer will go to a nonprofit organization are more common: Danone, a yogurt company, for example, announces that ten Mexican cents of each product sold goes to an organization whose mission is devoted to helping cancer patients, The Friendship House (Casa de la Amistad, A.C.). Therefore, the publicizing of amounts that are donated can frequently provide accountability about the resources that are provided for social causes and in that sense perhaps help to prevent misappropriation of funds donated for social causes.

Visibility and Recognition of Philanthropy

In order to increase the visibility and development of philanthropy in Mexico, prizes are awarded in public recognition of individual and corporate philanthropic activities. These prizes include the "Recognition of Assistance to Others 2003," awarded by CEMEFI; the "Luis Elizondo Award" given by the Tecnológico de Monterrey; the "National Prize to a Volunteer 2003," given under the leadership of the Mexican Volunteers' Association (Asociación Mexicana de Voluntarios, AMEVAC); the "Sharing Prize," authorized by the Compartir Fundación Social; and the "First Reason of Being," by the Fundación Merced.

Professionalization

One hopes that the organizations in the philanthropic sector in Mexico have an efficient, effective, and careful administration in order to take care of the causes that each of them has promised to aid. There is an interest in advancing philanthropic works in a manner that becomes more professional. This fact has generated a demand for training that has translated into the creation of courses, seminars, and workshops that are beginning to be recognized by universities. In this area, the Universidad Tecnológica y de Estudios Superiores de Monterrey (ITESM) offers a virtual undergraduate degree program in which twenty campuses are simultaneously connected in different cities of Mexico and Latin America to receive the signal for the teleconferences (via a closed-circuit TV program).[14] Distance learning has also been used as an instrument by the Ministry of Social Development (Secretaría de Desarrollo Social, SEDESOL), which, using the Social Development Institute (Instituto de Desarrollo Social, INDESOL), has organized six teleconferences directed at civil society organizations.[15]

Networks

Just as a group of people does not necessarily form a team, a group of organizations does not comprise a sector. In order to achieve a solid nonprofit sector, it is necessary to have a joint vision of the sector that would allow the establishment of defined goals and objectives. It is therefore very important to create the necessary synergies by melding organizations with diverse points of view into networks. Some examples of networks are the University Emergency Network for Aid in Case of Natural Disasters (Red Universitaria de Emergencias para la Atención de Casos de Desastres Naturales), Network for Childhood and Adolescence (Red por la Infancia y la Adolescencia), Network for Sustainable Rural Development in Mexico (Red para el Desarrollo Rural Sustentable), and the National Network of Civil Organizations or "All Rights for All People" (Red Nacional de Organismos Civiles, "Todos los Derechos para Todos").

It is also important to mention the initiative of major business organizations. This network is called "The Alliance of Social Responsibility of Businesses in Mexico" (Alianza por la Responsabilidad Social Empresarial en México, AliaRSE), whose members include the Administration by Values (Administración por Valores, AVAL), whose title incorporates the double meaning of *valores* in Spanish, which may mean "market stocks" as well as "spiritual values"; the Confederation of Chambers of Industry of Mexico (Confederación de Cámaras Industriales de los Estados Unidos Mexicanos, CONCAMIN); the Business Coordinating Council (Consejo Coordinador Empresarial, CCE); the Mexican Business Employers Confederation (Confederación Patronal de la República Mexicana, COPARMEX); Social Union of Mexican Businessmen (Unión Social de Empresarios de México, USEM); Impulse (Impulsa); and the Mexican Center on Philantrhopy (Centro Mexicano para la Filantropía, CEMEFI).

Similarly, a network of business and other organizations is being created in the Western hemisphere under the name RedeAmerica, in which ten countries participate: Argentina, Bolivia, Brazil, Chile, Colombia, Ecuador, the United States, Mexico, Uruguay and Venezuela. We believe that using these networks will increase cooperation at various levels of society and create a bond that will facilitate broad participation to ensure greater impact of philanthropic activities.

Government and Philanthropy

During the nineties, federal and state governments entered into a dialogue with philanthropic organizations by the creation of councils and other programs. Various government ministries have invited the participation of nonprofit organizations, such as the Citizens' Advisory Council (Consejo Consultivo Ciudadano); the National Counsel for the Prevention and Control of AIDS (Consejo Nacional para la Prevención y Control del Síndrome de Inmunodeficiencia Adquirida, CONASIDA) of the Ministry of Health (Secretaría de Salud, SS); SEDESOL; and the National Council for Sustainable Development (Consejo Nacional para el Desarrollo Sustenable) of the Ministry of Environment and Natural Resources (Secretaría de Medio Ambiente y Recursos Naturales, SEMARNAT).

This has created a space for dialogue on citizens' demands and proposals that are brought to the government by civil society organizations.[16] Within the nonprofit sector, there is a current of opinion that would like these councils to have a greater decision-making than consultative role in the future because of the belief that nonprofit organizations have more contact with the community needs and problems and therefore more ideas on how to solve them. Notwithstanding, we believe that the participation of nonprofit organizations in the already existing governmental councils and programs up to now represent a step forward in regard to organizations' participation in creating public policy.

State and federal governments have also aided in the work of nonprofit organizations by providing economic resources. Depending on the case, these resources have increased or decreased. For example, the total budget for projects of the Mexican Institute for Youth (Instituto Mexicano de la Juventud, INJUVE) has decreased by US$1,030,465 million (equivalent to 11.5 million pesos) in 2001, to US$940,860 (equivalent to 10.5 million pesos) in 2002 and to US$492,831 (equivalent to 5.5 million pesos) in 2003.

Another example is the National System for the Development of Integral Family Life (DIF). In the Federal District, the DIF implemented a project called "From the Street to Life" to aid organizations whose purpose is the prevention of children living in the street and research into this topic. This project had a budget in 2002 of US$421,146 (equivalent to 4.7 million pesos) for 27 organizations. In 2003, the budget was US$358,422 (equivalent to 4 million pesos) to aid 22 organizations.[17]

In contrast, the National Institute for Social Development (INDESOL) has increased the amounts it gives to organizations under the concept of "social co-investment." In 2002, it gave almost US$13,440,860 (equivalent to 150 million pesos), which aided 765 projects, and in 2003 it aided 1,249 projects with a total of US$19,175,627 (equivalent to 214 million pesos).

Challenges for the Future and Conclusion

The principal objective of this chapter has been to provide a general overview of the current situation of the nonprofit sector in Mexico. The dynamic of the vertiginous growth this sector implies meeting challenges for the future. These challenges are related to the necessity of creating spaces for thought about and promotion of joint initiatives for a greater impact on diverse social projects that are undertaken, of creating mechanisms to include citizens in the resolution of social problems as well as the search for mechanisms that allow the sustainability of these organizations.

The philanthropy sector by itself does not replace the urgently needed social and economic policies that until now have not adequately addressed the inequalities in our nation and that clearly reflect that more than 70 million people currently live in poverty.[18] That is to say, the philanthropy sector does not answer the need to consolidate a democratic system that would guarantee citizens' rights, and even less the need to have economic models that lead not only to growth but also to truly sustainable development. The philanthropy sector, however, represents a sign of hope for development in Mexico.

Notes

1. The list of organizations that are authorized to receive tax-deductible donations is published in Anexo 14 of the "Federal Tax Rules, Except for those on Foreign Trade" (also called "Resolución Miscelánia Fiscal" [Miscellaneous Resolutions or Omnibus Tax Rules]).
2. See *CEMEFI Informa* (2003).
3. See the foundation's Web page: www.fechac.org.
4. Piñar Mañas, José Luis (2001, 635).
5. See Article 95 of the Income Tax Law (Nueva ley del impuesto sobre la renta).
6. See Article 97 of the Income Tax Law.
7. See Article 96 of the Income Tax Law.
8. See Article 97 of the Income Tax Law.
9. See Article 98 of the Income Tax Law.
10. The group of active organizations is integrated by Convergencia de Organismos Civiles por la Democracia, Foro de Apoyo Mutuo, Centro Mexicano para la Filantropía, and Fundación Miguel Alemán.
11. See Web pages: http://gaceta.cddhcu.gob.mx or http://www.cemefi.org.
12. See Web page: www.teleton.org.mx.
13. The amount was calculated at the exchange rate of $11.16 pesos per dollar according to the *Diario Oficial de la Federación* published December 10, 2003.
14. See Web page: www.ruv.itesm.mx.
15. See web page www.indesol.gob.mx/.hdesol/formacion.html
16. See Sarvide (2003, 18–21).
17. Programa "De la Calle a la Vida," *Informe de Resultados,* DIF, CEMEFI-THAIS, México, D.F., 2002.
18. Carbonell (2000, 68).

References

Carbonell, Miguel. 2000. "Contexto y alternativas del desarrollo social." *Desarrollo social: Modelos, tendencias y marco normativo.* México: Comisión de Desarrollo Social de la Cámara de Diputados.

CEMEFI. 2003a. *CEMEFI Informa.* México: CEMEFI (June–August).

———. 2003b. *Directorio de Instituciones Filantrópicas, 1996–2003.* México: Centro Mexicano para la Filantropía.

Diario Oficial de la Federación. 2002. "Nueva ley del impuesto sobre la renta" (January 1).

Piñar Mañas, José Luis, ed. 1997. *Las fundaciones en Iberoamérica.* Spain: McGraw-Hill.

———. 2001. *El tercer sector iberoamericano: Fundaciones, asociaciones y ONGs.* Spain: Tirant Lo Blanch.

Sarvide, Laura. 2003. *Relación entre gobierno y sociedad Civil.* México: Espiral.

27

ANA LANGER AND JENNIFER CATINO

The Health of Women in Mexico

Opportunities and Challenges

In this chapter,[1] Langer and Catino write that although Mexico counts on sound epidemiological surveillance systems and international conferences and recommendations that have called for improved health care, there is a continuing failure to bring the HIV/AIDS pandemic under control, while other sexually transmitted infections are emerging or reemerging in epidemic proportions. This is a result of a lack of access to affordable high-quality reproductive health services and contraceptives. This has been blamed on rich nations not fulfilling their financial commitments toward implementing the global health and social agendas.

In Mexico, progress has occurred despite the power of the Catholic Church, which has challenged family planning, access to safe and legal abortion services, and services for adolescent sexual and reproductive health.

As a result of conservative influence by President Bush's administration, and other groups in the United States, large United Nations–convened conferences have been replaced by smaller and less influential regional and country meetings. Focus on women's health has been subdivided into thematic blocks, which makes it more difficult to garner the support to improve it.

Health care reform in Mexico included decentralization, which had a negative impact on formerly effective singularly focused, centrally managed programs, such as family planning and HIV/AIDS prevention. The health care system in Mexico continues to show evidence of insufficient coverage, especially in rural areas, inequitable distribution, and inefficiency. To remedy some of these deficiencies, the government recently established the National Center for Gender Equity and Reproductive Health, and the Fox administration plans to ensure universal access to antiretrovirals and high-quality HIV/AIDS care for all Mexicans by 2006. There also has been a liberalization of laws regarding abortion and the inclusion of emergency contraception (e.g., the "morning after" pill) in the national norms so that public health and family planning clinics are now obliged to provide this method of contraception. There has been less success in regard to screening for cervical cancer because the women at higher risk for cervical cancer are older and no longer use the public health system for maternal and child health services. Moreover, frequent gender bias in the care of women for health includes later diagnosis and less effective treatment than that provided for men of cardiovascular conditions and some cancers (in particular, lung cancer). Attention to women's health requires attention throughout their life, not only during their reproductive years.

Mexican Women's Health in the Global Context

Women's health, including that of women in Mexico, has traditionally been conceptualized within the relatively narrow purview of reproduction and fertility regulation. While this focus has been beneficial in many ways, it has restricted the focus of women's health needs to their reproductive years and reproductive systems. A more inclusive definition that moves beyond a woman's reproductive functions to include other dimensions of health and social aspects of her life is long overdue. One such definition reads, "a woman's health is her total well-being, not determined solely by biological factors and reproduction, but also by the effects of poverty, nutrition, stress, work load and conditions, among other factors" (Koblinsky, Timyan, and Gay, eds., 1993, 33). The definition of women's health, while recognizing the reality of a woman's reproductive and nurturing functions, should include all aspects of her life and make legitimate demands for services that meet her needs and take into account her life stage and sociocultural status, among other influential factors (Koblinsky, Timyan, and Gay 1993).

The "life-cycle approach" to women's health anticipates and aims to meet a woman's needs from infancy through old age (Family Care International 2000). Factors such as poverty, malnutrition, and violence against girls and women begin to influence the health of females even before birth and across the entire lifespan. Discriminatory practices that occur in some cultures, such as aborting female fetuses or abandoning female infants, are some of the extreme examples of gender-based violence that effect girls during infancy and childhood.

Early and unplanned pregnancy, sexually transmitted infections, unsafe abortions, and complications related to pregnancy and malnutrition continue to plague many women in developing countries from puberty through menopause. Research from around the world has demonstrated that women bear a heavier health burden and have greater needs for health services as a result of their reproductive capacity and child-rearing responsibilities; women are known to spend more time in hospitals and clinics than men, particularly during the reproductive years (Fathalla online). However, some research has also shown that health services for poor women are often of low quality, which can sometimes add to and aggravate women's health problems rather than remedy them (Miller et al. 2002; WHO 2000). There is also evidence of frequent gender bias in the care of women for health problems other than those related to reproductive health; indeed, cardiovascular conditions and some cancers (for example, lung cancer) tend to be diagnosed and treated later and less effectively among women than men.

Because women's health status in many countries in the world, including Mexico, is a product of the disadvantaged conditions of their environment coupled with a greater demand for health services, there is an urgent need for holistic women's health services that effectively address gender-specific needs across the life cycle. Such an approach was legitimized and adopted by the international community at the International Conference on Population and Development, which took place in Cairo, Egypt, in 1994 and is discussed in greater detail below.

This chapter focuses on the shift toward a more integrated approach to women's health in Mexico, presenting some of the most important advances that have been made over the past ten years and the challenges that remain. As an introduction, we begin with some background about the international context of women's health in the twenty-first century and Mexico's positioning vis-à-vis women's health over the past decade.

The mid-1990s were watershed years for global women's sexual and reproductive health (SRH). The United Nations–sponsored International Conference on Population and Development (ICPD) held in Cairo in 1994 and the Fourth World Conference on Women held in Beijing in 1995 represented progressive culminations of a long series of international meetings and country and global activities around themes related to women's status and rights, gender equality and equity, and reproductive rights and health (United Nations 1995).

In Cairo, 179 country delegations reached an historic agreement that recognized a shift from the concept of population control through reaching demographic targets to the importance of meeting the holistic health and social needs of individual women and men, and comprehensive definitions of sexual and reproductive health and rights were endorsed by the international community.[2] The comprehensive twenty-year plan laid out in the International Conference on Population and Development Programme of Action (ICPD) asserts the interdependence of population and development and calls for the empowerment of women as both a matter of social justice and the key to improving global quality of life (United Nations 1995). The Cairo consensus states that by meeting people's needs for family planning and other SRH services, population goals will be met by choice and opportunity rather than coercion and control (Catino 1999).

The Beijing conference, convened the year after Cairo, played an important complementary role in the positioning of global women's health and helped elevate the cause of gender equality to the center of the global development agenda. It was the largest gathering of government and NGO representatives ever held, with 17,000 in attendance, including representatives of 189 governments. The conference unanimously adopted the Beijing Declaration and Platform for Action (Fourth World Conference on Women: Beijing Declaration and Platform for Action 1995), which stands as a milestone for the advancement of women in the twenty-first century.

Both of these conferences helped to unify the international community behind a set of common objectives and they concluded with concrete plans for the advancement of women everywhere, in all spheres of public and private life. Also significant is that the meetings were convened at the apex of an international financial boom, led by the United States.

There have been important review exercises to evaluate how effectively both the Cairo and Beijing agendas are being implemented around the world. Most notably, the activities that culminated in a five-year review of the International Conference on Population and Development in New York in 1999 revealed some evidence of positive change, but more obstacles than advances (Catino 1999). Examples of national and regional deficiencies include the failure to bring the HIV/AIDS pandemic under control, particularly in sub-Saharan Africa. Other sexually transmitted infections (STIs), such as human papilloma virus (HPV) and syphilis, were acknowledged as emerging or reemerging in epidemic proportions. Continued lack of access to contraceptives and affordable high-quality reproductive health services, particularly for adolescents, were recognized as other critical problems in most countries in the developing world. Fueling these issues was the collective failure of donors, mainly from the developed world, to meet their financial commitments toward implementing the global health and social agendas.

A five-year review of the influence of the Beijing Platform of Action was also undertaken at the 23rd Special Session of the UN General Assembly in 2000. While it was difficult to measure progress at the national and international levels, there was an 80 percent governmental response rate to questionnaires asking them to evaluate the status of women in their countries across sectors. Many countries reported that women had entered the labor force in unprecedented numbers, increasing the potential for their ability to participate in economic decision making at various levels, starting with the household. Reports also demonstrated how women, individually and collectively, had become major actors in the rise of civil society throughout the world, stimulating pressure for increased awareness of gender equality in all issues and demanding a role in national and global decision-making processes (United Nations Division for the Advancement of Women 2000).

Unlike some countries in Latin America and the Caribbean (LAC), such as Guatemala, Honduras, and Argentina, which have consistently opposed the progressive agendas for women's health and rights ratified in Cairo and Beijing, Mexico signed on to the agreements and was considered among the most progressive countries in the region. Progress occurred despite the political and social power of the Catholic Church, which has historically presented challenges to women's health issues considered morally controversial, such as family planning, access to safe and legal abortion services, and adolescent sexual and reproductive health.

An important challenge to both implementing and reviewing the Cairo and Beijing conferences at the international level has been the negative influence of conservative groups, often linked to the religious right, that use the review processes as opportunities to undo, undermine, and weaken the progressive gains that were made and the language used to describe them in the conference documents. As a result of this influence, ten years after Cairo and Beijing, large United Nations–convened meetings that gather the full range of stakeholders (governments, NGOs, health and population scientists, multilateral and other donors) have been replaced by smaller regional and country meetings, which inherently have a more limited impact. Additional references to the hampering effect of political conservatism on women's health in Mexico and in general follow below.

The Millennium Development Goals (MDGs), approved by the United Nations in 2000, followed the Cairo and Beijing resolutions, but they moved far beyond the more focused women's health and empowerment agendas. In many ways, these broad new development guidelines have superseded the importance of the Cairo and Beijing agendas for women's health and rights. The MDGs commit the international community to an expanded vision of social progress, one that promotes human development as the key to sustaining social and economic progress in all countries and recognizes the importance of creating global alliances for development (The World Bank Group 2000). The eight MDGs focus on: eradicating poverty; achieving universal primary education; promoting gender equity and women's empowerment; reducing child mortality; improving maternal health; combating HIV, malaria, and other diseases; ensuring environmental sustainability; and achieving global partnership for development.

Within these goals, the holistic focus on a life-cycle approach to women's health in general and to sexual and reproductive health in particular has been replaced by goals that subdivide women's health into separate thematic blocks: gender, maternal health, HIV; this subdivision makes it more difficult to assess the overall condition of women's health, as well as garner the support to improve it. The MDGs, however, have been commonly accepted as a framework for investing in and measuring development progress by most governments and development agencies around the world.

In addition to the global shift toward the MDGs, several other complex and challenging processes have contributed to the decreasing priority of women's health. Among the most important are those discussed immediately below.

Global Challenges Affecting the Sexual and Reproductive Health of Women in Mexico

Conservatism

A surge in political and social conservatism has been sweeping many regions in recent years. Most notable are the actions of the Bush administration in the United States, which have had a powerful negative influence internationally on attitudes toward and resources available for women's health and development. In a symbolic gesture on his first day in office, U.S. president George W. Bush reinstated the "global gag rule," which prohibits any organization that receives development aid from the U.S. government from providing any abortion-related information or services (IPPF/WHR 2001). The Bush administration has been characterized by its ideological social views and consistent series of political maneuvers that have weakened progressive social policies and laws and diverted funding away from the types of services and approaches promoted by the Cairo and Beijing conferences. The potential for similar retrograde actions exists in Mexico today, which is led by a political party renowned for its social conservatism. However, the setbacks in Mexico have not been as profound as expected at the beginning of the current Fox administration (described below).

International Attention and Financial Assistance

The U.S.-led prioritization of combating terrorism since the attacks on September 11, 2001, has created an obvious shift in international priorities and financial resources away from the realm of international development. U.S.–Mexico cross-border issues, for example, were dropped from a high spot on the U.S. political and economic priority list as a consequence of "the war on terror." The economic downturn in the wake of the attacks on the United States has also had a powerfully negative impact on public and private resources available for global women's health. These global phenomena have played into the massive failure of donor countries to meet their financial commitments in support of women's health programs and services. In addition, the traditionally more liberal donors from private (mainly U.S.) foundations have had their financial assets limited by the economic recession in the United States and have gone though exercises in geographic re-prioritization based on the global political and health situation. The combination is taking a hard toll on Mexico and other countries in Latin America and the Caribbean, which have been deemed by many international donors as "middle-income" (based on aggregate national statistics that do not illustrate the vast disparity of wealth within and between countries) and therefore ineligible for external financial assistance.

Globalization

Globalization is characterized as the technology-assisted process of "de-nationalization" of markets, policies, and legal systems, or the rise of a "global economy." The consequences of this political and economic restructuring on local economies, human welfare, and the environment are the subject of an open debate among international organizations, governmental institutions, and the academic community. Some view it as an inevitable and beneficial process, while others fear that it increases inequality within and between nations, threatens employment and living standards, and thwarts social progress. The potentially negative aspects of globalization have been directly associated with developing countries, which, as a whole, have not been able to keep up with the integrating markets of more developed countries.

Increasing financial, health, and social gaps within Mexico's population have a major negative impact on women's health. A classic example is the case of maternal mortality. Poor Mexican women are three to four times more likely to die from pregnancy-related causes than middle-income women because their general health is poor to begin with (malnutrition, other diseases present, heavy physical work burden) and they lack access to quality health services and skilled attendance during pregnancy, delivery, and the post-partum period (Comisión Nacional para el Desarrollo de los Pueblos Indígenas 2004). The link between poverty and maternal death is cyclical because the impact of a maternal death on the surviving children and family make it more likely that those disadvantaged children will experience the same deficient conditions that led to their mothers' deaths (Miller et al. 2003).

Health Sector Reform

Most countries in LAC are to a greater or lesser degree undertaking processes of health sector reform. In theory, health sector reform is intended to improve the health status of populations by promoting and enhancing access, equity, quality, sustainability, and efficiency in the delivery of health care services to the largest possible number of people. The priorities of women's health advocates theoretically resemble those of health sector reform in a variety of ways. For example, both groups advocate improved health status through equitable access to high-quality care, integrated approaches to primary health care, and decentralization of authority through participatory processes that involve the public in setting priorities on health care spending, service design, and delivery (Langer, Nigenda, and Catino 2000). However, key questions remain about the effects these movements are having on one another in practice.

Health sector reform processes have important implications for reproductive health and can represent both barriers and opportunities. Indeed, they offer the opportunity to reposition women's health within the gamut of health services and perhaps elevate it as a priority from both policy and financial perspectives. However, women's and reproductive health can just as easily fade from attention and may be considered less of a priority, especially through processes of decentralization that leave thematic and funding decisions in the hands of personnel at lower levels of the health system who may not be adequately informed to make them (Merrick 1999). In addition, health sector reform has in some cases had a negative impact on formerly effective "vertical programs" (singularly focused, centrally managed), such as family planning and HIV/AIDS, which have become less efficient through decentralization. The health care system in Mexico, in its present struggle with reform, continues to show evidence of insufficient coverage, especially in rural areas, as well as inequitable distribution and inefficiency.

Mexican Women's Health Over the Past Decade (1994–2004): Examples of Positive Change

In spite of this challenging environment, over the past ten years there have been some important improvements in the public programs in place to support women's health. In 1993, the Department of Reproductive Health of the federal Ministry of Health (Departamento de Salud Reproductiva, which is currently known as *Cento Nacional de Equidad, Género y Salud Reproductiva*, MOH, Secretaría de Salud, SSA) was created. Under this department, important advances were made in areas including integration of women's health services, increased access for adolescents to sexual and reproductive health information and services, promotion of positive male involvement in women's and family health, strong links with NGOs, and active multisectoral delegate participation in global conferences like those mentioned above.

When Vicente Fox, a representative of one of Mexico's more conservative political parties (the Partido Acción Nacional or PAN) was elected president in 2000, the power and influence of the most conservative political and social groups in Mexico increased substantially. With this political pressure, efforts have been made to reverse some of the progress made in Mexico following Cairo and Beijing. For example, there has been a severe cutback in the availability of SRH services for adolescents in Mexico in the past few years. However, Mexico's long history of consistently progressive population policies coupled with the strength of civil society and advocacy organizations has helped to offset the power and influence of political and religious ideologues.

More recently, other new government programs were formed, including the national Women and Health Program that was later subsumed into the larger National Center for Gender Equity and Reproductive Health. These institutions, together with Mexico's strong women's rights movement and nongovernmental advocacy groups, have helped bring about the positive changes described below.

Liberalized Abortion Laws in Mexico City

In LAC, more than 95 percent of induced abortions are performed illegally, often under unsafe conditions. Unsafe abortions occur at a higher rate in this region than in any other region in the world (Becker, García, and Larsen 2002). In Mexico, abortion laws vary by state, but every state's law permits abortion in some circumstances (Becker, García, and Larsen 2002). The most widely legal circumstance to obtain an abortion is when the pregnancy results from rape (González de León Aguirre, and Billings 2002). In 2000, there was an unprecedented liberalization of the abortion laws in Mexico City (spearheaded by members of the left-leaning Partido de la Revolución Démocratica [PRD], with mayoral power in Mexico City), which increased the number of conditions under which a woman can obtain a legal abortion. Before 2000, abortion in Mexico City was allowed in cases of rape or risk of pregnancy to the woman's life. Decriminalization reforms were put in place to also include fetal impairment and risk to the woman's health (Lamas and Bissell 2000). This major progressive shift was in part the result of the tireless and systematic work of women's groups and advocacy initiatives that mobilized citizens and worked closely with government officials. These same groups helped draw national attention to events related to the violation of reproductive rights, such as in the case of "Paulina," a young girl from Mexicali who was raped and then obstructed by moralizing local government and legal forces from obtaining the legal abortion to which she was entitled under both federal and state laws.

There has also been an increasing body of advocacy research conducted and published in Mexico to understand public opinion about abortion. For example, one study found that 54 percent of participants did not know the legal status of abortion in their state. Contrary to conventional wisdom in a country where 92 percent of people profess to be Catholic (Instituto Nacional de Estadística Geográfica e Informática 2000), the same study found that some 70–83 percent of Mexican study respondents supported legal abortions when pregnancies result from rape or endanger a woman's life or health (Becker, García, and Larsen 2002). In a series of Gallup polls conducted in Mexico, the majority of respondents stated that decisions about how to handle an unwanted pregnancy should be that of the woman or the couple (GIRE 2004).

Inclusion of Emergency Contraception in National Norms

Emergency contraception (EC) is a contraceptive method used to prevent pregnancy after unprotected intercourse. In Mexico as elsewhere, there exists considerable public confusion about the difference between emergency contraception and medical abortion, largely because of misinformation disseminated by opposition groups. Emergency contraception helps *prevent* pregnancy; medical abortion *terminates* pregnancy. In spite of progressive and consistent population policies and highly promoted family planning services firmly established in Mexico more than thirty years ago, EC had not been included in the official family planning guidelines until very recently (January 2004) due to governmental authorities' fear of negative reactions from anti-choice groups and the Catholic Church. NGOs had been advocating for its inclusion for more than seven years with no success. National normative inclusion of EC in Mexico followed extensive preparatory activities by organizations such as the Consortium for Emergency Contraception, the Population Council, and local civil society organizations in Mexico. Research and public health efforts including an evaluation of the acceptability of EC, elaboration of education and advocacy strategies for health personnel and clients, dissemination of information to the media, and inclusion of EC in medical and nursing school curricula have helped to increase the acceptance of and support for EC use in Mexico (International Medical Advisory Panel Statement on Emergency Contraception, IPPF Medical Bulletin 2004).

Inclusion of EC in the national norms means that public health and family planning clinics are now obligated to provide the method, and that public sector providers receive training on method provision. This boon for women's health did not come without criticism and backlash. As elsewhere in Latin America, conservative religious groups have posed legal and political obstacles to the availability and distribution of EC. However, the MOH approval provided an important signal of government support for the contraceptive method to the public and commercial sectors. In the past year, four brands of EC have been registered for sale at pharmacies in Mexico.

Universal Availability of Antiretrovirals for HIV/AIDS Patients

HIV prevalence in Mexico remains concentrated in high-risk behavior groups (sex workers, men who have sex with men, intravenous drug users) and relatively low overall (0.3 percent in adults). However, an estimated 150,000 of Mexicans are known to be living with HIV/AIDS (Rodríguez, Bravo-García, and Uribe Zúñiga 2003). Access to treatment and care, including antiretrovirals* (ARVs), has varied considerably across socioeconomic groups. In 1999, 55 percent of people known to be living with AIDS in Mexico were thought to have regular access to ARVs.

While ARVs have dramatically improved the health and lives of people living with HIV/AIDS (PLHA) in high-income countries, the cost and clinical requirements of drug provision have put them out of reach for most PLHA in low- and middle-income countries. Despite the known challenges, there has been a public health interest and commitment in Mexico to expand access to ARVs in resource-poor settings. Notable in the LAC region, Brazil has long been a champion of providing wide-scale access to ARVs, and representatives of Brazil's National AIDS Program claim that it has saved more in health care costs than it has spent on ARVs.

Mexican MOH services for the uninsured have not typically included ARV treatment. However, this issue has become a priority for the Fox administration, which plans to ensure universal access to ARVs and high-quality HIV/AIDS care for all Mexican PLHA by 2006 (Bautista et al. 2004). Significant increases have been made in the federal budget to cover the uninsured and provide free ARV therapies.

If treatment services become available on a universal scale, the results would be favorable for Mexican women's health. Women bear a unique HIV/AIDS transmission burden as a result of their reproductive role. Unlike any other vulnerable subpopulation, women can transmit HIV not only to their sexual partners, but also to the fetus during pregnancy and the newborn during delivery and/or through breastfeeding. In addition to the misery of HIV infection inflicted on women themselves, their illness and death also have devastating consequences on their families and communities. Due to the unique biological and social roles that women play in Mexico and elsewhere, all activities aimed at preventing and managing HIV/AIDS will have a positive impact on women themselves, as well as their children, families, and communities.

---

*The human immunodeficiency virus (HIV) belongs to a class of viruses called retroviruses. Antiretrovirals are drugs that work by interfering with the HIV life cycle. Antiretroviral drugs do not cure HIV and they do not prevent HIV transmission. When used in combination, these medications reduce the amount of virus in the blood and help to delay the progress of disease.

There are important ongoing challenges in this ambitious MOH commitment, however, including frequent shortages of ARVs, distribution difficulties at the national level, and compliance/adherence issues in patients undergoing drug therapy.

Improved Program for Detection and Treatment of Cervical Cancer

Cervical cancer is the second leading cause of death for Mexican women and the principal cause of death in women of reproductive age. In 1992, Mexico had the highest cervical cancer mortality rate in the world (Flores et al. 2003). Each year more than 4,000 Mexican women die from this disease and the current mortality rate is 18.2 per 100,000 women (Hernández-Ávila et al. 1998). Risk of cervical cancer increases with age; 74 percent of deaths occur between the ages of thirty and sixty-four (Flores 2003).

Despite improved epidemiological surveillance and detection, mortality rates in Mexican women have been fairly consistent, without large decreases over the past fifteen years. Studies have shown that the limited effectiveness of cervical cancer reduction strategies in Mexico is mainly due to factors associated with poor quality and coverage (Lazcano-Ponce et al. 1999). There are complex challenges in reaching women in rural and isolated areas who have little access to or tendency to use the health system. Cultural barriers to the use of formal health services, such as language and modesty issues, may also play an important role (Watkins et al. 2002). Furthermore, many efforts of the national program have been directed toward women of reproductive age in the context of other women's health services, such as family planning, when most of the highest-risk women are older and no longer use the health system for maternal and child health services.

Efforts to restructure and strengthen Mexico's national cervical cancer screening program have been in effect for the past several years. In 1996, cervical cancer screening was incorporated into more comprehensive women's health services, and in 1998, cervical cancer policies were modified to adhere to international guidelines and emphasize increased and improved screening. Facilities and technical capacity for screening and treatment have increased and improved, as have measures for quality control (e.g., how cervical smears are obtained and interpreted). Over the last few years, cervical cancer mortality rates have shown a decrease in Mexico. This trend is likely to become more important in ten to twenty years, when the improvements in early detection and treatment of cancer precursors have an impact on cervical cancer–associated morbidity and mortality in the mid- and long-term (Secretaría de Salud 2004).

Conclusion

Important efforts to improve Mexican women's health are undeniable. As illustrated in this chapter, over the past decade Mexico has responded consistently well to international women's health and rights mandates with an obvious growth in national governmental structures (in the form of various interrelated women's health programs) to help ensure future improvements. Mexico's active and influential civil society has been a constant and strong force in advocating for women's health and rights. Over time, women's groups and NGOs in Mexico have become better organized, increasingly supported, and have broadened their constituencies. Currently, these groups constitute a more united voice for positive change in women's health and work vigilantly with the public health sector and other actors toward this end. Mexico also counts on sound epidemiological surveillance systems, reliable and timely information, and higher-quality research data for decision making than many other countries in the region.

Despite these strengths, however, positive measurable results on women's health outcomes are still elusive in most areas, including the reduction of maternal mortality and the control of cervical cancer. Hence, while Mexico has made important strides both in comparison with other countries in LAC and its own women's health history, there is still a long way to go in ensuring that all Mexican women have access to high-quality integrated services that respond to their holistic health needs (including sexual and reproductive health) at all stages of life.

Notes

1. This is a revision of a chapter that appeared in the first edition of this book.

2. "Sexual and reproductive health" is defined as a state of complete physical, mental, and social well-being, and not merely the absence of disease or infirmity, in all physical and emotional matters related to sexuality, the reproductive system, and its functions and processes. People should be able to have a satisfying and safe sex life and have the capability to reproduce and the freedom to decide if, when, and how often to do so. Males and females have the right to be informed and to have access to safe, effective, affordable, legal, and acceptable methods of their choice for the regulation of fertility, as well as the right of access to health care for safe pregnancy and childbirth. Sexual and reproductive health care is defined as the constellation of methods, techniques, and services that contribute to reproductive health and well-being by preventing and solving sexual and reproductive health problems (adapted from Alcalá 1995).

References

Alcalá, M.J. 1995. "Commitments to Sexual and Reproductive Rights for All." *Family Care International,* New York.

Bautista, S. et al. 2004. *HIV/AIDS Care in Mexico in the Era of HAART.* Cuernavaca, Mexico: National Institute of Public Health.

Becker, D., S. García, and U. Larsen. 2002. "Knowledge and Opinions About Abortion Law Among Mexican Youth." *International Family Planning Perspectives* 28, no. 4.

Catino, J. 1999. *Meeting the Cairo Challenge: Progress in Sexual and Reproductive Health.* New York: Family Care International.

Comisión Nacional para el Desarrollo de los Pueblos Indígenas. 2004. *La situación de los pueblos indígenas: ¿Dónde estamos?* Mexico City. Available at www.cdi.gob.mx.

Family Care International. 2000. *Sexual and Reproductive Health Briefing Cards.* New York, NY.

Fathalla, M. 2004. *Health and Being a Woman: Issues in Reproductive Health.* United Nations. Available at www.un.org/womanwatch/daw/csw/issues.htm. September.

Flores, Y. 2003. "Improving Cervical Screening in México: Results from the Morelos HPV Study." *Salud pública de México* 45 (suplemento 3).

Fourth World Conference on Women: Beijing Declaration and Platform for Action. 1995. Available at www.un.org/womenwatch/daw/beijing/platform/plat1.htm.

FUNDAR, Centro de Análisis e Investigación. 2004. *Tendencias alarmantes en el gasto etiquetado para las mujeres.* Mexico City: FUNDAR.

GIRE. 2004. *Cifras sobre el aborto.* Mexico City: GIRE (Grupo de Información en Reproducción Elegida). Available at www.gire.org.mx.

González de León Aguirre, D., and D. Billings. 2002. *El aborto en México.* Mexico City: Ipas.

Hernández-Avila, M., E.C. Lazcano-Ponce, P. Alonzo-de Ruiz, and I. Romieu. 1998. "Evaluation of the Cervical Cancer Screening Program in Mexico: A Population-based Case-Control Study." *International Journal of Epidemiology* 27.

Instituto Nacional de Estadistíca Geográfica e Informática. 2000. Available at www.inegi.gob.mx/est/.

International Medical Advisory Panel Statement on Emergency Contraception. 2004. *IPPF Medical Bulletin* 38, no. 1. London: International Planned Parenthood Federation, London, March.

IPPF Western Hemisphere Region. 2001. *Free Choice Saves Lives Campaign.* Available at www.freechoicesaveslives.org.

Koblinsky, M., J. Timyan, and J. Gay. 1993. *The Health of Women: A Global Perspective.* Boulder, CO: Westview Press.

Lamas, M., and S. Bissell. 2000. "Abortion and Politics in Mexico: Context Is All." *Reproductive Health Matters* 8, no. 16 (November).

Langer, A., G. Nigenda, and J. Catino. 2000. "Health Sector Reform and Reproductive Health in Latin America and the Caribbean: Strengthening the Links." *Bulletin of the World Health Organization* 78, no. 5.

Lazcano-Ponce, E.C., S. Moss, P. Alonso de Ruiz, Castro J. Salieron, and Avila M. Hernández. 1999. "Cervical Cancer Screening in Developing Countries. Why Is It Ineffective? The Case of Mexico." *Archives of Medical Research* 30, no. 3 (May–June).

Merrick, T. 1999. "Delivering Reproductive Health Services in Health Reform Settings." Washington, DC: World Bank (unpublished document).

Miller S, Tejada A, Murgueytio P. et al. 2002. "Strategic Assessment of Reproductive Health in the Dominican Republic." Mimeo. Santo Domingo, Dominican Republic. February 15.

Miller, S., N. Sloan, B. Winikoff, A. Langer, and F. Fikree. 2003. "Where Is the "E" in MCH? The Need for an Evidence-based Approach in Safe Motherhood." *Journal of Midwifery and Women's Health* 48, no. 1.

Population and Development. 1995. Programme of Action Adopted at the International Conference on Population and Development, Cairo 5–13 September 1994. New York: United Nations, Department for Economic and Social Information and Policy Analysis.

Rodríguez, C.M., E. Bravo-García, and P. Uribe Zúñiga. 2003. *Dos décadas de la epidemia del SIDA en México.* Mexico City: Centro Nacional de la Prevención y Control del SIDA.

Secretaría de Salud, Dirección General de Evaluación de Desempeño. 2004. *Información para la rendición de cuentas.* Mexico.

Tendencias alarmantes en el gasto etiquetado para las mujeres. 2004. Mexico City: FUNDAR.

United Nations. 1995. *Programme of Action Adopted at the International Conference on Population and Development, Cairo, 5–13 September 1994.* New York: Department for Economic and Social Information and Policy Analysis, United Nations.

United Nations Division for the Advancement of Women, On-line reference: www.un.org/womenwatch/daw.

Watkins, M.M., C. Gabali, M. Winkleby, E. Gaona, and S. Lebaron. 2002. "Barriers to Cervical Cancer Screening in Rural Mexico." *International Journal of Gynecological Cancer* 12, no. 5 (September–October).

Women of South-East Asia: A Health Profile. 2002. WHO (World Health Organization), Geneva, Switzerland.

The World Bank Group. 2000. *Millennium Development Goals, 2000.* Available at www.developmentgoals.org.

28

FERNANDA SOMUANO

Nongovernmental Organizations and the Changing Structure of Mexican Politics

The Cases of Environmental and Human Rights Policy

In 2000, there were twice as many Mexican nongovernmental organizations (NGOs) as in 1994 because of the decline in importance of the traditional influence of labor unions and peasant and business groups as Mexico diversified. Mexican participation in nongovernmental groups other than political parties increased from 4.6 percent of adults in 1990 to 6.1 percent in 2000. Their participation in organizations for the environment, Third World issues, and human rights grew more rapidly than in other groups, while participation in political parties fell. Participation in cultural groups was strongest by the young, and that in church groups was strongest by the old.

The new nongovernmental organizations formed important networks among sectors such as human rights, environment protection, housing, community health, and in many cases, among social movements, grassroots economic-development support work, and alternative public policy at the local and national level.

Fernanda Somuano writes that environmental protection and human rights nongovernmental organizations are especially successful because only 15 percent of the NGOs related to the defense and protection of the environment did not have a relationship with any level of government in 1991. As well, the NGOs' presence in the Mexican Action Network Against Free Trade (Red Mexicana de Acción Frente al Libre Comercio, RMALC) facilitated environmental agreements among Mexico, Canada, and the United States.

Human rights NGOs emerged from 1977 to 1982 to defend the rights of political prisoners taken in Mexico's 1970s counterinsurgency campaigns. Major changes in attitude began in 1997 as a result of the Mexican government's wish to obtain an Economic Association, Political Cooperation Agreement with the European Union and obtain a general free trade agreement with it. The inclusion of the "democratic clause," which made explicit reference to democratic governance and human rights, was an essential part of the agreement. Mexican and international pressure by several NGOs forced the Mexican government to change from rejecting the democratic clause to accepting it. A few months later, Mexico joined the International Criminal Court, accepting its authority to provide surveillance of human rights and punish those who violated them.

It is not certain whether nongovernmental organizations represent the values of all Mexicans: members of NGOs in Mexico tend to be men with more than average resources and education. As a result, the views of NGOs in some cases may not be those of all citizens.

What has been the role of nongovernmental organizations (NGOs) in Mexico's political change? Have these organizations had real influence in the process of agenda setting? To what extent have they been successful in advancing their goals? What have their strategies been? The goal of this chapter is to analyze the impact of NGOs in policymaking in two sectors where these organizations have claimed that they are quite successful: environmental protection and human rights.[1] Moreover, I try to identify the determinants of this success.

Since the early 1980s the public sector in Latin America has undergone a process of redefinition as democratization occurred and economic adjustment was implemented. Along with these changes, there has been a boom of popular associations and NGOs in the region that are helping municipal and local governments with the implementation and even shaping of social policy and services (Reilly 1995; Clark 1991; Landim 1996). Moreover, besides the increase in number, these new NGOs are different from those that existed prior to the debt crisis of the 1980s. Previously, NGOs were charity-oriented, paternalistic, and apolitical. The new ones claim to be more participatory and politically oriented. New NGOs are now much more professional and have not only widened the political agenda of governments, but have also moved into portions of the informal space vacated by government and traditional political institutions.

In Mexico, as in other Latin American countries (Brazil, Costa Rica, Nicaragua, Panama) the first NGOs were closely linked to the Catholic Church, which directly or indirectly managed many welfare and educational institutions. By the 1950s and 1960s, the Church's Social Secretariat played a crucial role in founding NGOs that worked in the areas of revolving credit funds, popular education, food distribution, health, and urban problems. Nevertheless, it was not until the spread of liberation theology that these institutions mushroomed.[2] By the 1970s, many foundations and centers were set up to accompany and finance efforts at *concientización* (consciousness raising), developed as part of the progressive Church doctrine of the "preferential option for the poor." In the discourse of the time, the prevailing goal called for the poor to discover their oppression and find a path to liberation. NGOs appeared in communities in several different Mexican states such as Morelos, Veracruz, and Jalisco (Hernández and Fox 1995).

This "promotional" approach quickly showed its virtues and limitations. Many of the production-oriented projects failed. Economic projects were limited by the egalitarian approach of the promoters, who were very distrustful of any activity that led to a differentiation of classes, a condition presumed to interfere with raising consciousness on egalitarian issues. The extreme politicization of organizing work led to repeated cycles of desertion by the promoters themselves.

This approach was also limited by its emphasis on the formation of small nuclei, while most mainstream grassroots organizers stress mass mobilization. Many of these small groups were parish-based and depended on charismatic leaders. Some of the popular education promoters, secular as well as religious, were distrustful of the mainstream popular movements, perhaps fearing that an alliance could lead to a loss of influence over their community groups. At the same time, many of the key regional and national social movements had serious reservations about many of the NGOs.

It was not until much later—the early 1980s—that more secular, technical, and politically oriented professionals began to set up NGOs in large numbers. Since that date, NGOs have been making important advances at the sectoral level. In some cases, they have formed important networks among sectors (i.e., human rights, environment protection, housing, community health), and in many cases alliances have been among social movements, grassroots economic-development support work, and alternative public policy at the local and national levels (Lopezllera 1990).[3]

Recent Development of NGOs in Mexico

As can be seen in Figure 28.1, the number of NGOs[4] in Mexico increased substantially in a period of six years. In 2000 there were twice as many NGOs as in 1994. This increment is due to several causes. According to Leonardo Avritzer (2001), it occurs because of an important breakdown of the historical model of collective action—characterized by the great influence of syndicalism and its incorporation in the structure of the state through corporatism.

The economic crisis of 1983 and the Mexico City earthquake of 1985 contributed to this collapse, which was provoked by three significant elements: (1) urban social movements that sought the constitution of identities independent from the state; (2) an increase in the participation of the middle classes; and (3) the formation of a coordinated network of civic associations that modified the control of the relationship between state and political society.

Most NGOs in Mexico are issue-specific in focus, although many work in both urban and rural areas, and quite a few deal with several issues at once. In this study, I concentrate on two of the NGO sectors that have been considered as the

Figure 28.1   **Number of Registered NGOs, 1994–2000**

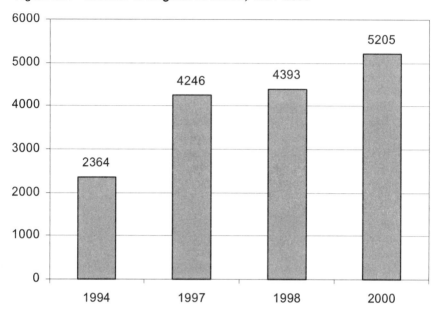

Source: Secretaría de Gobernación (2002), Encuesta Nacional de Cultura Política y Prácticas Ciudadanas 2001, Poder Ejecutivo Federal, Ciudad de México.

most influential in the process of policymaking in the context of a nation undergoing considerable change.

This chapter is organized as follows: I first describe the development of environmental NGOs during the last three decades, including their strategies and the level of success in the advancement of their goals. The second part analyzes the development and influence of human rights NGOs in the political agenda of the Mexican government during that same period. The last section provides some concluding remarks, identifying the factors that determine NGOs' impact on making policy or setting agendas.

Environmentalist NGOs and Networks

Most environmental NGOs are of relatively recent origin, although the Mexican ecological movement dates back to the late 1960s. In fact, according to a study carried out by Toledo and Velázquez (1995), 83 percent of the environmentalist NGOs were created between 1985 and 1994. The environmental organizations grew during this period. Examples of this growth are the anti-nuclear plant struggles in Pátzcuaro and Laguna Verde, the establishment of alliances with the Pact of Ecological Groups, and the development of environmental conflicts within peasants and indigenous people's groups in several parts of the country.

Through the 1970s and early 1980s, most environmental groups were urban, middle-class membership organizations rather than NGOs in the sense of their grassroots support. Even now, many are still weak and narrowly based, since they have been unable to form sufficiently broad or consolidated networks to represent the movement as a whole. Unlike other NGOs, environmentalist organizations tend to have important links with the governmental sector. According to Kürsinger-Wiemman and associates (1991), only 15 percent of the NGOs related to the defense and protection of the environment did not have a relationship with any level of government.

The participation and relationship of NGOs with the environmentalist movement has been diverse: some of them have led these fights, others have provided advice and support to community organizations, and some others have been mediators between the state and civil society.

The relationship between the state and environmentalist NGOs has been ambivalent. On the one hand, these organizations have constantly used an anti-state discourse (rejection of the state and its environmental policy); on the other, they have continuously looked for state support (many NGOs maintain important links with public officials, and they are often invited to participate in the public administration).

The impact that NGOs have had upon national and international environmental policies can be analyzed, for example, through their participation in the Global Forum in Rio de Janeiro in 1992, which provided an important and well-publicized opportunity to present the views of various representatives of civil society. As well, the NGOs' presence in the Mexican Action Network Against Free Trade (Red Mexicana de Acción Frente al Libre Comercio, RMALC) allowed the introduction of the environmental agreements among Mexico, Canada, and the United States. This last case may serve as an illustration of the main strategies used by these organizations in advancing their goals.

RMALC was formally constituted in April 1991. Although it is not an environmental network, one of RMALC's main wings includes environmental activists and their organizations, and one of its key concerns was the environmental impact on Mexico of the North American Free Trade Agreement (NAFTA).[5] RMALC's concern about NAFTA was based both on the negative experience of Canadian workers with the earlier U.S.–Canada free trade agreement, and on the fact that the Mexican government had already begun free trade negotiations with the United States. Many Mexican NGOs and social organizations saw the need to open debate in their country and to improve existing information channels with their North American counterparts.

Besides that, the stated goals of RMALC were: to call for national debate and public participation in the free trade agreement (FTA); to spread information among social organizations about economic integration and its potential costs; to open a permanent space for civil society to reflect on alternative development and to express its opinions and demands; to analyze the impact of free trade on specific sectors; and to define common strategies to influence public opinion and demand of government minimum guarantees that the FTA would not damage the rights or sovereignty of the Mexican people.[6]

In March 1992, three prominent Mexican intellectuals revealed a draft of the FTA (the "Dallas draft," named for the ministry-level trade negotiations in that city), which had been "filtered" to them through the Canada Action Network (CAN). RMALC brought the document to the Mexican Congress and to the attention of the public, analyzing its contents by early April and publicizing its reasons for judging NAFTA to be unfavorable to Mexico (Umlas 1996). The network's most important activity, outside of fomenting regular, informal contact among its Mexican members and its counterparts in the Americas, was its organization or co-sponsorship, with U.S. and Canadian networks, of tri-national and international conferences parallel to official or ministerial meetings. This activity is best understood as part of RMALC's set of strategies, as several of the conferences were planned and undertaken simultaneously and in the same city as official ministerial negotiations of NAFTA.

RMALC rejected NAFTA because of its lack of consultation with society and lack of public information, and for the damage it would do to Mexico's "capacity for self-determination," as well as to particular Mexican sectors. In the medium and long term, RMALC's strategy included the building of a "continental social pact" that was to extend the tri-national solidarity of networks formed around free trade to the rest of the continent. RMALC made extensive use of these ties in Canada, the United States, and Latin America to enable it both to secure documents and data and to help increase the circle of debate about free trade and development throughout the Americas.

With regard to relations with the Mexican government, RMALC also pursued a specific strategy that consisted in recognizing the need to seek a relationship with the state and to influence political parties. In May 1994, RMALC and several Mexican environmental NGOs and networks called a meeting to discuss the composition and functions of the National Consultative Committee, which was provided for in the environmental sidebar agreement of NAFTA, and which in theory would enable citizens to bring environmental complaints to the North American Commission on Environment Cooperation (NACEC), also created in 1994 as part of the environmental sidebar (Umlas 1996).

After the passage of NAFTA, in addition to its work with environmental organizations to influence NACEC proceedings, RMALC began to monitor NAFTA's effects on environment, labor, and other indicators, and continued to call for the treaty's renegotiation. Moreover, the network formed new goals since NAFTA became a reality. These goals included sharing lessons of RMALC's NAFTA experience with other networks in the region, building a more systematic tri-national movement, and strengthening efforts to modify international trade regulations.

Despite a decline in participation in the network since 1994 (because of the natural discouragement due to the passage of NAFTA); the scarcity of resources;

the lack of outreach in the Mexican provinces; and the network's inability, due to the lack of funds, to capitalize on its relations with groups abroad, RMALC provides interesting lessons. It has lasted well beyond the passage of NAFTA. It joined many diverse groups, sectors, and themes, and can be seen as an example of an important multisectoral space for debate, and a provider of information and communication linkages (Umlas 1996). So, while RMALC could not prevent the passage of NAFTA, it definitely modified the government's agenda on environmental issues and became an actor that government could not easily ignore.

The building of Cancún's Home Port is a more recent case of how environmentalist NGOs could influence the process of setting an agenda by opposing the proposed construction of a pier in the region.[7] Cancún has seen one of the biggest growth rates in Mexico in the last few years. Hotels, malls, bars, and other tourist attractions have flourished along the shore. Yet, when the construction of a new pier for cruises was announced, an unlikely alliance was formed between environmentalists, Mayan rights activists, and entrepreneurs. Although their interests may seem to be opposed, together they have managed to stop the project (Williams 2003).

The main argument that these allies stated against the project is that it represents a threat to sea life, land, and lifestyles. Moreover, indigenous rights activists argue that this type of huge construction project attracts only unskilled jobless workers to the region, making it more populous and poorer. Finally, the main concern for hotel entrepreneurs is that, since the pier would be a departure base for large cruises, "travelers destined for the cruise ships will cut into the capacity of Cancún's airport, taking up airline seats and landing slots. That will reduce the number of visitors who can get to the region's 46,000 hotel rooms."[8] With 80 percent of the local economy dependent on tourism, any drop in occupancy could mean a loss of jobs, spreading poverty in the region.

Home Port's promoters argue that cruise ships will be visiting anyway and that failure to build a departure base will only reduce Mexico's share of the fastest-growing sector of the tourism market. As of March 2005, the project is on hold.

Human Rights NGOs

The first human rights NGOs appeared in the period from 1977 to 1982. They emerged to defend the rights of political prisoners taken in Mexico's counterinsurgency campaigns of early and mid-1970, when illegal arrests, torture, and disappearances were not unusual in the country. During this period, the human rights movement included individual efforts of people who were willing to provide legal defense for the political detainees. It also included members of illegal leftist political parties, some of Mexico's political exiles from Chile, Argentina, Uruguay, and Brazil, foreign diplomatic staff, and other individuals who discretely shared information about human rights issues with foreign organizations such as Amnesty International (Welna 1977).

Finally, the participants in this movement also included individuals and organizations that were openly or covertly linked to the ruling party or government agencies (including the army, a secret police force, or the government ministry that oversaw the police and all political activity). The participants in this loose human rights movement were generally linked by limited and furtive exchanges of information about government repression of labor and party activism in Mexico, and by more abundant and open discussion of human rights abuses in foreign countries, especially in South America's Southern Cone countries. For the most part, this movement was tiny, unorganized, and unnoticed.

The human rights movement began to grow in the early 1980s, in part through the defense of the rights of large waves of political refugees from El Salvador and Guatemala. By the late 1980s, at the same time that protest against electoral violence and police abuse grew sharply, the movement began to spread and broaden its presence throughout the country (Hernández and Fox 1995).

The rise of human rights NGOs in Mexico took place in the period from 1989 to 1993. Interestingly, more than a half of these NGOs are located in places other than Mexico City, and they are predominant in local municipalities rather than in capitals. In this period, NGO staff began more formal coordination among organizations, creating four networks among themselves (Welna 1997).

Of all the NGO sectors, the human rights network is one of the broadest based, including many church-oriented groups and spanning the political spectrum. At the national level, the Mexican Human Rights Academy, the "Fray Francisco de Vitoria" Human Rights Center, and the "Miguel Pro" Human Rights Center are perhaps the most prominent groups.

The degree of organizational consolidation that the human rights movement has attained at the local level remains uneven, though. Important advances have taken place in the Chiapas highlands under the auspices of Bishop Samuel Ruiz, but major gaps still exists in other states with significant problems of poverty and political violence, such as Guerrero, Hidalgo, and Veracuz, among others. Church-linked human rights groups (not only Catholic, but also Protestant and Jehovah's Witnesses) working in the indigenous Tarahumara highlands in Chihuahua have also made some advances. Cross-border alliances with United States environmental NGOs such as the Texas Center for Policy Studies led to widespread critical discussion of a World Trade Bank–funded forestry project, contributing to its suspension in 1991 when large-scale logging enterprises undermined community forestry initiatives and indigenous rights to ejidal lands. Increased attention to the problems of police abuse and political violence, internationally as well as domestically, led to the creation of a governmental National Human Rights Commission, which is nominally committed to working with the NGO sector (Hernández and Fox 1995).

International attention and links have been crucial for the growth and consolidation of the human rights movement. However, the issue of the relationship of these organizations to foreign countries (especially with regards to the donations they receive from abroad) is also the aspect most criticized and questioned by the Mexican authorities.

There have been some studies that argue that human rights organizations and civil associations have induced significant changes in foreign policy during the last decade (Covarrubias 1999; Treviño 2003). The economic liberalization promoted by Carlos Salinas de Gortari (1988–1994) and Ernesto Zedillo (1994–2000) gave birth to the transformation of the international priorities of the Mexican government; specifically, economic issues became the main focus of foreign policy. Since those years, the priority issues in the Mexican agenda turned out to be commercial and financial. Mexico had to be seen by the world as a stable and secure partner.

Zedillo began his presidency in a complicated scenario, amid one of the worst economic crisis in the recent years, an indigenous uprising demanding basic social rights, and a very expensive financial rescue carried out by President Bill Clinton without the U.S. Congress's consent. Due to all these circumstances, the international image of Mexico was seriously damaged. Human rights NGOs capitalized on this situation by putting pressure on the government to advance their goals and demands, creating new networks and strengthening those that already existed, and denouncing the human rights violations of indigenous communities internationally.

The first response of the Mexican government to this adverse situation was to officially invite international organizations to follow the status of human rights protection in Mexico. This was particularly striking since it implied giving official permission for external actors to participate in domestic affairs. One of the first visits was that of the Inter-American Commission of Human Rights in July 1996. A second important visit was in 1997, when Nigel Rodley—special rapporteur against torture at the Human Rights Commission of United Nations—came to Mexico and met with different NGOs. Interestingly, the Mexican authorities declared they would accept any recommendations made by Rodley regarding human rights protection.

Last, but not least, Pierre Sané—the secretary general of Amnesty International—also visited Mexico in that same year. Nevertheless, since the Mexican government did not promote the visit, Zedillo did not accept an interview with Sané (Amnesty International 1997). This situation was perceived by the human rights movement and organizations as a big step back in the achievement of their agenda. Knowing its relative power, Amnesty International threatened the Mexican government, arguing it would initiate an international campaign to denounce rights violations occurring within Mexican territory.

The contradictions in the Mexican government's attitudes toward the human rights issue changed radically in 1997 when a new situation arose that NGOs could use in their favor: the Mexican government approved the Economic Association, Political Cooperation Agreement with the European Union and initiated the negotiations to sign a general free trade agreement with this entity (a process that concluded in 1999). The main difficulties during the negotiations were those related to the inclusion of the "democratic clause," which made explicit reference to democratic governance and human rights as essential parts of the agreement. Again, the domestic and international lobbying of several NGOs forced the Mexican government to change its initial rejection of the democratic clause to an acceptance of its inclusion in the agreement.

The most important success for the NGOs was when the Mexican authorities recognized the jurisdiction of the Human Rights Inter-American Court. NGOs gained such an important role that the Minister of Foreign Policy created a special office to coordinate the relations between the Mexican government and these organizations (Treviño 2003).

On March 23, 2000, despite initial reservations about accepting the democratic clause, the Mexican president declared the successful conclusion of the free trade agreement with the European Union (González 2000). Some months later, Mexico joined the International Criminal Court. This was very significant, since it implied that Mexican authorities recognized the Court as a supranational juridical mechanism with the authority to watch over human rights and punish those who violate them.

Moreover, the most recent accomplishment of the human rights network is the assessment that the United Nations high commissioner for human rights carried out in Mexico, under the supervision of a committee constituted by human rights NGOs.

Concluding Remarks

The cases analyzed above show that the optimal conditions for NGOs to have a substantial impact on policy, on increasing the opportunity for dialogue with civic groups, and on strengthening citizens' organizations include: forming networks and coalescing around well-defined and politically sensitive issues (especially when there is increased awareness of and international attention to Mexico); linking their interests and stakes to those that are considered most important in the governmental agenda; and making strategic use of network identity and resources (both material and symbolic) and political opportunities, including connections to government officials or other crucial actors (e.g., businessmen). As the cases show, when NGOs fulfill most of these conditions—even for a brief time—they are most effective in producing an impact on the variables mentioned above.

It is important to mention that even where NGOs have neither aimed at nor succeeded in influencing policy, they still play an important though less visible role by serving as a forum for debate and project planning. Formally constituted networks have also played an important part in allowing the transfer of knowledge, lessons, and ideas from one NGO, network, or even sector of society to another.

However, as stated by Fiorina (1999), the relationship between civil society, particularly NGOs and the nation's civic engagement, and social welfare, is not necessarily positive. In his view, intermediate levels of political participation may well lead to outcomes that are inferior not just to outcomes produced by higher levels of civic engagement, but also to those produced by lower levels. Civic engagement in the form of NGOs can be expected to have positive consequences if those engaged represent of the interests and values of the larger community. That is true by definition if everyone is engaged, but when engagement is largely the domain of minority viewpoints, obvious problems of unrepresentativeness arise. Results of an earlier work (Somuano 2003) show that members of NGOs in Mexico tend to be men and to have a certain level of resources such as political sophistication and education; therefore, since they are more active than others, the elites are in some danger of mistaking the pressures of these groups for the views of the citizenry as a whole. All these shortcomings may not apply to the cases studied here, but they have clearly come into play many times in recent Mexican politics.

Notes

1. The author of this article gratefully acknowledges Alonso Cerdán and Froylan Enciso for their excellent research assistance.

2. Liberation theology originated in Latin America around the 1960s as a movement committed to identifying and ameliorating the sources of spiritual and physical oppression of the poor. The movement takes its name from the title of a book by Gustavo Gutiérrez that was published in Spanish in 1971 and in English two years later. Gutiérrez cited one among the approaches that was to be central to the future development of liberation theology—the literacy programs of the Brazilian educator Paulo Freire, which involved a process of *concientización* by which the oppressed person becomes aware of her situation and is encouraged to find a language that makes her less dependent and more free as she commits herself to the transformation and building up of society (Freire 1973). The liberationists borrowed from the Left a belief in conflicting interests and structural oppression as an explanation for poverty and oppression. Yet they also shared the Christian belief in community and charity. Liberation theology stresses the importance of *comunidades eclesiales de base* (church base communities), which are "small lay-led communities, motivated by Christian faith, that see themselves as part of the church and that are committed to working together to improve their communities and to establish a more just society." See Rubenstein and Roth 1988; Levine 1985; Burdick 1994.

3. The networks' members worked in nineteen states, and their leaders estimated they identified and provided services or support to as many as one in ten low-income Mexicans.

4. In this study I define NGOs as private and self-governing organizations that provide members and nonmembers services or goods, are publicly registered (i.e., have legal status), and are subsidized with volunteer donations rather than in exchange for market-value fees, dues, membership, or political votes. The sources of financial support are almost always nongovernmental organizations themselves, sometimes based in industrialized countries, operating in the framework of international development cooperation.

5. Negotiations for NAFTA (which was passed by the U.S. Congress on November 17, 1993, and entered into force on January 1, 1994) began not long after President Salinas took office in 1988.

6. Taken from various undated documents of RMALC and its Web page (www.rmalc.org.mx).

7. The pier is a joint venture between the owners of Cancún-Xcaret theme park and Carnival Cruise Lines, one of the biggest cruise companies in the world. If the pier were to be fully operational, by 2007 it would offer four departures every week, and day visits for more than two dozen other vessels, implying an additional 800,000 visitors per year.

8. "Cruise ships don't have locally based employees, so they don't pay the same taxes we do, and that will hurt the community development budgets through the country," continues the argument. "Cruise ship passengers don't stay in hotels, they stay in their staterooms. When they come ashore, they might buy a beer or a t-shirt, but for the most part they spend their time and money on board" (Williams 2003).

References

Amnesty International. 1997. *Amnesty International Annual Report.* London.

Avritzer, Leonardo. 2001. "El nuevo asociacionismo latinoamericano y sus formas públicas: Propuestas para un diseño institucional. In *La Sociedad Civil: De la teoría a la realidad,* coord. Alberto Olvera. México: El Colegio de México.

Burdick, John. 1994. "The Progressive Catholic Church in Latin America." *Latin American Research Review* 29, no. 1.

Clark, John. 1991. *Democratizing Development. The Role of Voluntary Organizations.* London: Earthscan Publications.

Covarrubias, Ana. 1999. "El problema de los derechos humanos y los cambios en la política exterior." *Foro Internacional* 39.

Fiorina, Morris. 1999. "A Dark Side of Civic Engagement." In *Civic Engagement in American Democracy,* ed. Theda Skocpol and Morris Fiorina. Washington, DC: Brookings/ Russell Sage Foundation.

Freire, Paulo. 1973. "Desmitificación de la concientización." Cuernavaca, Morelos: Centro Intercultural de Documentación.

González, Roberto. 2000. "El TLCUE, relación estratégica." *La Jornada,* March 23.

Hernández, Luis, and Jonathan Fox. 1995. "Mexico's Difficult Democracy: Grassroots Movements, NGOs, and Local Government." In *New Paths to Democratic Development in Latin America: The Rise of NGO-Municipal Collaboration,* ed. Charles A. Reilly. Boulder, CO: Lynne Rienner.

Kürsinger-Wiemman, Edith, F. Hess, J. Lange, H. Lingau, H. Mercker, and A. Vermehren. 1991. *Política ambiental en México: El papel de las ONGs.* Mexico City: Instituto Alemán de Desarrollo.

Landim, Leilah. 1996. "Non-governmental Organizations in Latin America." In *Democracy in Latin America. Patterns and Cycles,* ed. Roderic A. Camp. Wilmington, DE: Jaguar Books on Latin America.

Levine, Daniel. 1985. "Religion and Politics: Drawing Lines, Understanding Change." *Latin American Research Review* 20, no. 1.

Lopezllera Méndez, Luis. 1990. "Las organizaciones civiles por la autogestión de los pueblos." IFDA dossier 77.

Reilly, Charles A., ed. 1995. *New Paths to Democratic Development in Latin America: The Rise of NGO-Municipal Collaboration.* Boulder, CO: Lynne Rienner.

Rubenstein, Richard L., and John K. Roth, eds. 1988. *The Politics of Latin American Liberation Theology: The Challenge to US Public Policy.* Washington, DC: Washington Institute Press.

Secretaría de Gobernación. 2002. *Encuesta nacional de cultura política y prácticas ciudadanas 2001.* México: Poder Ejecutivo Federal.

Somuano, María Fernanda. 2003. "The Role of NGOS in the Process of Democratization: The Case of Mexico." Unpublished Ph.D. dissertation University of Iowa.

Toledo, Víctor, and Enrique Velázquez. 1995. "Levadura verde: Las organizaciones no gubernamentales en México." Mexico. Typescript.

Treviño, Javier. 2003. "De cómo las ONG de derechos humanos redefinieron la soberanía del estado mexicano durante su transición democrática, 1998–2000," Unpublished Ph.D. dissertation. El Colegio de México.

Umlas, Elizabeth. 1996. "Environmental Nongovernmental Networks: The Mexican Case in Theory and Practice." Unpublished Ph.D. dissertation Yale University.

Welna, Christopher James. 1997. "Explaining Non-governmental Organizations (NGOs): Human Rights NGOs and Institutions of Justice in Mexico." Unpublished Ph.D. dissertation Duke University.

Williams, Carol. 2003. "An Ugly Fight at a Pretty Site." *Los Angeles Times,* January 20.

29

SARA GORDON RAPOPORT

Change and Continuity in Attention to Poverty in Mexico

People are poor either because they do not receive income or because they do not know how to create it. Sarah Gordon R. relates Mexican policies to alleviate poverty to the changes in economic conditions and policies in Mexico.

When an entire society has little income, policies to alleviate poverty are those that promote economic development. In the past, the poor were often thought to be incapable of saving, investing, or contributing to economic growth. Investment would take place by channeling funds to those thought to be capable of investment, either the government or private entrepreneurs. A wide variety of measures to obtain savings, create credit, and protect industry were used in Mexico. The high prices that resulted from this policy were partially offset by general subsidies for basic food, transport, water, electricity, and some rural credit. Poverty alleviation policies focused on providing the ability to afford a minimum level of living. Benefits beyond basic assistance were given to unions in exchange for their political support; these benefits were later extended to other groups. Despite intermittent rhetoric, increasing the ability of the poor to create income by improving their education and health took place mainly in large cities, and increased gradually. Health benefits from the Mexican Social Security Institute (IMSS) were obtained by salaried workers, while other workers depended on the Ministry of Health and other groups.

The expense of general subsidies and the need to have better information to identify those in the worst conditions led to the creation of an "index of marginalization." Toward the end of the 1970s, some assistance was given to small and communal farmers; poverty alleviation in urban areas took the form of school breakfasts and low-priced milk. Reforms in the 1980s and 1990s shifted poverty alleviation to groups living in extreme poverty. The National Solidarity Program (1988–1994) provided several kinds of assistance to groups that helped build and maintain schools, pave streets, and construct houses, and so forth. Benefits were channeled to areas in which the Institutional Revolutionary Party (PRI) hoped to regain votes lost to the Democratic Revolution Party (PRD, Partido de la Revolución

Democrática), but these expenditures did not significantly change votes in the presidential elections.

The National Solidarity Program (Programa Nacional de Solidaridad, or PRONASOL) was replaced by PROGRESA (the Program for Education, Health and Food (Programa de Educación, Salud y Alimentación, PROGRESA) (1997–2001). Health benefits were decentralized; several programs were established to improve education. PROGRESA was renamed OPORTUNIDADES by the Vicente Fox administration and extended to semi-urban and urban areas. Voluntary group medical insurance was established, which is especially important because in 2004, according to its directors, the IMSS spent more on pensions than on medicine and other medical materials for its patients. The Fox government proposed legislation that would prohibit IMSS from using its operating budget to fund pensions and would require that pensions be funded by deductions from the paychecks of workers.

Federal policy alleviation policies now require external evaluations to receive fiscal resources. However, funds provided to state governments for alleviation of poverty were not always spent according to federal criteria, because state governments respond to their greater knowledge of local conditions and to their own political needs.

Public opinion increasingly was focused on health and problems of the elderly, which will become more important as life expectancy increases. The Fox government's initiatives are consistent with the increase from 35 percent to 45 percent, between 1990 and 2000, of Mexicans who state that people should take more responsibility for themselves, and also from 47 percent to 54 percent who believe that the church gives adequate answers to social problems. These views are most frequently held by those who have the least education and income.

The analysis of the way in which the state regulates and takes care of poverty is fundamentally important within the framework of the economic and political change that is taking place in Mexico, as much because it is part of a group of transformations of social policy as because the means used toward this end have played a central role in the legitimization of the Mexican government.

In this context, and in that of democratization, we are interested in exploring the forms of government intervention and the criteria applied to reduce poverty, and in reflecting on whether they give rise to new ways of relating the government and the beneficiary poor population, and whether these new relations contribute to forming rationales of cohesion and social inclusion that differ from those predominating during the national revolutionary period (1940–1982). (The beginning date for the national revolutionary period for the purposes of social welfare policy is 1940 rather than 1917, because at the beginning the revolutionary regime did not make important advances in social welfare.)

We are also interested in studying the new objectives of the design and implementation of policies and the parameters to which they are subject, as well as the tensions generated as a product of these changes and conflicting rationales. Given that we are analyzing criteria, concepts, and forms of intervention, we will develop our analysis at a general level, based on both aggregated and disaggregated empirical data.

Today, a little more than twenty years after the beginning of the reforms designed to change the Mexican growth model and social policy paradigm, we can attempt a general evaluation of the basic aspects of the process, given that despite the fact that some features are not fully developed, there are signs of consolidation and institutionalization of some means or criteria of alleviating poverty that have gained legitimacy in public opinion. We distinguish two broad periods: before and after the changes. During the first (1940–1982), the social welfare model based on the interventionist state develops; during the second, from 1983 on, reform takes place to install a model based on market regulation. This led to the development of a different framework that should be kept in mind to understand the social benefit policies in each period. We begin with a brief exposition of the basic characteristics of the former. We will indicate general features, without claiming that there were no differences in the means used by the government during different presidencies.

The National Revolutionary Model (1940–1982)

We can identify two broad sources that contributed to the delineation of welfare policy during the national revolutionary government, using ideas of the elite that determined the solutions that policymakers could adopt, and that were anchored in the paradigm of the centrality of the state (Campbell 2001). On the one hand, the vision of welfare was based on the idea that economic growth would bring with it the welfare of the population. The intervention of the state in the economy was indispensable to achieve these objectives, and public investment was needed to increase productive capacity. On the other hand, the conception of the unrenounceable tutelary role of the state, sanctioned by the Constitution of 1917, affirmed that it was responsible for guaranteeing adequate social conditions, which gave rise to the corresponding basic responsibility for attending to social welfare (Gordon 1993, 1995).

Both ideas implied a strict relationship between economic policies and welfare policies, which was favored by the development of industrialization by means of import substitution. Under a macroeconomic focus, this model stimulated consumption in order to broaden the domestic market by increasing demand and maintaining low salaries; this was possible by using tariff protection that shielded domestic industry from international competition, therefore guaranteeing domestic industry's dominance of the internal market. The generalized subsidies of basic foods, transport, water, and electricity, the guaranteed prices for agricultural products and low interest credits for some sections of the rural population played a double role: giving access to consumption to broad strata of the population and promoting industrial production; for this reason, the action of the government enterprises dedicated to subsidizing prices was seen as part of economic policy and not part of social policy. The most important institution for attending to health and social protection, the IMSS, was founded in 1943 and was organized around salaried labor in private firms. Thus, the state impelled social cohesion and its own legitimacy. In exchange, the protection of the unemployed population was left to the Secretary of Health, whose budget was reduced, and to public welfare assistance, and, to a much smaller extent, to the private sector.

Although welfare policy was based on universal objectives, above all in regard to basic education and public health, it did not develop a welfare model with methods intended to provide universal protection for the population, such as protection from natural risks (disability, old age) and social risks (unemployment, lack of access to basic necessities), based on generalized taxes that would permit the financing of universal provision of services. The expansion of education and health services took place gradually, and those services were first provided in the biggest cities on the base of a highly centralized system.

The enjoyment of benefits beyond those of basic assistance was tied to formal employment and gave priority to unions, under the rationale of the exchange of political approval for welfare benefits. This rationale was based on a centralized structure in which the state was the hegemonic social actor that oriented the party system, and the official party exercised a monopoly of power by means of a sectoral structure—workers, peasants, and popular sectors in corporative organizations—that represented the interests of the lower classes, but did not represent the interests of all subgroups equitably. The state made itself the social representative of the people and authorized privileges to select corporative groups, and labor union control assured the political loyalty of broad sections of the population in exchange for favorable salary and employment policies, and for access to certain forms of material welfare (housing, health, and education). The state's fulfillment of its administrative functions (provision of urban infrastructure, authorization of credit, etc.) was subject to the same rationale. The exchange of political aid for the fulfillment of needs favored the reproduction of clientelistic relations, and those with rural and urban political bosses, as well as the development of a culture of exchange characterized by thankfulness of the individual or group, benefited. This developed the legitimacy of the political system that was identified or confounded with the aid of the then-hegemonic party (PRI, Partido Revolucionario Institucional), or of the person who embodied it. This led to the continual attempt by politicians to broaden their support among popular sectors by use of welfare policies.

Giving priority to aiding salary sectors that were organized in sectoral groups had two kinds of repercussions: on the one hand, it established a segmented and stratified aid system in which the quality of aid and the access to a large variety of benefits (day nurseries, discount stores, low-interest loans, vacation centers, etc.) depended on one's place of work and the union to which a worker belonged, which contributed to extending and deepening the narrow and segmented social structure. On the other hand, this implied paying very limited attention to the welfare of the population that was outside of formal labor markets, who were placed in the category of "undeserving" beneficiaries. Only gradually, to the extent that knowledge was developed, were specialized professionals trained, and did international organizations spread awareness of the necessity of taking care of specified problems and groups of the population. Thus, social aid programs began to be initiated, such as the Federal District's school breakfast program, which began in 1949. Similarly, diagnoses of specific needs were begun during the late 1950s by the National Nutrition Institute (Instituto Nacional de Nutrición) and the Department of Industry and Commerce (Secretaría de Industria y Comercio) (Valencia and Aguirre 1998), but it was not until the end of the 1970s that a diagnosis of the needs of the entire country's population was carried out, which resulted in the creation of an "index of marginalization" that was constructed by the general Coordination Group of the National Plan for Deprived Areas and Marginalized Groups (Coordinación General del Plan Nacional de Zonas Deprimidas y Grupos Marginados, or COPLAMAR), which was established in 1977 to fight the marginalization of the poor population.

In general terms, the population's needs were viewed as stemming from a lack of development, and it was thought that to the extent that development was extended and deepened, marginal sectors would be able to satisfy their basic needs. This led to the problem that welfare was approached as the gradual achievement of the benefits of growth and not as the diminution of poverty, and that the means of achieving it basically consisted in developing the agricultural production of small and communal farmers, whether by means of technical assistance or investment in physical infrastructure such as roads, electrification, school rooms, health centers, and drinking water—programs of rural employment that were, in small measure, productive. The programs were directed at productive sectors, not to population groups. It should be pointed out that this vision also predominated in the staff of international organizations such as the World Bank, which wished to increase incomes in rural—and often indigenous—areas. To approach the situation of backwardness of these regions and their heterogeneous problems, numerous government organizations, commissions, committees, and organizations to promote development were created in the 1970s. Their large number exposed the growing difficulty of coordination that confronted them. Coordination of attempts to alleviate rural poverty was attempted by centralizing decision making and designing of policies that went from the center to the periphery, from the federal government to the population covered by these programs. In the context of a system in which the state exercised power by means of a structure of sectoral organizations, the unit of intervention, or the recipient of benefits, was not the individual, but the community or the organized groups. The only special urban programs were breakfast for schoolchildren and milk at lower prices, because urban poverty was mainly seen as a problem of marginalization of entire areas, and there was rapid migration to cities from rural areas, which made construction of urban infrastructure especially important.

The economic model was incapable of incorporating broad groups of the population into the process of development. Despite an average annual growth rate of 6.3 percent between 1941 and 1982 (Ortiz Mena 1998), despite the regular increase in real salary between 1952 and 1976, which grew from 27.9 percent to 46.2 percent of national income during this period (Hernández Laos 1992), and despite the impact of social development programs in rural areas, toward the end of the period, in 1981, the share of all homes in poverty-stricken conditions was 52.5 percent, of which 30.9 percent were living in extreme poverty and 21.6 percent in moderate poverty (Hernández Laos 1992).

The estimates of poverty are based on statistics that combined estimates of income below that required to satisfy basic needs and alternate estimates of income below the poverty line, which includes income needed to satisfy both basic and additional needs (see Chapter 13 in this volume and Boltvinik 2001). Other sources only include one of the two measures, and therefore estimate that a smaller share of the population lives in poverty. For example, CEPAL, the Economic Commission for Latin America (Comisión Económica pava América Latina) used the unsatisfied basic needs approach and estimated that for 1970, 34 percent of the Mexican population was poor, of which 12 percent lived in extreme poverty, while the figures as modified by Hernández Laos (1992) indicated that in this year 74.2 percent of the population was poor and 58.2 percent lived in extreme poverty toward the end of the national revolutionary period.

However, during that period, the structure of employment changed: in 1940, 65 percent of the population worked in the primary sector, 15 percent in industry, and 19 percent in services. In 1980, the percentages were as follows: 28 percent, 22.9 percent, and 49.1 percent, respectively (Couriel 1984).

The Change in the Development Model, 1983–2004

The reforms that occurred during the 1980s and 1990s indicated the abandonment of the tutelary character of the state. The objective was to create a competitive economy and to replace the interventionist state by a regulatory state, which involved developing the market, as well as new foreign relations. The fiscal crisis of 1982 gave rise to measures for rationalizing spending, and to structural adjustment and the opening of trade. The rapid opening, initiated by adherence to the General Agreement on Tariffs and Trade (GATT) in 1986, would continue with the signing of free trade agreements, first with the United States and Canada (NAFTA) and later with European and Asian nations. Regarding state intervention in the economy, the gradual suppression of policies, organisms, and programs through which state economic action was carried out implied the sale or liquidation of numerous state firms and properties. In order to prevent state compensatory programs from interfering with the functioning of the market, diverse universal subsidy programs began to be withdrawn in 1984 and to be replaced by subsidies provided to target populations, initially to unionized workers; alternatively, the universal subsidy programs were placed within the operation of the distribution center of the Compañía Nacional de Subsistencias Populares (CONASUPO), which was in charge of distributing the subsidies. The diminution of generalized subsidies would continue throughout this period and culminate during the government of President Ernesto Zedillo (1994–2000), when the subsidy of the production-to-consumption chain of tortillas was ended in 1995. The Program of Subsidy of Tortilla Consumption, which had provided a kilogram a day of free tortillas to unionized workers distributed by their organizations, was converted into a selective subsidy that benefited families whose income was less than two minimum salaries in cities with more than 10,000 inhabitants (for information on minimum salaries and changes in them, see Chapter 24 in this volume). By 1998 the daily minimum wage was US$3.06, and one kilogram of tortillas cost $0.25; with one minimum wage you could purchase 12.7 kg (INEGI 2004). The same happened to the subsidized milk program, which was reoriented toward the regions with the greatest levels of poverty and its budget increased (Zedillo 1996).

In the period immediately after the crisis, the scarcity of financial resources brought with it the diminution of investment in social development; in the 1988 budget, 57 percent of spending was for the payment of the internal and external public debt (Carrasco and Provencio 1988) at the same time that the demand for public services was increasing because of the impoverishment of the population. The fall in federal social spending was calculated to be around 50 percent between 1982 and 1988 (author's calculations in constant prices based on Salinas de Gortari 1994). The reduction in funds available for domestic needs affected the poorest above all, given that the funds provided for regional and rural development suffered the largest reductions (Friedmann, Lustig, and Legovini 1997). For 1988, the share of households in poverty increased to 62.5 percent (Hernández Laos 1992). It is necessary to keep in mind that the economic model adopted in the framework of globalization of markets was not able to guarantee sustained economic growth, and that in addition to very low rates of growth, there were recurrent crises as a result of which new groups became impoverished. At the end of the 1980s, economic growth resumed, but in 1994 there was a new financial crisis that was a factor in the decline in the level of living of the majority of the population.

The objective of modifying the role of the state brought with it the impulse toward the decentralization of health and educational services, and their associated functions, attributions, and resources, to the state and municipal governments. Decentralization was carried out by a gradual and discontinuous process that did not in all cases have the objective of ridding the federal government of these responsibilities. The first decentralizations took place after the debt crisis broke out, under the pressure of the strong reduction of budgetary resources; without these decentralizations there would have been claims on government entities for aid in the areas for which the federal government had previously been responsible. The first wave of decentralizations included modifications of the Constitution (Article 115) that allowed the transfer to the *municipios* of the provision of some services and the transfer of health services to the states. The Department of Heath and Welfare (Secretaría de Salubridad y Asistencia) was empowered to coordinate the transfers to the states. In 1985, this transfer began to be implemented with funds provided by the World Bank, in entities that were believed to have adequate infrastructure and economic and human resources to provide health services (Brachet-Márquez 2002). This transfer would be suspended during the presidency of Carlos Salinas de Gortari (1988–1994), whose most important social policy, the National Solidarity Program (Programa Nacional de Solidaridad, or PRONASOL, initiated in December 1988) implied centralized units at least during the first stage. Salinas made decisions about how PRONASOL resources were spent, suspended the decentralization of health services, and increased the decentralization of education. The second stage of decentralization took place in a political and social context that was very different from the first stage, as we will see in a later section of this chapter.

The National Solidarity Program (PRONASOL), 1988–1994

The earlier economic model had not paid enough attention to the marginalization of the population, and the fight against poverty had begun to dominate social policy. This policy emphasis was part of the social policy favored by international organizations such as the World Bank and the OECD (Organization for Economic Cooperation and Development), which recommended providing selective attention to groups living in extreme poverty. This shift of focus took place in an atmosphere of growing interest by various nongovernmental organizations, volunteers, masses, citizens' networks, and so forth, in providing public and private goods and services. In the framework of economic restructuring and of social effects produced by the economic adjustment and reform of the state, the creation of PRONASOL claimed to address two aspects of these problems: in the economic sphere, by designing a compensatory microeconomic program with targeted expenditure, and in the political sphere, by preserving popular approval of the government in a context in which important changes in the tutelary character of the state were occurring, and making the population accept the change from universalist policies to those oriented to favoring only specified groups. As a result, paralleling the objectives related to welfare in both areas, PRONASOL was conceived as an instrument of governability.

PRONASOL's objective of regaining and/or broadening the great volume of votes in favor of the PRI has been demonstrated by an analysis of this program's expenditures. The authors who analyzed it concluded that the assignment of PRONASOL's resources was not based on objective indices of poverty, such as that of marginalization, but that the criteria of distribution of its budget were directed to the recovery of votes favoring the PRI, which had been lost in 1988. It also has been demonstrated, for example, that the social spending and production subsidies were significantly greater in regions that supported the PRD, which was toward the Left of the political spectrum (Dion 2000), although this spending had no significant effect on votes for the PRI presidential candidate in 1994.

The program's objectives were improving social welfare, both in rural and urban areas, encouraging production in depressed areas, aiding agricultural, agro-industrial, micro-industrial, and fishing activities, and encouraging regional development by "the construction of infrastructure work that had a regional impact and execution of development programs in specified regions" (Consejo Consultivo 1991). In addition, PRONASOL suggested the implementation of welfare programs in the following areas: health, by constructing and rehabilitating rural medical units, hospitals, and health centers; nutrition, by installing subsidized stores for basic foodstuffs in highly marginalized rural areas, including dairies and "soup kitchens"; education, encouraging the construction and renovation of school grounds, authorizing economic incentives, medical services, and basic provisions to students, primarily but not only for the elementary school level; housing, authorizing credit for the construction and repair of houses and encouraging construction by those who would live in the houses; basic services, by means of broadening the provision of drinking and sewage system water, and rural and urban electrification; paving streets; land reform, which was intended to legalize urban property ownership located in ejidal and communal properties; and road and highway infrastructure. The largest share of the budget was directed to infrastructure that aided production (42 percent), and a smaller amount was directed to the direct promotion of production. The programs for production were initially intended to aid production by small coffee producers, above all in indigenous zones, river fishing and small mining (Dion 2000), and, later, to develop cooperatives.

In a first stage, the federal government centralized the assignment of resources, but as a result of the strong criticism it received, it began to decentralize the carrying out of the programs to the state and municipal governments by means of "agreements for social development." Accords were also signed with diverse social groups to carry out social assistance (health care) and social welfare activities (transport) (Aguilar 1998). The groups presented projects, including their budgets. PRONASOL's officials decided whether or not to approve the projects.

In order to carry out its aim of aiding only the neediest groups in the population, PRONASOL had two important features: its already mentioned targeted assistance policy, and its reliance on the participation of its beneficiaries in constructing houses with materials provided by PRONASOL, street paving, drainage, repairing hospitals, painting schools, and so on. Its policy of targeted assistance was carried out by means of requests from organized groups that assumed a specified responsibility for obtaining the good or service, which indicated that targeting went beyond technical criteria, such as measurement of needs, and was a means of structuring social demands. The vast range of areas in which PRONASOL operated indicates that its objective of aiding only the neediest was limited by the type of targeting that was used. This leads us to conclude that although PRONASOL was the first market-oriented assistance program, its manner of operation justifies considering it as the last social program of the nationalist revolutionary regime. In effect, PRONASOL signified giving continuity to the way in which social programs operated from the 1970s onward, promoting the organization of the beneficiaries, their participation, and provision of work by the entire community, building on the strong tradition in indigenous communities of working without pay on the common lands or in the religious ceremonies.

Although PRONASOL increased the availability of basic services, these are only one component of goods and services included in disposable income, and therefore of income distribution as measured by the poverty line. From 1989 to 1992, the share of the first eight deciles in monetary income fell. Only the share of the two highest deciles increased (Cortés 2001). The difficulty of raising income above the poverty line by providing basic services without creating jobs or other sources of income was shown by the evaluations made under the Comité Técnico de Evaluación de PRONASOL that evaluated PRONASOL (Chávez, Moctezuma, and Rodríguez 1994). It concluded that PRONASOL did not make a substantial contribution to the reduction of extreme poverty.

Decentralization and Democracy, 1995–

PRONASOL was discontinued in 1995, after President Salinas's term of office ended. The new program, PROGRESA, which began in 1997, would show a greater consistency between the objectives and operating methods of the policy of combating poverty because it used technical methods to select its beneficiaries, in contrast to PRONASOL's selection of beneficiaries to channel social demands. This phase coincided with the increasing democratization of Mexico (see Chapter 21 in this book), expressed by an increase in the state and municipal entities governed by opposition parties, with the weakening of the presidency and the affirmation of an anti-poverty policy based on technical criteria directed to aiding individuals more than organized groups. It should be remembered that Ernesto Zedillo assumed the presidency in the context of the armed rising in Chiapas and strong battles within the PRI, as a result of which the president lacked the unanimous aid that his predecessors had obtained from PRI. These factors influenced the growing demand for decentralization by the states and *municipios* on behalf of both PRI governors and the opposition. This demand was favored by the requirements of international organizations (World Bank, OECD), which emphasized that resources should be managed in a decentralized manner, and by pressure from citizens' groups.

The policy of relieving poverty was included in President Zedillo's decentralization efforts under the name of New Federalism, and it resumed the process that had begun in 1983 using new methods—above all, local decision making. The explicit objective of the decentralization was to increase the efficiency and equity in the distribution and application of public expenditure. It was thought that if public problems were identified and decisions taken emanated from needs expressed by local governments, there would be greater citizen participation, which in turn would develop democratization of public management and release the federal government from its obligation of carrying out these tasks. This led to the redistribution of attributions, authorizing functions, responsibilities, and resources to the municipal governments (Zedillo 1996); the Chamber of Deputies was given the responsibility of supervising the income, expenditure, management, and application of the federal funds on behalf of the states and the Federal District. Similarly, explicit rules were established for the operation of the programs.

The decentralization of health services resumed in 1996 by means of the strengthening of a National Health Council (Consejo Nacional de Salud) as a permanent coordinating body between the federal government, the states, and the Federal District. This process implied the transfer of economic resources and physical capital (Zedillo 1996). In states with the greatest needs, the Program for Broadening of Coverage (Programa de Ampliación de Cobertura, PAC) was begun, with the aim of strengthening the health centers in small towns. Moreover, the Basic Packet of Health Services (Paquete Básico de Servicios de Salud, PABSS), which included twelve essential health services was introduced for marginalized zones in eleven federal entities (Zedillo 1996). Similarly, four programs were designed in order to aid the most backward schools, not targeted by other programs: the Program to Reduce Educational Backwardness (Programa para Abatir el Rezago Educativo, PARE); the Program to Reduce Educational Backwardness in Basic Education (Programa para Abatir el Rezago en Educación Básica, PAREB); the Integral Program to Reduce Educational Backwardness (Programa Integral para Abatir el Rezago Educativo, PIARE); and the Program to Aid Disadvantaged Schools (Programa de Apoyo a Escuelas en Desventaja, PAED) (Zedillo 1996). These programs finance teaching materials, school supplies, training and economic stimuli for teachers who worked in remote regions, and construction and rehabilitation of areas for preschool, primary, and secondary education (Zedillo 2000).

Reform of organizations and programs related to relieving poverty was also undertaken. This included the reform of the Department of Social Development (Secretaría de Desarrollo Social, SEDESOL), whose function had been planning, carrying out, and maintaining infrastructure works. After the reform, SEDESOL is only responsible for coordination and collaboration with the states' and municipal governments' tasks. The functions of planning, carrying out and maintaining infrastructure works are now carried out by municipal governments. Similarly, the latter were given the resources and attributions of the funds for basic social infrastructure (*Fondos de Desarrollo Social*).

SEDESOL included several programs: drinking water; sewage systems; drainage and construction of latrines; electrification; urbanization; assistance for education infrastructure; telephone communications for rural areas; construction and conservation of infrastructure for basic education; construction and maintenance of infrastructure for health services; road construction; and rural infrastructure. The local districts, along with the Municipal Development Councils, could approve works that cost less than 100,000 pesos (on average, US$15,576.00 in 1995) (Banco de Mexico 2004).

The transfer of anti-poverty infrastructure efforts from the federal government to the municipalities took place gradually: 50 percent of the budget was transferred in 1995, and a total of 65 percent had been transferred in 1996 (Zedillo 1996). This decentralization culminated in 1998 with the creation of the Budget Item 33, called "Federal Contributions for State and Municipal Entities" (Aportaciones Federales para Entidades Federativas y Municipios), under the item called the Contributions for Social Infrastructure (Fondo de Aportaciones para la Infraestructura Social, FAIS) (Zedillo 1998).

Beginning in 1996, a mathematical formula based on state and local poverty indicators was used to distribute these funds (Zedillo 1996). These means suppressed the mechanisms of direct relationship between public federal administration and the beneficiaries, which signified separating policy from administrative functions, placing them in different entities.

PROGRESA, 1997–2001, and OPORTUNIDADES, 2002–

Within the framework of the close relationship between democratization in Mexico and the de-politicization of anti-poverty programs, a new anti-poverty program (1997–2001) was designed, the Program for Education, Health and Food (Programa de Educación, Salud y Alimentación, PROGRESA). It should be remembered that because of the balance-of-payments crisis at the end of 1994, the economy decreased by 6.2 percent in real terms—the largest decrease since 1932—from 1994 to 1995. Economic activity contracted in all sectors: the worst declines occurred in building (23.5 percent); commerce, restaurants, and hotels (15.5 percent); and manufacture (4.9 percent).

In this process, the unequal concentration of income increased. The share of total income received by the four lowest deciles of the population fell from 14.4 percent in 1984 to 12.7 percent in 1994, and the share of total income of the middle (the fifth to seventh deciles) fell from 24.4 percent to 21.7 percent during the same period. The three deciles with the highest income increased their share of total income from 61.3 percent to 65.6 percent (González Gómez 1998).

The new program sought to establish technical criteria based on specialized sociodemographic knowledge to select its beneficiaries (PROGRESA 2000). This was done by using a three-stage methodology: first, localities were chosen; then households to benefit within these areas were selected; and then the list of these households was refined in community assemblies. A specialized evaluation carried out by researchers coordinated by the IFPRI (International Food Policies Research Institute) in 1999 stated that the targeting procedure was correct, both in its selection of localities and of households (Behrman and Todd 2000).

The design of SEDESOL had included three principle areas emphasized in the international discussion of poverty: (1) strengthening of personal capabilities, above all education and health (human capital); (2) productive capacities; and (3) social participation, based on the definition of poverty elaborated by Amartya Sen, who took a firm stand that it was important for people to develop their capabilities in order to escape from poverty.

Within this framework, the relationship between socioeconomic and demographic variables and poverty was clear, as, for example, the relation between infant mortality and mother's education. This vision placed special attention on mothers and identified the key role that they played in the welfare of the home, and it emphasized the most vulnerable groups: Indians, children, the disabled, and those over sixty years of age.

PROGRESA began to carry out its activities in August 1997, to benefit households in extreme poverty (with incomes of less than one minimum salary each month), located in highly marginal rural areas, with fewer than 2,500 inhabitants and at least 5 kilometers from a school or a health center. Using an integral perspective of the distinct individual and household factors (human capital) that led to poverty, the central idea was, and continued to be, to offer incentives to parents by means of scholarships beginning in the third grade of primary school in order to guarantee the continued attendance of their children in school until they completed basic education (which consists of basic and secondary education—ten years of schooling) and to take care of their health and that of the family. In order to counteract the tendency of rural families to withdraw their girls from school in the secondary level, the scholarship amount for girls was a little higher than that for boys. Moreover, a small sum was given to households to improve their nutrition, including food supplements for pregnant women and children under five years of age. Assistance was provided for health and preventive services as well. Participation in PROGRESA was conceived of as a co-responsibility of the parents, who had to promise to enroll and send their child to school on a regular basis. Children who received a scholarship from PROGRESA/OPORTUNIDADES had to attend school on at least 85 percent of the days in the school year (PROGRESA 2000). Both parents and children had to make periodic visits to clinics and to orientation talks on health care. There are talks for children and for parents (PROGRESA 1999). Thus, the incentive was accompanied by an implicit sanction, in the case the co-responsibility was not carried out: If they did not visit the clinics periodically or attend the school 85 percent of the school days, the scholarship was taken away.

In Mexico, programs are often coterminous with the presidency of their creator. PROGRESA continued to exist after the presidency of Ernesto Zedillo because the first evaluation of this program, carried out by an international group in which the International Institute for Food Policies (Instituto Internacional de Políticas Alimentarias, IFPRI) and various Mexican analysts participated (PROGRESA 2000), recognized its specialized character as a program that successfully achieved it objectives. It continued to operate under the same basic structures and was renamed "OPORTUNIDADES" in 2002; the area in which it operated was extended to semi-urban and urban zones, where poverty had increased. In effect, from 1984 to 1995, city households in poverty increased from 53.2 percent to 57.6 percent (Tuirán and Ávila 2002). The number of families benefited by PROGRESA/OPORTUNIDADES increased from 300,000 to 700,000 in 1997, then to 4,240,000 in 2002. The budget increased in real terms by 11.3 percent between 2003 and 2004 (SHCP 2003, 2004). The importance of this program since its creation is illustrated not only by the fact that it continued to operate after the end of government that created it, and even was expanded, but also by the fact that it has been submitted to evaluations that have been used to modify some of its aspects. Yet, to the extent that this program has been broadened, others intended to aid "human capital," such as the food program, have been reduced. Thus, for example, the program of subsidizing the consumption of tortillas, which had benefited 2.8 million families daily in 1996, reduced the number of its beneficiaries to 1.7 million families a day in 1998, to 633,172 families in 2002, and was terminated by the Chamber of Deputies at the end of 2003. Even though there was no official explanation, some officials indicated that the design of the program did not indicate the impact of the program or include the co-responsibility of the beneficiaries. A report indicated that the change in the foods people eat was another reason for ending the program, because families used the tortillas to feed animals (Cardozo 2004).

On the other hand, other programs of targeted subsidies for strengthening capabilities, such as the already mentioned subsidy of milk for children under twelve years of age whose families earned income less than two minimum wages, continued to be applied, even though according to the objectives of efficiency, there had been a firm stand taken on targeting areas of high and very high marginalization, and families were not allowed to participate in both OPORTUNIDADES and the subsidized milk program. If families applied to obtain both programs, their name was removed from both. The benefits of the milk program were extended to those over sixty years of age in extreme poverty; for the latter, it was anticipated that economic aid would be provided. The program of supply of basic foods at low prices in rural areas of high and very high marginalization (Abasto Popular), which began in the seventies and increased under the Salinas government, was also maintained.

Half of Mexico's population does not have medical insurance. In order to protect their health, the Fox administration designed the Popular Insurance (Seguro Popular) program, based on the voluntary affiliation of people located in urban and semi-urban areas. Participants in Seguro Popular make monthly payments based on family income, or income of the group with which they are affiliated: there are both family and group insurance policies. It is anticipated that those who are covered by Seguro Popular will be treated in public state government hospitals for which the federal government provided special funds (*Diario Oficial* 2003).

In rural areas, programs for those in extreme poverty, linked to OPORTUNIDADES, are provided; the Department of Health has special programs such as mobile surgery, for highly marginalized areas. In general, these programs encompass basic health assistance, treatment for infants' illnesses, reproductive health, and preventive medicine.

If the state hospitals lack the ability to treat a patient, the patient is sent to Nuevo León or Jalisco, which have highly developed medical facilities, for the required special treatment. Patients are also sent to the Federal District, although the demand for medical services in the Federal District is greater than the ability to provide them. By December 2003, the Seguro Popular Insurance program was functioning in twenty-five states, serving 641,000 families in 938 health centers and 111 hospitals (*La Jornada,* January 7, 2004).

The Fox government inaugurated a new program, Habitat, whose means of operation have not been clarified. It proposed to contribute to overcoming urban poverty, improve the habitat of the poor, and convert cities and their neighborhoods into organized, secure, and livable spaces. It is expected that this program will be applied to benefit poor people who live in selected neighborhoods and urban marginalized zones.

In contrast to the programs designed to strengthen human capital (food, education, and health), those directed at strengthening the sources of income have received very small budgets. This has happened not only because of monetary restrictions, but also because the government did not wish to replace the market in determining demand and wanted instead to stimulate a culture of entrepreneurship in the population. Examples of this kind of programs are those of temporary employment in rural areas, based on a design of stimulating self-selection by setting rural wages. These programs are designed to help rural workers who are temporarily unemployed; participants are paid the minimum wage. Construction of rural infrastructure was undertaken in order to increase the demand for rural labor. Those employed in these programs obtained jobs that lasted a maximum of eighty-eight working days, approximately three months. They were carried out only in zones of extreme poverty, in the states of Oaxaca, Yucatán, Guerrero, Michoacán, and Chiapas (Dávila, Levy, and López Calva 1996). These programs, similar to others designed to increase income, such as Productive Options (Opciones Productivas), Agricultural Day Laborers (Jornaleros Agrícolas), and Social Co-investment (Coinversión Social), have had limited budgets that have tended to be stable. The stability of the limited budgets has taken place with various programs created under the governments of the national revolutionary period that have continued to exist because of inertia. Among others, these include aid to farmers in rainy, low-productivity or disaster-stricken zones; aid to individuals, families, and social groups and productive organizations in rural areas for the development of productive projects and the generation of self-employment; and production credit for women.

The share of production programs in the expenditures to combat poverty between 1997 and 2002 oscillated between 16 and 18 percent, while those devoted to the development of human capital varied between 46 and 49 percent, and those for infrastructure around 35 percent (Fox 2002; SHCP 2002).

Conclusion

The anti-poverty policies put into operation as a result of the change in the economic growth model and in the tutelary role of the state have been characterized by relating to various dilemmas that imply ideological/political policies and principles. These dilemmas continue to be debated and carried out in the framework of democratization and of the continually increasing specialized knowledge about poverty.

A first tension is that existing between methods that claim to compensate needs and develop individual capabilities by means of transfers, on the one hand, and those that emphasize opening opportunities for the poor by increasing their productivity by using productive programs, on the other. The latter provides direct stimulation of production of goods and services. Despite the fact that both types of methods are needed to overcome poverty, there has been much greater emphasis on the development of individual capabilities, as we have seen.

Related to the first tension, another tension exists between universal methods and those targeted to specified sectors of the population, a tension that continues to be the subject of debate, even though the main programs have chosen to aid a targeted population, whether by technical criteria or by self-selection by the beneficiaries. Notwithstanding the debate, Mexicans view preferential attention to the poorest sectors as having legitimacy. However, universal programs to meet the health needs of the majority of the population are not rejected, and it is not unlikely that in the future there will be a new effort to obtain greater health coverage, whether or not based on individual contributions to paying medical costs or health insurance.

A third tension, of the highest importance, emanates from the fact that reduction of poverty is a very politicized topic, given that it was the touchstone of social policy in the national revolutionary period, which featured the exchange of political loyalty and assistance for welfare. The process of democratization in Mexico has brought with it the requirement of legitimacy for the entire system and not just for some of its parts. Currently, in the context of growing plurality and democratization, the institutionalization of policies is needed, especially those affecting poverty, and this is tending to occur, as indicated by the Congress's requirements that external evaluations be made of all programs that receive fiscal resources starting with the 2001 fiscal year, and that in all federal programs, a highly visible statement must be included certifying that the programs did not come from only one political party, but from the government as a whole. Paradoxically, electoral competition, in the framework of exchange of favors, contributed to the design and use of the programs by interest groups at the same time that the objectives of equity sought to obtain neutrality in the operation of the programs. The same party that in a *municipio* or state presided over the particularist use of a given program denounced the politicized management of a program in another *municipio* or state.

An additional tension is the ambiguous way in which participation was conceptualized as the basis of anti-poverty programs, above all in subsidy programs, which are those that received the largest share of funds. In these, the co-responsibility of individual beneficiaries is stipulated, and assumes various forms: in PROGRESA/OPORTUNIDADES, parents promise to enroll and regularly send their child to school, to visit medical clinics, and attend talks about health care; in other programs, they are obliged to provide personal data, or to use assistance for authorized purposes, under the sanction of losing the subsidy. This is designed to change the culture of the poor, with the aim of promoting a culture of co-responsibility in overcoming poverty by means of incentives and sanctions applied to individuals; however, it is not very clear if these new forms bring with them autonomous citizenship behavior or, on the contrary, stimulate dependence.

The evaluations of these programs do not provide public information about the number of their beneficiaries who, once enrolled, were later excluded because they did not comply with their co-responsibility obligations; the evaluations only provide judgments about the fulfillment of the original objectives of each program. The most recent evaluation of PROGRESA/OPORTUNIDADES recognized that the program did not have an impact on increasing student assistance in primary school (grades 1–6) because it already was greater than 90 percent before the program began. However, the evaluation indicated that the program had positive impact on attendance in secondary schools (grades 7 to 9) in rural areas, where attendance increased by 24 percent, and in high school (grades 10 to 12), which increased attendance by 84.7 percent in the 2002–2003 school year (Parker 2004). Regarding the effects of decentralization, the asymmetries between states has been emphasized, given that those with higher relative levels of development are also those that have the greater technical-administrative capacities in state and local government, and also are better able to coordinate their efforts with those of federal government organizations. Moreover, it should be remembered that only municipal funds are distributed using a formula that takes into account "poverty variables." The proposals to distribute other resources according to these variables have not been approved. Although the federal government offers incentives to those states that assign their own resources to programs, among them anti-poverty programs, they do not seem to be sufficient because of the penury of resources.

Finally, the provision of funds from the federal to the state governments for overcoming poverty took for granted that the state governments would assign these resources according to the criteria and priorities based on the federal measurements of poverty, and that state governments had the technical and administrative capability that is needed to effectively implement these programs according to the stated criteria. This did not necessarily happen, in as much as the state governments had a better understanding of local needs; their actions also resulted from local political pressures.

Note

The author is very grateful to Fiorella Mancini for providing excellent research assistance in the preparation of this chapter.

References

Aguilar, Luis Fernando. 1996. "Reformas y retos de la administración pública mexicana (1988–1994)." *Foro Internacional* 36, nos. 143–144 (January–June).

Banco de México. 2004. *Indicadores económicos.* Mexico. March 24. Available at www.banxico.gob.mx

Barajas, Gabriela. 2000. "Política y administración pública: un análisis de programas y agencias de atención a la pobreza en México, 1970–1994." Unpublished master's thesis. FLACSO.

Behrman, Jere R., and Petra E. Todd. 2000. "Aleatoriedad en las muestras experimentales del Programa de Educación, Salud y Alimentación," Progresa (Programa de Educación, Salud y Alimentación). *Más oportunidades para las familias pobres. Evaluación de resultados del Programa de Educación, Salud y Alimentación. Metodología de la evaluación de Progresa.* México: Secretaría de Desarrollo Social.

Boltvinik, Julio. 2001. "Conceptos y medidas de pobreza." In *Pobreza y distribución del ingreso en México,* ed. Julio Boltvinik and Enrique Hernández Laos. México: Siglo XXI.

Brachet-Márquez, Viviane. 2002. "Elementos para investigar la capacidad estatal político-administrativa en materia de salud pública. Los casos de Guanajuato, Oaxaca y Sonora." *Estudios Sociológicos* 20, no. 58 (January–April).

Campbell, John. 2001. "The Role of Ideas." In *The Rise of Neoliberalism and Institutional Analysis,* ed. John Campbell, and Ove K. Pedersen. Princeton and Oxford: Princeton University Press.

Cardozo Brum, Myriam. 2004. "Hacia el desarrollo de una cultura de la evaluación de políticas y programas sociales en México." Unpublished Ph.D. dissertation. México: FCPyS (Facultad de Ciencias Políticas y Sociales), UNAM (Universidad Nacíonal Autónoma de México).

Carrasco, Rosalía, and Enrique Provencio. 1988. "La política social, 1983–1988 y sus principales consecuencias." *Investigación Económica,* México, IIE-UNAM.

Chávez, Ana María, David Moctezuma Navarro, and Francisco Rodríguez Hernández. 1994. *El combate a la pobreza en Morelos. Aciertos y desaciertos de Solidaridad.* Cuernavaca: CRIM-UNAM.

Consejo Consultivo del Programa Nacional de Solidaridad. 1991. *El combate a la pobreza.* México: El Nacional.

Cortés, Fernando. 2001. "El ingreso y su desigualdad en la distribución: México 1997–2000." *Papeles de población,* no. 35. México: UAEM.

Cortés, Fernando, Daniel Hernández, Enrique Hernández, Miguel Székely, and Hadid Vera. 2002. "Evolución y características de la pobreza en México en la última década del siglo XX." In *La situación demográfica de México, 2002,* ed. CONAPO. México.

Couriel, Alberto. 1984. "Pobreza y subempleo en América Latina." *Revista de la Cepal,* no. 24, (December).

Cruz, Angeles, and Ciro Pénez Silva. 2004. "Responsabiliza Fox a diputados por el efecto de recortes al sector salvd." *La Jornada,* January 7.

Dávila, E., S. Levy, and L.F. López Calva. 1996. "Empleo rural y combate a la pobreza: Una propuesta de política." *Economía Mexicana* 4, no. 2, CIDE.

Dion, Michell. 2000. "La economía política del gasto social: El Programa de Solidaridad en México, 1988–1994." *Estudios sociológicos de El Colegio de México* 18, 53 (May–August).

Fox, Jonathan. 1992. *The Politics of Food in Mexico: State Power and Social Mobilitzation.* Ithaca and Londen: Cornell University Press.

———. 2002. *Segundo informe de gobierno.* México, Presidencia de la República.

Friedmann, Santiago, Nora Lustig, and Adriana Legovini. 1997. "México: gasto social y subsidios alimentarios durante el ajuste de los años ochenta." In *El desafío de la austeridad, pobreza y desigualdad en la América Latina,* comp. Nora Lustig. México: FCE.

González Gómez, Mauricio A. 1998. "Crisis and Economic Change." In *Mexico Under Zedillo,* Susan Kaufman and Luis Rubio. Boulder, CO: Americas Society.

Gordon, Sara. 1993. "La política social y el Programa Nacional de Solidaridad." *Revista mexicana de sociología* 55, no. 2.

———. 1995. "El Programa Nacional de Solidaridad en la modernización del estado mexicano." In *Estado y políticas sociales después del ajuste,* comp. Carlos Vilas. México: UNAM–Nueva Sociedad.

Hernández Laos, Enrique. 1992. *Crecimiento económico y pobreza en México. Una agenda para la investigación.* México: CIIH-UNAM.

INEGI. 2004. Available at www.inegi.gob.mx. July 13.

Parker, Susan. 2004. "Evaluación del impacto de Oportunidades sobre la inscripción, reprobación y abandono escolar." In *Resultados de la Evaluación Externa del Programa de Desarrollo Humano Oportunidades 2003.* Documentos finales, Instituto Nacional de Salud Pública Oportunidades, Centro de Investigaciones y Estudios sobre Antropología. México.

Programa para un Nuevo Federalismo 1995–2000. 2000. *Diario Oficial de la Federación,* México.

PROGRESA (Programa de Educación, Salud y Alimentación). 1999. *Más oportunidades para las familias pobres. Evaluación de resultados del Programa de Educación, Salud y Alimentación. Primeros avances.* México: Secretaría de Desarrollo Social.

———. 2000. *Más oportunidades para las familias pobres. Evaluación de resultados del Programa de Educación, Salud y Alimentación. Metodología de la evaluación de PROGRESA.* México: Secretaría de Desarrollo Social.

Rodríguez Noboa, P. 1991. "La selectividad como eje de las políticas sociales." *Revista de la CEPAL,* no. 44, (August), Santiago de Chile.

Salinas de Gortari, Carlos. 1994. *Sexto informe de gobierno.* México, Presidencia de la República.

Secretaría de Desarrollo Social (SEDESOL). 1998. *PROGRESA,* México.

———. 1998. *Informe de ejecución 1997 del Plan Nacional de Desarrollo.* México: SEDESOL.

SHCP (Secretaría de Hacienda y Crédito Público). 2003. *Cuenta pública,* Presupuesto Aprobado. México.

———. 2004. *Cuenta Pública,* Presupuesto Aprobado. México.

Sen, Amartya. 1992. *Inequality Reexamined.* New York: Russell Sage Foundation; Cambridge, MA: Harvard University Press.

Tuirán, R., and J.L. Ávila. 2002. "Población, pobreza y mercado de trabajo en México, 1970–1997." In *Población, pobreza y mercado de trabajo en América Latina,* ed. J. Boltvinik and E. Hernández Laos. Mexico: Siglo XXI.

Valencia Lomelí, Enrique, and Rodolfo Aguirre Riveles. 1998. "Discursos, acciones y controversias de la política gubernamental frente a la pobreza." In *Los rostros de la pobreza. El debate,* ed. Rigoberto Gallardo and Joaquín Osorio. México: ITESO-UIA.

Zedillo, Ernesto. 1995. *Primer informe de gobierno.* México, Presidencia de la República.

———. 1996. *Segundo informe de gobierno.* México, Presidencia de la República.

———. 1998. *Cuarto informe de gobierno.* México, Presidencia de la República.

———. 2000. *Sexto informe de gobierno.* México, Presidencia de la República.

Index

About the Editor

Laura Randall is professor emerita of the Department of Economics of Hunter College of the City University of New York. She is the author of *Factors Affecting Learning and Cost Effective Schooling in Primary Schools in Latin America* (2005); author of *The Political Economy of Brazilian Oil* (1993); *The Political Economy of Mexican Oil* (1989); *The Political Economy of Venezuelan Oil* (1987); *An Economic History of Argentina in the Twentieth Century* (1978) (published in Spanish as *Historia Económica de la Argentina en el Siglo XX)* (1983); *A Comparative Economic History of Latin America 1500–1914* (4 vols.): *Mexico, Argentina, Brazil and Peru* (1997).

She is the editor of the first edition of *Changing Structure of Mexico;* of *Reforming Mexico's Agrarian Reform* (1996) (published in Spanish as *Reformando la Reforma Agraria Mexicana* [1999]); of *The Political Economy of Latin America in the Post War Period* (1997); co-editor of *Schooling for Success: Preventing Repetition and Dropout in Latin American Primary Schools* (1999), and *Economic Development, Evolution or Revolution* (1964), and is the author of journal articles.

tutorial: software management

DONALD J. REIFER

(Third Edition)

IEEE Computer Society Order Number 678
Library of Congress Number 86-80073
IEEE Catalog Number EHO243-6
ISBN 0-8186-0678-9

IEEE COMPUTER SOCIETY

THE INSTITUTE OF ELECTRICAL AND ELECTRONICS ENGINEERS, INC.

IEEE
COMPUTER
SOCIETY
PRESS

Published by IEEE Computer Society Press
1730 Massachusetts Avenue, N.W.
Washington, D.C. 20036-1903

COVER DESIGNED BY JACK I. BALLESTERO

IEEE Computer Society Order Number 678
Library of Congress Number 86-80073
IEEE Catalog Number EH0243-6
ISBN 0-8186-0678-9 (Paper)
ISBN 0-8186-4678-0 (Microfiche)

Order from: IEEE Computer Society   IEEE Service Center
            Post Office Box 80452   44 Hoes Lane
            Worldway Postal Center   Piscataway, NJ 08854
            Los Angeles, CA 90080

 THE INSTITUTE OF ELECTRICAL AND ELECTRONICS ENGINEERS, INC.